ADULT DEVELOPMENT & AGING

The Canadian Experience

LORI HARPER
MACEWAN UNIVERSITY
VILLA CARITAS HOSPITAL

BONNIE DOBBS
UNIVERSITY OF ALBERTA

NELSON

NELSON

Adult Development and Aging, First Edition

by Lori Harper and Bonnie Dobbs

VP, Product and Partnership Solutions:
Claudine O'Donnell

Publisher, Digital and Print Content:
Lenore Taylor-Atkins

Marketing Manager:
Ann Byford

Content Development Manager:
Lisa Peterson and Liisa Kelly

Photo and Permissions Researcher:
Jessie Coffey

Production Project Manager:
Jaime Smith

Production Service:
SPi Global

Copy Editor:
Christina Maria Jelinek

Proofreader:
SPi Global

Indexer:
SPi Global

Design Director:
Ken Phipps

Higher Education Design PM:
Pamela Johnston

Interior Design:
Sharon Lucas Creative

Cover Design:
Sharon Lucas Creative

Cover Image:
Jupiterimages/Thinkstock

Art Coordinator:
Suzanne Peden

Illustrator(s):
Articulate Graphics LLC

Compositor:
SPi Global

Library and Archives Canada Cataloguing in Publication Data

Harper, Lori, 1959-, author Adult development & aging / Lori Harper (MacEwan University), Bonnie Dobbs (University of Alberta).

Includes bibliographical references and index.ISBN 978-0-17-659413-8 (softcover)

1. Adulthood--Psychological aspects--Textbooks. 2. Aging--Psychological aspects--Textbooks. 3. Older people--Psychology--Textbooks. 4. Textbooks. I. Dobbs, Bonnie Marie, 1952-, author II. Title. III. Title: Adult development and aging.

BF724.5.H37 2017
155.6   C2017-904141-X
ISBN-13: 978-0-17-659413-8
ISBN-10: 0-17-659413-2

Dedication
To my mom and dad. I miss them every single day.
Lori Harper

To my parents, who taught me about the challenges
and the many blessings of growing old.
Bonnie Dobbs

BRIEF CONTENTS

TABLE OF CONTENTS

PREFACE

As you look around your neighbourhood, you may be starting to notice that there are more older people. As a society, we are aging. In fact, this is a phenomenon that is occurring in most countries in the world. As you will soon learn, the over-85 age group is the fastest-growing segment of the population with more and more people reaching 100 years of age than ever before. This is really quite something when you think about it. In addition, the proportion of older adults who are immigrants, particularly those from the Philippines and China, will increase considerably in the decades to come, changing the face of aging in Canada. A lot of research and work is needed in many key areas (e.g., healthcare, pension reform, age-friendly environments, housing) in order for us to meet the challenges of an aging society.

As you read this book, you will learn about the cohort of individuals called the "baby boomers." Individuals who are a part of the baby-boom generation first began turning 65 in 2011, with the last wave of baby boomers turning 65 in 2030. This generation will change what we know about aging. This should come as no surprise. These are the same individuals who shook things up in the 1960s and 1970s by challenging the underlying values and attitudes of the social order. They were the first generation to do this, and they had a tremendous impact on all aspects of society including hair length, fashion, music, views of marriage, and patriotism. Baby boomers are healthier, are more educated, and have more money than generations before. They have high expectations for retirement and they are certainly not going to quietly age. Importantly, they will challenge the negative stereotypes associated with getting older that are so pervasive today.

This is an exciting time to be learning about aging in Canada. For example, there are more and more training programs offered at Canadian universities that prepare students to work with older adults in a variety of disciplines. In fact, as you read through this book and explore the website, you will be introduced to many individuals from different disciplines (e.g., psychology, social work, nursing) whose specialty is working with older adults. They will share with you the many reasons that they chose to work with older persons. Another exciting aspect of studying adult development and aging in Canada is that there are many researchers in this country whose programs of research are devoted to aging—you will read the results from much of their work in this book. There also are national studies going on as we speak, with Canadian researchers collecting data on older adults on a wide variety of variables (e.g., health, lifestyle, education, retirement). The Canadian Longitudinal Study on Aging is the largest and most comprehensive study on health and aging in Canada, following more than 50 000 individuals between the ages of 45 and 85 (at the time of recruitment), for a period of 20 years. We will learn so much about aging in Canada from the results of this study. Gerontology truly is evolving in this country.

So, why did we decide to write a textbook about adult development and aging? There are many reasons. First of all, we wanted to create a textbook that is relevant for Canadian students and one that is based primarily on Canadian content. More importantly, though, we wanted to write a book that changes the way most people think about aging. If you buy into the stereotypes, aging is perceived as all doom and gloom with nothing to look forward to but decline. We are here to tell you that aging is not all doom and gloom. As you will learn, there is tremendous variability in the aging process and this process is influenced by a host of factors. Aging is a very individual process, with some 75-year-olds who look and feel like 50-year-olds and vice versa. We also want to get students interested in and excited about working and interacting with older adults. At the very least we hope that after you have read this book, you will have a more balanced understanding of what it is like to get older including many of the positive features of aging. Welcome to *Adult Development and Aging: The Canadian Experience*—prepare to be enlightened, inspired, and challenged!

To see how much you may already know about aging, go to www.timegoesby.net/weblog/2004/09/dr_erdmans_amaz.html and take the quiz.

FEATURES

Adult Development and Aging is designed to meet the needs of Canadian students enrolled in psychology, healthcare, and social science courses with a focus on the older adult and boasts a uniquely positive perspective on aging through relatable examples, up-to-date research, and engaging pedagogy.

- **Case Study** and **Lived Experience** boxes bring core concepts to life through down-to-earth scenarios that explore the experience of aging, or of caring for someone who is aging.
- **Figures, Tables, and Photos** enrich the student experience through contemporary research and examples.
- The **Good Practice** boxes at the end of each chapter awaken students to career options in geriatric mental health by profiling diverse practitioners from across the country.

Adult Development and Aging comes with a full set of in-text features to help students retain information and supplement their learning. The chapters are designed to have all the information students will need at their disposal.

- **Learning Objectives** at the start of major sections promote a focused reading experience for maximum comprehension.
- **Reflective questions** throughout each chapter provoke students to think critically and consider content through a personal lens.
- **End-of-chapter study tools** including a **chapter summary** and **key terms** encourage students to reflect on what they've learned and retain key concepts.

INSTRUCTOR
RESOURCES

SUPPORT FOR INSTRUCTORS AND STUDENTS

The Nelson Education Teaching Advantage (NETA) program delivers research-based instructor resources that promote student engagement and higher-order thinking to enable the success of Canadian students and educators. Visit Nelson Education's **Inspired Instruction** website at nelson.com/inspired/ to find out more about NETA.

The following instructor resources have been created for *Adult Development and Aging*. Instructors can access these ultimate tools for customizing lectures and presentations at nelson.com/instructor.

NETA TEST BANK

The NETA Test Bank for *Adult Development and Aging* has been created by a carefully selected subject-matter expert who is trained in the guidelines of NETA (the Nelson Education Teaching Advantage), a system for effective construction and development of high-quality test questions. The test bank contains an assortment of multiple-choice, true/false, short-answer, and essay questions.

NETA POWERPOINT

Microsoft® PowerPoint® lecture slides have been created for every chapter in *Adult Development and Aging*, with many of the slides featuring key figures, tables, and photographs from the text. The NETA principles of clear design and engaging content have been incorporated throughout so that customizing the deck for their courses will be simple for instructors.

COURSEMATE

The CourseMate for *Adult Development and Aging* brings course concepts to life with interactive learning and exam-preparation tools that integrate with the printed textbook. Students activate their knowledge through quizzes, games, and flashcards, among many other tools.

CourseMate provides immediate feedback that enables students to connect results to the work they have just produced, increasing their learning efficiency. It encourages contact between students and faculty: Instructors can opt to monitor their students' level of engagement with CourseMate, correlating their efforts to their outcomes. Instructors can even use CourseMate's quizzes to practise "Just in Time" teaching by tracking students' results in the Engagement Tracker and customizing their lesson plans to address students' learning needs.

As their class engages with CourseMate, instructors can watch student comprehension and engagement soar. Ask your Nelson Learning Solutions consultant for a demo today.

ABOUT THE AUTHORS

Courtesy of Lori Harper

LORI HARPER

Dr. Lori Harper is a clinical psychologist in geriatric psychiatry at Villa Caritas Hospital in Edmonton, Alberta, a clinical lecturer at the University of Alberta, and an instructor and field placement coordinator at MacEwan University. She was the Director of Training of the Edmonton Consortium Predoctoral Clinical Psychology training program for five years and still supervises graduate students, clinical and counselling psychology residents, as well as psychiatric residents. She is an accreditation site visitor for the Canadian Psychology Association. Over the last 20 years, Dr. Harper has focused her practice on geriatric psychiatry. Dr. Harper holds a Ph.D. in clinical psychology from the University of Calgary.

Larry Wong/Edmonton Journal

BONNIE DOBBS

Dr. Bonnie Dobbs is a full professor in the Department of Family Medicine, the Director of the Medically At-Risk Driver Centre, and the Director of Research for the Division of Care of the Elderly at the University of Alberta. Her primary research interests include the effects of medical conditions on driving, the consequences of driving cessation for medically impaired drivers and their families, and the role of alternate transportation in maintaining the mobility, independence, and safety of medically at-risk/impaired drivers and for the older population in general. Dr. Dobbs holds a Ph.D. in gerontology with specialization in psychology, human ecology, and medicine from the University of Alberta.

ACKNOWLEDGMENTS

This has been an incredible undertaking and one that we are very proud of. However, this book would not have been possible without the unfailing encouragement of the following individuals: Lori Harper would like to thank her husband Doug for all his love and support, and her boys, Matthew and Liam, for fending for themselves while this book was being written. She also would like to send a huge thank you to her boss, Gail Tricker, for supporting all her endeavours and for giving her the flexibility to write this book. Finally, Lori would like to thank Dr. Allen Dobbs for his mentorship, friendship, and support over many years. Bonnie Dobbs would like to thank her husband Al who is a constant source of inspiration, for his encouragement and unwavering support while writing this book.

We both would like to thank Mary Ellen Lepionka for sharing with us her valuable resources on pedagogy and Dr. Russ Powell whose smiley faces behavioural program kept us on track. A very special thank you to Tara Pidborochynski for her keen eye, superb attention to detail, and overall enthusiasm while reviewing our chapters. And a big thank you to Kayla Lucas and Emily Hussey for numerous proofreadings of the chapters and for always being available and eager to help, especially when deadlines were looming. Thank you to Trish Chatterley for her uncanny ability to find articles that no one else could find. Many thanks to our reviewers whose constructive criticism and insightful comments made this a much better book. Finally, to our team at Nelson (Lenore Taylor-Atkins, Lisa Peterson, Liisa Kelly, Christina Maria Jelinek, Jaime Smith, and Hemalatha Loganathan), thank you. There is no way we could have done this without your considerable patience and guidance. You truly made this an enjoyable experience.

— Dr. Lori Harper and Dr. Bonnie Dobbs

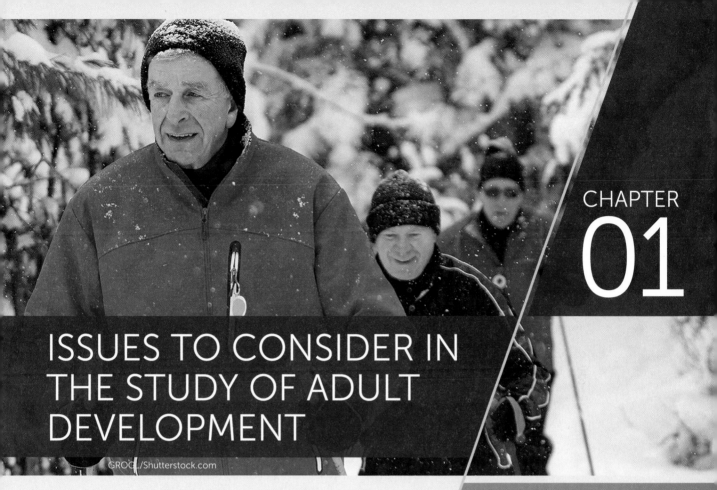

GROCL/Shutterstock.com

ISSUES TO CONSIDER IN THE STUDY OF ADULT DEVELOPMENT

CHAPTER OUTLINE

"Aging is not lost youth but a new stage of opportunity and strength."

Betty Friedan (1921–2006)

So . . . live your life and forget your age.

1.1 FOOD FOR THOUGHT IN THE STUDY OF ADULT DEVELOPMENT

LEARNING OBJECTIVES

To understand:

- the new terminology used to refer to "senior citizen"
- the historical beginnings of the study of adult development in Canada

A WORD ON TERMINOLOGY

According to the British Columbia Law Institute (BCLI), a positive, appropriate way to reference aging in the English language is missing. There does not appear to be a word that recognizes the wisdom, strength, and, often, the opportunities associated with getting older (Taylor, 2011). According to Taylor, the term "elderly" brings to mind frailty and the term "senior" is too limiting. "Older adult" or "older person" might be better terms as they are thought to be more neutral and acknowledge that the experience of aging varies from person to person. The American Psychological Association also endorses using the term older adult rather than elderly or senior in their publications for similar reasons (see Puryear-Keita, 2014). Recently, SeniorMarketing.com surveyed 1114 adults on their feelings about the language used to describe older adults. The participants ranged from under the age of 39 to 80 years of age or older, with 35 percent aged 50 to 59 and 40 percent aged 60 to 69 years old. Just over 50 percent of those surveyed responded that they are not comfortable with the term senior and preferred older adult. Interestingly, 71 percent of respondents indicated that they were comfortable with the term "baby boomer" because this name represents influence, individualism, idealism, success, and resilience (Seniormark, 2013). You will learn about the boomer generation as you read this book. The cohort is truly changing how we think and feel about aging! So, in keeping with current terminology, we will use the terms older adult, older person, or boomer when referring to those over the age of 65.

HISTORICAL ASPECTS OF THE STUDY OF ADULT DEVELOPMENT

Before we begin a brief review of the history of the study of adult development in Canada, it is important to become familiar with the term "gerontology." **Gerontology** is the scientific study of aging. This includes the biological, psychological, and sociological changes that individuals face as they age. Also included in the study of gerontology are the social and economic impacts of the aging of the world's population. Importantly, aging is not all about decline. Aging also brings many opportunities for individuals and societies.

Even though getting older is a very normal part of development, interest in the study of aging has only increased in the last 70 years or so. Historically, the focus of research from a developmental perspective has been on children and adolescence. For example, both Piaget's stage theory of cognitive development and Freud's psychosexual stages of development were completed by adolescence. Interestingly, the American psychologist who wrote the first major work on aging was a pioneer in the field of child and adolescent development. G. Stanley Hall, who was the first president of the American Psychological Association, published *Senescence: The Last Half of Life* in 1922 at the age of 78. However, it would be many years later before the interest in studying adult development really took hold. In the United States, in 1946, the National Institutes of Health established a large-scale research centre and the Gerontological Society of America (GSA) also was founded that year with representation from disciplines such as medicine, biology, and nursing, as well as psychology. Research journals and organizations that focused on aging soon followed.

In Canada, systematic research on aging began around the same time. In 1944, the Gerontology Research Unit at McGill University was founded. During the 1950s, the Canadian Welfare Council formed the Committee on Aging, which began research in social gerontology. Beginning in 1957, research on aging was being promoted by several provincial conferences that focused exclusively on aging. In 1966, the first provincial office on aging was created in Ontario, and the final report of the Senate's Special Committee on Aging was published (Andrews, Campbell, Denton, & McGilton, 2009). That same year, the first Canadian Conference on Aging was held in Toronto. At that time, Canadian gerontologists were becoming increasingly involved in international gerontology associations. This led to the establishment of the *Canadian Association on Gerontology* (CAG) in 1971, which today has more than 2000 members. CAG continues to be the major forum for aging research in Canada. This organization provides opportunities for professionals interested in aging to share information through annual conferences and a newsletter. In 1982, CAG began publishing the *Canadian Journal on Aging*, a refereed journal which is published quarterly (Andrews et al., 2009).

The Canadian Geriatrics Society (CGS), initially called the Canadian Society of Geriatric Medicine, was established in 1981. The objective of the CGS is to promote excellence in the medical care of older Canadians. CGS also holds an annual conference and publishes a quarterly refereed journal titled *Geriatrics Today: Journal of the Canadian Geriatrics Society*. In 1988, the Canadian Gerontological Nursing Association was founded. The mandate of this organization is to provide education and support to the nurses who participate with older adults in care of their health and to address the health of older Canadians (Sheets & Gallagher, 2013). More recently, the Canadian Coalition for Seniors' Mental Health was founded. This organization's mission is to ensure that the mental health of older adults is recognized as a key Canadian health and wellness issue.

From the late 1970s until the mid-1980s, extensive support was provided for research and research training on population aging by the Strategic Grants Program of the Social Sciences and Humanities Research Council of Canada (SSHRC). This included support for new research centres including the Gerontology Research Centre at Simon Fraser University, the Centre on Aging at the University of Manitoba, the Institute for Life Course and Aging at the University of Toronto, as well as centres in Guelph, Moncton, Victoria, and St. Johns (Andrews et al., 2009). In fact, there are approximately 44 gerontology research and education centres across Canada (Sheets & Gallagher, 2013). Aging is now a topic of interest!

Perhaps the most significant change to the study of aging in the past decade has come through the establishment of the Canadian Institutes of Health Research (CIHR). Because of active involvement and feedback from the Canadian gerontological community, the Institute of Aging (IA) became one of the 13 grant-awarding agencies that comprise the CIHR (Andrews et al., 2009). The IA has prioritized research on aging in five areas: biological mechanisms of aging, maintenance of functional autonomy, healthy and successful aging, cognitive impairment in aging, and health services and policy related to older adults. The IA has been a key factor to the growth of research investigating health and aging in Canada. Many multidisciplinary projects have been funded through the IA including the Canadian Longitudinal Study on Aging (CLSA). With a team of more than 200 investigators and collaborators from 26 Canadian universities, co-principal investigators Drs. Raina (McMaster University), Wolfson (McGill University), and Kirkland (Dalhousie University) are following 50 000 Canadian men and women nationally between the ages of 45 and 85 for a period of 20 years. Data collected will include information on the changing biological, psychological, medical, and socio-economic aspects of the lives of Canadian people as they age (Andrews et al., 2009).

Another exciting aspect in the development of the study of aging in Canada is that, in the last decade, there has been a growth of doctoral graduate programs in gerontology including a PhD in gerontology at Sherbrooke University as well as at Simon Fraser University. The University of Regina and the University of Sherbrooke offer a master's degree program in gerontology as well. Interestingly, McMaster University offers a mixed master's degree in Health and Aging (Andrews et al., 2009). As you can see, it is a very exciting time to study aging in Canada. These types of programs also are widely available in the United States, and in 2014, Bottiggi Dassel and her colleagues wrote an article called "*What Can I Do with a Doctoral Degree in Gerontology? Expanding Your Options*" (Bottiggi Dassel et al., 2014). Visit http://dx.doi.org/10.1080/0270196 0.2013.870901 if you would like to have a look at this article.

1.2 THE DEVELOPMENTAL PERSPECTIVE OF AGING

LEARNING OBJECTIVES

To understand:
- the lifespan developmental perspective of aging
- what can influence development over the lifespan

THE LIFESPAN DEVELOPMENTAL PERSPECTIVE

Today, the idea that human development occurs throughout one's life is widely accepted by researchers, although, as you have just learned, this was not always the case. Paul B. Baltes and his colleagues (e.g., Baltes, 1987; Baltes & Baltes, 1990; Baltes & Smith, 2004) really championed the study of development *across* the lifespan, rather than just focusing on children and adolescents. In their seminal research, these researchers identified four key principles to lifelong development. These key principles are presented in Table 1.1.

Baltes also identified three types of influences that interact with each other to produce developmental change over the lifespan. Let's look at these now.

WHAT INFLUENCES LIFESPAN DEVELOPMENT?

The first type of influences on development is called **normative age-graded influences**. These normative changes tend to affect most people at a particular age. For example, turning 18 in many parts of the world is seen as the start of adulthood. Although this is changing, people tend to start careers or finish university, get married, and start a family in their 20s or 30s. Another age-graded influence is the timing of retirement, with age 65 largely accepted as the

TABLE 1.1

KEY PRINCIPLES TO THE STUDY OF DEVELOPMENT	
History and Context	All individuals develop within a certain set of circumstances that are influenced by the time in which we live as well as the culture in which we live.
Plasticity	It is possible to improve functioning at any age. Many skills can be taught or will improve with practice throughout one's life, although there are some limits to the degree of improvement.
Multiple Causality	How an individual develops is shaped by biological, psychological, sociocultural, and life cycle factors.
Multi-directionality	Development can involve both increases and decreases and this varies not only within persons but from person to person as well. As people gain in one area like expertise, for example, they may lose in other areas such as cognitive processing speed.

Source: Adapted from Baltes, P.B. (1987). Theoretical propositions of lifespan developmental psychology: On the dynamics between growth and decline. *Developmental Psychology, 23*(5), 611–626.

age to retire. However, as you will soon learn, this is changing. Other great examples of normative age-graded influences are puberty and menopause. Normative age-graded influences are a way to structure your life in terms of knowing where you are on your biological or social clock. The significance of normative age-grade changes are influenced by the larger society or culture you live in.

Normative history-graded influences are influences that are experienced by most people in a specific area or culture at the same time. These tend to be large in scale like the current war in Syria, the Paris attacks that occurred in 2015, or the suicide bombings in Belgium in 2016. These events have changed the way most people think about travel abroad in terms of safety and security. Similarly, the attack on the twin towers of the World Trade Center on September 11, 2001, made the world seem unsafe to many. Other examples of history-graded events that have had a tremendous impact on many societies worldwide are the arrival of the Internet and personal technologies like cellphones, as well as social media such as Facebook and Twitter. These technologies have had a huge effect on how we communicate information. Knowing the influences of normative age-graded and normative history-graded events may appear to make the development course for a particular individual somewhat predictable. However, there is a wild card that needs to be considered and this is non-normative influences.

Non-normative influences are random, unexpected events that are unique to an individual. Winning the lottery would be an example of a non-normative event. However, these events are not always positive. Getting in a serious car accident and developing a serious illness are examples of negative non-normative events.

REFLECTIVE QUESTION

As you ponder the influences on lifespan development, what normative history-graded and non-normative influences have you experienced?

1.3 AGE: THERE IS MORE TO THE WORD THAN YOU MAY THINK

LEARNING OBJECTIVES

To understand:
- the chronological, biological, psychological and sociological aspects of aging
- the difference between primary, secondary, and tertiary aging

CHRONOLOGICAL, BIOLOGICAL, PSYCHOLOGICAL, AND SOCIAL AGE

There are many ways in which age can be measured. However, when we think about how old another person is, we typically think about **chronological age**. This term refers to the number of years a person has lived. Because this is the most familiar way to measure age, many programs or rites of passage are based on chronological age. For example, in North America, chronological age determines when we can drink, drive, and vote legally. But is chronological age the best way to measure development? Is a person who is 40 years of age different from a person who is 60 years of age? The answer is yes! However, these numbers on their own tell us only that these two people were born 20 years apart. They do not tell us anything else. Interestingly, the need to go beyond a chronological definition of age was recognized way back in the 1980s. In their seminal paper, Barak and Shiffman (1981) noted that although chronological age stood out as the most frequently used variable in aging research at the time, age often has nothing to do with how people see themselves. In fact, these researchers found that people often perceive themselves to be at an age younger than their birth age. This may explain why it is not uncommon to hear older adults say, "But I don't feel like I am 70 [or 75 or 80]; I feel much younger!" In more recent research, Montepare (2009) and Mock and Eibach (2011) found that the older adults in their samples tended to feel younger than their chronological age and this finding can be seen across cultures. For example, Barak (2009) found that across 18 culturally different countries, the chronological age of the participants was much older than the age that the participants felt.

In fact, the age that you feel may be the most important factor that has an effect on your health and happiness. Rippon and Steptoe (2015) found that self-perceived age predicted all-cause and cardiovascular mortality in an eight-year follow-up of a sample of 6489 individuals aged 52 years and older. After statistically adjusting for health behaviour, physical disability, and health at baseline, there remained a 41 percent greater hazard of death in those individuals who felt older than their actual age compared to those who felt younger than their actual age. In addition, research evidence suggests that those individuals who are happiest and better adjusted in old age do not worry about age as a number. Instead, they focus on their individual strengths (Rippon & Steptoe, 2015; Stephan, Demulier, & Terracciano, 2012). It seems that baseball legend Satchel Paige (1906–1982) had it right. He believed that many people were so obsessed with age that they allowed age to define their identities. He encouraged people to break out of the mindset that makes you think of your age first and your identity second. His famous quote, "How old would you be if you didn't know how old you were?" is a good question indeed (www.brainyquote.com/quotes/quotes/s/satchelpai103901.html).

Biological age is a description of a person's development based on the aging of various physical systems. From this perspective, age is an index of biological health. It is important to remember though that one individual's physical health may be very different from another individual's physical health who is of the same age. For example, a 50-year-old who has regular cardiovascular exercise is likely to be biologically younger than a 50-year old who does not exercise. Bone density scans are one way to measure biological health as are lung function tests.

Age also can be thought of in terms of a person's ability to adapt to change compared with others. This is known as **psychological age**. Theoretically speaking, psychological age can be measured through stage theories such as those proposed by Erickson or Piaget. It is an attempt to understand development by how an individual thinks, reasons, and acts independently of chronological age.

Finally, **social age** is a measure of how well a person's behaviour fits with the norms or expectations that society has for a person of a particular age. For example, a 20-year-old widow would have a relatively advanced social age, and a man who becomes a father for the first time at the age of 60 would have a younger social age than many of his peers. Sometimes psychological age, social age, and biological age are all considered when determining **functional age**. This is a measure of how well an individual can function in his or her environment. In terms of studying adult development, this may be the most useful measure of age. Because there is considerable variability in how people age, knowing only their chronological age is not very helpful, especially if you consider that, to help older adults remain active and engaged in the community, it is much better to know their functional age.

PRIMARY, SECONDARY, AND TERTIARY AGING

Much like there is more to age than a number, there also is more to aging itself. In fact, there are three different processes involved. **Primary aging** is normal, disease-free development during adulthood. It is the typical and gradual changes that happen to most people as they age. **Secondary aging** is the physical and/or cognitive changes that are related to lifestyle, disease, or injury and are *not* part of the normal aging process. Diseases such as cardiovascular disease or dementia are examples of secondary aging. Secondary aging can affect the rate at which primary aging occurs. Finally, **tertiary aging** is the rapid decrease in cognitive and functional ability in the years prior to death.

AGE 65 YEARS OF AGE AND OLDER: ONE HOMOGENEOUS GROUP?

Traditionally, a person enters into "old age" at the age of 65. If you are wondering how 65 became a marker for old age, it may be because of Otto von Bismarck. You may be thinking, Otto von who? Well, he was the Chancellor of Germany, and in the early 1880s, he had a bit of a problem. Marxist unrest was spreading across Europe and many of his own countrymen were calling for socialist reforms. In 1889, to stave off more radical policies, Bismarck came up with the very first social insurance program in which the national government would contribute to the pensions of older Germans. While this may seem like a generous idea, very few people lived to be age 65 at the time! More about retirement in Chapter 11.

Is everyone who turns 65 the same? As you will learn as you read through this book, there is tremendous variability in the cognitive and physical abilities of those individuals who are 65 years of age or older (World Health Organization, 2015a). Researchers who study adult development have known this for many years. When you read research involving older adults, more and more you will see those 65 years of age and older divided into groups. Typically, the groupings will comprise young-old (those who are 65 to 74 years of age), old-old (those 75 to

84 years of age), and the oldest-old (those 85 years of age and older). Another way older adults are grouped is by calling those between ages 50 and 75 the **third age** and those older than 75 the **fourth age**. As an aside, you may be wondering what the first and second ages are. The **first age** represents youth to roughly the early 20s and the **second age** refers to individuals from the early 20s through to the 40s. We have learned a considerable amount about older adults in the third age but we don't know as much about older adults in the fourth age. This is because most people in the past typically did not live into their 80s and 90s. However, this is no longer the case.

1.4 WORLDWIDE POPULATION AGING
LEARNING OBJECTIVES

To understand:

- changes in the population pyramid in Canada and around the world
- why there was a decline in fertility rates
- what a baby boom is
- who the baby boomers are
- the significance and contributions of the baby boom generation
- the diversity of the Canadian older adult population

CHANGES IN THE POPULATION PYRAMID IN CANADA AND AROUND THE WORLD

If you take a moment and look around the local mall or grocery store, you may notice something has changed in the past five years or so. What could it be? The difference you will likely find is that you are now seeing more older adults as compared to people of other ages. This is not only happening in your neighbourhood; it also is happening around the world. We are an aging society. In fact, population aging is going to become one of the most significant social changes of the 21st century. The aging of the global population will influence nearly every segment of society including the demand for goods and services, such as transportation and housing, as well as family structures and intergenerational ties (United Nations, Department of Economic and Social Affairs, Population Division, 2015a).

According to data from *World Population Prospects: The 2015 Revision* (United Nations, Department of Economic and Social Affairs, Population Division, 2015b), the number of adults aged 60 years and over has increased substantially in recent years in most countries and regions, and this growth is expected to continue to increase in future decades. For example, between 2015 and 2030, the number of people in the world aged 60 years and over is projected to grow by 56 percent, from 901 million to 1.4 billion. By 2050, the global population of older persons is projected to more than double in size reaching nearly 2.1 billion. Globally, adults over the age of 80 are growing even faster than the number of older persons overall. Projections indicate that in 2050, those over 80 will number 434 million worldwide, having more than tripled in number since 2015 when there were 125 million people worldwide over age 80. In fact, **centenarians**, or those individuals who live to be 100 years of age or older, are growing in large numbers as well. This is quite something!

Japan is home to the world's oldest population. Incredibly, 33 percent of Japan's population was aged 60 years or over in 2015. Because of China's one-child policy, it has been projected that by the year 2036, there will be 200 million more older adults in China than children under the age of 15. Over the next 15 years, the number of older persons is expected to grow the fastest in

Latin America and the Caribbean, with a projected 71 percent increase in the population aged 60 years or over. Interestingly, the number of older adults is growing faster in urban areas than rural areas (United Nations, 2015a).

What do you think accounts for the aging of the world population?

So why is the population aging globally? There have been several reasons put forth. Better healthcare, improved access to healthcare, and eradication of childhood diseases have contributed to our aging population, but perhaps the most important reason is the significant decline in the global birth rate (United Nations, Department of Economic and Social Affairs, 2015a). You can get a good look at the decline in birth rates occurring in **G8 countries** over the last 60 years in Figure 1.1 (Statistics Canada, 2016a).

Fertility replacement level refers to the number of children born per woman necessary for the population to replace itself taking into account mortality between birth and age 15 in the absence of migration. The fertility replacement level is roughly 2.1 children per woman for most countries, although it may modestly vary with mortality rates. As shown in Figure 1.1, Canada's current fertility rate of 1.61 is in the mid-range for G8 countries. Among G8 countries, France

FIGURE 1.1

FERTILITY RATES IN G8 COUNTRIES, 1950–2011

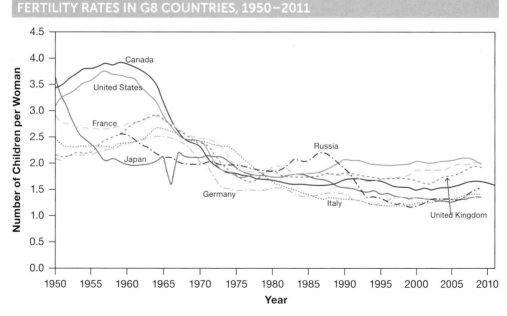

Source: Statistics Canada. (2016a). *Canadian demographics at a glance: Second edition* (Catalogue no. 91-003-X). Retrieved from http://www.statcan.gc.ca/pub/91-003-x/91-003-x2014001-eng.pdf.

FIGURE 1.2

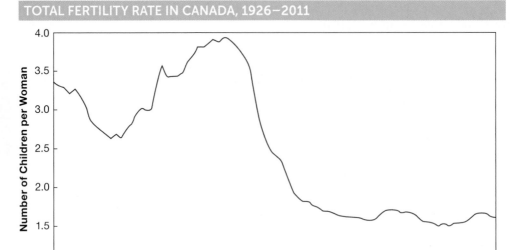

Source: Statistics Canada. (2016a). *Canadian demographics at a glance: Second edition* (Catalogue no. 91-003-X). Retrieved from http://www.statcan.gc.ca/pub/91-003-x/91-003-x2014001-eng.pdf.

and the United States have a fertility rate of 2.00, which is very close to the replacement level. As you can see, Russia, Italy, Germany, and Japan all have fertility levels well below the replacement level.

In Canada, since 1971, the total fertility rate has been below the replacement level. This means that, on average, couples are no longer having enough children to replace themselves. As mentioned previously, and as you can see from Figure 1.2, in 2011, Canada's fertility rate was 1.61 children per woman (Milan, 2014), a striking difference when you consider that, at the turn of the century, Canadian women were having five children on average (Statistics Canada, 2016a).

REFLECTIVE QUESTION

What do you think some of the challenges are to families and to social structures as a result of a population that is aging?

While population aging is a global phenomenon, it is more advanced in developed nations compared to countries where the developmental process started later (United Nations, 2015a). A population pyramid illustrates the age and sex structure of a country's population. The population is distributed along the horizontal axis, with males shown on the right and females on the left. Figure 1.3 shows the changes to the population pyramid in Canada from 1971 to 2011, and projected changes for the year 2030 (Department of Finance Canada, 2012).

FIGURE 1.3

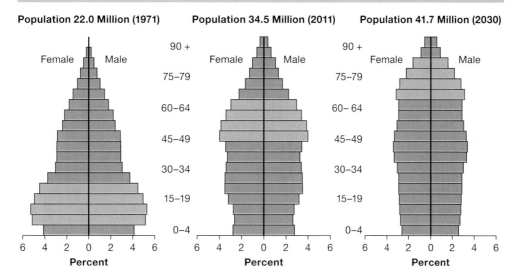

Economic and fiscal implications of Canada's aging population. The blue bulge in each pyramid denotes the baby boomers.

Source: Department of Finance Canada. (2012). *Economic and fiscal implications of Canada's aging population* (Catalogue no. F2-217/2012E-PDF). Reproduced with the permission of the Department of Finance Canada, 2017. Retrieved from https://www.fin.gc.ca/pub/eficap-rebvpc/eficap-rebvpc-eng.pdf.

Population pyramids are called "pyramids" because that is what one typically looks like. Usually, the number of younger people in a country is much greater than the number of older people. However, as you can see from Figure 1.3, the pyramids are beginning to look more like rectangular columns because of the aging of the population. In fact, in 2015, the Canadian population over 65 years of age exceeded the population under 14 years of age for the first time in history (Department of Finance Canada, 2012). If you look again at the pyramids, you will see a blue bulge that started at the bottom of the pyramid in 1970 moving toward the top of the pyramid in 2030. This bulge is due to the baby boom cohort. Let's find out about this cohort now.

THE BABY BOOMERS

By definition, a **baby boom** is a sudden rise in the number of births from year to year. Between 1946 and 1965, Canada experienced a baby boom. This occurred because of a strong postwar economy, the reunion of families following World War II, and high marriage rates. In fact, from 1946 to 1965, Canada had the largest annual increase in the number of births since 1921; more than 8.2 million babies were born during this time, which, on average, is close to 412 000 a year (Statistics Canada, 2012a). To give you some perspective, in 1941, only 264 000 Canadian babies were born (Beaujot & McQuillan, 1982). The baby boom in Canada peaked in 1959 at 479 000 births when the total fertility rate reached 3.94 children per woman (Carrière, Martel, Légaré, & Picard, 2016). This phenomenon also occurred in the United States, the United Kingdom, and parts of Europe, but the baby boom was largest in Canada (Statistics Canada, 2016a). However, by the end of the 1960s, the baby boom was over and fertility rates declined significantly. In fact, in 2011, the fertility rate for women aged 20 to 24 was at a record low. You might be interested to know that, in 2010, the fertility rate for women aged 35 to 39 was higher than for women aged 20 to 24 years of age. This gap widened in 2011 (Statistics Canada, 2016b).

REFLECTIVE QUESTION

What do you think accounts for the decline in fertility rates by the end of the 1960s?

So what could have influenced a decline in birth rates? Well, the influence of religion on daily life declined, contraception was now more effective and more easily accessed, and the participation of women in higher education and in the paid labour force was on the rise. All these factors are thought to have contributed to the decline of fertility levels in North America and in many developed countries in the world (Statistics Canada, 2016b).

Children born in the postwar baby boom (1946–1965) are called **baby boomers**. The first of the baby boomers turned 65 in 2011 and, depending on what research you read, it is estimated that in the United States, at least, 8000 to 10 000 individuals turn 65 every day (Pruchno, 2012). By 2031, the baby boomers will range in age from 65 to 85. This generation is like no other generation before it. Not only is it significant for its size, but also baby boomers are more highly educated than previous generations and, as a result, more likely to be in professional careers and managerial positions. They also are more likely to work past the retirement age of 65. They have more money to spend than previous generations. They are more ethnically and racially diverse than previous generations (Frey, 2010). And, the baby boomers have higher rates of separation and divorce, lower rates of marriage, and, as we have just discussed, fewer children. They also are unique in that they are the first generation to challenge the underlying values and attitudes of the social order. The baby boomers have influenced just about every facet of society including fashion, music, race relations, and child rearing (Pruchno, 2012). In addition, research in Canada has shown that baby boomers have higher expectations of public services than previous generations and will demand the most from these services (Guberman, Lavoie, Blein, & Olazabal, 2012). They also have a better understanding of their rights as citizens, and they continue to question the rules and regulations that govern society even today (Steinhorn, 2007).

DIVERSITY IN OLDER ADULTS

One important fact that we hope stays with you after you read this book is that older adults are not all the same. As mentioned previously, there is a good deal of variability in the physical and cognitive abilities of individuals who are 65 years of age and over. In fact, there is probably more variability among those aged 65 and older than any other age group (Findsen & Formosa, 2011). Lifestyle and socio-economic factors, as well as ethnic background, will influence the way we age and, in turn, influence the overall physical and cognitive health of older adults. Older adults also are becoming different in another way. The older adult population as a whole is becoming more ethnically diverse. Immigration contributes significantly to the ethno-cultural diversity observed in those aged 65 and over.

According to the Canadian 2006 Census, 30 percent (900 000) of older adults were immigrants (Ng, Lai, Rudner, & Orpana, 2012). However, most of the older adults who were surveyed in 2006 were **established immigrants**. Established immigrants are those who have been permanent residents of Canada for more than 10 years. Approximately 6 percent of the older adult immigrants (80 000) were **recent immigrants** who have been permanent residents of Canada for less than 10 years. Most are **family class immigrants** in that they are sponsored by their family to come to Canada. Recent immigrants who are older adults face many barriers.

What types of challenges do you think older adult immigrants who have recently migrated to Canada face?

For example, as family class immigrants, older adults do not have access to economic resources and they are not eligible for pension programs. Individuals must live in Canada for 10 years before they are eligible for government pensions. This can be an incredible challenge for families if an older family member develops an illness or dementia before the 10-year period is up and he or she needs a higher level of care than the family can provide. Without a pension, the burden of this expense falls on the family of the sponsored older adult. If the family can't afford to pay for this type of care, who will?

Interestingly, the home countries that older immigrants have come from have changed substantially over the last three decades. Almost one half of older adult immigrants who arrived in Canada in recent years are from South and East Asian countries instead of from the United Kingdom and Western Europe, which was the trend in Canada's earlier years. These changes in the profile of Canada's older population will have many implications for developing public policies and programs aimed at older adults, particularly regarding healthcare services and home support, which, traditionally, have been developed for older adults who came to Canada from Western European countries (Carrière et al., 2016).

Of note is that the Aboriginal populations of Canada and the United States are much younger and growing faster than the overall Canadian and American populations. In Canada, in 2011, Aboriginals aged 65 and over accounted for 5.9 percent of the Aboriginal population, which is much lower than the percentage (14.2 percent) of older adults in the non-Aboriginal population in Canada (Statistics Canada, 2013a). More about our culturally diverse nation is discussed in Chapter 8.

1.5 EAST VERSUS WEST: CHANGING VIEWS OF OLDER ADULTS?

LEARNING OBJECTIVES

- To understand Eastern and Western views of aging and older adults

Research on the influence of cultural values and beliefs on attitudes toward older adults and aging has been dominated by comparisons between Eastern and Western cultures. Traditionally, Eastern collectivist cultures are perceived to adopt a more positive view of aging in general and older adults in particular. But what do we mean when we say Eastern cultures? In research studies, typically the East is made up of both East Asian countries (China, Japan, and Korea) as well as South/Southeast Asian countries (India, Malaysia, and the Philippines). The West is comprised of English-speaking and Western European countries that are more geographically spread out but culturally similar. For example, Australia, New Zealand, Canada, the United States, the United Kingdom, and Western Europe are classified as Western cultures (North & Fisk, 2015). It is believed that in Eastern cultures, age is associated with increased reverence and respect (Yun & Lackman, 2006). These beliefs are thought to stem from the principles of **Confucianism**, which give older members an esteemed role within both social and familial contexts, and from the stronger collectivist tradition of **filial piety**. Filial piety compels younger people to obey, respect, maintain contact with, and take care of the older adults in their family (North & Fisk, 2015). In contrast, Western cultures, which hold more individualistic values, appear to adhere to a more youth-oriented society and hold more negative beliefs about aging (Nelson, 2011).

So, is it really that simple? Do Eastern collectivist cultures hold older adults in high esteem and Western cultures, where the emphasis is on individualism, hold negative beliefs about older adults and aging? While there is empirical evidence supporting this East–West cultural difference, the research that is available appears to be mixed (Zhang et al., 2016). Some studies fail to find any significant cultural differences between the East and the West (see Boduroglu, Yoon, Luo, & Park, 2006; McCann, Cargile, Giles, & Bui, 2004), while other studies have found support for the notion that aging attitudes are more positive in Eastern compared to Western cultures (see Chung & Lin, 2012; Tan, Zhang, & Fan, 2004). Yet, other researchers have found negative attitudes toward aging and older adults in Eastern cultures (Luo, Zhou, Jin, Newman, & Liang, 2013; Zhou, 2007). For example, North and Fisk (2015) conducted a meta-analysis comparing Eastern and Western attitudes about aging and older adults and found that Eastern cultures hold greater negative attitudes toward older adults than Western cultures.

To try to make sense of the inconsistencies in the findings, Zhang and colleagues (2016) looked at the effect that personal and cultural values had on the attitudes toward older adults. Using data from the sixth wave of the *World Population Survey*, they found that, regardless of culture, attitudes toward older adults were influenced more by personal values than by cultural values. These researchers found that across cultures, people tended to hold more positive attitudes toward older adults when they scored high in communal values when compared to those who scored low in communal values (e.g., friendliness, warmth, and love). So, in the end, it may not be cultural values that influence an individual's attitude toward older adults but, rather, personal values.

REFLECTIVE QUESTION

What might account for the shift in Eastern cultures' views about older adults and aging?

So what is the bottom line? Ng (2002) suggests that it is an exaggeration to say that Eastern cultures look up to and respect their elders while Western cultures abandon them. As you have just learned, there is variability in Eastern attitudes toward older adults. Löckenhoff and her colleagues (Löckenhoff et al., 2009) argue that some of the negative attitudes found in the research studies may be related to differences in population structure. Recall that although the world, in general, is aging, this is occurring more quickly in some Eastern cultures, which puts pressure on societies that are ill prepared to manage an older population. Luo and his colleagues (2013) argue that the negative attitudes that are being observed in Eastern cultures toward aging and older people are a result of a combination of educational, social, and economic factors. For example, in China, there are high levels of geographical, social, and intellectual segregation between young and old adults. There is tremendous caregiver burden as a result of the one-child generation in China, which is compounded by a lack of governmental support for caregiving. Further, there is a lack of education about aging in the school systems (although this is true of Western school systems as well). It also could be the case that, in the future, as Eastern cultures become more modernized and feel the influence of Western cultures, capitalism, and individualistic values, younger adults may begin to feel less obligated to maintain traditions of filial piety (Nelson, 2011). In addition, access to education, as well as increasing literacy among young people, has undermined the traditional elder roles of prime knowledge holder and storyteller (Nelson 2011; North & Fisk, 2015).

Closer to home, changing traditional roles is echoed in a Canadian study in which 17 Somali elders were interviewed about their views of aging in Canada and Somalia (Lagacé, Charmarkeh, & Grandena, 2012). Through focus groups and interviews, these researchers asked the participants about their views of aging. They found that participants worried about an intergenerational gap in their views of aging compared to their Canadian-born and -raised children. A prominent theme in the interviews with participants was that in Somalia, elders are seen as useful and have opportunities to continuously contribute to society. Consider the following comment from an elder male participant:

> In Somali culture, as you age, you become more prominent because of your experience. All aspects [of experience], whether it be financial or otherwise, are put back into your family, relatives, and cousins. Here [in Canada], aging is an inconvenience. Back home, [older adults] are taking care of themselves, they are part of a leading group . . . they are connected to society . . . there is a system of integrating the elderly. (Lagacé et al., 2012, p. 418)

Another participant commented that "respecting elders was a norm in Somalia, not so in Canada . . . the miscommunication may cause problems for the family unit" (Lagacé et al., 2012, p. 418). It appears that it is not only Eastern cultures that are experiencing changing attitudes toward older adults. It will be interesting to see what the future holds in terms of the attitudes people of different cultures hold toward older adults and aging.

REFLECTIVE QUESTION

When you consider your own family situation, do you feel you have an obligation to look after your parents or grandparents now or in the coming years?

1.6 MYTHS AND STEREOTYPES OF AGING

LEARNING OBJECTIVES

To understand:

- what ageism is
- that the myths and stereotypes of old age are just that—myths and stereotypes
- the media's influence in perpetuating the stereotypes of older adults
- how stereotypes affect older adults' performance in laboratory and community settings
- what can be done to reduce ageism

AGEISM

Before we begin a discussion of the myths and stereotypes associated with aging, it is important to become familiar with the term **ageism**. Robert Butler coined this term in 1969. Ageism refers to the "systematic stereotyping of, and discrimination against, people because they are old, just as racism and sexism accomplish this with skin colour and gender" (Butler, 1969, p. 243). According to the Ontario Human Rights Commission (2016), ageism has two components. The first is that ageism is a "socially constructed way of thinking about older persons based on negative attitudes and stereotypes" (p. 1). The second part is that because of ageist beliefs, there is a "tendency to structure society based on an assumption that everyone is young" (p. 1). In fact, Palmore (2004) and Bennett and Gaines (2010) call ageism the third greatest "ism" in our society after racism and sexism. According to the *Revera Report on Ageism: A look at gender differences* (International Federation on Ageing and Revera Inc., 2012), 52 percent of Canadians believe that ageism is the most tolerated form of social prejudice. According to Fisk and North (2015), aged-based biases have cast older adults as largely irrelevant to the rest of society. Ageism stems from the myths and negative stereotypes of older adults.

According to the International Federation on Aging and Revera Inc. (2014), older Canadian adults experience a good deal of ageism. In 2013, 1500 Canadians aged 18 to 32 (Gen Y), 33 to 45 (Gen X), 46 to 65 (baby boomers), 66 to 74, and 75 and older were polled to find out their attitudes about aging and to assess their level of awareness and experience with ageism. Of those surveyed, 6 in 10 older adults aged 66 and older believed that they have been treated unfairly because of their age. Furthermore, 35 percent of those polled admitted that they have treated an older adult differently because of his or her age. According to the survey, the three most common forms of age discrimination faced by Canadian older adults are being ignored or treated as invisible, being treated like they have nothing to contribute, and others assuming they are incompetent simply because of their age.

Not surprisingly, there are gender differences when it comes to ageism. According to the International Federation on Aging and Revera Inc. (2012), Canadian women 66 years of age and older are more likely than men to say they have been treated unfairly because of their age and they are more likely to say that others view them as incompetent.

As Nelson (2011) points out, ageism is very strange indeed. Think about it for a moment. It is prejudice against an older you! And it is an "ism" that many of us will personally experience one day (Bennett & Gaines, 2010). Why do we mock what we will one day become ourselves? According to **Terror Management Theory** (Martens, Goldenberg, & Greenberg, 2005), we hold negative stereotypes and beliefs about older adults because it helps us to deal with or avoid the anxiety that most people feel about their own death. This leads younger adults to associate negative qualities and feelings with older adults because older adults remind us that we cannot live forever (Nelson, 2011). This bias toward older persons only serves to create a continuous cycle of ever-growing prejudice against older adults (Martens et al., 2005). According to Nelson (2011), there is a good deal of evidence that supports this theory as it is applied toward our understanding of the origins of ageism. Levy and colleagues (2011) give us some food for thought:

> Imagine if every year, along with a medical check-up, we were encouraged to get another check-up, a social-cognitive check-up at which those beliefs that are most likely to affect health were assessed. This check-up would be administered by an expert who could give prescriptions consisting of age-appropriate mental exercises to bolster beneficial beliefs and resist harmful beliefs. Although scientists' findings do not yet support such prescriptions, they are a worthy goal of research. (p. 437)

Scheidt (2017) agrees. He suggests that, regardless of our age, it is important for all of us to develop personal strategies that preserve our integrity against the ageism seen in ourselves and in society.

STEREOTYPES OF AGING

The stereotypes and myths about older adults stem from ageism. Some of the stereotypes of older adults that you have likely heard are older adults will lose their memory, develop dementia, and become cranky, lonely, and socially isolated; older adults certainly won't be interested in sex; and, for sure, they can't learn anything new. According to Yeh (2015), these stereotypes are the result of the so-called arc of life in which it is falsely believed that all of life's joys and discoveries peak in middle-adulthood followed by a very long, steady decline in physical and cognitive abilities. She believes that this type of thinking reduces all individuals to a sort of bystander status where age is something that happens *to us* rather than a more empowering view that aging occurs with our guidance (Yeh, 2015). Of course, we have positive stereotypes of older adults as well: wise, generous, and responsible, for example. Unfortunately, there are far more negative stereotypes than positive stereotypes (Hummert, 2011). The portrayal of older adults in the media fuels these stereotypes. In fact, a recent Google search of *cerebral atrophy* led us to a Wikipedia page that suggested that "cerebral atrophy, as you get older . . . results in the typical characteristic of elderly adults engaging in inappropriate or offensive behaviours." Yikes! Let us assure you that inappropriate and offensive behaviours are not typical of an older adult.

You might be surprised to learn that Facebook also is a site for negative age stereotypes. Levy, Chung, Bedford, and Navrazhina (2014) did a content analysis of publically accessible

Facebook groups that concentrated on older adults. Eighty-four groups with a total of 25 489 members were analyzed. These researchers found that all but one of the sites focused on negative age stereotypes. In fact, 37 percent of the sites analyzed advocated banning older adults from shopping online. What?? Really? Levy and her colleagues (2014) point out that while Facebook has the potential to break down barriers between generations, it also has the potential to create new ones.

In a review of children's attitudes toward older adults, Gilbert and Ricketts (2008) found that various forms of media, particularly children's books (think *Snow White* or *Sleeping Beauty*) and television shows, provide children with negative views of older adults. These researchers found that children as young as five held negative stereotypes of older adults.

Older adults on television often are portrayed as incompetent and asexual. Although this often is accompanied by humour, it is not a realistic portrayal of older adults. Consider Abe Simpson, who is Bart Simpson's grandfather on the critically acclaimed television series *The Simpsons*. Abe is typically portrayed as a senile person who is not only a burden to his son Homer but very dependent on Homer as well. When older adults see themselves depicted this way, they do not like it. For example, Canadian researchers (Horton, Baker, Côté, & Deakin, 2008) conducted semi-structured qualitative interviews with older adults that addressed this topic. One of the questions participants were asked in the study was, "How do you see older adults portrayed on television?" One participant replied, "Sometimes [older adults] are portrayed as almost helpless. That bothers me. They're not all that way. Just because you get older, doesn't mean you've got to be told what to do, what to say, how to do everything. So I think the media exploit that" (Horton et al., 2008, p. 1003).

In addition, the media can be a very powerful tool in pressuring older adults to look or act in a particular way. Hurd Clark and Griffin (2008) interviewed 44 Canadian women who ranged in age from 50 to 70 about their experiences and attitudes toward a broad range of beauty work interventions. They found that 42 out of the 44 women they interviewed used beauty work interventions such as cosmetic surgeries and non-surgical cosmetic procedures, as well as hair dye and makeup, as a way to respond to the perceived social pressures to look young. In other words, these women altered their appearances to hide their chronological age. If you believe the messages you receive from the media, youth is seen as the only acceptable age to be. Box 1.1 contains some of the comments made by the Canadian women in this study.

Let's think about birthday cards for a moment. Birthday cards often communicate a single message and this message can be understood as "I am sorry you are another year older." Birthday themes for middle-aged adults often include the caption "over the hill" and often included in "over the hill" party packs are items such as black balloons and even, on occasion, a plastic gravestone (Nelson, 2011)! According to Nelson, the message is clear: "Ageing is bad, and we have a tendency to make fun of people who are getting older" (Nelson, 2011, p. 41). You may not have thought of this before but this is a perfect example of ageism. You can see this for yourself the next time you buy a birthday card!

Balazs (2014) argues that in order to persuade older adults to buy products, advertisers will need to incorporate more women and members of a minority group into advertisements; portray older adults more accurately in their work, leisure, and relationship roles; limit the use of unrealistic, ageless models; and connect with the value systems of older adults. You can see the change of the portrayal of older adults beginning already. For example, in the last 10 years or so, new magazines have been developed that are geared to older adults. In Canada, *Zoomer* is one such magazine. Topics found in this magazine range from money management to tips for a healthy sex life to where to travel. It always includes information about the Canadian

BOX 1.1

PRESSURE TO LOOK YOUNG

The media has always impacted me. I've never been able to ignore it or distance myself from it. I've incorporated the values of our mainstream media. So it's been a continual struggle for me to counter those values. As I grow older, it's very difficult to see the wrinkles appearing and the skin losing its elasticity. My radical feminism, on the one hand, is saying, "Don't be so absurd." The other side of me struggles. When I look through magazines and see all of these advertisements for wrinkle creams and the amount of cosmetic surgeons there are out there now, I am just absolutely appalled at what's going on . . . but I've considered getting rid of these wrinkles, and the facelifts and all that. Whether I'll ever do it or not, I don't know, but certainly I've considered it.

—Comments made by a 65-year-old woman in the Hurd Clark and Griffin (2008) study.

> *I do feel pressure to look younger. My boyfriend is younger than me and I wouldn't want to get too old looking because of the age difference between us. He's 53, and I'm 60. I think he could be dating someone who is 40 quite easily. So there's pressure on me to look good. . . .*

—Comments from a 60-year-old woman in the same study.

Association of Retired Persons (CARP) and the current issues that the group is lobbying for. In television, you can see shows that portray older adults as healthy, engaged with life, and dating (e.g., Betty White on the hit show *Hot in Cleveland*). Perhaps change is occurring (although s-l-o-w-l-y) regarding what society considers beautiful. Consider, for example, that at the age of 69, Susan Sarandon was chosen as one of the world's most beautiful people by *People* magazine in 2016, and in that same year, she became the new face of L'Oréal Paris. It is not much but it is a beginning. Marketers believe that over the next few years, more older adults will be seen in commercials and will be portrayed more realistically (see Figure 1.4). Hopefully, this more realistic portrayal of older adults in the media will help to decrease ageism. Over the next few years, it will be interesting to see if the portrayal of older adults in the media really does improve.

You might be surprised to find that negative stereotypes of aging can be endorsed by older adults themselves. The process is termed **negative self-stereotyping** (Kruse & Schmitt, 2006). Many older adults will take the explicit and implicit stereotypes of aging that they have carried with them throughout their lives and apply these stereotypes to themselves. In other words, the stereotypes that younger adults have held toward older adults while growing up they now apply to themselves. In laboratory settings, these internalized stereotypes have been shown to negatively affect the functioning of older adults in many domains such as cognitive performance, especially memory. For example, Canadian researchers Chasteen and her colleagues (2015) found that older adults' negative views of aging predicted their performance in the domains of memory and hearing abilities. In addition, the detrimental effects of internalized negative stereotypes has been shown to affect the functioning of older adults in the community in terms of decreases

FIGURE 1.4

Horsche/Thinkstock

Realistic and positive views of older adults will help to reduce ageism.

in self-efficacy, poorer health, and perceived well-being (Bennett & Gaines, 2010; Coudin & Alexopoulos, 2010; Sargent-Cox & Anstey, 2015). Levy, Zonderman, Slade, and Ferrucci (2012) found that people who had internalized negative aging stereotypes at mid-life had an increased probability of experiencing a cardiovascular event nearly 20 years later. So how does internalizing negative stereotypes lead to greater risk of having a cardiovascular event? It appears that people who endorse aging stereotypes believe that debilitating health problems are inevitable in older adulthood. Such negative perceptions of aging result in unhealthy lifestyle behaviours and become self-fulfilling prophecies as a result (Levy et al., 2012).

Canadian researchers Genoe and Whyte (2015) argue that discriminatory attitudes and assumptions of old age have deep consequences on older adults' participation in meaningful leisure experiences. Often, older adults have internalized the message that they are too old to engage in activities that they enjoyed in the past and even though they may still be able to participate, they do not because of internalized stereotypes.

Bennett and Gaines (2010) identify other ways in which stereotypes can affect the functioning of older adults. The first is a phenomenon called **stereotyped threat**, which has been widely studied in the field of social psychology. "Stereotyped threat" refers to the fear of being judged in accordance with a negative stereotype of the group you belong to. This fear creates anxiety which results in underperformance on a particular task, which, in turn, reinforces the negative stereotype of the larger group to which you belong. There is substantial research evidence that shows that stereotyped threat occurs in older adults and negatively affects cognitive performance, especially on tasks of memory (Krendl, Ambady, & Kensinger, 2015; Levy et al., 2012).

Can these internalized stereotypes that many older adults have of aging be modified? It seems that having a positive view of your own aging may help. Fernández-Ballesteros, Bustillos, and Huici (2015) found that, in their sample of 112 adults aged 55 to 78, those individuals who had a positive perception of their own aging were less vulnerable to an activation of a negative stereotype in the stereotyped threat condition in a memory task than their same-aged counterparts who had a negative perception of their own aging. As a result, those who had a more positive view of aging showed better memory performance than those who had a poor perception of aging.

1.7 INTERVENTIONS TO DECREASE AGEISM
LEARNING OBJECTIVES

• To understand what can be done to decrease ageism and stereotypes of older adults

So, what can we do to eliminate ageism and aging stereotypes? Like other forms of social prejudice, ageism most often is imbedded in a lack of understanding and awareness of older adults. This lack of understanding can develop into inaccurate and unfair assumptions based on age (Sheridan Centre for Elder Research and Revera Inc., 2016). Spending time with older adults is a valuable way to combat ageist beliefs (see Figure 1.5). In fact, research has shown that early education about aging and providing opportunities for intergenerational experiences are keys to reducing ageism (Chorn Dunham & Casadonte, 2009; Fair & Delaplane, 2015; Gilbert & Ricketts, 2008). For example, Fair and Delaplane (2015) conducted a longitudinal study in which 31 second-grade children (Mean age = 7.6 years) participated in a year-long intergenerational service learning project. Children made monthly visits to older adults who lived in retirement communities. The teachers referred to these older adults as "grand friends." Students visited their grand friends over the course of a year. These researchers found that participating in the intergenerational service learning project over the course of a year positively influenced the young children's impressions of older adults. One 7-year-old reflected that "it is good to spend time with older adults. You can teach them; they can teach you."

Even playing a game can generate more positive views about aging. Researchers in Australia developed The Game of Late Life, a novel educational activity. They introduced students to this game in an undergraduate psychology of aging course (Brinker, Roberts, & Radnidge, 2014). The game was designed to provide transformational learning where students imagine themselves as older adults and move through late life via a game board, encountering various life events along the way. One of the key features of the game is that several of the life event outcomes (moves on the board) are dependent on how the player interprets and responds to that event. Playing the game produced significantly more positive attitudes among the students toward aging, and it also significantly reduced the anxiety that students had about aging.

It turns out that hanging out with and having quality relationships with grandparents also have a positive effect on younger adults' views of older adults. Using an online survey, Hakoyama

FIGURE 1.5

CHILDREN WITH OLDER ADULTS

Jeanette Dietl/Shutterstock.com

Having children interact with older adults on a regular basis positively influenced children's perceptions of older adults.

and MaloneBeach (2014) explored the impact of perceptions of grandparent and grandchild (GP–GC) closeness on young adults' views toward older adults in general. In a survey of 534 undergraduates who had at least one grandparent living, they rated several aspects of GP–GC relationships and their views about older adults. They found that young adult grandchildren who reported higher levels of GP–GC closeness viewed their grandparents as knowledgeable and wise. They also found that the belief that one's grandparents are knowledgeable and wise was significantly correlated with rating older adults in general as knowledgeable and wise. These authors suggest that cultivating positive relationships between GP and GC can create a pathway for decreasing the stereotypes that lead to ageism.

Finally, Sheridan Centre for Elder Research and Rivera Inc. (2016) argue that it is essential to incorporate the concept of ageism into elementary and secondary school curriculums. As a society, we need to change our way of thinking about what it means to age in the same way that society has come together to fight racism and sexism and, more recently, bullying. It also is very important to become aware of your own stereotypes of aging and challenge these beliefs. Hopefully, we all will be old some day. Would you not like to live in a society that cares for and values people at every age?

1.8 GOOD PRACTICE

Anne Lyle, B.A.
Clinic for Alzheimer's Disease and Related Disorders, University of British Columbia (UBC) Hospital
NeuroHealth Clinic

WHERE DID YOU TRAIN?

I trained at Concordia University College of Alberta in Edmonton—they offered a B.A. in applied psychology. This means that in addition to the regular psychology courses, I took a course in psychometrics and had a field placement with a brain injury rehabilitation organization. I also volunteered for about a year in Dr. Scott Purdon's lab at Alberta Hospital Edmonton. In addition to this, I worked at Alberta Hospital Edmonton as a psychiatric aide, which gave me great exposure to a variety of populations with mental health issues.

WHERE DO YOU WORK?

I currently work at the Clinic for Alzheimer's Disease and Related Disorders at the Djavad Mowafaghian Centre for Brain Health at UBC. I also work in private practice for the NeuroHealth Clinic.

WHAT DO YOU DO?

The bulk of my work is administering and scoring neuropsychological tests. The rest of my time is spent triaging the patient waitlist, ordering test materials, and researching tests and norms.

WHY DO YOU LIKE WORKING WITH AN OLDER-ADULT POPULATION?

I've always enjoyed working with older adults and it probably has something to do with me being very close to my grandparents. I value what older adults have to offer and I think this is one of the reasons we work well together as our fast-paced world doesn't always take the time to listen to what older adults have to say. I hear the best stories and have learned incredible things from them. Also, aging is a fascinating process that often is ignored or treated as something negative. This is a shame as it's part of the life cycle and a part of one's journey. Not examining aging would be like getting partway through a complex algebraic equation and stopping before you try to work out the answer.

DO YOU HAVE ADVICE FOR STUDENTS WHO WANT TO GET INTO THE FIELD?

Truthfully, I think if a student is interested in working with older adults, they should probably try to volunteer or work with organizations that cater to this population, such as nursing homes or seniors' centres. Also, it would be a good idea to take as many aging courses as they can.

Robert Frerichs, Ph.D.
Glenrose Rehabilitation Hospital, Edmonton, Alberta

WHERE DID YOU TRAIN?

University of Victoria, Victoria, British Columbia

WHERE DO YOU WORK?

The Glenrose Rehabilitation Hospital (GRH), a tertiary care facility in Edmonton, Alberta. The GRH has many services dedicated to older adults including in-patient units, day programs, outpatient geriatric assessment clinics, and a host of specialized programs run by physicians and allied healthcare professionals.

WHAT DO YOU DO?

I work as a geriatric clinical neuropsychologist. My job mostly involves conducting comprehensive neuropsychological investigations of older adults for the purpose of identifying and diagnosing different forms of cognitive impairment. I also provide education and support for individuals with dementia and their families, teach cognitive strategies for

individuals with milder forms of cognitive problems, and have a role in training soon-to-be neuropsychologists and other healthcare professionals.

WHY DO YOU LIKE WORKING WITH AN OLDER-ADULT POPULATION?

Helping others and delivering a valued healthcare service is a pretty rewarding experience regardless of the population you serve. For me, one of the reasons I particularly enjoy working with older adults is the diversity I encounter. Every person comes with their own set of strengths and challenges as well as a range of life experiences. My patients and their families, many of who are caregivers, inspire me and continually help shape my own views.

DO YOU HAVE ADVICE FOR STUDENTS WHO WANT TO GET INTO THE FIELD?

A book on aging is a fine start but I recommend reaching beyond and making contact with professionals in the field. Ask questions, job shadow, and volunteer or get involved in research with older adults to help determine if it's a good fit for you.

Colleen Bamber, B.Sc., O.T.
Villa Caritas, Geriatric Psychiatry, Edmonton, Alberta

WHERE DID YOU TRAIN?

Occupational Therapy Program, Department of Rehabilitation Medicine, University of Alberta

WHERE DO YOU WORK?

I work in the Organic Disorders units at Villa Caritas.

WHAT DO YOU DO?

I assess functional status in patients with organic disorders such as a dementia. For example, I assess the functional abilities that are needed to manage one's daily life. I provide programs (psychosocial, cognitive, and physical) to patients, and I provide appropriate equipment for patients such as wheelchairs and footwear. I also assist with the identification of the level of care a patient needs once discharged.

WHY DO YOU LIKE WORKING WITH AN OLDER-ADULT POPULATION?

I enjoy working with older adults. There is a mix of physical and mental components to the work I do in assessment and treatment. Our older adults have a wealth of experience even though some have a dementia. They are a very special population and they deserve to be treated with respect and dignity. I like working with older adults because I feel I am able to make a significant difference

(positive although time limited) in patients' lives. I use my skills to work towards the goal of functional improvement and/or maintenance. My aim is to maximize the patient's well-being through an adapted environment, personal contact, and supportive activities as well as to provide skills training.

DO YOU HAVE ADVICE FOR STUDENTS WHO WANT TO GET INTO THE FIELD?

Occupational therapy offers a variety of skills in many areas to improve mental and physical capacity. You can make a difference! Treat people with dementia as unique individuals who have similar needs to individuals who do not have a dementia: the need to be respected and recognized, and the need to maintain self-worth.

1.9 SUMMARY

- Gerontology, from the Greek words for "old man" and "study of," was coined by Ilya Ilyich Mechnikov in 1903. It is the study of the social, psychological, cognitive, and biological aspects of aging.

- In Canada, systematic research on aging began around 1944. The Canadian Association on Gerontology, the Canadian Geriatrics Society, and the Canadian Gerontological Nursing Association are important aging organizations in Canada as is the Canadian Coalition for Seniors' Mental Health.

- The Institute of Aging has been a key factor in the growth of research investigating health and aging in Canada. It is funding a Canada-wide research project called the Canadian Longitudinal Study on Aging.

- Lifespan development is influenced by four factors: age-graded

influences, history-graded influences, normative influences, and non-normative influences.

- Age can be measured in various ways. Although chronological age is the most widely used, it is not the best measure. Other ways to measure age are by looking at the biological, psychological, and sociological age of individuals. However, the best way to measure age is by understanding a person's functional age.

- There are three different processes involved in aging: primary aging, secondary aging, and tertiary aging.

- There is tremendous variability in the cognitive and physical abilities of those individuals who are 65 years of age or older.

- Some researchers divide those 65 years of age and older into groupings of young-old, old-old, and the oldest-old. Other researchers divide older adults into third age (between 50 and 75 years of age) and fourth age (76 years and older). In general, we know a considerable amount about "young older adults" (young-old or third age) but not about old-older adults (old-old and oldest-old, or fourth age).

- Immigration contributes significantly to the ethno-cultural diversity observed in those aged 65 and over.

- We are an aging society. In fact, population aging is going to become one of the most significant social changes of the 21st century. Globally, the oldest-old are growing even faster than the number of older persons overall. Japan is home to the world's oldest population.

- A significant decline in the global birth rate has been put forth to explain global aging. Currently in Canada, the total fertility rate is below the replacement level. Population pyramids are starting to look more like columns, and for the first time in many countries, there will be more older adults than children.

- A baby boom is a sudden rise in the number of births from year to year. Between 1946 and 1965, Canada experienced a postwar baby boom; people born during this time are called baby boomers. Of note is that the baby boom generation does not like the term seniors and prefers to be called older adults, older persons, or boomers.

- Traditionally, it was believed that Eastern collectivist cultures adopt a more positive view of aging and respect and honour older adults, while Western cultures hold more individualistic values and more negative beliefs of old age. However, the research supporting these differences is mixed with some studies finding more negative views of aging among Eastern cultures.

- *Ageism* refers to the "systematic stereotyping of, and discrimination against, people because they are old." Many Canadians believe that ageism is the most tolerated form of social prejudice ranking above racism and sexism.

- The three most common forms of age discrimination faced by Canadian older adults are being ignored, being thought of as having nothing to contribute, and others assuming that they are incompetent simply because of age. Canadian women 66 years of age and older are more likely than men to say they have been treated unfairly because of their age.

- According to Terror Management Theory, we hold negative stereotypes and beliefs about older adults because it helps us to deal with or avoid the anxiety that is associated with our own death.

- Ageism breeds the stereotypes and myths about older adults. Ageism often is fueled by the media. However, this is slowly starting to change as businesses change their marketing strategies in order to tap into this large cohort which has more money to spend than previous generations.

- Negative self-stereotyping is the process where older adults internalize aging stereotypes. This can negatively affect an older adult's cognitive performance, self-efficacy, and health.

- Stereotyped threat refers to the fear of being judged in accordance with a negative stereotype of the group you belong to. Having a positive view of aging can counteract the effects of stereotypes.

- Early education about aging and providing opportunities for intergenerational experiences are key to reducing ageism.

Key Terms

Ageism
A form of discrimination against older adults based on age alone.

Baby Boom
A sudden rise in the number of births observed from year to year.

Baby Boomers
People born in the postwar baby boom (1946–1965).

Biological Age
A description of a person's development based on the aging of various physical systems.

Centenarian
An individual who lives to be 100 to 110 years.

Chronological Age
The number of years a person has lived.

Confucianism
A system of philosophical and ethical teachings founded by Confucius.

Established Immigrants
An individual who has been a permanent resident of Canada for more than 10 years.

Family Class Immigrants
Immigrants who were sponsored by their families to come to Canada.

Fertility Replacement Level
The average number of children born per woman at which a population exactly replaces itself from one generation to the next, without migration. This rate is roughly 2.1 children per woman for most countries, although it may modestly vary with mortality rates.

Filial Piety
In Confucian philosophy, filial piety is a virtue of respect for one's parents, elders, and ancestors.

First Age
One of the four ages of life, with this age described as from youth to the early 20s.

Fourth Age
One of the four ages of life, with this age described as older than 75 years of age.

Functional Age
A measure of how well an individual can function in his or her environment. This measure takes into account biological, psychological, and social age, as well as the environmental influences.

G8 Countries
Refers to the group of eight highly industrialized nations—Canada, France, Germany, Italy, Japan, the United Kingdom, the United States, and Russia—that hold an annual meeting to foster consensus on global issues like economic growth and crisis management, global security, energy, and terrorism.

Gerontology
The scientific study of aging.

Negative Self-Stereotyping
When an older adult believes the negative stereotypes associated with aging and integrates these concepts into his or her self-concept.

Non-normative Influences
Random, unexpected events that are unique to an individual. Winning the lottery would be an example of a non-normative event.

Normative Age-Graded Influences
Normal age-related changes that most people experience. Puberty and menopause are examples of normative age-graded influences.

Normative History-Graded Influences
Influences that are experienced by most people in a specific area or culture at the same time. These tend to be large in scale like

the recent war in Syria or the terrorist attacks in Belgium in 2016.

Primary Aging
Normal, disease-free development during adulthood.

Psychological Age
An attempt to understand development by how an individual thinks, reasons, and acts independent of chronological age.

Recent Immigrants
Individuals who have been a permanent resident of Canada for less than 10 years.

Second Age z
One of the four ages of life, with this age described as from the early 20s through the 40s.

Secondary Aging
The physical or cognitive changes that are related to lifestyle, disease, or injury and are not part of the normal aging process.

Social Age
A measure of how well a person's behaviour fits with the norms or expectations that society has for a person of a particular age.

Stereotyped Threat
Fear of being judged in accordance with a negative stereotype of the group you belong to.

Terror Management Theory
A theory that proposes a basic psychological conflict that results from having a desire to live but realizing that death is inevitable. This conflict produces terror, and is believed to be unique to human beings. It explains why people engage in certain behaviours to reduce this conflict.

Tertiary Aging
The rapid decrease in cognitive and functional ability in the years prior to death.

Third Age
One of the four ages of life, with this age described as from roughly 50 to 75 years of age.

CHAPTER
02

RESEARCH DESIGNS AND ETHICAL ISSUES

Jim West/Alamy Stock Photo

CHAPTER OUTLINE

"Research is to see what everybody else has seen, and to think what nobody else has thought."

Albert Szent-Györgyi

Adults aged 65 and over are one of the fastest-growing segments of the Canadian population, with an anticipated 10 million individuals 65 and older in Canada by 2035 (Statistics Canada, 2015). This demographic change has widespread implications in many areas of our society including the economy (e.g., changes in labour force participation), the healthcare system (e.g., delivery of healthcare services to meet the demands of an aging population), and social structures (e.g., appropriate housing to meet the needs of an aging population). A commonality among all these areas is the need for research to better understand the impact of, and prepare for, the changes that will occur because of our aging population. In this chapter, you will learn about the methods used to study the process of aging, as well as the ethical issues that have relevance for aging research.

2.1 RESEARCH ON AGING AND THE AGING PROCESS

LEARNING OBJECTIVES

To understand:

- research designs to study the process of aging
- the advantages and disadvantages of each of the research designs in the context of aging research

RESEARCH DESIGNS TO STUDY THE PROCESS OF AGING

The study of aging (**gerontology**) is multidisciplinary involving three core disciplines—biology, psychology, and sociology. However, many other disciplines such as anthropology, criminology, geography, linguistics, and political science also contribute to the knowledge base. Research on aging across the disciplines not only helps us to understand adult development in general; it also helps to dispel common misconceptions about aging (Tergesen, 2014, November 30; see Box 2.1).

After reading Box 2.1, you can see that research plays an important role in dispelling myths about aging. There are three basic research designs used when conducting research on older adults: cross-sectional, longitudinal, and sequential. Every study of adult development is built on three building blocks: age, cohort, and time of measurement (Cavanaugh & Whitbourne, 2003). **Age effects** reflect differences, such as biological, psychological, or sociocultural changes, as the consequences of growing older. **Cohort effects** are differences as a result of having been born in a certain time or region, or having experienced the same life experience (in the same time period), with these experiences or circumstances unique to the group in question. **Time of measurement effects** reflect differences due to cultural, historical, environmental, or other events at the time that the data are collected. As you will soon learn, different research designs used in aging research attempt to identify and separate out these three effects.

BOX 2.1

STEREOTYPES OF AGING

Everyone knows that as we age, our minds and bodies decline—and life inevitably becomes less satisfying and enjoyable. Everyone knows that cognitive decline is inevitable. Everyone knows that as we get older, we become less productive at work. Everyone, it seems, is wrong.

Contrary to the stereotype of later life as a time of loneliness, depression, and decline, a growing body of scientific research shows that, in many ways, life gets better as we get older. "The story used to be that satisfaction with life went downhill, but the remarkable thing that researchers are finding is that doesn't seem to be the case," says Timothy Salthouse, a professor of psychology at the University of Virginia. In fact, a growing body of evidence indicates that our moods and overall sense of well-being improve with age. Friendships tend to grow more intimate, too, as older adults prioritize what matters most to them, says Karen Fingerman, a professor of human development and family sciences at the University of Texas at Austin. Other academics have found that knowledge and certain types of intelligence continue to develop in ways that can even offset age-related declines in the brain's ability to process new information and reason abstractly. Expertise deepens, which can enhance productivity and creativity. Some go so far as to say that wisdom—defined, in part, as the ability to resolve conflicts by seeing problems from multiple perspectives—flourishes. To be sure, growing older has its share of challenges. Some people do not age as well as others. And especially at advanced ages, chronic conditions including diabetes, hypertension, and dementia become increasingly common and can take a toll on mental, as well as physical, health. Still, those who fall into the "stereotype of being depressed, cranky, irritable and obsessed with their alimentary canal" constitute "no more than 10 percent of the older population," says Paul Costa, a scientist emeritus at the National Institutes of Health, who for more than three decades directed the personality program of the long-running Baltimore Longitudinal Study of Aging. "The other 90 percent of the population isn't like that at all." Dr. Costa says.

Source: Tergesen, A. (2014, November 30). Why everything you think about aging may be wrong. *The Wall Street Journal*. Retrieved from http://www.wsj.com/articles/why-everything-you-think-about-aging-may-be-wrong-1417408057.

REFLECTIVE QUESTION

As you ponder the statements above, does it challenge any ideas you may have about getting older?

CROSS-SECTIONAL DESIGNS

In studies using the **cross-sectional design**, data are gathered from a cross-section (a slice of the population) at a specific point in time. The data are collected at the same time or during the same time period (e.g., 2016) from people who are similar on a number of characteristics (e.g., community-dwelling Canadians, place of residence in Canada) but who differ on other key

FIGURE 2.1

Cross-Sectional Design

Cohort	Time of Measurement			
---	1980	1990	2000	2010
1925	65	75	85	95
1935	55	65	75	85
1945	45	55	65	75
1955	35	45	55	65
1965	25	35	45	55

characteristics (e.g., age, income levels, and gender). When using the cross-sectional design in research on aging, participants usually are separated into groups or **cohorts** (e.g., participants born in 1925, 1935, 1945, 1955 and 1965), with the results reported for each of the cohorts being studied (see Figure 2.1).

There are both advantages and disadvantages to the cross-sectional design. The advantages are that this design allows for a comparison across different age groups at a single point in time. As such, studies using a cross-sectional design take less time to carry out and often are less costly to perform than studies using longitudinal or sequential designs. Studies using a cross-sectional design also allow researchers to compare many different **variables** from different age groups/ cohorts at the same time.

One of the major disadvantages of the cross-sectional design in the context of aging research is that the results tell us only about **age differences** and not about **age changes**. For example, if we measured the heights of different men aged 20 to 80, we likely would find, on average, that men in their 20s are taller than men in their 80s. We could conclude that there are significant age differences in height. However, even though we shrink with age, the height of older men is very similar to their height when they were younger. Thus, very little of the difference in height between younger and older men is due to changes in height because of the aging process (e.g., age changes). Rather, the difference in height between the younger and older men in our study is most likely due to changes in diet and health over the years with younger men on average much taller than their grandfathers (Kausler, Kausler, & Krupsaw, 2007).

The second major disadvantage of a cross-sectional design in terms of aging research is the presence of cohort effects. For example, let's suppose we conduct a study on whether older individuals take longer to learn how to use the computer than do younger individuals. We enroll individuals aged 25 and younger and individuals aged 65 and older and test them on how to use a "new" computer. The results indicate that the older participants take longer to learn how to use the computer than do younger participants. Can we conclude that older adults are slower learners when it comes to computers? Not necessarily. That is, we need to think about what factors other than age might be responsible for these differences. One of the factors that likely affects our findings is familiarity with computers. That is, individuals younger than 45 grew up with computers or were still relatively young when the computer was introduced. On the other hand, individuals 65 years of age and older spent most of their lives (45 years or more) without a computer. Having not grown up in a technologically centred age, many older adults have had less training, less knowledge, and far less experience with a computer compared to individuals who are younger. This difference in exposure (cohort effect), rather than age per se, most likely accounts for the differences in the time taken to learn to use the "new" computer between the two age groups. Can you see how using cross-sectional designs can be problematic? One of the major problems with this design is that it's difficult to know for certain if changes that are seen between an older and a younger sample of participants are due to cohort effects or age effects.

LONGITUDINAL DESIGNS

Unlike cross-sectional designs, **longitudinal designs** involve following the same group of people over an extended period of time, collecting data on the same measures of interest at two or more points in time (see Figure 2.2). One of the major advantages of this design is that it allows for assessment of age changes because the same participants are tested over time. Another advantage of this design is that, typically, all the participants are from the same cohort (e.g., all born in the year 1925), which increases the probability that the changes that are identified are age-related and not due to cohort effects.

A major disadvantage of studies using a longitudinal design is that the researchers cannot separate out **maturation effects** (e.g., age effects) from **time of measurement effects**. The amount of time required to conduct studies using a longitudinal design also is a disadvantage (for the participants and the researchers!). These types of studies also are very expensive to conduct. As you can imagine, following research participants for years and collecting data on a regular basis (every year for a number of years) is both time consuming and expensive (see Box 2.2). Another disadvantage of this type of design is that **practice effects** may threaten the validity of a study in that participants who are repeatedly tested and interviewed may become increasingly familiar with the study measures. As a result, there may be improvements in performance that are unrelated to the normal patterns of development. Also, this type of research design is subject to high drop-out rates (known as participant **attrition**), which can result in smaller and non-representative samples. This, in turn, can weaken the **internal validity** of the study. Another limitation of the longitudinal research design is the uniqueness of the study environment. This uniqueness may affect the **external validity** of the study such that the findings are not **generalizable**.

The Nun Study, portrayed in Box 2.3, is an example of a longitudinal design (Snowdon, 1997). One of the advantages of studying the sisters from the School Sisters of Notre Dame is

FIGURE 2.2

EXAMPLE OF A LONGITUDINAL RESEARCH DESIGN

Longitudinal Design				
Cohort	Time of Measurement			
---	1980	1990	2000	2010
1925	65	75	85	95
1935	55	65	75	85
1945	45	55	65	75
1955	35	45	55	65
1965	25	35	45	55

BOX 2.2

THE CHALLENGES OF LONGITU-DINAL RESEARCH DESIGNS

Longitudinal studies are not for the faint of heart! For example, once the study is designed, numerous procedures must be put into place to ensure that the data are collected with fidelity to the scientific goals. These steps can take weeks to months or even longer. In studies that involve cohorts from multiple centres, it is typical to spend a year or more developing and beginning to implement the study design before actually launching the study. Time is needed to hire and train staff and to lay the groundwork for recruitment. The ethics application needs to be written and submitted, with approval sometimes taking months. Participant recruitment often is a challenge in any study, and even more so in longitudinal studies. A successful longitudinal study is proactive in retaining participants. Numerous aspects of study operation lead to successful retention. For example, regular contacts for follow-up, newsletters, and birthday and holiday cards maintain the relationship between partici-pants and research staff over the course of the study. There also is the need for regular tracking of data collection, and processes need to be in place for identifying poten-tial problems related to data collection and generating solutions. Ongoing data entry is critical, and keeping up with data entry and running quality checks on the data can consume enormous amounts of time and study resources. And, the process of writing up the results and submitting for publication can take months and sometimes years!

Source: Newman, A. (2010). An overview of the design, implementation, and analyses of longi-tudinal studies on aging. *Journal of the Amer-ican Geriatrics Society, 58*(Suppl 2), S287–S291. doi:10.1111/j.1532-5415.2010.02916.x

BOX 2.3

CASE STUDY THE NUN STUDY

One of the most interesting longitudinal studies to date is what is affectionately known as the Nun Study. This research, which began in 1986 as a pilot study using data collected from the covenant of School Sisters of Notre Dame living in Mankato, Minnesota, was expanded in 1990 to include nuns of the order living in other convents in the Midwestern, Eastern, and Southern regions of the United States. One of the main goals of the research, carried out by Dr. David A. Snowdon and his colleagues, was to identify the causes of Alzheimer's disease and other brain diseases, as well as to develop a better understanding of the cognitive and physical changes associated with normal aging. Over the years, the 678 nuns who participated in the study agreed to repeated examina-tion of their physical and cognitive abilities, as well as providing regular blood samples for genetic and nutritional studies. In addi-tion, the diaries that the nuns kept since they took their first vows at a very early age were regularly inspected for depth and com-plexity of writing. Each nun who participated agreed to donate their brain upon death for further study. The Nun Study has resulted in researchers finding out more than was ever known before about the developmental pat-tern of Alzheimer's disease as well as valuable knowledge about the cognitive and physical changes that occur in normal aging.

Source: Snowdon, D.A. (1997). Aging and Alzheimer's disease: Lessons from the Nun's Study. *The Geron-tologist, 37*(2), 150–156. doi:10.1093/geront/37.2.150

that the participants have homogeneous lifestyles and background. That is, they had the same reproductive history and marital status; were non-smokers and did not drink excessive amounts of alcoholic beverages; had similar occupations, income, and socioeconomic status; had similar social activities and support; and had access to similar preventive, nursing, and other medical-care services. This meant that many of the factors that confound most epidemiologic studies were eliminated or minimized in this study.

Before discussing sequential designs, consider longitudinal studies that have been conducted on aging. How many do you think have been done worldwide? How many in Canada? Given the complexity and expense of longitudinal studies, the numbers might surprise you. To the best of our knowledge, there have been 132 longitudinal studies conducted worldwide and seven in Canada. (see Table 2.1). If you are interested in seeing all 132 longitudinal studies, go to http://www.ncbi.nlm.nih.gov/pmc/articles/PMC3483563/#SD1.

SEQUENTIAL DESIGNS

One of the challenges of studying aging is that age cannot be manipulated—meaning that the variable that we are most interested in can never be a true **independent variable**. Also, it's difficult to isolate the effects of aging from other effects because aging does not occur in a vacuum. Rather, the process of aging is surrounded by historical, social, and economic events that influence the lives of individuals and groups as they age. **Sequential designs**, which were the brainchild of K. Warner Schaie in the 1960s, allow researchers to separate out at least some of the effects of aging from cohort and time of measurement effects. This is done by combining cross-sectional and longitudinal designs in the same

TABLE 2.1

LONGITUDINAL STUDIES ON AGING IN CANADA			
STUDY NAME	ACRONYM	NUMBER OF PARTICIPANTS	INFORMATION SITE
Aging in Manitoba Longitudinal Study	AIM	350	http://www.statcan.gc.ca/pub/82-581-x/2006001/projects/4078827-eng.htm
Canadian Multicentre Osteoporosis Study	CaMos	9423	http://camos.org
Canadian Longitudinal Study on Aging	CLSA	50 000	http://www.clsa-elcv.ca
Canadian Study of Health and Aging	CSHA	10 263	http://www.csha.ca
Manitoba Follow-Up Study	MFUS	3983	http://www.mfus.ca
Ontario Longitudinal Study of Aging	OLSA	2000	No link found
Victoria Longitudinal Study	VLS	1064	http://www.ualberta.ca/~vlslab

Source: Erten-Lyons, D., Sherbakov, L.O., Piccinin, A.M., Hofer, S.M., Dodge, H.H., Quinn, J.F., . . . Kaye, J.A. (2012). Review of selected databases of longitudinal studies. *Alzheimer's & Dementia, 8*(6), 584–589. doi:10.1016/j.jalz.2011.09.232. Retrieved from http://www.ncbi.nlm.nih.gov/pmc/articles/PMC3483563/#SD1.

study (Schaie & Caskie, 2005). There are different types of sequential designs. The three that we discuss are the **cohort-sequential design**, the **time-sequential design**, and the **cross-sequential design**. Each has advantages and disadvantages. Let's turn now and look at the cohort-sequential designs.

The cohort-sequential design consists of two or more cross-sectional studies done at two different time periods. The advantage of this design is that it separates (isolates) age and cohort effects. However, time of measurement effects cannot be separated out, so this type of design is best when time of measurement effects are expected to be minimal or trivial. In our example (see Figure 2.3), two different cohorts (1925 and 1935) are compared at two different ages (65 and 75). At the end of the study, if there are significant differences between the two cohorts on the measures of interest, we can conclude that the time of birth influences the variable/variables being measured. On the other hand, if both cohorts show similar scores (or similar patterns of consistency *or* change) on the variable/variables of interest. We can conclude that the results reflect the intrinsic aging process. We also could find that the differences in performance between the two cohorts across the two time periods are different. This pattern would lead us to look for whether there were other differences between the two cohorts (e.g., different early life experiences) that affected their later life performance on the variable/variables of interest.

As noted earlier, the other types of sequential designs are the time-sequential and cross-sequential. The time-sequential design compares two or more cross-sectional samples at two or more times of measurement. As such, this sequential design is useful for distinguishing between age and time of measurement effects. The cross-sequential design combines a cross-sectional and a longitudinal design. Although this design is an improvement over independent cross-sectional and longitudinal designs, there still is a confound between age and time of measurement.

In this section of the chapter, we have discussed several advantages and disadvantages of cross-sectional, longitudinal, and sequential designs in aging research, which are summarized in Table 2.2.

Decisions on which design you wish to use when conducting research with older adults will depend on many factors including your research questions, the population you wish to study, recruitment, the expertise of your research team, funding availability, and ethical approval. Let's turn now and look at ethical considerations in research with older adults.

FIGURE 2.3

EXAMPLE OF A COHORT-SEQUENTIAL DESIGN

Cross-Sequential Design				
Cohort	Time of Measurement			
---	1980	1990	2000	2010
1925	65	75	85	95
1935	55	65	75	85
1945	45	55	65	75
1955	35	45	55	65
1965	25	35	45	55

TABLE 2.2

ADVANTAGES AND DISADVANTAGES OF THE THREE MAIN RESEARCH DESIGNS IN AGING RESEARCH		
	ADVANTAGES	**DISADVANTAGES**
Cross-sectional	• Useful for examining age differences.	• Does not allow for identification of age changes. • Age and cohort effects are confounded.
Longitudinal	• Useful for examining age changes. • May allow for separating out age and cohort effects.	• Age and time of measurement effects are confounded.
Sequential		
• Cohort-sequential	• Useful for separating out age and cohort effects.	• Time of measurement effects cannot be separated out.
• Time-sequential	• Useful for separating out age and time of measurement effects.	• Cohort and time of measurement effects are confounded.
• Cross-sequential	• Eliminates age as a factor.	• Age and time of measurement effects are confounded.

2.2 ETHICAL ISSUES IN THE CONTEXT OF AGING RESEARCH

LEARNING OBJECTIVES

To understand:

- ethical issues in the context of aging
- the concepts of informed consent, the right to withdraw, and confidentiality of data

There are a number of ethical issues when conducting research with human participants. The three ethical issues that we discuss, in the context of conducting research with older adults, are informed consent, the right to withdraw, and confidentiality of data.

INFORMED CONSENT

Informed consent is a mandatory and basic right of all individuals who participate in research. As defined by the Government of Canada's Panel on Research Ethics, consent to participate in research is defined as "free, informed, and ongoing consent" (Government of Canada, 2014a), with the terms "free" and "voluntary" used interchangeably. One of the key issues related to informed consent is how it is obtained. That is, *who* approaches the individual, *how* an individual is approached, and *when* the individual is approached are important considerations. Elements of trust and dependency in relationships can affect voluntary consent. For example, the individual being recruited may feel pressured to follow the wishes of those who have some form of control over them. This control can be professional, physical, psychological, or financial (e.g., physician–patient relationship; adult child–parent relationships). **Coercion**, which is a more extreme form of **undue influence**, can negate the voluntariness of a decision to participate or remain in a research study. Large or very attractive incentives (monetary or otherwise) for participation in research also can result in undue influence and negate voluntary participation. The key to informed consent is that prospective participants understand the information being conveyed to them by researchers. As such, information on the study, its purpose, how participants are selected, the methods and procedures, and possible risks and benefits are foundational to voluntary participation in research, with research beginning only after the participants (or their authorized third parties) have provided their consent. The 2014 Tri-Council Policy Statement (TCPS): Ethical Conduct for Research Involving Humans (Government of Canada, 2014b) stipulates that evidence of consent is demonstrated either in a signed consent form or in documentation by the researcher of another appropriate means of consent.

An important consideration in research on aging is the inclusion of individuals who lack the capacity to decide for themselves as to whether they wish to participate in research. Individuals with a progressive dementia such as Alzheimer's disease are, by definition, on a path of declining capacity to consent to research. Yet, research in this population is needed to further our understanding about the cause(s), treatment(s), and prevention of the disease. Moreover, the TCPS 2 (2014) (also known as the TCPS-2) has indicated that "those who lack the capacity to decide on their own behalf must neither be unfairly excluded from the potential benefits of research participation, nor may their lack of decision-making capacity be used to inappropriately include them in research" (see Government of Canada, 2014b, Section C, p. 43). The challenge for Research Ethics Boards (REBs) (and researchers) is to be aware of these ethical considerations and seek to find a balance between the benefits and potential risks for prospective participants (Government of Canada, 2104b). In instances where a participant lacks capacity to understand informed consent, **proxies** can serve as substitute decision makers and provide consent.

RIGHT TO WITHDRAW

If you were to look at a consent form for participation in research, you most likely would find a sentence that says, "You have a right to withdraw from this study at any time without penalty." The right to withdraw from participation in research is recognized in virtually all national and international guidelines for research on human subjects (Schaefer & Wertheimer, 2010). In addition to including a statement on the right to withdraw from the study, a statement about whether withdrawal of data is possible should be included. For example, in some regulated clinical trials, when a participant withdraws from the study, the data collected from the participant to the point of withdrawal remain as part of the study database. If data withdrawal is not possible—at all, or after a certain time point—this should be communicated in the Information Letter provided to participants.

CONFIDENTIALITY OF DATA

Confidentiality of data also is an important consideration when conducting research with human subjects. Participants need to be informed about how confidentiality or anonymity (if applicable) will be achieved and/or maintained. Participants also need to be informed on issues such as who will have access to the research data and where it will be kept (e.g., on a password-protected computer, with the file encrypted) and how the results of the study will be disseminated (e.g., presented at academic conferences or published in academic journals). In addition, participants should be informed about **anonymity**. Finally, participants need to be informed about how long the data will be kept and how it will be destroyed.

Earlier in this chapter, we discussed the importance of having vulnerable populations, such as those with dementia, participate in research. And we discussed some ethical considerations for research participation from the perspective of the individual with dementia. In 2015, Pachana, Liddle, Peel, Juang, & Knight (2015) did an interesting study in which they reviewed 157 researchers' experiences in Australia and the United States with regard to submitting ethical proposals using older adults with and without a dementia. Six main issues were raised by the Ethical Review Boards. These are listed in Table 2.3. As you can see, informed consent was a main issue for almost two-thirds of the Ethical Review Boards.

In addition to the issues identified above, Pachana and her colleagues (2015) also found that the main area of concern from the researchers was "not hearing older adults' voices: exclusions based on assumptions" (Pachana et al., 2015, p. 703). That is, the researchers described how restrictions and delays in trying to move their research using older adults through the ethics process often resulted in a loss of older adult participants. They also stated that the overly restrictive practices of conducting research with older adults, and particularly those older adults with a dementia, impede the participation of the very people needed for the development of clinical interventions. There was a general consensus among the researchers that many of the ethics boards made assumptions about older adults that were not realistic and that were overly protective and potentially ageist. As you can see, individuals who sit on ethics boards are subjected to the same biases and stereotypes present in the general population. Pachana and colleagues concluded that the ethics boards involved in the survey tended to see all older adults as vulnerable because of their age. They also pointed out that it may be helpful for those who sit on ethics boards to remember that all older adults are not in poor health or cognitively impaired. Pachana and colleagues also suggested that an important guideline for committees when looking at ethics applications involving older adults is self-reflection on potential biases and stereotypes that committee members may have, which may, in turn, influence their decision to approve the research.

TABLE 2.3

ISSUES RAISED BY ETHICAL REVIEW BOARDS ON RESEARCH APPLICATIONS THAT INCLUDED OLDER ADULTS WITH AND WITHOUT A DEMENTIA	
MAIN ISSUES RAISED BY ETHICAL REVIEW BOARDS	**PERCENT**
Consent and Information Requirements	61.0
Participant Vulnerability	58.6
Participant Burden	44.6
Data Access	29.3
Study Methodology	25.5

Source: Pachana, N.A., Liddle, J., Peel, N.M., Juang, C., & Knight, B.G. (2015). Can we do better? Researchers' experience with ethical review boards on projects with a late life focus. *Journal of Alzheimer's Disease, 43*(3), 701–707. doi: 10.3233/JAD-141956.

Can you think of other ethical issues that might arise when conducting research with older adults?

Earlier, we mentioned the 2014 Tri-Council Policy Statement: Ethical Conduct for Research Involving Humans (Government of Canada, 2014b). This document reflects the work of the Canadian Institutes of Health Research, the Natural Sciences and Engineering Research Council of Canada, and the Social Sciences and Humanities Research Council of Canada. The TCPS 2 (2014), as it is commonly known, is an updated and expanded version of the 1998 TCPS. An underlying value of the TCPS 2 (2014) is that researchers have a respect for human dignity when conducting research. However, the TCPS 2 (2014) also recognizes that both researchers and REB members navigate a "sometimes difficult course between the two main goals of providing the necessary protection of participants and serving the legitimate requirements of research" (Government of Canada, 2014b, p. 9). The TCPS 2 (2014) guidelines, which are based on the three core principles of respect for persons, concern for welfare, and justice, are designed to assist researchers and REB members in this journey. One of the changes that is most relevant to research on older adults is the clarification that consent is based on decision-making capacity and not chronological age. Many of you reading this may go on to participate in research or conduct research yourselves. You can learn more about the guidelines for conducting research by going to http://www.pre.ethics.gc.ca/eng/policy-politique/initiatives/tcps2-eptc2/Default/. The guidelines really are an interesting read.

As you continue to read this book, you will see that much more research needs to be done in most areas of aging. Conducting ethical research is paramount and the central role of ethics boards is to ensure that ethical research is conducted. Notably, given the current and projected increases in the number of individuals with dementia, the development of a national strategy regarding policies for research with older adults with and without a dementia is much needed.

2.3 GOOD PRACTICE

Stacy Podetz, Psy.D.
Saskatoon Health Region, Department of Seniors' Health and Continuing Care, Saskatoon, Saskatchewan

WHERE DID YOU TRAIN?

I received a Bachelor of Science (Honours in psychology) at St. Francis Xavier University in Antigonish, Nova Scotia in 2005. I completed a Master of Arts in clinical psychology at Saint Michael's College in Burlington, Vermont, in 2008. I then went on to complete my Doctor of Psychology in clinical psychology (Psy.D.) at Antioch University, New England, in 2013. I completed my pre-doctoral residency with the Saskatoon Health Region in 2013.

WHERE DO YOU WORK?

Currently, I work within all the 30 long-term-care (LTC) homes in the Saskatoon

Health Region, which are home to a diverse and complex population of residents. Individuals who live in these 30 LTC homes are unable to live independently in the community for a variety of health, mental health, cognitive, and/or behavioural reasons. The conditions with which individuals suffer include dementia, acquired brain injuries, and complex medical conditions such as quadriplegia, morbid obesity, and post-stroke syndromes. Common to residents living in care are neuro-degenerative conditions such as Huntington's disease, Parkinson's disease, other degenerative dementias, as well as genetic/congenital disorders (e.g., Prader-Willi syndrome, spina bifida, and cerebral palsy). As with any community, there is a full range of mental health issues and diagnoses, including bipolar disorder, schizophrenia, depression, anxiety, as well as personality disorders. The full lifespan is represented with people ranging in age from 3 to 105 years old. However, I primarily work with the adult population. Some residents have lived in long-term care for all or most of their lives; for others, LTC is a new experience.

WHAT DO YOU DO?

Within my role as psychologist, I provide adult therapy with an emphasis on geriatrics and complex medical needs. I am involved with diagnostic assessments, consultation, and education regarding individuals with dementia, trauma, grief and loss, personality disorders, and other cognitive and/or co-morbid mental health disorders. I have the opportunity to work within several multidisciplinary teams including physicians, nursing, psychiatry, social work, occupational therapy, physical therapy, and speech–language pathology.

WHY DO YOU LIKE WORKING WITH AN OLDER-ADULT POPULATION?

The great degree of variety and complexity within the aging population was initially appealing to me as a new graduate. My expectations did not disappoint as I have been afforded the opportunity of an expansive clinical experience with a wide range of severity and symptomatology.

On a more personal note, I have always been drawn to working with the aging and elderly population as the healthcare field underserves and overlooks mental health in this population. Simply providing a space to be heard can be an incredibly powerful intervention for those who have faced such oppression within the healthcare setting. Furthermore, helping other care providers see the benefit of providing space to be heard enriches the quality of life of those living in long-term care.

DO YOU HAVE ADVICE FOR STUDENTS WHO WANT TO GET INTO THE FIELD?

Working within after long-term care (LTC) challenges our traditional boundaries as psychologists. We meet in our clients' homes and join their communities of family, caregivers, and friends. A resident who has been living in LTC for over 40 years once asked if I planned to bring in a picture from my recent wedding. He explained that although I am his psychologist for one hour each week, I am an important part of his and others' community the rest of the week. They were excited for me, just as other members of my community were, and wanted to join in my joy. The significance of our roles in residents' lives is greater than simply our roles as psychologists. This presents the challenge of dual roles and a need for transparency and clarity within those roles. From this challenge, however, some of the most meaningful personal and professional experiences emerge.

Leslie Pisani, M.S.W.
Hys Centre Medical Clinic, Community Geriatrics, Edmonton, Alberta

WHERE DID YOU TRAIN?

I received my Bachelor of Social Work degree in 1983 and my Master of Social Work with a clinical specialization in 2011, both from the University of Calgary–Edmonton Program.

WHERE DO YOU WORK?

I work for Covenant Health in community geriatric psychiatry.

WHAT DO YOU DO?

I see patients in consultation with psychiatrists or community therapists and I carry a caseload of individuals for whom I am their therapist. In addition, I am the co-therapist for various groups. My clients are older adults with psychiatric conditions and complex personal, family, social, legal, and/or financial concerns.

WHY DO YOU LIKE WORKING WITH AN OLDER-ADULT POPULATION?

I have always appreciated the wisdom my clients have shared with me. They are usually very appreciative of empathetic efforts to help them help themselves.

DO YOU HAVE ADVICE FOR STUDENTS WHO WANT TO GET INTO THE FIELD?

Expose yourself to many learning opportunities as they will be useful throughout your career. Seeking the strengths in yourself and your clients will keep hope in your life and their lives.

Fern Stockdale-Winder, Ph.D.
Saskatoon Health Region, Saskatoon, Saskatchewan

WHERE DID YOU TRAIN?

I completed my master's and my Ph.D. training at the University of Saskatchewan in Saskatoon, Saskatchewan. I had the good fortune of doing my pre-doctoral internship at the Nova Scotia Hospital in Dartmouth, Nova Scotia, from 1994 to 1995. While I was there I had the chance to work with the Seniors Mental Health Team, one of the first in the country. One of the highlights of my training was driving out to rural Nova Scotia and doing home visits with seniors and their families.

WHERE DO YOU WORK?

I work at Saskatoon City Hospital in Saskatoon, Saskatchewan.

WHAT DO YOU DO?

I am currently a psychologist at the Rehabilitation Centre, Saskatoon City Hospital, Saskatoon Health Region. I provide psychology services to a 34-bed in-patient unit. I see patients who range in age from 12 to 94, and approximately 25 percent of my caseload is over the age of 65. Patients who attend our unit are generally here for several weeks, and are recovering from a variety of medical events including stroke, spinal cord injury, brain injury, amputation, and other neurological disorders. I do very little assessment and a great deal of talk therapy to assist with grieving loss of function, building hope for whatever recovery is possible, and finding new sources of meaning in a sometimes dramatically changed way of being in the world. I have also been challenged to rethink how to conduct therapy when people's speech or cognition has been changed, but the need to emotionally express themselves and to heal is still very much present.

WHY DO YOU LIKE WORKING WITH AN OLDER-ADULT POPULATION?

I enjoy working with an older-adult population because of the richness of life experience that living several decades often brings. An older adult usually has a personal narrative of interesting life events, hard-won life lessons, multiple relationships, and some level of resilience after having weathered many storms. I appreciate being able to draw on these many strengths to assist the person and their family or friends in finding their way forward through whatever challenge has currently presented itself. I also find the work of assisting the person in coming to a sense of peace about whatever has been left undone to be authentic and satisfying work.

DO YOU HAVE ADVICE FOR STUDENTS WHO WANT TO GET INTO THE FIELD?
I started building experience with older adults by volunteering at a LTC facility. What was to be a four-month volunteer experience of weekly visits turned into a friendship that lasted for years. Those types of experiences can provide empathy and understanding that is an important foundation for later work as a clinician.

2.4 SUMMARY

- Three basic research designs used in aging research are cross-sectional, longitudinal, and sequential. Each has advantages and disadvantages.

- There are a number of ethical issues when conducting research with human participants. The three primary ethical issues in the context of aging research are informed consent, the right to withdraw, and confidentiality of data. These issues are particularly important when conducting research with cognitively impaired older adults.

- The 2014 Tri-Council Policy Statement: Ethical Conduct for Research Involving Humans (Government of Canada, 2014b) guidelines are based on the three core principles of respect for persons, concern for welfare, and justice, and is designed to assist researchers and REB members in conducting research with humans.

Key Terms

Age Changes
Changes in an individual due to the aging process.

Age Differences
Differences between age groups due to differences in experiences and not due to the aging process.

Age Effect(s)
Differences, such as biological, psychological, or sociocultural changes, as the consequences of growing older.

Anonymity
Refers to either not collecting identifying information from research participants (e.g., name, address, email address, etc.) or not linking individual responses with participants' identities.

Attrition
Occurs in research when participants who have been recruited for a study drop out. Attrition threatens the internal validity of a study.

Coercion

Threat of harm or punishment for failure to participate in research. Coercion exists if individuals do not feel they can refuse to participate in research, if refusal causes a perceived substantial loss to the individual, or if individuals believe that participation is not truly voluntary.

Cohort(s)

Refers to an aggregate (group/groups) of individuals within a given population who experience the same event within the same time interval.

Cohort Effect(s)

The effect that having been born in a certain time, region, or period, or having experienced the same life experience (in the same time period) has on the development or perceptions of a particular group. These perceptions, characteristics, or effects are unique to the group in question.

Cohort-Sequential Design

A research design consisting of two or more cross-sectional studies done at two different time periods.

Confidentiality

Refers to the protection of participant information and/or responses collected in research studies, with this information available only to the investigator(s) or members of the research team. The easiest way to protect participants is through the collection and use of anonymous or anonymized data.

Cross-Sectional Design

A research design where individuals of different ages are compared at a single point in time.

Cross-Sequential Design

A research design that combines a cross-sectional and a longitudinal design.

External Validity

The extent to which results of a study can be generalized to other people (population validity), to other settings (ecological validity), or over time (historical validity).

Generalizable

The extension of research findings and conclusions from a study conducted on a sample population to the population at large or to other settings.

Gerontology

Gerontology, from the Greek words for "old man" and "study of," was coined by Ilya Ilyich Mechnikov in 1903. It is the study of the biological, psychological, and sociological aspects of aging.

Independent Variable

The variable that is manipulated in a research study.

Informed Consent

Indication of agreement by an individual to become a participant in a research project.

Internal Validity

Effects observed in the research study are due to the manipulation of the independent variable and not due to extraneous or confounding variables.

Longitudinal Design

A research design where data are collected from the same participants over time (often several years).

Maturation Effect(s)

Changes that can occur in a participant due to normal development processes as a function of time. These effects can threaten the internal validity of the study.

Practice Effects

Outcomes that can occur when participants are tested more than once on the same measure of interest.

Proxy/Proxies

A person/persons authorized to act on behalf of someone else.

Sequential Design

A type of research design that involves a combination of longitudinal and cross-sectional designs and that follows several cohorts of different ages over time.

Time of Measurement Effect(s)
Differences due to cultural, historical, environmental, or other events at the time that the data are collected.

Time-Sequential Design
A research design that compares two or more cross-sectional samples at two or more times of measurement.

Undue Influence
Can occur when participants are recruited to participate in research by those who have some form of control over them.

This influence may cause the participant to act otherwise than by their own free will or without adequate attention to the consequences.

Variable
In research, a variable is any attribute, characteristic, or phenomenon that can be controlled or changed. There are three types of variables in research: the independent variable, the dependent variable, and the control variable, also known as the constant variable.

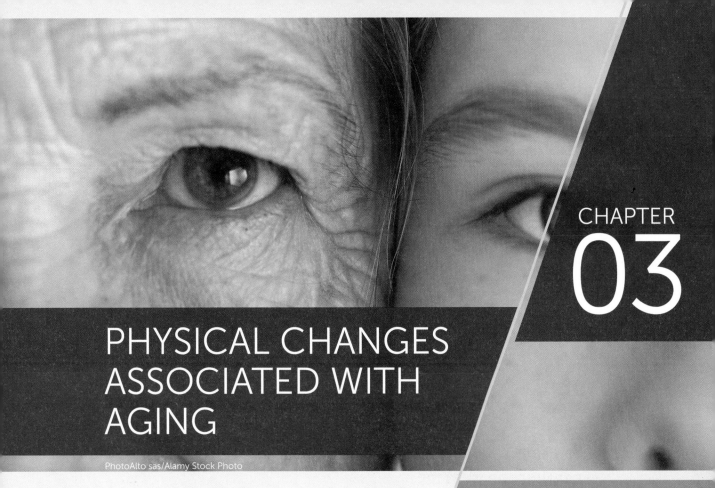

CHAPTER
03

PHYSICAL CHANGES ASSOCIATED WITH AGING

CHAPTER OUTLINE

*"Those who think they have no time for bodily exercise will sooner or later
have to find time for illness."*

Edward Stanley (1826–1893)

Many of the physical changes with aging that are described in this chapter
are part of the normal aging process (e.g., changes in vision, hearing, taste,
smell, and touch). On the other hand, many physical changes that occur with
age are *not* part of the normal aging process. Specifically, many diseases
that are associated with aging such as heart disease and osteoporosis can
either be minimized or avoided by lifestyle decisions. As you read through
this chapter, think about the changes with age that are preventable or can
be postponed by the adoption of healthier lifestyle choices and behaviours.

3.1 PHYSICAL CHANGES WITH AGING: OLD AND NEW CONCEPTS

LEARNING OBJECTIVES

To understand and be able to describe

- the primary theories of aging
- the physical changes in appearance as a result of the aging process
- the changes in sensory and motor abilities with aging
- the impact of these age-associated changes in appearance and the stereotypes associated
  with these changes

Why do we age? The question seems simple, but in fact it is quite complex. Did you know that
there are more than 300 theories that have been developed to explain the aging process? Several of
the more common aging theories are **programmed theories of aging**, **cellular theories of aging**,
and **error theories of aging** (Weinert & Timiras, 2003). Programmed theories of aging argue that
aging is dependent on a biological clock—that is, aging is genetically programmed to occur with the
passage of time. Researchers believe that even when cell death is thought to be random, cell death
may be part of a master genetic program that governs the aging process (Mackenzie, 2012). Currently, researchers do not clearly understand what mechanism(s) activate(s) the destruction of cells.

One of the more popular cellular theories of aging comes from a discovery made by Leonard
Hayflick in 1996. He discovered that cells grown in laboratory Petri dishes divide only a finite number
of times before they die. This is known as the **Hayflick limit**. Furthermore, Hayflick found that the
number of divisions a cell is able to make depends on the age of the cell. For example, fetal tissue cells are
capable of dividing 40 to 60 times while adult cells are capable of dividing only approximately 20 times.
There is evidence to suggest that the limit placed on cell division is due to the shortening of telomeres,
which are the end tips of chromosomes. According to Lin, Epel, and Blackburn (2012), telomeres play

an important role in aging by regulating the cell's response to stress and damage to DNA molecules. It also has been shown that telomere shortening and dysfunction are associated with age-related diseases including cardiovascular disease, Type 2 diabetes mellitus, and cancer (Armanios, 2013).

Unlike the programmed theories of aging, error theories of aging argue that aging is due to environmental insults that result in progressive damage to living organisms. Examples of error theories of aging include the **wear and tear theory** (Weisman, 1882) and the **free radical theory of aging** (Gerschman, 1981; Harman, 1956).

While not a theory of aging per se, one approach to longevity that is getting a good deal of attention is **caloric restriction**. The idea that reducing calories, without malnutrition, can extend life is not a new idea. In 1935, McCay, Crowell, and Maynard published the first paper showing that a 25 to 30 percent reduction in caloric intake, without malnutrition, extends the average and maximum life spans in rats. This classic study with rats was followed by numerous caloric restriction (CR) studies with a variety of species including fish, monkeys, dogs, hamsters, flies, primates, humans, as well as yeast (Chung et al., 2013). Interestingly, CR does not only extend the life of the species that have been studied, but CR also has been shown to lower the risk of developing cancer, diabetes, and cardiovascular diseases in these various species (Fontana, Meyer, Klein, & Holloszy, 2004; Meyer et al., 2006). CR, or dietary restriction, is the only established anti-aging paradigm to serve as the gold standard in research studies that assess aging interventions. CR has become a priority research focus of the National Institute on Aging in the United States (Willcox & Willcox, 2014). The question is, can the effects seen in CR in other species be consistently replicated in humans? As it turns out, not a lot of research has evaluated the effects of CR in humans but the research that has been done looks promising.

The Okinawans of Japan are a group of people who are of particular interest to CR researchers as they were known to have the longest life expectancy in the world. This increased longevity seemed to be a result of the Okinawans' diet, which was low in fat and sugar, had fewer calories, was rich in antioxidants and seafood, and was high in legumes and soy (Willcox & Willcox, 2013). However, recently, there has been a tendency for the indices of longevity to decline in the Okinawan due to changes in dietary habits (Miyagi, Iwama, Kawabata, & Hasegawa, 2003) as well as changes in smoking habits and alcohol consumption, and higher rates of obesity, particularly for the Okinawan men (Willcox, Willcox, Yasura, Ashitomi, & Suzuki 2012).

> Can you see any difficulties that might arise when trying to do caloric restriction research with humans?

REFLECTIVE QUESTION

Despite the fact that very little scientific evidence shows that CR extends life and reduces the likelihood of developing chronic illness in humans, people are practising CR. The Calorie Restriction Society International has over 7000 members and this membership is growing every day. In addition, the Society has conferences every two years. Individuals who follow a CR diet aim to eat 25 to 30 percent fewer calories than recommended. However, the food sources of the calories are very important. A CR diet must include nutrient-dense food that fulfills all the recommended daily nutrient requirements. Several CR diets have been developed and an individual may restrict calorie intake every day or alternate fasting days. For example, an individual may fast every other day or several days a week and then eat what he or she would like on non-fasting days. It is a very interesting concept and one that is certainly drawing the attention of laypeople and researchers alike. The question is, how long could an individual follow such a diet? What is important to remember is that none of these theories explains aging in such a way that all researchers agree on. As you can see, many theories have been put forth to explain the aging process.

In addition to developing theories of aging to help us to better understand why we age, researchers also have distinguished between primary and secondary aging. **Primary aging** is defined as the gradual and inevitable process of bodily deterioration that takes place throughout life. It is argued that this accumulation of biochemical damage leads to changes such as impaired vision and hearing, slowed movements, decreased resistance to infections, and a reduced ability to adapt to stress. **Secondary aging**, on the other hand, is believed to be the result of disease and poor health practices such as not exercising, smoking, and an unhealthy diet. Unlike primary aging, secondary aging is believed to be preventable either through lifestyle choice or modern medicine. We will turn now and discuss changes in appearance, as well as changes in sensory and motor abilities, associated with aging.

3.2 CHANGES IN APPEARANCE (SKIN, VOICE, AND HAIR) WITH AGE

LEARNING OBJECTIVES

To understand and be able to describe:

- the changes in the skin with age and procedures to prevent or delay these age-associated changes
- the changes in voice with age
- the changes in hair with age

CHANGES IN SKIN WITH AGE

Have you thought about how you might look when you are 65? 75? 85? One of the most visible signs of aging is wrinkling of the skin. Skin is the largest organ in the body, consisting of the epidermis and the dermis, with loose connective tissue and fat (the hypodermis) underlying the dermis (see Figure 3.1). The **epidermis** is the outer layer of the skin. It is made up of mostly flat, scale-like cells called squamous cells. Under the squamous cells are round cells called basal cells. The deepest part of the epidermis also contains melanocytes. Melanocytes produce melanin which gives skin its colour. Another main layer of the skin is the **dermis**. This inner layer of skin, which lies below the epidermis, contains blood and lymph vessels, hair follicles, and glands. These glands produce sweat, which helps regulate body temperature, and sebum, an oily substance that helps keep the skin from drying out. Sweat and sebum reach the skin's surface through tiny openings called pores. The **hypodermis** (subcutaneous layer) lies between the dermis and underlying tissues and organs. It consists of mostly adipose tissue and is the storage site of most body fat.

Aging of the skin, also known as **cutaneous aging**, is the result of both intrinsic and extrinsic aging. **Intrinsic aging**, which takes place over the years and occurs irrespective of extrinsic factors, is defined as the gradual irreversible changes in structure and function of an organism that occur due to the passage of time (Bergfeld, 1997). **Extrinsic aging**, on the other hand, is due to external factors such as exercise, diet, exposure to sunlight, and smoking (Bergfeld, 1997). With intrinsic aging, the skin becomes pale, thinner, and more fragile. Fine wrinkles and exaggerated

FIGURE 3.1

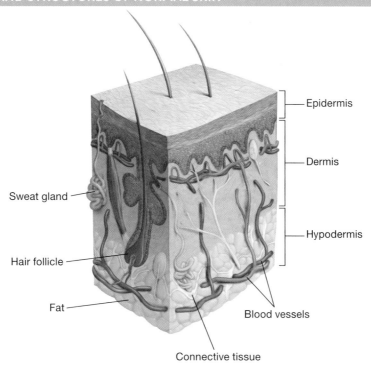

Epidermis

Dermis

Hypodermis

Sweat gland

Hair follicle

Fat

Blood vessels

Connective tissue

expression lines are apparent (see Figure 3.2), and the skin becomes dry and less elastic. These changes are due to reductions in the amount of **collagen** produced, diminished functioning of the sweat and oil glands, reductions in the amount of elastin that is produced, and reductions in the formation of glycosaminoglycan (polysaccharides) that exist naturally in the dermis of the skin as natural moisture factors. Of interest, of all the wrinkles that occur with age, few are due to this intrinsic aging process. It also is important to note that intrinsic aging of the skin, although universal, is significantly different among different populations, with Caucasians having an earlier onset and greater skin wrinkling and sagging than other skin types (Makrantonaki, Bekou, & Zouboulis, 2012). There also are gender differences in intrinsic aging of the skin. For example, skin becomes less elastic with age, with changes in elasticity more pronounced in older women than older men. In addition, skin thickness decreases with age, with this decrease thought to be due to reduction in collagen with age. This decrease is faster in older women than older men due primarily to estrogen deficiency during and after menopause. However, the post-menopausal use of estrogen increases collagen content, dermal thickness, and elasticity, and it decreases the likelihood of senile dry skin (Calleja-Agius & Brincat, 2012; Farage et al., 2012).

Extrinsic aging of the skin, on the other hand, is due to environmental factors such as sun, tobacco use, exposure to pollution, and other lifestyle factors such as diet, sleeping habits, and overall health. The two major environmental influences leading to aging of the skin are chronic exposure to solar ultraviolet (UV) irradiation and smoking (Langton, Sherratt, Griffiths, & Watson, 2010), with exposure to sunlight accounting for up to 90 percent of visible skin aging (U.S. Environmental Protection Agency, 2015; World Health Organization [WHO], 2003).

Signs of extrinsic aging include a thickening of the cornified layer of the skin (the top layer of the epidermis), freckles, and sunspot formation; precancerous changes such as **actinic keratosis**;

FIGURE 3.2

frantab/Shutterstock.com

and skin cancers including **basal cell carcinoma**, **squamous cell carcinoma**, and **melanoma**. Alone or in combination, these changes result in skin that is thin with deep wrinkles, is rough in appearance, is of uneven tone, and has the presence of brown patches.

If you were reading carefully, you will have noticed that the majority of the changes to the skin with age are preventable (e.g., due to extrinsic factors). One of the best ways to minimize wrinkles and reduce the other changes to your skin previously described above is to protect your skin against both UVA and UVB rays. Protection against UVA and UVB rays also helps to minimize the risk of skin cancer. Skin cancer is currently the most common type of cancer—it also is one of the most preventable types of cancer (Canadian Cancer Society, 2012). Recommendations for protection against skin cancer include the use of a broad-spectrum sunscreen that has a sun protection factor (SPF) of 15 or higher. Limiting exposure to UV radiation, whether it is from the sun or from artificial sources such as sunlamps and tanning beds, can reduce the risk of developing skin cancer. Of interest, results from a recent review of 19 studies over a 25-year span on indoor tanning equipment revealed that there is an association between indoor tanning and two types of skin cancer: squamous cell carcinoma and melanoma. Results also indicated that risk of melanoma, one of the deadliest skin cancers, increases by 75 percent when tanning-bed use starts before age 35. Finally, the results from this same report also found that there is an association between UV-emitting tanning devices and cancer of the eye (ocular melanoma) (El Ghissassi et al., 2009).

REFLECTIVE QUESTION

In thinking about your own aging, does knowing the strong association between use of tanning beds and skin cancer influence your decision to use a tanning bed?

In addition to reducing exposure to UV radiation, there also is good evidence that the regular use of topical **retinoids** can rejuvenate premature aging of the skin due to repeated exposure to ultraviolet radiation. Retin-A, a prescription skin cream that is a vitamin A derivative, increases the collagen content in the upper dermis. Applied nightly, epidermal thickening and improvement in fine wrinkles can be seen as early as three months following use, with improvements in fine and coarse wrinkling, sallowness, discolouration, roughness, and looseness of the skin (Hubbard, Unger, & Rohrich, 2014). As with many medications, there are side effects to Retin-A cream, including redness, peeling, and flaking. These side effects are dose-dependent and have a tendency to decrease in severity over time. We will have more to say about other procedures currently in vogue to reduce the effects of aging later in the chapter.

REVERSING THE SIGNS OF AGING

In the early 1990s, the **baby boomers** began to enter middle age. Importantly, this baby-boomer cohort is the first generation with expectations of leisure time, good health, and an increased desire for preservation of a youthful appearance (Harkin & Huber, 2004). The desire for beauty is not new, dating back to Cleopatra whose most famous beauty secret was bathing in milk and honey. Historically, both men and women have gone to great lengths to beautify themselves, but beauty practices have been mainly the domain of women (Honigman & Castle, 2006). Although preoccupation with one's appearance extends across the lifespan, the onset of middle age is associated with an increase in this preoccupation because of negative stereotypes and myths associated with aging (Honigman & Castle, 2006). This obsession with a youthful appearance, as well as factors such as self-esteem, perceptions of body, and life satisfaction, has resulted in proliferation of and demand for surgical and non-surgical cosmetic procedures that are designed to reverse the aging process (Ching, Thoma, McCabe, & Antony, 2003).

Cosmetic surgery is concerned with the "maintenance, restoration, or enhancement of an individual's physical appearance through surgical and medical techniques" (Swami, Chamorro-Premuzic, Bridges, & Furnham, 2009, p. 7). Not surprisingly, middle- and upper-class women who are middle- and older-aged are major consumers of cosmetic surgeries such as tummy tucks, breast lifts, blepharoplasty (eyelid surgery), and facelifts. But younger women and younger and older men are increasingly becoming major consumers of cosmetic surgeries as well (American Society of Plastic Surgeons, 2017a). Unfortunately, data on the number of cosmetic surgeries done in Canada are lacking. However, data from the American Society of Plastic Surgeons indicate that almost 1.8 million cosmetic surgical procedures such as breast augmentation, eyelid surgery, and facelifts were done in 2016, with more than 15.4 million minimally invasive cosmetic procedures such as botulinum toxin Type A (Botox), soft tissue fillers (also called dermal fillers), and chemical peels done in this same time period (American Society of Plastic Surgeons, 2017a).

Recall that we previously mentioned that the baby boomers are the first generation with an increased desire for preservation of youthfulness. You might be wondering whether this is reflected in an increase in the number of cosmetic procedures that are being done. Indeed, the number of cosmetic procedures described above that have been done since 2000 has increased significantly. For example, the number of injections of botulinum toxin in the United States increased from 786 911 in 2000 to more than 7 million in 2016, a 797 percent increase! During this same period, soft tissue fillers increased from 652 885 in 2000 to more than 2.6 million in 2016, a 298 percent increase (American Society of Plastic Surgeons, 2017a). Preserving a youthful appearance is not without cost. In the United States, more than $16 million was spent on cosmetic procedures in 2016 (American Society of Plastic Surgeons, 2017b) (see Figure 3.3).

The aging of the baby boomer cohort also has fuelled the development of commercial skin products such as anti-aging moisturizers, serums, or treatments that are marketed to reverse the signs of intrinsic skin aging (Harkin & Huber, 2004). It has been estimated that the total market for anti-aging products and services was $249.3 billion in 2012, with this total expected to increase to $261.9 billion by the end of 2013, and to $345.8 billion by 2018 (PRNewswire, 2015).

Currently, there is an interesting debate in the literature as to whether the consumption of cosmetic surgeries and other non-invasive cosmetic procedures is a means of self-care designed to look "better, not younger" versus "hiding the effects of aging" (Garnham, 2013). Similar arguments

FIGURE 3.3

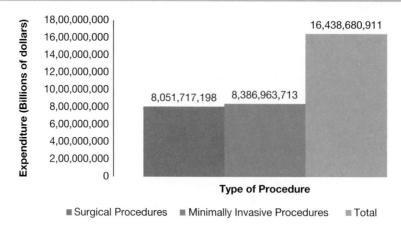

Source: American Society of Plastic Surgeons. (2017a). *New statistics reflect the changing nature of plastic surgery. American Society of Plastic Surgeons.* Retrieved from http://www.plasticsurgery.org/news/press-releases/new-statistics-reflect-the-changing-face-of-plastic-surgery. American Society of Plastic Surgeons. (2017b). *More than $16 billion spent in cosmetic plastic surgery.* Retrieved from http://www.plasticsurgery.org/news/press-releases/more-than-16-billion-spent-on-cosmetic-plastic-surgery.

have been advanced by others, with the debate positioned as "tensions between agency and determinism as women exercise choice in a social context that is shaped and constrained by societal obsessions with youth and appearance" (Hurd Clarke, Repta, & Griffin, 2007, p. 84). From a philosophical perspective, **agency** is the capacity for human beings to make choices. **Determinism**, on the other hand, presumes that all events are completely determined by previously existing causes. In a study on perceptions and experiences of non-surgical cosmetic procedures in women aged 50 to 70 years, Hurd Clarke and colleagues (2007) found that some of the women expressed positive feelings toward non-surgical cosmetic procedures, seeing the procedures as an enhancement to their bodies and their self (e.g., an expression of agency). This group of women was satisfied with the results and indicated that they were willing to consider additional procedures in the future. Other women in the study (none of whom had had non-surgical cosmetic procedures done) indicated that they were opposed to all forms of non-surgical cosmetic procedures, with their opposition based on what they saw as a social devaluation of women, a form of female oppression, and devaluation of aging (e.g., determinism) (Hurd Clarke et al., 2007).

As the baby boomers move through their senior years, the use of cosmetic surgical and non-surgical procedures will undoubtedly continue to surge as middle-aged and older individuals increasingly turn to these procedures to erase the vestiges of time, as well as to prevent or delay age-associated declines. It will be interesting to see whether these procedures soon become a normative aspect of modern aging.

REFLECTIVE QUESTIONS

What are your thoughts on cosmetic surgical and non-surgical procedures?

Have you thought about having any of these procedures done now?

Would you consider having any of these procedures done as you get older?

CHANGES IN VOICE WITH AGE

In addition to changes in the skin with age, there also are changes in the voice with age. With age, we lose muscle mass, our mucous membranes thin and become drier, and we lose fine coordination. These changes occur in the **larynx** as well as the vocal cords, resulting in **presbyphonia**, a term used to describe the changes associated with the aging voice. These changes include a higher pitch in men and a lower pitch in women, reductions in volume and projection (a thin voice), tremor or shakiness in the voice, reduced vocal endurance, and, for those who sing, reduced vocal endurance (Gregory, Chandran, Lurie, & Sataloff, 2012).

CHANGES IN HAIR WITH AGE

The most obvious sign of aging is a change in hair colour. Greying of the hair is due to a reduction in melanocytes. These cells, which produce **melanin**, are located in the lower region of hair follicles. Greying of the hair, which is closely related to chronological age, often begins in the 30s, appearing first at the temples and extending to the top of the scalp. Of interest, greying for individuals of Asian and African descent occurs about five to 10 years later than it does for Caucasians, possibly because of genetics. Body and facial hair also turn grey with age, but this change usually occurs later than greying of scalp hair. Other body hair (armpits, chest, and pubic) may or may not turn grey.

Hair also becomes thinner with age and hair loss is common. Hair loss with age occurs in both men and women, with this loss being more noticeable in men. **Androgenetic alopecia** (commonly known as male pattern baldness) is an age-dependent hair-loss disorder, affecting more than 80 percent and 42 percent of 70-year-old Caucasian men and women, respectively (Gan & Sinclair, 2005). For men, male pattern baldness is due to sensitivity of the hair follicle to androgens (principally dihydrotestosterone), as well as to genetics (Vary, 2015). In women, the role of androgens in female pattern baldness is less clear (Unger, Unger, & Wesley, 2013). For men with male pattern baldness, the hair begins to recede at the temples and starts to thin on the top of the head. A bald patch gradually develops in the middle of the scalp. With time, the bald patch gradually enlarges, leaving a rim of hair around the back and the sides of the scalp. For women, androgenetic alopecia tends to affect the top of the head but there also may be a more general thinning of hair all over the head. It is commonly believed that the hair loss associated with androgenetic alopecia in men is passed down on the mother's side. While it is true that a key gene for male pattern baldness is on the X chromosome, male pattern baldness has what is called a polygenetic inheritance (determined by many genes) (Unger et al., 2013). Another common misconception is that male pattern baldness skips a generation. Again, there is no evidence for this.

What are the psychological effects of going bald? Surprisingly, there is very little research in this area. Results from an older study indicate that androgenetic alopecia can be stressful for both men and women, but substantially more stressful for women (Cash, Price, & Savin, 1993). The market for global alopecia treatment was valued at more than $7.3 million (USD) in 2015, with this market expected to exceed $11.8 billion (USD) by 2024 (Business Wire, 2016). Despite the prevalence of androgenetic alopecia, there are few effective treatments available for this disorder. Recently, Varothai and Bergfeld (2014) reviewed published medical and non-medical treatment for androgenetic alopecia in both men and women. Results of that review indicate that the best evidence-based treatments for males are an oral medication called finasteride (brand name is Propecia) and a topical solution of a medication called minoxidal (brand name Rogaine). For women, topical minoxidal was seen as the most effective and safest treatment solution (Varothai & Bergfled, 2014). Of interest, there is less evidence for the effectiveness of many of the non-pharmaceutical products that are marketed for treatment of androgenetic alopecia such as aloe vera, topical caffeine, ginseng, and melatonin. Hair replacement surgery, in which plugs of skin and hair are transplanted from another area of the body (e.g., back of the head or from the beard) to the scalp, is another method of treating male pattern baldness. However, the success rate of hair replacement surgery is variable due to differences in surgical techniques and skills of the surgical team, as well as individual differences in those receiving the surgery.

3.3 CHANGES IN THE SENSORY SYSTEMS (VISION, HEARING, TASTE, SMELL, AND TOUCH) WITH AGE

LEARNING OBJECTIVE

- To understand and be able to describe the changes in each of the sensory systems with age

In addition to changes in the skin, hair, and voice with age, the aging process also is associated with changes in the sensory systems: vision, hearing, taste, smell, and touch. In general, these changes begin around 50 years of age. Often, once these changes have been recognized and accepted, adjustments or adaptations can be made that help in overcoming many of the losses.

CHANGES IN VISION WITH NORMAL AGING AND DUE TO DISEASE

In Canada, normal vision is recorded as 20/20 (Imperial system) or 6/6 (Metric system). What this means is that an individual can see at 20 feet (six metres) what a person with normal vision can see at 20 feet (six metres). Vision loss is measured similarly. That is, an individual with 20/40 vision loss is able to clearly see an object at 20 feet (but no more) that an individual with unimpaired vision can see at 40 feet (but no more).

Vision declines with age. That is, during the normal aging process, the pupil become smaller and less responsive to variations in light, the lens begins to lose elasticity and thickens and yellows, and the muscles that control both pupil size and the reaction to light lose strength (see Figure 3.4). These changes affect our vision in a number of ways. First, the decrease in the

FIGURE 3.4

DIAGRAM OF THE EYE

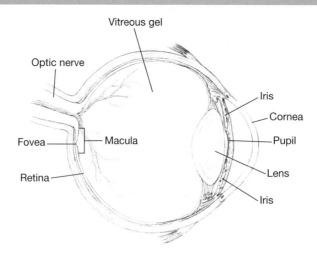

diameter of the pupil makes seeing in dim light more difficult. The decreased ability of the pupil to adjust to varying light conditions also results in a gradual loss in **dark adaptation**, which makes it more difficult to adapt from darkness to bright light (or vice versa). Changes in dark adaptation with age make it more difficult to read a menu in dimly lit restaurants or find your seat in a dark movie theatre. Changes in dark adaptation also increase sensitivity to glare, making it more difficult to drive at night, particularly on dark pavement when it is raining.

The loss of elasticity in the lens results in difficulties in **accommodation**. With normal aging, this loss of elasticity results in a condition called **presbyopia**. Presbyopia, which typically becomes noticeable in individuals beginning around age 40, is part of the natural aging process. As such, presbyopia is not a disease and cannot be prevented. Symptoms of presbyopia include difficulty reading small print, needing to hold material at arm's length to properly focus on it, eyestrain or headaches after reading or doing close work, and a need for brighter lighting when reading or doing close work. Presbyopia is easily corrected through wearing of prescription glasses (e.g., reading glasses, bifocals, or progressive lenses) or contact lenses. More recently, corneal inlays (implants) are being used to correct presbyopia. These implants, which are placed in the corneal stroma (the middle layer of the cornea) result in improvements in near and inter-mediate vision without a significant loss of distance vision, contrast sensitivity, or stereopsis (depth perception) (Lindstrom, MacRae, Pepose, & Hoopes, 2013).

Finally, the yellowing of the lens with age affects colour perception. This yellowing results in dulling of colours and difficulties differentiating between colours and between colour shades (e.g., blue, green, and violet). Yellowing of the lens also can create difficulties in determining where an object ends and its background begins.

The impact of all these visual changes for everyday life can be profound. As noted above, difficulties seeing in dim light can affect the ability to read menus in dimly lit restaurants or to safely navigate the dimly lit aisles in movie theatres; increased sensitivity to glare can affect one's safety and comfort level when driving at night or in the rain; presbyopia results in the inability to read a newspaper or book with small print (see Figure 3.5); difficulties in colour perception can result in wearing clothing that does not match (this may explain the colourful clothing you see out on the golf course.); and the yellowing of the lens can increase the risk of falls due to the inability to differentiate between where a curb ends and the pavement begins or where a stair ends and the floor begins. Proper lighting, increasing the amount of ambient light in the home, and avoiding highly polished surfaces in the home (e.g., covering shiny floors with carpets and changing from high-gloss- to matte-finished countertops) can help to compensate for the changes in accommodation and dark adaptation. Regular visits to an eye specialist and use of reading

FIGURE 3.5

THE USE OF VISUAL AIDS ENABLES READING FINE PRINT

Clynt Garnham Medical/Alamy Stock Photo

FIGURE 3.6

Cordelia Molloy/Science Source

Cordelia Molloy/Science Source

glasses, bifocals, trifocals, progressive lenses, or contacts can help with vision changes due to presbyopia. The use of halogen or fluorescent light bulbs; the selection of warm colours such as yellow, orange, and red in the home; and placement of coloured tape on the edge of steps can all help to minimize the effects that yellowing of the lens produces.

In addition to the changes in vision due to the normal aging process, there are changes in vision due to disease. Three common age-associated diseases are macular degeneration, cataracts, and glaucoma. **Age-related macular degeneration (AMD)** is a leading cause of vision loss among people 50 years of age and older and is the leading cause of vision loss in Canada (CNIB, 2015a). AMD causes damage to the photoreceptors in the macula, a small spot near the centre of the retina (See Figure 3.4). The macula is the part of the eye needed for sharp, central vision, and damage to this area results in blank spots when the person is looking directly ahead (see Figure 3.6). As such, AMD can interfere with simple everyday activities such as the ability to read, write, see faces, fix things around the house, or drive. There are two types of AMD—wet and dry. Wet AMD, which accounts for two-thirds of all AMD, occurs when abnormal blood vessels start to grow under the macula behind the retina. Often, these new blood vessels are very fragile and leak blood and fluid, which causes the macula to bulge or lift from its normal place in the back of the eye. Damage to the macula often occurs rapidly and is severe. In the early stages, thermal laser surgery may prevent severe damage for some individuals. Dry AMD, which accounts for the remaining one-third of all AMD, is the result of thinning of the macula. The degree of vision loss with dry AMD depends on the location and amount of thinning of the lining of the retina. Currently, there are no treatments or cures for dry AMD (National Eye Institute, 2015).

A **cataract** is an opacification (clouding) of the crystalline lens of the eye, which blocks light from reaching the retina of the eye (see Figure 3.7). Cataracts are a leading cause of vision loss and the most common cause of reversible blindness in the world (Asbell et al., 2005). More than 2.5 million Canadians have cataracts (CNIB, 2015b). The presence of cataracts increases with age. In 2010, one-fifth (21 percent) of Canadians 65 to 79 years of age were diagnosed as having cataracts, with this percentage increasing to 32 percent for Canadians 80 years of age and older (Public Health Agency of Canada [PHAC], 2010a). Cataracts may be due to a variety of causes: some are **congenital**, a few occur during the early years of life, but most cataracts are the result

FIGURE 3.7

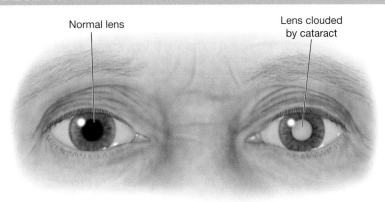

Normal lens

Lens clouded
by cataract

of the aging process. Risk factors for age-related cataracts include increasing age, family history, diabetes, prolonged exposure to the sun, tobacco and/or alcohol use, and previous eye injuries such as cuts, punctures, or chemical burns to the eye. Long-term use of some medications, such as steroids or diuretics, also can increase an individual's risk for cataracts. Cataract surgery can be done to improve vision. With cataract surgery, the cloudy lens is removed and replaced with an artificial lens. Most cataract surgery is done today on an outpatient basis without general anesthetic, with a recovery period of about six weeks. In general, few individuals have complications from the surgery, and most individuals have improved vision and quality of life following surgery (Hildreth, Burke, & Glass, 2009).

Regular visits to an eye specialist as well as the adoption of a healthy lifestyle may help to protect the lens of the eye and reduce the risk of conditions such as cataracts. A diet rich in Vitamins C and E and consumption of foods containing **carotenoids** has been found to reduce the risk of cataracts in older individuals (Christen, Liu, Glynn, Gaziano, & Buring, 2008; Ravindran et al., 2011).

Glaucoma, a group of diseases characterized by increased **intraocular pressure**, also is more common with age. With glaucoma, the normal fluid pressure inside the eye (intraocular pressure) increases, which can result in damage to the optic nerve, leading to blindness. The most common type of glaucoma is primary open-angle glaucoma. Early detection and treatment are important for the prevention of damage to the optic nerve and vision loss. There are a number of common tests for glaucoma. One of those tests (tonometry) involves measuring the pressure in the eye by delivering a small puff of air. There are a number of medications available to treat glaucoma. Eye drops, which help to promote the drainage of the aqueous fluid and/or decrease the amount of fluid production, often are the first choice for treating the condition. There also are oral medications that facilitate the outflow of aqueous fluid and reduce the production of fluid. Laser surgery has been shown to be a safe and effective alternative to treatment with medications (National Eye Institute, 2015).

CHANGES IN HEARING WITH AGE

The effects of noise, aging, disease, and heredity combine to make hearing loss a common problem in modern society. Hearing loss occurs when there is a problem with, or damage to, one or more parts of the ear or the nerve pathways in the brain involved in hearing (see Figure 3.8 for anatomy of the ear).

FIGURE 3.8

THE EAR

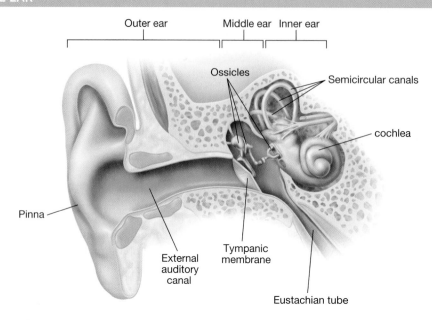

Outer ear   Middle ear   Inner ear

Ossicles

Semicircular canals

cochlea

Pinna

External auditory canal

Tympanic membrane

Eustachian tube

There are two main types of hearing loss: conductive hearing loss and sensorineural hearing loss. **Conductive hearing loss** is caused by abnormalities or damage to the middle ear (e.g., eardrum or ossicles). **Sensorineural hearing loss** typically results from permanent damage to the inner ear (cochlea) or the auditory nerve. Ninety percent of hearing loss is sensorineural, with this type of hearing loss caused by impaired functioning of the cochlear hair cells. Age-related hearing loss (**presbycusis**) is a progressive and irreversible sensorineural hearing loss resulting from degeneration of the cochlea or associated structures of the inner ear or auditory nerves. Age-related hearing loss (ARHL), which is most marked at higher frequencies, occurs gradually, most often occurs in both ears, and affects each ear equally. It also is one of the most common chronic conditions in older adults, with one in three adults 65 years of age and older having this type of hearing loss (WHO, 2012a). However, ARHL can occur as early as age 40 in males and a decade later in females (Sharashenidze, Schacht, & Kevanishvili, 2007). Results from the 2012 and 2013 Canadian Health Measures Survey (CHMS) indicated that adults aged 60 to 79 years were significantly more likely to have hearing loss (47 percent) compared with younger adults aged 40 to 59 years (16 percent) and 19 to 39 years (7 percent). In this study, hearing loss was defined as loss of hearing that was at least mild (> 25 decibels in adults age 19 to 79). Males (25 percent) were significantly more likely to have hearing loss compared with females (14 percent) (Statistics Canada, 2015b).

What causes ARHL? Although you might think that ARHL is simply due to the effects of aging on the ability to hear, ARHL is due to a combination of factors. One of the risk factors for ARHL is long-term repeated exposure to noise resulting in gradual, irreversible damage to the sensory cells and other structures, which in turn leads to permanent hearing loss. In the current population of older adults, this may be the result of working with noisy machinery. However, for the baby boomer cohort (and in younger cohorts as well), regular and/or prolonged exposure to noise as a result of listening to loud music (on their iPhones, for example) is a risk factor for ARHL, with this type of exposure more harmful to the cochlea than the natural process of aging (Gonçalves, Mota & Marques, 2009). Until recently, genetics were not believed to play a role in ARHL. However, results from a nine-year study have confirmed a link between a gene (the glutamate metabotropic receptor 7 [*GRM7*] gene) that produces a key protein in the inner ear and impairments in pure-tone thresholds and difficulties in speech perception in older individuals (Newman et al., 2012). These findings reinforce observations in older people that genetics and environment interact, linking ARHL to other neurodegenerative risk factors such as medical conditions including diabetes, hypertension, renal failure, tobacco use, and illicit drug use (Walling & Dickson, 2012).

As mentioned earlier, one of the defining characteristics of ARHL is a gradual loss of the ability to hear high-frequency sounds (over 2 KHz). For example, the consonants s, z, t, f, and g are high-frequency, high-pitched sounds that are "soft." Conversely, vowels (e.g., a, e, i, o, and u) are low-frequency, low-pitched, "loud" sounds. The majority of speech information is carried by the consonant sounds. These differences affect an older person's ability to understand what is being said. That is, individuals with ARHL will be able to hear *when* someone is speaking (from being able to hear the louder, low-frequency vowels) but will not be able to understand *what* is said due to the loss of consonant information. For example, try to understand what is being said in the following sentences:

Oe uo a ie ee a a ie i. e ae a oio. e a oe ai. Oe ay oio a ai i e oe. e a a oue a oe o e oo. e e iie. ooy a ee. oio a ee o o e ae. e a uy. "i oie i oo o! i oie i oo o!"

Now try figuring out what is being said in these sentences:

nc pn a tme thr ws lttle grl. Hr nm ws Gldlcks. h hd gldn hr. n d Gldlcks ws wlkng n th frst. h sw hs nd knckd n th dr. Sh wnt nsd. Nbd ws thr. Gldlcks sw thr bwls n th tabl. h ws hngr. "Ths prrdg s t ht! Ths prrdg s t cld!" (see end of chapter for complete paragraph)

You likely were able to figure out the second set of sentences but found it next to impossible to figure out the first set of sentences! This gives you a better sense of what it is like for someone with ARHL to understand what is being said—that is, if all that a person hears are the low-frequency vowels, without the advantage of hearing the consonants to fill in the blanks, this person will have difficulty determining what is being said.

In addition to the differences between vowels and consonants described above, consonants also are more likely to be drowned out by background noise. Thus, older individuals with ARHL will be able to carry on a conversation one-on-one in a quiet room but will have difficulty hearing in a noisy setting. Individuals with ARHL also have more difficult hearing women than men because women's voices tend to be of higher pitch than men's voices. You can well imagine how that affects conversations between an older man and his wife!

One of the most common complaints of older adults with ARHL is that although they hear the speech, they have trouble understanding what is being said, particularly in the presence of noise. Two longitudinal studies have shown a relationship between hearing loss and cognitive decline. The first, the Health ABC study, showed that individuals with normal hearing performed much better on tests of cognitive functioning than individuals with hearing loss (Lin et al., 2013). The results from the second longitudinal study (The Baltimore Longitudinal Study on Aging), involving 639 individuals who were followed for more than 10 years, indicated that those individuals with hearing loss had a higher probability of developing dementia, with the probability of developing dementia increasing as the severity of hearing loss increased (Lin, Metter et al., 2011). These and other similar findings in this area have important implications for how older adults are assessed for hearing loss. For example, the inclusion of measures of cognitive function in assessments of hearing loss in older individuals, the type of hearing aid selected, and instructions on the use of the hearing aids (e.g., hearing aids with fewer programs and instructions on hearing-aid use that are not overly complicated) all are important assessment factors (Pichora-Fuller & Singh, 2006). Finally, as noted by Pichora-Fuller and Singh (2006), "Although it is true that there are well-known declines in hearing and in cognitive processing that are associated with age, it also is important not to forget that there is great heterogeneity in the older population" (p. 53). As such, it is important to make decisions about an individual's functional ability based on performance and not on the date of birth on their birth certificate.

Now, take a moment and think about your communication every day and how much of it is dependent upon your ability to hear—talking with a cashier at the store or a server in a restaurant, following conversations at a social function, communicating during a doctor's appointment or during medical testing, and going to a movie. Now, think about what your world would be like if you were unable to hear. Helen Keller often is credited with noting that "blindness cuts us off from things, but deafness cuts us off from people" (Harrington, 2000). ARHL negatively impacts a person's ability to communicate with others (Davis et al., 2016). It also is not surprising, then, that studies have found that hearing loss in older adults can lead to depression, isolation, social withdrawal, and reductions in overall quality of life (Ciorba, Bianchini, Pelucchi, & Pastore, 2012; Dalton et al., 2003; Mener, Betz, Genther, Chen, & Lin, 2013; Mick & Pichora-Fuller, 2016).

You might be wondering if there are strategies that you can use when conversing with an older individual with hearing loss. Strategies that are helpful include facing the person and maintaining eye contact (or positioning yourself at eye level) in that facial expressions and body language are important sources of information in communication. Speaking at a normal rate in a clear voice also is helpful. It is important that you not shout as shouting not only distorts your words but also can be demeaning. If the individual has difficulty understanding what is said, rephrase rather than repeat the same words over and over again. Reducing the background noise (turning off the television or turning down the radio) when conversing with an older individual can be helpful.

In addition to the strategies identified above, hearing loss can be minimized by the use of hearing aids. In one of the largest studies ever done in this area, Kochkin and Rogin (2000) surveyed 2069 hearing-impaired individuals 50 years of age and older and 1710 of their family members. The results indicated that the use of hearing aids was associated with improvements in physical, emotional, mental, and social well-being. Of interest, these benefits were more noticeable to family members and friends than to the actual users themselves! Despite the benefits of hearing aids, a minority of hearing-impaired individuals use hearing aids. In a recent Canadian study, Feder and colleagues (2015) found that only 24 percent of Canadians aged 70 to 79 wear a hearing aid or aids. This percentage is similar to results from a large population-based survey in the United States, where only 19 percent of Americans 70 years of age and older reported wearing a hearing aid (Lin, Thorpe, Gordon-Salant, & Ferruci, 2011). Why do older adults who are hard of hearing not wear hearing aids? For some, denial that they have a hearing problem is a major reason, whereas for others, belief that "nothing can be done" is a major barrier to hearing aid use. Vanity, cost, difficulty in handling hearing aids, and bad experiences (e.g., poor quality sound and/or squealing sounds) are additional barriers to hearing-aid use in the elderly.

Do you know someone who is hard of hearing and who will not use their hearing aids?

If so, what reasons do they give for not wearing their hearing aids?

Advances in technology have resulted in improvements in hearing aids. Prior to the introduction of digital hearing aids in 1996, modern hearing aids were of the analogue type (Bauman, 2015). With **analogue hearing aids**, sound is converted to an electric signal and amplified. Compared to the older analogue hearing aids, not only do the newer digital hearing aids have improved sound quality, they also are smaller in size, are more comfortable to wear, and have reductions in the amount of feedback (McCormack & Fortnum, 2013). Some of the digital hearing aids also can sync up wirelessly with Bluetooth to a smart phone, enabling the individual to hear calls through the hearing aid. The phone also can be used to adjust the settings on the hearing aid. There are even accessories that allow the individual to stream audio from an MP3 player, laptop, or TV right to the hearing aid! It will be interesting to see if these advantages translate into an increased use of hearing aids in the older adult population. As you can see from Figures 3.9a and 3.9b, today's hearing aids also are significantly smaller than the hearing aids of the past. Some are so small that they fit in the ear canal and are barely visible. However, the smaller size can be associated with a loss of power and features. Unfortunately, the newer hearing aids can be expensive (ranging from $1000 to $6000), with the cost of the hearing aids borne by the individual.

Finally, there has been some interesting research done in Canada that may revolutionize the treatment of hearing loss. In this research, Dr. Claude Alain and his colleagues (Du, Buchsbaum, Grady, & Alain, 2016) have pinpointed the specific part of the brain that older adults rely on to differentiate speech sounds in background noise. As you learned earlier, changes occur in the peripheral and central auditory systems of the brain with age, with hearing aids or assistive listening devices used to compensate for these age-related declines in

FIGURE 3.9a

ORIGINAL HEARING AID

SPL/Science Source

(a)

FIGURE 3.9b

MODERN HEARING AID

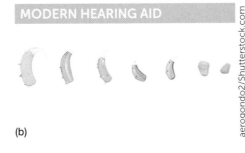

aerogondo2/Shutterstock.com

(b)

hearing. However, there now is evidence that changes occur in the speech motor area of the brain (Broca's area) to help older adults identify speech embedded in noise. The recognition that there are other areas of the brain that can affect hearing is important in that it suggests that training programs can be devised to target these brain areas and/or to adapt the way that hearing aids are developed.

CHANGES IN TASTE AND SMELL WITH AGE

The tastes that we experience as human beings are dependent on how our taste receptors are stimulated. Our taste receptors are located in small oval structures called **taste buds,** which are situated mainly on the tongue, as well as in the mouth and throat. When the chemicals in food activate the taste receptors, signals are sent to processing regions in the brain and decoded, and we perceive the taste of food (Keast & Costanzo, 2015). A common misconception is that the taste receptors that respond to different tastes are located in separate regions of the tongue (e.g., taste receptors for sweet on the tip of the tongue, taste receptors for bitter on the back of the tongue, etc.). Rather, we now know that taste receptors in humans are scattered throughout the tongue. Another misconception was (and perhaps still is) the belief that there are four distinct tastes: sweet, salty, bitter, and sour. A fifth taste, umami, has been identified with this taste described as rounded, rich, and savoury (Lindermann, Ogiwara, & Ninomiya, 2002). There is a growing body of evidence for the existence of a sixth taste – fat (Keast & Costanzo, 2015). Although the existence of this sixth taste has yet to be confirmed, its existence is particularly important given the increasing prevalence of overweight and obesity. In the last 30 years in Canada alone, the prevalence of obesity has increased by 200 percent, with the prediction that about one in five Canadian adults (21 percent) will be obese by 2019 (Twells, Gregory, Reddigan, & Midodzi, 2014).

Does taste change with age? Currently, the research on changes in taste perception with age is contradictory, with some studies indicating no decline and other studies indicating declines but not necessarily for all types of taste. In general, the majority of the studies show a decline in taste sensitivity with age (Mojet, 2004). In addition to normal aging, diseases or conditions such as upper respiratory and middle ear infections; radiation therapy for cancers of the head and neck; head injury; and surgeries to the ear, nose, and throat are associated with disorders in taste, as are common drugs such as antibiotics and antihistamines. Poor oral hygiene and dental problems also can contribute to taste disorders in older adults (National Institute on Deafness and Other Communicative Disorders, 2014).

Smell also changes with age. The sense of smell depends on sensory receptors that are located in the olfactory epithelium lining the roof, superior conchae, and septum of the nasal cavity. In a recent review, Doty and Kamath (2014) reported that decreased olfactory function is present in over half of individuals between the ages of 65 and 80 years, and in over three quarters of those over the age of 80. As noted by Boyce and Shone (2006), "the world is a different place without the sense of smell" (p. 239).

REFLECTIVE QUESTION

Can you imagine **not** being able to smell the flowers in the spring, the aroma of freshly baked bread, or the scent of your favourite cologne?

Not only does smell provide us with pleasant experiences, it also plays an important role in safety. For example, an inability to smell a fire or to detect leaking natural gas poses safety issues for many older adults due to declines in smell with age. Of interest, an age-related decline in the sense of smell is associated with an increased risk of developing dementia (Devanand et al., 2015). A recent study also found that a reduction in the sense of smell was a good predictor of death (Pinto, Wroblewski, Kern, Schumm, & McClintock, 2014). Specifically, in this study, older individuals who had lost their sense of smell (**anosmia**) had three times the odds of death as those with a normal sense of smell (**normosmic**). Why is a decline in smell a good predictor of death? The belief is that the olfactory system is an early indicator of overall physiological declines and, as such, the decline in smell serves as the "canary in the coal mine."

The senses of smell and taste are closely related in that smell plays an important role in the ability to identify different tastes—think about how bland food tastes when you have a cold. Loss of taste and smell with age can result in older individuals losing an interest in food, which in turn can lead to malnutrition (Ramage-Morin & Garriguet, 2013). However, food can be made more interesting with the addition of herbs and spices, rather than salt. Did you know that Canadians consume about 3400 mg of sodium each day? This is more than double the amount that we need! There now is ample evidence that too much sodium is associated with high blood pressure, which is a major risk factor for stroke, heart disease, and kidney disease, with excessive sodium intake linked to an increased risk of osteoporosis (Strazzullo, D'Elia, Kandala, & Cappuccio, 2009). So, ditching the salt shaker is good advice for not only older individuals but for all of us. Declines in sense of smell and taste also pose a safety risk in that older individuals may eat food that is spoiled. Have you noticed spoiled food in your grandparents' fridge? If so, what measures do you think you could take to prevent your grandparents from eating this food?

CHANGES IN TOUCH WITH AGE

The sensation of touch is part of the somatosensory system. Somatosensory function refers to the detection, discrimination, and recognition of touch sensation and **proprioception** (Dinse, Tegenthoff, Heinisch, & Kalisch, 2009). Of interest, there is less research on changes in touch with age as compared to the other senses. Research that has been done indicates that tactile thresholds increase significantly with age, as do thresholds for pain and temperature (Wickremaratchi & Llewelyn, 2006). These changes have important implications for everyday living. For example, decreased temperature sensitivity can make it hard for an older person to tell the difference between cool and cold water and warm and hot water. This can result in an increased risk of injury from burns or from hypothermia and frostbite. The reduced ability to detect touch and pressure can lead to pressure ulcers (the breakdown of an area of the skin due to constant rubbing or pressure against the skin). A reduced sensitivity to pain can result in older adults not knowing how severe an injury is after burning themselves or after falling down the stairs because they do not perceive the pain. There are a number of techniques that older individuals can use to minimize the risk of injury due to changes in touch with age. These techniques include adjusting the water temperature on the water heater to reduce the risk of burns, regular inspection of the skin for signs of a pressure sore or injury, and frequent monitoring of the thermostat in the home to prevent overheating or becoming too chilled.

3.4 CHANGES IN THE CARDIOVASCULAR SYSTEM WITH AGE

LEARNING OBJECTIVE

- To understand and be able to describe the changes in the cardiovascular system with age

CARDIOVASCULAR DISEASE

Cardiovascular disease (CVD) is an umbrella term used to describe many diseases of the cardiovascular system, including diseases of the heart (e.g., **arteriosclerosis**, **coronary artery disease**, **valvular heart disease**, **heart failure**) as well as diseases throughout the body (e.g., **peripheral vascular disease**). Stroke, which is the result of an interruption of blood flow to the brain or rupture of blood vessels in the brain, also is classified as a disease of the cardiovascular system. Did you know that someone in Canada dies every seven minutes from heart disease or stroke (Heart and Stroke Foundation, 2015)? A person having a heart attack may experience one or more of the following symptoms: pressure, tightness, pain, or a squeezing or aching sensation in the chest or arms, which may spread to the neck, jaw, or back; nausea, indigestion, heartburn, or abdominal pain; shortness of breath; breaking out into a cold sweat; fatigue; and lightheadedness or sudden dizziness.

As shown in Figure 3.10, the risk of death from cardiovascular disease increases dramatically with age. That is, for both men and women, the risk of death from cardiovascular diseases increases from 7.4 percent for both men and women 25 to 34 years of age to 42.4 percent for both men and women 85 years of age and older. You also can see from Figure 3.10 that, in general, men are far more likely to die from cardiovascular disease than are their same-aged female counterparts.

FIGURE 3.10

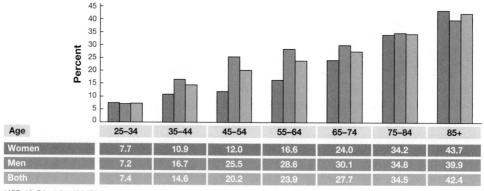

PERCENTAGE OF DEATHS DUE TO CVD*, BY SEX AND AGE GROUP, CANADA, 2004

Age	25–34	35–44	45–54	55–64	65–74	75–84	85+
Women	7.7	10.9	12.0	16.6	24.0	34.2	43.7
Men	7.2	16.7	25.5	28.6	30.1	34.8	39.9
Both	7.4	14.6	20.2	23.9	27.7	34.5	42.4

* ICD-10-CA codes: I00–I99.

Why do you think men are more likely to die from cardiovascular disease than are their same-aged female counterparts?

STROKE

Stroke (also known as cerebrovascular accident or CVA) is the third-leading cause of death in Canada, accounting for almost six percent of all deaths in the same time period (Statistics Canada, 2012b). A stroke is the result of the rupture of blood vessels in the brain (hemorrhagic stroke) or the interruption of flow to the brain due to a narrowed or blocked artery (ischemic stroke). Most strokes are ischemic strokes. With both hemorrhagic and ischemic strokes, blood supply to the brain is reduced or interrupted, which can result in the death of brain cells. Symptoms that someone may be having a stroke include sudden numbness, weakness, or paralysis in the face, arm, or leg (especially on one side of the body); slurring of words or difficulty in understanding speech; trouble seeing from one or both eyes (sudden blurring or vision or seeing double); a sudden severe headache that may include vomiting or dizziness; and/or difficulty walking (loss of balance or loss of coordination). Strokes are a medical emergency and anyone having signs or symptoms of a stroke should seek immediate medical attention.

As you can see in Figure 3.11, the risk of death due to an acute stroke increases significantly with age. That is, the rate of death due to a stroke is very low for individuals below 65 years of age. However, the rates of death from stroke increase dramatically after age 65 (PHAC, 2009).

FIGURE 3.11

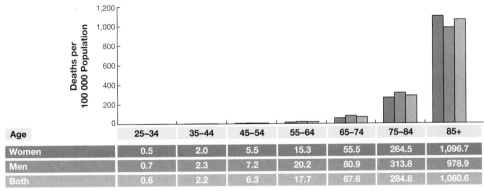

RATES OF DEATH DUE TO ACUTE STROKE*, BY SEX AND AGE GROUP, CANADA, 2004

Age	25–34	35–44	45–54	55–64	65–74	75–84	85+
Women	0.5	2.0	5.5	15.3	55.5	264.5	1,096.7
Men	0.7	2.3	7.2	20.2	80.9	313.8	978.9
Both	0.6	2.2	6.3	17.7	67.6	284.8	1,060.6

* ICD-10-CA codes: I60, I61, I63, I64.

Source: © All rights reserved. *Tracking heart disease and stroke in Canada.* Public Health Agency of Canada, 2009. Adapted and reproduced with permission from the Minister of Health, 2017.

TABLE 3.1

MODIFIABLE AND UNMODIFIABLE RISK FACTORS FOR CARDIOVASCULAR DISEASE

MODIFIABLE RISK FACTORS	UNMODIFIABLE RISK FACTORS
Hypertension	Family history of cardiovascular disease
High cholesterol	Ethnicity
High triglycerides	Gender
High levels of low-density lipoprotein	Age
Low levels of high-density lipoprotein	Diabetes (Type 1)
Tobacco use	Socioeconomic status
Physical inactivity	
Obesity	
Diabetes (Type 2)	
Diet high in saturated fats	
Excessive use of alcohol	

Source: World Heart Federation. (2015). *Cardiovascular risk factors*. Retrieved from www.world-heart-federation.org/cardiovascular-health/cardiovascular-disease-risk-factors.

You might be wondering what factors increase a person's risk for heart disease and stroke. Although some of these risk factors cannot be changed (unmodifiable risk factors), the majority of risk factors can be either treated or changed (modifiable risk factors) (see Table 3.1). Modifiable risk factors include **hypertension**, high cholesterol levels, tobacco use, physical activity, obesity, diabetes, an unhealthy diet, and excessive use of alcohol (World Heart Federation, 2015). Unmodifiable risk factors include family history of cardiovascular disease, ethnicity, gender, age, diabetes and socioeconomic status . That is, individuals with a family history of heart disease, people of African or Asian ancestry, females, individuals who are 55 years of age and older, those with Type 1 diabetes, and being poor are at increased risk for heart disease and/or stroke (World Heart Federation, 2015).

The good news is that, overall, the rates of death due to cardiovascular disease and stroke have been decreasing over the years (see Figure 3.12). That is, over the past 60 years, death rates for cardiovascular disease and stroke have declined by more than 75 percent (PHAC, 2009). Reasons for a reduction in these death rates are the result of many factors including improvements in diagnosis, treatments, and drug therapies, as well as changes in lifestyle such as lower rates of smoking, increased physical activity, and increased consumption of fruit and vegetables.

Although there have been incredible gains in the diagnosis, treatment, and outcomes of cardiovascular disease and stroke in the last 60 years, there also is cause for concern going forward. Heart disease continues to be a leading cause of death in many countries worldwide. In Canada, heart disease was the second-leading cause of death in 2009, accounting for just over 20 percent of all deaths (PHAC, 2009). The aging of the population, the high percentage (60 percent) of adults who are overweight or obese, the tripling of obesity rates in children, the skyrocketing rates of diabetes in individuals who have had heart attacks, and the poor diets and

FIGURE 3.12

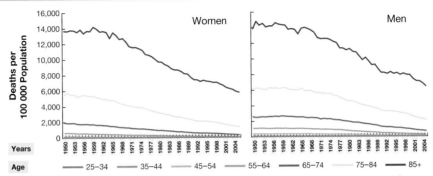

* ICD-10-CA codes: I00-I99. Note: The coding schemes for this condition changed in 1958, 1969, 1979, and 2000, and this may influence trends.

lack of physical activity of many Canadians threaten to undo many of the gains realized in this area over the last six decades (Heart and Stroke Foundation, 2015; PHAC, 2009).

> What can you do to reduce your risk of developing cardiovascular disease and stroke as you get older?

REFLECTIVE QUESTION

3.5 CHANGES IN THE DIGESTIVE SYSTEM WITH AGE
LEARNING OBJECTIVE

- To understand and be able to describe the changes in the digestive system with age

The digestive tract (gastrointestinal tract) is a long twisting tube that begins at the mouth and ends at the anus. The digestive tract, which is about nine metres in length, has two important functions: the digestion and absorption of food. Other organs that are needed for digestion are the liver, gallbladder, and pancreas. As with other bodily systems, changes in the digestive system do occur with age. Changes include a sluggish metabolism that can result in weight gain and constipation. Older adults also are more susceptible to a condition called diverticulitis, which is the development of small pouches in the lining of the colon. For some older adults, diverticulitis can result in constipation and discomfort. If these small pouches become inflamed, the person may experience pain, fever, and abdominal discomfort. Changes in the digestive system with age also can affect the foods that an older person is able to eat. For example, many older adults find that they can no longer tolerate coffee, alcohol, or spicy foods in the same quantity as when they were younger. Heartburn, dyspepsia (indigestion), and intestinal gas also are more common with age (National Institute of Diabetes and Digestive and Kidney Diseases, 2015).

There are a number of lifestyle behaviours that can help to reduce many of the changes in the digestive system with age. These behaviours include eating a low-fat, high-fibre diet rich in fruits and vegetables; drinking plenty of water to stay hydrated; engaging in regular exercise such as walking, biking, or swimming; and practising moderation by not overindulging in food or drinks (Concordia University, n.d.).

3.6 CHANGES IN THE IMMUNE SYSTEM WITH AGE
LEARNING OBJECTIVE

- To understand and be able to describe the changes in the immune system with age

The immune system is the body's natural defense against diseases and infections. There are two major components of the immune system—the **innate immune system** and the adaptive immune system. The innate immune system, which is present at birth, has set strategies for identifying and dealing with certain kinds of infections without having to be trained on how to identify them. This typically involves the activation of white blood cells such as neutrophils, eosinophils, and macrocytes in response to infectious microbes such as bacteria or viruses or non-infectious agents such as sunburn or cancer (National Institute of Allergy and Infectious Diseases, 2013). The **adaptive immune system**, on the other hand, develops over time through the exposure to a specific pathogen. Following exposure, the B or T cells that have been activated are retained in the body as memory cells, creating an **immunological memory**, leading to an enhanced response to subsequent encounters with that pathogen (National Institute of Allergy and Infectious Diseases, 2013). This learned response to pathogens is the basis of **vaccination**.

Both of the innate and the adaptive immune systems change with age, with these changes contributing to the increased susceptibility of older individuals to infectious diseases, vaccine failure, and possibly autoimmunity and cancer (Castle, 2000). Although Canadian data are lacking, results from the United States indicate that infectious diseases account for one-third of all deaths in people 65 years and older with an estimated 90 percent of deaths resulting from pneumonia occurring in people 65 years and older (Mouton, Bazaldua, Pierce, & Espino, 2001). In this paper, the authors note that death resulting from influenza also occurs primarily in the elderly.

As you will learn in Chapter 5, older individuals are more likely than younger individuals to spend time in hospitals and other institutional settings (e.g., lodges, long-term-care care facilities). This results in older individuals having an increased exposure to infections in hospital and institutional settings. These hospital-acquired infections are called **nosocomial infections**. Two of the bugs that can be acquired in the hospital are *Clostridium difficile* and methicillin-resistant *Staphylococcus aureus* (MRSA). Both of these infections are difficult to treat and are more common in patients 65 years of age and over (Miller et al., 2010).

Is there anything older people can do to boost their immunity? Of interest, there are many products on store shelves that claim to boost immunity. These products include aloe vera, echinacea, garlic, ginseng, and probiotics (see www.health.harvard.edu/staying-healthy/how-to-boost-your-immune-system). The idea that we can boost our immune system is enticing but, to date, there are no scientifically proven direct links between lifestyle and improved immune function (Munkyong, Meydani, & Wu, 2012). The good news is that this is an area that is being actively researched, with studies investigating the effects of diet, exercise, herbal supplements, etc., on immune system functioning. In general, adoption of a healthy lifestyle such as engaging in regular exercise; eating a diet high in fruits, vegetables, and whole grains and low in saturated fat; maintaining a healthy weight; avoiding smoking; limiting the use of alcohol; getting adequate sleep; controlling your blood pressure; and engaging in regular medical screening for conditions in your age group and risk category are recommended as steps toward keeping your immune system strong and healthy.

3.7 CHANGES IN THE METABOLIC SYSTEM WITH AGE

LEARNING OBJECTIVE

- To understand and be able to describe the changes in the metabolic system with age

The metabolic system includes the pancreas, liver, thyroid, and hypothalamus. Diabetes, which is a chronic metabolic disorder, is one of the most common chronic diseases in Canada, with the percent of Canadians living with diabetes increasing with age (PHAC, 2016).

DIABETES

Diabetes mellitus is a chronic disease characterized by hyperglycemia (high blood sugar). Typically, the disease is categorized into two forms: Type 1 diabetes (previously called insulin-dependent diabetes mellitus and/or juvenile diabetes) and Type 2 diabetes (previously called non-insulin-dependent diabetes mellitus and adult-onset diabetes). Type 1 diabetes can occur at any age, but it most often occurs before the age of 30 years. Type 2 diabetes, on the other hand, usually occurs in individuals over the age of 40 years. Type 1 diabetes usually is more severe and is characterized by the body's impaired ability to produce **insulin**. Daily insulin injections are required to manage Type 1 diabetes. Type 2 diabetes, on the other hand, is typically less severe and is marked by the body's impaired ability to recognize and utilize insulin. Type 2 diabetes can be managed by diet alone or in combination with **oral hypoglycemic agents**. Some individuals with Type 2 diabetes, are, however, treated with insulin. Canadians were central to the discovery of the treatment for Type 2 diabetes. For more information, read Box 3.1.

Due to population growth, the aging of the population, increasing rates of obesity, and an increase in a sedentary lifestyle, the number of people with diabetes is rapidly increasing in many countries worldwide (Wild, Roglic, Green, Sicree, & King, 2004). In 2008/2009, nearly 2.4 million Canadians (6.8 percent) were living with diagnosed diabetes. Importantly, the overall **prevalence** of diagnosed diabetes increased by 70 percent since 1998/1999 (PHAC, 2011a). As can be seen in Figure 3.13, the prevalence of diabetes increases significantly with age. This is due in large part to the decreased ability of the body to produce and use insulin with age, placing older individuals at an increased risk of developing Type 2 diabetes. As shown in Figure 3.13, the 75- to 79-year-old age group had the highest proportion of individuals with diagnosed diabetes (23 percent of females and almost 29 percent of males), with those aged 80 to 84 having the second-highest proportion of individuals with diagnosed diabetes.

Long-term complications of both Type 1 and Type 2 diabetes include an increased risk of cardiovascular disease (e.g., heart attacks, strokes, and high blood pressure); kidney disease; damage

FIGURE 3.13

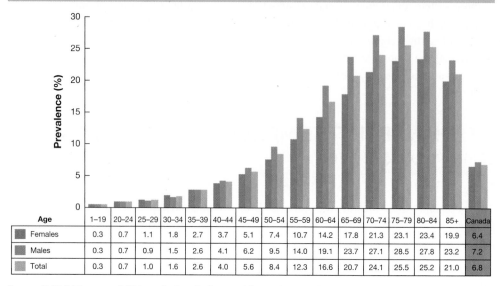

Age	1–19	20–24	25–29	30–34	35–39	40–44	45–49	50–54	55–59	60–64	65–69	70–74	75–79	80–84	85+	Canada
Females	0.3	0.7	1.1	1.8	2.7	3.7	5.1	7.4	10.7	14.2	17.8	21.3	23.1	23.4	19.9	6.4
Males	0.3	0.7	0.9	1.5	2.6	4.1	6.2	9.5	14.0	19.1	23.7	27.1	28.5	27.8	23.2	7.2
Total	0.3	0.7	1.0	1.6	2.6	4.0	5.6	8.4	12.3	16.6	20.7	24.1	25.5	25.2	21.0	6.8

to the eye (retinopathy), which can result in blindness, as well as an increased risk for other eye disorders such as cataracts and glaucoma; and nerve damage (neuropathy) resulting in tingling, numbness, burning, and pain, particularly in the lower limbs. Nerve damage to the feet and reduced blood flow to the lower limbs can result in amputations of the toe, foot, or leg. However, with effective management of blood sugar levels, individuals with both Type 1 and Type 2 diabetes can reduce the risk of long-term complications. What does "effective management of blood sugar levels" mean? In general, the blood sugar level for healthy individuals (e.g., those without diabetes) is about 4 mmol/L (millimoles per litre). Recommended target levels for individuals with diabetes are 4 to 7 mmol/L for individuals with Type 1 and 2 diabetes before meals and 5 to 10 mmol/L for people with Type 1 and Type 2 after meals (Canadian Diabetes Association, 2013).

As noted above, Type 2 diabetes is associated with older age, obesity, and physical inactivity. As such, many cases of Type 2 diabetes can be prevented through the adoption of a healthy lifestyle (e.g., regular exercise; a diet high in fruits, vegetables, and whole grains and low in saturated fat; maintaining a healthy weight) (Penn et al., 2013; Tay et al., 2014; Wannamethee, Thomas, Whincup, & Sattar, 2009).

3.8 CHANGES IN THE MUSCULOSKELETAL SYSTEM WITH AGE

LEARNING OBJECTIVE

- To understand and be able to describe the changes in the musculoskeletal system with age

THE DISCOVERY OF INSULIN: A LASTING CANADIAN CONTRIBUTION

Before the discovery of insulin, diabetes was a feared disease that most certainly led to death. Physicians knew that sugar worsened the condition of patients with diabetes and that the most effective treatment was to put the patients on very strict diets where sugar intake was kept to a minimum. At best, this treatment could buy patients a few extra years, but it never saved them. In some cases, the harsh diets even caused patients to die of starvation.

During the 19th century, observations of patients who died of diabetes often showed that the pancreas was damaged. In 1869, a German medical student, Paul Langerhans, found that there were clusters of cells within the pancreatic tissue that produce digestive juices but the function of these cells was unknown. Some of these cells were eventually shown to be the insulin-producing beta cells. Later, these cell clusters were named the *islets of Langerhans* in honour of the person who discovered them.

In 1921, a Canadian surgeon Frederick Banting and medical student Charles H. Best were credited with discovering the hormone insulin in the pancreatic extracts of dogs. The pair then developed insulin for human treatment with the help of Canadian chemist James B. Collip (a professor at the University of Alberta who helped by developing an improved process for extracting the insulin from the pancreas) and Scottish physiologist J.J.R. Macleod. The first medical success was with a boy with Type 1 diabetes—14-year-old Leonard Thompson—who was successfully treated in 1922. Close to death before treatment, Leonard bounced back to life with the insulin. This news rapidly spread beyond Canada, and in 1923 the Nobel Committee decided to award Banting and Macleod (a leading figure in the study of diabetes in Canada) the Nobel Prize in Physiology or Medicine. Since that time, scientists and medical historians have been more inclined to view the discovery of insulin as a collaborative effort by a team of scientists including Banting, Best, Collip, Macleod, and others.

Source: © Nobel Media AB.

The musculoskeletal system consists of bones, muscles, tendons, ligaments, joints, cartilage, and other connective tissues.

MUSCLE STRENGTH, HEIGHT, AND WEIGHT

The aging process is associated with progressive declines in muscle mass and strength (sarcopenia), with these changes beginning as early as the fourth decade of life, with up to 50 percent of mass being lost by the eighth decade of life (Watson, 2012). There also are declines in aerobic capacity with age (Crane, Macneil, & Tarnopolsky, 2013). These age-associated changes in skeletal muscle and aerobic capacity have important implications for everyday activities such as declines in mobility (walking, climbing stairs), functional impairments (opening jars, rising from a chair), increases in fatigability, and reductions in overall quality of life. The good news is that long-term participation in aerobic exercise appears to lessen the age-related reductions in muscle strength in addition to providing cardiorespiratory and metabolic benefits (Crane et al., 2013).

In addition to the changes listed above, changes in height and weight occur with age. The loss of height with age is related to changes in the bones, muscles, and joints. As we noted in Chapter 2, in general, individuals typically lose about one centimetre (almost one-half inch) every 10 years after age 40, with loss in height occurring even more rapidly after age 70. Changes in total body weight with age differ for men and women. Men often gain weight until about age 55, and then begin to lose weight later in life. This may be related to a drop in the male sex hormone testosterone. Women usually gain weight until age 65, and then begin to lose weight. Weight loss later in life occurs partly because fat replaces lean muscle tissue, and fat weighs less than muscle. Lifestyle choices that can reduce these age-related body changes include getting regular exercise, eating a healthy diet that includes fruits and vegetables, whole grains, and the right amounts of healthy fats; limiting alcohol use; and avoiding smoking (Minaker, 2011).

OSTEOARTHRITIS AND RHEUMATOID ARTHRITIS

Arthritis is a condition that is common with age. It is an umbrella term referring to a group of more than 100 medical conditions affecting the musculoskeletal system. Although arthritis often is seen as an old person's disease, nearly three out of five Canadians with arthritis are younger than 65 years of age (PHAC, 2010b). Two of the most common forms of arthritis are osteoarthritis and rheumatoid arthritis. Both of these chronic conditions are common in older adults, affecting 44 percent of this population in Canada in 2009 (PHAC, 2010b).

Osteoarthritis also is condition that is common with age. It is characterized by irreversible damage to joint structures, such as cartilage, bone, and joint capsules (Felson & Neogi, 2004). Osteoarthritis usually develops in the smaller joints of the fingers, the weight-bearing joints of the leg (e.g., hip, knee, toes), and the movable portions of the spine. **Rheumatoid arthritis** is a chronic inflammatory condition affecting the joints as well as other tissues in the body. See Figure 3.14 for images of a normal joint, a joint with osteoarthritis, and one with rheumatoid arthritis. Symptoms include stiffness in one or more of the joints, which is usually accompanied by pain upon movement and joint tenderness. Joints in the fingers, wrists, shoulders, feet, and ankles are commonly affected. Currently, there is no cure for arthritis. Drugs called non-steroidal anti-inflammatories (NSAIDs) are typically used to reduce the pain and swelling associated with arthritis.

OSTEOPOROSIS

Osteoporosis is a disease in which the bones become thin and porous, resulting in decreased bone strength and an increased risk for fractures. Osteoporosis is estimated to have affected 29 percent of women and six percent of men 65 years of age and older in Canada in 2009 (PHAC, 2010c). Common sites of fracture associated with osteoporosis include the wrist, spine, hip, and shoulder, with approximately 70 percent of hip fractures in Canadians 45 years and older attributed to osteoporosis (PHAC, 2010c). Osteoporosis often is known as the "silent thief" because these changes in the bone occur without symptoms—until a fracture takes place. Although both men and women lose bone mass beginning in their mid-30s, women lose bone at a greater rate around the time of the menopause. One of the best preventions for osteoporosis is the development of strong bones during childhood and adolescence,

FIGURE 3.14

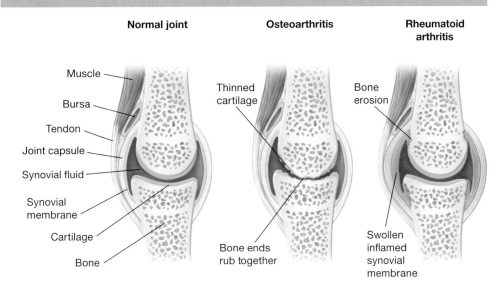

with special attention to the intake of calcium and Vitamin D. Dairy products are good sources of calcium (remember hearing your mother telling you to drink your milk!). The recommended daily dose of calcium is 1000 mgs for males aged 51 to 70 years and 1200 mgs for women aged 51 to 70 years, with a recommended daily dose of 1200 mgs of calcium for both males and females older than 70 years (Health Canada, 2012a). Vitamin D improves the absorption of calcium. Surprisingly, few foods naturally contain Vitamin D. Fatty fish (such as tuna, salmon, and mackerel), as well as fish liver oils (e.g., cod liver oil) are among the best sources of Vitamin D. In many countries in the world, fortified foods provide most of the Vitamin D in our diets. In Canada, the addition of Vitamin D to milk (e.g., fortification) became mandatory in 1965 (Canadian Public Health Association, n.d.). In addition to milk, margarine is fortified by law in Canada ($\geq$ 530 IU/100 g) (National Institutes of Health, 2014). Other food sources that often are fortified with Vitamin D include ready-to-eat breakfast cereals, orange juices, and yogurt. The recommended daily dose of Vitamin D for adults up to and including 70 years of age is 600 IU, increasing to 800 IU for adults over the age of 70 (Health Canada, 2012a).

Vitamin D also is produced in the body through exposure to ultraviolet rays from the sun. However, as was outlined in the beginning of this chapter (see Changes in Appearance section) exposure to the sun's ultraviolet rays increases the risk for skin cancer. Because Vitamin D is readily available in fortified foods and from oral supplements, it makes sense to rely on alternate sources of Vitamin D for meeting daily requirements. However, this area is not without controversy. In addition to Vitamin D intake, adoption of regular resistance training and stretching also is important in helping to prevent the development of osteoporosis in that these two forms of exercise help to build muscle mass and strength.

3.9 CHANGES IN THE NERVOUS SYSTEM WITH AGE

LEARNING OBJECTIVE

- To understand and be able to describe the changes in the nervous system with age

The nervous system consists of neurons, nerves, tracts, and other tissues. Along with the endocrine system, the nervous system controls and integrates the activities and responses to environmental and internal and external stimulations (Kiernan & Rajakumar, 2013). Common age-related anatomical changes in the nervous system include a reduction in both the size of the brain and its weight due primarily to a decrease in the volume of the cerebral cortex. Other anatomical changes include a reduction in neurons, a decrease in the number of dendrite branches and interconnections, changes in synaptic organization, and a decline in the rate of neurotransmitter production (Knight & Nigam, 2008). With aging, abnormal intracellular deposits or plaques begin to accumulate in the neurons. An excessive accumulation of these plaques results in clinical features that are similar to those seen in Alzheimer's disease. The anatomical changes described above are linked to various functional changes, many of which have been described in the sections above (e.g., hearing, vision, smell, taste).

3.10 CHANGES IN THE REPRODUCTIVE SYSTEM WITH AGE

LEARNING OBJECTIVE

- To understand and be able to describe the changes in the reproductive system with age

The reproductive system consists of the ovaries, uterus, and vagina in females and the testes, penis, and scrotum in males. As with the other systems of the body, age-related changes occur in the reproductive system (and genitals) for both men and women.

MENOPAUSE

For women, a reduction in the secretion of estrogen and progesterone, and permanent cessation of menstruation, which results in loss of fertility, are two of the major changes with age. The onset of menopause typically begins in the mid- to late- 40s (Grady, 2006) and lasts for about four years for most women. For men, the changes in fertility are not as major or as rapid as with women. Rather, the changes in the production of testosterone and sperm occur gradually during a process called andropause.

Symptoms of menopause include hot flashes and night sweats, vaginal changes, and trouble sleeping (Dennerstein, Dudley, Hopper, Guthrie, & Burger, 2000; Nelson et al., 2005). Estrogen replacement therapy, which was first approved in 1941 by the U.S. Food and Drug Administration (Stefanick, 2005), was commonly used to treat menopausal symptoms until the mid-1970s. At that time, studies emerged linking the use of estrogen to endometrial cancer (cancer that begins in the endometrium, which is the inner lining of the uterus). Beginning in the early 1980s, progesterone was added to estrogen therapy to reduce the risk of endometrial cancer, with this combination of drugs called **hormone replacement therapy** (HRT). The use of HRT increased throughout the 1990s and 2000s due in part to the lowered risk of endometrial cancer with the combination therapy and publication of new studies documenting the benefits of HRT in reducing the risk of coronary artery disease and hip fractures.

However, the use of HRT began to decline in 2002 with the publication of results from a large study that started in 1991. Results from this study, called the Women's Health Initiative, indicated that the use of HRT was associated with increasing rates of cardiovascular disease and breast cancer in healthy post-menopausal women (Chlebowski et al., 2003; Manson et al., 2003). Since that time, HRT use has continued, with the recommendation that it be used in the management of moderate to severe menopausal symptoms (Martin & Barbieri, 2015). In addition to its use in management of menopausal symptoms, HRT has been used for prevention of fractures.

PHYSICAL CHANGES IN THE GENITAL SYSTEM

Physical changes in the female and male genital systems also occur with age. For women, in addition to the changes associated with menopause described above, the breasts begin to atrophy and the labia (external genital tissue) decrease and thin with age. The vaginal walls also become thinner, dryer, and less elastic, and may become irritated—a condition known as atrophic vaginitis. Sexual intercourse can become painful due to these vaginal changes. The level of normal microorganisms in the vagina also changes with age, increasing the risk of vaginal yeast infections.

For men, decreases in testicular tissue occur with age. Enlargement of the prostate gland also is common as men get older and can interfere with urination. This condition, called benign prostatic hypertrophy, affects approximately 50 percent of men. Notably, prostate function does not affect fertility, and a man can father a child even after his prostate gland has been removed. Prostate and bladder cancer also are more common with age. On the other hand, testicular cancer (cancer that starts in the testes) is more common in younger men.

Erectile dysfunction, which is the inability of a man to attain and maintain an adequate erection for satisfactory sexual intercourse, is more common with age (Gareri, Castagna, Francomano, Cerminara, & De Fazio, 2014). Importantly, however, erectile dysfunction most often is due to medical reasons rather than aging. Illnesses such as diabetes and drugs (e.g., those used to treat high blood pressure) can cause erectile dysfunction (Solomon, Man, & Jackson, 2003). Medications commonly used for erectile dysfunction in men include Viagra, Cialis, or Levitra. You likely have seen advertisements for these drugs on television. Finally, sex drive (libido) also decreases in both men and women with age. However, reductions in libido are more common in women, due in part to the physical changes associated with menopause (e.g., vaginal dryness, hot flashes, night sweats) (Garefalakis & Hickey, 2008). Despite these changes, many older adults continue to have and to enjoy sexual intercourse.

3.11 CHANGES IN THE URINARY SYSTEM WITH AGE
LEARNING OBJECTIVE

- To understand and be able to describe the changes in the urinary system with age

The urinary system consists of the kidneys, ureters, bladder, and urethra. The function of the urinary system is to remove waste and extra fluid from the body through the production and excretion of urine. There are a number of changes to the urinary system with age. Specifically, the kidneys get smaller and the blood flow to the kidneys decreases. These changes affect the kidneys' ability to filter out waste and extra fluid. With age, the kidneys also lose the ability to balance the amount of salt and acid in the body. The tissue in the bladder loses its elasticity, which reduces the amount of urine that the bladder can hold. The muscles of the bladder also become weaker, which results in more urine being left in the bladder after a person urinates. Both of these changes may result in an older person having to urinate more often. There also are changes in the sensation of needing to urinate, which can lead to the need to urinate suddenly and urgently. The muscles in the pelvic floor get weaker with age, particularly in women. This change can lead to involuntary loss of urine (incontinence). In men, the flow of urine can be blocked by an enlarged prostate gland. As mentioned earlier, this condition is called benign prostatic hypertrophy and is common with age.

Urinary incontinence (UI), which is defined as involuntary leakage of urine, is a prevalent health condition which increases with age (Swanson, Kaczorowski, Skelly, & Finkelstein, 2005). The condition is more common in women (The Canadian Continence Foundation, 2014). In a recent Canadian study, Ramage-Morin & Gilmour (2013) found that more than half a million adults aged 65 and older experienced UI in 2008/2009. UI is due to the loss of bladder control as a result of changes in the underlying muscles and/or nerves (The Canadian Continence Foundation, 2014). UI can be transient or established. Transient UI is triggered by reversible factors such as waiting too long to urinate. The main causes of established UI are coughing, sneezing, straining, exercise, or any other type of exertion (stress urinary incontinence), the leaking of urine associated with the sudden uncontrollable urge to empty the bladder (urge incontinence), the constant leaking or dribbling from a full bladder (overflow incontinence), and a combination of stress and urge incontinence (mixed urinary incontinence) (The Canadian Continence Foundation, 2014). The good news is that there are a number of treatments available for UI. These include behavioural treatments (e.g., bladder retraining such as timed voiding, pelvic muscle exercises), medical treatments (e.g., drugs such as anti-cholinergics/anti-spasmodics), mechanical treatments (e.g., **pessaries**), and surgical treatments (e.g., stitches, slings, transurethral resection of the prostate) (The Canadian Continence Foundation, 2014). What are the effects of UI on older adults? UI can affect quality of life; for example, Ramage-Morin and Gilmour (2013) found that men and women aged 65 and older had higher odds of being lonely than their same-aged counterparts without UI.

Finally, urinary tract infections are the most common bacterial infection in older adults (Mouton et al. 2001). Diabetes, as well as the use of urinary catheters, can increase the risk for urinary tract infections in older people.

3.12 CHANGES IN SLEEP WITH AGE
LEARNING OBJECTIVE

- To understand and be able to describe the changes in sleep with age

Sleep, like many of the other bodily processes, changes with age. The common belief is that the amount of sleep needed decreases as one gets older. When examined across the age range, total sleep time does decrease with age—from 10 to 14 hours a night for toddlers to 6.5 to 8.5 hours a night for young adults to five to seven hours for adults 65 years of age and older (Gooneratne & Vitiello, 2014). Other changes in sleep with age include time spent awake at night (with older adults spending more time awake than younger age groups) and time spent in REM sleep (with older adults spending less time in REM sleep than younger age groups). Although it is commonly believed that time to fall asleep at the beginning of the night is longer for older adults, this is generally not the case (Ohayon et al., 2004). Interestingly, although studies have shown that there are objective changes in sleep with age (such as those described above), other studies that have looked at subjective perspectives of sleep indicate that complaints of sleep disturbances decrease with age (Gooneratne & Vitiello, 2014).

TABLE 3.2

STEPS TO IMPROVE SLEEP	
Limit the intake of caffeine late in the day.	Avoid caffeine (from coffee, tea, soft drinks, and chocolate) late in the day.
Avoid the intake of alcohol before bedtime.	Alcohol should not be used as a sleeping aid. Although it might seem to make you sleepy, its use can disrupt your sleep.
Avoid big meals or spicy foods just before bedtime	Large or spicy meals may lead to indigestion or discomfort. Try to eat a modest-size dinner at least three hours before bedtime.
Minimize liquid intake before sleep.	Limit what you drink within an hour and a half before bedtime.
Engage in regular exercise.	Participate in moderate aerobic activity on a regular basis.
Ensure your bedroom is conducive to sleep.	Ensure that your bed is comfortable, and minimize the amount of noise and light in the room. A cool room is more conducive to sleep than a hot room.
Eliminate distractions.	Eliminate distractions such as having a television or radio on before going to sleep. Avoid using a computer in bed.
Keep a regular bed-time routine.	Maintain a consistent sleep schedule by going to bed and getting up at the same time every day.
Avoid or limit the use of sleeping pills.	Consistent use of sleeping pills can interfere with the sleep cycle. Avoiding or limiting their use is recommended.

Insomnia, which is characterized by difficulty in getting to sleep or in staying asleep, is the most common sleep disorder (Neikrug & Ancoli-Israel, 2010). It has been estimated that insomnia affects almost half of individuals 65 years of age and older (Ohayon, Carskadon, Guilleminault, & Vitiello, 2004). Results from a large-scale study in Canada involving 2000 individuals between 18 and 99 years of age indicated that individuals aged 60 years of age and older had lower rates of insomnia than those below the age of 50 (Morin et al., 2011). However, other studies suggest that the prevalence of insomnia increases with age, from 10 percent between ages 15 and 24 to almost 20 percent at age 75 and older (Tjepkema, 2005).

There are a number of steps that older adults can adopt to improve their sleep (see Table 3.2). As you can see, most of these steps require only a small change in everyday behaviours, are easy to implement, and are not costly.

3.13 IMPACT OF CHANGES IN APPEARANCE AND STEREOTYPES ASSOCIATED WITH AGING

In this chapter, we have reviewed many of the physical changes that occur with age and the impact of those changes on everyday functioning. Because many of the age-related declines affect not only our physical appearance but also our functional abilities, there are many stereotypes that are associated with the aging process, which in turn can have psychological effects on older individuals and decrease their self-esteem. Older adults may have feelings of worthlessness and devaluation because of negative views that many people have about getting old. As a result of studying this chapter, we hope that you are better able to understand and interact with older adults who are likely to have many of the physical changes discussed in this chapter.

Which stereotypes do you think are the most demeaning for an older person?

Which stereotypes do you think will change over the next several decades because of the advancements in medicine or technology?

Has learning about the normal changes with age changed your beliefs or attitudes toward older people?

3.14 GOOD PRACTICE

Ronak Patel, Ph.D.
Health Sciences Centre, Winnipeg, Manitoba

WHERE DID YOU TRAIN?

I completed my M.A. and Ph.D. in the clinical psychology program at Ryerson University in Toronto, Ontario.

WHERE DO YOU WORK?

Most of my work is based out of the Health Sciences Centre, which is one of the main teaching hospitals in Manitoba.

WHAT DO YOU DO?

I am a clinical neuropsychologist and assistant professor within the College of Medicine at the University of Manitoba.

WHY DO YOU LIKE WORKING WITH AN OLDER-ADULT POPULATION?

I have had a long-standing interest in working with older adults. What I find particularly interesting is examining how the culmination of varied experiences over the lifespan ultimately affects people's behaviour as they get older. These experiences might have a significant impact on how an individual manages their overall mental and physical health over the course of the aging process. There is still much about the aging brain that remains unknown, and this provides many exciting opportunities for scientific research. Finally, I like working with older adults because they often enjoy sharing their life experiences and wisdom, and they usually have a great sense of humour!

DO YOU HAVE ADVICE FOR STUDENTS WHO WANT TO GET INTO THE FIELD?

Always pursue what genuinely interests you. The overarching umbrella of aging is quite broad. One could study aging from any number of perspectives (e.g., emotional, physical, cognitive, neurobiological, environmental, healthcare policy). Take the time to figure out what really piques your interest. Draw from your own personal experiences and from the people around you to develop and foster your interests. I believe we never stop learning as human beings; thus, challenge yourself to see what you can learn from our older adults.

Christine Knight, Ph.D.
Alberta Health Services, Calgary, Alberta

WHERE DID YOU TRAIN?

I obtained an undergraduate degree in psychology from McGill University, Montreal. Quebec, a joint master's degree in applied psychology and gerontology from the University of Waterloo, Ontario and a Ph.D. in clinical psychology from Lakehead University, Thunder Bay, Ontario. Throughout my training, I sought out research and clinical opportunities in areas related to aging such as chronic pain, physical medicine and rehabilitation, grief and loss, geriatric neuropsychology, and the promotion of healthy aging.

WHERE DO YOU WORK?

I work for Alberta Health Services as a consulting psychologist for all the programs that fall under the umbrella of geriatric mental health in the Calgary area.

WHAT DO YOU DO?

I provide assessment, diagnostic, and treatment services to older adults with mental health conditions, including those presenting with complex psychiatric and medical co-morbidities, such as chronic pain and suspected cognitive impairment or dementia. I act as a regional resource, working in partnership with and providing consultation to families, physicians, and professional and para-professional staff along the continuum of healthcare, including outreach, day treatment, a psychiatric in-patient unit, supported housing, and long-term care. In one day I can go from doing psychotherapy with a depressed and housebound client in her living room to conducting an assessment of decision-making capacity with a resident living in long-term care. I also conduct research, as well as teach and supervise graduate students through the Department of Psychology at the University of Calgary.

WHY DO YOU LIKE WORKING WITH AN OLDER-ADULT POPULATION?

I love the challenge and complexity of the clients I serve. Their life experiences are so diverse, and the cohort differences are fascinating, but the wisdom and resiliency that I witness every day is priceless.

DO YOU HAVE ADVICE FOR STUDENTS WHO WANT TO GET INTO THE FIELD?

Be creative and persistent about seeking out opportunities to work with older adults. They are not always well advertised, but there is a psychologist in just about every community who loves working with older adults, and they are probably very excited to hear that you are too. We might be a rare breed, but we tend to be very passionate about what we do.

Angela Vandervelde, R.SLP
Villa Caritas, Geriatric Psychiatry, Edmonton, Alberta

WHERE DID YOU TRAIN?

University of Alberta, Edmonton, Alberta

WHERE DO YOU WORK?

Villa Caritas Hospital in Edmonton, Alberta

WHAT DO YOU DO?

I do swallowing assessments to determine the safest and most appropriate consistency of food and fluid for patients experiencing swallowing difficulty. I also do communication (speech–language) assessments to determine how individuals with cognitive–communication impairment can most effectively communicate and engage in meaningful interactions. I also run an interdisciplinary group to maintain voice quality in older adults.

WHY DO YOU LIKE WORKING WITH AN OLDER-ADULT POPULATION?

It is incredibly rewarding to help older adults with cognitive–communication impairment share their life stories one way or another, whether it be by speaking, looking at photographs, or some other creative means. It is inspiring to learn about their experiences and accomplishments, and it makes the older adult feel great to share their wisdom and knowledge with younger generations. It is the privilege (and challenge) of a speech–language pathologist to try to extract this wisdom and knowledge from older adults with communication impairment.

DO YOU HAVE ADVICE FOR STUDENTS WHO WANT TO GET INTO THE FIELD?
Get a strong academic foundation but don't forget to think outside the box and be creative when working with older adults.

3.15 SUMMARY

- Many of the physical changes that occur with aging are part of the aging process, but many can either be minimized or avoided by lifestyle decisions. Now that you have read the chapter, what changes can you make to help you age well?

- Several of the more commonly used aging theories are programmed theories of aging, cellular theories of aging, and error theories of aging. One aging theory that is getting a good deal of attention is caloric restriction (CR).

- Researchers have distinguished between primary and secondary aging. Primary aging is defined as the gradual and inevitable process of bodily deterioration that takes place throughout life. Secondary aging, on the other hand, is believed to be the result of disease and poor health practices such as not exercising, smoking, and eating an unhealthy diet. The good news is that secondary aging is preventable.

- With regard to changes in the skin, of all the wrinkles that occur with age, few are due to this intrinsic aging process. The two major environmental influences leading to aging of the skin are chronic exposure to solar ultraviolet (UV) irradiation and smoking, with exposure to

sunlight accounting for up to 90 percent of visible skin aging.

- The baby-boomer cohort is the first generation with an increased desire for preservation of a youthful appearance. There currently is an interesting debate in the literature as to whether the consumption of cosmetic surgeries and other non-invasive cosmetic procedures are a means of self-care designed to look "better, not younger" versus "hiding the effects of aging."

- Presbyphonia is a term that is used to describe the changes associated with the aging voice. These changes include a higher pitch in men and a lower pitch in women, reductions in volume and projection (a thin voice), and a tremor or shakiness in the voice.

- Hair colour becomes grey with age due to a reduction in melanocytes. Body and facial hair also turn grey with age, but this change usually occurs later than greying of scalp hair. Hair also becomes thinner with age and hair loss is common, with this loss being more noticeable in men.

- Vision changes with age. The pupils become smaller and less responsive to variations in light, the lens begins to lose elasticity and thickens and yellows with age, and the muscles that control pupil size and the reaction to light lose strength. These changes affect our vision in a number of ways. There also are changes in vision due to age-associated diseases such as macular degeneration, cataracts, and glaucoma.

• There are two main types of hearing loss—conductive hearing loss and sensorineural hearing loss. The most common cause of age-related hearing loss (ARHL—also known as presbycusis) is the loss of the sensory receptors in the inner ear due to the aging process. However, long-term repeated exposure to noise, illnesses such as diabetes and hypertension, as well as genetics, are associated with ARHL. Recent studies have shown a relationship between hearing loss and cognitive decline. There has been some interesting research done in Canada that may revolutionize the treatment of hearing loss.

• The research on changes in taste perception with age is contradictory, but in general, there seems to be a decline in taste sensitivity with age. Many illnesses and injuries can affect taste. Smell changes with age. The senses of smell and taste are closely related in that smell plays an important role in the ability to identify different tastes.

• The risk of death from cardiovascular disease increases dramatically with age for both men and women. The good news is that most risk factors can either be treated or changed.

• Changes in the digestive system with age include a sluggish metabolism, which can result in weight gain and constipation. Older adults also are more susceptible to a condition called diverticulitis.

• Both of the innate and the adaptive immune systems change with age, with these changes contributing to the increased susceptibility of older individuals to infectious diseases, vaccine failure, and possibly autoimmunity and cancer.

• Diabetes mellitus is a chronic disease characterized by high blood sugar. There are two types of diabetes: Type 1 diabetes and Type 2 diabetes. Type 1 diabetes can occur at any age, but it most often occurs before the age of 30 years. Type 2 diabetes, on the other hand, usually occurs in individuals over the age of 40 years.

• The aging process is associated with progressive declines in muscle mass and strength (sarcopenia), with these changes beginning as early as the fourth decade of life. There also are declines in aerobic capacity with age. The good news is that long-term participation in aerobic exercise appears to lessen the age-related reductions.

• Changes in height and weight occur with age. Lifestyle choices can reduce these age-related body changes.

• Two of the most common forms of arthritis are osteoarthritis and rheumatoid arthritis. Both of these chronic conditions are common in older adults, affecting 44 percent of older adults in Canada.

• Osteoporosis is a disease in which the bones become thin and porous, resulting in decreased bone strength and an increased risk for fractures. Getting enough exercise and enough calcium and vitamins each day are important preventive measures.

• Age-related changes occur in the reproductive system, the genital system, and the urinary system for both men and women. Menopause and a reduction in the secretion of estrogen and progesterone are two of the major changes for women. For men, enlargement of the prostate gland is common with age and can interfere with urination. There are a number of changes to the urinary system with age. Incontinence can occur because of these changes. The good news is that there are interventions that can minimize these changes.

- Sleep time declines with age, from an average of 8.9 hours in younger individuals to 7.4 hours in older adults. Insomnia, which is characterized by difficulty in getting to sleep or in staying asleep, is the most common sleep disorder. However, older adults have lower rates of insomnia.

- Because many of the age-related declines affect not only our physical appearance but also our functional abilities, there are many stereotypes that are associated with the aging process, which in turn can have psychological effects on older individuals and decrease their self-esteem.

Key Terms

Accommodation
The ability of the lens of the eye to change focus from distant to near objects (and vice versa).

Actinic Keratosis
An actinic keratosis is a rough, scaly patch on the skin that develops as a result of years of exposure to the sun. It is most commonly found on the face, lips, ears, back of the hands, forearms, scalp, or neck. A small percentage of actinic keratosis lesions can become cancerous.

Adaptive Immune System
The adaptive immune system, which is more complex than the innate immune system, includes the thymus, spleen, tonsils, bone marrow, circulatory system, and lymphatic system.

Agency
A philosophical term referring to the capacity for human beings to make choices.

Age-Related Macular Degeneration (AMD)
A chronic eye disease that causes vision loss in the centre of an individual's field of vision. There are two types of AMD—wet and dry macular degeneration.

Analogue Hearing Aid
A form of hearing aid. With analogue hearing aids, sound is processed as an electrical signal by a microphone. Analogue sound is like making a photocopy—the sound is registered and you get an overall picture. But the actual processing is like re-copying a photocopy—it can only be done to a certain extent because it causes a deterioration of the original imprint.

Androgenetic Alopecia
A common type of hair loss in men, with a typical pattern of receding hairline and hair thinning on the crown of the head. It commonly is known as male pattern baldness.

Anosmia
Loss of the sense of smell.

Arteriosclerosis
Thickening and hardening of the walls of the arteries, occurring typically in old age.

Baby Boomers
Individuals born between 1946 and 1965.

Basal Cell Carcinoma
A type of skin cancer that begins in the basal cells—a type of cell within the skin that produces new skin cells as old ones die off. Most basal cell carcinomas are thought to be caused by long-term exposure to ultraviolet (UV) radiation from sunlight. Basal cell carcinomas are the least dangerous of skin cancers in that they rarely metastasize (spread) or become life-threatening. However, they should be treated.

Caloric Restriction
A strategy to increase longevity by reducing calories, without malnutrition.

Carotenoids
Plant pigments responsible for bright red, yellow, and orange hues in many fruits and vegetables. Dietary carotenoids are thought to provide health benefits by decreasing the risk of disease, particularly certain cancers and eye disease.

Cataract
A clouding of the crystalline lens of the eye.

Cellular Theories of Aging
Theories of aging that propose that human aging is the result of cellular aging, whereby an increasing proportion of cells reach senescence, a terminal stage at which cells will cease to divide.

Collagen
A fibrous protein that provides strength and elasticity to skin, bones, cartilage, and connective tissue.

Conductive Hearing Loss
Hearing loss that occurs when sound is not conducted efficiently through the outer ear canal to the ear drum and the tiny bones (ossicles) in the middle ear.

Congenital
Existing at or dating from birth.

Coronary Artery Disease
A disease of the coronary arteries—the major blood vessels that supply your heart with blood, oxygen, and nutrients. The presence of cholesterol-containing deposits (plaque) in the arteries and inflammation usually are to blame for coronary artery disease.

Cutaneous Aging
Aging of the skin.

Dark Adaptation
The ability of the pupil to adjust to changes in the amount of available light through reflex pupil dilation and activation of rod cells in preference to the cone cells.

Dermis
The inner layer of the skin that lies below the epidermis.

Determinism
A philosophical term that presumes that all events are completely determined by previously existing causes.

Epidermis
The outer layer of the skin.

Error Theories of Aging
Theories that argue that aging is due to environmental insults that result in progressive damage to living organisms. The wear and tear theory and free radical theory are two examples of error theories of aging.

Extrinsic Aging
Aging due to external factors such as exercise, diet, exposure to sunlight, and smoking.

Free Radical Theory of Aging
A theory that argues that organisms age because cells accumulate free radical damage over time. Free radicals, which are formed naturally in the body, are highly reactive and have the potential to cause damage to cells.

Glaucoma
A group of eye conditions that damage the optic nerve. This damage often is the result of an abnormally high pressure in the eye.

Hayflick Limit Theory
A theory that argues that the human cell is limited in the number of times it can divide. The argument is that human cells divide approximately 50 times, after which they stop dividing and die.

Heart Failure
A common condition that develops after the heart has become damaged (e.g., a heart attack) or weakened by other medical conditions such as high blood pressure that is undiagnosed or untreated for a long period of time.

Hormone Replacement Therapy (HRT)
Therapy that involves treating symptoms of menopause with estrogen and progesterone.

Hypertension
High blood pressure, which is defined by a systolic blood pressure greater than 140 mmHg (millimetres of mercury) and a diastolic blood pressure greater than 90 mmHg.

Hypodermis
The hypodermis lies between the dermis and underlying tissues and organs.

Immunological Memory
The ability of the immune system to respond more rapidly and effectively to a pathogen that has been encountered previously.

Innate Immune System
The immune system that is present at birth and includes our skin, the cough reflex, mucous membranes, and stomach acid.

Insomnia
A sleep disorder characterized by difficulty in getting to sleep or in staying asleep.

Insulin
A hormone that is important for metabolism and utilization of energy from the ingested nutrients—especially glucose.

Intraocular Pressure
Fluid pressure inside the eye.

Intrinsic Aging
A form of aging that takes place over the years and occurs irrespective of extrinsic factors; the gradual irreversible changes in structure and function of an organism.

Larynx
Also known as the voicebox, the larynx is a hollow, tubular organ connected to the top of the windpipe (trachea); air passes through the larynx on its way to the lungs. The larynx also produces vocal sounds and prevents the passage of food and other foreign particles into the lower respiratory tract.

Melanin
A natural substance produced by hair follicles that gives colour to hair, skin, and eyes.

Melanoma
The most serious type of skin cancer. It develops in the cells that produce melanin. Exposure to ultraviolet (UV) radiation from sunlight or from tanning lights or beds increases the risk of developing melanoma.

Normosmic
A normal sense of smell.

Nosocomial Infections
Also known as a hospital-acquired infections (HAIs), nosocomial infections are infections that are acquired in a hospital or other health care facility.

Oral Hypoglycemic Agents
Drugs used in the treatment of diabetes mellitus. These drugs are taken orally and are used to lower glucose levels in the blood.

Osteoarthritis
A type of arthritis that occurs when the protective cartilage on the ends of the bones wears down over time. It is the most common form of arthritis, affecting millions of people worldwide.

Osteoporosis
A disease characterized by low bone mass and deterioration of bone tissue.

Peripheral Vascular Diseases
Diseases of the blood vessels (arteries and veins) located outside the heart and brain.

Pessaries
A plastic device inserted into the vagina that may help prevent urine leakage by supporting the neck of the bladder.

Presbycusis
An age-related hearing loss characterized by a gradual and progressive inability to hear, particularly high-frequency sounds.

Presbyopia
The gradual loss of the ability to focus actively on nearby objects (e.g., loss of near vision).

Presbyphonia
Changes associated with the aging voice.

Prevalence
A statistical concept referring to the number of cases of a disease that are present in a particular population at a given time.

Primary Aging
The gradual and inevitable process of bodily deterioration that takes place throughout life.

Programmed Theories of Aging
Theories that argue that aging is genetically programmed to occur with time, and this process of deterioration eventually leads to death.

Proprioception
The ability to sense stimuli arising within the body regarding position, motion, and equilibrium.

Retinoids
A class of chemical compounds that are forms of vitamin A or are chemically related to it. Retinoids minimize the appearance of wrinkles, bolster the thickness and elasticity of the skin, slow the breakdown of collagen, and lighten brown spots caused by sun exposure.

Rheumatoid Arthritis
A chronic inflammatory disorder that typically affects the small joints in hands and feet. Unlike the wear-and-tear damage of osteoarthritis, rheumatoid arthritis affects the lining of the joints, causing a painful swelling that can eventually result in bone erosion and joint deformity.

Secondary Aging
Believed to be the result of disease and poor health practices such as not exercising, smoking, and an unhealthy diet.

Sensorineural Hearing Loss
Hearing loss that occurs as a result of damage to the inner ear (cochlea) or the nerve pathways from the inner ear to the brain. Sensorineural hearing loss is progressive and irreversible and is the most common type of permanent hearing loss.

Squamous Cell Carcinoma
A common form of skin cancer that develops in the thin, flat squamous cells that make up the outer layer of the skin. If not adequately treated at an early stage, squamous cell carcinoma can become life-threatening.

Stroke
A medical condition that occurs when the blood supply to a part of the brain is interrupted or severely reduced, depriving the brain tissue of oxygen and nutrients. Because brain cells begin to die within minutes, a stroke is a medical emergency.

Taste buds
Sensory organs that are found on the tongue and allow us to experience tastes that are sweet, salty, sour, bitter, and umami.

Vaccination
Involves the injection of a killed microbe in order to stimulate the immune system against the microbe, thereby preventing disease. Vaccination (also called immunization) against viral diseases involves injection of a virus that has been weakened or killed. Vaccination against bacterial diseases generally involves using only a small portion of the dead bacteria to stimulate the formation of antibodies against the whole bacteria.

Valvular Heart Disease
A type of heart disease that occurs when one or more of the four valves (tricuspid, pulmonary, mitral, and aortic) of the heart do not work correctly.

Wear and Tear Theory
A theory that argues that the effects of aging are caused by damage done to cells and body systems over time. Essentially, the body systems "wear out" due to use, and, once they wear out, these body systems can no longer function correctly.

Once upon a time there was a little girl. Her name was Goldilocks. She had golden hair. One day Goldilocks was walking in the forest. She saw a house and knocked on the door. She went inside. Nobody was there. Goldilocks saw three bowls on the table. She was hungry. "This porridge is too hot! This porridge is too cold!"

From "LearnEnglish Kids—Goldilocks and the Three Bears," British Council, https://learnenglishkids.britishcouncil.org/sites/kids/files/attachment/stories-goldilocks-and-the-three-bears-transcript_2012_07_13_0.pdf. Reprinted by permission of the British Council.

Public Health Agency of Canada. (2016). *Health Status of Canadians 2016: Report of the Chief Public Health Officer.* Retrieved from: https://www.canada.ca/en/public-health/corporate/publications/chief-public-health-officer-reports-state-public-health-canada/2016-health-status-canadians.html?_ga=2.256046219.121967560.1504308153-23641325.1500934741

CHAPTER

04

COGNITIVE CHANGES, POST-FORMAL THOUGHT, AND WISDOM

XiFotos/E+/Getty Images

CHAPTER OUTLINE

"There is nothing either good or bad, but thinking makes it so."

Shakespeare (*Hamlet*)

One of the myths of aging is that older adults become dim-witted. While there are structural changes to the brain in normal aging, these are not significant enough to interfere with day-to-day functioning. Similarly, there are changes in memory in normal aging, but, again, these changes do not greatly interfere with daily life. While older adults may experience some changes in language capabilities with age, what is more of a concern is that people tend to change how they converse with older adults. Do you become wise with age? Well, this is not a given and, as you will learn, wisdom is not strongly correlated with age. The good news is that a healthy diet and exercise are related to good brain health. Let's start by looking at some techniques that have significantly influenced researchers' knowledge of the aging brain.

4.1 NEUROIMAGING TECHNIQUES
LEARNING OBJECTIVES

To understand:

- the techniques used to study changes in the brain with age
- what researchers have learned about the aging brain using neuroimaging techniques

Neuroimaging is an umbrella term that refers to a variety of methods and technologies for investigating the brain in both humans and animals. Within the past 20 years or so, neuroimaging methods have revolutionized the study of cognition and aging. There are two neuroimaging techniques that are most often used in neurocognitive research. The first technique is called **structural neuroimaging**. This method provides detailed images of the brain's anatomical structure at a certain point in time. These images look like photographs. This type of imaging helps to identify changes to the structure of the brain that occur after stroke or if, for example, a tumour is present. The most common of the structural imaging techniques are x-rays, **computerized tomography** (CT scans), and **magnetic resonance imaging** (MRI). The other type of neuroimaging is called **functional neuroimaging**. Functional neuroimaging provides information about brain activity rather than brain structure. In this method, researchers monitor brain activity as individuals engage in a variety of tasks such as reading or responding to stimuli like auditory sounds. The areas of the brain that are involved in doing the tasks illuminate, giving researchers a great view of the parts of the brain involved with each type of task. There are several types of functional neuroimaging. For example, there is **positron emission tomography** (PET), **single photo emission computerized tomography** (SPECT), **near infrared spectroscopic imaging** (NIRSI), and **diffusion tensor imaging**. However, it is **functional magnetic resonance imaging** (fMRI) that is used most widely to understand the function of the brain during particular tasks. If you would like to know what it would be like to be in an fMRI study, go to this link: https://fission.sas.upenn.edu/psychex/

Neuroimaging techniques have become key to our understanding of normal age-related changes to the brain, as well as disease processes that can occur with age such as Parkinson's disease and Alzheimer's disease. These techniques also have become very important to the field of rehabilitation (e.g., stroke rehabilitation). According to Crosson and his colleagues (2010), functional neuroimaging could be central in defining how brain systems reorganize during rehabilitation, and, as a result, it may be possible to design treatments that can boost reorganization and thereby enhance rehabilitation.

WHAT DO NEUROIMAGING STUDIES TELL US?

Neuroimaging studies have shown us that older adults activate more and different areas of the brain than younger adults do when doing the same cognitive tasks. In particular, younger adults show evidence for focal, left prefrontal activity whereas older adults show activation in both the left and right prefrontal areas when engaged in a cognitive task (Reuter-Lorenz & Park, 2010). These findings challenge the prevailing idea that specific brain regions control specific brain functions. This led to the development of a theory known as HAROLD, which stands for **Hemispheric Asymmetry Reduction in Older Adults** (Cabeza, Andersen, Locantore, & MacIntosh, 2002; Cabeza et al., 2004). According to this theory, the higher level of bilateral activations in the prefrontal cortex of aging brains demonstrates a compensatory strategy for numerous cognitive tasks (Cabeza et al., 2002). **Bilateralization**, in this case, refers to evidence that, in older brains, activations for cognitive tasks spread out to both hemispheres of the prefrontal cortex, whereas in the young, they are typically confined to a single hemisphere. This is known as **compensation**. When older adults perform the same task as younger adults, they use different neural circuitry, which, in turn, enhances their performance on these tasks (Reuter-Lorenz & Park, 2010). Another theory known as the CRUNCH model (**Compensation-Related Utilization of Neural Circuit Hypothesis**) also attempts to explain compensatory activity in older adults (Reuter-Lorenz & Cappell, 2008). In this model, the older brain will work harder and broaden its search for available resources to use in a particular cognitive task (Stanley et al., 2015). However, according to the CRUNCH theory, more brain activation occurs in older adults as compared to younger adults on only those tasks that are easier to do. On the other hand, on those tasks that are harder for older adults to do, this compensatory mechanism no longer is effective, which leads to equal or less activation in older adults relative to young adults.

Although there is support for both of these models, neither are very good at explaining when or why compensation breaks down. Interestingly, other researchers have found evidence that over-recruitment of brain activity does not necessarily lead to better task performance. For example, some researchers (Rypma, Eldreth, & Rebbechi, 2007; Zarahn, Rakitin, Abela, Flynn, & Stern, 2007) have suggested that when performance is matched between age groups, over-recruitment reflects less efficient use of neural resources by older adults rather than compensation.

According to Park and Reuter-Lorenz (2009), the dilemma for cognitive neuroscientists is not so much in clarifying age-related decline in cognitive abilities. Rather, it is trying to understand that a high level of cognitive success can be maintained by older adults in the face of significant neurobiological change (as you will soon learn). In an attempt to understand this success, Park and Reuter-Lorenz (2009) proposed the **scaffolding theory of cognitive aging** (STAC). According to these researchers, performance on various tasks of cognition is maintained due to the continuous engagement of compensatory scaffolding by the brain. According to this theory, the brain recruits additional brain circuitry to support those cognitive structures in which functioning may have become inefficient. In other words, as the brain develops, more efficient neural circuits are created to handle those tasks that are well learned and have become automatic. Rather than discarding the less efficient effort-intensive circuits, the aging brain drafts them into its compensatory systems as a means of reducing deficits. One important idea in STAC is that scaffolding is not a process that simply begins in older age. Rather, across the lifespan, the individual is confronted with cognitive challenges to which the brain must adapt (Reuter-Lorenz & Park, 2010). In their most recent model, Reuter-Lorenz and Park (2014) have added life-course factors that can enhance (e.g., exercise, meditation, cognitive training) or deplete (e.g., cardiovascular disease) neural structures. Although there is a growing consensus that the aging brain retains considerable plasticity of function, it is less clear how age differences in brain activity relate to cognitive performance. According to Grady (2012), the aging process is complex and the many factors that are influenced by age hamper research in this area. Grady argues that longitudinal studies from childhood to old age that investigate cognitive processes, as well as the brain mechanisms that underlie them, are much needed. The few longitudinal studies of brain functioning in older adults that have been done have shown mixed results with one study showing decreased task-related brain activity over time and others showing both increases and decreases in brain activity depending on the specific brain region and cognitive demands assessed (Beason-Held, Kraut, & Resnick, 2008a; Beason-Held, Kraut, & Resnick, 2008b). Let's turn now and look more in depth at age-related changes to the brain.

4.2 NORMAL AGE-RELATED CHANGES TO THE BRAIN

LEARNING OBJECTIVES

To understand:
- the changes in brain structure with age
- cognitive reserve
- the effects of bilingualism on cognitive reserve

CHANGES IN BRAIN STRUCTURE WITH AGE

From reading the previous section, it is pretty clear that aging is associated with changes to the brain. Importantly, while normal aging is associated with loss of brain volume (shrinkage) and weight, not all areas of the brain are affected equally, and there is variability in age-related brain change across individuals (Persson et al., 2016). The frontal cortex (especially the prefrontal cortex), hippocampus, and parietal lobes experience considerable shrinkage with age (see Figure 4.1). These areas are important to learning, memory, planning, and other complex mental activities. In fact, poor performance on tasks measuring **executive functions** has been associated with decreased volume in the prefrontal cortex (Juraska & Lowry, 2012), while decreases in the hippocampus have been associated with deficits in episodic memory (Shi, Liu, Zhou, Yu, & Jiang, 2009). On the other hand, the occipital lobe shows very little age-related changes. Interestingly, although shrinkage in the brain with age is well documented, researchers do not fully understand why this shrinkage occurs. Initially, shrinkage of the brain was thought to be due to the death of neurons (Juraska & Lowry, 2012), but other research has shown that the loss of neurons in most brain areas is minimal in normal aging (Yankner, Lu, & Loerch, 2008). Other factors such as neuronal shrinkage, loss of **glial cells**, and reduction in **myelination** may be contributing to the reduction in brain volume (Salthouse, 2011). Widening of the grooves (sulci) in the brain and shrinking of the convolutions of the brain (gyri) also occur with age, secondary to loss of volume. The **white matter** of the brain consists of bundles of axons that connect areas of **grey matter** (the neuronal cell bodies) in the brain to each other and carry nerve impulses between neurons (Fields, 2010). A thin layer of fat,

FIGURE 4.1

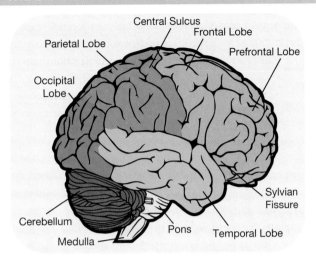

known as **myelin**, surrounds the axons providing electrical insulation, which is white in colour, giving rise to the name "white matter." The loss of grey-matter volume begins in early adulthood and continues throughout adulthood; the death of neurons has been identified as a possible cause of grey-matter volume loss (Harada, Natelson-Love, & Triebel, 2013). However, as mentioned previously, this loss in volume may better be explained by a decrease in the size and number of connections between the neurons (Salthouse, 2011). By contrast, total white-matter volume change is regarded to have a nonlinear relationship with age, with an increase until approximately the fifth decade of life and a decline thereafter (Giorgio et al., 2010). The health of white matter also declines with age. Diffusion tensor imaging, which diffuses water through the white matter, is used to determine the health of this part of the brain. These changes to the white matter are seen as abnormal areas of **signal intensity** on MRIs and are clinical markers of increased risk of depression, impaired gait and mobility, stroke, and dementia in both cross-sectional and longitudinal studies (Wardlaw, Valdes-Hernandez, & Munoz-Maniega, 2015).

Changes in neurotransmitters, most notably dopamine, serotonin, and acetylcholine, also occur with age (Peters, 2006). Declines in dopamine have been associated with declines in short-term memory and working memory (Nyberg, Lövdén, Riklund, Lindenberger, & Bäckman, 2012). Changes in the way the brain processes serotonin have been associated with cognitive decline in normal aging and dementia such as Alzheimer's disease. Decreases in acetylcholine in the hippocampus also have been commonly associated with Alzheimer's disease, but decreases in acetylcholine have not been consistently found during normal aging (Juraska & Lowry, 2012). In addition, there is evidence of alterations in the size, number, and density of blood vessels in the brain with age (Desjardins, 2015). It should be noted that researchers who have done systematic reviews of the literature on the relationship between structural change and cognitive functioning note that there still is considerable uncertainty about the role of the characteristics of specific brain structures on the age differences and age changes observed in cognitive functioning (Raz & Kennedy, 2009; Salthouse, 2011). Salthouse (2011) points to several methodological limitations of the existing research, and these limitations need to be addressed before strong conclusions can be drawn. Limitations include small sample sizes, narrow age ranges (i.e., young and older adults but no middle-aged adults), and, in many prior studies, separate consideration of different types of structural variables when there is evidence that they are not independent of each other. As just mentioned, there is variability in structural changes in the brain associated with normal aging. Also, age-related changes in cognition are not the same across all **cognitive domains** or across all older individuals. As you will learn in this chapter, some aspects of cognition do not change with age, some decline with age, whereas others improve with age. In addition, some older adults show no signs of cognitive decline prior to death, but upon autopsy, researchers find neuropathological features of advanced Alzheimer's disease (Bennett et al., 2006). The findings suggest that there are factors that reduce or control the clinical aspect of brain changes. How can this be so? We now introduce you to the concept of **cognitive reserve** (Stern, 2002).

COGNITIVE RESERVE

The concept of cognitive reserve (CR) arose after numerous research findings showed that the degree of damage to the brain does not always correlate with cognitive and functional abilities. In other words, two people with similar levels of brain damage or pathology do not necessarily function at the same level (Duncan, Phillips, Nicoladis, & Montanari, 2016). The idea is that the brain can continue to perform at its best for a longer period because of factors such as higher educational attainment, complex work experiences, and an active lifestyle (Grotz, Seron, Van Wissen, & Adam, 2017). As a result, the most common way to measure CR is by measuring occupation, number of years of education, and the amount of leisure activities an individual engages in, usually within the last year (Grotz et al., 2017). Opdebeek, Martyr, and Clare (2016) conducted a meta-analysis of 135 cross-sectional studies and pointed out that drawing conclusions about CR research is difficult because of the different measures used to determine CR. However, these researchers did identify that educational level was the most common index of CR. To try to get a better understanding of the best way to measure CR, Grotz and her colleagues (2017) developed the Index of Cognitive Reserve (ICR). It is a retrospective self-report tool designed to fully assess experiences and activities across the lifespan. The ICR has two components: ICR-standard and ICR-detailed. ICR-standard is an index of CR that uses educational attainment, primary occupation, and amount of current participation in stimulating activities as measures. CR-detailed is an index of CR that encompasses the highest level of education combined with the number of training courses, last occupation worked at, and the amount of current participation in social and intellectual activities. These researchers found that higher levels of both ICR-standard and ICR-detailed were associated with a greater minimization of normal age-related effects on cognition but that the ICR-detailed was more strongly related to this minimization than the ICR-standard. One shortcoming of this study is that most of the 204 participants had retired from white-collar jobs so the results are likely not generalizable. However, the ICR shows promise as a measure of CR, and the researchers call for more studies on larger and more representative samples. Whalley, Staff, Fox, and Murray (2016) also found that a high educational attainment and occupational level contributed positively to cognitive functioning in late life, suggesting to these researchers that modifying life-course factors may reduce the risk of developing a dementia. It will be interesting to see what future research shows. Identifying factors that reduce the risk of developing a dementia is paramount given the increasing prevalence of dementia in societies today.

EFFECTS OF BILINGUALISM ON COGNITIVE RESERVE

Before moving on, we would like to say a few words about the effects of bilingualism on cognitive reserve. Bilingual or multilingual individuals are those who systematically use two or more languages in everyday life (Omidvar, Jafari, Tahaei, & Salehi, 2013). Researchers have found that fluent bilinguals know thousands of words in each language that they speak, but rarely do they make errors when they read or listen or speak in either language (Kroll, Bobb, Misra, & Guo, 2008; Kroll, Van Hell, Tokowicz, & Green, 2010). This notable accomplishment has been attributed to the fact that individuals who are bilingual have an ability to maximize executive control in resolving cross-language conflict. Maximizing executive control has led many researchers to hypothesize that bilingual individuals should perform better on measures of executive control than those individuals who speak only one language. In a review of the literature, Baum and Titone (2014), who carry out research on bilingualism at McGill University, found a great deal of evidence to support this hypothesis. There also is evidence that knowing more than one language can delay the onset of Alzheimer's disease (Bialystok, Craik, & Freedman, 2007; Chertkow et al., 2010). From their review of the literature, Baum and Titone (2014) note that more research is needed to sort out the mechanisms underlying the neuroanatomical and neurophysiological changes associated with being bilingual. Let's move on now and look at the changes in memory and attention in normal aging.

4.3 CHANGES IN MEMORY AND ATTENTION IN NORMAL AGING

LEARNING OBJECTIVES

To understand:
- the changes in memory abilities with normal aging
- the memory abilities that do not change with age
- how the effects of memory changes in normal aging affect everyday functioning
- the changes in attention with normal aging
- the types of attention that do not change with age
- how changes in attention due to normal aging affect everyday functioning

Two of the most basic cognitive functions affected by age are memory and attention. But before we look at age-related changes in memory and attention, we want to let you know that Canadian researchers have made significant contributions to the field of cognitive neuroscience and aging. Their work alone would take many textbooks to discuss. Drs. Nicole Anderson, Fergus Craik, Meredyth Daneman, Cheryl Grady, Lynn Hasher, Morris Moscovitch, Jennifer Ryan, and Endyl Tulving are some of the researchers at the Rotman Institute in Toronto who continue to add to our knowledge about changes in normal and pathological aging. Please go to www.baycrest.org/research/rotman-research-institute/ to find out what kind of research they are currently doing and to meet other Canadian researchers in this field. In addition, here is a website that lists Canadian universities offering cognitive science programs:

http://www.canadian-universities.net/Universities/Programs/Cognitive_Science.html.

MEMORY CHANGES IN NORMAL AGING

Memory is one of the basic cognitive functions affected by age. Before we begin to discuss those changes, it is important to consider the question, what is memory? This may seem to be an odd question to ask in that, intuitively, we all have a sense of what memory is. Broadly speaking, memory is the capacity for storing and retrieving information. That is, our memory allows us to remember all kinds of information—personal experiences and specific events as well as common knowledge such as the names of colours, the capitals of countries, and other historical information. Memory also allows us to hold, process, and manipulate information for a short time as well as store information over a very long period of time.

As you can see from the description above, human memory is not a single unitary system. Rather, there are many types of memory and many ways in which to categorize memory. Three main types of memory are sensory memory, short-term/working memory, and long-term memory.

SENSORY MEMORY

Sensory memory refers to the initial process of storing information perceived through our senses, with this information stored in an almost identical representation of the stimuli that exists in the observable environment. Our sensory memory systems hold information in a relatively raw, uninterpreted form for a very brief time. Sensory memory is divided into five memory types (one for each of the senses). The three most-studied forms of sensory memory are **iconic memory** (visual), **echoic memory** (sound), and **tactile memory** (touch). Sensory memory decays very quickly after perception of the stimuli (typically in the region of 200 to 500 msecs [milliseconds]). Unlike other types of memory that we will discuss in this chapter, sensory memory typically does not change with age (Poon, 1985). For example, in a landmark experiment in the 1960s, younger and older adults were shown a series or grid of letters for a brief time (50 msecs) and then asked to recall the letters. The results showed that older adults typically were able to recall as many letters as the younger adults (Sperling, 1960). However, since that time, Ruzzoli, Pirulli, Brignani, Maioli, and Miniussi (2012) have shown that although the auditory encoding of information does not change with age, the maintenance of this information is impaired with age.

Information is passed from our sensory memory to our short-term memory through the process of **attention**. Importantly, sensory memory often is confused with short-term memory but there is a significant difference between the two. Sensory memory, which cannot be controlled, lasts only a few seconds at most, whereas information in short-term memory can last for approximately 20 seconds.

SHORT-TERM MEMORY / WORKING MEMORY

A comprehensive overview of the history of short-term and working memory is beyond the scope of this chapter. However, a brief overview of memory (with a focus on short-term and working memory) is provided to help you in understanding the changes in the conceptualization of memory over time. The scientific study of memory is usually traced back to Hermann Ebbinghaus who, in 1885, studied his own acquisition and forgetting of new information over time (an English version of his 1885 manuscript was printed in 1913). He found that memory loss is greater in the first few days after learning new information, with the rate of forgetting much slower as the days progress. This has come to be known as the **forgetting curve**. Five years later, William James (1890) proposed the distinction between **primary memory**, the small amount of information that is immediately held in consciousness (something akin to an afterimage) and **secondary memory**, the vast body of knowledge stored over a lifetime. In 1968, Atkinson and Shiffrin proposed what is known as the **information-processing model**. In this model, which is based on a computer metaphor, there are three main storage compartments or stores that hold information at different points during processing of that information.

As shown in Figure 4.2, information from the external environment is first detected by the sense organs and enters sensory memory. If attended to, the information then enters the short-term store (short-term memory). Information is then transferred from this short-term store to the long-term

FIGURE 4.2

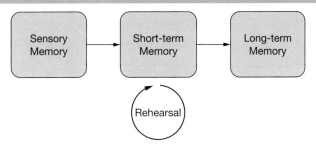

Source: http://thepeakperformancecenter.com/educational-learning/learning/memory/classification-of-memory/.

store (long-term memory) through **rehearsal**. Atkinson and Shiffrin (1968) argued that if rehearsal does not occur, then information is forgotten (e.g., lost from short-term memory) through the processes of displacement or decay. The information-processing model has been influential in that it generated a great deal of research in memory. However, weaknesses of the model led to the development of the **working-memory model** (Baddeley & Hitch, 1974; Baddeley, 1986; 2006).

As conceptualized by Baddeley and Hitch (1974) and revised by Baddeley in 1986 and again in 2006, working memory consists of two slave systems, an episodic buffer and a central executive. The two systems, which hold information in a relatively passive manner, consist of a **phonological loop** for storage of auditory information and a **visuospatial sketchpad** for storage and manipulation of visual and spatial information (see Figure 4.3). The **episodic buffer** holds information from the phonological loop and the visuospatial sketchpad, as well as from long-term memory. The **central executive** (the boss) controls and coordinates the other three components of working memory (think of an air traffic controller who is responsible for planes taking off and landing at airports). As such, it is responsible for the manipulation of information within working memory and for controlling the two less-important storage subsystems (the phonological loop and the visuospatial sketchpad) and the episodic buffer. (see Figure 4.4 for a picture of Dr. Baddeley). In general, working memory can be thought of as a mental blackboard—that is, a workspace that allows us to temporarily hold information while we use that information to solve a problem, make a decision, remember to complete a task, or learn new information.

FIGURE 4.3

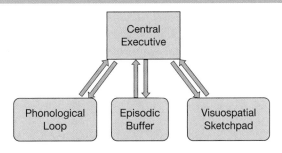

Source: Repovš, G., & Baddeley, A. (2006). The multi-component model of working memory: Explorations in experimental cognitive psychology. *Neuroscience, 139*, 5–21. doi:10.1016/j.neuroscience.2005.12.061.

FIGURE 4.4

Wikimedia Commons

Does working memory change with age? In general, there are few, if any, changes in the phonological loop, the visuospatial sketchpad, and the episodic buffer with age (Braver & West, 2008). However, changes in central executive function with age have been identified as a key contributor to age-related declines across a range of cognitive tasks (Glisky, 2007; Peters, 2006). That is, many complex cognitive tasks depend on the central executive for managing and coordinating the different components of the task. For example, working memory is needed for everyday abilities such as managing finances, shopping, and cooking, as well as for everyday activities such as following spoken directions, actively participating in group discussion, and organizing materials and activities.

There are a number of tasks that have been developed to assess working-memory changes with age. One of these tasks is a reading-span task that was developed by Canadian researcher Meredyth Daneman and her colleague Patricia Carpenter in 1980. This measure of working memory has been widely cited, and it has been adapted for research on working memory, reading comprehension, and cognitive processing. It is a dual-task paradigm, combining a memory-span measure with a concurrent processing task. The task requires participants to read or listen to a series of two to six sentences. Participants are then required to recall, in the correct order, the last word for each of the sentences read. The number of words one is able to correctly recall is called one's "reading span." Of interest, complex span tasks such as the one discussed above have recently been automated, with these tasks contributing to our knowledge of working memory (Redick et al., 2012).

FIGURE 4.5

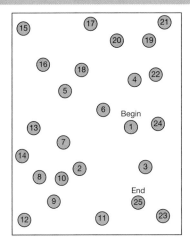
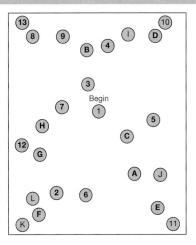

Source: Reitan, R.M. (1958). Validity of the Trail Making Test as an indicator of organic brain damage. *Perceptual and Motor Skills, 8,* 271–276. doi:10.2466/pms.1958.8.3.271.

Two other commonly used tasks are the Trail-Making Task and digit-span tasks. The Trail-Making Test has two components—Trails A and Trails B. Trails A requires an individual to connect a sequence of 25 encircled numbers distributed on a sheet of paper. Trails B is similar except that the person must alternate between numbers and letters (1, A, 2, B, 3, C, etc.) (Reitan, 1958; see Figure 4.5). The goal is to complete each of the tasks as quickly and accurately as possible. The primary outcome measure is time to completion. Although both of these tasks look relatively simple, performance on the each of the tasks changes with age. In 2003, a Canadian researcher (Tombaugh, 2004) administered Trails A and B to 911 community-dwelling, cognitively intact individuals aged 18 years and older. As you can see in Figure 4.6, the time taken to complete both Trails A and B increases with age and fewer years of education, with the difference in time to complete between young and old even greater on Trails B.

Studies that have been done with digit-span tasks also reveal differences in performance with age. In a typical digit-span task, a series of digits are read out loud to participants, with participants immediately repeating them back. The task begins with a length of two digits (e.g., 8, 5), with the number of digits increasing in length with each subsequent presentation (9, 2, 4; 7, 3, 6; . . . .). Testing ends when the participant fails to accurately report back the digits or when the maximum list length is reached (typically nine digits for forward-span tasks and eight for backward-span tasks). In the forward-digit-span tasks, participants are asked to repeat the digits in the order in which they are given, whereas in the backward-digit-span task, the participant needs to reverse the order of the numbers. The central executive component of working memory is seen as playing an important role in the performance of both reading- and digit-span tasks. Results from a study examining the effects of age on forward- and backward-span tasks are shown in Figure 4.7 (Hester, Kinsella, & Ong, 2004). As you can see, there is a significant age-related decline in the average number of digits (digit-span tasks) and blocks (spatial-span tasks) recalled, with older participants recalling significantly fewer digits and blocks than younger participants. Similar findings have been reported in a recent meta-analysis of 123 studies on

FIGURE 4.6

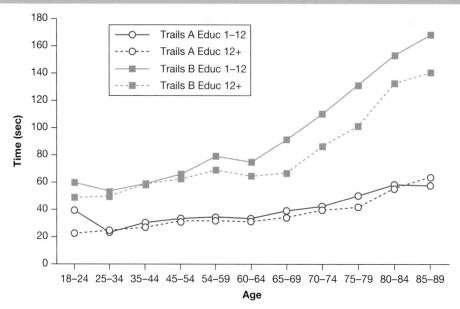

Source: Republished with permission of Elsevier Science and Technology Journals, from Tombaugh, T.N. (2004). Trail Making Test A and B: Normative data stratified by age and education. *Archives of Clinical Neuropsychology, 19*(2); permission conveyed through Copyright Clearance Center, Inc.

memory span and aging (Bopp & Verhaeghen, 2005). That is, the authors found that there are differences on all span tasks as a result of age (e.g., with older participants performing more poorly), with simple span tasks (e.g., forward-digit span) showing smaller age differences than more complex span tasks (e.g., reading-span tasks, computation-span tasks).

An interesting development in the study of working memory and age is the introduction of virtual reality to assess performance on everyday tasks. One such example is the Virtual Multiple Errands Test (VMET) (Rand, Weiss, & Katz, 2009). In the VMET, participants navigate a virtual supermarket to obtain items from a predetermined shopping list. In addition to obtaining the items, they also must obtain information (e.g., time the store closes) and obey rules to promote planning and efficiency (e.g., they cannot go to the same aisle twice). Studies have found that results on the VMET are strongly correlated with other measures of executive function and attention (Parsey & Schmitter-Edgecombe, 2013).

You might be wondering why working memory abilities change with age. Although it is not entirely clear, a number of theories have been generated to account for these changes. The most prominent theories are a reduction in processing resources (Craik & Byrd, 1982), a general slowing in the speed of processing information (Salthouse, 1995), and difficulties in inhibiting irrelevant information (Hasher & Zacks, 1988).

The reduction of processing resources theory hypothesizes that older adults do not have as many processing resources available as younger adults, and this leads to less efficient encoding and retrieval of information (Craik & Byrd, 1982; Craik, 1986). That is, research has shown that older adults show impairments on tasks with high attentional demands, with relatively no signs of impairment on tasks that are less demanding. The speed of processing theory, on the other

FIGURE 4.7

MEAN FORWARD- AND BACKWARD-SPAN PERFORMANCE ACROSS AGE GROUPS

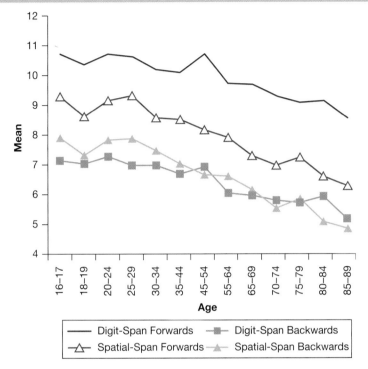

Source: *Journal of the International Neuropsychological Society*: KINS by INTERNATIONAL NEUROPSYCHOLOGICAL SOCIETY. Reproduced with permission of CAMBRIDGE UNIVERSITY PRESS in the format reuse in a book/textbook via Copyright Clearance Center.

hand, hypothesizes that increased age is associated with a decrease in the speed with which many processing operations can be executed and that this reduction in speed leads to impairments in cognitive functioning (Salthouse, 1995; 1996). There is a substantial body of research documenting that older adults are slower than younger adults on many tasks, with older adults showing greater decrements in performance on complex tasks than their younger counterparts (Hof & Mobbs, 2009). The inhibition theory proposed by Hasher and Zacks (1988) theorizes that inhibitory processes, which are responsible for regulating the information that enters and leaves working memory, weakens with age. As a result, a lot of irrelevant information that gains entry into working memory is not deleted and, as such, creates interference.

As mentioned earlier, Canadian researchers have made significant contributions to the field of cognitive neuroscience and aging. One of the very fruitful developments stemmed from applying the concepts and methods of cognitive psychology to patients with brain impairment, an approach termed "cognitive neuropsychology" (Baddeley, 2010). That is, while most brain-damaged patients typically suffer from a number of deficits, cases occasionally occur in which a single isolated cognitive function is impaired, while other cognitive functions are preserved. This allows researchers to test theories of cognitive function directly. A very influential case was that of HM (see Box 4.1). Of interest to our discussion of working memory, HM's pattern of memory deficits was influential in Baddeley and Hitch's (1974) initial conceptualization of working memory.

BOX 4.1

THE STORY OF HM

HM is likely the best-known patient in the history of neuroscience. HM had been knocked down by a bicycle at the age of 7, began to have minor seizures at age 10, and had major seizures after age 16. At the age of 27, he became so incapacitated by his seizures, despite high doses of anti-convulsant medication, that he could not work or lead a normal life. HM underwent an experimental procedure in which the front half of his hippocampus (on both sides) was removed along with most of his amygdala. The operation was successful in that it significantly reduced HM's seizures but it left him with severe memory loss.

HM was referred to Dr. Wilder Penfield and neuropsychologist Dr. Brenda Milner at the Montreal Neurological Institute for assessment of his memory loss. When Milner first visited HM, she saw "someone who forgot daily events nearly as fast as they occurred, apparently in the absence of any general intellectual loss or perceptual disorder. He underestimated his own age, apologized for forgetting the names of persons to whom he had just been introduced, and described his state as "like waking from a dream . . . every day is alone in itself. . . ." (Milner, Corkin, & Teuber, 1968, p. 217). HM died December 2, 2008, at the age of 82. One of HM's legacies is that the descriptions of his memory loss initiated the modern era of memory research.

Milner's work with HM established her reputation as one of the most important neuroscientists of the 20th century (and made HM famous). Dr. Milner has been inducted into the Canadian Medical Hall of Fame, as a fellow of the Royal Society of London, and the Royal Society of Canada. Currently in her 90s, Milner is still teaching and researching at the Montreal Neurological Institute (see Figure 4.8).

Source: Adapted from Squire, L.R. (2009). The legacy of patient H.M. for neuroscience. *Neuron, 61*(1), 6–9. doi: 10.1016/j.neuron.2008.12.023.

FIGURE 4.8

BRENDA MILNER, 2011, AGED 94

Eva Blue, https://creativecommons.org/licenses/by/2.0/.

LONG-TERM MEMORY (EPISODIC AND SEMANTIC MEMORY)

Unlike working memory, long-term memory allows us to store large amounts of information for indefinite periods of time. Our short-term memories can become long-term memories through a process of consolidation that involves rehearsal and creating meaningful associations. And, unlike short-term memory, which relies on storing information via acoustic and visual codes, information is stored in long-term memory primarily based on meaning and association (e.g., **semantically**). The two primary forms of long-term memory are episodic and semantic memory. **Episodic memory** is a part of long-term memory responsible for storing personally experienced information about a specific event (e.g., your first day of school; what you had for breakfast). **Semantic memory**, on the other hand, is a part of long-term memory responsible for storing information about the world (e.g., the names of colours, sounds of letters, capitals of countries in the world, and other basic facts).

In thinking about the descriptions of episodic and semantic memory, do you think that either or both of these types of memory change with age?

There is ample evidence that episodic memory changes significantly with age. Episodic memory problems that occur as a part of normal aging can occur as a result of deficiencies in **encoding**, **storage**, or **retrieval**. Encoding refers to the initial process of getting information into the memory system for storage and later retrieval. Storage refers to the ability to retain information in the memory system over time. Retrieval, on the other hand, refers to the ability to get information out of the memory system when needed. In terms of encoding, there is a large body of research that indicates that older individuals have more difficulty in encoding compared to younger individuals. Perhaps you have heard your grandmother say, "Where have I put my keys?" or "What was the name of your friend who came to dinner last month?"

Why do older individuals have difficulty in encoding? One of the reasons for failing to encode information is failure to attend to the event while it is happening. That is, if a person is distracted, the process of encoding information is weaker, resulting in failures in remembering the information. For example, research has shown that older individuals are more susceptible to the disruptive effects of distraction than are younger individuals (Hasher & Zacks, 1988). This is one of the reasons that older individuals prefer working in a quieter environment. The way that the information is processed also can affect the ability to remember information. An influential theory, called the **levels of processing theory** (Craik & Lockhart, 1972), argues that the depth of mental processing affects the ability to recall information. Based on this theory, superficial or shallow mental processing at the perceptual level results in weak memory traces, whereas deeper (semantic level) processing results in stronger memory traces. Craik and Lockhart (1972) also theorize that how information is rehearsed can affect the ability to recall information; the researchers argue that shallow processing involves what is called **maintenance rehearsal** (e.g., simply repeating a word to hold the information in your short-term memory) and **elaborative rehearsal** (e.g., processing information at a deeper level through linking the information with previous knowledge through associations or images) is associated with better recall. Think about meeting someone for the first time. If you want to remember that person's name, you will have a better chance of doing that if you use elaborative rehearsal (e.g., Jane rhymes with brain) as opposed to simply rehearsing the name.

Research also shows that older individuals have more difficulty with consolidating and retrieving information. Specifically, older individuals tend to show more deficits on tests of free recall as compared to deficits on recognition memory (Morcom & Friston, 2012). However, how the information is presented to older adults affects episodic memory recall. For example, if the items to be remembered are presented with cues and at a slowed pace, and if older adults have some familiarity with the information to be remembered, their recall performance improves (Light, 2012). In contrast to episodic memory, results from years of research indicate that semantic memory changes little with age. That is, although older adults often report difficulties in recalling the names of common objects or other well-learned information, semantic memory stays relatively stable with the normal aging process. The one change that does occur in semantic memory as part of normal aging is an increased difficulty in retrieving information that is otherwise accessible. This experience, called **tip-of-the-tongue** phenomena, refers to the experience of being unable to produce a name or a word despite the experience of feeling confident of your knowledge of the name or word. We will talk more about TOT experiences later in the language section of this chapter.

ATTENTIONAL CHANGES IN NORMAL AGING

William James, one of the leading thinkers of the late 19th century and believed by many to be the father of American psychology (Fadul, 2017), stated "everyone knows what attention is" (James, 1890). Operationally, attention refers to how we actively attend to and process specific information in the environment. There are different types of attention. Three main types of attention that we will discuss in this chapter are selective attention, divided attention, and sustained attention. As with memory, some types of attention change in normal aging, while others remain relatively stable. In the following section, we define each of these types of attention and describe the effects of age on attentional abilities.

SELECTIVE ATTENTION

Selective attention refers to the ability to attend to some stimuli in the environment while disregarding other stimuli that are irrelevant to the task at hand (Glisky, 2007). A common method of studying selective attention is to ask individuals to search for a target letter that is surrounded by other non-target letters (distractors) (see Figure 4.9). As you can see in Figure 4.9, the complexity of the task can vary—the search for the target image (the Red T) in the figure on the left is easy, whereas the search for the Red T in the figure on the right is more difficult.

The Stroop task is another commonly used task to assess selective attention. In this task, individuals are asked to name the colour of the font of the word, and not what the word says (see Figure 4.10). In this case, the word information interferes with the naming of the colour of the font,

FIGURE 4.9

AN EXAMPLE OF A SELECTIVE ATTENTION TASK

Find the Red T:

L L L L
L L L L
L L L L
L L T L

Find the Red T:

L L T L
T L T T
T T L L
L L T L

FIGURE 4.10

PURPLE   YELLOW   RED

BLACK   RED   GREEN

RED   YELLOW   ORANGE

BLUE   PURPLE   BLACK

RED   GREEN   ORANGE

resulting in errors and an increase in **response time**. In general, older adults are slower than younger adults in their response times to the targets, with these age differences attributed to general slowing of information processing in older adults rather than due to changes in selective attention with age (Verhaeghen & Cerella, 2002). However, Ben-David and Schneider (2010) suggest that age-related changes in colour perception can contribute to the differences in Stroop effects observed with age. These researchers had 88 younger adults do the Stroop task with two colour sets: one saturated and the other de-saturated to simulate age-related changes in colour perception. They found that the colour manipulation was sufficient to create errors and a slower response time that mimics age effects. This is an important consideration as this is a measure that is often used diagnostically.

DIVIDED ATTENTION

Do you ever do two things at once? You likely do that a lot (hopefully, it's not texting while behind the wheel!). Divided attention refers to the allocation of available attentional resources to coordinate the performance of more than one task at a time (Sternberg, Sternberg, & Mio, 2012). A typical way that researchers study divided attention is by using a dual-task paradigm in which the participant has to perform two or more tasks at the same time or process two or more sources of information concurrently. To determine the cost of dividing attention, performance under the dual-task condition is compared to performance when the tasks are performed separately. For example, using a computer, participants may be asked to do a tracking task (e.g., keep a dot inside a box). During this tracking task, letters are then presented on a screen and if a target letter appears (e.g., the letter x), the participant is required to respond by clicking the mouse. Results from a meta-analysis involving studies with younger and older individuals indicate that older adults are more affected by the division of attention than are younger adults, and particularly so when the demands of the task are high (Verhaeghen, Steitz, Sliwinski, & Cerella, 2003).

> Can you think of an everyday situation in which older individuals may be more affected by having to perform under dual-task conditions than younger individuals? A hint is to go back and read the beginning of this section.

REFLECTIVE QUESTION

SUSTAINED ATTENTION

Sustained attention refers to the ability to maintain concentration on a task over an extended period. Typically, sustained attention is measured through performance on vigilance tasks. The Mockworth clock task is an example of a task used to measure simple vigilance. With this task, participants are required to monitor the movement of a pointer on a clock-like device. The pointer, which is like the second hand of a clock, moves in discrete steps of one per second. However, at irregular intervals, the pointer makes a double jump, and the participant is expected to detect and record the number of double jumps of the pointer in a defined time period. The continuous performance test (CPT) is an example of today's version of a vigilance task (Connor, 2001). Results of studies using simple vigilance tasks indicate that there are no differences in performance with age. For example, in an early study on changes in vigilance with age, Surwillo and Quilter (1964) found that there was no difference in the detection of double jumps of the pointer over a period of one hour between younger and older participants. Specifically, 82 percent of the double jumps (23 of the 3600 movements of the pointer over one hour) were detected by younger participants, with 78 percent of the double jumps detected by older participants. However, there are age differences on more complex vigilance tasks, with older adults performing more poorly than their younger counterparts. With complex vigilance tasks, stimuli (e.g., a large letter such as a *p*) or a distractor letter (e.g., the letter *d*) appear on a screen in the same location with randomly changing time intervals (between 0.5 and 5 seconds). Over the course of the task, the target letter is presented 110 times and the distractor letter is presented 220 times. The participant is required to press a computer key when the target letter appears. Outcome measures include correct detection of the target letter, false alarms (identifying the distractor letter as the target letter), **omission errors** (failing to identify the target letter), **commission errors** (responding to non-targets), and reaction time (time to respond to the stimulus). Results indicate that while older adults are not significantly slower at responding to stimuli on complex vigilance tasks, older adults have more false alarms and make significantly more omission and commission errors as compared to younger individuals (Mani, Bedwell, & Miller, 2005). Of interest, tests of vigilance have been used on the International Space Station and on three NASA missions to assist crew members in identifying changes in sustained attention due to various fatigue-related conditions (e.g., acute and chronic sleep restrictions, abrupt shifts in work/rest cycles).

REFLECTIVE QUESTION

In thinking about this monitoring of vigilance in astronauts, what do you think is the potential for changes in sustained attention and the impact of those changes in older adults who have sleep disturbances or changes in their everyday work/rest cycles due to illness?

4.4 LANGUAGE CHANGES WITH AGE

LEARNING OBJECTIVES

To understand:
- the language change that occurs with age
- elderspeak
- what factors to consider when speaking with an older adult

While you are having a conversation with an older adult, you likely will not notice any obvious differences at all in their speech. Vocabulary knowledge is well maintained across the lifespan, and there is evidence that older adults have a more diverse vocabulary and use more uncommon words than do younger adults (Rabaglia & Salthouse, 2011). However, you may find it interesting to know that, even though it may not be readily observed, there are several normal age-related changes that occur to spoken language.

WORD-FINDING DIFFICULTIES

A common complaint among older adults is an increase in word-finding difficulty or tip-of-the-tongue states (TOT). TOT states are defined as difficulty in retrieving a well-known word or familiar name, even though there is a strong feeling that the word is known. This is the meaning of the phrase "it's on the tip of my tongue." In their seminal work, Burke and her colleagues (Burke & Laver, 1990; Burke, MacKay, Worthley, & Wade, 1991) proposed that word-finding problems arise from a breakdown in the access to phonological information. The transmission deficit hypothesis (TDH) holds that the mental connections linking an idea to its phonology (which is an ordered sequence of consonants and vowels) is very important in the process of linking an idea, such as *an evil villain living in another galaxy who represents the dark side of the force*, to the words, *Darth Vader*. If any links in the word's phonology are broken, the individual will be able to retrieve the idea but not the word (Kemper, 2015). Furthermore, the speaker may retrieve part of the word she is looking for and say, "It starts with a *D*," but the individual will not be able to access all the letters of the searched-for word, which results in a tip-of-the-tongue state. So how do the links become broken? Burke and Shafto (2004) argue that the links are maintained through frequent and regular use but will degrade over time if not used.

Although TOT experiences can occur at any age, they occur most often in older adults. Results from diary studies, in which people of different ages record the number of their TOT experiences, indicate that older adults report about twice as many TOT experiences per week as compared to younger adults. Of interest, there also is evidence that older adults are about as successful as younger adults in gaining access to the missing word when they exert the effort to do so (Kausler, Kausler, & Krupsaw, 2007). Older adults also are more likely to use **circumlocutions**, a roundabout or indirect way of speaking in which the person uses more words than necessary to express an idea (Theocharopoulou, Cocks, Pring, & Dipper, 2015). These researchers found that circumlocutions occurred more often in older adults in a TOT state than the younger participants in their study.

SENTENCE PRODUCTION

There is substantial support that there is a decrease across the lifespan in the production of complex sentences using subordinate, embedded, and **left-branching clauses**, and that older adults are less likely to produce sentences rich in prepositions (Rabaglia & Salthouse, 2011). These changes in sentence production are thought to be due to a decrease in working memory capacity. For example, greater levels of clausal embedding may place greater demands on a speaker's ability to hold all the components of a sentence in mind, particularly during the effort to produce left-branching clauses (e.g., the girl who runs the nursery school of our church is very young) compared to right-branching clauses (e.g., She is really young to be running a nursery school for our church). With a left-branching clause, there is a delay between the association of subject (the girl) and the predicate (very young), which is thought to tax working memory (Nippold, Cramond, & Hayward-Mayhew, 2014). However, finding age differences may depend on how sentence complexity is being measured. In a recent study, Nippold and her colleagues (2014) investigated sentence complexity in young, middle-aged, and older adults by using two tasks. The first was a conversational language task in which the participant was asked to talk about a variety of topics such as family, friends, and hobbies. The second task was a peer-resolution task in which participants were asked to listen to two hypothetical scenarios involving conflict. After each scenario was presented, the participant was asked to retell the story and reflect upon it and then the participant answered a series of questions. Each sample was transcribed and coded into mean length of utterances, clausal density, and the use of left-branching clauses. These researchers found that all groups produced greater sentence complexity during the conflict scenarios than the conversational language task and that the groups did not differ on any syntactic measure for either task. Nippold and her colleagues (2014) concluded that syntactic complexity in sentence production exhibited a pattern of stability across the lifespan. These researchers argue that, to completely understand an individual's syntactic competence, tasks such as conflict scenarios should be used. These types of tasks encourage reflection on complex topics rather than simply involving participants in conversations about everyday topics. Conversations about everyday topics place fewer demands on an individual's cognitive and linguistic resources, so that a true picture of sentence production capabilities may be missed in older adults. These researchers also point to the fact that there were large individual differences on both tasks. It will be interesting to see what information further research in this area will bring.

ELDERSPEAK

As we have said previously, although there are normal age-related changes that occur in speech, these changes do not really affect an older adult's ability to converse with others or let their opinions or needs be known. What seems to change is how people in general converse with older adults. Because of the numerous stereotypes associated with aging, many people, especially if they have not had much exposure to older adults, adopt a style of communication that is demeaning. In their seminal research, Ryan, Giles, Bartolucci, and Henwood (1986) identified two patterns of communicating with older adults. **Under-accommodation** occurs when a communication partner fails to consider how normal age-related changes affect speaking and listening. **Over-accommodation** occurs when the communication partner relies on negative stereotypes of the older adult to guide communication. Both involve speaking to an older adult as though they were incompetent and helpless. Under-accommodation can create social isolation (even in a room full of people) and over-accommodation is perceived by older adults as insulting and patronizing and may discourage them from fully participating in a conversation (Kemper, 2015; Ryan et al., 1986; Ryan, Hummert, & Boich, 1995; Mohlman et al., 2012).

"Elderspeak" is an over-accommodation and a type of speech used with older adults. Also called "secondary baby talk," this type of speech is characterized by a slow rate of speaking, exaggerated intonation, simplified vocabulary and grammar, and a higher pitch (Kemper, 2015). Other aspects of elderspeak include using terms of endearment like "sweety" or "honey" and exclaiming to an older adult, "Oh, you are so cute!" Elderspeak resembles the kind of speech one might use with small children. As mentioned previously, older adults do not like to be addressed this way as it gives them the impression that they are seen as being cognitively impaired and/or having significant communication problems (Kemper, 2015). In fact, in one study, older adults viewed elderspeak as "degrading, disrespectful, and demeaning" (Hummel, 2012, p. 23). Next time you are at the grocery store or the bank or just out and about, see if you can spot someone who is speaking to an older adult using elderspeak. It happens more often than you might think!

One place you will, for certain, find elderspeak is in long-term-care (LTC) facilities, as it is often used by nursing staff while providing care to older adults in these facilities

(Herman & Williams, 2009; Williams, Herman, Gajewski, & Wilson, 2009). These researchers have found that using elderspeak increased negative vocalizations (e.g., yelling out, wailing, crying) and resistance to care, which distresses both residents and staff. Healthcare providers, as well as family members, may benefit from education programs aimed at eliminating this type of communication.

In an early study, Whitbourne, Culgin, and Cassidy (1995) found that cognitively intact residents in LTC were less bothered by elderspeak than their community-dwelling counterparts. These researchers suggested that because older adults in LTC were more often exposed to elder-speak, they were less bothered by it. However, it could be the case that the participants in their study downplayed the effects of elderspeak because they did not want to rock the boat. A recent study by Couslon, Harper, Galenza, Bratt, and Hasse (2015) found that older adults in long-term care often do not speak their minds because it is more important to fit in and not cause trouble. To assist individuals in their interactions with older adults, the Gerontological Society of America (2012) has created recommendations for communicating with older adults. Those recommendations are provided in Box 4.2.

BOX 4.2

RECOMMENDATIONS FOR COMMUNICATING WITH OLDER ADULTS

- First, consider your own stereotypes of aging. Is this affecting your communication style with older adults?
- There is much diversity in the older adult population, so you will need to adjust how you verbally interact with an older adult on a case-by-case basis.
- Avoid elderspeak!
- Directly face an older adult when you are speaking to him or her.
- Make eye contact.
- Minimize background noise.
- Consider hearing and vision impairment in the person you are speaking with but don't assume that they cannot hear you or see you.
- If the person you are speaking to is hard of hearing, increase your speech volume *slightly*, speak clearly, and speak a bit more slowly. Don't shout and don't raise the tone of your voice.

- If conveying critical information or a lot of information, break the information into chunks. Consider the following statement: "You have arthritis of the hip which is making it painful for you to walk and may eventually require hip-replacement surgery if we cannot control your pain with medications." To understand this sentence, the listener must retain the word "arthritis" in short-term memory while processing that (1) arthritis is causing pain while walking, and (2) surgery may be necessary if medication therapy is ineffective in controlling the pain. You already know that older adults have difficulty following and remembering information presented this way because of changes in working memory. A better way to present this same information would be something like this: "You have arthritis of the hip. The arthritis is causing pain when you walk. Taking medication should help to control your pain. If the pain continues, we might need to consider hip-replacement surgery."

4.5 CAN TRAINING MODIFY AGE-RELATED COGNITIVE CHANGES?

LEARNING OBJECTIVES

To understand:

- the types of cognitive training programs that have been developed to prevent or minimize age-related cognitive decline
- the effectiveness of the different cognitive training programs

Interest in developing effective intervention strategies to minimize age-related cognitive decline has grown rapidly. There seems to be two main types of training programs in the literature: cognitive training programs that consist of directed practice of specific cognitive tasks and cognitive stimulation programs, which are designed to increase general cognitive functioning. These programs are thought to prevent or minimize the effects of age-related cognitive decline (Reijinders, van Heugten, & van Boxtel, 2012). Dr. Sherry Willis, along with Dr. K. Werner Schaie and Dr. Paul Baltes, have long championed cognitive training as a method to improve or prevent age-related cognitive decline in older adults. The question is, are these training programs effective? According to Lustig, Shah, Seidler, and Reuter-Lorenz (2009), some of these interventions show strong potential for improving older adults' cognitive abilities but other studies make exaggerated claims. In addition, the pattern of results has been inconsistent.

One reason for the inconsistent pattern of results may be that there are large differences across studies in the duration of the training program as well as the type and intensity of the training program. For example, cognitive training programs have ranged from a few days to months in duration, and trained individuals have been compared with active control groups in some studies and with passive, no-contact groups in others (Noack, Lövdén, & Schmiedek, 2014).

In their review of the literature on the effectiveness of cognitive training, Reijinders and colleagues (2012) found that cognitive training was effective in improving performance in executive functioning, processing speed, memory, attention, and fluid intelligence. Furthermore, improvements were seen in self-rated performance on cognitive tasks. The Advanced Cognitive Training for Independent and Vital Elderly (ACTIVE) study focuses on improving memory, processing speed, and reasoning in community-dwelling older adults. The findings showed that this training improved cognitive skills in these targeted domains but this training did not transfer to other cognitive domains. Nonetheless, these improvements could still be observed up to five years later in many of the participants (Ball et al., 2006; Willis et al., 2006). However, Gross and his colleagues (2012) found somewhat different results when they conducted a meta-analysis of 35 studies investigating the effectiveness of memory training alone. They found that older adults who were trained in a variety of memory strategies (rather than just one or two) had greater gains in memory capability, but this trend was not significant. These researchers' inclusion criteria were much stricter than previous reviews of memory training, which may explain the discrepancy in findings. Gross and his colleagues (2012) argue that, even though their findings were not significant, their review demonstrates that memory training has the *potential* to improve memory ability in older adults.

In an interesting study, Au and colleagues (2015) trained older adults in a real-time strategy video game for 23.5 hours in an effort to improve cognitive functioning. A battery of cognitive tasks, including tasks of executive control and visuospatial skills, were assessed before, during, and after video-game training. These researchers found that the participants improved significantly in the measures of game performance. They also improved significantly more than the control participants in executive control functions, such as task switching, working memory, visual short-term memory, and reasoning (Au et al., 2015). Although more research in the area is needed, it could be really beneficial to sit down with your parents or grandparents and play a video game.

An interesting research question is, does improved performance on cognitive tasks transfer to improved day-to-day functioning? The ACTIVE study is the first study to show transfer of improved cognitive functioning to improvements in daily functioning. Ten to 14 weeks of organized training sessions given to community-dwelling older adults in memory, reasoning, and speed of processing resulted in better preserved functional status than in the control group, even 10 years later (Rebok et al., 2014). However, the degree of difference between the experimental and control groups was modest. We also should mention that in 2016, the creators and marketers of the *Lumosity* brain-training program agreed to settle U.S. Federal Trade Commission (FTC) charges alleging that they deceived consumers with unfounded claims that playing *Lumosity* games could improve cognitive performance and delay cognitive impairment associated with age and other serious health conditions (FTC, 2016). According to Jessica Rich, director of the FTC's Bureau of Consumer Protection, *Lumosity* preyed on consumer's fears about age-related cognitive decline when the company suggested that their games could prevent memory loss and the development of dementia. She went on further to say that *Lumosity* simply did not have the science to back up its advertisements.

There are important obstacles to overcome, especially with regard to identifying clear, large, and durable effects of cognitive training on everyday cognitive tasks, functional status, and quality of life. However, considerable advances and new research tools are bringing us closer to identifying efficient training that has the potential to bring real benefits to day-to-day life. This is important research to help keep older adults independent in the community (Lustig et al., 2009).

EFFECTS OF LIFESTYLE FACTORS ON COGNITION

It is well documented that lifestyle factors play an important role in the cognitive vitality of older individuals. One such factor is physical activity. In a recent review of the literature on the effects of physical activity and exercise on cognitive and brain functions in older adults, Bherer and colleagues (2013) found that older adults who participate in any type of regular physical activity show less decline in cognitive abilities such as working memory, attention, processing speed, and general mental functioning than those not participating in regular physical activity. Studies also have shown that other types of exercise such as resistance training are associated with improvements in cognitive function (e.g., improved memory, verbal reasoning) in older adults (Cassilhas et al., 2007). In a review and meta-analysis of studies, Lehert and colleagues (2015) found that engaging in tai chi exercise improved overall cognitive functioning. These researchers also found that following a **Mediterranean diet** that was supplemented with olive oil improved global cognition and memory, although there was only one study that fit their inclusion criteria. However, in a recent clinical trial, Valls-Pedret and colleagues (2015) found that a Mediterranean diet supplemented with olive oil or nuts was associated with improved cognitive function in their sample of 447 older adults ($M = 66.9$ years). Collectively, these results indicate that eating healthily and exercising can positively affect an individual's cognitive functioning. The good news is that these two variables are in a person's control—so get moving and start eating healthy foods!

Another health-related factor that can affect cognitive functioning in later life is the medications that many older adults take. Confusion is a serious side effect that can occur from some medications or the interactions of several medications. If an older adult is overmedicated, this also can cause confusion and cognitive decline. The good news is that when medications are properly managed, there is little chance that adverse side effects such as confusion will occur. Other factors to consider that can affect cognitive functions in older adults are poor nutrition as well as alcohol abuse. In fact, significant alcohol abuse can cause dementia. More about this in the neurocognitive chapter.

4.6 INTELLIGENCE
LEARNING OBJECTIVES

To understand:
- what intelligence is as well as the key theories of intelligence
- the classic aging pattern in intellectual functioning as well as cohort differences
- that intellectual changes can be modified with training
- the benefits of lifelong learning
- the challenges faced by older adult learners

WHAT IS INTELLIGENCE?

David Wechsler (1939) defined intelligence as "the aggregate or global capacity of the individual to act purposefully, think rationally, and to deal effectively with the environment" (p. 3). There have been many other definitions of intelligence put forth, but, today, there is general agreement among scholars and laypeople alike that an intelligent person is one who can reason, has the capacity to acquire language, and has the ability to problem solve. For many years, psychologists have argued about whether intellectual ability is acquired or inherited. Currently, there is a consensus that both nature and nurture play an important role in intellectual development. However, questions remain: what exactly is intelligence and what is the best way to measure it?

A FEW KEY THEORIES OF INTELLIGENCE

People make informal judgments about intelligence every day. Comments about intelligence such as "Fred is smarter than Connor" or "Madison is not very bright" imply that intelligence is something that individuals have in lesser and greater amounts and, therefore, it is something that can be measured. Indeed, this is the basic assumption that underlies the **psychometric approach** to intelligence. This approach has dominated the study of intelligence since the 19th century.

SPEARMAN'S G

There have been numerous theories of intelligence put forth in which the number of cognitive abilities thought to make up intelligence are quite different from one another. The earliest theory of intelligence was proposed by Dr. Charles Spearman (1904). Spearman observed that individuals who do well on one kind of mental test tend to do well on other types of mental tests and, conversely, if an individual does poorly on a test of mental abilities, it is most likely that this person will do poorly on other mental tests. This finding suggested to Spearman that all mental tests measure a global element of intellectual ability in addition to specific cognitive skills. He called this global component general intelligence, or *g*. He argued that general intelligence formed the foundation from which all other mental abilities developed. His theory had a tremendous impact on how psychologists measure intelligence. In fact, intelligence tests today are intended to measure *g* as defined by Spearman. The Wechsler Adult Intelligence Test (WAIS-IV) (Wechsler, 2008), originally developed by David Wechsler in 1939, is the most widely used intelligence test today. The WAIS-IV provides a full-scale IQ based on an individual's performance on four indexes: verbal comprehension (verbal scales), perceptual reasoning (performance scales), processing speed, and working memory. Each of these indexes is made up of a variety of subtests thought to measure each domain. Performance on these four indexes will provide an **Intelligence Quotient** (IQ), which is a single score that measures a person's intelligence in relation to their age group.

PRIMARY MENTAL ABILITIES AND MULTIPLE INTELLIGENCES

L.L. Thurstone was one of several scholars who disagreed with Spearman about the existence of *g* and he maintained that intelligence does not come from a single, general factor. In fact, he argued that *g* was a statistical artifact resulting from the mathematical procedures used to study it. Instead, Thurstone (1938) proposed that intelligence is the result of seven independent factors that he called *"primary abilities."* These primary abilities are presented in Table 4.1. Primary mental abilities are thought to be organized into clusters of secondary mental abilities. Two secondary mental abilities that have received the greatest research attention are fluid and crystallized intelligence. These constructs will be reviewed later on in this chapter.

More recently, Howard Gardner (1983) also challenged the idea that *g* can accurately depict all the components of intelligence. His 1983 book *Frames of Mind: The Theory of Multiple Intelligences* outlines his theory and his eight major types of intelligence. Gardner's theory had a tremendous impact on the field of education where it has inspired educators to look at novel ways of teaching directed at the various types of intelligence proposed by Gardner. His multiple intelligences are presented in Figure 4.11.

FLUID AND CRYSTALLIZED INTELLIGENCE AND THE CATTELL-HORN-CARROLL MODEL (CHC)

The concepts of **fluid** and **crystallized intelligence** (Gf-Gc) were originally put forth by Raymond Cattell (1963) and then further developed by Cattell's student, John L. Horn (Horn & Cattell, 1966). Horn and Cattell argued that *g* should be divided into fluid and

TABLE 4.1

L. L. THURSTONE'S PRIMARY MENTAL ABILITIES	
MENTAL ABILITY	**DESCRIPTION**
Word Fluency	The ability to express oneself easily and articulately.
Verbal Comprehension	The ability to understand words.
Spatial Visualization	The ability to organize and manipulate spatial patterns.
Numerical Ability	The ability to understand basic math.
Memory	The ability to recall previously experienced or learned materials.
Reasoning	The ability to think logically.
Perceptual Speed	The ability to quickly perform simple cognitive tasks quickly and efficiently.

Source: Thurstone, L.L. (1938). *Primary mental abilities.* Chicago, IL: University of Chicago Press.

FIGURE 4.11

GARDNER'S MULTIPLE INTELLIGENCES

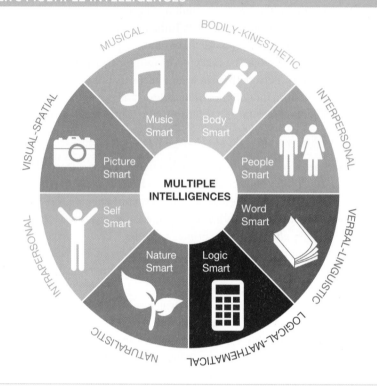

crystallized intelligence. "Fluid intelligence" refers to those intellectual abilities needed for problem solving in novel situations and includes such abilities as pattern recognition, abstract reasoning, and problem solving (Cattell, 1963). "Crystallized intelligence" refers to an individual's accumulated skills, knowledge, and life experience, and it is influenced by culture (Horn & Cattell, 1966). The Perceptual Reasoning Index of the WAIS is thought to be a measure of fluid intelligence while the Verbal Comprehension Index of the WAIS is thought to measure crystallized intelligence. Studies have consistently shown that fluid intelligence decreases with age while crystallized intelligence increases with age and only begins to show modest, if any, declines after the age of 70 (Schaie, 2013). This is known as the **classic aging pattern**.

However, Salthouse took issue with the idea that crystallized intelligence declines after the age of 70. He argues that crystallized intelligence may continue to grow into a person's 80s or 90s but there is not a good way to measure this intellectual growth. Currently, the tests that measure crystallized intelligence have been designed to assess general, culturally shared knowledge. One's crystallized knowledge contains these aspects but also most likely contains knowledge that is unique to that individual (Salthouse, 2010).

The general consensus among researchers is that fluid intelligence is influenced by biology and therefore subject to early decline, whereas crystallized abilities are acquired through experience, learning, and culture, and are thought to grow and develop with age. Of note is that the concepts of fluid and crystallized intelligence have become so ingrained in the field of intelligence that they have become arguably the most used terms in the psychological literature (Salthouse, 2010).

You may think that after all this time, interest in research exploring what intelligence is and how to measure it would have declined. However, this is definitely not the case. In his seminal, highly acclaimed work, John Carroll undertook a comprehensive review of 70 years of research on the nature, classification, and structure of cognitive abilities. Based on the results of his factor analysis, he proposed a three-stratum structure of intelligence in his book *Human Cognitive Abilities* (Carroll, 1993). He called this the Cattell-Horn-Caroll (CHC) model of intelligence. Factors such as induction, numerical facility, and visualization are located in the first stratum. Fluid and crystallized intelligence are located in the second stratum while *g* comprises the third stratum. His model is presented in Figure 4.12.

His work has had tremendous influence on the study of intelligence. In fact, Google Scholar reports that his book has been cited over 5000 times! Although this seminal work has been widely acclaimed, it too has been revised. Extensions of the three-stratum model are summarized in Schneider and McGrew (2012). Many psychologists today believe that the CHC model of intelligence is the most comprehensive and empirically supported psychometric theory of the structure of cognitive abilities to date (James, Jacobs, & Roodenburg, 2015; McGrew, 2009; Schneider & McGrew, 2012).

FIGURE 4.12

THE CATTELL-HORN-CARROLL (CHC) MODEL OF INTELLIGENCE

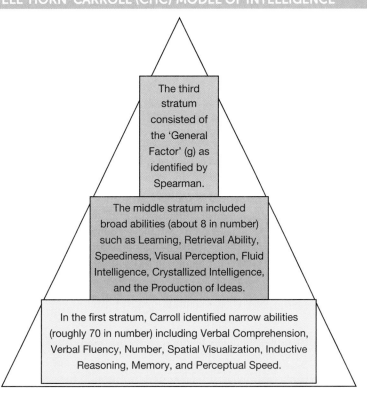

The third stratum consisted of the 'General Factor' (g) as identified by Spearman.

The middle stratum included broad abilities (about 8 in number) such as Learning, Retrieval Ability, Speediness, Visual Perception, Fluid Intelligence, Crystallized Intelligence, and the Production of Ideas.

In the first stratum, Carroll identified narrow abilities (roughly 70 in number) including Verbal Comprehension, Verbal Fluency, Number, Spatial Visualization, Inductive Reasoning, Memory, and Perceptual Speed.

Source: Carroll, J.B. (1993). *Human cognitive abilities: A survey of factor analytic studies.* New York, NY: Cambridge University Press. Reprinted by permission of the publisher.

DOES INTELLIGENCE CHANGE WITH AGE?

Do you think that intelligence changes with age? Well, the results from early research investigating age-related changes in intelligence were really quite dismal, and researchers would have you believe that with age, significant cognitive declines in intelligence occur. However, early researchers used data from cross-sectional studies and the observed changes might have been due to cohort effects rather than the effects of age.

Although there have been several longitudinal studies looking at age-related changes in intelligence scores over the years (e.g., Baltimore Longitudinal Study on Aging, Iowa State Study, The Victoria Longitudinal Study, and The Canadian Study of Health and Aging), the landmark research study investigating changes in performance on intelligence tests associated with age is the Seattle Longitudinal Study (SLS), which was first initiated in 1956 and began as K. Warner Schaie's doctoral dissertation. The SLS has provided an abundance of information on the changes that occur in intelligence with age. Data collection is ongoing and occurs every seven years. To date, over 6000 adults from 22 to over 100 years of age have participated in the study. Schaie uses the Primary Mental Abilities Test (PMAT) (Thurstone, 1938) to measure intellectual change. This measure based on the primary mental abilities identified by Thurstone was presented in Table 4.1.

So, what did we learn from the SLS? Contrary to earlier beliefs that intelligence declined significantly with age, study results over the years have consistently shown that there is no uniform pattern of age-related decline in intellectual abilities (Schaie & Willis, 2010). While the findings did lend support to the Classic Aging Pattern, the rate of decline in fluid intelligence was much slower than originally thought. Moreover, there were significant individual differences in performance across measures of both fluid and crystallized intelligence (Schaie & Willis, 2010). In addition, a recent, more comprehensive examination of individual differences in intellectual change showed that, at the age of 81 years, less than half of all participants showed reliable declines in intellectual functioning in the preceding seven years (Schaie & Willis, 2010).

COHORT DIFFERENCES IN INTELLECTUAL ABILITIES

Several longitudinal studies have investigated cohort differences in intellectual abilities but the results have been mixed (Bowles, Grimme, & McArdle, 2005; Finkel, Reynolds, McArdle, Gatz, & Pederson, 2003; Zelinski & Kennison, 2007). Using data from the SLS, Gerstorf and his colleagues (2011) found substantial cohort differences in cognitive abilities. Figure 4.13 shows the changes in PMAT scores for two cohorts; those reaching old age in the 1960s and 1970s and those reaching old age in the 1980s and 1990s. As you can see, relative to those born earlier, individuals in the later-born cohort showed, on average, considerable better cognitive functioning at age 70 as well as lower rates of cognitive decline from ages 50 to 80. The cohort that was born later had higher scores throughout the entire age range on all abilities assessed with the exception of number ability.

REFLECTIVE QUESTION

What may account for cohort differences in intellectual functioning?

FIGURE 4.13

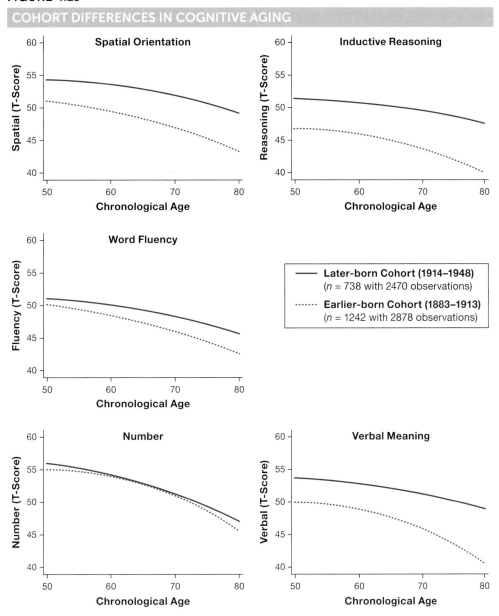

Source: Gerstorf, D., Ram, N., Hoppmann, C., Willis, S.L., & Schaie, K.W. (2011). Cohort differences in cognitive ageing and terminal decline in the Seattle Longitudinal Study. *Developmental Psychology, 47*(4), 1026-1041. doi:10.1037/a0023426.

Gerstorf and his colleagues (2011) put forth several explanations for their findings. Higher educational attainment as well as access to a higher quality of education in the later-born cohort was thought to account for much of the cohort differences. This makes sense when you think about it. It was not unusual for later-born cohorts of children to leave school as early as grade four or five as children were needed to work on the farm or go to work to help their families make ends meet. Also included in the explanation of the observed cohort differences in intellectual functioning were advances in, and access to, technology, workplaces requiring individuals to use increasingly complex cognitive skills, and greater participation of women in the labour force. Let's turn now to look at the effects of other variables on intelligence.

FACTORS THAT CAN AFFECT INTELLIGENCE SCORES IN OLDER ADULTS

HEALTH

The field of study that focuses on intelligence and health outcomes is called **cognitive epidemiology**. There is evidence from over 50 years of research that IQ scores are a sensitive and predictive marker of increased mortality (Aichele, Rabbit, & Ghisletta, 2015; Deary, Weiss, & Batty, 2010; Maenner, Greenberg, and Mailick, 2015). This has been found cross-culturally in samples from the United States, Australia, Sweden, and Scotland (Batty, Deary, & Gottfredson, 2007). Recall the phenomenon known as **terminal drop** in which there is rapid decline in cognitive functioning just prior to death. Some researchers may argue that the predictive validity of IQ scores in determining mortality is hampered by reverse causality in that diseases such as diabetes or hypertension can cause cognitive decline, especially in older adults. However, studies in which the participants had their IQ assessed in childhood or early adulthood, which represents **premorbid functioning**, and had higher mortality rates at follow-up in the absence of disease, minimize this concern (Batty et al., 2007).

Researchers have demonstrated that, regardless of age, lower IQ scores do appear to be associated with an elevated risk of cardiovascular disease (CVD), obesity, and stroke (Batty, Deary, Benzeval, & Der, 2008). In fact, Batty and his colleagues (2007) found that lower intelligence scores were associated with increased rates of CVD at a level of magnitude greater than most of the established risk factors (e.g., high blood pressure, body mass index).

REFLECTIVE QUESTION

What do you think might account for this relationship between lower IQ scores and increased mortality risk?

As you ponder the question above, it is not yet entirely clear how intelligence influences mortality. It could be the case that higher intelligence reduces mortality in that individuals with higher intelligence engage in more healthful behaviours (Batty et al., 2007). Conversely, those individuals with lower IQ test scores likely experience numerous disadvantages all through their lives that contribute to an increased rate of mortality (Maenner et al., 2015). Interestingly, the effects of social class, income, and the role of education, when adjusted statistically, have been shown to reduce (but not eliminate) the effect of intelligence on mortality (Kilgour, Starr, & Whalley, 2010). However, this finding is being debated by other researchers (Aichele, et al., 2015; Deary, Weiss, & Batty, 2010). Clearly, this is another area of research that needs more investigation.

Factors that are thought to be associated with the maintenance of intelligence in older adults are average to high socio-economic status, engagement in and exposure to stimulating environments, high intellectual status of spouse, strong social connections, as well as the maintenance of high levels of perceptual processing speed (Schaie, 2013; Schaie & Willis, 2010). Furthermore, personality traits have been associated with higher levels of intelligence in later life. For example, positive beliefs, a flexible attitude (Willis & Boron, 2008), and the personality trait of openness to experience (Zeigler, Cengia, Mussel, & Gerstorf, 2015) all have been associated with higher intelligence in older adults.

4.7 POST-FORMAL THOUGHT: MOVING BEYOND PIAGET

LEARNING OBJECTIVES

To understand:

- post-formal thought
- the developmental stages in post-formal thought

Jean Piaget had a tremendous impact on how psychologists conceptualize intellectual development. According to Piaget, intellectual development is adaptation through activity. Two very basic concepts in his theory are assimilation and accommodation. Assimilation occurs when new experiences are incorporated into existing schemas. Accommodation occurs when an individual's new experience causes existing schemas to change. For example, a baby is first fed with a bottle and later with a spoon. The introduction of a spoon fits into the baby's schema of eating. Eventually, as the baby grows, he will learn to feed himself with a spoon. This will cause the baby's existing schema of eating to change. Piaget argues that the development of thought is gradual and occurs over four developmental stages. These stages are presented in Table 4.2 for your review.

Researchers now believe that a qualitatively different type of thinking emerges in adulthood that is entirely distinct from the Formal Operations stage proposed by Piaget (King & Strohm Kitchener, 2002; Strohm Kitchener, King, & DeLuca, 2006; Lemieux, 2012). Post-formal thinkers expect that there will be ambiguity and contradiction when seeking the correct answer, and that the truth or the correct answer will most likely vary based on the situation (King & Strohm Kitchener, 2002; Strohm Kitchener et al., 2006). There also is recognition that emotional and subjective factors play a role in thinking. Post-formal thinkers are not black and white thinkers and are much more accepting of the grey areas, where the answer to a problem is not so clear.

There have been limited studies investigating post-formal thinking abilities, and there is some controversy regarding the theoretical definition of concepts (Kallio, 2011). However, based on the results of several cross-sectional and longitudinal research studies, King and her colleagues (King & Strohm Kitchener, 2002; Strohm Kitchener et al., 2006) have been able to identify a systematic progression of reflective judgment that begins in young adulthood. According to Strohm Kitchener and colleagues (2006), the conceptual framework for reflective judgment is a stage model in which there are seven distinct but developmentally related sets

TABLE 4.2

STAGE OF DEVELOPMENT	AGE RANGE	DESCRIPTION
Sensorimotor	Birth to 2 years of age	At this age, the infant experiences the world through the senses (e.g., grasping, placing objects in mouth).
Preoperational	2–7 years of age	Basic mental operations replace sensorimotor activities as the primary way to learn. Symbolic thinking increases. It is still difficult at this stage for children to take another's perspective. Children believe that inanimate objects have the same perception/senses that they do. Abstract thinking is not developed.
Concrete Operational	7–11 years of age	Children in this stage learn complex problem solving and can reason logically about concrete events. Hypothetical thinking is difficult at this stage.
Formal Operations	11–15 years of age	Children can think logically about abstract propositions. Deductive reasoning develops.

Source: Based on www.psychologynoteshq.com/jean-piaget-theory/http://normaveronicatoapantaflores.blogspot.ca/2012/07/cognitive-development-theory-of-jean.html.

of assumptions about the process of knowing and how knowing is acquired. As an individual moves throughout each stage, knowledge of what is true becomes less certain. The seven developmental stages of the reflective judgment model may be broadly summarized into three distinct levels of thinking: pre-reflective (Stages 1–3), quasi-reflective (Stages 4 and 5), and reflective (Stages 6 and 7).

In the pre-reflective thinking stages, individuals hold the belief that knowledge is gained through the word of an authority figure or through first-hand observation rather than, for example, through the evaluation of evidence. Individuals in this stage of thinking believe that what they know is correct and, furthermore, they know this with complete certainty (King & Strohm Kitchener, 2002). If you are a pre-reflective thinker, most issues are assumed to have a right answer so there is very little conflict in making decisions. This is where you would find those individuals who are black or white thinkers. According to King and Strohm Kitchener (2002), once an individual has reached the second developmental stage, there is a realization that knowledge can be quite subjective and, therefore, holds a measure of uncertainty. Therefore, individuals in the quasi-reflective stages of development tend to view judgments as highly personal. In the final stages of reflective reasoning, individuals show true reflective judgment. Individuals recognize that knowledge claims can't be made with certainty. Interestingly, individuals in this stage aren't stressed out by this realization. Rather, they try to make judgments that are reasonable and about which they are relatively certain, based on their evaluation of the information available. As new evidence becomes available, individuals re-evaluate their belief system (King & Strohm Kitchener, 2002).

Based on the above stages, what type of thinker are you?

4.8 WISDOM

LEARNING OBJECTIVES

To understand:

- the challenges in defining and measuring wisdom
- the three dimensions of personal wisdom
- the relationship between wisdom and well-being

VARIATIONS IN THE DEFINITION OF WISDOM

Although the concept of wisdom has been around since ancient times, it has been only recently that an increased interest in studying wisdom has occurred. Despite this increase in interest, there still is no single consensus definition of wisdom to date, despite the development of many definitions and several assessment measures (Jeste et al., 2010). Also of note is a recent suggestion in the wisdom literature to make a distinction between **personal wisdom** (wisdom about one's own life) and **general wisdom** (wisdom concerning life in general) (Staudinger, Dörner, & Mickler, 2005; Staudinger & Glück, 2011). Experts in the field of wisdom as well as laypersons tend to describe personal wisdom as having a combination of cognitive, reflective, and affective components (Ardelt, 2011; Bangen, Meeks, & Jeste, 2013; Jeste et al., 2010).

According to Ardelt (2015), the cognitive dimension of wisdom includes a need for a deep and thorough understanding of both interpersonal and intrapersonal aspects of life. While there is a desire to know the truth, there is recognition that knowledge has its limits. There also is an appreciation of life's uncertainties. In the cognitive dimension, an individual is very much aware of, and accepts, both the positive and negative aspects of human nature. The reflective dimension of wisdom enables an individual to have profound insight as well as an ability to self-reflect or perceive events from multiple viewpoints. According to Ardelt (2015), individuals learn to control their feelings through the practice of self-examination and self-awareness and, little by little, rise above their subjectivity and the tendency to blame external factors for one's shortcomings. This does not mean that wise individuals hold back or deny negative emotions; rather, they are able to acknowledge, regulate, and eventually dissolve negative emotions (Ardelt, 2015). Finally, the affective dimension of wisdom includes empathy, social connectedness, and generativity (Jeste et al., 2010). Interestingly, Jeste and Oswald (2014) point out that it is not clear whether it is the reflective, affective, or cognitive dimension of wisdom that is the most important and that the level of importance may differ depending on the culture or context. These researchers also point out that behaviour or action should be a critical part of wisdom. Jeste and Oswald (2014) argue that a wise individual not only "thinks wisely, but also acts wisely" (p. 319).

It also should be pointed out that there is controversy around the role of spirituality in the concept of wisdom. Many religious traditions such as Judaism, Hinduism, and Buddhism emphasize religiosity, or at least spirituality, as an attribute of wise people. However, Western definitions of wisdom often exclude spirituality (Jeste et al., 2010). Interestingly, there is some research that suggests that traditional religiosity and religious practices are unrelated to wisdom (Ardelt, 2008; Le, 2008).

Of the three dimensions of wisdom presented above, do you think that one dimension holds more importance than another?

If so, which one is more important and why?

DOES WISDOM OCCUR NATURALLY WITH AGE?

In most societies, wisdom has traditionally been associated with older age (Jeste & Vahia, 2008). However, the available research does not always support a consistent relationship between age and wisdom (Ardelt, 2010; Brugman, 2006). While growing old may provide you with the time to grow wise, it is no guarantee that you will become wise!

MEASURING WISDOM

Not surprisingly, measuring wisdom has proven to be very difficult because a common definition of wisdom has been elusive. In addition, the correlations among the various measures of wisdom are low, which again reflects the differences in researchers' definitions of wisdom. Furthermore, none of these measures seem to be best suited to assess the affective, cognitive, and reflective domains of personal wisdom (Redzanowski & Glück, 2013).

Can you think of a person in your life who you consider to be wise?

If so, what specific characteristics led you to believe that he or she is wise?

Interestingly, there is evidence to suggest that, regardless of the measure used to assess personal wisdom, it has been positively associated with psychological well-being (Etezadi & Pushkar, 2013), subjective well-being (Bergsma & Ardelt, 2012; Zacher, McKenna, & Rooney, 2013), and physical health (Ardelt, 2003). As the majority of these studies are cross-sectional, Ardelt (2015) conducted a two-wave, 10-month longitudinal study with 123 older adults aged 55 to 87. The three-dimensional wisdom scale was used to measure the cognitive, reflective, and affective dimensions of wisdom. She found that the presence of personal wisdom in an individual was positively correlated with subjective well-being, mastery, and purpose in life. Based on these results, Ardelt concluded that providing opportunities for older adults to acquire the cognitive, reflective, and affective dimensions of wisdom may be helpful for increasing subjective well-being in this population. Ardelt also argues that, because the development of wisdom takes time, individuals should be encouraged to grow in wisdom throughout life, in particular, the later years of life when older adults might have extra time to pursue activities that enhance psychosocial growth.

Heather Royan, B.A.
Villa Caritas, Geriatric Psychiatry, Edmonton, Alberta

WHERE DID YOU TRAIN?

I did two years of general studies at MacEwan University, Edmonton, Alberta and then transferred to the University of Alberta, Edmonton, Alberta to finish my major in psychology. In addition, through a special program at the University of Alberta, I did a one-year work experience placement in seniors' mental health at the Centennial Centre for Mental Health and Brain Injury in Ponoka, Alberta, and ended up working there for three more years as a psychometrist and program facilitator.

WHERE DO YOU WORK?

I work at Villa Caritas Hospital in Edmonton, Alberta. It is a specialized psychiatric in-patient facility for older adults with complex mental health issues.

WHAT DO YOU DO?

I'm a psychometrist. I perform psychological assessments (which are SUPER interesting to do) under the supervision of a clinical psychologist. I also partake in research projects, work with students from many disciplines, and am a member of an amazing interdisciplinary team.

WHY DO YOU LIKE WORKING WITH AN OLDER-ADULT POPULATION?

I honestly never imagined myself working with older adults, as I initially wanted to be a teacher and work in early education. But looking back, almost all of my jobs have involved older people in some way. I was extremely close to my late grandfather growing up, so I think working with older adults makes me feel a little closer to

him. I find that this population is incredibly dynamic and so varied. Age really is just a number and my patients prove that to me day in and day out! I am constantly challenged, learning, and growing—both as a professional and as a person. There's nothing stagnant about this field!

DO YOU HAVE ADVICE FOR STUDENTS WHO WANT TO GET INTO THE FIELD?

Volunteering is a great way to get your foot in the door—drop-in facilities, living facilities for older adults, or local community programs for older adults are great places to start. Check with your instructors to see if there are field placement options offered through your school. Do an independent study on a topic related to older adults. Working with older adults is definitely becoming the "sexy" field to get into, given the advancing age of the population worldwide. There are so many changes in this population that we can already see, such as older adults with very young attitudes and ways of life. Imagine, hippies are becoming the old people?! Get in as soon as you can!

John Fisk, Ph.D.
Nova Scotia Health Authority, Halifax, Nova Scotia
QUEII Health Science Centre, Halifax, Nova Scotia
Dalhousie University, Halifax, Nova Scotia

WHERE DID YOU TRAIN?

I trained at the University of Western Ontario, London, Ontario (B.Sc. Honours Physiology & Psychology, 1978; M.A. Psychology, 1979; Ph.D. Psychology, 1984) and at Brandies University, Waltham, Massachusetts (NSERC post-doctoral fellowship 1984–1985).

WHERE DO YOU WORK?

I am employed by the Nova Scotia Health Authority and my clinical practice is based at the QEII Health Sciences Centre in Halifax, Nova Scotia. I hold an academic appointment as an associate professor in the Department of Psychiatry at Dalhousie University with a cross-listing in the Department of Psychology and Neuroscience, as well as an appointment as assistant professor in the Department of Medicine, Division of Geriatric Medicine.

WHAT DO YOU DO?

I am a clinical neuropsychologist and I run a neuropsychological assessment service for people with known or suspected neurodegenerative disorders in Nova Scotia. Much of my clinical work is focused on neuropsychological assessment for the purposes of the diagnosis of atypical or complex presentations of cognitive problems seen in association with neurodegenerative disorders. For those with established diagnoses, my assessments serve to assist in management decision making, such as suitability for specific treatments or interventions and personal decision making by patients and their families, such as work continuation. My research is focused on the clinical populations that I serve and includes studies of dementia, multiple sclerosis, systemic lupus erythematosus, and Parkinson's disease, among others. In my research I examine the epidemiology and outcomes of these disorders as well as early signs of cognitive problems, associations with MRI and other clinical and pathological measures, and the effects of these disorders on mental health and health-related quality of life. In addition, I supervise graduate students in the Clinical Psychology Program at Dalhousie University in their thesis research and clinical practicum training, and I supervise pre-doctoral residents in

clinical psychology in our hospital-based internship/residency training program.

WHY DO YOU LIKE WORKING WITH AN OLDER-ADULT POPULATION?

I have always enjoyed working with an older-adult population because of the opportunity to learn from their experiences. I have met many truly remarkable people whose breadth of life experiences and accomplishments amaze me. You learn quickly not to underestimate people and to appreciate that there is much more to people than their diagnosis. When I talk to the people that I meet in my practice, I often am astounded by what they have had to deal with and overcome in their lives. It gives me a great appreciation of the resiliency of human beings and helps put in perspective any problems that I face in my own everyday life. My work can be challenging in that more often than not I often am providing people with diagnostic information that no one ever wants to hear. Despite this, the opportunity to be able to educate and help people and their families deal with the challenges of a neurodegenerative disorder is a privilege, and I am grateful that I have the chance to do this work. Without this opportunity, I would not have done the research that I have done. The ideas for research questions always come from my clinical work. The people that I see every day in my clinical practice tell me the important questions that need to be answered and for their insights I am truly grateful.

DO YOU HAVE ADVICE FOR STUDENTS WHO WANT TO GET INTO THE FIELD?

Acceptance into a graduate program in clinical psychology is very challenging due to the small class sizes of most of these programs in Canada. Persistence and flexibility are important. Not all will have faculty with research programs focused on older-aged populations. Look for opportunities in clinical practicum training, elective coursework, or other research project requirements that can provide exposure to older age groups if this is not available in your thesis research. For those specifically interested in clinical neuropsychology, keep in mind that there can be opportunities to obtain all of the requirements for specialization in this field within general clinical programs. This may require a bit more work on your part to seek out opportunities to fulfill those training requirements, however.

4.10 SUMMARY

- Healthy aging is associated with loss of brain density and weight in the frontal and temporal lobes, as well as in the hippocampus. Selected neuronal death occurs as well as widening of the grooves and shrinking of convolutions. A reduction in some neurotransmitters occurs as well as a decrease in cerebral blood flow with age. Senile plaques and neurofibrillary tangles begin to form.

- With age come changes in cognition. However, age-related changes in cognition are not the same across all cognitive domains or across all older individuals. A concept called "cognitive reserve" has been used to explain some of the age-related changes to cognition. Bilingualism also has been shown to act as a protective factor for cognitive decline.

- Atkinson and Shiffrin proposed the information-processing model of memory, which is based on a computer metaphor. This model has three stages: sensory memory, short-term memory, and long-term memory. Because of weaknesses in this model, the concept of working memory became widely accepted.

- Age-related changes in working memory might be due to a reduction in processing resources, a general slowing in the speed of processing information, and/or difficulties in inhibiting irrelevant information.

- The two primary forms of long-term memory are episodic and semantic memory. A large body of research shows that episodic memory changes with age. On the other hand, semantic memory remains relatively intact but what seems to change is retrieval of information in this memory store.

- There are three types of attentional processes: selective, divided, and sustained. In general, older adults perform slower on tests of selective and divided attention, which is thought to be due to a decrease in processing speed. There are not huge differences between young and older adults on sustained attention tasks.

- A common complaint among older adults is an increase in word-finding difficulty or tip-of-the-tongue states. There also is a decrease across the lifespan in the production of complex sentences. However, finding age differences may depend on how sentence complexity is being measured.

- "Elderspeak" is a type of communication used with old adults. Also called "secondary baby talk," this type of speech is characterized by a slow rate of speaking, exaggerated intonation, simplified vocabulary and grammar, and a higher pitch.

- Cognitive training programs have been developed to try to increase general cognitive functioning or prevent or minimize the effects of cognitive decline with age. Some of the interventions show strong potential for improving older adults' cognitive abilities, but other studies make exaggerated claims about the effectiveness of these programs.

- Lifestyle factors such as physical activity and diet play a role in the cognitive abilities of older adults.

- There have been numerous theories of intelligence put forth in which the number of cognitive abilities thought to make up intelligence are quite different from one another.

- John Carroll revised model of intelligence is the most comprehensive and empirically supported psychometric theory of intelligence

- Studies have consistently shown that fluid intelligence decreases with age while crystallized intelligence increases with age and begins to show modest declines only after the age of 70. However, there are considerable individual differences.

- Findings show that there is no uniform pattern of age-related decline in intellectual abilities. Moreover, there are significant individual differences in performance across measures of both fluid and crystallized intelligence.

- There are substantial cohort differences in intelligence. Cohorts born later show higher scores throughout the entire age range on all abilities assessed with the exception of number ability.

- Regardless of age, lower IQ scores do appear to be associated with an elevated risk of cardiovascular disease, obesity, stroke, and mortality.

- Certain personality traits, such as being open to new experiences and having a flexible attitude, are thought to maintain intelligence in older adults.

- The baby boom generation is better educated than previous generations and many older adults, particularly women, engage in lifelong learning. Older adults prefer intergenerational learning to age-segregated learning because there is a strong belief that older and younger students can learn from each other. Barriers to lifelong learning include such factors as time, age, accessibility, and ageism.

- Researchers believe that a qualitatively different type of thinking emerges in adulthood. Researchers also have identified a systematic progression of reflective judgment that begins in young adulthood.

- Contrary to popular opinion, wisdom does not come automatically with age. To date, there is no agreement among scholars about how to define wisdom. Interestingly, regardless of how you measure wisdom, it has been positively associated with well-being, physical health, mastery, and having a purpose in life among older adults.

Key Terms

Attention
The cognitive process of selectively concentrating on one aspect of the environment while ignoring other things.

Bilateralization
A term that refers to evidence that in older brains, activations for cognitive tasks spread out to both hemispheres of the prefrontal

cortex, whereas in the young, activations are typically confined to a single hemisphere.

Cognitive Capacity
The total cognitive resources available at any given time.

Central Executive
A part of the working memory model, proposed by Baddeley (2000), that controls and coordinates the three other components of working memory.

Circumlocutions
A roundabout or indirect way of speaking; the use of more words than necessary to express an idea.

Classic Aging Pattern
The developmental trend in which crystallized intelligence increases with age while fluid intelligence declines with age.

Cognitive Domains
Cognitive domains include attention, memory, perception, language, problem solving, and creativity.

Cognitive Epidemiology
A field of research that investigates the relationship between intelligence and health.

Cognitive Reserve
The idea that certain factors help to maintain cognitive functioning in the risk of accumulating brain pathology. These characteristics are thought to be high education level, complex work, and engaging in stimulating leisure and social activities.

Commission Errors
Errors that result from doing something wrong (e.g., pressing a button twice instead of once on a psychological task).

Compensation
In older adults, activations for cognitive tasks spread out to both hemispheres of the prefrontal cortex, whereas in the young, they are typically confined to a single hemisphere.

Computerized Tomography
A neuroimaging technique that creates detailed images of internal organs, bones, soft tissue, and blood vessels.

Compensation-Related Utilization of Neural Circuit Hypothesis (CRUNCH)
A model that explains that older brains will work harder to search for available resources to use in a particular cognitive task.

Crystallized Intelligence
An individual's accumulated skills, knowledge, and life experiences.

Diffusion Tensor Imaging
A neuroimaging technique that uses the diffusion of water molecules to determine the health of the white matter in the brain.

Echoic Memory
A component of sensory memory that is specific to retaining auditory information.

Elaborative Rehearsal
A type of rehearsal, as defined by Craik and Lockhart (1972) in relation to their levels of processing theory, that involves linking new information to information that already is in long-term memory to assist in retention of that information.

Encoding
The initial process of getting information into the memory system for storage and later retrieval.

Episodic Buffer
A part of the working memory model, proposed by Baddeley (2000), that holds information from the phonological loop and the visuospatial sketchpad, as well as information from long-term memory.

Episodic Memory
The part of long-term memory that is responsible for storing personally experienced events or episodes.

Executive Functions

A set of cognitive processes (attention, inhibitory control, working memory, problem solving, reasoning, and planning) that are necessary for the cognitive control of behaviour.

Fluid Intelligence

Those intellectual abilities needed for problem solving in novel situations.

Forgetting Curve

A term, based on research by Ebbinghaus (1885; 1913), that is used to describe the rapid loss of information after it is learned and the role of rehearsal in retaining information.

Functional Magnetic Resonance

A neuroimaging technique that measures brain activity by detecting changes associated with blood flow.

Functional Neuroimaging

A neuroimaging technique that provides information about brain activity rather than brain structure.

General Wisdom

The body of ideas or explanations generally accepted as true by the public or by experts in a field.

Glial Cells

Cells in the brain that provide support and protection for neurons in the central and peripheral nervous systems.

Grey Matter

Composed of neuronal cell bodies and unmyelinated axons, grey matter serves to process information in the brain. Structures within the grey matter process signals generated in the sensory organs or other areas of the grey matter.

Hemispheric Asymmetry Reduction (HAROLD)

A theory that claims that the higher level of bilateral activations in the prefrontal cortex of aging brains demonstrate a compensatory strategy for numerous cognitive tasks.

Iconic Memory

A type of sensory memory for visual information that fades very rapidly.

Information-Processing Model

A model of memory proposed by Atkinson and Shiffrin (1968). Based on a computer metaphor, the model is hypothesized to have three main storage compartments (sensory, short-term, and long-term memory) that hold information at different points during the processing of information.

Intelligence Quotient

A single score derived from a set of standardized tests developed to measure cognitive abilities in relation to one's age group.

Left-Branching Sentences

A sentence in which subordinate elements of the sentence appear before the main meaning of the sentence (e.g., sweating in the noon heat, the man cut down the tree).

Levels of Processing Theory

A theory, proposed by Craik and Lockhart in 1972, that hypothesizes that the depth of memory processing affects memory function. The authors argued that deep processing leads to longer-lasting memories whereas shallow processing leads to memories that decay easily.

Magnetic Resonance Imaging

A neuroimaging technique that uses a magnetic field and pulses of radio wave energy to make pictures of organs and structures inside the body. MRI also may show problems that cannot be seen with other imaging methods such as CT scans.

Maintenance Rehearsal

A type of rehearsal, as defined by Craik and Lockhart (1972) in relation to their levels of processing theory, that involves repeating information over and over again in a short period of time to assist in retention of that information.

Mediterranean Diet
A diet found in Mediterranean countries such as Greece that emphasizes consumption of fruits, vegetables, nuts, grains, olive oil (as opposed to butter), and grilled or steamed chicken and seafood (as opposed to red meat), plus a glass or two of red wine.

Meta-analysis
A systematic method that takes data from several independent studies and integrates those data using statistical analysis.

Myelin
An insulating layer that forms around nerves, including those in the brain and spinal cord. It is made up of protein and fatty substances. Myelin allows electrical impulses to transmit quickly and efficiently along the nerve cells.

Myelination
The process of coating the axon of each neuron with a fatty coating called myelin, which protects the neuron and helps it conduct signals more efficiently.

Near Infrared Spectroscopic Imaging
A neuroimaging technique that allows functional imaging of brain activity (or activation) through monitoring of blood oxygenation and blood volume in the prefrontal cortex.

Neuroimaging
An umbrella term that refers to a variety of methods and technologies for investigating the brain in both humans and animals.

Neurotransmitters
A chemical substance, released at the end of a nerve fibre following the arrival of a nerve impulse, that diffuses across the synapse, resulting in the transfer of the impulse to another nerve or muscle fibre, or some other structure.

Omission Errors
Failure to identify the target letter in a distractor task.

Over-Accommodation
Relying on negative stereotypes of older adults to guide communication.

Personal Wisdom
Knowledge that is gained through experience.

Phonological Loop
A part of the working memory model, proposed by Baddeley (2000), that stores and rehearses speech-based information, and deals with spoken and written material.

Positron Emission Tomography
A neuroimaging technique that uses small amounts of radioactive materials (called radiotracers), a special camera, and a computer to help evaluate organ and tissue functions. PET may detect the early onset of disease before it is evident on other imaging tests.

Premorbid Functioning
How a person was functioning before the onset of physical or emotional illness.

Primary Memory
A former description of memory used to define memory that is retained for only a very short period of time. It has since been referred to as short-term memory in the dual store model of memory.

Psychometric Approach
The branch of psychology that deals with the design, administration, and interpretation of quantitative tests for the measurement of psychological variables such as intelligence, aptitude, and personality traits.

Rehearsal
The process of continuously repeating to-be-remembered information. This method is effective in maintaining information over a short period of time.

Response Time
The time that passes between the introduction of a stimulus and the reaction by the individual (subject) to that stimulus.

Retrieval
Refers to the ability to get information out of the memory system when needed.

Scaffolding Theory of Cognitive Aging (STAC)
According to this theory, performance on various tasks of cognition is maintained due to the continuous engagement of compensatory scaffolding by the brain.

Secondary Memory
The vast body of knowledge stored over a lifetime.

Semantic Memory
The part of long-term memory that is responsible for storing information about the world (e.g., the names of colours, the sounds of letters, capitals of countries in the world, and other basic facts).

Signal Intensity
A measure of areas of abnormal tissue in the brain. When the brain is injured a scar will form over the injury. During MRI scanning, this scarring will give off a high signal that differentiates it from normal (unscarred) tissue.

Single Photo Emission Computerized Tomography
A nuclear neuroimaging technique that uses gamma rays.

Storage
The ability to retain information in the memory system over time.

Structural Neuroimaging
A neuroimaging technique that provides detailed images of the brain's anatomical structure at a certain point in time.

Tactile Memory
Memory that is collected through feeling or touching something. It also is known as haptic memory.

Terminal Drop
A rapid decline in cognitive functioning just prior to death.

Tip-of-the-Tongue Phenomena
Refers to the experience of being unable to produce a name or a word despite the experience of feeling confident of one's knowledge of the name or word.

Under-Accommodation
Failure to consider how normal age-related changes affect speaking and listening.

Visuospatial Sketchpad
A part of the working memory model, proposed by Baddeley (2000), that stores and manipulates visual and spatial information.

White Matter
Composed of bundles of axons that connect various grey matter areas of the brain to each other and carry nerve impulses between neurons.

Working Memory Model
A model of working memory proposed by Baddeley and Hitch (1974) and revised by Baddeley in 2000. It is a model that has replaced what used to be called short-term memory. Working memory is conceptualized as consisting of a central executive, a phonological loop, a visuospatial sketchpad, and an episodic buffer. All the components play an important part in the temporary storage of information.

Photo by Colin McConnell/Toronto Star via Getty Images

CHAPTER

05

LONGEVITY, HEALTH, AND FUNCTIONING

"It's paradoxical that the idea of living a long life appeals to everyone but the idea of getting old doesn't appeal to anyone."

Andy Rooney

Canadians are living longer. In fact, the fastest-growing age group consists of those over the age of 85. Women are still outliving men but the gap is narrowing. Have you thought about your own aging? It may seem a long way off but how you care for yourself as you age has a big influence on how you will function as an older adult.

How long do you think you will live? Find out by playing the Longevity Game at http://media.nmfn.com/flash/longevity-game/finish.html.

5.1 HOW LONG WILL YOU LIVE?
LEARNING OBJECTIVES

To understand:

- the average and maximum longevity for humans
- the gender differences in longevity
- genetic and environmental factors that influence longevity
- the meaning of the healthy immigrant effect

LONGEVITY

Have you ever wondered how long you will live? Today, more people than ever before are living well into old age. While today's young and middle-aged adults can look forward to a longer lifespan, it should be kept in mind that the lifestyle choices we make as we age will influence the quality of life we experience in older adulthood. More about this later in the chapter.

Why is it important to know how long you will live? Identifying how long one can expect to live is important for several reasons. For example, it has implications for health and service programs, retirement programs, and the development of age-appropriate housing. Living longer will certainly present challenges in all these areas. For example, in Canada, we currently are experiencing a need for supportive housing that helps older adults remain independent in the community for as long as they can. If this shortage is not addressed soon, where will older adults who need assistance live?

Longevity is influenced by genetic and environmental factors. **Average longevity** (also known as life expectancy) is a statistical measure that refers to the age at which half of the individuals born in a given year will have died. Life expectancies are increasing rapidly. For example, between 1921 and 2011, the gain in overall life expectancy for Canadians was nearly 25 years, with almost half of the gains in life expectancy occurring between 1921 and 1951 due to decreases in infant mortality (Decady & Greenberg, 2014).

ORMA SLACK

In 2015, the oldest living Canadian was Orma Slack, who lived to be almost 115 years of age. She was born on February 19, 1903, in Bracebridge, Ontario. She married William Slack in 1926 and eventually moved to Belleville in 1950. She was just a few months old when Orville Wright flew the first airplane! She was 12 years old when the *Titanic* sank and she was in her 20s for much of the Great Depression. Mrs. Slack lived on her own until five years ago when she moved to the Westgate Lodge. She remained active and, amazingly, the last time she was on skis was on her 100th birthday! She volunteered at the Belleville General Hospital Foundation's Opportunity Shop thrift store until the age of 104. She stopped only because she couldn't find a ride. Her secret? As stated by Orma, *"Ever since I was a child, the world did not change for better or worse. Things don't change, so go with the flow. I've never done anything special to help me get to my age, but the secret may be my positive attitude to people and life. I don't recall ever saying a bad thing about a neighbour, family member, or a friend."* For more information go to http://www.intelligencer .ca/2014/02/18/orma-celebrates-111th -birthday-wednesday (Mountney-Lessard, 2014). Do you want to know if Mrs. Slack is still the oldest living Canadian? Go to https://en.wikipedia.org/wiki/List_of _Canadian_supercentenarians to find out.

In 2011, the average Canadian life expectancy at birth was estimated to be 81.76 years of age (Martel, 2013). Canadian national and provincial estimates for longevity at birth and at age 65 are presented in Table 5.1. As can be seen, if you live in British Columbia, Alberta, Ontario, or Quebec, you are expected to live somewhat longer than Canadians in other provinces. Nunavut has the lowest life expectancy at birth (Martel, 2013). If you were born in the United States, you can expect to live to an average age of 78.7 years (Arias, 2015).

You might be wondering if Canada's population is aging in a similar way across the provinces and territories. As you can see from Table 5.2, the age structure of the three Prairie provinces is very different from the age structure of the other seven provinces. There are more young people in the Prairies than in other provinces. Alberta has the youngest median age of the provinces at 36.3 years, while Saskatchewan and Manitoba have populations much younger than the national average. This is thought to be due in part to higher fertility rates, international immigration, and interprovincial migration. Nunavut has the youngest population with a median age of 26.1 and almost 31 percent of its population under the age of 15. In contrast, the four Atlantic provinces have the highest percentage of people over the age of 65 years in Canada (Statistics Canada, 2014).

GENDER DIFFERENCES IN LONGEVITY IN CANADA AND AROUND THE WORLD

According to the World Health Organization (WHO, 2014a), women in all countries around the world outlive men. In 2012, global life expectancy at birth was 72.7 years for women and 68.1 years for men. As you can see from Table 5.3, women in Japan have the longest life expectancy in the world followed by women in Spain, Switzerland, and Singapore. Life expectancy among men was 80 years or more in nine countries in the world, with the longest male life expectancies in Iceland, Switzerland, and Australia (WHO, 2014a). Although not

TABLE 5.1

LIFE EXPECTANCY AT BIRTH AND AT AGE 65, CANADA, PROVINCES AND TERRITORIES, 2009–2011

REGION	AT BIRTH		AT AGE 65	
	Males	Females	Males	Females
Canada	79.33	83.60	18.82	21.73
Alberta	79.06	83.45	18.81	21.83
British Columbia	80.25	84.40	19.65	22.32
Manitoba	77.72	82.19	18.12	21.25
New Brunswick	78.36	83.14	18.36	21.24
Newfoundland and Labrador	77.09	82.00	17.28	20.39
Northwest Territories	76.28	80.07	17.76	20.23
Nova Scotia	78.05	82.64	17.92	20.83
Nunavut	68.75	73.91	14.55	15.39
Ontario	79.77	83.92	19.00	21.89
Prince Edward Island	78.15	82.90	17.95	20.96
Quebec	79.43	83.55	18.60	21.56
Saskatchewan	77.20	82.20	18.28	21.42
Yukon	75.19	79.61	16.24	18.87

Source: Martel, L. (2013). *Mortality: Overview, 2010 and 2011* (Catalogue No. 91-209-X). Ottawa, ON: Statistics Canada.

shown in Table 5.3, in Canada in 2016, life expectancy at birth was 83.6 years for women and 79.4 years for men (Statistics Canada, 2016c). However, this gap between men and women is getting smaller. For example, during the years 1994 to 1996, the gap in life expectancy at birth between men and women was 6.1 years, whereas in 2006 to 2008, it was 4.6 years (Statistics Canada, 2012c).

Results from the WHO report (2014a) indicate that life expectancy for both men and women is still less than 55 years in nine sub-Saharan African countries: Angola, Central African Republic, Chad, Côte d'Ivoire, Democratic Republic of the Congo, Lesotho, Mozambique, Nigeria, and Sierra Leone (WHO, 2014a). In fact, Africa is the youngest continent in the world. As you can see in Figure 5.1, there are dramatic differences in longevity around the world.

REFLECTIVE QUESTION

Why do you think Africa is the youngest country in the world?

TABLE 5.2

POPULATION ESTIMATES, AGE DISTRIBUTION, AND MEDIAN AGE AS OF JULY 1, 2016, CANADA, PROVINCES AND TERRITORIES

	POPULATION	0 TO 14 YEARS	15 TO 64 YEARS	65 YEARS AND OVER	MEDIAN AGE
	Number	Percentage			Years
Canada	36 286 425	16.10	67.40	16.50	40.60
Alberta	4 252 879	18.50	69.60	11.90	36.30
British Columbia	4 751 612	14.60	67.50	17.90	42.10
Manitoba	1 318 128	18.70	66.20	15.00	37.50
Newfoundland and Labrador	530 128	14.10	66.80	19.10	45.30
New Brunswick	756 780	14.60	65.90	19.50	45.00
Northwest Territories	44 469	21.80	71.10	7.10	33.30
Nova Scotia	949 501	14.10	66.50	19.40	44.60
Nunavut	37 082	30.70	65.40	4.00	26.10
Ontario	13 982 984	15.90	67.80	16.40	40.60
Prince Edward Island	148 649	15.70	65.40	18.90	43.90
Quebec	8 326 089	15.60	66.40	18.10	42.10
Saskatchewan	1 150 632	19.20	65.90	14.80	36.90
Yukon	37 082	17.00	71.40	11.60	39.50

Source: Statistics Canada. (2016c). *Annual demographic estimates: Canada, provinces and territories* (Catalogue No. 91-215-X). Ottawa, ON: Statistics Canada.

Why do women live longer than men? Many reasons have been offered to explain gender differences, but it is likely that a combination of biological, social, and genetic factors account for the difference (Newman & Brach, 2001; Rieker & Bird, 2005). As you will see later in this chapter, the rate of men dying from the top three causes of death in Canada is significantly higher than the rate for women. Some of the illnesses such as heart disease are associated with lifestyle factors such as cigarette smoking and alcohol consumption. In terms of gender differences, men are thought to smoke and drink alcohol more than women. Also, women have two X chromosomes (men only have one), and this is thought to be a protective factor against heart disease in women. Men see their physicians less often than do women. Men also have higher rates of violence than women and are more likely to die prematurely (e.g., work-related accidents, motor vehicle crashes, victims of war). Finally, although more male than female babies are born, men are more susceptible to infectious diseases. However, none of the factors listed above can fully account for age differences in longevity between males and females (Rieker & Bird, 2005).

TABLE 5.3

LIFE EXPECTANCY AT BIRTH AMONG MEN AND WOMEN IN 2012 IN THE 10 TOP-RANKED COUNTRIES

MEN			WOMEN		
Rank	Country	Life Expectancy	Rank	Country	Life Expectancy
1	Iceland	81.20	1	Japan	87.00
2	Switzerland	80.70	2	Spain	85.10
3	Australia	80.50	3	Switzerland	85.10
4	Israel	80.20	4	Singapore	85.10
5	Singapore	80.20	5	Italy	85.00
6	New Zealand	80.20	6	France	84.90
7	Italy	80.20	7	Australia	84.60
8	Japan	80.00	8	Republic of Korea	84.60
9	Sweden	80.00	9	Luxembourg	84.10
10	Luxembourg	79.70	10	Portugal	84.00

Source: World Health Organization Media Centre. (2014, May 15). *World health statistics 2014: Large gains in life expectancy*. Retrieved from http://www.who.int/mediacentre/news/releases/2014/world-health-statistics-2014/en/. Reprinted by permission of the World Health Organization (WHO).

FIGURE 5.1

WORLD MAP DEPICTING LIFE EXPECTANCY IN YEARS

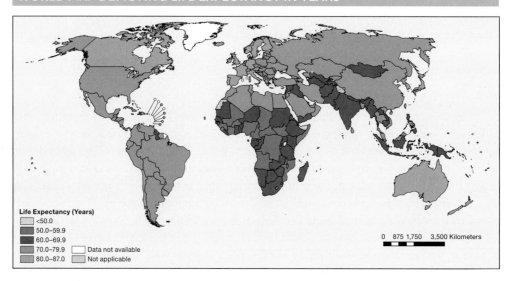

Source: World Health Organization. (2016a). *Global life expectancy, both sexes, 2015*. Retrieved from http://gamapserver.who.int/mapLibrary/Files/Maps/Global_LifeExpectancy_bothsexes_2015.png. Reprinted with permission from the World Health Organization.

What other factors do you think might account for gender differences in longevity?

AGING BABY BOOMERS

As mentioned in Chapter 1, the baby boomers are aging at an unprecedented rate. According to the United Nations, the number of persons 65 years of age and older worldwide was 841 million in 2013, which is four times higher than the 202 million who were 65 and older in 1950. It is projected that the older population will almost triple by 2050, when it is expected to surpass the two billion mark (United Nations Department of Economic and Social Affairs Population Division, 2013). It is further estimated that the number of Canadians 65 years of age and over should reach 20 percent in 2036 and 25 percent in 2061 (Statistics Canada, 2016c). And, for the first time in history, Canada now has more individuals 65 and older than children aged 14 and younger (Statistics Canada, 2016c).

You may be surprised to learn that of those 65 years of age and older, it is the 85 years and older age group that is growing the fastest. Consider that in July 1984, there were only 202 300 individuals 85 years or older. In 2016, this number had more than tripled to 787 492 (Statistics Canada, 2016c).

CENTENARIANS IN CANADA AND AROUND THE WORLD

Individuals who live to be 100 to 110 years of age are called **centenarians**. Recent statistics indicate that there were 7345 centenarians in Canada as of July 1, 2016, or roughly 20 centenarians per 100 000 population. In comparison, there were only 11 centenarians per 100 000 population in Canada in 2001 (Statistics Canada, 2016c). To put being 100 years of age or older in context, these individuals were just children at the start of World War I in 1914. They likely married, had children of their own, and endured economic struggles during the Great Depression of the 1930s. Most of them likely retired in the 1970s. More women than men reached the age of 100, with recent Statistics Canada (2016c) estimates showing that there are 13 male per 100 female centenarians. Statistics Canada population projections also show that the number of centenarians will likely continue to rise. By 2061, this number could reach more than 78 300 Statistics Canada, (2015c)! As shown in Figure 5.2, provincially, Saskatchewan has the highest rate of individuals over the age of 100 while the three Territories as a group, as well as Newfoundland and Labrador, have the lowest rates (Statistics Canada, 2011a).

You might wonder how Canada compares to other countries in the world in terms of the number of centenarians. Among G7 countries, Canada currently has one of the lowest proportions of individuals 65 years of age and older (16.5%) (see Figure 5.3). In contrast, Japan has one of the oldest populations in the world and the highest proportion of people 65 years and older of any G7 country (27%), or just over one in four people. The United States is the only G7 country where the proportion aged 65 and older is lower (15%) than in Canada (Statistics Canada, 2016c).

FIGURE 5.2

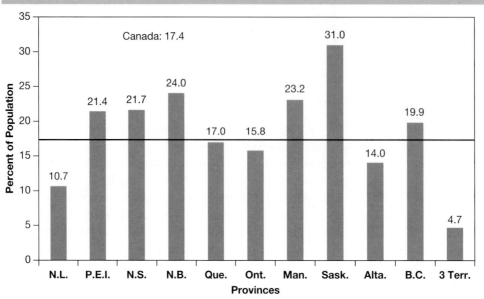

Note: "3 Terr." indicates Yukon, Northwest Territories, and Nunavut.

Source: Statistics Canada. (2011a). *Centenarians in Canada: Age and sex, 2011 census* (Catalogue No. 98-311-X2011003). Ottawa, ON: Author.

A similar pattern is evident when looking at centenarians across countries. Canada's rate of centenarians in 2011 was 17.40 per 100 000 (Statistics Canada, 2016c), which is slightly below the average of 19.7 per 100 000 among **G8 countries**. France, Italy, and the United Kingdom all have higher rates of centenarians than Canada (Statistics Canada, 2011a).

FIGURE 5.3

CENTENARIANS IN G8 COUNTRIES

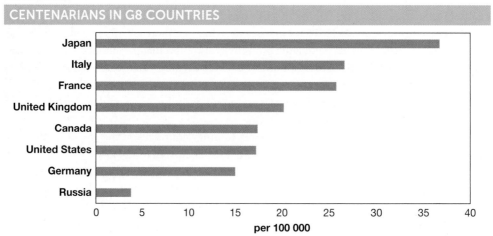

Source: Statistics Canada. (2011a). *Centenarians in Canada: Age and sex, 2011 census* (Catalogue No. 98-311-X2011003). Ottawa, ON: Author.

MAXIMUM LONGEVITY

Maximum longevity is the oldest age one can possibly live. **Supercentenarians** are a special group of people who live beyond 110 years. You may not recognize the name but Jeanne Louise Calment was a supercentenarian who has lived the longest of any human to date. She lived to the **authenticated** age of 122 years, 164 days. Jeanne died in Arles in southern France on August 4, 1997. When asked on her 120th birthday what she expected of the future, she replied, "A very short one" (Whitney, February 22, 1995). Gerontologists originally thought that 110 to 120 years of age was the longest a person could live, but, today, the idea that life cannot extend past 120 years is being reconsidered. With improvements in healthcare and better management of chronic conditions, we just may see more people living past 100 years of age.

What do you think accounts for the differences in longevity in G8 countries?

What are some of the implications of living past 100 years of age?

Is it a good idea to extend life indefinitely?

Would you want to live to be 100? 110? or longer?

REFLECTIVE QUESTIONS

ETHNIC DIFFERENCES IN LONGEVITY

Determining ethnic differences in longevity is quite complex because of a lack of longitudinal data in many countries in the world (Newbold, 2006). In Canada and the United States, foreign-born individuals tend to live longer and are in better health than those who are native-born. This is known as the **healthy immigrant effect** (Cunningham, Ruben, & Narayan, 2008; Kennedy, McDonald, & Biddle, 2007). The three main reasons given for this effect are the healthy habits and behaviours practised by immigrants prior to leaving their home country, immigrant self-selection in that a country's healthiest and wealthiest have the financial and physical means to migrate, and strict health screening by authorities in the host country prior to immigration (Gee, Kobayashi, & Prus, 2004; Kennedy et al., 2007). This healthy immigrant effect is even higher when you compare foreign-born individuals to native-born individuals from the same ethnic group (Cunningham et al., 2008; Trovato & Odynak, 2011). Interestingly, there is some evidence to suggest that the longer an immigrant lives in the host country, the more his or her health resembles the health of people born in the host country. This increased similarity between immigrants and native-born residents' health is attributed to the adoption of the behaviours and eating habits of the host country by the immigrant population (Cunningham et al., 2008; Gee et al., 2007). Trovato and Odynak (2011) did one of the very few studies that looked at sex differences in Canadian immigrant mortality. It is no surprise that they found immigrant females enjoy a higher life expectancy than immigrant males. However, they also found that immigrants have a smaller gap between female–male life expectancy compared to Canadian-born individuals. This smaller gap has been attributed to a smaller sex difference in suicides and mortality from cancer, particularly lung cancer. As the immigrant population continues to grow, more research will be needed to understand how changes in health status occur over time to better address the needs of an increasingly diverse aging population.

With respect to Aboriginal peoples, it is very difficult to obtain accurate information on this segment of the Canadian population due to scarcity of data. For example, in some remote reserves in Canada, birth and death certificates are not kept. In some cases, a birth or a death may not be recorded at all, and in other cases, although rarely, a birth or a death may be recorded multiple times. In addition, in remote Aboriginal communities, most individuals are required to travel outside of their home community to receive medical care, which may or may not be documented. To complicate matters further, there often is a lack of information about Aboriginal identity on medical, birth, and death records, which also contributes to inaccurate health information (Statistics Canada, 2011b).

Having said that, what we do know is that the Aboriginal populations of Canada are much younger and growing faster than the overall Canadian non-Aboriginal population. Data from the National Household Survey (Statistics Canada, 2013a) show that in 2011, the median age of the total Aboriginal population was 28 years, which is 13 years younger than the median age of 41 years for non-Aboriginal Canadians. Further, in 2011, it was estimated that there were 82 690 Aboriginal people who were aged 65 and over, accounting for almost 6 percent of the total Aboriginal population. Compare this to the non-Aboriginal older adult population, which was almost 14 percent of the total Canadian population in 2011 (Statistics Canada, 2013a). Because the Aboriginal population is much younger and smaller than the non-Aboriginal populations in Canada, aging in general has not been a focus of concern among Aboriginal health organizations until recently (Statistics Canada, 2013a).

OTHER FACTORS AFFECTING LONGEVITY

What do you think influences how long a person will live? As you may have guessed, several factors influence longevity. Let's start with genetics. You might think that if your parents live a long life, the chances of you living a long life are greater. However, twin studies have shown that genetic factors account for only 25 to 30 percent of the individual differences in lifespan (Herskind et al., 1996; Hjelmborg et al., 2006; Ljungquist, Berg, Lanke, McClearn, & Pedersen, 1998; McGue, Vaupel, Holm, & Harvald, 1993). We are learning more and more about genes and their effect on both longevity and disease thanks to the Human Genome Project (HGP) (National Human Genome Research Institute, 2014), which was completed in April of 2003. For the first time in history, we have the ability to read the genetic blueprint needed to build a human being. The results that are being generated are really quite amazing. For example, because the sequencing of DNA is now understood, we can now begin to identify genes and mutations linked to different forms of cancer. We now are beginning to understand the genotypes of specific viruses that will help to identify appropriate treatment. For more information about the HGP, go to www.genome .gov/10001772.

REFLECTIVE QUESTION

What might be some of the ethical and social implications of knowing how to build a human being?

Environmental factors, as well as lifestyle and socio-economic factors, can influence how long a person will live (Public Health Agency of Canada, [PHAC], 2013a). For example, air and water pollution may contribute to a shorter life as may the carcinogens present in some of the food we eat. Smoking, as well as the abuse of drugs and alcohol, are lifestyle factors that can contribute to a shorter life. Having a lower socio-economic status has been linked to a decrease in lifespan because of reduced opportunities to eat healthily and exercise. Reduced access to healthcare services also is a factor. While there is equal access to healthcare in Canada, some Canadians may not be able to afford prescriptions or health and/or visual aids that they may need (e.g., glasses). Fortunately, many of these factors are in our control and changes can be made at both the individual and the societal level.

5.2 ILLNESS AND DISABILITY

LEARNING OBJECTIVES

To understand:
- the definition of health
- the health of older Canadians
- the factors that affect health
- patterns of illness and disability in older Canadians
- the consequences of co-morbidity and polypharmacy
- the compression and expansion of morbidity hypotheses
- the dynamic equilibrium hypothesis

THE HEALTH OF OLDER CANADIANS

DEFINITIONS OF HEALTH

What do we mean when we ask someone about their **health**? That is, are we asking them about their physical health? their mental health? or their social well-being? Because there are many *dimensions* to health, it is not surprising that there are many *definitions* of health. One of the most frequently used definitions, formulated by the WHO and still in use today, describes health

CASE STUDY — A SNAPSHOT OF SUCCESSFUL AGING

Mary is an 83-year-old lady who lives with her husband in the home that they bought as a young married couple. Like several of her friends, Mary volunteers at the local hospital gift shop one morning a week, as well as once a week at the local Older Adult Centre. Although Mary still is relatively active, she has cut back on her volunteer hours the past few years because of changes in her health. Similar to many of her friends who are the same age, Mary has several chronic conditions, including high blood pressure, osteoporosis, arthritis, and cataracts. She had cataract surgery a year ago in both of her eyes and has enjoyed good vision since that time. Her blood pressure is well controlled with medication, and she takes her calcium and vitamin D pills regularly for her osteoporosis, as well as a prescribed drug for her arthritis. Mary also makes sure that she gets her flu shot every year. Despite her chronic health conditions, Mary says that, overall, her health is very good, and she enjoys spending time with family and friends and being active in the community.

as "a state of complete physical, mental, and social well-being and not merely the absence of disease or infirmity" (WHO, 1948, p. 100). However, this definition of health is increasingly being criticized. First, the requirement of complete physical, mental, and social well-being would undoubtedly leave the majority of us unhealthy most of the time (Smith, 2008). Second, the **epidemiological** pattern of diseases has shifted over time, from high rates of death from **acute diseases** (e.g., infectious, parasitic diseases) and short life expectancy to high rates of **chronic disease** and longer life expectancy (Goulding, Rogers, & Smith, 2003; Harper & Armelagos, 2010; Omran, 2005). As such, the number of people living with chronic diseases is continuing to increase worldwide, making the WHO definition of health counterproductive in that it characterizes individuals with chronic diseases (and with a **disability** or disabilities) as definitely ill (Huber et al., 2011).

Because of limitations to the current WHO definition of health, there have been a number of proposals for a new definition of health. The most well-known revised definition of **health** is the one found in the *Ottawa Charter for Health Promotion* in which health is seen as "a resource for everyday life, not the objective of living. Health is a positive concept emphasizing social and personal resources, as well as physical capacities" (retrieved from http://www.who.int/healthpromotion/conferences/previous/ottawa/en/).

MEASURING THE HEALTH STATUS OF OLDER ADULTS

In looking at the health status of older adults, we see that, overall, today's older adults are living longer and are healthier than older adults from previous generations. But even so, chronic diseases increase with age. As shown in Figure 5.4, the percentage of the population with one or more chronic diseases increases with age (PHAC, 2010d). Specifically, if we compare the percentage of individuals with chronic diseases in the 45 to 64 age range to the percentage of individuals with

FIGURE 5.4

THE PROPORTION OF THE POPULATION WITH ONE OR MORE CHRONIC DISEASES BY SELECTED AGE GROUPS, CANADA, 2009

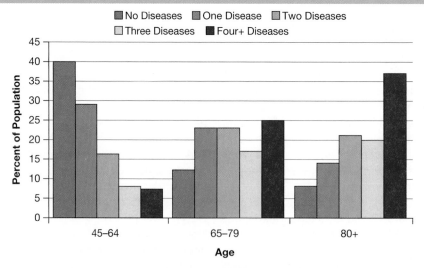

chronic diseases in the other two older-age categories, you can see that the percentage of individuals with one, two, three, and four or more chronic diseases increases significantly across the three age groupings. Another way of looking at these data is to look at the percentage of individuals with no diseases across the three age groupings. As you can see, 40 percent of individuals 45 to 64 years of age have no chronic diseases. In comparison, only 12 percent of individuals in the 65 to 79 age group and only 8 percent of Canadians in the 80+ age group have no chronic disease.

Another way of measuring health is to have people simply rate their health on a scale from poor to excellent. When health is measured in this way, approximately 60 percent of males and females in Canada 12 years of age and older rated their health as "very good" or "excellent." However, as shown in Figure 5.5, the percentage of both men and women rating their health as very good or excellent decreases with age (Statistics Canada, 2011c). Interestingly, although the self-ratings of health are slightly higher than ratings of health as measured by number of chronic conditions, the general pattern is one of decline in health across the age ranges, irrespective of how health is measured. However, this decline in health is not universal among older adults and there is much variability in the aging process. You may wonder about the validity of self-ratings of health. That is, how accurate are people when rating their own health? It turns out that self-ratings of health are pretty good predictors of health, with lower self-ratings of health associated with an increased risk of mortality (DeSalvo, Fan, McDonell, & Fihn, 2005) and morbidity (Mavaddat, Parker, Sanderson, Mant, & Kinmonth, 2014), as well as lower functional status (Idler & Kasl, 1995).

FIGURE 5.5

PERCENTAGE OF INDIVIDUALS REPORTING VERY GOOD OR EXCELLENT HEALTH, HOUSEHOLD POPULATION AGED 12 OR OLDER, BY AGE GROUP AND SEX, CANADA, 2011

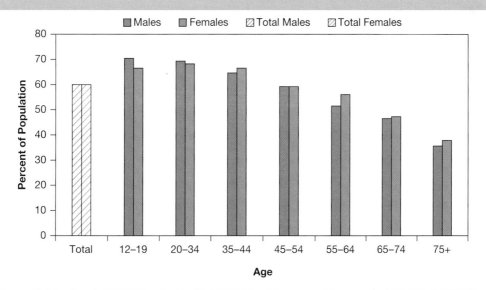

Source: Statistics Canada. (2011c). *Perceived health, 2011*. Retrieved from www.statcan.gc.ca/pub/82-625-x/2012001/article/11665-eng.htm.

You may be wondering if self-ratings of mental health are similar to overall self-ratings of physical health. As shown in Figure 5.6, the majority of Canadians, including older adults, report their mental health as very good or excellent (PHAC, 2014a). We will have more to say about mental health in older adults in Chapter 6.

FACTORS AFFECTING HEALTH

Many factors affect a person's health. These factors or determinants of health include the physical environment, the social and economic environments, and individual characteristics and behaviours (WHO, 2015b). Genetics play a role in determining not only lifespan but also healthiness and the likelihood of developing certain illnesses. By now you know that age and health status are strongly related, with older individuals more likely to have poorer health status. Gender and health status also are strongly related, with the pattern of diseases different for men and women across the age range. In the older adult population, women are more likely than males to have arthritis, asthma, hypertension, mood disorders, and urinary incontinence. Older men, on the other hand, are more likely to have cancer, diabetes, and heart disease as compared to older women. There also is a strong relationship between both education and income and health status across all age groups, with lower levels of education and lower income associated with poorer health status (Gilmour, 2012). And, as you know by now, immigrant status also can affect health.

Individual behaviours such as eating habits, level of physical activity, smoking and drinking habits, and ways of coping with stress also affect health status. In older adults, healthy eating habits and consuming foods high in nutrition can help to prevent illness. However, like many younger Canadians, many older Canadians fail to eat a balanced diet. For example, in Canada in 2004, 52 percent of men and 60 percent of women 71 years of age and older did not consume

FIGURE 5.6

PERCENTAGE OF INDIVIDUALS REPORTING VERY GOOD OR EXCELLENT SELF-PERCEIVED MENTAL HEALTH BY AGE GROUP, CANADA, 2003 AND 2012

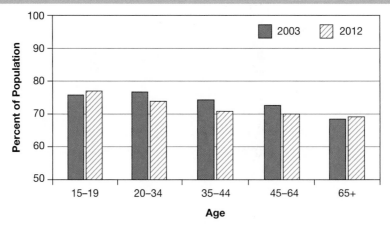

the recommended daily minimum of five servings of fruits and vegetables (Garriguet, 2006). Decreased appetite, dietary restrictions, medications, and illness are factors that can lead to malnutrition in an older adult. Economics also affects access to nutritious food. Although some older adults are economically disadvantaged, most older Canadians are thought to have sufficient physical and economic access to nutritious food (PHAC, 2014a). Regular physical activity plays a role in preventing illness and enhancing mental health. However, the majority of older adults are physically inactive and activity levels tend to decrease across the upper age range (Edwards & Mawani, 2006). Regular physical activity helps older adults in maintaining muscle and bone strength, as well as assisting with coordination and flexibility. Participation in physical activities also helps older adults maintain their social connectedness with others. Smoking and consumption of alcohol are less common in the older adult population as compared to other adult age groups. Based on self-reports, 9 percent of Canadian older adults indicate that they are current smokers, with 47 percent reporting being a former smoker (PHAC, 2010d). Compared to younger age groups, the rate of alcohol use also is lower in the older adult population.

It is well established that stress can negatively affect health status. Chronic illness or the loss of partners, family members, and friends are just some of the many difficult issues that older adults face. Methods of coping with stress also can affect health status. Positive mental health can help older adults cope with these life challenges. Poor mental health can not only affect physical well-being but also negatively affect emotional and social well-being (PHAC, 2010d). Older adults also provide a significant amount of care to fellow older adults with long-term physical, cognitive (e.g., dementia), and mental health disorders, as well as during temporarily difficult times. These older adults caring for other older adults are more likely to report feeling stressed by helping others, with older women more likely to report being stressed than men (Penning & Wu, 2016). We will talk more about stress and methods of coping with stress in Chapter 6.

Two factors affecting health status in older adults that you may not have thought about are the degree of social support that they receive and their level of social engagement. Using data from the 2008/2009 Canadian Community Health Survey, Gilmour (2012) found that older adults with low levels of social support were less likely to report positive self-perceived health, and more likely to be lonely and dissatisfied with life compared to older adults with high social support. Participation in social activities also was associated with self-perceived health status such that ratings of self-perceived health increased as the number of social activities increased. Conversely, the likelihood of reporting loneliness or dissatisfaction with life decreased. Finally, the extent to which individuals participate in their community and feel that they belong can influence their long-term physical and mental health. Based on data from the Canadian Community Health Surveys, at least two-thirds of adults 65 years of age and older rated their sense of community belonging as very strong (Sheilds, 2008).

How would you define health?

What are the implications of defining health as the absence of disease?

What are the implications of defining health as a resource for everyday life?

REFLECTIVE QUESTIONS

ILLNESSES AND DISEASES COMMON IN OLDER CANADIANS

ACUTE ILLNESSES

Mary, the 83-year-old lady portrayed in the case study earlier, is typical of older individuals in that she has several chronic diseases. Mary also minimizes the risk of getting infectious diseases such as the flu by getting the influenza vaccine annually. In Canada, as in most developed countries in the world, acute diseases such as tuberculosis, small pox, poliomyelitis, diphtheria, and tetanus have ceased to be major causes of death. The control of these, and other infectious diseases, is due in large part to vaccines. Canada was certified as polio-free in 1994, and diseases such as diphtheria, tetanus, and German measles are rare in Canada. Smallpox has been eliminated worldwide. The absence of some infectious diseases and low rates of other infectious diseases is due, in large part, to routine immunizations for children. However, some of these infectious diseases are reappearing in Canada and other developed countries due, in part, to public perceptions that vaccines are unsafe. Currently, the anti-vaccine movement has been fuelled by the belief that the vaccine for measles, mumps, and rubella (MMR) causes autism. Notably, research indicates that the MMR vaccine is *not* linked to autism spectrum disorder (www.cdc.gov/ncbddd/autism/topics.html). Of interest, a research article published in the *Lancet* in 1998 linking the MMR vaccine to autism often is used as evidence that the MMR vaccine causes autism (Wakefield et al., 1998). However, this article has recently been retracted because the results could not be replicated (see Flaherty, 2001; Godlee, Smith, & Marcovitch, 2011).

In addition to children, adults require immunization. In Canada, influenza is a major cause of hospitalization and mortality among older adults. In 2009 to 2010, approximately 2300 individuals 65 years of age and older were admitted to hospital for influenza and approximately 10 percent of them died (Canadian Institute for Health Information, 2011a). Influenza can be prevented, with vaccination for influenza recommended worldwide, particularly for high-risk groups such as adults 65 and older. Influenza vaccinations also are recommended for people who live and work with older adults because of the risk of their spreading the flu to their older patients. To facilitate access, public health programs across Canada provide publicly funded vaccinations to people aged 65 and older. In addition, priority for vaccination is given to healthcare and social service workers who work with high-risk groups such as older individuals. Despite these efforts, vaccination rates in Canada frequently remain below set targets (PHAC, 2014b), with Canada having one of the lowest rates of vaccination for adults age 65 and older in OECD countries (Snowdon, Schnarr, Hussein, & Alessi, 2012). To assist Canadians in keeping track of and managing their immunization records more easily, a bilingual mobile application (app) has been developed by the Public Health Agency of Canada and collaborating partners. The new CANImmunize app is available for iOS & Android with availability for Mac / PC coming soon (see https://www.canimmunize.ca/en/home).

CHRONIC ILLNESSES

Chronic illnesses are now responsible for more than 80 percent of all deaths and a leading cause of disability worldwide (WHO, 2010). In addition to classifying illnesses in terms of "acute" and "chronic," we also can distinguish illnesses in terms of communicable disease (often referred to as infectious disease), non-communicable disease (often referred to as chronic disease), and injuries (WHO, 2010). Of the 57 million deaths that occurred globally in 2008, almost two-thirds (36 million) were due to non-communicable diseases consisting mainly of cardiovascular diseases, cancers, diabetes, and chronic lung diseases. Other diseases included in the non-communicable disease category were gastrointestinal diseases, renal diseases, and neurological and mental health disorders (WHO, 2010).

The main causes of death due to communicable and non-communicable diseases and injuries in Canada are shown in Figure 5.7 (Statistics Canada, 2015d). As you can see, the main causes of death for younger Canadians are quite different than those for older adults. For younger Canadians aged 0 to 24 years and 25 to 44 years, a large proportion of all deaths are due to accidents, cancer, and suicide. Conversely, the main causes of death for adults aged 65 and older in 2012 were due to cancer, heart disease, and stroke (Statistics Canada, 2015d). Although the overall percentage of deaths due to injuries as a main cause of death in the population 65 years of age and older is lower than for those below 65 years of age, the number of deaths among older adults due to both intentional and unintentional injuries is still significant, ranking eighth in overall causes of death for Canadian older adults in 2006 (data not shown). Of these deaths due to injury in older adults, 10 percent were due to motor vehicle crashes and almost one-half were caused by falls (41 percent) (PHAC, 2010d).

FIGURE 5.7

PERCENTAGE DISTRIBUTION FOR THE 5 LEADING CAUSES OF DEATH IN CANADA, 2012

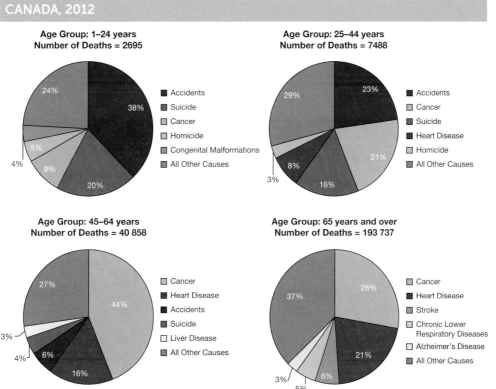

Source: Statistics Canada. (2015d). *Health fact sheets: The 10 leading causes of death, 2012* (Catalogue No. 82-625-X). Ottawa, ON: Author. Retrieved from http://www.statcan.gc.ca/pub/82-625-x/2015001/article/14296-eng.htm.

In 2009/2010, more than one-quarter of a million Canadian adults reported experiencing a fall-related injury (PHAC, 2014c). Falls are the leading cause of injury-related hospitalizations among Canadian older adults, with hospital stays for older adults who fall nine days longer than hospital stays for any other cause. This difference highlights the disproportionate healthcare costs of fall-related injuries compared to causes of hospitalization. Risk factors for falls in older adults are multifactorial and include chronic and acute health conditions, balance or gait deficits, sensory factors, inadequate nutrition, social isolation, as well as factors related to the built and social environments. Research also shows that over one-third of older adults who are hospitalized for a fall are discharged to long-term care. Finally, falls in older adults also lead to negative mental health outcomes (e.g., fear of falling, loss of autonomy and greater isolation, confusion, immobilization, and depression) (PHAC, 2014c).

REFLECTIVE QUESTION

What do you think can be done to reduce the risk of falls in the older adult population?

DISABILITY

Disability often is the result of living with a chronic medical condition. Surprisingly, there is not one universally accepted definition of disability or model to understand it (Palmer & Harley, 2012). According to the WHO (1980), a disability is "any restriction or lack of ability (resulting from an impairment) to perform an activity in the manner or within the range considered normal for a human being" (p. 143). The prevalence of disability is affected by age and gender, with the number of individuals with disability increasing with age (Statistics Canada, 2013c; see Figure 5.8). Women also experience more disability than men and this pattern holds across the

FIGURE 5.8

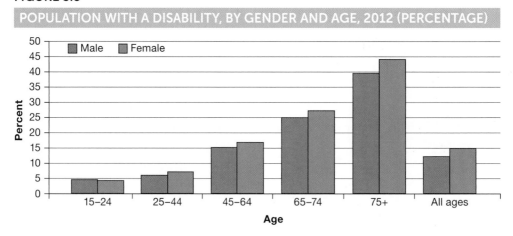

POPULATION WITH A DISABILITY, BY GENDER AND AGE, 2012 (PERCENTAGE)

Source: Statistics Canada. (2013c). *Disability in Canada: Initial findings from the Canadian Survey* (Catalogue No. 89-654-X—No 002). Ottawa, ON: Statistics Canada

lifespan. The reason that more women have disabilities than men is only now being determined, but this seems partially related to women's roles in society (e.g., caregiving responsibilities) and partially associated with women's genetics (e.g., greater chances of developing osteoporosis and arthritis). In some countries, older women experience prejudice and are denied equal access to healthcare (WHO, 2014a), which undoubtedly has a negative impact on health.

There are two components to disability. The first is **Activities of Daily Living** (ADLs) (Katz, Ford, Moskowitz, Jackson, & Jaffe, 1963). ADLs are basic self-care activities such as bathing, dressing, eating, and using the toilet. The second is **Instrumental Activities of Daily Living** or IADLs (Lawton & Brody, 1969). These involve more complex everyday tasks such as shopping, banking, taking medication, and preparing meals.

MODELS OF DISABILITY

There are two major models of disability. The first is the medical model, which views disability as being caused by a disease, injury, or health condition (Barnes & Mercer, 2003). In this model, an intervention is needed to correct the problem within the individual. The social model understands disability as a socially created problem and not an attribute of the individual and, therefore, something in the political environment must change (WHO, 2002). Verbrugge and Jette (1994) developed a comprehensive model of disability that includes both sociocultural factors such as the social and physical environment and personal factors such as attitudes and lifestyle factors. Also included in this model (see Figure 5.9) are risk factors and two types of intervention strategies. One of the advantages of this model of disability is that you can better understand the individual in the context of his or her total environment, which allows for interventions tailored to the individual's needs.

In an effort to develop an internationally comparable model of disability, the WHO (2002) put forth the International Classification of Functioning, Disability, and Health (ICF). The ICF is a multidimensional classification system that provides a framework for health and disability, with more of an emphasis on health. Because everyone can experience a decrement in health and thereby a disability, ICF normalizes the experience of disability (WHO, 2002). If adopted widely, it would facilitate communication and research in the field (Jette, 2006).

FRAILTY

Frailty is a term that is used to loosely describe a state of increased vulnerability as a result of age-associated declines in reserve and function, which results in a reduced ability of the individual to cope with everyday stressors (Xue, 2011). There is a strong association between frailty and age, with frailty affecting approximately 15.7 percent of adults 80 to 84 years of age and 26.1 percent of those 85 years of age and older (Collard, Boter, Schoevers, & Oude Voshaar, 2012). Despite its prevalence, frailty is challenging to identify and often goes unrecognized by healthcare professionals. There are many instruments or measures that have been developed to assess fraility in older adults. The Frailty Index is a suitable measure for identifying frailty (Jones, Song, & Rockwood, 2004; Mitnitski, Mogilner, & Rockwood, 2001).

FUNCTIONAL HEALTH

An important consideration is the impact of chronic conditions and disabilities on an older adult's functional health status. Functional health status is how well a person is functioning in daily life. Assessing functional health status helps to identify older adults who need assistance with everyday activities. In hospitals, functional assessments often are conducted by occupational

FIGURE 5.9

A MODEL OF DISABLEMENT

EXTRA-INDIVIDUAL FACTORS

MEDICAL CARE & REHABILITATION
(Surgery, physical therapy, speech therapy, counselling, health education, job retraining, etc.)

MEDICATIONS & OTHER THERAPEUTIC REGIMES
(Drugs, recreational therapy/aquatic exercise, biofeedback/meditation, rest/energy conservation, etc.)

EXTERNAL SUPPORTS
(Personal assistance, special equipment and devices, standby assistance/supervision, day care, respite care, meals-on-wheels, etc.)

BUILT, PHYSICAL, & SOCIAL ENVIRONMENT
(Structural modifications at job/home, access to buildings and to public transportation, improvement of air quality, reduction of noise and glare, health insurance & access to medical care, laws & regulations, employment discrimination, etc.)

THE MAIN PATHWAY

PATHOLOGY → **IMPAIRMENTS** → **FUNCTIONAL LIMITATIONS** → **DISABILITY**

(Diagnoses of disease, injury, congenital/ developmental condition)

(Dysfunctions and structural abnormalities in specific body systems: Musculoskeletal, cardiovascular, neurological, etc.)

(Restrictions in basic physical and mental actions: Ambulate, reach, stoop, climb stairs, produce intelligible speech, see standard print, etc.)

(Difficulty doing activities of daily life: Job, household management, personal care, hobbies, active recreation, clubs, socializing with friends and kin, childcare, errands, sleep, trips, etc.)

RISK FACTORS
(Predisposing characteristics: Demographic, social, lifestyle, behavioural, psychological, environmental, biological)

INTRA-INDIVIDUAL FACTORS

LIFESTYLE & BEHAVIOUR CHANGES
(Overt changes to alter disease activity and impact)

PSYCHOSOCIAL ATTRIBUTES & COPING
(Positive affect & emotional vigour, prayer, locus of control, cognitive adaptation to one's situation, confident, peer support groups, etc.)

ACTIVITY ACCOMMODATIONS
(Changes in kinds of activities, procedures for doing them, frequency or length of time doing them)

Source: Social science & medicine by PERGAMON. Reproduced with permission of PERGAMON in the format Book via Copyright Clearance Center.

FIGURE 5.10

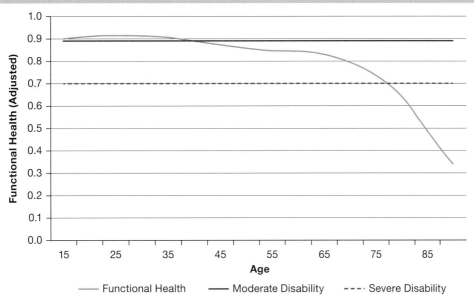

FUNCTIONAL HEALTH OF CANADIANS, 2009–2015

Source: Decady, Y., & Greenberg, L. (2014). *Health at a glance: Ninety years of change in life expectancy* (Catalogue No. 82-624-X). Ottawa, ON: Statistics Canada. www.statcan.gc.ca/pub/82-624-x/2014001/article/14009-eng.htm.

therapists who assess abilities such as cooking, banking, and knowledge of safety issues. Generally speaking, older Canadian adults report themselves to be in good functional health (Decady & Greenberg, 2014; see Figure 5.10). Despite these positive self-reports, many older adults do experience limitations as a result of long-term physical conditions caused by injury and disease. In addition, multiple disabilities can be caused by one condition. For example, a person who has arthritis might develop pain and mobility impairment. As you can see by the data in Figure 5.10, for many people, the older you get, the more likely it is that you will have a disability. Results from the Canadian Study of Health and Aging showed that pain, foot problems, arthritis, mobility, cognitive impairment, and vision problems contributed to ADL- and IADL-related functional disabilities (Griffith, Raina, Wu, Zhu, & Stathokostas, 2010). However, overall, there is tremendous variability in the reported limitations in the functional health status of older adults, emphasizing the diversity in health status within this large group (Canadian Institute for Health Information, 2011a).

TRENDS IN ILLNESS AND DISABILITY

Non-communicable diseases contribute significantly to death rates. Notably, a large percentage of non-communicable diseases are preventable through the reduction of behavioural risk factors. The four most common risk factors identified are tobacco use, physical inactivity, harmful use of alcohol, and an unhealthy diet. Currently, there is a worldwide epidemic of obesity (WHO, 2015c). **Obesity**, defined as a **Body Mass Index** (BMI) greater than or equal to 30, has more than doubled since 1980 (WHO, 2015c). As with other age groups, obesity contributes to an increased risk of poor health outcomes in older adults, including Type 2 diabetes, hypertension, and heart disease.

As you learned earlier, the number of years that we can expect to live has increased dramatically over the last 100 years. We also noted in sections of this chapter that there is a very strong relationship between age and the presence of illness and disability. You might wonder if we have not simply traded off a longer life for a longer period of illness and disability! In 1980, James Fries hypothesized that because of increased prevention and improved treatment of acute and chronic illnesses, the time (e.g., years) spent in disease and disability would be delayed or compressed into a shorter period before the time of death. Specifically, the **compression of morbidity hypothesis** proposes that the average age at which one becomes disabled for the first time is postponed, causing the time between the onset of disability and death to be compressed into a shorter period (i.e., people will stay healthier for a longer time and will be in poor health for a shorter time) (Fries, 1980). There also is the possibility that there will be an expansion of morbidity such that people will be living longer in poor health (**expansion of morbidity hypothesis**) (Gruenberg, 1977; Kramer, 1980). The third possibility, which takes a stance between the two extremes, proposes a **dynamic equilibrium hypothsis** in which the postponement of death is accompanied by delays in disability such that the relative time in poor health remains the same (Manton, 1982). Supporting evidence for the three theories is mixed due in part to differences in the way that disability is measured, as well as to differences in findings across countries. It also is important to note that many health trends and issues that are of concern in Canada today have their foundation in younger age groups (PHAC, 2014a). For example, the emerging epidemic of obesity among the younger and middle-aged populations may reverse any gains in reducing late-life functional decline, resulting in increased rates of functional decline in future populations of older individuals.

Based on what you have learned about the trends in illness and disability, which theory do you think will have the most support over the next several decades?

5.3 CO-MORBIDITY AND POLYPHARMACY
LEARNING OBJECTIVES

To understand:
- the consequences of co-morbidity and polypharmacy
- the compression and expansion of morbidity hypotheses
- the dynamic equilibrium hypothesis

The term **co-morbidity** is used to describe the co-occurrence of multiple chronic or acute diseases and medical conditions in an individual (Bayliss, Edwards, Steiner, & Main, 2008). With increased age, the chance of having more than one chronic condition increases. As a result, older adults are more likely to take several medications. Based on combined data from the Canadian Health Measures Surveys between 2007 and 2011, prescription drug use increases with age, increasing from 12 percent among 6- to 14-year-olds to 83 percent among 65- to 79-year-olds (Rotermann, Sanmartin, Hennessy, & Arthur, 2014). The *number* of prescription drugs also increases with age. That is, using data from the same surveys, the percentage of Canadians taking more than one medication increased from 3 percent for those aged 6 to 14 to 70 percent for those aged 65 to 79 (Rotermann et al., 2014). **Polypharmacy**, typically defined as the use of five or more medications, also is more common in the adult population and is becoming even more common (Reason, Terner, McKeag, Tipper, & Webster, 2012). In their study, Rotermann and colleagues (2014) found that polypharmacy was highest among older adults, with approximately 30 percent of the 65- to 70-year-old age group taking five or more medications. This compares to 11 percent of individuals 45 to 64 and 1.5 percent or less of children and young adults using five or more prescription medications. In addition, polypharmacy in the adult population is becoming more common. That is, between 1998 and 2008, the percentage of Canadian older adults taking more than five prescription medications doubled from 13 percent (1998) to approximately 30 percent (2008) (Rotermann et al., 2014). More recent data indicate that 23 percent of Canadians older than 65 years of age and 30 percent older than 85 years of age had claims for 10 or more drug classes in 2009 (Canadian Institute for Health Information, 2011a).

> Since baby boomers are generally healthier than previous generations, as they become older adults, do you think they will use fewer medications?

REFLECTIVE QUESTION

Earlier in this chapter, we talked about the number of centenarians in Canada and the increase in centenarians over the past several decades. You might wonder how healthy these centenarians are. In a recent study in Ontario, Rochon and colleagues (2014) found that of the 1842 centenarians living in Ontario in 2010, 45 percent were living independently in the community, 54 percent were in long-term care, and 1 percent were in an acute-care hospital. Relevant to this discussion, the average number of prescription medications taken in the previous year was 9.2, with this number the same for men and women. Prescription drugs commonly taken by older adults include those that act on the nervous system (e.g., anxiolytics, hypnotics, sedatives, and antipsychotics), the alimentary system (e.g., laxatives, antacids, and drugs for the treatment of peptic ulcers and flatulence), and the metabolic system (e.g., drugs for diabetes) (Ramage-Morin, 2009).

AGING AND MEDICATIONS

Polypharmacy in the older adult population can have negative consequences including adverse drug reactions. Older adults are particularly at risk for adverse drug reactions because of the physiological changes that occur with aging. These changes affect both **pharmacokinetics** and **pharmacodynamics**. Pharmacokinetics includes absorption, distribution, and clearance of a drug. In older adults, absorption is generally slower, particularly for drugs that are administered orally. Distribution of a drug, into either fat or water depending on the drug's chemical characteristics, also changes with age. That is, as one gets older, the percentage of body fat typically increases and the proportion of body water decreases. As such, drugs that are lipid soluble (e.g., diazepam

[Valium]) may stay in the body longer because there are more fat stores into which they can be distributed. For drugs that are water soluble, the concentration of the drugs may be higher in older adults because there is less body water in older individuals. Aging also can affect the metabolism of and clearance of drugs due to the changes in the liver and kidneys with age. As we age, blood flow through the liver decreases, which can reduce the clearance of drugs from the body. Metabolism of drugs also can be affected in some older adults due to changes in the cytochrome P450 system, a major enzyme system by which the liver metabolizes drugs. Reductions in renal blood flow with age, resulting in decreased kidney function, can affect clearance of drugs in the older population (for an excellent review, see Wooten & Galavais, 2005). So, the rule of thumb when prescribing medications for older adults is to start with a low dosage and increase slowly if needed.

Pharmacodynamics also is affected by aging. That is, changes to drug receptors can make older adults more sensitive to certain medications. Changes in the blood-brain barrier can affect drugs that act on the central nervous system. The changes in both pharmacokinetics and pharmacodynamics increase an older adult's risk for both drug–drug and drug–disease interactions. In addition to an increased risk of adverse drug reactions, polypharmacy in older adults increases the risk for cognitive impairment and elevates their risk for falls. In terms of cost, overall, prescription medications are the second-most costly component of the Canadian healthcare system, accounting for 14 percent ($29 billion) of annual healthcare spending in 2013 (Rotermann et al., 2014).

Pharmacists play an important role in informing older adults about their medications and in reducing drug-related problems in this segment of our population. That is, pharmacists are well positioned to identify potentially inappropriate medications and to determine which medications are still providing benefit and which medications are no longer necessary and, as such, should be stopped. Pharmacists also play an important role in making it easier for older adults to take their medications by properly labelling medications, and by packaging and organizing prescription drugs better. **Multi-compartment compliance aids** and **blister packs** have become a common method of packaging medications for patients with complex medication regimes and/or for patients perceived as having problems taking medications at home. However, there is little evidence to support the effectiveness of these aids (Nunney & Raynor, 2001). Problems associated with older adults using these aids include difficulty opening the compartments, inadequate labelling due to lack of space on labels, and an inability to accommodate dose forms such as liquids and drops. In addition, separating tablets and capsules from their original containers (e.g., larger pill bottles) can result in patients losing track of what medications they are taking and why (i.e., what each pill is for). Finally, there are some older individuals who do not take their prescribed medication. That is, older adults with dementia may forget to take their medications and low-income older adults may not have the money to buy the medications that have been prescribed. For the older adult with dementia, use of a pill organizer and having someone oversee their medication adherence can help to reduce the number of missed medication doses. For low-income older adults, the use of generic, rather than brand-name, drugs may help to eliminate or reduce the number of missed doses.

REFLECTIVE QUESTION

Can you think of ways to reduce polypharmacy in the older adult population?

5.4 QUALITY OF LIFE

LEARNING OBJECTIVE

- To understand factors that affect quality of life

DEFINING QUALITY OF LIFE

Quality of life (QOL), which is assessed through self-report, is defined as an "individual's perception of their position in life in the context of the culture and value systems in which they live and in relation to their goals, expectations, standards and concerns" (WHO, 1997, p. 1).

FACTORS AFFECTING QUALITY OF LIFE

Many factors are thought to affect quality of life such as health status, economic status, and physical activity. Most of the research has focused on how illness or disability affects quality of life. Based on the results of their study, King and her colleagues (2012) developed a model of quality of life in late-life disability. They conducted semi-structured interviews with 62 community-dwelling, ethnically diverse participants who were members of the On Lock Lifeways in the United States. This program provides all-inclusive care to older adults in their communities. The average age of those interviewed was 78 years and 63 percent were women. King and colleagues found that four broad categories contribute to quality of life: psychological, social, physical, and spiritual or religious. This model is presented in Figure 5.11.

As you can see, many factors contribute to quality of life, but these researchers found that dignity and having a sense of control in some aspect of daily life was central to quality of life in the participants. Maintaining current level of functioning, a positive attitude, and having positive social relationships also contributed to a higher quality of life. Participants also explained a process where they first struggled with the loss of a particular ability but then found a sense of peace through acceptance of the disability. King and her colleagues (2012) suggest that as older adults are faced with greater disability, they become less focused on what they cannot do and more focused on what they can do.

5.5 CANADA'S HEALTHCARE SYSTEM

LEARNING OBJECTIVES

To understand:
- the Canadian healthcare system
- the differences between the Canadian and the American healthcare systems
- factors that may improve the healthcare system

OVERVIEW OF CANADA'S HEALTHCARE SYSTEM

Canada's healthcare system is a hallmark of identity for many Canadians. Known as Medicare, the publicly funded system provides universal health insurance coverage to all Canadian citizens and permanent residents. As a brief history, Saskatchewan was the first province to establish public, universal hospital insurance in 1947. Ten years later, the federal government passed legislation to share in the cost of provincial hospital insurance plans. By 1961, all 10 Canadian provinces and 2 territories had public insurance plans that covered in-hospital care. In 1962, Saskatchewan

FIGURE 5.11

A MODEL OF QUALITY OF LIFE IN LATE-LIFE DISABILITY

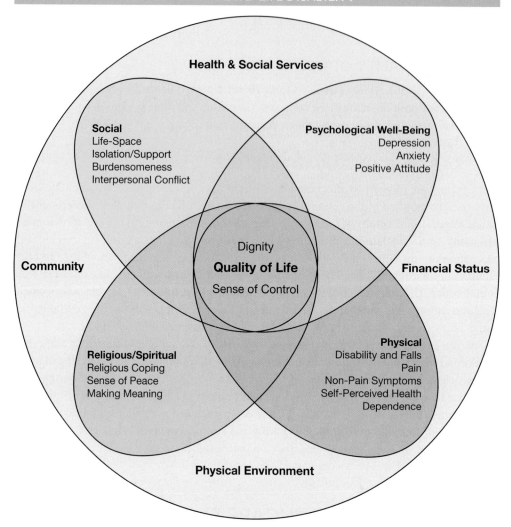

Source: King et al. (2012). Quality of life in late-life disability: "I don't feel bitter because I am in a wheelchair." *Journal of the American Geriatrics Society, 60*(3), 572. Journal of the American Geriatrics Society by AMERICAN GERIATRICS SOCIETY; AMERICAN THERAPEUTIC SOCIETY; TEXAS GERIATRICS SOCIETY. Reproduced with permission of BLACKWELL PUBLISHING LTD. in the format Book via Copyright Clearance Center.

again played a pioneering role by providing insurance for physicians' services outside hospitals. Shortly thereafter, the remaining provinces and territories followed suit, and by 1962, all provincial and territorial plans included insurance coverage for physicians' services.

In 1979, a review of Canadian health services was undertaken by Justice Emmett Hall. In his report, he indicated that healthcare in Canada ranked among the best in the world, but warned that extra billing by physicians and user fees levied by hospitals were creating a two-tiered system that threatened the accessibility of care (Hall, 1980). In response to these concerns, Parliament passed the **Canada Health Act** in 1984 to discourage user charges while in hospital and extra billing by physicians. To encourage compliance, the Act has an automatic dollar-for-dollar penalty if any province permits such charges for insured health services (University of Ottawa, 2014).

The Canadian healthcare system is based on five principles. These founding principles (which translate to the mnemonic **UPPAC**) are as follows:

Universality: All eligible residents are entitled to public health insurance coverage on uniform terms and conditions;

Portability: Coverage for insured services must be maintained when an insured person moves or travels within Canada or travels outside the country;

Public administration: The health insurance plan of a province or territory must be administered on a nonprofit basis by a public authority;

Accessibility: Reasonable access by insured persons to medically necessary hospital and physician services must not be impeded by financial or other barriers; and

Comprehensiveness: All medically necessary services provided by hospitals and doctors must be insured.

In terms of funding, the Canadian federal government provides cash and tax transfers to the provinces and territories to support health systems. The federal government also provides equalization payments to less prosperous provinces and territorial financing to the territories. In the Canadian system, healthcare providers are predominantly private but receive funding for their services via public monies via provincial budgets. Hospitals in Canada are largely private, nonprofit organizations run by community boards or voluntary organizations. However, provincial governments have considerable authority over the operation of hospitals, not only in terms of setting the overall budgets but also in reviewing large financial decisions made by hospital boards. Provincial governments also have the power to determine scope of services offered and to close hospitals that are deemed unnecessary (Makarenko, 2010).

In Canada, physicians are, primarily, in private practice and remunerated on a fee-for-service basis. The fees that they can charge are based on a predetermined pricing system. Physicians who opt out of the system cannot bill above the predetermined pricing system for services that they provide. Currently, universal coverage for health services in Canada does not fund preventive health programs, home care, dental care, or prescription drugs. However, there is considerable variation across the provinces/territories as to which services are covered (e.g., hospital prescription medications, physical therapy, long-term care, dental care, and ambulance services) (Snowdon et al., 2012). Of interest, areas and services that fall outside the scope of the Canada Health Act have more than tripled their share of the **gross domestic product (GDP)** since 1990 (Scully, 2012).

Canadians' ratings on their values of the healthcare system have changed over time. As can be seen in Figure 5.12 and based on ratings over five time periods between 1991 and 2000, the principle of universality has been viewed as highest in importance, followed by the principles of portability and accessibility. The provision of administration of healthcare services on a "nonprofit basis by a public authority" (e.g., public administration) consistently has received the lowest ratings of importance over the five time periods.

How important are the five principles of the Canada Health Act to you? your family? your grandparents?

FIGURE 5.12

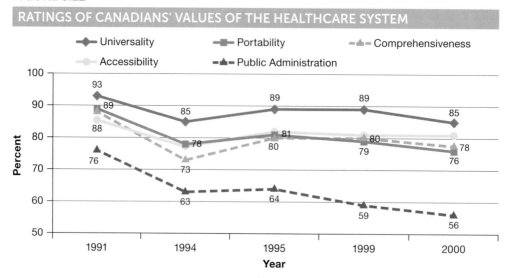

RATINGS OF CANADIANS' VALUES OF THE HEALTHCARE SYSTEM

Source: The Hay Health Care Consulting Group. (2001, March). *The Berger Population Health Monitor. Survey #22.*

Recommendations made to achieve greater value for health system costs in the 2012 Snowdon report include:

1. Re-designing health care systems to focus on healthy active living that mitigates risk of chronic illness and has the added benefit of achieving quality of life;
2. Giving patients and families the tools to manage their own health and wellness, including complete transparency and access to personal health information to support health decisions that achieve quality of life;
3. Re-configuring health professional practice models and approaches from single discipline to inter-professional models of practice that fully engage the unique scope of practice and expertise each professional brings to the healthcare team;
4. Designing integrated services across the continuum of care, supported by cooperative models of health system leadership, whereby organizations and their leaders are incentivized and held accountable for achieving quality of life outcomes for the populations they serve; and
5. Aligning reimbursement models for health professionals with Canadians' values, such that professionals are reimbursed based on achieving best-practice quality outcomes, rather than reimbursement focused on health service transactions (Snowdon et al., 2012, pp. 5–6).

COMPARISON OF HEALTHCARE SYSTEMS IN CANADA AND THE UNITED STATES

In contrast to Canada, the United States had no single nationwide healthcare system until 2012. That is, prior to 2012, health insurance in the United States was purchased in the private marketplace or provided by the government but only to certain groups (Ridic, Gleason, & Ridic, 2012). About 84% of the population is covered by either public (26%) or private (70%) health insurance, with approximately 61% of health insurance coverage employment related (Ridic et al.,

2012). The two major types of private health insurance in the United States, initiated in 1966, are **Medicare** and **Medicaid**. There also is a provision to purchase private health insurance, known as **Medigap**. Medicaid covers approximately 12 percent of the American population. It is estimated that approximately 16 percent (approximately 40 million) of Americans are uninsured at any given time. Many of these individuals receive healthcare services through public clinics and hospitals, state and local health programs, or charity organizations (see Ridic et al., 2012, for an excellent comparison of healthcare systems in Canada, the United States, and Germany).

The Affordable Care Act (ACA), which also is known as **ObamaCare**, was introduced in the United States in 2012. It is designed to give more Americans access to affordable, quality health insurance and to reduce the increases in healthcare spending. Some of the key features of ObamaCare are the elimination of preexisting conditions, expansion of free preventive services and health benefits, expansion of Medicaid, improvements to Medicare, and elimination of insurance companies from "dropping policy holders when they are sick" (U.S. Department of Health and Human Services, 2015). Recent statistics indicate that the introduction of ObamaCare has resulted in significantly improved trends in self-reported coverage, access to primary care and medications, affordability, and health (Sommers, Gunja, Finegold, & Musco, 2015). However, in 2017, with Donald Trump as president, there are ongoing attempts to repeal or replace many parts of the ACA.

The cost of providing healthcare is a concern in jurisdictions worldwide. How does Canada compare to other countries? A comparison of the costs of the healthcare systems across countries is informative. In 1971, both the United States and Canada spent approximately 7.4 percent of their GDP on healthcare. Estimates for 1990 indicate that Canada spent more than 9 percent of its GDP, or $60 billion, on healthcare, whereas the United States contributed $660 billion or 12 percent of its GDP (Madore, 1992). A more recent comparison of the total expenditure of healthcare per capita between Canada and the United States, as well as six other **OECD countries**, is shown in Figure 5.13. As can be seen, the United States has the highest rate

FIGURE 5.13

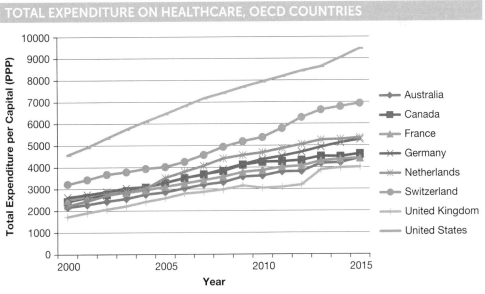

Source: OECD.Stat. (2016). *Total expenditure on health care OECD countries*. Retrieved from http://stats.oecd.org/Index.aspx#.

of total expenditure in healthcare per capita, with Canada's median expenditure of $3442 (US, **PPP**) over the 10-year period ranking third highest (Snowdon et al., 2012). The high expenditures of the United States' healthcare system are primarily due to the heavy reliance on technology and over-provision of care in a heavily privatized healthcare system (Snowdon et al., 2012).

OLDER ADULTS' USE OF THE CANADIAN HEALTHCARE SYSTEM

In Canada, older adults are frequent users of the healthcare system. Their use consists of hospital services as well as as other sectors of the healthcare system including hospital-based continuing-care beds, home care, visits to family physicians, and greater use of prescription drugs (Canadian Institute for Health Information, 2011b). Despite the frequent use of the healthcare system by older adults, the overall per capita spending on older adults 65 years of age and older in Canada *decreased* between 1998 and 2009 (see Figure 5.14), suggesting that the baby boomers are healthier than previous cohorts. It seems that the general growth in the population, increased costs of delivering healthcare (e.g., increased wages of healthcare professionals, increased physician fees), and increases in utilization of general health services (e.g., increased use of diagnostic services) across *all* age ranges have contributed to increases in health expenditures (Canadian Institute for Health Information, 2011b). So, as you can see from the statistics above and contrary to popular belief, older adults are *not* the reason for increases in health expenditures. Rather, this belief may be due to ageism.

Notably, use of healthcare services by older adults is strongly associated with the number of chronic conditions and not by age. Specifically, older adults with three or more chronic

FIGURE 5.14

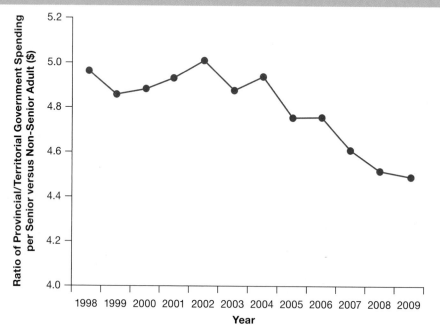

PER CAPITA SPENDING ON OLDER ADULTS VERSUS YOUNGER ADULTS, 1998 TO 2009, CANADA

Source: Canadian Institute for Health Information. (2011a). *Health care in Canada, 2011: A focus on older adults and aging.* Ottawa, ON: CIHI. Reprinted by permission of the Canadian Institute for Health Information (CIHI).

conditions had almost three times the number of healthcare visits than older adults with no chronic conditions (Canadian Institute for Health Information, 2011a). Older adults with three or more chronic conditions also reported significantly more visits to allied healthcare professionals such as nurses, physiotherapists, social workers, and counsellors and nearly twice the rate of visits to specialist physicians, pharmacists, and dietitians as older adults who self-reported only one chronic condition (Canadian Institute for Health Information, 2011a).

RATIONING OF HEALTHCARE

Prolonging life is desirable to many people but it is expensive. If we are to experience a healthcare crisis down the road, what shall we do? Who should get healthcare dollars? Some answers that have been given are controversial. One of the most controversial answers came from philosopher Daniel Callahan (1987); he suggested that healthcare should be rationed to people based on age. In other words, once you got to be a certain age, you would not receive heroic measures to save your life. He is not alone. More recently Daniels (2013) has called for the rationing of healthcare based on age. If you are wondering if rationing healthcare has been done before, the answer is yes. In Britain, for example, kidney dialysis routinely was withheld from people over the age of 55 in the early days of chronic dialysis (Schwartz & Aaron, 1984). However, as this became known to British citizens, there was public outcry and the practice of withholding kidney dialysis to those in need over the age of 55 was stopped.

Would age-based rationing of care be acceptable? Public opinion surveys have shown that in the United States, people are in favour of withholding *heroic measures* to save critically ill older adults at the end of life, but few people would withhold care based on age alone (Hoffman, 2012). As we move through the phenomenon of living with an aging population, there is no doubt that the debate will continue. Is every 75-year-old the same? As you have learned, there is tremendous diversity in old age.

REFLECTIVE QUESTIONS

Do you think rationing of healthcare should be based on age?

Should families look after their own?

Do you think there will be generational wars regarding tax dollars and healthcare?

5.6 SUCCESSFUL AGING

LEARNING OBJECTIVES

To understand:
- models of successful aging and how older adults view successful aging
- the criticisms of successful aging models
- that there is no special way to age successfully
- the differences between ADLs and IADLs

MODELS OF SUCCESSFUL AGING

The ability to live in reasonably good health and remain independent and productive has become very much a reality. Over the last 60 years, many researchers have put forth definitions and criteria regarding what it means to age successfully. What is interesting is that the definition has changed significantly over time. For example, Cumming and Henry (1961) regarded successful aging as the desire of older people to disengage from active life in order to prepare themselves for death. This is quite different from Ryff's (1989) model in which aging is seen as a developmental process in which continued personal growth is very much possible in old age.

International interest in successful aging has grown significantly since Rowe and Kahn introduced their widely used model of successful aging in 1997. These researchers argue that there are three key components to successful aging: the avoidance of disease and disability, the maintenance of cognitive and physical function, and engagement with life. Another model of successful aging is the Selective Optimization with Compensation (SOC) model developed by Baltes and Baltes (1990). According to this model, aging is a heterogeneous process with many different pathways and outcomes. Successful agers select areas of their life that are important to them and then make the most of the available resources that aid success in these areas. At the same time, according to this model, people compensate for the losses they experience in order to create an environment where aging successfully can be attained.

Over the years, other models have been developed to describe successful aging (see Vaillant, 2002), but there remains much disagreement and criticism regarding the models to date. A criticism of the SOC model is that compensation and optimization strategies may become increasingly difficult to use because of age-related losses in resources (Ouwehand, de Ridder, & Bensing, 2007). A difficulty with Rowe and Kahn's model is that very few older adults meet their successful aging criteria. That is, the complete absence of disease as we age is unrealistic for many people (Bowling & Dieppe, 2005; Martinson & Berridge, 2015). McLaughlin, Connell, Heeringa, Li, and Roberts (2010) used Rowe and Kahn's criteria to calculate the prevalence of successful aging in the United States using data from the Health and Retirement Survey. These researchers found that only 11.9 percent of participants met the criteria of successful aging in any of the four time points measured. Using 2009 data from the Canadian Community Health Survey, Meng and D'Arcy (2014) found that only 35 percent of participants were deemed to be aging successfully based on Rowe and Kahn's criteria.

Another criticism of the successful aging models in general is that they neglect the structural forces that influence functioning later in life and assume that older adults have the resources to age successfully such as having access to healthcare and living above the poverty line (Stowe & Cooney, 2015). Also absent from successful aging models are the opinions from different cultures. How do people from other ethnic backgrounds define successful aging? Chung and Park (2008) conducted one of the few studies investigating the definition of successful aging in another culture. Interestingly, low-income older adults from North Korea named "success of adult children" as a factor in successful aging. People in North Korea still tend to believe that the "children's success is the parent's success." (Chung & Park, 2008, p. 1071).

In addition, some researchers are concerned that many of the models of successful aging promote, rather than reduce, ageism. For example, categorizing total health as good aging and the presence of disease or disability as bad aging creates a very simplistic either/or category that does not capture the diversity in which we age (Martinson & Berridge, 2015; Morell, 2003; Rozanova, Northcott, & McDaniel, 2006; Stone, 2003).

Can you guess what another major criticism of successful aging models is? There is a key piece that is missing. You would be absolutely correct if you said that what is missing are criteria generated by older adults themselves. How do older adults define successful aging? Studies that have compared self-ratings of successful aging to the criteria set out by Rowe and Khan (1997) have found that self-ratings from older adults are considerably higher than the successful aging ratings they would have attained using Rowe and Kahn's criteria

(Cernin, Lysack, & Lichtenberg, 2011). For example, Montross and colleagues (2006) found that the older adults in their study viewed themselves as aging successfully even though the majority experienced disability and chronic illness. Not only do more older adults age successfully when using self-ratings but also the criteria for successful aging that older adults consider important is different than the criteria set out in Rowe and Kahn's model. That is, a sample of 72 community-dwelling older adults stated that a balance between self-acceptance, contentedness, self-growth, and engagement in life were key components to aging successfully (Reichstadt, Sengupta, Depp, Palinkas, & Jeste, 2010). Other findings suggest that having financial resources, a positive attitude, a realistic perspective, and the ability to adapt to change are key components to aging successfully (Reichstadt, Depp, Plainkas, & Jeste, 2007). Data from the Manitoba Follow-Up Study (Tate, Lah, & Cuddy, 2003), which followed a cohort of 3983 World War II veterans, showed that having goals and interests and being engaged with family are important to successful aging. As you can see from the results presented above, the responses given by older adults are very diverse, indicating that aging successfully is very personal and has multiple meanings.

It is not hard to find celebrities who are thought to be aging well: Queen Elizabeth and her husband Prince Phillip, Michael J. Fox, Donald Sutherland (President Snow in *The Hunger Games*), William Shatner (a.k.a., Captain Kirk, for all you Trekkies out there), Madonna, Betty White, and Jane Fonda are some who come to mind. All remain active despite aches and pains and a chronic illness or two. But it is not only celebrities who are aging well. There are many older adults who are not in the spotlight but who are engaged with life and who are active and giving back to their communities. Florence Storch was one very active older adult. Please see Box 5.2 to read about her interesting choice of an activity as she got older.

BOX 5.2

FLORENCE STORCH, ALBERTA'S JAVELIN-THROWING CENTENARIAN

Did you know that Canada has a nation-wide sports program for people 55 years and older? The Canadian Adult Population Games Association held its first games in Regina in 1996 and they have been growing strong ever since. The Canada 55+ Games are held every second year and allow older adults to compete in 19 events that include golf, bowling, bridge, track and field, swimming, hockey, curling, lawn bowling, badminton, slo-pitch softball, and horseshoes. The 1500 or so who compete in the Games represent over 100 000 older Canadian adults who actively participate in local events leading up to the national games. Florence Storch was an active participant in these Games.

Florence lived in the family farm home and became an athlete at the age of 90. Her sport of choice? Javelin throwing. She won many medals and for several years was the oldest athlete at the Games. And, at the 2014 Games held near Edmonton, a 101-year-old Storch captured a silver medal. Florence died peacefully in her sleep on 21 October, 2015 at the age of 102.

THE CANADIAN PRESS/Jason Franson

How do you think your parents or grandparents would define successful aging?

There is no special formula for aging successfully. Aging is a lifelong process and it would make sense that it would be important to make good lifestyle choices, not only at a young age but also as you age. There is a good deal of evidence that would suggest that eating healthily, watching your cholesterol, keeping your brain active, exercising, getting enough sleep, and drinking in moderation will help you to age successfully. In addition, psychological factors such as feeling connected to others, staying involved in some capacity, being able to learn new things, and continuing to grow as a person also are very important. It looks somewhat easy on paper, but the truth of the matter is that life is full of surprises and challenges that can sometimes get in the way of taking the best care of yourself. As a busy university student, we are sure you can relate. As you look forward, how will you age?

5.7 HEALTH PROMOTION ACTIVITIES FOR OLDER ADULTS

LEARNING OBJECTIVE

- To understand health promotion internationally and nationally

Given that the population of the world is becoming older, healthy aging initiatives have come to the forefront around the world, including Canada. The European Union declared 2012 as the European Year for Active Aging and Solidarity between Generations (Eurostat European Commission, 2011), with the aim to establish a culture across Europe of people remaining active into older adulthood. This initiative has helped convey a more positive image of population aging in Europe by highlighting the potentials of older people and promoting their active participation in society and in the economy. Reversing the belief that older adults are a burden on society is the biggest aim of the *European Year for Active Aging and Solidarity Declaration*. As Europeans live longer and healthier lives, European governments are looking for ways to involve older persons more in society and to keep them active. The hope is that these initiatives will result in economic benefits for society as a whole, while at the same time promoting the mental, social, and physical well-being of older adults. For more information on the results, go to www.aepumayores.org/sites/default/files/KS-EP-11-001-EN.pd.

In 2006, the Canadian provincial and federal governments developed a *Vision for Healthy Aging in Canada*. Efforts are being made to recognize, value, and support the contributions made by older adults. The hope is to reduce ageism and inequities and provide age-friendly environments and opportunities for older Canadians to make healthy choices (Healthy Aging and Wellness Working Group of the Federal/Provincial/Territorial Committee of Officials [Seniors], 2006). In addition, the Canadian government has reintroduced its ParticipACTION program. **ParticipACTION** was originally launched as a Canadian government program in the 1970s to promote healthy living and physical fitness. It ended in 2001 due to financial cutbacks but was revived in 2007. Valuable ParticipACTION resources for older adults include Canadian physical activity guidelines for adults 65 and older, physical activity tips, guides to healthy eating, and advice for safety in the home (Government of Canada, 2015a).

Frank Brodhecker, B.S.W.
Villa Caritas, Geriatric Psychiatry, Edmonton, Alberta

WHERE DID YOU TRAIN?

University of Calgary Faculty of Social Work extension campus on the University of Alberta campus

WHAT DO YOU DO?

I do initial assessment on in-patients. This includes assessing where they live, financial status, legal directives, and level of family support. I also collect collateral information from family or friends to determine level of care and placement if required. I create a care plan for each of my patients. This lays out the dynamic stressors the individual has, as well as the supports and resources he or she may need once discharged.

WHY DO YOU LIKE WORKING WITH OLDER ADULTS?

Older adults have a lot of life experience and I learn a lot from working with them. I want to be supportive in the time of their lives when they are feeling the most vulnerable. I like the complexity of each case, and I enjoy working with the families and the never-ending family dynamics.

DO YOU HAVE ADVICE FOR STUDENTS WHO WANT TO GET INTO THE FIELD?

Get a good understanding of development over the lifespan. It is important to understand that the person is influenced by their life experience and choices. To get started, I would recommend getting volunteer experience.

Mun Tran, Ph.D.
St. John's Hospital, Thunder Bay, Ontario

WHERE DID YOU TRAIN?

I obtained an M.A. and a Ph.D. in clinical psychology from Lakehead University, Thunder Bay, Ontario. I completed graduate-level clinical training in various settings, including hospitals, correctional facilities, and outpatient mental health clinics.

WHERE DO YOU WORK?

Currently, I work in a rehabilitation and complex care hospital in Thunder Bay, Ontario.

WHAT DO YOU DO?

The programs I cover are diverse and include hospice/palliative care, reactivation, transitional care, extensive services, as well as geriatric assessment and rehabilitative care. The majority of clients that I serve are older adults with complex medical conditions and a range of cognitive and mental health issues. My role involves conducting cognitive and psychological assessments as well as providing psychotherapy. I also provide in-service support and training to hospital staff, education to families, and clinical consultation services to allied healthcare professionals. Additionally, I contribute to hospital-wide program development and quality improvement initiatives related to geriatric care (e.g., delirium screening and prevention).

WHY DO YOU LIKE WORKING WITH AN OLDER-ADULT POPULATION?

My career in the field of geriatric psychology has many challenges that I find highly rewarding. I value the problem solving required to modify assessment and treatment techniques to address sensory impairments and other prevalent changes associated with aging. Working with an older-adult population often necessitates collaborating with family members and other healthcare providers and I enjoy this aspect of my work. Furthermore, older adults have a wealth of experience and wisdom, and I derive considerable satisfaction from listening to their life stories.

DO YOU HAVE ADVICE FOR STUDENTS WHO WANT TO GET INTO THE FIELD?

Given the specialized knowledge and specific skills needed to work within this field, my advice to students is to gain varied clinical exposure and research experience with older adults to understand the complexities of this unique population.

Kevin Lawless, M.D., F.R.C.P.C.
Villa Caritas, Geriatric Psychiatry, Edmonton, Alberta and University of Alberta, Edmonton, Alberta

WHERE DID YOU TRAIN?

I did my undergraduate training as well as medical school and my psychiatry residency at the University of Alberta.

WHAT DO YOU DO?

As the clinical lead for a multidisciplinary team, I provide assessment and treatment for a diverse population of older adults. Included in this is the general medical care of patients. As an assistant clinical professor, I supervise aspects of psychiatric training of undergraduate medical students and I provide postgraduate training to residents in general psychiatry and residents in the new sub-specialty of geriatric psychiatry. I provide after-hours consultation services to various crisis teams in the Edmonton area regarding their interactions with older adults.

WHY DO YOU LIKE WORKING WITH OLDER ADULTS?

I believe that older adults are worthy of the best care we can provide because they have contributed to society, raised families, and kept the wheels of industry going. As a psychiatrist, I enjoy the challenge of sorting out the various etiologies of illness in this population including medical, neurological, psychiatric, and social. As a psychiatrist medical doctor, I can utilize most aspects of my training to assess and treat this population. I find it a challenge and a reward, and I feel quite privileged to work with this population. I value individuals who have entered their elder years.

DO YOU HAVE ADVICE FOR STUDENTS WHO WANT TO GET INTO THE FIELD?

Students who want to get into geriatric medicine should do electives with older adults and volunteer at organizations that are involved with older adults. Talk to older adults; they have a wealth of information!

5.9 SUMMARY

- Along with the rest of the world's population, Canadians are getting older. It is important to remember that the older adult population is very diverse. How well we take care of ourselves while we are aging contributes to this diversity as well.

- For the first time in history, Canada now has more individuals 65 and older than children aged 14 and younger. Longevity is influenced by several factors. Although women live, on average, about four years longer than men, the age gap between women and men is getting smaller. While the epidemiological pattern of diseases has shifted over time, overall, today's older adults are living longer and are healthier than older adults from previous generations.

- Two factors affecting health status in older adults that you may not have thought about are the degree of social support that older adults receive and their level of social engagement.

- Influenza is a major cause of hospitalization and mortality among Canadian older adults. Despite awareness programs and publically funded vaccinations, vaccinations for people aged 65 and older remain low.

- The main causes of death for older adults are cancer, heart disease, and stroke. The prevalence of disability is affected by age and gender, with the number of individuals with disability increasing with age. Women also suffer more disability than men and this pattern holds across the lifespan. However, in general, older Canadian adults report themselves to be in good functional health.

- Chronic conditions in older adults also are more common with the number of chronic conditions often increasing with age.

- The number of prescription drugs used also increases with age. Older adults are at a higher risk for adverse drug reactions because of the physiological changes that occur with aging.

- Older adults have identified that maintaining independence, having a sense of control in some aspect of daily life, having a positive attitude, and having positive social relationships are some factors that contribute to a higher quality of life.

- Canada has a publicly funded system which provides universal health insurance to all Canadian citizens and permanent residents. In contrast to Canada, the United States had no single nationwide healthcare system until recently. The two major types of private health insurance in the United States are Medicare and Medicaid. One of the major reforms of the healthcare system in the United States recently was the introduction of the Affordable Care Act (ACA) which also is known as ObamaCare. However, under the Donald Trump administration, there are ongoing attempts to repeal or replace many parts of the ACA.

- Although older adults are thought to be heavy users of hospital services, the overall per capita spending on adults 65 years of age and older in Canada decreased between 1998 and 2009.

- Overall, the theories of successful aging have been criticized for not being realistic and for inadvertently promoting ageism. Not surprisingly, older adults' definitions of what it means to age successfully is very different than the models.

- Because of global aging, many countries in the world, including Canada, have developed or are developing initiatives to recognize, value, and support older adults. These activities include health promotion activities such as ParticipACTION.

Key Terms

Activities of Daily Living (ADL)
Basic self-care activities such as bathing, dressing, eating, and using the toilet.

Acute Diseases
Diseases characterized by a relatively sudden onset of symptoms that are usually severe.

Authenticated
Proof of age by birth certificate.

Average Longevity
A statistical measure that refers to the age at which half of the individuals born in a given year will have died.

Blister Packs
A special method of packing medications, where each dose of medication is placed in a small plastic bubble and backed by a sheet of foil. Medications are organized by day, usually for up to a week at a time. This method of packaging medications allows the patient to see which doses of medication(s) he or she has taken. Blister packages are prepared by a pharmacist.

Body Mass Index (BMI)
BMI is a simple calculation using a person's height and weight. The formula is BMI = kg/m2 where kg is a person's weight in kilograms and m2 is their height in metres squared.

Canada Health Act
Legislation adopted in 1984 that specifies conditions required by provinces and territories to receive funding for healthcare.

Centenarian
Individuals who live to be 100 to 110 years.

Chronic Diseases
Diseases that persist over a long period. The symptoms of chronic diseases are sometimes less severe than those of the acute phase of the same disease.

Co-morbidity
Co-occurrence of multiple chronic or acute diseases and medical conditions in an individual.

Compression of Morbidity Hypothesis
Hypothesis that proposes that the average age that one becomes disabled for the first time is postponed, therefore decreasing the time between onset of disease and death.

Disability
An umbrella term, covering impairments, activity limitations, and participation restrictions. An *impairment* is a problem in a body function or structure; an *activity limitation* is a difficulty encountered by an individual in executing a task or action; while a *participation restriction* is a problem experienced by an individual in involvement in life situations.

Dynamic Equilibrium
Hypothesis that proposes that postponement of death is accompanied by delays in disability so that the relative time in poor health remains the same.

Epidemiological
Relating to the study of the causes and effects of health conditions and diseases in defined populations.

Expansion of Morbidity Hypothesis
Hypothesis that proposes people will live longer in poor health.

G7 Countries
Canada, France, Germany, Italy, Japan, the United Kingdom, and the United States. The European Union is also represented within the G7. These countries are the seven major advanced economies as reported by the International Monetary Fund.

G8 Countries
Refers to the group of eight highly industrialized nations—France, Germany, Italy, the United Kingdom, Japan, the United States, Canada, and Russia—that hold an annual meeting to foster consensus on global issues like economic growth and crisis management, global security, energy, and terrorism.

Gross Domestic Product (GDP)
The value of all the goods and services produced in a country within a time period, usually calculated annually.

Health
A state of complete physical, mental, and social well-being and not merely the absence of disease or infirmity (WHO, 1948).

Healthy Immigrant Effect
Foreign-born individuals tend to live longer and are in better health than those who are native-born; also known as the foreign-born health advantage.

Immigrant seniors
Refers to individuals 65 years of age and older and who were not born in Canada and/or did not have Canadian citizenship at birth.

Instrumental Activities of Daily Living (IADLs)
Complex everyday tasks such as shopping, banking, taking medication, and preparing meals.

Maximum Longevity
The oldest age one can possibly live.

Medicaid
The second type of public health insurance in the United States; provides coverage for certain economically disadvantaged groups (e.g., older adults, blind, people with disabilities, or members of families with dependent children). Medicaid is jointly financed by the federal and state governments and is administered by each state.

Medicare
A national public health insurance program for aged and disabled individuals in the United States that is administered by the federal government. There are different components of Medicare (Part A and Part B), with each component providing coverage for different services and each has a different funding stream.

Medigap
An extra health insurance that Americans can buy from a private company to pay healthcare costs not covered by Original Medicare, such as co-payments, deductibles, and healthcare for travelling outside the United States. Medigap policies do not cover long-term care, such as stays in a nursing facility, dental care, or vision care.

Multi-compartment Compliance Aids
Containers that have different compartments with the medications organized by time of day (e.g., morning, noon, afternoon, and bedtime), usually for up to a week at a time. Typically, MCAs are filled by the individual.

ObamaCare
A law in the United States enacted in 2012 that aims to reform the American healthcare system by providing affordable healthcare to more Americans; also known as the Affordable Care Act.

Obesity
Body mass index greater than or equal to 30.

OECD Countries
The Organization for Economic Cooperation and Development (OECD) countries are a group of 20 countries that collaborate information to promote policies that aim to improve the social well-being of the global population.

ParticipACTION
A national nonprofit organization whose mission is to help Canadians sit less and move more. ParticipACTION, which was originally established in 1971, was re-established in 2007 with a goal of making physical activity a vital part of everyday life in Canada.

Pharmacodynamics
The study of the effects of drugs and the mechanism of their action.

Pharmacokinetics
The study of the absorption, distribution, metabolism, and excretion of drugs.

Polypharmacy
The simultaneous use of multiple medications by one patient.

PPP
Public healthcare expenditure per person.

Supercentenarian
Individuals who live over 110 years.

UPPAC
Mnemonic for the five principles that the Canadian healthcare system is based on: Universality, Portability, Public administration, Accessibility, and Comprehensiveness.

Marmion/Shutterstock.com

MENTAL HEALTH AND MENTAL HEALTH DISORDERS

CHAPTER OUTLINE

"Grow old along with me! The best is yet to be."

Robert Browning

One of the biggest myths about aging is that the mental health of older adults deteriorates. This myth appears to be fuelled by the losses experienced as we age. And while many older adults do experience some form of loss, in general, the majority of older adults experience these changes without major disruption to their lives. As you will learn in this chapter, although older adults experience many of the same mental illnesses as young adults, the rates of mental illness, overall, are not higher in the older adult population. In fact, the Mental Health Commission of Canada (2015) found that roughly 70 percent of Canadians aged 65 and over reported their mental health to be very good or excellent. In general, those older adults that do suffer from a mental illness seem to have chronic and recurring illnesses that began at a younger age (Zarit, 2009). As the quote above suggests, good things can and often do happen in old age.

6.1 DEFINING MENTAL HEALTH
LEARNING OBJECTIVES

To understand:
- what mental health is
- what affects an individual's mental health
- what psychopathology is
- where older adults are treated for mental illness
- some of the different places psychologists work with older adults

WHAT IS MENTAL HEALTH?

Mental health has long been recognized by the World Health Organization (WHO) as an integral and essential component of well-being. More specifically, mental health is "a state of well-being in which the individual realizes his or her own abilities, can cope with the normal stresses of life, can work productively and fruitfully, and is able to make a contribution to his or her community" (WHO, 2005, p. 2). The Public Health Agency of Canada (PHAC) has a somewhat more complex definition of mental health:

> The capacity of each of us to feel, think, and act in ways that enhance our ability to enjoy life and deal with the challenges we face. It is a positive sense of emotional and spiritual well-being that respects the importance of culture, equity, social justice, interconnections, and personal dignity. (PHAC, 2006, p. 3)

As far as definitions go, these sound straightforward, right? However, as it turns out, there is controversy as to what constitutes mental health. With regard to the often-cited WHO definition, Galderisi, Heinz, Kastrup, Beezhold, and Sartorius (2015) argue that people in good mental health can be angry or unhappy or ill because these are normal aspects of life. These researchers also take exception to the criteria of being able to work "productively and fruitfully," which by the WHO's definition is required for a person to be in good mental health. What if the individual is retired? What if the individual has a physical disability that interferes with his or her ability to work? Does this mean that neither of these individuals is in good mental health? Canadian researcher Laurie Manwell and her colleagues (2015) suggest that the lack of a consensus definition of mental health interferes with the integration of mental health initiatives into global health programs. However, the WHO argues that the differences in values across cultures, gender, and classes may be too large to allow for agreement on a definition. The WHO further suggests that the term "mental health" can be understood across cultures, social class, and gender without one universal meaning. For example, age and wealth have different expressions around the world and yet have a core common-sense universal meaning (WHO, 2004).

Regardless of how you define mental health, the awareness of the importance of mental health is gaining ground. For example, in 2013, the WHO released the Mental Health Action Plan 2013–2020 (MHAP), which acknowledges the important role that mental health plays in achieving overall health for all individuals. The *WHO Mental Health Atlas 2014* (WHO, 2014b) is the most comprehensive and widely used source of information on global mental health, and is a valuable source of mental health resources available to prevent and treat mental disorders and help protect the human rights of people living with mental illness. Data are presented in the *Atlas* from 184 WHO member states, covering 98 percent of the world's population. Through the *Atlas*, the WHO is able to track the progress made toward the goals laid out in the MHAP. Unfortunately, the information presented in the *Atlas* indicates that resources for improving or maintaining mental health remain scarce. In fact, you may be surprised by the findings. If you want to have a closer look, use this link: www.who.int/mental_health/evidence/atlas/mental_health_atlas_2014/en/.

The Mental Health Commission of Canada released *Changing Directions, Changing Lives,* the first-ever *Mental Health Strategy for Canada* in 2012. The goal of this strategy is to increase awareness of mental illness and decrease the stigma associated with mental health disorders, as well as to provide appropriate, accessible mental health services for everyone. In 2016, the Mental Health Commission of Canada released *Advancing the Mental Health Strategy for Canada: A Framework for Action (2017–2022)* (www.mentalhealthcommission.ca/sites/default/files/2016-08/

advancing_the_mental_health_strategy_for_canada_a_framework_for_action.pdf). The main objective of the framework is to implement many of the goals laid out in the 2012 Mental Health Strategy within the next five years.

DETERMINANTS OF MENTAL HEALTH

Mental health professionals are now beginning to understand that an individual's mental health is determined by many psychological, biological, and social factors. For example, factors such as an unhealthy lifestyle, rapid social change, and poverty are associated with poor mental health. Stressful work conditions, social exclusion, risks of violence, ill physical health, and human rights violations also are associated with poor mental health (WHO, 2014c). Before we explore mental illnesses in older adults, it is important to understand that there is more than one classification system used to diagnose a mental illness. Let's look at these two primary classification systems now.

A WORD ABOUT THE *DIAGNOSTIC AND STATISTICAL MANUAL* AND THE *INTERNATIONAL CLASSIFICATION OF DISEASES*

In terms of defining and diagnosing a mental illness, the *Diagnostic and Statistical Manual* (*DSM*), published by the American Psychiatric Association (APA), is the most widely used classification system of mental disorders in North America. The latest version of the *DSM (DSM-5)* was published in 2013. In other parts of the world, mental illness is understood in terms of the criteria put forth in the *International Classification of Diseases* (*ICD*), which is developed by the WHO. The *ICD-10* is currently under revision with a planned release for the *ICD-11* in 2018. Over the years, there has been much controversy about which diagnostic system is better, and heated debates between British and America psychiatrists often could be found in research journals such as the *British Journal of Psychiatry*. Some of the controversy stems from differences in diagnostic criteria for the same disorder across the two systems, with this occurring for several disorders. This has happened because, initially, there was very little collaboration between the APA and the WHO in the development of the classification systems. Another difficulty is that the *DSM* is a book that focuses on mental disorders alone. In the *ICD*, however, mental disorders are only a chapter among many chapters in a book that includes all physical ailments as well as mortality rates. This difference in approach means that the *DSM* can be updated relatively quickly (for example, when research clarifies some aspect of a particular mental disorder). Not so with the *ICD* because the entire book requires revision. For the current *DSM-5* and *ICD-10* revisions, both organizations have worked closely together, which has resulted in very similar diagnostic criteria. This has helped to reduce, but not completely eliminate, the controversy.

So, what differences remain between the two classification systems? The *ICD* is approved by the World Health Assembly and, as such, is the official world classification system. A major reason for the creation of the *ICD* is to establish a comprehensive manual for determining causes of mortality, thus enhancing efforts at improving public health (Cuthbert & Insel, 2013). More attention is given to *primary* care in low- and middle-income countries in the *ICD* as compared to the *DSM*. As well, the *ICD*'s development is global, multidisciplinary, multilingual, and has been created for *all* healthcare providers to use (International Advisory Group for the Revision of *ICD-10 Mental and Behavioural Disorder*, 2011). As a result, it has to be simple in language so that all healthcare providers, including those in low-income countries who may have little formal qualifications, can use it (Tyrer, 2014). A major focus for the *ICD* is on ease of use by clinicians and a reduction in the number of diagnoses.

On the other hand, the *DSM* is really a North American classification system and, although it is used in other countries outside North America, it is primarily used in Canada and the United States. It is used mainly by psychiatrists, but psychologists, family physicians, and other healthcare providers use its criteria as well to diagnose a mental health disorder. Unlike the *ICD*, the focus of the *DSM* is on *secondary* psychiatric care in high-income countries. As well, there tends to be more disorders with each revision of the *DSM* as compared to the *ICD* (Tyrer, 2014). So, will one system win over the other in the end? This is an interesting question. Of note, there now is a rather ambitious plan being initiated by the National Institute of Mental Health in the United States to replace the *DSM* classification system with a new system of Research Domain Criteria (RDoC). These criteria will be linked more closely to the neurobiological correlates of mental illness (Cuthbert & Insel, 2013). The idea is to develop a classification system for mental disorders based upon dimensions of neurobiology and observable behaviour. Research is currently underway and if you would like more information, Google "Research Domain Criteria". We will now turn to a discussion of mental illness in the context of the *DSM-5*.

WHAT IS MENTAL ILLNESS?

The *DSM-5* defines mental illness as "a syndrome characterized by clinically significant disturbances in an individual's cognition, emotion regulation, or behaviour that reflects a dysfunction in the psychological, biological, or developmental processes underlying mental functioning" (APA, 2013, p. 20). Mental disorders are associated with significant impairment in social and/or occupational functioning.

There are three criteria that mental health professionals consider when determining if an individual has a mental illness. The first is, how different is the behaviour from what is considered socially acceptable? Culture plays a very important role here because what is considered socially acceptable behaviour can be different depending on the cultural context. The second is, how disruptive is the behaviour? Does it significantly interfere with a person's ability to function on a day-to-day basis? The last criterion is distress. To what degree is the person distressed by the behaviour? This last criterion is a little tricky because having a mental illness often impairs a person's **insight** and judgment, so the behaviour may be more distressing to family and friends than to the individual. When you think about mental illness, it also is important to consider historical context. For example, in the 1980s, the *DSM-III* (APA, 1980) included homosexuality as a mental disorder. However, homosexuality was not considered a mental disorder in the *DSM-IV* (APA, 1994) and has not been included in the *DSM* since then.

MENTAL HEALTH FACILITIES IN CANADA WITH A GERIATRIC SPECIALTY SERVICE

In Canada, there are numerous facilities where an older adult can get specialized psychiatric care. Some facilities, such as the Douglas Mental Health Centre in Montreal Quebec, have geriatric psychiatric units for people 65 years of age and older. These units are integrated with other medical services in a general hospital. Other facilities, such as the Baycrest Hospital in Toronto, Ontario, offer many specialty services (e.g., outpatient, in-patient, day program, and resident) to older adults including specialized care to those who have a mental illness or dementia. Over 2500 older adults are seen each day at this facility! In Nova Scotia, the Centre for Health Care of the Elderly provides comprehensive geriatric assessment and treatment to older persons and their families. In Alberta, we have a hospital dedicated to geriatric mental health. Edmonton's Villa Caritas Hospital (VCH) provides psychiatric services for adults aged 65 and older with a severe mental health concern. As with other psychiatric facilities, patients admitted to VCH must be medically stable on admission. In addition, patients who are admitted will have **acute** psychiatric symptoms and/or moderate to severe behavioural difficulties that significantly compromise their physical or mental well-being. Individuals can be admitted formally or informally (voluntarily). Formal patients must meet the criteria to be admitted under the Mental Health Act. Each province and territory has its own Mental Health Act but, essentially, each of these Acts includes these three criteria: 1) the individual has a mental disorder, 2) the individual is likely to cause serious harm to himself/herself or another, and 3) the individual suffers substantial mental or physical deterioration or serious physical impairment.

6.2 ASSESSMENT METHODS FOR MENTAL HEALTH DISORDERS

LEARNING OBJECTIVES

To understand:

- what assessment is and why it is important
- different assessment methods
- what factors can influence assessment

WHAT IS ASSESSMENT AND WHY IS IT IMPORTANT?

Essentially, assessment is a formal process where some type of behaviour or emotion is understood, measured, and predicted. According to Gould, Edelstein, and Gerolimatos (2012), as well as speaking from clinical experience, a multidimensional approach to assessment has the most benefit. A good assessment involves gathering data from several sources such as family members and healthcare professionals. Conducting a thorough assessment is important for several reasons. It is very difficult to provide appropriate care or develop an accurate treatment plan without accurate assessment. Imagine if you will that a 72-year-old woman is having difficulty with her memory. She is confused, not making much sense, and is very anxious or nervous as a result. Without doing a thorough assessment, the Emergency Room physician assumes, because of her age, that she must have a dementia. She is given medication to help with her anxiety and is sent home with her family. However, in reality, what she has is a delirium caused by an interaction between two medications that she has been taking. The importance of doing a thorough assessment is highlighted in the Case Study box. Believe it or not, this is a true story!

ISSUES IN ASSESSMENT

Before we go into some of the issues that are important when assessing older adults, it is important to note that a definite diagnosis of a mental illness or a dementia should not be made using only *one* assessment method. In addition, when selecting a psychological test for use with an older adult, it is very important that the test that is selected included older adults in its development. For example, the Beck Depression Inventory-II (Beck, Steer, & Brown, 1996) is a measure commonly used to screen for depressive symptoms in younger and middle-age adults. However, this measure of depressive symptoms includes questions about fatigue, loss of interest in sex, and sleeping patterns. As a result, it is not the best measure to use with older adults as these symptoms can be the result of normal aging. When using a screen to assess depressive symptoms in an older

Mrs. Smith was admitted to Midwest Hospital with significant confusion and an inability to care for herself. Her house was unsafe to live in because there was garbage all over and she had been ripping apart the walls of her home. During a clinical interview, she could not provide much information about herself. She was diagnosed with dementia. She was transferred to a psychiatric hospital as her behaviour was difficult to manage and she had become aggressive. Plans were being made to have her live in a long-term-care facility. However, after a few days in the psychiatric hospital, it became clear that she had been significantly abusing multiple over-the-counter medications. So, in the end she didn't have a dementia; she had a delirium! This was successfully treated and she returned to independent living in the community with supports in place.

adult, the Geriatric Depression Scale (GDS) (Yesavage et al., 1982–1983) should be used as the types of questions provided above are not included in the GDS. As a result, artificially inflated scores in older adults are less likely when using the GDS.

Of all the assessment measures available, the clinical interview is the most widely used (Gould et al., 2012). In addition to obtaining verbal information from the individual, important nonverbal information can be observed as well. Through a clinical interview, the mental health professional can begin to understand the amount of insight and judgment the individual has about his or her mental illness and current situation. In addition, clinical interviews give healthcare professionals an opportunity to build trusting relationships with patients.

REFLECTIVE QUESTION

What kind of nonverbal information would be important to look for when doing a clinical interview?

In addition to the clinical interview, a thorough physical examination is necessary to rule out an underlying medical cause that might explain the individual's emotions, thinking, or behaviour. For example, an older adult who has a urinary tract infection (UTI) may become very confused, and it may actually look like he or she has a dementia. However, once the UTI has been treated successfully, the confusion will clear.

Performance-based assessment also is an important method of assessment in that it allows the clinician to observe how a person functions in his or her own environment. For example, can a person safely prepare meals? Is he or she aware of safety issues? Can he or she pay bills? These activities are known as **Instrumental Activities of Daily Living** (IADLs) (Lawton & Brody, 1969). **Activities of Daily Living** (ADLs) (Katz, 1983) also are assessed. ADLs include such activities as brushing one's teeth, washing one's face, or toileting independently.

FACTORS THAT CAN INFLUENCE ASSESSMENT

Positive and negative biases that healthcare professionals may have about the individuals that they care for is a factor that can influence assessment. An example of a negative bias is not assessing an older adult's sexual behaviours because of the belief that older adults are asexual. A positive bias that can lead to inaccurate assessment is assuming that "little old ladies" are sweet and kind and never become violent. How would this bias affect your assessment of an older woman who is accused of spousal abuse? These biases stem from ageism which we discussed in Chapter 1. It is very important that healthcare professionals have the appropriate knowledge of the population they are working with because information can easily be missed or misunderstood.

The second factor that can influence the assessment process is the environment that the assessment occurs in. For example, older adults often have an age-associated hearing loss. If the assessment takes place in a room with a lot of background noise, the individual may answer questions in such a way that may lead the healthcare professional to believe that the individual is confused when, in fact, all that person has is a hearing impairment. This example underscores the importance of healthcare professionals having a solid understanding of the physical and sensory changes that occur with normal aging. Other issues that can significantly interfere with an accurate psychological assessment in older adults are not considering such factors as English as a second language or not having appropriate norms to compare the cognitive performance of the individual being assessed. Recall that the over-85 age group is the fastest-growing age group in our population today. Although several psychological measures now have norms up to the age of 90, more and more referrals are made for people over the age of 90.

When assessing people of any age, it is important for the healthcare professional to get an individual's best performance. However, medical appointments and investigations, psychological assessments, and other types of work-up can be very stressful for individuals of any age. This stress will certainly interfere with getting the individual's best performance. In order to reduce the stress that older adults might experience during an assessment, Canadian researchers Sonia Lupien and her colleagues (2012) developed the *Guidelines for Health Professionals and Scientists Working with Older Adults*. If you are interested in learning more about these guidelines, please access this resource: www.humanstress.ca/documents/pdf/KT/KT_document_EN.pdf.

6.3 MENTAL ILLNESSES IN OLDER ADULTHOOD
LEARNING OBJECTIVES

To understand:
- the mental illnesses that most commonly occur in older adults and the challenges that can occur with diagnosis
- gender differences in mental illness in older adults
- what might account for lower levels of depression in older adults
- the risk factors associated with the development of late-life depression
- the medical conditions associated with depression and anxiety in older adults
- suicide rates of older adults in Canada

In any given year, one in five (or about 20 percent) Canadians over the age of 15 is living with a mental illness (Pearson, Janz, & Ali, 2013). Mood and anxiety disorders are the most common mental illnesses and, combined, these two disorders account for approximately 70 percent of all

FIGURE 6.1

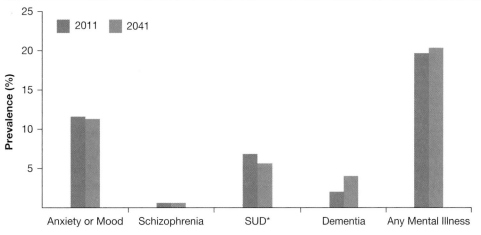

* Substance use disorders

Source: Mental Health Commission of Canada. (2013). *Making the case for investing in mental health in Canada.* http:// www.mentalhealthcommission.ca/English/system/files/private/document/Investing_in_Mental_Health_FINAL_Version_ENG.pdf. Reprinted by permission of the Mental Health Commission of Canada.

mental disorders in Canada (PHAC, 2015). The prevalence rates of specific mental disorders in Canada are shown in Figure 6.1.

As discussed earlier in this chapter, the introduction of the *DSM-5* (APA, 2013) resulted in changes in the classification of a number of mental illnesses. In the next section, rather than reviewing all the mental disorders that are presented in the *DSM-5*, only those mental illnesses most commonly found in older adults will be examined. It should be noted that there have been significant changes to the diagnostic criteria for many of these mental disorders. As mentioned before, the *DSM* usually adds to its list of disorders with each new edition and the *DSM-5* is no exception. The diagnostic changes in the *DSM-5* for a number of mental health disorders in older adults will be briefly discussed in the next sections where relevant.

MAJOR DEPRESSIVE DISORDER (DEPRESSION)

Disruptive mood dysregulation disorder, premenstrual dysphoric disorder, and substance-/ medication-induced depressive disorder have been added to the *DSM-5* Mood Disorders chapter. Bipolar and related disorders are now in a separate chapter. Although the formal name of depression is "major depressive disorder"(MDD), we will refer to the disorder as "depression" in this chapter. Important for older adults, the *DSM-5* (APA, 2013) now considers a few age-related features of depression. For example, memory impairment now is acknowledged as a common feature of depression in older adults (although memory impairment can sometimes be mistaken for dementia).

A main feature of depression is loss of interest in activities that one previously enjoyed, and this symptom is one of two symptoms that must be present for a formal diagnosis of depression. Not surprisingly, the other symptom is low mood. While the following list of symptoms is not exhaustive, other symptoms of depression include feelings of hopelessness and worthlessness, excessive guilt, lack of motivation, and weight loss. Thoughts of suicide are not uncommon in individuals with depression. In 1967, Beck argued that the main features of depression are negative thoughts about oneself, the world, and the future. He coined this the "negative triad". Since then, negative thinking has been considered an important feature of depression.

PREVALENCE RATES OF DEPRESSION IN OLDER ADULTS

Research using community surveys has consistently found lower levels of depression in older adults, as compared to younger adults, in countries around the world (Gum, King-Kallimanis, & Kohn, 2009; Kessler et al., 2010a; Kessler et al., 2010b; Patten et al., 2015; Reynolds, Pietrzak, El-Gabalawy, Mackenize, & Sareen, 2015), and this pattern of findings is no different in Canada (Caron et al., 2012; Mosier et al., 2010; Streiner, Cairney, & Veldhuizen, 2006). For example, Patten and his colleagues (2015) used data from the Canadian Community Health Survey to examine the last-year prevalence rate of depression in a household sample of 25 113 Canadians. Their findings are presented in Figure 6.2. As you can see, depression is not as prevalent in the older age groups as it is in the young- and middle-aged groups. Interestingly, although depression is higher in women, prevalence rates between men and women tend to even out among the oldest-old.

REFLECTIVE QUESTION

Why do you think the prevalence rates of depression even out among the oldest-old?

FIGURE 6.2

AGE- AND SEX-SPECIFIC PREVALENCE OF PAST-YEAR MAJOR DEPRESSIVE DISORDER

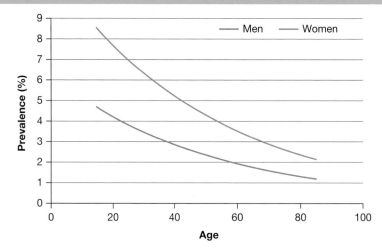

Source: Patten, S., et al. (2015). Descriptive epidemiology of major depressive disorder in Canada in 2012. *The Canadian Journal of Psychiatry*, *60*(1), 23–30. Copyright © 2015 by the Authors. Reprinted by permission of SAGE Publications, Inc.

Although rates of depression are lower among older adults in community samples, the rate of depression in long-term-care (LTC) facilities is alarming (Snowdon, 2010). Hoover and colleagues (2010) examined the outcomes from 634 060 assessments based on what is referred to as the **Minimum Data Set** (MDS) from approximately 4000 LTC facilities across the United States. These researchers found that 54 percent of residents in LTC facilities were diagnosed with depression within the first year of living in an LTC facility. According to the Canadian Institute for Health Information (2015), prevalence estimates of depression among LTC residents in Canada range from 14 to 44 percent. In a recent study, Neufeld, Freeman, Joling, and Hirdes (2014) examined over 60 000 anonymous MDS assessments from LTC facilities in Ontario, Canada. They looked at the prevalence of depressive symptoms and diagnoses among older adults newly admitted to LTC facilities and then again at three-month follow-up. These researchers found that depressive symptoms were present in 53 cases per 100 residents at admission, and by follow-up, this had increased to almost 61 cases per 100 residents! On a more hopeful note, these researchers also found that 1 in 10 residents went from expressing high levels of depressive symptoms at admission to showing no signs of depression at follow-up.

> What do you think can be done to reduce the rates of depressive symptoms in LTC facilities?

REFLECTIVE QUESTION

WHY ARE THERE LOWER LEVELS OF DEPRESSION IN OLDER ADULTS LIVING IN THE COMMUNITY?

Several reasons have been given to explain the lower rates of depression found in older adult populations living in the community but, to date, there has been no consensus. Because most of the research is cross-sectional, the findings may be due to cohort factors rather than age (see Chapter 2). Some researchers have argued that lower rates of depression can be accounted for by selective attrition in which those individuals who have depression earlier in life are less likely to live to old age because of suicide, and/or alcohol and drug abuse (Cuijpers et al., 2014a; Lawrence, Hancock, & Kisely, 2013; Moustgaard, Joutsenniemi, Sihvo, & Martikainen, 2013). As you recall, some of the data on the prevalence rates of depression come from household surveys. This method of data collection may create a selection bias in that there may be age groups that are more willing than others to report psychiatric symptoms (Kessler et al., 2010a). Another explanation is that older adults may experience depression differently than do young- and middle-age adults. For example, older adults are less likely to endorse cognitive-affective symptoms of depression, including dysphoria and worthlessness/guilt, than are younger adults (Fiske, Wetherell, & Gatz, 2009). The issue here is that, maybe, researchers are *missing* clinically relevant depressive symptoms in older adults. For example, older adults may be more likely than other age groups to present with **sub-syndromal depressive symptoms** (SSD) that do not quite meet the *DSM*-5 (APA, 2013) diagnostic criteria for MDD (Büchtemann, Luppa, Bramesfeld, & Reidel-Heller, 2012; Edelstein, Bamonti, Gregg, & Gerolimatos, 2015). In other words, older adults may display less severe symptoms of depression that nonetheless interfere with daily functioning. In fact, SSD is associated with medical co-morbidities, suicidal ideation, healthcare use, and decreases in quality of life in older adults (Büchtemann et al., 2012; Meeks, Vahia, Lavretsky, Kulkarni, & Jeste, 2011). In 2015, Laborde-Lahoz teamed up with researchers from the University of Manitoba and other colleagues to investigate the prevalence, co-morbidity, and risk for new-onset psychiatric disorders in those older adults with SSD. Using data from a nationally representative sample of adults from the United States, these researchers found that SSD is as prevalent as depression among those 55 years of age and older and that SSD is associated with an increased risk of developing a new-onset depressive disorder and an anxiety disorder over a three-year follow up. It would seem that late-life depression is much more diverse in its presentation than when it occurs in middle-age and young adults. Even though SSD does not meet *DSM-5* criteria for a formal diagnosis of MDD, SSD appears to be just as debilitating as MDD. As a result, researchers are calling for a more comprehensive approach to the diagnosis of depression in older adults.

This has been a lot of information to digest. We have explored several reasons that might account for the lower rates of depression among older adults. However, there may be other reasons worthy of consideration. Perhaps there are fewer cases of mental illness in general and depression in particular in older adults today because older adults have different types of stress and different types of coping styles than do younger adults. It also could be the case that older adults engage in less negative thinking than do younger adults. Perhaps it's who older adults choose to hang out with that lowers the rate of depression in this population. Let's now consider these possibilities.

The Stress and Coping paradigm developed by Lazarus and Folkman (1984) has given us a framework to understand **coping** strategies. A key aspect of this model is that it is not the *event* itself that causes stress but how a person *interprets* the event. According to this framework, there are two ways an individual can cope with stressful life events: problem-focused coping and emotion-focused coping. Problem-focused coping involves using coping strategies that attempt to change the problem in some way. Emotion-focused coping involves coping strategies that deal with the feelings associated with the problem. Sometimes a stressful situation cannot be changed (e.g., loss of driving privileges due to a dementia). When this happens, to effectively cope with the event, the person would use emotion-focused coping. If you apply the framework from a developmental perspective, two differences appear to emerge between younger and older adults. First of all, there is a difference in the type and amount of stress experienced as we age. Overall, older adults experience less stress than younger or middle-aged adults and the source of the stress in older adults usually is due to health issues. On the other hand, stress for younger adults typically centres on work, finances, personal concerns, and family (Almeida, Piazza, Stawski, & Klein, 2011). Another difference between young and older adults in coping with stress is the type of coping strategy used. In general, younger adults tend to use more problem-focused coping strategies where a direct approach is taken to change the event causing the stress. On the other hand, older adults tend to use emotion-focused coping strategies, which include managing the thoughts and feelings associated with the event (Meléndez, Mayordomo, Sancho, & Tomás, 2012; Zarit, 2009). In addition, older adults have typically had a lifetime of stressors and so, presumably, they would rely on past experience to deal with current stressors. So, it appears that, generally, older adults tend to take things in stride (Armstrong, Wuthrich, Knight, & Joiner, 2014) as compared to their younger counterparts.

Thinking style also may help older adults cope differently with stress. Support for this comes from a study by Armstrong and her colleagues (2014). These researchers looked at self-report differences in habitual negative thinking (the negative triad) between university students and older adults in Australia. They found that older adults engaged in significantly less habitual negative thinking than the younger adults, which led these researchers to conclude that this thinking style contributes to lower stress and the lower prevalence rates of depression found among older adults.

Finally, older adults also are thought to be more selective in who they spend time with. Carstensen and her colleagues (Carstensen, 1992; Carstensen, Fung, & Charles, 2003; Carstensen, Isaacowitz, & Charles, 1999) argue that as we age, we become increasingly aware that we have a finite amount of time left on the planet. As a result, older adults want to spend more time with people that they positively interact with and avoid those individuals in which they share negative interactions with. This temporal perspective is the basis of the socio-emotional selectivity theory (Carstensen et al., 1999). It seems that this strategy would go a long way to reduce the problems and stress that can arise from unhealthy relationships for both older and younger adults!

RISK FACTORS FOR THE DEVELOPMENT OF DEPRESSION IN OLDER ADULTS

Physical illness, in particular cardiovascular disease, stroke, and diabetes, can influence the development of depression in older adults (Valkanona & Ebmeier, 2013). Other factors that have been found to be related to the development of depression in late life include low social support and isolation (Edelstein et al., 2015; Karg, Burmeister, Shedden, & Sen, 2011).

SUICIDE IN THE WORLD

An estimated 804 000 suicidal deaths occurred worldwide in 2012, representing an annual global **age-standardized** suicide rate of 15.0 for males and 8.0 for females per 100 000 population. However, since suicide is a sensitive issue, and even illegal in some countries, it is very likely that suicide is underreported with suicide deaths likely being much higher than current estimates. Even in countries where accurate birth and death records are kept, suicide often may be misclassified as an accident or another cause of death (WHO, 2014d). For example, in an urban teaching hospital in Canada, clinicians estimated the prevalence of deliberate self-poisoning to be 63 percent higher than the prevalence determined by **E-Codes** (Rhodes et al., 2002). This discrepancy was much larger among the older age groups. Registering a suicide also is a complicated procedure involving several different authorities, including law enforcement, which may deter family and friends from reporting a death as a suicide.

Why do you think more males commit suicide than females?

REFLECTIVE QUESTION

SUICIDE IN CANADA

The Canadian rate of suicide per 100 000 population was 10.8 in 2011 (Mental Health Commission of Canada, 2015). In Canada, males have a higher males have a higher rate of suicide completion than do females (approximately 18 percent versus 5 percent, respectively) (Statistics Canada, 2009). Figure 6.3 shows the rates of suicide by Canadian provinces and territories

FIGURE 6.3

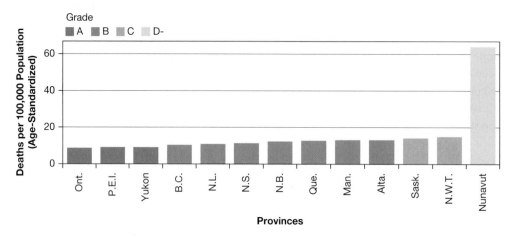

Suicides, 2009–2011

Source: The Conference Board of Canada, (2015). *Provincial and territorial ranking: Suicides*. Retrieved from http://www.conferenceboard.ca/hcp/provincial/health/suicide.aspx. Reprinted by permission of the Conference Board of Canada.

between the years 2009 and 2011. As you can see, Nunavut's has the highest suicide rate in Canada and these rates are significantly higher than the rates of all other provinces and territories in Canada.

REFLECTIVE QUESTION

Which age group do you think has the highest suicide rate?

As you reflect on the question above, we bet you are thinking that adolescents have the highest rate of suicide. This is a common misconception. You might be surprised to learn that suicide rates are highest in those 70 years of age and older for both men and women in most regions of the world. In fact, in Canada, the suicide rate for men over the age of 85 is 29 suicides per 100 000 population. Compare this to the rate for adolescents, which is 22 suicides per 100 000 population (Mental Health Commission of Canada, 2015).

Unfortunately, there is evidence to suggest that older adults who have committed suicide have visited a physician in days to months before taking their own life but rarely sought services from a mental health professional. Juurlink and his colleagues (2004) used data from the province of Ontario's coroner's records to identify those adults 66 years of age and older who committed suicide. Of the 1354 older adults who committed suicide, almost half had visited a physician in the preceding week. Luoma, Martin, and Pearson (2002) found that 45 percent of older adults in their sample who committed suicide had seen a physician in the last month of their life.

PREVENTIVE MEASURES FOR DEPRESSION

It would seem that primary care physicians and other healthcare professionals need much more support and education about suicidal ideation and depressive symptom presentation in their older adult patients. However, there is limited research with regard to the proper assessment of suicidal ideation in older adults. Huh and colleagues (2012) found that training physicians and other healthcare professionals about suicidal thoughts and behaviours in older adults increased their awareness of the importance of suicide in this population as well as improved their competency in assessing and treating older adults with suicidal ideation. The Canadian Coalition on Seniors' Mental Health (2006) developed national guidelines for the assessment of suicide risk and prevention of suicide in older adults. As part of this initiative, a toolkit for suicide prevention in late life has been developed for use by mental health professionals. This toolkit includes information about the identification of suicidal thoughts and behaviours and steps for prevention. For more information on the toolkit, go to www.ccsmh.ca/en/projects/suicide.cfm.

Promoting and strengthening connectedness with family, friends, and community are important to lowering the risk of suicide in older adults. In a recent study, Purcell and her colleagues (2012) found that participants who reported a greater sense of connection with family members were significantly less likely to report suicidal ideation. Canadian researcher Isaac and his colleagues (2009) reviewed Gatekeeper training and found that it holds promise as a strategy to reduce suicide in older adults. The purpose of the Gatekeeper model is to support the well-being and independence of older adults by educating laypeople in the community on how to identify at-risk older adults and refer them to an appropriate agency. Neufeld and her colleagues (2015) believe that home-care workers are well situated to recognize potential suicide risk among their older clients. Using data from the home-care sector in Ontario, they found an increased risk of intentional self-harm was associated with depression, indicators of alcohol abuse, and loneliness. Neufeld and her colleagues (2015) propose that these factors could be targeted for immediate intervention by properly trained home-care providers. The good news is that by increasing education and awareness among healthcare professionals and members of the community, suicidal behaviour in this population may decrease.

TREATMENT OF DEPRESSION

A combination of **pharmacotherapy** and psychotherapy are usually very effective in the treatment of depression, although some individuals benefit from psychotherapy alone. In terms of pharmacotherapy, selective serotonin reuptake inhibitors (SSRIs), which belong to the class of medications known as anti-depressants, are the first medication of choice for the pharmacological treatment of depression in older adults (Diaez, Nunes, Machado-Vieira, & Forlenza, 2011). This type of antidepressant helps to restore normal levels of the neurotransmitter serotonin. However, physicians must be careful when prescribing any **psychotropic** medication to older individuals. This is because psychotropic medications may interact with other medications, resulting in very serious side effects as older adults are more susceptible to drug-induced side effects (Andreescu & Varon, 2015). Prescribing medications for older adults is not an exact science and sometimes several medications and dosing levels are tried before one is found that works the best. The rule of thumb in prescribing medication for an older adult is "Start low, Go slow."

Electroconvulsive therapy (ECT) also can be very effective for severe depression in older adults, especially if the individual does not respond to antidepressant medication. Older adults also respond well to psychotherapy interventions and, as mentioned before, these interventions often are combined with antidepressant medication. Several meta-analyses and review studies have provided support for the efficacy of cognitive behavioural therapy (CBT) as an individual therapy for depression in older adults (Peng, Huang, Chen, & Lu, 2009; Pinquart, Duberstein, & Lyness, 2007; Kiosses, Leon, & Areán, 2011; Shah, Scogin, & Floyd, 2010), as well as group therapy for depression in older adults (Cuijpers, Karyotaki, Pot, Park, & Reynolds, 2014b; Feng et al., 2011). For older adults, modifications can be made to CBT such as shortening sessions, presenting information at a slower pace, and involving family members if need be (Bower & Loebach-Wetherell, 2015; DiNapoli, LaRocca, & Scogin, 2015). Problem-solving therapy (PST), which is another cognitive behavioural approach, has been adapted specifically to treat depression in older adults. In this type of therapy, older adults receive training in problem identification, problem-solving skills, formulating goals, evaluating the pros and cons of a potential solution, and then choosing an appropriate solution (Simon, Cordás, & Bottino, 2014). PST has shown good results in decreasing depressive symptoms in older adults (Cuijpers et al., 2014b; Kiosses & Alexopoulos, 2014). Other researchers have shown that older adults also benefit from interpersonal psychotherapy (Diaez et al., 2011; Heisel, Talbot, King, Tu, & Duberstein, 2015). Finally, the results from a pilot study conducted in Canada show promise for the effectiveness of mindfulness-based cognitive therapy in reducing depressive symptoms in older adults (Labbé et al., 2016). The take-home message here is that older adults can benefit greatly from psychotherapy.

ANXIETY DISORDERS

As with depression, there have been changes to the Anxiety Disorders chapter in the *DSM-5* (APA, 2013) as well. One of the biggest changes is that obsessive-compulsive disorder and post-traumatic stress disorder are no longer included and each now has its own chapter.

While depression is the most common mood disorder, anxiety disorders are the most common mental disorder (Mental Health Commission of Canada, 2015). Anxiety disorders are a group of disorders that have at their core nervousness, fear, apprehension, and worry, and these symptoms interfere with an individual's ability to function. The actual likelihood of the stressor the person is worried about happening does not match the intensity, duration, and frequency of these symptoms (APA, 2013). The physical symptoms that accompany anxiety disorders can be debilitating and include increased heart rate, sweating, dry mouth, chest pain, hyperventilation, diarrhea, insomnia, and headaches (Byers, Yaffe, Covinsky, Freidman, & Bruce, 2010).

The majority of anxiety disorders in the older population have an onset at an earlier age (Andreescu & Varon, 2015; Le Roux, Gatz, & Wetherell, 2005; Zhang et al., 2015). However, almost half of older adults with generalized anxiety disorder (GAD) experience their first onset after age 50 (Chou, 2009; Le Roux et al., 2005). Of interest, GAD appears to be the most common anxiety disorder found in older adults (Bryant, Jackson, & Ames, 2008). Older adults who experience GAD have significant levels of impaired quality of life and disability when compared to same-aged healthy controls (Poresnsky et al., 2009).

REFLECTIVE QUESTION

Why do you think GAD might occur for the first time in an older adult?

PREVALENCE RATES OF ANXIETY DISORDERS IN OLDER ADULTS

There is variability regarding the prevalence rates reported for GAD in older adults. GAD prevalence rates range from 1 percent to 12.5 percent with higher rates in women than men; this variability is consistent in studies around the world including Canada (Byers et al., 2010; Gonçalves, Pachana, & Byrne, 2011; Mackenzie, Reynolds, Chou, Pagura, & Sareen, 2011; Zhang et al., 2015). In a review of the literature from 1980 to 2007, Bryant and her colleagues (2008) found the prevalence rates of GAD in clinical samples of older adults to be twice as high as prevalence rates of GAD in clinical samples of younger adults.

DIFFICULTY ASSESSING ANXIETY DISORDERS IN OLDER ADULTS

Diagnosing anxiety in older adults is challenging. The majority of the screening tools used to measure GAD are not appropriate for use with older populations (Therrien & Hunsley, 2012; Wetherell & Gatz, 2005). This is because the content of older adults' worry is different than younger adults. That is, older adults tend to worry more about health issues, family-related problems, and world concerns. Middle-age adults, on the other hand, tend to worry about work-related issues (Gonçalves & Byrne, 2013; Wuthrich, Johnco, & Loebach-Wetherell, 2015).

Other difficulties in recognizing symptoms of anxiety in older adults are that anxiety can be masked by co-morbid medical conditions and medication side effects. In addition, many older adults who have anxiety may not recognize the symptoms they experience as anxiety and assume that it is a part of normal aging (Bower & Loebach-Wetherell, 2015). This means that when asked about being anxious, older adults are more likely to report that they are not anxious. Finally, a large percentage of older adults with GAD also have depression and differentiating between the two disorders can be difficult (Chou, 2009; Wuthrich et al., 2015). Let's turn now to look at the relationship between medical conditions and anxiety disorders.

RELATIONSHIP BETWEEN ANXIETY DISORDERS AND MEDICAL CONDITIONS

Most studies with older adults do not differentiate between the types of anxiety disorders when investigating the relationship between anxiety and medical conditions. A few that have looked at GAD specifically have found that this disorder is associated with a higher risk of coronary heart disease (Batelaan, ten Have, van Balkom, Tuithorf, & de Graaf, 2014; Martens et al., 2010; Roest, Zuidersma, & De Jonge, 2012; Tully, Cosh, & Baune, 2013), greater disability and functional impairment, and lower health-related quality of life (Brenes et al., 2005; Gonçalves et al., 2011; Poresnsky et al., 2009). Using data from the Canadian Community Health Survey, El-Gabalawy and her colleagues (2011) looked at which physical health conditions are more likely to co-occur with anxiety disorders in general. They analyzed data from 12 792 participants and found that anxiety disorders were significantly associated with cardiovascular disease, arthritis, migraine headaches, lung disease, and gastrointestinal problems. They also found that those older adults who had both a physical illness and co-morbid anxiety rated their health as poorer that those who had a physical illness or anxiety alone. When co-morbid anxiety and depression appear together, older adults suffer a more chronic course of illness (Almeida et al., 2011). Given these associations, accurately recognizing and treating an anxiety disorder in an older adult is very important.

TREATMENT OF ANXIETY DISORDERS

Anxiety disorders in older adults are treated with medication as well as psychotherapy. For older adults, SSRIs are the medication of choice for both short-term and long-term treatment of anxiety disorders in general (Lenze et al., 2009; Andreescu & Varon, 2015). CBT for older adults has been shown to be an effective treatment (Gonçalves & Byrne, 2012; Gould, Coulson, & Howard, 2012; Rosnick, Wetherell, White, & Andreescu, 2016) as well as other interventions such as supportive discussion groups, relaxation therapy, and worry groups (Bower & Loebach-Wetherell, 2015). Of interest is the growing literature on the effectiveness of internet-delivered CBT with older adults (Staples, Fogliati, Dear, Nielssen, & Titov, 2016; Zhou, Xue, & Kong, 2016). A recent Canadian study showed that Internet-delivered CBT for older adults who had GAD as well as concurrent depressive symptoms was effective in symptom reduction, even at a one-month follow up (Jones, Hadjistavropoulos, & Soucy, 2016). This is an exciting finding as internet-delivered CBT shows potential as a method to treat isolated older adults in rural areas where mental health services are minimal. Internet-delivered CBT also may be very helpful to those older adults who have mobility issues and who may not be able to easily access mental health services.

6.4 SUBSTANCE USE DISORDERS
LEARNING OBJECTIVE

- To understand alcohol use and alcohol and drug abuse

ALCOHOL USE

According to the WHO (2015d), the worldwide consumption of alcohol in the year 2010 was equal to 6.2 litres of pure alcohol consumed per person age 15 years or older. This number would be higher but the WHO estimates that approximately 25 percent of alcohol intake goes unrecorded because of the consumption of homemade alcohol and alcohol that is sold illegally. In all WHO regions, females are more likely to be lifetime **abstainers**; that is to say, females are more likely to not drink at all. However, there is considerable variability in alcohol consumption by region. In general, the wealthier a country is, the more alcohol is consumed and the number of abstainers is lower (WHO, 2015d).

The Canadian Tobacco, Alcohol, and Drug Survey (CTADS) is a biennial general population survey that produces estimates of the rates of alcohol, tobacco, and illicit drug use in Canadians 15 years and older. Results are based on data collected from 14 565 respondents across all 10 provinces in 2013. Data show that 76 percent of Canadians surveyed reported drinking alcohol in the last year with males reporting higher consumption than women (81 percent versus 71 percent). Unfortunately, there was no specific data reported for older adults (Statistics Canada, 2015e).

According to the *Chief Public Health Officer's Report on the State of Public Health in Canada* (Government of Canada, 2016a), the highest percentage of past-year drinkers were found to be 30- to 34-year- olds. The highest percentage of risky drinkers, based on drinking over the previous week, was found in young adults (ages 20 to 29). However, these data only capture risky drinking in the week previous to the survey, meaning that the these data provide only a limited snapshot of risky drinkers in Canada. Data from this same report, from April 2013 to March 2014, showed Canadians bought almost 76 litres of beer, 16 litres of wine, 5 litres of spirits, and 4 litres of other alcoholic beverages per person. Proportionally, Canadians drink more beer (51 percent) than spirits (27 percent) or wine (22 percent) (Government of Canada, 2016a).

So, where do older adults fit in? Do older adults drink more than younger adults? The research would suggest that older adults do not have higher rates of alcohol use when compared to younger adults. They have not been treated in great numbers in substance abuse programs either (Cummings, Bride, & Rawlins-Shaw; 2006; Substance Abuse and Mental Health Services Administration, 2013). This has led to the belief that, in general, alcohol consumption does decrease for reasons such as health problems, fixed income, and decreased social opportunities (Babatunde, Outlaw, Forbes, & Gay, 2014; Platt, Sloan, & Costanzo, 2010). In fact, alcohol abuse by older adults was rare in the 1960s and 1970s (Atkinson, Turner, Kofoed, & Tolson, 1985). However, it seems that, relative to young adults, the frequency of alcohol use among a number of middle-aged and older adults is increasing, although it is still not as prevalent as in younger age groups (Choi, DiNitto, & Marti, 2015; Kuerbis, Sacco, Blazer, & Moore, 2014). There seems to be a variety of reasons to account for the increasing use of alcohol in today's older age groups. Remember that the baby boomer generation is quite different from other generations before them. Baby boomers came of age during the 60s and 70s, which was a period of upheaval and transformation in the social order. During this time, attitudes toward alcohol and drug use became much more socially acceptable. In addition, the baby boomers have more money to spend on alcohol than previous generations and, as a result, have developed very different drinking habits. (see Figure 6.4).

FIGURE 6.4

DRINKING ALCOHOL HAS BECOME MUCH MORE ACCEPTABLE AMONG BABY BOOMERS

bikeriderlondon/Shutterstock.com

It also is the case that the media likely has something to do with the increase in alcohol use among older adults. If advertisements about alcohol are to be believed, drinking certain alcoholic beverages makes one more attractive, play better sports, drive a better car, and have more friends than those who do not! In addition, there is a growing body of research that would suggest that moderate alcohol consumption is a protective factor for many age-related diseases such as cardiovascular disease, stroke, and diabetes, and that moderate drinkers have better overall health than their heavier drinking and abstinent peers (Di Castelnuovo et al., 2006; Kaplan et al., 2012; Mukamal et al., 2006; Ronksley, Brein, Turner, Mukamal, & Ghali, 2011). Babatunde and colleagues (2014) suggest that a moderate drinker is one who drinks within the recommended guidelines (which we will get to shortly). According to researchers from the University of Montreal, because of the protective health factors associated with moderate drinking, as well as the promotion of diets such as the **Mediterranean diet**, which includes a moderate consumption of red wine, drinking alcoholic beverages has become more favourable among Canadians, especially for those adults aged 55 and over (Moriconi, Nadeau, & Demers, 2012). In fact, alcohol remains the most commonly used substance in this age group (Arndt, Clayton, & Shultz, 2011). It is interesting to note that, the use of illicit drugs also is increasing among older adults.

Before we can begin a discussion on the abuse of alcohol, we need to know what is considered a reasonable amount of alcohol to consume. According to the Canadian Centre on Substance Use and Addiction (2017; Butt, Beirness, Gliksman, Paradis, & Stockwell, 2011), the recommended daily consumption of alcohol for women is no more than two standard drinks per day on most days or 10 standard drinks per week. The recommended daily consumption for men is no more than 3 standard drinks a day on most days or 15 standard drinks per week. See Figure 6.5 for the Canadian Centre on Substance Use and Addiction amounts for a standard drink.

FIGURE 6.5

STANDARD DRINKING GUIDELINES

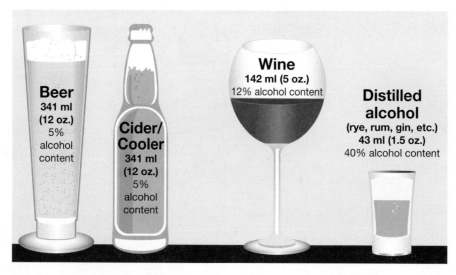

Source: Canadian Centre on Substance Use and Addiction. (2017). Canada's low-risk alcohol drinking guidelines. http://www.ccsa.ca/Resource%20Library/2012-Canada-Low-Risk-Alcohol-Drinking-Guidelines-Brochure-en.pdf. Reprinted by permission of the Canadian Centre on Substance Use and Addiction.

The American Geriatric Society (2003) recommends that older adults drink *less* than that recommended for other age groups. This organization suggests that older adults in general should drink no more than seven standard drinks per week. This makes sense, especially if you recall the physical changes that occur with age. That is, older adults become more sensitive to the effects of alcohol because alcohol is metabolized more slowly with age, which means it remains in the body longer (Babatunde et al., 2014). The outcome of this for older adults is a higher blood alcohol concentration than younger adults for the same amount of ingested alcohol. Older adults also have less lean body mass, which results in less water available to dilute the alcohol that is consumed.

PREVALENCE OF SUBSTANCE USE DISORDERS

The *DSM-5* (APA, 2013) has made significant changes to the Substance-Related and Addictive Disorders chapter. The categories of **substance abuse** and **substance dependence** are now combined into a single disorder called substance use disorder. Substance use disorder is now measured on a continuum from mild to severe. One of the diagnostic criteria in the *DSM-5* is a failure to fulfill obligations at work, home, or school. However, these criteria are not very helpful for detecting substance abuse in older adults because they have fewer obligations. As we are sure you have suspected, some of the symptoms of alcohol abuse can be mistaken for other problems such as medical illness or self-neglect (Caputo et al., 2012).

So, how many Canadians have a substance use disorder? The most recent data from the Canadian Community Health Survey (Pearson et al., 2013) indicate that 21 percent of Canadians (approximately 6 million) 15 years of age and older met the criteria for a substance use disorder in their lifetime. If you look at rates of substance abuse over the last year in these same individuals, the number is 4.4 percent. Alcohol is the most commonly abused substance at 3.2 percent. Men have higher rates of alcohol abuse than women. The most recent Canadian statistics suggest that six to ten percent of older adults over the age of 65 have an alcohol use disorder (PHAC, 2006). Han, Gfroerer, Colliver, and Penne (2009) suggest that the number of adults aged 50 years or older with a past-year substance use disorder will substantially increase in the next several decades because of the number of older adults in the baby boomer generation.

PATTERNS OF ALCOHOL ABUSE IN OLDER ADULTS

There appears to be two patterns of alcohol abuse in the older adult population; one in which alcohol abuse started before the age of 60 and the other in which alcohol abuse started after the age of 60. The latter is commonly known as late-onset alcohol-use disorder (Trevisan, 2014). Those older adults who have been abusing alcohol before 60 years old appear to have a poorer outcome. Typically, this group consists of males who have been abusing alcohol for a long period of time and, as a result, have burned bridges between family and friends. They also likely have chronic physical impairments, alcohol-related medical impairments, and some level of cognitive impairment (Babatunde et al., 2014). According to Kinney (2011), approximately two-thirds of older adult alcoholics fall into this category.

The clinical picture associated with late-onset alcohol misuse is usually milder. This group includes more women (Kuerbis et al., 2014). For this group of individuals, the alcohol abuse may have started after a stressful life event such as the loss of a spouse or an ill-planned retirement (Offsay, 2007).

DIFFICULTIES ASSOCIATED WITH ALCOHOL ABUSE

Excessive drinking is associated with a host of difficulties for people of all ages. For example, alcohol can interact with several medications such as aspirin and antidepressant medication in such a way that the medications will not work properly (Babatunde et al., 2014). Alcohol abuse is highly correlated with depression and anxiety disorders as many people self-medicate in an attempt to ease psychological or physical pain (Trevisan, 2008). Heavy drinking also has been linked to cardiovascular disease, dementia, high blood pressure, osteoporosis, cirrhosis of the liver, an inability of the body to properly absorb nutrients, and an increased injury from falls (Caputo et al., 2012; Kuerbis & Sacco, 2012; Di Castelnuovo et al., 2006; Kaplan et al., 2012; Ronksley et al., 2011). Interestingly, these researchers found that abstainers and heavy drinkers were at an increased risk of mortality compared to moderate drinkers. However, it is not clear why this is the case.

For older adults, there also appears to be a relationship between alcohol use and increased risk of placement in LTC facilities. Kaplan and his colleagues (2014) looked at data from the National Population Health Survey. This survey is conducted in Canada every two years by Statistics Canada. The data consisted of a sample of 5404 community-dwelling residents who lived in the provinces of Canada (excluding individuals on First Nation reserves and members of the military). The participants' patterns of alcohol use was followed from 1994/1995 to 2008/2009—a period of 14 years. These researchers found that lifetime abstainers, former drinkers, and infrequent drinkers were more likely to be placed in LTC than those participants who drank in moderation. We are starting to think that a glass of wine a day is a good thing!

SUBSTANCE USE OTHER THAN ALCOHOL

The Canadian Drug Use Monitoring Survey is an annual general population survey of substance use among Canadians 15 years of age and older. According to the 2012 survey, past-year cannabis use was approximately 10 percent among those surveyed (Health Canada, 2012b). However, with the upcoming legalization of cannabis, this number may change. Other than cannabis, the use of drugs such as cocaine, ecstasy, or heroin was reported by only two percent of those surveyed. Canadian data on older adults were not available. However, there are data from the United States that suggest that illicit drug use among the current cohort of older adults is quite low in the United States (Wang & Andrade, 2013; Blow & Barry, 2014). For example, national surveys conducted in the United States found that fewer than two percent of those aged 50 years and older used illicit drugs (Blow & Barry, 2012; Colliver, Compton, Gfroerer, & Condon, 2006). However, as the baby boomers age, this number likely will be significantly higher because they grew up when illicit drug use was more socially acceptable.

PRESCRIPTION DRUG MISUSE

There is a growing concern about the misuse of prescription medication among older adults (Blow & Barry, 2014). For example, Schonfield and his colleagues (2010) surveyed 3497 older adults in three social services agencies in the United States and found that medication misuse occurs in 18 to 41 percent of the older clients served in those agencies. This is significant because older adults use more prescription medicine than any other age group. As a result, there is a higher chance of adverse effects from medication interactions in older adults. According to the Canadian Centre for Addiction and Mental Health (2006), almost 20 percent of hospitalizations in individuals over the age of 50 are due to misuse of medications.

TREATMENT OF SUBSTANCE USE DISORDERS

Older adults who drink to excess often go into treatment emotionally exhausted, physically run-down, and socially depleted. Older adults seem to do better in treatment programs that involve age-appropriate care with healthcare professionals who are knowledgeable about aging issues. In addition, older adults will remain in treatment longer if the treatment is age-specific and offered at a slower pace (Farkas, 2006). Providing age-appropriate information about the issues older adults are likely to be facing, as well as the medical aspects of addictions and aging, is very helpful. **Motivational interviewing**, 12-step programs such as Alcoholics Anonymous, and CBT can be useful techniques but more so if they are age-specific (Blow & Barry, 2012). Motivational interviewing is thought to be well suited for those older adults who abuse alcohol but who do not meet the criteria for an alcohol-abuse problem (Satre & Leibowitz, 2015).

6.5 OTHER MENTAL HEALTH ISSUES
LEARNING OBJECTIVES

To understand:
- common conditions associated with psychotic disorders in older adults
- risk factors associated with developing a psychosis in older adulthood
- hoarding behaviours in older adults
- the characteristics of hoarders
- hoarding disorder in older adults

PRIMARY AND SECONDARY PSYCHOTIC DISORDERS

According to the *DSM-5* (APA, 2013), psychotic disorders include abnormalities in at least one of the following five domains: delusions, hallucinations, disorganized thinking (speech), grossly disorganized or abnormal motor behaviour (including catatonia), and negative symptoms. Psychosis can be caused by a psychiatric illness (primary psychosis) or a medical or neurologic condition (secondary psychosis). As a rule of thumb, physicians rule out any secondary causes of psychosis before considering the source of the symptoms to be primary. About 60 percent of psychotic disorders in older adults are due to a medical or neurological condition (Reinhardt & Cohen, 2015). The conditions commonly associated with psychosis in older adults are presented in Table 6.1. As you can see, dementia and depression account for the majority of psychoses in older adults. In fact, psychotic features occur in 20 to 45 percent of older adults hospitalized for depression (Reinhardt & Cohen, 2015). In addition, delusions are a common psychotic symptom in late-life depression. These delusions often are very paranoid in nature (Dr. K. Lawless, personal communication, December 5, 2015). Delusions also are very common in Alzheimer's disease.

> **REFLECTIVE QUESTION**
>
> Given the significant memory impairment in Alzheimer's disease, what do you think a common delusion would be?

TABLE 6.1

THE SIX D'S OF PSYCHOTIC DISORDERS			
DISORDER	**COURSE**	**PROPORTION OF ALL CAUSES OF PSYCHOSES**	**TYPE OF PSYCHOSES**
Delirium	Days to weeks	10%	Secondary
Drugs, alcohol, toxins	Days to months	11%	Secondary
Disease	Days to months	10%	Secondary
Depression and other affective disorders	Weeks to months	33% (Depression) 5% (Bipolar)	Primary
Dementia	Months to years	40%	Primary
Delusional disorder and schizophrenia-spectrum disorders	Months to decades	2% (Delusions) 1% (Schizophrenia)	Primary

Source: Reinhardt, M.M., & Cohen, C.I. (2015). Late-life psychosis: Diagnosis and treatment. *Current Psychiatry Reports*, *17*(1), 1–13. doi:10.1007/s11920-014-0542-0. Current psychiatry reports by CURRENT SCIENCE INC. Reproduced with permission of CURRENT SCIENCE INC. in the format Book via Copyright Clearance Center.

Have you had a chance to reflect on this question? A very common delusion in individuals who have Alzheimer's disease is that others are stealing from them. If you can't find an item because you can't remember where you put it, you might think someone stole the item from you too! The difference is, of course, that you will eventually find the misplaced item. This is not necessarily the case when a person has memory deficits. In addition, delusions of infidelity are not uncommon in individuals who have Alzheimer's disease.

Another delusional disorder that has been observed in patients with Alzheimer's disease and other dementias is called Capgras Syndrome. This syndrome is a delusion in which the patient believes that a family member such as a spouse, sibling, or child has been replaced by an impostor. The remarkable feature of a Capgras delusion is that patients are able to recognize the related person's face but believe that their relative has been replaced by look-alike imposters (Thiel, Studte, Hildebrandt, Huster, & Weerda, 2014). The cause of this syndrome is not well understood but there is recent research that suggests that it is the result of lesions in the right middle frontal gyrus (Thiel et al., 2014). Visual hallucinations are the most common type of hallucination in Alzheimer's disease and they typically involve intruders in the home, and the presence of animals and deceased relatives (Ropacki & Jeste, 2005).

There is a host of risk factors associated with aging that may increase the probability of an older adult becoming psychotic. In a systematic review of studies in this area, Canadian researchers identified poor health status, cognitive problems, visual impairment, and negative life events as risk factors for psychosis (Brunelle, Cole, & Elie, 2011). Polypharmacy also may cause psychotic symptoms in older adults.

SCHIZOPHRENIA IN OLDER ADULTS

As you already may know, schizophrenia is a type of psychotic disorder. An important change in the *DSM-5* with regard to this disorder is the removal of the subtypes of schizophrenia (e.g., disorganized, paranoid) because of poor validity (APA, 2013). One way to think about schizophrenia is in terms of positive and negative symptoms. To make it easier to remember what positive and negative symptoms are, we think about positive symptoms as something that is added to the person. For example, the psychotic symptoms of hallucinations and delusions are not there when the person is well. Negative symptoms can be thought of as something that is taken away from the individual. Negative symptoms include a reduction in the amount of thinking (poverty of thought), and reductions in motivation and the ability to show emotion (affective flattening). It is the negative symptoms that are the hardest to treat in schizophrenia. Of interest, the age of onset of schizophrenia is not a diagnostic criterion in either the *DSM-5* or the *ICD-10* (Iglewicz, Meeks, & Jeste, 2011). This, in turn, affects research in the area because there is a lack of a consistent age cut-off for diagnosing schizophrenia that occurs in late life for the first time (Iglewicz et al., 2011).

The prevalence of late-onset schizophrenia (LOS) is generally believed to be relatively uncommon (Howard & Jeste, 2011). It has commonly been thought that with age, the symptoms of schizophrenia become worse. Unfortunately, this appears to be true for those who are chronically institutionalized (Harvey, 2005). However, Harding (2003) summarized 10 longitudinal studies with a combined sample size of 2439 community-dwelling individuals with schizophrenia who were followed on average over 28 years. He found considerable improvement in their schizophrenia with age, especially regarding a reduction of positive symptoms. Cohen, Pathak, Ramirez, and Vahia (2009) found that there is a wide range of favourable outcomes for individuals who have schizophrenia, but it depends on the conceptual model that is being used. For example, in looking at symptoms alone, roughly 49 percent of Cohen and colleagues' sample of older adults attained symptom reduction. However, in looking at measures of successful aging and integration into the community, older individuals with schizophrenia had poorer outcomes.

An interesting study on older individuals with schizophrenia was conducted by Shepherd and her colleagues (2012). They wanted to know how community-dwelling individuals with schizophrenia would describe the course of their illness over the years. They interviewed 32 adults over the age of 50 who had a mean duration of schizophrenia of 35 years. All but one of the 32 participants they interviewed felt that their symptoms of schizophrenia (especially the positive symptoms) were more severe at the start of their illness. As you can see from Figure 6.6, symptom improvement was seen in the middle course of the illness. The participants attributed this improvement to active development of self-management skills and strategies to deal with hallucinations and delusions. As you can see, however, participants differed in their outlook on the future. Participant responses could be divided into three categories: those who were optimistic and empowered by the improvements they experienced so far, those that experienced dismay over the discrepancy between their current situation and life goals, and those who were resigned to accept their current level of independence and functioning. Future research using a larger sample with groups stratified by age would help to clarify the perspectives about the experience of schizophrenia across the lifespan.

TREATMENT OF PSYCHOSIS

Atypical **antipsychotic medications**, such as risperidone or olanzapine, are typically used to treat psychosis, including schizophrenia, in older adults. However, these types of medications are associated with adverse metabolic effects such as weight gain, an increase in cholesterol, and the onset of diabetes. As such, close monitoring of an older adult taking antipsychotic medications is needed (Iglewicz et al., 2011). The aim of antipsychotic medication is to reduce symptom burden but this doesn't always improve functioning. Older adults can benefit as well as younger adults from psychosocial skills training such as functional adaptive skills training, which aims to improve everyday life skills (Patterson et al., 2006). In addition, CBT, in combination with social skills training (CBSST), has been shown to lead to better skill acquisition and

FIGURE 6.6

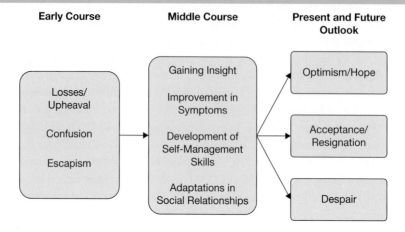

Source: Republished with permission of Oxford University Press, from S. Shepherd et al. (2012). Perspectives on schizophrenia over the lifespan: A qualitative study. *Schizophrenia Bulletin, 38*(2), 295–303; permission conveyed through Copyright Clearance Center, Inc.

self-reported improved functioning in older adults with the benefits continuing at 12-month follow-up (Granholm et al., 2007).

HOARDING DISORDER

Originally, hoarding behavior was thought to be part of **obsessive-compulsive disorder** (OCD), and it wasn't until the latest edition of the *DSM* (APA, 2013) that hoarding was recognized as its own disorder (APA, 2013). The *DSM-5* defines hoarding disorder (HD) as persistent difficulty in discarding or parting with possessions, regardless of their actual value. This difficulty is due to a perceived need to save the items and the intense distress associated with discarding items. The clutter associated with hoarding is to the degree that you are unable to use the space for what it was intended. This is clearly illustrated in Figure 6.7. You definitely could not use this kitchen!

The excessive acquiring of goods is not an inclusionary criterion for a diagnosis of HD, but a diagnosis of HD must specify whether or not excessive acquiring is a feature. Although this can happen by stealing items, in the majority of cases, the accumulation occurs because of excessive buying or picking up items for free (Frost & Muller, 2014). Although there are cases of hoarding in which excessive acquiring is not a feature (Mataix-Cols et al., 2010), Frost and colleagues (2009) found that this characteristic was evident in nearly 60 percent of the hoarding cases they reviewed. Interestingly, and maybe not surprisingly, people have hoarded since prehistoric times. According to Penzel (2014), the Collyer brothers were important for bringing hoarding behaviour into the public eye (see Box 6.1 for their story).

Despite this increased awareness of hoarding, it wasn't until 1993 that Frost and Gross published the first paper on hoarding followed by the groundbreaking paper published by Frost and Hartl in 1996, which outlined a cognitive behavioural model of hoarding. As we are sure you are aware, the media has brought a lot of attention to HD. For example, A&E produced *Hoarders* in 2009, which was the first reality show about people who hoard. This was followed by TLC's show called *Hoarding: Buried Alive*. These shows sensationalize severe hoarding behaviour, and it is not

FIGURE 6.7

As you can see, plenty of clutter. The space is no longer functional.

© John Gibbins/San Diego Union-Tribune via ZUMA Wire/Alamy Stock Photo

BOX 6.1

THE COLLYER BROTHERS: THE STORY OF HARLEM'S HOARDING HERMITS

In the early 1930s, Homer and Langley Collyer lived together in New York City. They came from a wealthy family and were well educated. After their parents died, they continued to live in the family home. Over the years, they began to live in isolation and, eventually, they lived without gas, telephone service, and running water. One day, Homer, the oldest brother, suffered a stroke and became bedridden. As Langley was caring for his older brother, he began to collect all sorts of items such as cardboard boxes, newspapers, metal cans, tree branches, and almost any other item he could find. The neighbours thought the pair to be quite odd and reclusive and they began to wonder what was going on inside the brothers' home. Kids began to throw rocks at the windows and Langley, scared someone would break in, boarded up many of the windows. He also began to booby trap the entrances to the trails that ran through the debris in the house. Although the police had been to the home on several occasions because of complaints from neighbours about its rundown condition, they never actually got inside the house. This all changed in the spring of 1947. A terrible smell was coming from the house which resulted in an anonymous phone call to police suggesting that there

MENTAL HEALTH AND MENTAL HEALTH DISORDERS **195**

must be a dead body inside the house. Finally, the police were able to enter the house but not through the front door. As you can see from Figure 6.8, the house was so full of debris that the police could only enter through the top windows.

When they finally entered, the police found the body of Homer right away but they could not find Langley. His body was found a month later crushed to death under a mountain of debris. Apparently, Homer starved to death after his brother was killed by falling debris. As you can see, the amount of clutter in the home was incredible. Among the 120 tons of debris, the police found a boat, 14 grand pianos, and over 3000 books. The story became a major media event and hundreds of people showed up daily to watch in amazement as the junk was brought out of the house. The name Collyer became a symbol of "uncontrolled and pathological collecting" (Penzel, 2014, p. 14).

FIGURE 6.8

THE COLLYER BROTHERS' HOME WHEN POLICE FINALLY WERE ABLE TO ENTER

New York Daily News/Contributor/Getty Images

New York Daily News/Contributor/Getty Images

New York Daily News/Contributor/Getty Images

unusual to find people talking about what happened on the last episode. Unfortunately, these programs do not address the underlying psychological problems that contribute to hoarding. Ninety percent of the hoarders who are forced to clean up their homes (as depicted in the shows) fill their homes again within a year (Dr. Peggy Richter, as cited in *The Globe and Mail*, 2012; retrieved from www.theglobeandmail.com/life/health-and-fitness/advsunnybrook/sunnybrookfeatures/inside-the-hoarders-mind/article4098750/; C. Dirksen, personal communication, November 16, 2015). It is important to note that hoarding symptoms range from mild to the more severe cases, which are the ones that are most commonly shown on TV.

PREVALENCE RATES OF HOARDING DISORDERS

Prevalence rates for hoarding have been difficult to determine for several reasons. First, there have been a multitude of sample and measurement problems due to the absence of a consistent definition of the illness (Steketee & Frost, 2014). In fact, Ayers, Namji, Mayes, and Dozier (2015) suggest that prevalence rates should be interpreted cautiously because the *DSM-5* (APA, 2013) criteria are relatively new and studies prior to 2013 would not have used the new formalized criteria. Another difficulty is that **insight** appears to be impaired in most hoarders and, as a result, few seek treatment. However, it is unclear if it is actually insight that is impaired or if the disease is due to overvalued ideas about the importance of possessions (Tolin, Frost, Steketee, & Fitch, 2008). Estimates of HD, using the most recent research, would indicate that the prevalence rate of HD in the general population ranges from 2.3 percent (Iervolino et al., 2009) to 5.8 percent (Samuels et al., 2008; Timpano, Keough, Traeger, & Schmidt, 2011). In Canada, prevalence data are not available but the rate is estimated to be about the same as reported above. However, it appears that where you are collecting the data may influence prevalence rates. For example, a study that investigated the prevalence of HD in a New York not-for-profit service that provides support to individuals who were facing eviction found the prevalence rate of HD to be 22 percent, a rate that is considerably higher than the rate found in the general population (Rodriguez et al., 2012). This finding suggested to Rodriguez and colleagues that not-for-profit agencies would be well suited to identify individuals with HD. This is because individuals with HD usually only come to the attention of mental health agencies via non-mental health agencies (e.g., fire, police, bylaw enforcement), which refer after an emergency such as pest infestation or fire.

CHARACTERISTICS OF HOARDERS

Adults who hoard tend to be unmarried, to live alone, and, often, to have lower incomes. Other important features are a strong affection for objects, emotional sensitivity, and perfectionism (Steketee & Frost, 2014). In addition, problems in executive functioning such as difficulty organizing, categorizing, and making decisions play a role in hoarding behaviour (Ayers et al., 2015). Historically, hoarding symptoms have been linked to OCD but, in actuality, co-morbid OCD affects only a minority of individuals. MDD is the most commonly occurring co-morbidity in people who hoard and is present in at least 50 percent of cases (Deifenbach, Di Mauro, Frost, Steketee, & Tolin, 2013; Otte & Steketee, 2011). Other common co-morbid disorders associated with HD are anxiety disorders, impulse control disorders, and attention deficit/hyperactivity disorder (Wheaton & Van Meter, 2014).

Although identification of and treatment for HD does not typically start until the individual is in his or her 50s, HD is a chronic condition that usually begins in childhood or adolescence.

According to Tolin and her colleagues (2010), hoarding behaviours in childhood or adolescence often are described as mild. The prominence of severe symptoms tends not to occur until after age 40. These researchers suggest that severe hoarding symptoms (especially clutter in the home) take several years to develop because the presence of others in the home (e.g., parents, spouse) limits the acquisition of items, assists with discarding items, and forces removal of the clutter.

One factor that may affect the onset of HD is traumatic or stressful life events. Hartl, Duffany, Allen, Steketee, and Frost (2005) found that the hoarders reported greater frequencies of trauma including having something taken from them by force. Tolin and her colleagues (2010) found that the majority of the hoarders experienced a loss or change in relationships, interpersonal violence, or loss or damage to their possessions earlier in their lifetime. The research on prevalence of HD is mixed regarding gender differences (Timpano et al., 2011; Tolin et al., 2010), but in clinical studies of hoarding cases, women predominate. This pattern suggested to Steketee and Frost (2014) that women are more likely than men to volunteer for research studies or seek treatment. Or, it could be the case that women are more likely to have experienced triggers for HD such as changes in a relationship, interpersonal violence, or loss or damage to possessions.

HOARDING DISORDER IN OLDER ADULTS

In terms of prevalence rates, Samuels and his colleagues (2008) found that hoarding symptoms were three times more prevalent among older adults in their study when compared to younger adults, but other studies have not found an increase in hoarding symptoms with age (Fullana et al., 2010, Timpano et al., 2011). Ayers and her colleagues (2015) suggest that one reason for this discrepancy is that older adults may normalize their hoarding symptoms as they age, which would make hoarding hard to detect using the self-report measures typically used to compare hoarding symptoms across the lifespan. Although the number of individuals with HD may not increase with age, studies indicate that the severity of hoarding does increase with age (Ayers, Saxena, Golshan, & Wetherell, 2010). The reasons for this are not clear. As such, longitudinal data are needed to clarify the course of hoarding across the lifespan.

Social isolation is common among older adults with HD and, although the evidence is anecdotal, friends and family members often cut off contact with their loved one who has HD because of frustration and ongoing conflict about the amount of clutter (Ayers et al., 2015). This isolation can have deadly consequences. Remember what happened to the Collyers? Their situation is not unusual and other older adults who have HD have been found dead weeks after being trapped by falling debris (Brakoulias & Milicevic, 2015). In addition to safety issues, HD in older adults can have serious functional consequences. Ayers, Scheisher, Liu, and Wetherell (2012) found that older adults with HD had moderate to severe difficulty finding important documents, moving around the house, eating at a table, using the washroom, using the kitchen sink or stove, and sleeping in a bed. Rodent infestation and food contamination are common as is an increased risk for fire. In fact, if you search the Internet using the term "hoarders and fires" you will no doubt be amazed at the challenges that occur trying to fight a fire in the home of an individual with HD! Because HD is accompanied by safety and health challenges, it makes it very difficult for older adults to age in place, and many may face eviction by either landlords or environmental health agencies. In fact, Canadian researchers found that premature moving or eviction occurs for many older adults who hoard (Whitfield, Daniels, Flesaker, & Simmons, 2012). With the development of formal diagnostic criteria, new information about this disorder will no doubt increase over the next few years.

ANIMAL HOARDING

One can't have a discussion of hoarding behavior without including animal hoarding. The *DSM-5* (APA, 2013) did not include animal hoarding as an official subtype because its diagnostic classification remains unclear due to limited research evidence (Mataix-Cols, 2014). However, animal hoarding is described in the *DSM-5* as a condition associated with HD. Animal hoarding is the collection of a large number of animals accompanied by a failure to provide minimum standards of care (e.g., nutrition, veterinary care) and a failure to act on the declining health of the animals. Severe overcrowding and extremely unsanitary conditions are key features of animal hoarding (APA, 2013). Animal control agencies and humane shelters in the United States estimate that there are approximately 3000 reportable cases of animal hoarding annually (Patronek, 2006). Interestingly, cats seem to be the most commonly hoarded animal (Frost, Patronek, Arluke, & Steketee, 2015). The Hoarding of Animals Research Consortium has identified three types of animal hoarders although more research is needed to confirm these classifications (Frost et al., 2015). These three types are presented in Table 6.2. Of the three types identified, exploiters present the most serious cases of animal hoarding.

The Canadian Veterinary Medical Association (2017) recommends the following website which has information about recognizing animal hoarders and tips to intervene: https://www.canadianveterinarians.net/policy-advocacy/recognizing-abuse-hoarding.

TABLE 6.2

TYPES OF ANIMAL HOARDERS

TYPES	DESCRIPTION
Overwhelmed Caregivers	Individuals who were reasonably caring for a large number of animals until a change in circumstances impaired their ability to care for the animals (e.g., loss of resources such as a job or a spouse). Attempts are made to provide adequate care but, eventually, these individuals become overwhelmed and their living conditions deteriorate. The collection of new animals tends to be passive with new animals coming from breeding of existing animals. Overwhelmed caregivers usually have an awareness of their problems with animal care and are more likely to comply with interventions than rescuers or exploiters.
Rescuers	Individuals who have a strong sense of mission characterize rescuers. These individuals strongly oppose euthanasia and demonstrate strong fears about the death of their own animals but fail to recognize the poor quality of care they are providing. The method of acquiring animals is much more active and often involves searches for animals they perceive to be in need of care. Mission-driven animal hoarders often go to great lengths to avoid authorities and it is not unusual to find these types of hoarders pretending to be from legitimate shelters.
Exploiters	Exploiters often are individuals who have sociopathic characteristics and acquire animals to serve their own needs. Lacking in empathy, exploiters have little to no attachment to their animals. They have no insight into their behaviour.

Source: Adapted from Frost, R.O., Patronek, G., Arluke, A., & Steketee, G. (2015). The hoarding of animals: An update. *Psychiatric Times, 32*(4). Retrieved from www.psychiatrictimes.com/addiction/hoarding-animals-update.

TREATMENT OF HOARDING DISORDER

To date, there are very few research studies that have looked at hoarding treatment for older adults. One study investigated multi-component CBT for hoarding based on a model proposed and manualized for treatment (Steketee & Frost, 2007). Treatment included education and case formulation, motivational interviewing, skills training for organizing and problem solving, direct exposure to non-acquiring and discarding, and cognitive therapy. After 26 multi-component CBT sessions, 71 percent of patients were considered to be improved by therapist ratings and 81 percent of patients rated themselves improved. Steketee and her colleague (2007) noted that, while the multicomponent CBT was effective in treating hoarding behaviour, treatment refusal and compliance remained a concern. Ayers and colleagues (2011) also used the same multi-component CBT protocol developed by Steketee and Frost (2007) in a smaller sample of 12 hoarders over the age of 65. While Ayers and her colleagues (2011) found statistically significant changes in hoarding severity, only three of the twelve participants were classified as treatment responders at post-treatment, and their gains were not maintained at six-month follow-up. There were no changes in measures of anxiety, disability, and clutter ratings at post-treatment and follow-up. While no participants dropped out, homework compliance was variable, but when homework was completed, it correlated with decreases in hoarding severity.

Although there are not many studies investigating the treatment outcomes for HD, the recognition that this disorder is disabling is evidenced by the growth of programs and services available to individuals with HD in Canada and the United States. For example, the Canadian Mental Health Association offers weekly drop-in support groups, pre-registered psychoeducational groups, and a monthly support group for family and friends of people with HD in several major cities in Canada. Now that HD has its own diagnostic criteria, future research will certainly help to shed more light on this interesting but debilitating disorder.

In terms of treatment for animal hoarders, to date, there is an absence of validated therapies (Frost et al., 2015). With recidivism rates as high as 100 percent in some studies, this is of great concern (Frost et al., 2015). According to researchers, successful interventions must include not only the welfare of the animals but also the animal hoarder's unmet physical and mental healthcare needs, the inhabitable conditions of the animal hoarder's home, as well as the legal and financial consequences of these cases (Nathanson, 2009; Patronek, 2006).

6.6 POSITIVE PSYCHOLOGY
LEARNING OBJECTIVES

To understand:
- what positive psychology is
- the research available that uses positive psychology interventions with older adults

WHAT IS POSITIVE PSYCHOLOGY?

Martin Seligman and Mihaly Csikszentmihalya coined the term "positive psychology" in the year 2000. These two psychologists argued that psychology had become too focused on pathology and disease. Reviewing positive psychology in clinical practice, Duckworth, Steen, and Seligman (2005) state that positive psychology is the scientific study of strengths, wellbeing and functioning ... the aim is to broaden the focus of clinical psychology beyond suffering and its direct alleviation ... viewing the most distressed persons as more than a sum of damaged habits or childhood conflicts ... positive psychology asks for more consideration of the individual's positive life experience, strength of character, and how these buffer against various mental illnesses. (p. 631)

The positive psychology movement de-emphasizes diagnostic labels such as defensiveness and neuroticism to describe how individuals do or do not cope with stressful situations. Rather, positive psychology scientifically explores affirmative person-centred approaches to address the difficulties that people are challenged by and encourages people to use their personal strengths to deal with these difficulties (Hill & Smith, 2015) (see Figure 6.9). Researchers have found that positive psychology interventions are effective for improving outcomes such as life satisfaction, psychological well-being, resilience, and hope. Interventions based on positive psychology also have been shown to decrease depressive symptoms and pessimism (Carson, Muir, Clark, Wakely, & Chander, 2010; Pietrowsky & Mikutta, 2012).

FIGURE 6.9

FOCUSING ON OLDER ADULTS' STRENGTHS ARE A PART OF POSITIVE PSYCHOLOGY

Rawpixel.com/Shutterstock.com

RESEARCH ON POSITIVE PSYCHOLOGY INTERVENTIONS WITH OLDER ADULTS

Despite the growth of research on positive psychology interventions, there is little research that has addressed the effectiveness of these types of interventions with older adults. Meaning-centred interventions such as forgiveness, gratitude, and altruism may be well suited to address age-related decline and age-associated loss (Hill & Smith, 2015). For example, Allemand, Steiner, and Hill (2013) randomized 78 older adults (mean age of 70 years) to an immediate treatment group (forgiveness intervention) or a waiting-list control condition. At pre-test, participants in both conditions were instructed to recall a serious interpersonal transgression that was still unresolved and to briefly describe it. Participants also were asked to answer questions related to the type of relationship between themselves and the transgressor as well as how emotionally painful the perceived transgression was and how long ago the transgression occurred. These researchers found that the forgiveness intervention reduced the level of perceived emotional pain and cognitions associated with the transgression. It is interesting that nearly half of the sample (47 percent) indicated that the serious transgression occurred 10 to 20 years ago. Allemand and colleagues suggest that their findings show promise for using forgiveness interventions for older adults to help clarify and deal with past or present interpersonal transgressions.

Another study that used a positive psychology intervention was conducted in Hong Kong and the results also look very promising. Participants consisted of mostly females between the ages of 65 and 105 years of age. None of the participants met the criteria for depression, but the number of depressive symptoms endorsed by each participant was recorded. The participants were divided into smaller groups of eight or nine people and each group met weekly for one and a half hours for a period of nine weeks. Each weekly session focused on a theme in positive psychology such as optimism, gratitude, courage, and meaning of life. A pre–post design was used. Ho and his colleagues (2014) found that this intervention reduced the number of depressive symptoms endorsed at baseline and increased the levels of life satisfaction, gratitude, and happiness following the intervention.

6.7 UNDERUTILIZATION OF MENTAL HEALTH SERVICES BY OLDER ADULTS

LEARNING OBJECTIVES

To understand:
- that older adults underuse mental health services
- some of the barriers associated with accessing mental health services

There is a good deal of evidence to suggest that worldwide, older adults underutilize mental health services when compared to younger adults (Cairney, Corna, & Streiner, 2010; Chaplin, Farquharson, Clapp, & Crawford, 2015; Gum, Hirsch, Dautovich, Ferrante, & Schonfeld, 2014; Sareen, Cox, Afifi, Yu, & Stein, 2005; Scott, Mackenzie, Chipperfield, & Sareen, 2010; Wang et al., 2005). Using data from the Canadian Community Health Survey: Mental Health and Well Being (Gravel & Béland, 2005), Cairney and colleagues (2010) found that more than 60 percent of the older adults surveyed and who met the diagnostic criteria for one of the five psychiatric disorders measured did not seek help for their mental health problems.

Another Canadian study compared patterns of mental health service utilization among those 45–64, 65–74, and aged 75 and older (total n = 59 302) (Crabb & Hunsley, 2006). These researchers found that help seeking for mental health issues decreased with age. For example, 8.5 percent of those 45–64 years sought treatment for a mental health problem in the last year compared to only 3.9 percent of 65- to 74-year-olds and only 2.8 percent of older adults over age 75. Adults aged 65 years and older were most likely to seek out their family physician for help. Age remained a significant predictor of mental health service utilization even after accounting for other relevant variables such as gender, marital status, years of education, and number of chronic medical conditions. These numbers are concerning. Consistent with research discussed earlier in the chapter, both groups of researchers found that the majority of older adults who sought treatment for mental health issues went to their family physician, not a psychologist or other healthcare professional. This underscores the need to integrate mental health services into primary or integrative care networks. In general, the strength of primary or integrated healthcare services is that this model emphasizes inter-professional collaboration and communication in all aspects of patient care. In fact, it appears that the best way to treat mental health issues in older adults is to take into account the individual's physical needs, as well as cognitive and functional status, when planning treatment interventions (MacCourt, Wilson, & Tourigny-Rivard, 2011).

REFLECTIVE QUESTION

Can you think of barriers that would prevent older adults from seeking mental health services?

BARRIERS TO TREATMENT FOR MENTAL HEALTH ISSUES

But what could be preventing older adults from seeking help for mental health issues? Stigma could be a factor, and studies have shown that it can significantly interfere with help seeking in younger populations. However, studies have found that older adults were no more likely to report stigma as a barrier to seeking treatment than other age groups (Cook & Wang, 2010; Pepin, Segal, and Coolidge, 2009). Pepin and colleagues (2009) found that the belief that it would be difficult to find a qualified psychotherapist was the highest-ranked barrier to seeking treatment. Unfortunately, this perception is true given the shortage of clinicians with specialized training in this area. These researchers also highlight that, while there are common barriers to treatment regardless of age such as cost of and access to services, transportation difficulties are a significant barrier to treatment, especially for 75- to 90-year-olds.

Cohort effects may be another factor affecting treatment for mental health issues. The current cohort of older adults has lived through wars and the Great Depression. The mantra often heard at the start of my sessions with older adults is that "you don't cry over spilled milk" or "when you fall off the horse, you get back on." For some older adults, feelings aren't seen as useful or relevant. This is somewhat similar to the research findings. Studies from both Canada (Scott et al., 2010) and Australia (Wuthrich & Frei, 2015) found that one of the major barriers to seeking treatment in the older adult population is that older adults did not perceive their symptoms as being significant enough to warrant treatment. For example, approximately 50 percent of older adults who had co-morbid anxiety and depression in the Australian study did not seek help because they thought their symptoms were normal given their current circumstances. A further 30 percent of the older adults reported that they had not sought help because they too thought their symptoms were normal given their age or health conditions or because they had felt this way all their lives! Other research also has shown that older adults, especially those over 75 years of age, believed that depression is a part of normal aging (Pepin et al., 2009). However, Canadian researchers, in a replication study done using data from the National Comorbidity Survey in the United States, found very different results. Mackenzie and colleagues (2008) found that compared to younger adults, those adults between the ages of 55 and 74 years were two to three more times likely to report *positive* attitudes toward getting help for mental health issues. Clearly, more research is needed but, in the meantime, what might be helpful is educating older adults about the symptoms of mental illnesses such as depression and anxiety. It also might be helpful to stress the fact that feeling this way is not part of the normal aging process and that it is important to seek help.

6.8 TRAINING PROGRAMS AND TREATMENT GUIDELINES FOR WORKING WITH MENTALLY ILL OLDER ADULTS

LEARNING OBJECTIVE

- To understand that training psychologists and other healthcare professionals to work with older adults is finally gaining some ground

We think by now that you have figured out that we are not very well prepared for the growing number of older adults who will need mental health services. There is a shortage of research and also a shortage of mental health professionals who are trained to work with older adults. This is not just in psychology but also across many other disciplines. In fact, one of the greatest challenges appears to be getting people interested in the field. We are hoping that this book will inspire many of you to work with older adults. As you will find when you read the profiles of mental health professionals in Canada who work with older adults, it is both a challenging and rewarding career.

REFLECTIVE QUESTION

Can you think of what might be personally rewarding in working with older adults?

Unfortunately, opportunities in geriatric training in many healthcare disciplines often are not well integrated into general training programs. This has resulted in a lack of even the basic skills required to work with older adults (Karel, Gatz, & Smyer, 2012). However, we seem to be moving in the right direction. In 2006, the Canadian Coalition for Seniors' Mental Health (CCSMH) established comprehensive treatment and assessment guidelines for depression, suicide, and delirium (Conn et al., 2006). In 2014, the guidelines for the management of the behavioural and mood symptoms that occur in individuals who reside in long-term-care facilities were updated (Conn, Gibson, & McCabe, 2014). The guidelines are research-based and are clearly written so that they can be used by a range of healthcare professionals. These guidelines are available on the CCSMH website. The Mental Health Commission of Canada also has published a more recent document titled *Guidelines for Comprehensive Mental Health Services for Older Adults in Canada* (MacCourt, Wilson, & Tourigny-Rivard, 2011). These authors present a framework for the development of an integrated model for mental health services for older adults. The APA (2014) also has published *Guidelines for Psychological Practice with Older Adults*. There now is a general consensus in the field of psychology regarding the importance of providing training opportunities at all levels of training in geropsychology (Karel, Molinari, Emery-Tiburcio, & Knight, 2015).

In the United States, the first conference on training in professional geropsychology was held in Boulder, Colorado in 2006. The purpose of the conference was to identify the core elements needed in geropsychology training and to provide specific guidelines for training at the graduate, internship, and post-licensure levels. Out of this conference came the Pikes Peak Model of geropsychology. The Pikes Peak competencies in geropsychology are organized into 10 domains of skill, knowledge, and attitude. There are far too many to list, but several of the domain areas are presented in Box 6.2. For an excellent description of the domains and a review of competency-based training in geropsychology, see Karel and his colleagues (2015).

BOX 6.2

THE PIKES PEAK MODEL COMPETENCIES

Attitudes

- Recognize how attitudes and beliefs about aging may influence the assessment of older adults.
- An awareness of the tremendous diversity represented in the older adult population is essential.

Knowledge Base

- Understand methodological issues in conducting or evaluating research on aging as well as the theory and research informing psychological assessment and the limitations of using assessment instruments created for younger adults.
- Recognize the changes that occur with normal aging versus abnormal aging.
- Knowledge of the neuroscience of aging including changes in cognition.

- Understand psychopathology in older adults including the prevalence, etiology, and illness presentation.
- Recognize the influence of illness and pharmacology on the assessment and treatment of late-life mental health problems including an awareness of how these factors may affect treatment outcomes.

Skill Competencies

- Understand how an older adult functions in daily life (e.g., managing finances, driving).
- Develop or carry out psychotherapeutic interventions based on empirical research, theory, and clinical judgment.
- Understand the distinct ethical and legal issues and practice standards that are part of professional psychology practice with older adults (e.g., decision making and functional capacities, advance-care planning and surrogate

decision making, respect for older clients' confidentiality when with families or caregivers, end of life).

Source: Adapted from Karel, M.J, Molinari, V., Emery-Tiburcio, E.E., & Knight, B.G. (2015). Pikes Peak conference and competency based training in professional geropsychology. In P.A. Lichtenberg & B.T. Mast (Eds.), *APA handbook of clinical geropsychology: History and status of the field and perspectives on aging, Vol. 1,* pp 19–43.

6.9 GOOD PRACTICE

Mychelle Blackwood, R.N.
Misericordia Community Hospital, Edmonton, Alberta

WHERE DID YOU TRAIN?

I completed my R.N. training in Sarnia, Ontario, and earned my diploma in nursing from Lambton College and then my B.Sc.N. from Ryerson University in Toronto 10 years later. I also have been granted specialty certification in gerontological nursing from the Canadian Nurses Association.

WHERE DO YOU WORK?

I work in the Geriatric Outpatient Clinic at the Misercordia Hospital in Edmonton, Alberta.

WHAT DO YOU DO?

I am a geriatric assessment nurse. I am part of an interdisciplinary team which does comprehensive geriatric assessments. We assess and address the specific problems an older adult may present with such as cognitive decline, falls/mobility issues, pain, nutrition concerns, bladder and bowel concerns, medication issues, and sensory problems.

WHY DO YOU LIKE WORKING WITH AN OLDER-ADULT POPULATION?

I love working with the older-adult population because I am truly inspired by their resilience as they encounter life's experiences and challenges.

DO YOU HAVE ADVICE FOR STUDENTS WHO WANT TO GET INTO THE FIELD?

If you love this population and are considering focusing your career on geriatrics, you will be richly rewarded and greatly appreciated by our older-adult population for all that you do to enrich their lives.

Terry Cooper, Ph.D.
Geriatric Outpatient Clinic, Hy's Centre, Edmonton, Alberta

WHERE DID YOU TRAIN?

B.A. Psychology, McGill University, Montreal, Quebec
Ph.D. Psychology, Concordia University, Montreal, Quebec

WHERE DO YOU WORK?

I work in an outpatient clinic which is part of the Community Geriatric Psychiatry Program, affiliated with a local psychiatric hospital.

WHAT DO YOU DO?

Currently, I am working as a clinical psychologist providing services in the community to an older-adult population in the greater Edmonton area. As part of a multidisciplinary team, the bulk of my work consists of conducting formal cognitive assessments usually for diagnostic purposes, as well as other psychological interventions if needed.

WHY DO YOU LIKE WORKING WITH AN OLDER-ADULT POPULATION?

An older population shows as much variety in clinical presentation as do younger populations, but they have a lot more years of life experience. This means that you often have more historical information with which you can follow the progression of psychiatric illnesses such as depression and bipolar disorder. You can gain a better understanding of how such illnesses can change people throughout the course of their lives, and how they can affect cognitive functioning (such as memory and concentration) as aging progresses. In working with this population, you also see much more clearly the interaction between physical and psychological well-being. For example, an acute medical condition such as a urinary tract infection can produce symptoms indistinguishable from an acute psychotic episode, and these symptoms usually show a complete remission when treated with antibiotics. Working with older adults does provide this unique life-long perspective of the impact of both physical and psychological factors across the years, which often is not always obvious when working with younger populations.

DO YOU HAVE ADVICE FOR STUDENTS WHO WANT TO GET INTO THE FIELD?

For younger students, if the majority of contact with the elderly population is through a clinical setting (such as an initial summer placement), you will likely come into contact with older adults who have various degrees of cognitive impairment. It will be important to resist making inaccurate generalizations about the population as a whole based on observations within a particular clinic, as this can lead to harmful stereotypes. Ageism still occurs in many forms, and actively working in this field will provide you with a better understanding of what should be the real focus of psychological–medical interventions as well as political agendas. It's important to get this right, as we will all experience being old one day.

Sherry Hayden, Ph.D.
UBC Hospital, Geriatric Psychiatry, Vancouver, British Columbia
Peace Arch Hospital, Vancouver, British Columbia

WHERE DID YOU TRAIN?

I received my B.A. at the University of Alberta followed by an M.Sc. and a Ph.D. at what is now Albizu University in Miami, Florida.

WHERE DO YOU WORK?

I work at the UBC Hospital at the clinic as well as on the geriatric psychiatric units in the Peace Arch Hospital. In addition, I have a private practice working with individuals who have concussions.

WHAT DO YOU DO?

I am a neuropsychologist at the Clinic for Alzheimer's Disease & Related Disorders. I have been here for 24 years. Along with my psychometrist, we assess outpatients with query dementia, particularly complex cases or those with co-morbidities (i.e., psychiatric disorders). In this clinic I treat some patients as well. I also provide sessional consultation work (contract) to a group of in-patient geriatric psychiatry units.

WHY DO YOU LIKE WORKING WITH AN OLDER-ADULT POPULATION?

I had been interested in this field since I was a teenager. My mother worked in a nursing home and took me with her to work many times. This exposed me to the population and I have loved it ever since.

DO YOU HAVE ADVICE FOR STUDENTS WHO WANT TO GET INTO THE FIELD?

Be sure this is what you love and want to do. It takes considerable patience working with this population, and a lack of real love and tolerance for what is seen can be an issue.

6.10 SUMMARY

- A number of older adults experience many of the mental illnesses found in other age groups, but on a much smaller scale.

- Medical co-morbidities and the changes that occur with normal aging can interfere with identifying a mental illness in an older adult. One difficulty is that age-appropriate diagnostic criteria for mental disorders are lacking.

- Compared to younger adults, substance abuse disorders are lower among older adults. However, excessive alcohol use can interfere with medication efficacy and is highly correlated with depression and anxiety disorders as well as many physical illnesses in older adults. Misuse of prescription medication in older adults is a growing concern.

- About 60 percent of psychotic disorders in older adults are due to a medical or neurological condition. Risk factors for developing a psychotic disorder are poor health status, cognitive problems, visual impairment, and negative life events.

- Hoarding disorder (HD) in older adults can have serious functional consequences as well as numerous health and safety issues. HD makes it extremely difficult for older adults to age in place.

- Positive psychology interventions are effective for improving life satisfaction, psychological well-being, resilience, and hope in older adults.

- Although it has been demonstrated that older adults can benefit just as much from psychological therapy as younger adults, older adults underutilize mental health services.

Abstainers
Individuals who drank fewer than two drinks in the previous year.

Activities of Daily Living
Basic self-care tasks such as dressing, brushing teeth, eating, and going to the washroom.

Acute
Requiring serious attention or action.

Age-Standardized
A statistical technique used to allow populations to be compared when the age profiles of the populations are quite different.

Antipsychotic Medication
Used to treat psychotic illness. Antipsychotic medications are generally divided into two categories. First-generation antipsychotics are called typical and second-generation antipsychotics are called atypical. The main difference between the two types is that the first-generation drugs block dopamine and the second-generation drugs block dopamine and also affect serotonin levels.

Coping
The actions people use to decrease stress. These can be positive actions such as running or deep breathing or negative actions such as drinking too much alcohol or spending too much money.

E-Codes
Documentation of cessation of treatment or care by hospital administration that is connected to deliberate self-harm is identified by the presence of an external cause of injury or poisoning code, an E-code, according to the *International Classification of Diseases (ICD-10)* system.

Insight
An understanding of the motivations behind one's thoughts or behaviour.

Instrumental Activities of Daily Living
Daily activities that require higher-order cognitive abilities such as planning.

Mediterranean Diet
A diet found in Mediterranean countries such as Greece that emphasizes fruits, vegetables, nuts, grains, olive oil (as opposed to butter), and grilled or steamed chicken and seafood (as opposed to red meat), plus a glass or two of red wine.

Minimum Data Set
A standardized assessment instrument developed for long-term-care settings that includes demographic information, medical diagnoses, as well as social and emotional functioning.

Motivational Interviewing
A technique in which the interviewer becomes a helper in the change process and expresses acceptance of her/his client.

Obsessive-Compulsive Disorder (OCD)
An anxiety disorder characterized by uncontrollable, unwanted thoughts and repetitive, ritualized behaviours that an individuals with OCD often recognize that their obsessive thoughts and compulsive behaviours are irrational but these thoughts and behaviours are very difficult to resist.

Performance-Based Assessment
Assessing an individual's ability to perform ADLs and IADLs.

Pharmacotherapy
Treatment of disease with medication.

Psychotropic
Medications used in the treatment of mental illness that have an effect on thinking, feeling, and behaviours.

Substance Abuse
The habitual misuse of alcohol or drugs.

Substance Dependence
An adaptive state that develops from repeated misuse of alcohol or drugs, which results in withdrawal upon cessation of drug or alcohol use.

Sub-syndromal Depressive Symptoms
A term that is used when an individual has some depressive symptoms but not enough to meet the criteria for a diagnosis of a major depressive episode.

Alexander Raths/Shutterstock.com

NEUROCOGNITIVE DISORDERS

"We are parents, grandparents, spouses and friends. We have had long and successful careers. When we were diagnosed with dementia, these experiences did not disappear; they are and will always be a part of us."

Mary Beth Wighton, Member, Ontario Dementia Advisory Group. Standing Senate Committee on Social Affairs, Science and Technology. (2016). *Dementia in Canada: A national strategy for dementia-friendly communities.* Retrieved from http://www.alzheimer.ca/~/media/Files/ national/Advocacy/SOCI_6thReport_DementiaInCanada-WEB_e.pdf. Reprinted by permission of the Senate of Canada.

One of the major objectives of this chapter is to dispel some of the myths about dementia and old age. Up until the last few decades, dementia was thought of as a normal part of aging. We want to make it perfectly clear that dementia is not a normal part of aging and not everyone will develop this disease. The baby boomers are healthier than previous generations, and there is evidence that the prevalence rates of dementia might actually be lower in the future (Matthews et al., 2013; Qiu, von Strauss, Bäckman, Winblad, & Fratiglioni, 2013). The good news is that many risk factors for developing dementia are within an individual's control. Often, caring for individuals who have a dementia can be extraordinarily difficult, but, as you will learn, there are several positives to caring for someone with dementia. You may not have considered the relationship between depression and dementia, or driving issues in dementia, or even older adults in prison who have a dementia. We will talk about these important issues in this chapter as well.

7.1 NEUROCOGNITIVE DISORDERS
LEARNING OBJECTIVES

To understand:

- the changes in the *DSM-5* regarding neurocognitive disorders
- the difference between dementia and Alzheimer's disease
- the signs and symptoms of Alzheimer's disease
- the changes in the brain associated with Alzheimer's disease
- the diagnostic challenges associated with Alzheimer's disease
- the causes of Alzheimer's disease
- the risk factors for developing Alzheimer's disease
- vascular and other neurocognitive disorders
- what mild cognitive impairment is

DEFINING DEMENTIA IN THE *DIAGNOSTIC AND STATISTICAL MANUAL OF MENTAL DISORDERS (DSM-5)*

The American Psychiatric Association (APA) has made some significant changes to its classification of dementia in the *DSM-5* (APA, 2013). Let's start with terminology. The term "dementia" has been replaced by the term "neurocognitive disorder." There are two reasons for this change.

First, dementia is not just a disease of old age. It also can occur in young adults as is the case with traumatic brain injury or HIV infection. In addition, neurocognitive disorder has a broader definition in that individuals who have a decline in only one area of cognitive functioning can receive this diagnosis. The old criteria used in the *DSM-IV-TR* required a decline in at least two areas of cognitive functioning such as memory and executive functioning (APA, 2000). However, the term dementia will likely remain in use because this term has been used for decades and is easily understood by everyone. Furthermore, the underlying dementia process that is causing the neurocognitive disorder must be identified. When using the new *DSM-5* diagnostic criteria, a healthcare professional also must determine whether the neurocognitive disorder is mild or major in terms of the degree of symptoms. For example, for a diagnosis of a mild neurocognitive disorder, there must be evidence of modest cognitive decline from a previous level of functioning. While this decline does not significantly interfere with a person's ability to look after themselves, greater effort, compensatory strategies, or accommodation may be required. In other words, the person may need some help with certain daily activities (APA, 2013). For a diagnosis of a major neurocognitive disorder, an individual must show a significant decline from a previous level of functioning, and the individual's cognitive deficits must significantly interfere with their ability to function day to day (APA, 2013).

What is the difference between dementia and Alzheimer's disease?

Another big change is that to meet diagnostic criteria for a dementia in the previous versions of the *DSM*, the individual had to exhibit impaired memory functioning. In the new classification system, memory does not have to be impaired to receive a diagnosis of a neurocognitive disorder. This makes sense if you consider that in a fronto-temporal dementia, the individual may experience language difficulties or symptoms such as apathy or disinhibition long before there is evidence of impaired memory.

It is important to point out that dementia is not a specific disease. Rather, it is an umbrella term that describes a wide range of symptoms. Some dementias are non-progressive and are secondary to underlying physical conditions such as infections, reduced oxygen flow to the brain, or a brain tumour. In addition, the side effects of some medications can be so severe that the individual may behave as if they have a dementia. Untreated depression also may look like a dementia in an older person. Therefore, a thorough assessment is so important when diagnosing a dementia, particularly because non-progressive dementias can be reversed with treatment. The Case Study Box 7.1 highlights the importance of a thorough assessment. Believe it or not, this is a true story!

However, most dementias are progressive and involve the eventual destruction of memory, learning, reasoning, and communicating, as well as the ability to carry out daily activities. When you think about your answer to the reflective question, you would have been correct if you said that Alzheimer's disease is a type of dementia just as Lewy body dementia or fronto-temporal dementia is a type of dementia. In the past, dementia was referred to as "senility" or "senile dementia" and it was widely believed by professionals and laypersons alike that developing dementia was inevitable, and part of the normal aging process. However, as we said previously, dementia is not inevitable nor is it a part of the normal aging process.

BOX 7.1

CASE STUDY: THE BENEFITS OF A THOROUGH ASSESSMENT

Mrs. Smith has a long history of depression and anxiety. Her anxiety has increased over the last two years. Most recently her depression and anxiety have been managed by her family physician. She was seen by psychiatry at the Central Hospital in December of 2015 and admitted. She had been over-medicating herself with prescription opiates and high-dose benzodiazepines. She was weaned off both the opiates and benzodiazepines during her admission, but after she was discharged, her anxiety seemed to have increased. Mrs. Smith was seen again on May 30, 2016, in the emergency room at the North Central Hospital after her son found her in her apartment confused, hyperventilating, anxious, and rocking back and forth on the floor. Her son reported a one-month history of this type of behaviour. In addition, her self-care was very poor and she was malnourished. She was admitted to the North Central Hospital for assessment and treatment. Her working diagnosis at that time was an atypical fronto-temporal dementia. When her behaviours did not improve, the healthcare team decided that she could not manage on her own at home and they were looking for a long-term-care bed. While waiting for a long-term bed to become available, Mrs. Smith developed a few behaviours that were difficult for the staff to manage. She was refusing to eat and she was disruptive and interfering with other patients' care. Arrangements were made to have her transferred to South Central Hospital, which is a geriatric psychiatric hospital. Once admitted, it took some time to understand Mrs. Smith's symptoms and she remained in the psychiatric hospital for almost eight months. Her medications were reviewed and changed a few times over the course of her admission. Slowly, she began to improve. Her confusion cleared and she could handle her self-care independently. She went home to her apartment over the course of several days accompanied by occupational therapy team members who did a functional assessment. The functional assessment revealed that she could manage her finances and pay bills and that she had knowledge of safety rules. She knew how to get around the city by bus. She could cook her own meals and was very familiar with her kitchen appliances. While in the geriatric psychiatric hospital, she also had her cognition assessed by a clinical psychologist. The report from psychology indicated that she did not have a dementia of any kind. In the end, she was diagnosed with a generalized anxiety disorder. So, rather than being placed in long-term care, she returned to independent living with community support and regular medical follow-up.

According to Prince, Comas-Herrera, Knapp, Guerchet, and Karagiannidou (2016), 46.8 million people were living with a dementia in 2015. Because of our aging population, this number is expected to rise to approximately 75 million people worldwide by 2030. Not that long in the future when you think about it. Also it is estimated that 68 percent of all people living with dementia will live in low- and middle-income countries, which is concerning because healthcare resources are very scarce in these countries (Prince et al., 2016).

According to the Alzheimer Society of Canada, as of 2016, there are an estimated 564 000 Canadians living with dementia. Each year, there are approximately 25 000 new cases diagnosed. By 2031, that number is expected to rise to 937 000 (Alzheimer Society of Canada, 2016a). Dementia is a devastating illness not only for the people who have this disease but also for their caregivers and families. Unfortunately, in most countries, there is a lack of awareness and understanding of dementia resulting in stigmatization and barriers to diagnosis and care (World Health Organization [WHO, 2012]). In an effort to reduce this stigma, the Canadian government, in collaboration with the Alzheimer Society of Canada, launched *Dementia Friends Canada* in 2015. This is a digitally based awareness program aimed at not only providing Canadians with information about dementia but also informing how each of us can be supportive of those affected by this disease (Standing Senate Committee on Social Affairs, Science and Technology, 2016). To become a dementia friend, go to https://www.dementiafriends.ca/.

Dementia also is a very expensive disease. According to the Alzheimer Society of Canada (2016b), the combined healthcare system costs and out-of-pocket caregiver costs amounted to approximately $10.4 billion in 2016.

Because of the aging population, there has been a tremendous interest and growth in dementia research in the last decade. In 2014, Canada's Minister of Health announced the launch of the *National Dementia Research and Prevention Plan* (NDRPP) in response to the goal set at the G8 Dementia Summit in 2013. The goal set at the summit was to find a cure for dementia or a disease-modifying treatment by 2025. The research component of the NDRPP is the Canadian Institute of Health Research's (CIHR) Dementia Research Strategy. The CIHR Dementia Research Strategy has two components: domestic and international. The domestic component is the Canadian Consortium on Neurodegeneration in Aging (CCNA). This consortium has 350 researchers working among 20 teams across Canada. The international component of the CIHR Dementia Research Strategy creates opportunities for Canadian researchers to collaborate with their colleagues from other countries (Standing Senate Committee on Social Affairs, Science and Technology, 2016). The Canadian government also launched a National Strategy for Dementia-Friendly Communities in 2016. We are now making progress! Let's move on to look at the most common of the neurocognitive disorders.

ALZHEIMER'S DISEASE

Alzheimer's disease was first identified in 1906 by Alois Alzheimer and it is the most common form of dementia, accounting for 60 to 80 percent of all cases (Alzheimer's Association, 2016a; WHO, 2012b). It is difficult to know for certain the incidence or prevalence rates of Alzheimer's disease because prevalence rates often include dementia of all types. In addition, people can be diagnosed with Alzheimer's disease and upon autopsy, findings show that it was another type of dementia (Beach, Monsell, Phillips, & Kukull, 2012; Bradford, Kunik, Shulz, Williams, & Singh, 2009).

SIGNS AND SYMPTOMS OF ALZHEIMER'S DISEASE

The onset of Alzheimer's disease is insidious in that it is not exactly clear when the disease process started. Although there is variability in disease progression and presentation, the development of Alzheimer's disease is usually gradual, and often the first symptoms are impaired memory and learning. This is accompanied by progressive decline in all areas of cognitive functioning including impairments in attention, reasoning, judgment, problem solving, language abilities, and visual perception (APA, 2013). Another symptom often reported early on in the course of the illness is getting lost while driving, even in familiar places. As the disease advances, it becomes increasingly difficult for individuals to engage in self-care routines without cuing and, eventually, individuals will need another person to do their care. Inappropriate social behaviour and changes in personality often occur with disease progression (APA, 2013). Life expectancy varies for each person with Alzheimer's disease. The average life expectancy after diagnosis is eight to 10 years. In some cases, however, it can be as short as three years or as long as 20 years. Unfortunately, researchers in Canada and the United Kingdom suspect that only 20 to 50 percent of individuals who have a dementia are diagnosed (Morgan et al., 2014).

BRAIN CHANGES ASSOCIATED WITH ALZHEIMER'S DISEASE

After decades of investigation, researchers have begun to understand more fully the neurological changes in the brain associated with Alzheimer's disease. Although the changes to the brain are microscopic, they are thoroughly destructive and interfere with the ability of the neurons in the brain to communicate with each other and repair themselves. Alzheimer's disease not only impedes communication between neurons but also impairs neuronal functioning to the point where the neurons eventually die (Alzheimer's Association, 2016a). While there is **atrophy** of the brain with normal aging, it is nowhere near the amount of shrinkage of the brain caused by the accumulated death of neurons as Alzheimer's disease progresses. Figure 7.1 shows the difference between atrophy in a normal aging brain and a brain affected by Alzheimer's disease.

The hallmark changes to the brain caused by Alzheimer's disease are the formation of **amyloid plaques** and **neurofibrillary tangles**. Amyloid plaques form outside the neuron. The starting point for the development of amyloid plaques is **amyloid precursor protein (APP)**, which is a

FIGURE 7.1

A HEALTHY BRAIN AND AN ALZHEIMER'S DISEASE BRAIN

Healthy Brain

Brain with Alzheimer's

Science Source

protein associated with the membrane that surrounds the cell. When APP is being made inside the cell, part of it remains inside the neuron and part of it remains outside the neuron. The part of APP that remains outside the cell is cut off by enzymes called **secretases**. There are three types of enzymes involved in this process: alpha-secretase, beta-secretase, and gamma-secretase. Normally, alpha-secretase cuts off the part of the APP that remains outside the cell that has the potential to become beta-amyloid. Scientists do not understand why, but in Alzheimer's disease, something goes wrong with this process and, instead, beta-secretase cuts APP off in the wrong place (National Institute on Aging, 2003). This causes beta-amyloid to form, which is a sticky substance. Eventually beta-amyloid forms plaques that cannot dissolve. These plaques begin to accumulate in the brain as the body has no way to get rid of these abnormal deposits (National Institute on Aging, 2003). Figure 7.2 depicts the process of the development of beta-amyloid plaque. In the first picture, you can see how the APP molecule sticks out of the neuron. In the second picture, the secretases enzymes clip the beta-amyloid protein. Finally, in the last picture, you can see how the pieces of beta-amyloid stick together and form plaques outside of the neuron.

Neurofibrillary tangles are the second major change to the brain in Alzheimer's disease. Unlike plaques that occur outside the neuron, tangles occur inside the neuron. The primary component of tangles is a protein called "tau." Each neuron has a transport system that is organized in parallel strands that looks like a railway track. Nutrients and other materials travel along the strands from the cell body down to the axon. Tau is a key component in maintaining the stability of microtubules which keep the strands straight. In Alzheimer's disease, tau collapses into twisted strands called tangles (Alzheimer's Association, 2016b). When this happens, the tracks can no longer stay straight. As a result, nutrients and other essential supplies can no longer move through the neuron, which eventually dies as a result (James, Doraiswamy, & Borges-Neto, 2015). How a neurofibrillary tangle develops in Alzheimer's disease is presented in Figure 7.3. If you would like to watch a video about the development of plaques and tangles, please see https://www.youtube.com/watch?v=NjgBnx1jVIU.

Another avenue of research investigating the changes in the brain associated with Alzheimer's disease focuses on the activation of inflammatory pathways. This research is based on evidence that shows that long-time use of anti-inflammatory drugs is associated with a reduced risk of developing the disease (Wyss-Coray & Rogers, 2012).

FIGURE 7.2

THE DEVELOPMENT OF BETA-AMYLOID PLAQUES

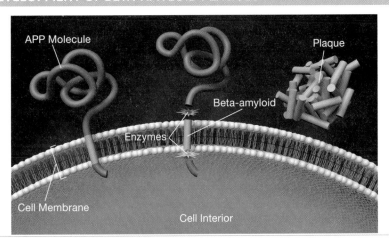

FIGURE 7.3

HOW A NEUROFIBRILLARY TANGLE DEVELOPS IN ALZHEIMER'S DISEASE

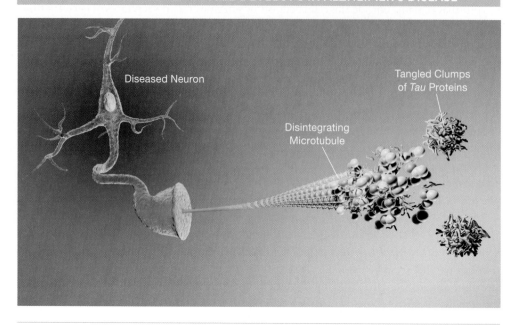

THE DIAGNOSTIC CHALLENGES ASSOCIATED WITH ALZHEIMER'S DISEASE

While the diagnosis of a neurocognitive disorder often is made by psychiatrists, neuropsy-chologists, or clinical psychologists, family physicians play an important role in identifying individuals who have a dementia. In fact, family physicians often are the first healthcare professionals that people turn to when there are concerns about memory or cognitive functioning. However, determining if patients have cognitive problems that warrant further investigation is time consuming for already-busy family physicians. As a result, cognitive impairment in an older adult is commonly screened using Mental Status Exams, which can be administered quickly in a physician's office. One common screening tool is the Mini Mental Status Exam (MMSE) (Folstein, Folstein, & McHugh, 1975). The total score in the original version is 30 points with low scores (< 24) suggestive of cognitive impairment. Another screening tool that is widely used is the Montreal Cognitive Assessment (MoCa). The MoCA was developed in Montreal by Nasreddine and colleagues (2005) to screen patients who present with cognitive complaints but who may still perform in the normal range on the MMSE. Cognitive impairment is suspected if the individual scores less than 26 points out of 30 on the MoCA. It is important to note, however, that a diagnosis of dementia should never be made based on screening measures alone. A complete medical workup and thorough neuropsychological assessment should be done. However, many clinicians do not conduct thorough assessments and family physicians, in particular, fail to accurately diagnose many cases of Alzheimer's disease (Bradford et al., 2009). If a dementia is suspected, physicians can refer their patients to memory clinics, which are available across Canada. For a list of memory clinics, go to http://alzheimersremedies.org/memory_clinics_in_canada.html.

In a thorough assessment, a diagnosis of Alzheimer's disease is determined through a process of exclusion. What this means is that all other treatable causes of the changes in cognitive status or behaviour are ruled out. If there is no underlying medical condition causing the symptoms, it is most likely Alzheimer's disease. This process of exclusion is used because there is no single test that can identify Alzheimer's disease. And, although diagnostic accuracy has improved considerably, autopsy continues to be the only way to know for certain if the neurocognitive disorder is indeed Alzheimer's disease.

In an effort to improve the diagnostic accuracy of Alzheimer's disease, the National Institute of Neurological and Communicative Disorders and Stroke (NINCDS) and the Alzheimer's Disease and Related Disorders Association (ADRDA) first established criteria for the clinical diagnosis of Alzheimer's disease in 1984. These criteria are commonly referred to as the NINCDS-ADRDA criteria for the diagnosis of Alzheimer's disease and other dementias. These criteria have been universally adopted and widely used in clinical trials and clinical research (Jack et al., 2011; McKhann et al., 2011). However, our knowledge of the clinical presentation and biology of Alzheimer's disease has increased significantly since 1984, and the NINCDS-ADRDA criteria had to be updated to reflect that knowledge. It should be noted that the original NINCDS-ADRDA criteria were developed on the belief that Alzheimer's disease is a **clinical-pathological** entity (McKhann et al., 1984). What this means is that individuals who have symptoms of Alzheimer's disease also will have the underlying pathology of plaques and tangles. However, over the last few decades, researchers have found that the pathology of plaques and tangles can be present in an individual's brain *without* the individual ever showing symptoms of Alzheimer's disease. In 2009, the National Institute on Aging (NIA) and the Alzheimer's Association (AA; NIA-AA) sponsored work groups to refine the 1984 diagnostic and research criteria for Alzheimer's disease. There are two significant differences between the new criteria developed and the criteria published in 1984. These differences are the incorporation of the **biomarkers** of Alzheimer's disease into the new criteria as well as the formal inclusion of the pre-dementia phase (mild cognitive impairment, or MCI) and the pre-clinical phase (where the diagnosis of Alzheimer's disease can be made *before* the individual exhibits any observable clinical symptoms) in the 2011 diagnostic criteria (Dubois et al., 2007; Jack et al., 2011; O'Brien, 2013).

If you are wondering how a diagnosis of Alzheimer's disease can possibly be made without observable symptoms, you are not alone and many medical professionals took exception to this criterion (Chiu & Brodaty, 2013). So, how can one be diagnosed with Alzheimer's disease without the presence of symptoms? By using biomarkers. It was Dubois and colleagues (2007, 2010) who first championed the inclusion of biomarkers in the diagnostic criteria for Alzheimer's disease. Consider that in 1984, the only biomarker available as evidence of Alzheimer's disease was progressive atrophy of the brain, which could be seen on **computerized tomography scans** (O'Brien, 2013). Currently, there are several developments in biomarkers research. For example, the presence of tau and amyloid protein in cerebrospinal fluid and the presence of hippocampal atrophy have been identified as biomarkers of Alzheimer's disease. Another advance is the development of **positron emission tomography (PET) imaging** tracers that can view tau protein in the brain (Sinha, Firbank, & O'Brien, 2012). This is of importance because neuropathology studies have previously demonstrated that clinical symptoms and disease stage are more strongly correlated with the distribution of tangles (created by tau protein) than plaques (created by amyloid protein), and early research suggests that the amount of tau protein in the brain is a better predictor of disease progression (Brier et al., 2016; James et al., 2015; Johnson et al., 2016.) As you can imagine, the idea of diagnosing Alzheimer's disease in an individual who has one or more biomarkers but who does not have any symptoms of Alzheimer's disease has caused a good deal of controversy and has raised many questions and ethical concerns.

For example, and as mentioned earlier, there is evidence that some individuals who have an abundance of plaques and tangles in their brains do *not* go on to develop clinical symptoms of Alzheimer's disease. Chiu and Brodaty (2013) argue that, because there currently is no treatment for Alzheimer's disease, early diagnosis using biomarkers may cause more harm than good as it may lead to personal distress and suffering for many years prior to any symptom development. Furthermore, what if symptoms never develop? At the end of the day, the research to date on the utility of biomarkers in the diagnosis of Alzheimer's disease, while promising, is conflicting and more validation research is needed (Chiu & Brodaty, 2013; Jack et al., 2011; Molin & Rockwood, 2016).

So, what will these different criteria mean for Canadian physicians and geriatricians? The Fourth Canadian Consensus Conference on the Diagnosis and Treatment of Dementia convened in 2012 in Montreal, with the purpose of updating the Canadian diagnostic approach to Alzheimer's disease in light of the new criteria. The consensus was that the new criteria would not change practice in primary-care facilities (e.g., family physician offices). And, although the inclusion of biomarkers in the diagnostic criteria is promising, the consensus was that their use would be limited to clinical trials and research in the area (Molin & Rockwood, 2016). We also should mention that, with all the technological advantages of late and the push for a cure for Alzheimer's disease, it is no surprise that researchers are looking at innovative ways to detect and diagnose the disease. Canadian researchers at the Toronto Rehabilitation Institute have developed a new technology that analyzes a person's natural speech to detect and monitor Alzheimer's disease and other cognitive disorders. Artificial intelligence has been developed that can identify variables such as rate of speech, pitch, prosody (rhythm), and tone as well as choice of words and how many pauses an individual makes when speaking. This technology has been shown to reliably identify Alzheimer's disease, Parkinson's disease, and aphasia with 85 to 100 percent accuracy (Fraser, Meltzer, & Rudzicz, 2016). It is for sure an exciting time for researchers!

WHAT CAUSES ALZHEIMER'S DISEASE?

This remains a difficult question to answer. We know that plaques and tangles are associated with Alzheimer's disease but researchers do not understand why. Researchers do know that Alzheimer's disease comes in two forms. The first is known as **early-onset familial Alzheimer's disease** and, as the term "familial" implies, this type of Alzheimer's disease is hereditary. This form of the disease occurs in individuals before the age of 65 who have had a positive family history of Alzheimer's disease for at least three generations (Shea et al., 2016). However, this type of Alzheimer's disease accounts for less than 1 to 5 percent of all cases (Alzheimer Society of Canada, 2014a; Panpalli Ates, Karaman, Guntekin, & Ergun, 2016; Shea et al., 2016). Approximately 50 percent of individuals who have the familial form of Alzheimer's disease carry mutations in one of three genes. These three genes are the presenilin genes PS1 (found on Chromosome 14), PS2 (found on chromosome 1), and amyloid precursor protein (APP; found on chromosome 21). If you have an alteration in any one of these genes, you are at greater risk to develop early-onset familial Alzheimer's disease (Alzheimer Society of Canada, 2014a).

As you might have guessed, Alzheimer's disease occurs most often in individuals 65 years of age and older. This form of Alzheimer's disease is called **sporadic Alzheimer's disease** or "late onset" because this form occurs in individuals after age 65. Sporadic Alzheimer's disease is due to a complex combination of our genes, our environment, and our lifestyle. There have been several genes under investigation for the role they may play in the development of sporadic Alzheimer's disease. However, the gene thought to be of most importance to the development of sporadic Alzheimer's disease is called apolipoprotein E (ApoE) and this gene is associated with chromosome 19. There are three different types of the ApoE gene—E2, E3, and E4. Everyone has two copies of the ApoE gene; one from each parent. ApoE2 is the rarest form of ApoE, and carrying even one copy appears to reduce the risk of developing Alzheimer's disease (Liu, Kanekiyo, Xu, & Bu, 2013; Wu & Zhao, 2016). ApoE3 is the most common type but having ApoE3 does not seem to influence the risk of developing Alzheimer's disease. However, ApoE4, which is found in only approximately 20 percent of the population, is present in almost half of individuals who have sporadic Alzheimer's disease (Wu & Zhao, 2016). Having one ApoE4 gene increases your risk of developing the disease and if you have two ApoE4 genes, your risk is even higher. Now, having said that, not everyone who has one or even two ApoE4 genes develops Alzheimer's disease. Further, Alzheimer's disease occurs in many people who don't even have the ApoE4 gene. This suggests that ApoE4 affects the risk of developing Alzheimer's disease but it is not a cause of Alzheimer's disease. Some people who worry about developing sporadic Alzheimer's disease might be interested in finding out if they carry an ApoE4 gene. According to the Alzheimer Society of Canada (2014a), advisory committees around the world have recommended against this type of genetic testing. This is because individuals who have an ApoE4 gene might never develop Alzheimer's disease, and individuals who do not have the ApoE4 gene can still develop Alzheimer's disease. So, in the end, genetics are not the whole story in the development of Alzheimer's disease.

As mentioned, early lifestyle and environmental factors play a role but many of these risk factors are not fully understood yet. One environmental factor that has received a good deal of research attention is aluminum. During the 1960s and 1970s, aluminum emerged as a possible risk factor for developing Alzheimer's disease (Martyn, Coggon, Inskip, Lacey, & Young, 1997). Concerns were raised about everyday exposure to aluminum through pots and pans, beverage cans, antiperspirants, and antacids, but early research was inconsistent and the concern about using aluminum seemed to fade away. However, epidemiological and experimental findings indicate that aluminum is not as harmless as was previously thought, and there is a growing and consistent body of evidence that points to a relationship between chronic exposure to aluminum and the development of Alzheimer's disease. A recent meta-analysis looked at aluminum levels in the brains of three cohort and five case control studies, with a total of 10 567 participants (Wang et al., 2016). These researchers investigated the association between chronic exposure to aluminum in drinking water and chronic exposure to aluminum due to occupation. This meta-analysis showed that chronic aluminum exposure was associated with a 71 percent increase in the risk of developing Alzheimer's disease. Another recent meta-analysis looked at 34 studies involving 1208 participants and 613 individual Alzheimer's disease cases. Compared to control subjects, those with Alzheimer's disease had significantly higher levels of aluminum in their brains and cerebrospinal fluid (Virk & Eslick, 2015). According to Tomljenovic (2011), a researcher at the University of British Columbia, the hypothesis that aluminum significantly contributes to the development of Alzheimer's disease is built upon solid experimental evidence and should not be dismissed. Despite the growing evidence, the issue as to whether the intake of aluminum from general environmental sources is enough to cause Alzheimer's disease remains controversial (Bondy, 2016; Exley, 2014)—another area where much more research is needed.

RISK FACTORS FOR THE DEVELOPMENT OF ALZHEIMER'S DISEASE

Although Alzheimer's disease is not a normal part of aging, age is the biggest risk factor for the development of this disease. The older you become, the higher the risk. In Canada, one in 20 individuals over age 65 and approximately one in four of those over age 85 has Alzheimer's disease (Alzheimer Society of Canada, 2014b). However, it must be made clear that not every older adult will develop this disease.

Recent estimates suggest that, for most world regions, almost two-thirds of individuals diagnosed with Alzheimer's disease are women (Alzheimer's Disease International, 2015). Initially, researchers thought this was because women live longer than men. Other researchers have suggested that it is the loss of estrogen through menopause that puts women at higher risk for developing Alzheimer's disease (Viña & Lloret, 2010). However, the reasons for higher rates of Alzheimer's disease found in women seem to be more complex than this. Regarding genetic findings, the results of a large prospective cohort study published in 2014 confirmed the results from previous case control studies—that women who are positive for ApoE4 are at greater risk of developing Alzheimer's disease than are men who are ApoE4 positive (Altmann, Tian, Henderson, & Greicius, 2014). Women who are diagnosed with Alzheimer's disease tend to experience quicker progression of atrophy in the hippocampus than do men (Ardekani, Convit, & Bachman, 2016). In addition, women have been shown to have a different clinical presentation in that men show more aggressive behaviours, more co-morbidities, and higher mortality than women. Women tend to have more affective symptoms and disability but live longer with the disease than do men (Sinforiani et al., 2010). Finally, broader societal factors also may play a role in the higher rates of Alzheimer's disease in women. For example, education and occupation level have been shown to be protective factors in the development of Alzheimer's disease. In previous generations and in many countries around the world today, significant inequalities exist between men and women in the attainment of higher education and occupational status such that women often are more disadvantaged (Mielke, Vemuri, & Rocca, 2014). Canevelli and his colleagues (2017) suggest a greater effort should be made to collect and report data on those factors that can interact with sex and gender and may significantly influence clinical manifestations, outcomes, and trajectories of the disease over time.

There are several other risk factors for developing Alzheimer's disease but the good news is that several of these risk factors are modifiable—meaning that an individual has control over them. In 2014, the World Dementia Council made a request to the Alzheimer's Association to evaluate and report on the state of the evidence on modifiable risk factors for cognitive decline and dementia. The Alzheimer's Association (United States) believes there is sufficient evidence to support the link between several modifiable risk factors and a reduced risk for cognitive decline, and these modifiable risk factors also may be associated with a reduced risk of developing

FIGURE 7.4

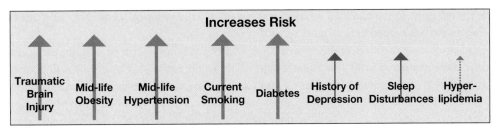

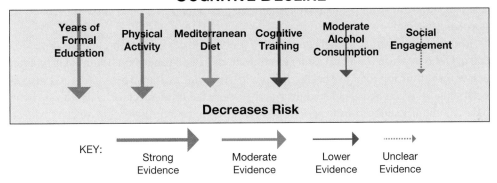

Source: Baumgart et al. (2015.) Summary of the evidence on modifiable risk factors for cognitive decline and dementia: A population-based perspective. *Alzheimer's & Dementia, 11*(6), 718-726. doi:10.1016/j.jaz.2015.05.016 *Alzheimer's & Dementia: The Journal of the Alzheimer's Association* by Alzheimer's Association. Reproduced with permission of ELSEVIER in the format Book via Copyright Clearance Center.

dementia. Specifically, regular physical activity and the management of cardiovascular risk factors (diabetes, obesity, smoking, and hypertension) reduce the risk of cognitive decline and may reduce the risk of dementia (Baumgart et al., 2015). Eating healthily and following the Mediterranean diet also appears to lower the risk of developing Alzheimer's disease. The strength of evidence on the risk factors that both increase and reduce the risk of developing Alzheimer's disease is presented in Figure 7.4.

MILD COGNITIVE IMPAIRMENT

Mild cognitive impairment (MCI) identifies a spectrum of disease that includes impairment in both memory and non-memory cognitive domains (Albert et al., 2011). This contrasts with the earlier criteria for MCI where memory impairment was a requirement for the diagnosis. Individuals who have MCI have mild but measurable changes in thinking abilities. Family, friends, and the person with MCI may notice these changes but the changes in cognitive abilities are not serious enough to interfere with daily life and independence (Alzheimer Society of Canada, 2014c). Approximately 15 to 20 percent of people age 65 or older have MCI (Roberts & Knopman, 2013).

The most common subtype of MCI is amnestic MCI, where memory loss is the main symptom. The second subtype is non-amnestic MCI, where an individual's memory is not impaired but other thinking abilities such as organizing and planning, or reasoning and judgment, may be affected. It appears that individuals who have impairments in memory are at a greater risk of developing Alzheimer's disease (Albert et al., 2011; Ritchie & Tuokko, 2010; Tampi, Tampi, Chandran, Ghori, & Durning, 2015). Using data from the Canadian Study of Health and Aging, Ritchie and Tuokko (2010) found that MCI was more common in women than men, but a study done in the United States found that MCI is more common in men than women (Langa & Levine, 2014). More research is needed to determine sex differences in MCI.

As previously mentioned, the revised NIA-AA 2011 diagnostic criteria and guidelines for Alzheimer's disease view MCI as an early stage of Alzheimer's disease. However, it is important to note that MCI can develop for other reasons (such as a reaction to medication), and MCI does not always lead to dementia. In some cases, people who have been diagnosed with MCI return to normal cognitive functioning or remain stable. In other cases, such as when a medication causes cognitive impairment, MCI is mistakenly diagnosed. Therefore, it's important that people experiencing cognitive impairment see a healthcare professional as soon as possible (Alzheimer's Association, 2016a).

Learning the Ropes for Living with MCI is a program that is offered through Baycrest Hospital in Ontario, which is a global leader in innovations in aging and brain health. This program focuses on optimizing cognitive health through lifestyle choices, memory training, and psychosocial support. It is aimed at older adults and their close family members/friends who are living in the community and who are experiencing MCI. Drs. Anderson, Troyer, and Murphy, who are neuropsychologists at Baycrest, have written the first comprehensive book on mild cognitive impairment. It's called *Living with Mild Cognitive Impairment: A Guide to Maximizing Brain Health and Reducing Risk of Dementia* (Anderson, Murphy, & Troyer, 2012).

VASCULAR DEMENTIA

Vascular dementia is the second-leading cause of dementia. In Canada, this form of dementia accounts for 15 to 20 percent of all cases of dementia (Standing Senate Committee on Social Affairs, Science and Technology, 2016). We know that vascular dementia can be caused by a large vessel **cerebral vascular accident**, which also is called a stroke. A stroke is a loss of brain function caused by a sudden brain blood vessel blockage (ischemic stroke) or rupture (hemorrhagic stroke). Ischemic stroke is the most common type of stroke. However, more recently, researchers have found that most vascular dementia is caused by cerebral **small vessel disease**. Small vessel disease is thought to arise from damage to small arteries, arterioles, capillaries, and small veins in the brain, which are often referred to as "white matter lesions" (Perneczky et al., 2016; Rincon & Wright, 2014). Therefore, there is much variability in presentation of vascular dementia depending on the extent and location of the lesions. Vascular dementia due to white matter lesions usually has a gradual onset with slow progression. However, vascular dementia due to a large vessel stroke has a sudden onset and may progress with a stepwise or fluctuating decline, depending on whether the individual experiences more strokes (APA, 2013). The prevalence of pure vascular dementia is low, especially in those aged 75 and older, and vascular dementia most often occurs with other dementias such as Alzheimer's disease (Perneczky et al., 2016; Snyder et al., 2015). When Alzheimer's disease and vascular dementia occur at the same time, the condition is called mixed dementia. Mixed dementia is thought to occur in at least 50 percent of all dementia cases (Alzheimer Society of Canada, 2015).

Interestingly, the risk factors for developing vascular dementia are similar to those for Alzheimer's disease (Alzheimer Society of Canada, 2016c; Perneczky et al., 2016). For example, established risk factors for vascular dementia are hypertension, diabetes, high cholesterol, low physical activity, smoking, and depression. This overlap in risk factors has influenced the direction that research on dementia has taken in recent years (Perneczky et al., 2016). Important questions researchers are trying to answer are, what proportion of the total burden of dementia is caused by vascular risk factors? And, second, if vascular factors are significant to the development of dementia including Alzheimer's disease, has improved cardiovascular health in recent decades influenced dementia occurrence? As you read in the beginning of this chapter, there is evidence that prevalence rates of dementia are indeed declining. These are very interesting and exciting questions, and future research is needed to fully understand the relationship between vascular changes and Alzheimer's disease.

PARKINSON'S DISEASE

Parkinson's disease is a chronic, progressive disorder of the nervous system that affects movement. Primary symptoms of Parkinson's disease include tremor of the hands, arms, legs, jaw, and face; slowness of movement; rigidity or stiffness of the limbs and trunk; and impaired balance and coordination. There is no known cause of Parkinson's disease, and presently there is no cure. In Canada, it has been estimated that 55 000 Canadians aged 18 or older living in private households have been diagnosed with Parkinson's disease. Approximately 79 percent of these individuals are over 65 years of age (Wong, Gilmour, & Ramage-Morin, 2014). Sometimes, individuals who have Parkinson's disease will develop dementia. For the dementia to be attributed to Parkinson's disease (and not another dementia such as Alzheimer's disease), the motor and other symptoms of Parkinson's disease must be present at least one year before there are symptoms of dementia (APA, 2013). Motor symptoms include slowness in movement; involuntary shaking or tremor at rest; stiffness of arms, legs, and trunk; and trouble with balance and walking. Of interest, the actor Michael J. Fox, who was born in Edmonton, Alberta, was diagnosed with early-onset Parkinson's disease in 1991, but did not share the news with the public until 1998. His public disclosure of his illness and creation of the Michael J. Fox Foundation for Parkinson's Research has raised awareness of the disease and increased the amount of research in this area (see https://www.michaeljfox.org/). For an inspirational true story about another Canadian with Parkinson's disease, please read the Lived Experience Box 7.2. If you want to learn more about Tim Hague, please go to https://www.youtube.com/watch?v=ZKkQciJD1hY.

BOX 7.2

LIVED EXPERIENCE: PARKINSON'S DISEASE DID NOT GET IN THE WAY OF TIM HAGUE'S DREAM

Tim Hague Sr. is a 55-year-old man who lives in Winnipeg, Manitoba. In 2010, at the age of 50, he was diagnosed with young-onset Parkinson's disease. He overcame the odds when he went from a diagnosis of Parkinson's disease to—just three years later—becoming the inaugural winner of CTV's *The Amazing Race Canada*. Since his diagnosis, Tim has become active in the promotion of Parkinson's issues, his experiences in living life with Parkinson's, and motivating others through his message of strength, perseverance, and courage. His mantra for life is to *Live Your Best*. You can visit Tim's website at https://www.timsr.ca/.

FIGURE 7.5

Courtesy of Tim Hague Sr.

FRONTO-TEMPORAL NEUROCOGNITIVE DISORDER

Fronto-temporal dementia (FTD) refers to a cluster of syndromes that result from degeneration of the frontal and temporal lobes. This dementia accounts for approximately 5 percent of all dementias and usually occurs in individuals before the age of 65 (APA, 2013; Onyike & Diehl-Schmid, 2013). The areas of the brain affected by FTD are generally associated with personality and behaviour. There are two major clinical forms of FTD: a behavioural type and a language type (Kurz, Kurz, Ellis, & Lautenschlager, 2014). In the behavioural type, a person can become withdrawn but often the person's behaviour becomes disinhibited in that he or she will say inappropriate things or behave in inappropriate ways. Simply stated, the person's mental filter is altered so that social rules are no longer considered when saying something or doing something. For example, a caregiver told us that she knew something was wrong with her husband when they were walking through a mall one day and he started shouting, "You're fat!" to people he passed who he perceived to be overweight! The behavioural variant seems to account for nearly 60 percent of cases of FTD, while the language variants are less common (Onyike & Diehl-Schmid, 2013). The language variants are subdivided into **non-fluent aphasia** and **primary progressive aphasia**. The average length of the disease can vary but survival from symptom onset usually is between six and 11 years (Seltman & Matthews, 2012). Diagnosis of FTD is challenging because behaviour and language changes are usually the first symptoms present while memory or other cognitive impairment may be absent and occur later in disease progression. While this may seem like a blessing, the behaviours associated with FTD are significant and distressing for caregivers.

NEUROCOGNITIVE DISORDER WITH LEWY BODIES

Lewy body dementia involves progressive cognitive impairment, which, in the early stages of the disease, appears to affect complex attention and executive function rather than learning and memory. Lewy body dementia is not common and prevalence estimates range from 0.1 percent to 5 percent in the United States (APA, 2013). Unfortunately, we could not find any Canadian prevalence rates. This dementia frequently is accompanied by very complex visual hallucinations and sleeping difficulties. Delusions often are seen. Individuals often experience repeated falls and fluctuations in cognitive abilities. The symptoms associated with Lewy body dementia can be a challenge to manage because almost 50 percent of individuals who have Lewy body dementia are very sensitive to the medications used to treat hallucinations and delusions. The individual also may experience Parkinson's disease-like symptoms such as rigid muscles, slow movement, and tremors. How can healthcare professionals differentiate between a Lewy body dementia and Parkinson's disease dementia? This is a complex question but one marker is that the cognitive deficits in a Lewy body dementia must be observed at least one year before the individual exhibits any Parkinson features (APA, 2013).

ALCOHOL-RELATED DEMENTIA

Research has shown that excessive and prolonged use of alcohol can lead to permanent damage to the structure and function of the brain (Harper, 2009). However, alcohol-related dementia (ARD) has not received much research attention due to the uncertainty of the exact pathophysiological profile of ARD. The controversy about ARD is that researchers are pondering if it is possible to have a dementia that is the direct result of ethanol neurotoxicity. This type of dementia could be caused by thiamine deficiency or a number of underlying factors such as neurotoxicity and nutritional deficiencies (Ridley, Draper, & Withall, 2013). The direct pathophysiology has been hard to determine because of many confounding factors. For example, individuals who abuse alcohol often have other co-morbidities such as psychiatric illness, higher rate of vascular risk factors, and head injury, which also may be contributing to the dementia (Gupta & Warner, 2008). Another confounding factor is that individuals who abuse alcohol also may be abusing other substances such as drugs. Prevalence rates are hard to determine because of variability in diagnostic criteria used by researchers. According to the American Psychiatric Association (2013), a major neurocognitive disorder that can be wholly attributed to alcohol abuse is rare. However, the rate of mild neurocognitive disorders in those who have been abstaining from alcohol for two months is approximately 30 to 40 percent. Interestingly, if the cognitive deficits are recognized early, they may be reduced or reversed if the individual stops drinking alcohol.

Irrespective of the type of dementia, support for individuals with a dementia and their caregivers is important. The Alzheimer Society of Canada, which is active in communities across the nation, offers programs and services to help individuals with dementia, their caregivers, and healthcare professionals with information, resources, and support. You can learn more about this organization and the services it provides by visiting the website at https://www.alzheimer.ca/en/We-can-help/Our-services.

7.2 DELIRIUM

LEARNING OBJECTIVES

To understand:
- what delirium is
- the significance of delirium in an older adult population

WHAT IS IT AND WHY IS IT IMPORTANT TO IDENTIFY?

Delirium is a serious and common condition that often goes undetected in older adults. It is characterized by acute deterioration of mental status in which an individual exhibits deficits in attention as well as altered levels of consciousness and psychotic features. However, the most significant abnormality is an inability to attend to even the simplest of conversations (Anand & MacLullich, 2017). Symptoms of delirium develop over a short time and tend to fluctuate throughout the day. Most cases of delirium are temporary and may resolve after a few days, but in some cases, the delirium persists for weeks or months (Anand & MacLullich, 2017). Delirium is the most common complication of hospital admission for older people, and it develops in up to one half of older patients after hip fracture and vascular surgery.

There is a strong relationship between delirium and dementia in that dementia is associated with an increased risk of developing delirium and delirium is associated with increased risk of developing dementia, although it is unclear whether the delirium is exposing an unrecognized dementia or starting a process of cognitive decline (Anand & MacLullich, 2017; Sepulveda et al., 2015). Distinguishing delirium from dementia is a common clinical problem and it can be particularly challenging to distinguish delirium from Lewy body dementia because some features such as hallucinations and fluctuation in symptoms are common to both disorders. According to Anand and MacLullich (2017), the safest clinical approach is to consider that until proven otherwise, all older adults exhibiting confusion have a delirium. In addition, performing routine cognitive assessment on older adults who are physically ill would improve detection rates. The non-modifiable risk factors for the development of delirium are increased age, dementia, and stroke. However, there are many reversible causes of delirium and this is another reason why a thorough assessment is so important. Reversible causes of delirium include infections, trauma, surgery, constipation, and adverse drug effects, which often co-occur (Anand & MacLullich, 2017).

Delirium has been associated with very poor outcomes for older adults including increased mortality, greater length of hospital stay, loss of independent living, and evidence of increased dementia risk (Tow et al., 2016). This is of concern because it has been estimated that approximately one-third of cases of delirium are preventable (Anand & MacLullich, 2013).

7.3 TREATMENT ISSUES RELATED TO NEUROCOGNITIVE DISORDERS

LEARNING OBJECTIVES

To understand:
- the use of cognitive enhancers and memory training in dementia
- the behavioural and psychological symptoms of dementia (BPSD)
- the treatment options available for BPSD and the limitations of the available literature investigating treatment of BPSD

COGNITIVE ENHANCERS AND MEMORY TRAINING

COGNITIVE ENHANCERS

A classification of drugs known as **acetylcholinesterase inhibitors (AChEIs)**, or cognitive enhancers, are used for the treatment of progressive dementias such as Alzheimer's disease. A recent meta-analysis done by Canadian researchers found no significant effects of cognitive enhancers on cognition (Tricco et al., 2013), which is similar to the findings of other reviews (Winslow, Onysko, Stob, & Hazlewood, 2011). Medications such as vitamin E, estrogen, or non-steroidal anti-inflammatory medications have not been shown to be effective in the treatment of dementia (Winslow et al., 2011). In short, there are no proven treatments that delay or stop the progression of dementia for any length of time (Alzheimer's Association, 2016a).

MEMORY TRAINING

You are probably wondering if there are other ways to treat the memory impairment that occurs in dementia. As a matter of fact, there is growing body of research evidence that supports the efficacy of non-pharmacological cognitive interventions. Kinsella and her colleagues (2016) found that older adults who had MCI benefited from learning the memory strategies taught in their study but not to the extent that the healthy older adult participants did, particularly at the six-month follow-up. However, a systematic review of cognitive strategies taught to individuals with MCI showed positive effects for both subjective and objective measure of memory, and these effects persisted from one month to five years (Hong, Jang, Hwang, Roh, & Lee, 2015).

BEHAVIOURAL AND PSYCHOLOGICAL SYMPTOMS OF DEMENTIA (BPSD)

The prevalence of BPSD is common in individuals who have Alzheimer's disease. It is estimated that agitation and aggression occur in approximately 20 to 30 percent of individuals who live in the community and approximately 40 to 60 percent of individuals with Alzheimer's disease who live in care facilities (Ballard, Corbett, Chitramohan, & Aarsland, 2009; Cipriani, Vedovello, Nuti, & Di Fiorino, 2011; Van der Mussele et al., 2015; Zhao et al., 2016). Disinhibition, apathy, and psychosis are all examples of BPSD, but it is agitation and aggression that are the most common and the most distressing (Lyketsos et al., 2011).

Agitation can be defined as inappropriate verbal, vocal, or motor activity that cannot be explained by apparent needs or confusion (Cohen-Mansfield & Billig, 1986). These researchers identified four types of agitation in their seminal study: aggressive-physical, non-aggressive-physical, aggressive-verbal, and non-aggressive-verbal. Agitation can be manifested as pacing, restlessness, and/or repetitive vocalizations, which can escalate to shouting, and verbal insults. Physical aggression can include biting, hitting, and pinching (Gallagher & Herrmann, 2014). BPSD is the most common reason for hospitalization in this population and can contribute to caregiver burnout, early institutionalization, and poor quality of life (Gallagher & Herrmann, 2014; Wetzels, Zuidema, de Jonghe, Verhey, & Koopmans, 2010).

TREATMENT OF AGITATION AND AGGRESSION

Numerous studies have shown that prescribing antipsychotic medication to treat agitated and aggressive behaviour in persons with dementia is not safe and associated with many side effects and mortality (Kales et al., 2012). As a result, the consensus is to use non-pharmacological approaches in the treatment of agitation and aggressive behaviours whenever possible

(Iglewicz, Meeks, & Jeste, 2011; Wang, Borisovskaya, Maxwell, & Pascualy, 2014). Music therapy is a type of non-pharmalogical approach that has been used to decrease agitation. Livingston and her colleagues (2014) reviewed 10 studies of group music therapy that followed a specific protocol where the groups were led by a trained therapist and included specific content. While they found promising results, this intervention was effective only for decreasing agitation levels while the individual with dementia was in the group setting and did not have long-term effects. **Reminiscent therapy** also has shown some promise in reducing agitation but the difficulty is that, in general, the studies investigating the effects of music and reminiscence therapy on agitation are of poor quality and, as a result, it is difficult to draw conclusions (Blackburn & Bradshaw, 2014; Cotelli, Manenti, & Zanetti, 2012; Livingston et al., 2014). However, music can have a significant effect on many individuals who have a dementia. For a very powerful example, go to https://www.youtube.com/watch?v=fyZQf0p73QM.

In their review, Livingston and her colleagues (2014) also looked at the effect of sensory interventions such as **multi-sensory stimulation** (MSS) on agitation. MSS occurs in special rooms that are designed to stimulate various senses using lighting effects, colour, music, sounds, and scents, for example. The person is usually accompanied by an aide or therapist. These researchers found that MSS reduced agitation during the intervention but, again, the intervention did not have a long-term effect on the agitated behaviour of individuals with dementia. These researchers also found that the research on pet therapy as an intervention is mixed. It also should be noted that, based on the results of their review, these researchers came to the conclusion that aromatherapy and light therapy do not work for agitation and should not be used. Interestingly, Livingston and her colleagues (2014) found strong evidence, both in the short term and the long term, that training paid caregivers in communication and person-centred care is effective in reducing agitation. According to Kong and Park (2015), future studies investigating non-pharmacological interventions for the treatment of agitation need to apply more rigorous research methods and provide more description of the research methods used in each study. Given that agitation significantly interferes with the quality of life in persons with a dementia, finding effective interventions is very important. In terms of treating aggression, the non-pharmalogical protocol often used is to remove the aggressive individual from the environment they are in and place them in an environment that is quiet and soothing.

7.4 THE CHALLENGES AND JOYS OF CAREGIVING
LEARNING OBJECTIVES

To understand:
- what informal caregiving is
- the characteristics of informal caregivers
- caregiver burden
- the joys and challenges that can occur when caregiving

INFORMAL CAREGIVING

An informal caregiver is a family member or friend who provides unpaid care for a loved one who is living with a mental or physical disability or illness (Turcotte, 2013). Informal care accounts for more than 80 percent of the care needed by people with long-term mental or physical conditions. This type of support reduces the demands and costs to our healthcare and social services systems, which are estimated to be more than $9 billion a year if not for the help of informal caregivers (Alberta Caregivers Association, 2014). As our population grows older, informal caregivers become increasingly important to the well-being of older adults. According to the 2012 *Canadian General Social Survey* (GSS) on *Caregiving and Care Receiving Survey* (Sinha, 2013), an estimated 8.1 million Canadians aged 15 years and older provided care to a chronically ill, disabled, or aging family member in 2012. Approximately half (45 percent) of those surveyed provided care to parents, and, often, the parent was their own mother. Interestingly, the second-most-common category of caregivers consisted of close friends, colleagues, and neighbours (16 percent).

Informal caregiving can include a variety of helping activities that vary in terms of the emotional or physical demands placed on the caregiver. These activities can consist of meal preparation, coordinating appointments, and providing personal care. As you can see from Figure 7.6, providing transportation and meal preparation were the two most common informal caregiving tasks provided to care-recipients in Canada in 2012 (Sinha, 2013). However, 88 percent of caregivers reported that they offer emotional support in addition to providing help with daily activities, and virtually all caregivers made sure the care-recipient was okay by either calling or visiting them. Of note, caregiving is not limited to one specific task or activity, and 73 percent of caregivers reported that they provided help with two or more tasks. In general, women are more likely to assist the care-recipient with medical treatments and personal care, and men are more likely to assist the care-recipient with home maintenance or outdoor work.

FIGURE 7.6

PROVIDING TRANSPORTATION AND PREPARING MEALS ARE THE TWO MOST COMMON CAREGIVING TASKS

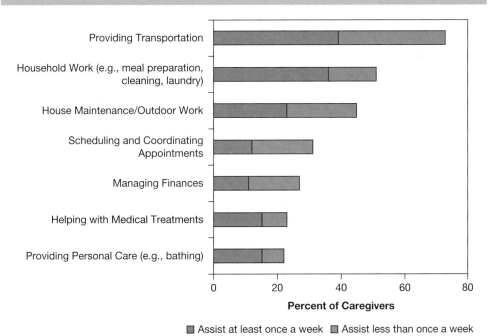

Source: Sinha, M. (2013). *Spotlight on Canadians: Results from the Canadian General Social Survey. Portrait of caregivers, 2012* (Catalogue No. 89-652-no.001). Ottawa, ON: Statistics Canada.

Consistent with the fact that many care-recipients are parents, caregivers often are between the ages of 45 and 54 years of age (24 percent) and 55 to 64 years of age (20 percent). Between the years 2007 and 2012, the number of caregivers in Canada aged 45 years and over increased by 760 000 to 4.5 million (Sinha, 2013). Table 7.1 shows the characteristics of care-recipients and the care provided by those caregivers age 45 and over surveyed in the 2008–2009 *Canadian Community Health Survey - Healthy Aging* (CCHS) (Turner & Findlay, 2012). As you can see, very few of the caregivers lived with the care-recipient. And, a sizeable percent of caregivers had been providing care for more than five years. It is further estimated that 20 to 25 percent of caregivers in Canada are aged over 65 years (Cranswick & Dosman, 2008), suggesting that a considerable proportion of caregivers are older adults themselves.

TABLE 7.1

PERCENT DISTRIBUTION OF CHARACTERISTICS OF CARE RECIPIENT AND CARE PROVIDED, HOUSEHOLD POPULATION AGED 45 OR OLDER, CANADA EXCLUDING THE TERRITORIES, 2008/2009

CARE RECIPIENT	PERCENT
Age Group	
65 to 74	21.6
75 to 84	45.9
85 or older	32.5
Relationship to Caregiver	
Parent/Parent-in-Law	55.8
Friend/Neighbour/Other	19.2
Spouse/Common-Law Partner	10.5
Other Relative	9.7
Child (Older than age 65)	4.8
Residence	
Another Household	69.6
Same Household	13.6
Healthcare Institution	12.0
Deceased	4.8
Health Condition	
Short-Term	13.4
Long-Term	83.5
Other	3.1
Type of Care Provided	
Transportation	38.8
Help with Activities Such as Housework	20.5
Personal Care	15.5
Meal Preparation and Delivery	11.2

CARE RECIPIENT	PERCENT
Other	14.0
Frequency	
Regular (Daily)	21.1
Regular (Less than Daily)	35.5
Occasionally/Rarely	43.4
Duration	
Less than 1 year	30.2
1 to less than 3 years	21.5
3 to less than 5 years	13.8
5 or more years	34.5

Source: Turner, A., & Findlay, L. (2012). Informal caregiving for seniors. *Health Reports, 23*(3) (Catalogue No. 82-003-XPE). Ottawa, ON: Statistics Canada.

REFLECTIVE QUESTION

Although there is considerable variability in how one ages, can you see any potential difficulties that can arise from older adults caring for other older adults?

THE CHALLENGES OF CAREGIVING

Even though families have traditionally been the primary caregivers for older adults, family care was largely overlooked by researchers until the early 1980s. Since then, we have begun to understand more about the demands associated with informal caregiving. Most of the early research studies explored caregiving in the context of caring for a person who has a dementia. However, as noted in more recent research, the majority of these studies focused on the negative aspects of caring (Carbonneau, Caron, & Desrosiers, 2010; Lou et al., 2015). What we have learned from these studies is that informal caregiving can pose significant challenges to a caregiver's psychological, physical, social, and financial well-being (Schoenmakers, Buntinx, & Delepeleire, 2010). Collectively, these negative aspects of caregiving are referred to as **caregiver burden**, and these challenges are especially pronounced when the care-recipient suffers from dementia. Caring for a person with dementia has been linked to a reduction in health-related quality of life (Berglund, Lytsy, & Westerling, 2015; Serrano-Aguilar, Lopez-Bastida, & Yanes-Lopez, 2006), an increase in physical health problems including heart disease (Vitaliano, Zhang, & Scanlan, 2003; von Känel et al., 2008), and an increased risk of mortality (Perkins et al., 2013). Indeed, a loss of self can occur as caregivers tend to give up many hobbies or activities they previously enjoyed in order to provide care. Anxiety and depressive disorders are much more common among informal caregivers when compared to those who are not caregiving (Alberts, Hadjistavropoulos, Pugh, & Jones, 2011; Schoenmakers et al., 2010). Alberts and her colleagues (2011) looked at the rates of **dementia anxiety** in a sample of 116 Canadian older adult caregivers (mean age = 73.3). These researchers found that dementia anxiety could be predicted by caregiver depression scores and whether the care-recipient had a diagnosis of dementia. They concluded that the anxiety that the caregiver participants felt about developing dementia themselves may exacerbate the stress of caregiving, which could be influencing both the amount and quality of care provided.

In addition, the presence of BPSD in care-recipients increases the chances of developing caregiver burden (García-Alberca et al., 2013). However, Lou and colleagues (2015) found that the length of time the caregiver spent with the care-recipient is a key factor in developing caregiver burden. In other words, if a caregiver is spending six hours a day with a care-recipient who is displaying BPSD, he or she will be more likely to develop caregiver burden than a caregiver who is spending six hours a week with the care-recipient.

Another significant source of stress for caregivers is challenges related to the organization of healthcare. Taylor and Quesnel-Vallée (2017) looked at the structural burden of caregiving in the United States and Canada. They found that caregiving was hampered in both countries by discontinuous and fragmented health and social care. They point out that even in a country where there is universal healthcare, inequalities can occur. For example, one of the researchers of the study was able to access a subsidized LTC bed for her mother. However, the researcher knew the process to acquire this bed only because of her aging research. Otherwise, her mother would not have gotten this bed. They use this as an example to show that inequities in both private and publicly paid formal services are likely shaped more by caregiver characteristics than the characteristics of the care-recipient. This means that disadvantaged caregivers need to spend a great deal of time and energy educating themselves about health and social care services and educating healthcare providers about the needs of the care-recipient in addition to advocating for the care-recipient. Taylor and Quesnel-Vallée call for more research to document structural burden as well as the development of theories to highlight the contributions of structural burden to caregiver burden.

Although the focus of the caregiving research has been on the negative aspects of caregiving, this research has had a tremendous impact on our understanding of the many challenges that informal caregivers experience. This has resulted in the organization of caregiver support groups across Canada and in the rest of the world where caregivers themselves can get support and information about caring for an individual who has a dementia. For example, the Alzheimer Society of Canada has resources for caregivers in each of its branches across Canada. A central message in these resources is that, as a caregiver, it is essential to find the time to also look after yourself! The growing number of agencies that offer **respite care** also can help to give caregivers some time to themselves by providing paid caregiving to the care-recipient. This type of caregiving can happen at the care-recipient's home or in a hospital or other formal setting that has beds that can be used for respite care.

The Government of Canada is now providing financial support to informal caregivers and you will learn about the specifics of this in Chapter 12. Supporting informal caregivers is very important for two reasons. Caregivers and those they care for prefer that their family member stays at home as long as possible before placement in a LTC facility. In addition, there is a growing shortage of available beds in LTC in Canada (Kuluski, Williams, Laporte, & Berta, 2012), which adds to the urgency of providing support for those that care for their family member at home.

REFLECTIVE QUESTION

Can you think of any positive aspects to caring for a parent or spouse who has a dementia?

THE JOYS OF CAREGIVING

Considering all the challenges that accompany caring for an individual with a dementia, why do informal caregivers continue to provide the care that they do? Well, it's because there are many benefits to providing care to an individual with dementia despite the many challenges that occur. Through a series of focus groups and personal interviews with Canadian informal caregivers from Manitoba, Ontario, and Saskatchewan, Peacock and her colleagues (2010) found several positive factors associated with caregiving. The participants in the study indicated that caring provides an "opportunity to give back" to the care-recipient. Many of the participants acknowledged that personal growth had occurred as a result of caregiving. Discovery of inner strengths, as well as feelings of accomplishment and competence, was experienced by many caregivers. This seems to stem from mastering the many challenges of caring for a person who has a dementia. Developing a closer relationship to the care-recipient also was seen as a positive aspect of caregiving. Interestingly, several of the participant caregivers who had children at home noted how caring for a parent with dementia was seen as positive role modelling for their own children.

7.5 SPECIAL CONSIDERATIONS FOR OLDER ADULTS WITH A NEUROCOGNITIVE DISORDER

LEARNING OBJECTIVES

To understand:
- the challenges that older adults and older adults with a dementia face in prison and the ethical implications of continued incarceration of a person with a dementia
- the association between dementia and depression
- the limitations of the research on dementia and depression
- the effects of dementia on the ability to drive
- issues related to identification of driving ability
- the consequences of not driving for the individual and family
- that programs and resources are available to support the individual and family in coping with the loss of driving privileges
- the effects of stigma in Alzheimer's disease
- the different types of stigma

INCARCERATED OLDER ADULTS WITH DEMENTIA

Before we discuss some of the issues that arise from caring for incarcerated older adults with a dementia, some general background information about adults and older adults in prison is required to "set the stage." The United States has the highest incarceration rate of any industrialized country with a rate of 707 per 100 000 population per year. The rate of incarceration in Canada is similar to most of the countries in the Organisation for Economic Co-operation and Development (OECD) and stands at 118 per 100 000 population per year. Iceland has the lowest incarceration rate of 45 persons per 100 000 population per year (Statistics Canada, 2015e). Maybe people are less inclined to engage in wrongdoing in Iceland because of the cold!

There are more men than women in prison in Canada. In the 10-year period between 2005 and 2015, the federal inmate population grew by 10 percent (The Correctional Investigator Canada, 2015). During this time, the percentage of the inmate population that is Aboriginal grew

FIGURE 7.7

Inmate Population Diversity

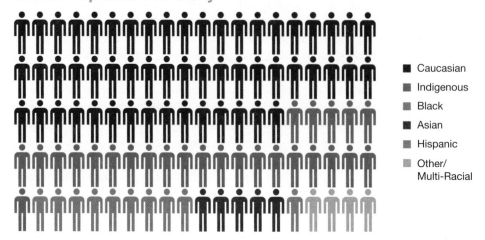

- ■ Caucasian
- ■ Indigenous
- ■ Black
- ■ Asian
- ■ Hispanic
- ■ Other/ Multi-Racial

Source: The Correctional Investigator Canada. (2016). *Annual report of the Office of the Correctional Investigator 2015–2016.* http://www.oci-bec.gc.ca/cnt/rpt/annrpt/annrpt20152016-eng.aspx. Reprinted by permission of The Office of the Correctional Investigator.

by more than 50 percent. The population of women incarcerated increased by over 50 percent and the number of Aboriginal women inmates almost doubled. In fact, Aboriginal women now comprise 35.5 percent of the population of women incarcerated (The Correctional Investigator Canada, 2015). Figure 7.7 gives you an idea of the diversity in the prison population.

What might be more surprising to you is the so-called greying of the prison population. Older adults represent the fastest-growing sector of the inmate population. In the United States, it has been projected that by 2030, the number of adults in prison over the age of 50 will have increased by 4400 percent since 1981 (American Civil Liberties Union [ACLU], 2012). In Canada, one in four of the federal incarcerated population is aged 50 or over (The Correctional Investigator Canada, 2016).

Are you wondering why the age of 50 and over is considered "old" in prison? It's because the physiological state of inmates has been estimated to be 10 to 15 years beyond their chronological years. Therefore, an individual who is 50 years of age in prison would have the physiology of a 60- to 65-year-old outside of prison. This acceleration is thought to be because of the lack of access to healthy living and healthcare prior to incarceration in addition to the stress of living in prison (ACLU, 2012). You may assume that this changing demographic in the prison system reflects the aging of our population, and this is certainly one of the reasons for the change but other explanations have been put forth. Another explanation for the growing number of older adults in the prison system in the United States is tougher sentencing laws—the passage of the three strikes law has led to an explosion of middle-age offenders serving long-term sentences (Moll, 2013).

REFLECTIVE QUESTION

Can you think of some of the issues that can arise from aging in prison?

Recently, researchers have turned their attention toward the aging prison population and the numerous challenges faced not only by inmates growing old in the prison system but also the challenges faced by the prisons that house them as well. Provincial and federal penitentiaries are not designed for the older prisoner in mind and are ill-equipped to handle the physical changes that can occur with aging. For example, older inmates may require assistive devices such as walkers or wheelchairs and they may require help with eating or showering. Dropping to the floor for alarms and/or getting into a top bunk to sleep may be difficult for some. The information in the Lived Experience Box 7.3 was taken from a participant in a study conducted by Crawley and Sparks (2005) in which they interviewed 80 inmates aged 65 to 85 years of age. This is an excellent illustration of some of the problems that can arise.

Older adults often have multiple co-morbid physical illnesses that cannot easily be treated in the prison infirmary. Consider that in one prison in Ontario, where more than half of the inmate population is age 50 or older, there are four dialysis machines running! (The Correctional Investigator Canada, 2016). As a result, healthcare costs are approximately three times higher for older inmates than the general population (Williams et al., 2010). Older adults often are victimized by younger cell mates because as a group, older inmates often have little social status within the prison order. Coupled with diminishing physical strength, they are more at risk for intimidation and bullying by younger, stronger, and more aggressive inmates (The Correctional Investigator Canada, 2012). The programming or rehabilitative programs offered tend to focus on developing vocational skills and social skills, which may not be relevant to most older adults who are close to retiring or long past retirement age.

Presently, correctional facilities across the world are grappling with the growing number of older adults, many of whom are in need of specialized care and re-entry into community programming (Stone, Papadopoulos, & Kelly, 2012). Despite the growing need, there is still no national strategy to address the healthcare concerns of the one-quarter of the inmate population that is now aged 50 or older. What is needed is more research on the dynamics of growing old in jail to inform the development of age-appropriate programs. Recent information from the United States shows that 13 states have built separate wings for older adult prisoners, nine states have specialist medical facilities including hospice care, and six states have entire correction facilities dedicated to older offenders (Davies, 2011; Sterns, Lax, Sed, Keohane, & Sterns, 2008). In Canada, we do not yet have designated prisons for older offenders.

BOX 7.3

EXERCISING IN PRISON: NOT AS EASY AS IT SOUNDS FOR SOME OLDER ADULTS

Now exercise, when you go out on exercise, you have to go out and stay out for the whole hour (Really?). Yes, because they lock the gate behind you, and they won't let you back in. And I mean, you know Albert don't you? Well I mean he's 82—can you imagine poor old Albert out there for an hour? So we don't go out ... I mean without being crude about it, you know, if you want to go to the toilet when you're out there you're in trouble aren't you? Cos there isn't one. And even if you wanted to go out to exercise for an hour, you've got to make sure you can get there before they shut the gate. Because if you're slow getting there, and they've already locked the gate, they send you back (Crawley & Sparks, 2005).

Crawley, E., & Sparks, R. (2005). Hidden injuries? Researching the experiences of older men in English prisons. *The Howard Journal of Criminal Justice, 44*(4), 345-356. doi: 10.1111/j.1468-2311.2005.00380.

FIGURE 7.8

blickwinkel/Alamy Stock Photo

Now that you have some context about older adults in the prison system, let's talk about individuals who have a dementia in the prison system. To date, there has been an absence of national studies conducted in the United States regarding the prevalence of dementia among older adult offenders (Maschi, Kwak, Ko, & Morrissey, 2012). There is an absence of such studies in Canada as well. Because of the accelerated process of aging that occurs in prison, there is reason to believe that the prevalence of dementia may be two to three times more frequent in prison than in the community (Wilson & Barboza, 2010).

There appear to be two types of prisoners who have dementia in prison: career criminals who have developed dementia while in prison and those who may have been incarcerated for a crime they committed while having an unrecognized dementia. Aday (2003) suggests that first-time offences committed in old age often are the manifestation of early dementia, which can weaken inhibitions and result in, for example, deviant sexual behaviour. Having a dementia may exacerbate the many challenges that occur as one ages in prison. A prisoner with dementia may no longer recognize the rules and regulations of the prison system, which puts these individuals at

REFLECTIVE QUESTION

Can you think of any ethical issues that may arise from keeping individuals with dementia in prison?

risk for receiving institutional charges (Maschi et al., 2012). There also are several ethical issues associated with keeping an older adult with dementia in the prison system.

Consider that there are four central components to punishment as laid out by law. The first component is to place convicted offenders in prison so that they will not continue to commit crimes. Prisons are thought to have some deterrent value both to the individual who committed the crime as well as to the larger society. Incarceration provides an opportunity to rehabilitate prisoners by providing educational and social programming. Finally, imprisonment provides retribution or punishment for wrongdoing. The reflective question below is a controversial one.

REFLECTIVE QUESTION

Should individuals who have an advanced dementia and who no longer know that they are in prison or what they are in prison for remain in prison?

A colleague of ours, Dr. Kevin Lawless, who is a geriatric psychiatrist, is a strong advocate for redirecting those individuals who have committed a crime because of a dementia from the criminal justice system into the mental health system, and he works with prosecutors in an effort to do this. Progress is slow but there is growing awareness that prison may not be the best place for individuals with dementia.

Here is more food for thought. Should older adults who have served time on their sentence and who are no longer a threat to public safety because of physical limitations and infirmity continue to be incarcerated? The topic of **compassionate release** typically results in opposing public opinion from punitive ("They did the crime so they should do the time") to more sympathetic responses such as letting the person die with dignity (Maschi et al., 2012). Hopefully, the development of a national strategy that includes policy and best practice components will occur in the near future to address the complexities that arise from older adults who are in prison with and without a dementia.

DEPRESSION IN DEMENTIA

It has been estimated that as many as 50 percent of individuals diagnosed with a dementia will develop depressive symptoms, and as many as 15 to 20 percent will develop a major depressive disorder (Fritze, Ehrt, Hortobagyi, Ballard, & Aarsland, 2011). The relationship between dementia and depression is complex and not well understood. The available data are inconclusive because of different dementia criteria used for inclusion into the various studies, the variability of assessment tools used to determine the presence of dementia or depression, and the length of follow-up (Bennett & Thomas, 2014; Cipriani, Lucetti, Carlesi, Danti, & Nuti, 2015).

What we do know is that depression commonly co-occurs with dementia and, in particular, individuals who have a vascular dementia. Depression also has been reported to be both a risk factor for developing Alzheimer's disease and an early symptom of Alzheimer's disease. For example, in a review of the literature, Cipriani and colleagues (2015) found convincing evidence that having a depression early in life was associated with an increased *risk* of developing Alzheimer's disease and that late-life depression was an early *symptom* of Alzheimer's disease.

Perhaps depression occurs after an individual has been given a diagnosis of Alzheimer's disease; however, Carpenter and colleagues (2008) concluded from their findings that this generally is not the case. It should be noted that depressive symptoms are difficult to assess in individuals who have a more advanced dementia as self-awareness and verbal skills diminish.

Individuals who have both a depression and a dementia are at an increased risk of hospitalization, placement in LTC facilities, further cognitive decline, and death (Fritze et al., 2011). Furthermore, Alzheimer's disease and co-morbid depression have been associated with an increase in aggressive and agitated behavior (Van der Mussele et al., 2013). Given the impact on quality of life that co-morbid dementia and depression have, a greater understanding of the relationship between the two is very important.

DRIVING AND DEMENTIA

EFFECTS OF DEMENTIA ON DRIVING ABILITY

Motor vehicle crashes are one of the leading causes of accidental deaths (Insurance Institute of Highway Safety, 2015). In looking at fatality rates due to motor vehicle crashes across the age range in the United States, younger drivers (aged 20–24) and older drivers (aged 80 and older) have the highest fatality rates (Insurance Institute of Highway Safety, 2015), with younger and older males having higher fatality rates than their same-aged female counterparts (see Figure 7.9). And, if we adjust for distance travelled, the fatality rates are higher for older drivers than for younger drivers, with drivers 80 years of age and older having the highest fatality rates (see Figure 7.10).

FIGURE 7.9

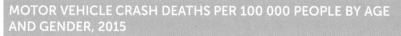

MOTOR VEHICLE CRASH DEATHS PER 100 000 PEOPLE BY AGE AND GENDER, 2015

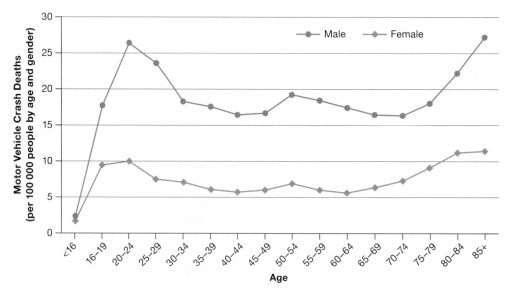

Source: Insurance Institute of Highway Safety. (2015). *Older drivers.* Retrieved from http://www.iihs.org/iihs/topics/t/older-drivers/fatalityfacts/older-people/2015. Reprinted by permission of the IIHS.

FIGURE 7.10

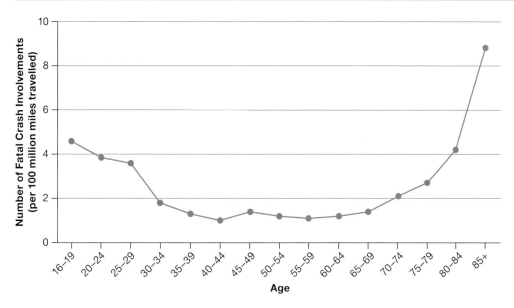

Source: Insurance Institute of Highway Safety. (2015). *Older drivers.* Retrieved from http://www.iihs.org/iihs/topics/t/older-drivers/fatalityfacts/older-people/2015. Reprinted by permission of the IIHS.

Part of the reason for older drivers having higher fatality rates is because of increased fragility with age. Importantly, the high crash rates of older drivers typically are not due to changes associated with the normal aging process. Rather, these crashes often are associated with health-related conditions such as dementia (Carr & Ott, 2010; Ott & Daiello, 2010). Closer to home, recent statistics from Transport Canada show a disturbing trend; that is, older drivers as a group have the highest rate of fatalities due to a motor vehicle crash of any age group irrespective of kilometres driven (Transport Canada, 2014).

How does dementia affect driving? As you learned earlier in this chapter, most dementias are progressive and involve impairments in cognitive abilities such as memory, attention, reasoning, judgement, and problem solving. If you stop and think about it, all of these abilities are needed for driving. However, not all drivers with a dementia are unsafe drivers. Early research in this area indicated that most individuals in the *early* stages of dementia are still safe to drive (Ott et al., 2008). However, at some point in the illness, all drivers with dementia will become unsafe to drive (Brown & Ott, 2004).

IDENTIFYING UNSAFE DRIVERS WITH DEMENTIAS

Physicians play an important role in identifying drivers with a dementia. In seven of the provinces and all three territories in Canada, physicians are required by law to report a "medically impaired" driver. In the remaining three provinces (Alberta, Quebec, and Nova Scotia), discretionary reporting is allowed, meaning that physicians can, but are not required to, report (Canadian Medical Protective Services, 2015).

TABLE 7.2

RED FLAGS THAT DRIVING MAY BE UNSAFE IN DRIVERS WITH A DEMENTIA
• Unaware of driving errors
• Getting lost or confused while driving
• Trouble navigating turns
• Difficulty staying in lane
• Missing traffic signs
• Near misses
• Unable to keep up with speed of traffic
• Other drivers honking
• Scrapes or dents on the car or garage

To assist physicians in identifying drivers with a dementia who may no longer be safe to drive, researchers at the University of Alberta developed a **screening tool** called the SIMARD (Screen for the Identification of cognitively impaired Medically At-Risk Drivers) MD (a Modification of the Demtect) (Dobbs & Schopflocher, 2010). The SIMARD MD is a brief, easy-to-administer paper-and-pencil test. It can be scored in a minute or two with no special training or clinical expertise needed. Importantly, it was developed and validated against actual driving performance using a driving evaluation scientifically developed to identify cognitively impaired drivers who are unsafe to drive (Dobbs, Heller, & Schopflocher, 1998). The SIMARD MD is available to healthcare professionals at no charge. Since its launch in 2011, the website at the University of Alberta for the SIMARD MD has been accessed by almost 4000 physicians and other healthcare professionals in Canada and around the world.

On-road assessments are considered to be the gold standard for assessing a driver with dementia who has been identified as being at risk for declines in driving competence (Wang, Kosinski, Schwartzberg, & Shanklin, 2003). Driving simulators also are used to assess declines in driving abilities, in part because they reduce the risk of crashes. However, the use of simulators is associated with simulator sickness, with older adults more susceptible to simulator sickness than younger age groups (Brooks et al., 2010; Roenker, Cissell, Ball, Wadley, & Edwards, 2003). For example, in a study examining left-hand turns, 40 percent of the older adults dropped out due to simulator sickness compared to only 14 percent of the younger adults (Edwards, Creaser, Caird, Lamsdale, & Chisholm, 2003).

Families also play an important role in identifying drivers with a dementia who may no longer be safe to drive. Once a diagnosis of dementia has been given, family members should begin monitoring driving closely. What should family members look for to see if their family member's driving has declined to an unsafe level? Red flags that driving may have declined are shown in Table 7.2.

As you can imagine, discussions with drivers with dementia about the need to stop driving are difficult given the importance of driving to independence and mobility. In addition, dementia not only robs the individual of his or her ability to drive; it also robs them of their insight that their driving has declined to an unsafe level. Hartford Insurance has developed a number of excellent resources to help individuals with dementia and their families cope with the loss of driving privileges, as well as ways to stay mobile. One of these publications is *At the Crossroads: Family Conversations about Alzheimer's Disease, Dementia, and Driving* (The Hartford, 2015: see https://www.thehartford.com/resources/

mature-market-excellence/publications-on-aging). Driving Cessation Support Groups (DCSGs) also have been developed to help individuals with dementia and their caregivers cope with the loss of driving privileges (Dobbs, Harper, & Wood, 2009). Individuals with dementia who attend the DCSGs show significant improvements in depression, increases in quality of life, and decreases in memory and behavioural disturbances compared to those individuals with dementia not attending the DCSGs. The specialized DCSGs are particularly effective in helping the caregivers deal with issues related to driving cessation (e.g., the repetitive questions from patients as to why they can't drive; the regular and ongoing anger and hostility associated with the loss of their license), as well as related concerns (e.g., reducing caregiver depression, improving caregiver quality of life, improving communication with family members) (Dobbs et al., 2009).

Loss of driving privileges is associated with loss of mobility and independence. For those with dementia, the inability to learn and remember bus schedules as well as the inability to understand spoken and written directions and to recognize previously familiar destinations make unescorted public transportation a safety issue. As such, transportation outside of the public transit system is needed to help individuals with dementia (and often their caregivers) stay mobile and safe. The University of Alberta's Medically At-Risk Driver (MARD) Centre has done a lot of work in this area including the development of regional and provincial surveys on alternate transportation for older adults, provincial listings of service providers in this area, the development of a *Transportation Toolkit for the Implementation of Alternate Transportation for Seniors in Alberta* (Dobbs, Pidborochynski, & Rehani, 2016) to help organizations in both rural and urban settings develop more responsive forms of transportation for seniors and persons with disabilities. Other valuable resources for enhancing the mobility of older adults who chose not to drive or who can no longer drive because of illnesses include publication of Mobility Guides that list service providers such as hairdressers, meal delivery, library services, and medical services who will come into the home. For an example of one of these guides, go to https://www.mard.ualberta.ca. The "sharing economy" is another one of the solutions to helping older adults to stay mobile. Ride-sharing companies like Lyft and Uber are changing the way that many younger and older adults today get around.

REFLECTIVE QUESTION

How would you get around if you could no longer drive?

STIGMA IN ALZHEIMER'S DISEASE

There is considerable evidence that the combined impact of having Alzheimer's disease and the negative response to diagnosis and symptoms significantly undermines psychosocial well-being and quality of life for individuals who are diagnosed with the disease. Loss of independence, status, identity, as well as diminished value and self-worth are commonly identified by people with Alzheimer's disease. In fact, shame and humiliation are the most common negative emotions experienced by individuals who have Alzheimer's disease (Werner, 2014). Stigma emphasizes and deepens the distress experienced by persons with dementia and, as an age-related disorder, older people with dementia are not only exposed to the stigma associated with dementia but to age discrimination as well—the so-called double whammy (Godfrey, Surr, Boyle, Townsend, & Brooker, 2005). We would expect, then, that an older person with dementia and a mental illness such as depression would experience a so-called triple whammy. Dementia has been so negatively portrayed in the media that many older adults in the Netherlands and Belgium are writing advance directives in which they refuse all medical treatment and request euthanasia in case they develop symptoms of dementia (de Boer et al., 2007).

According to Mary Schultz, who is a spokesperson for Alzheimer Canada, one of the most difficult things to overcome for individuals who are newly diagnosed with a dementia is not the diagnosis itself but getting used to how other people perceive them once they receive the dementia diagnosis (*CTV News,* January 5, 2016. Retrieved from https://www.ctvnews.ca/health/still-here-alzheimer-society-launches-campaign-to-end-disease-stigma-1.2724282).

Unfortunately, we know very little of the experience of dementia from the perspective of the person who has a dementia. This is because, until recently, it was a fairly common belief that individuals who have dementia could not possibly articulate the experience of having the disease. Consider the quotes in the Lived Experience Box 7.4 . These quotes are from a survey conducted by Alzheimer's Disease International (2012). Clearly, these individuals are able to discuss their experience of having Alzheimer's disease.

To add to the quotes above, here is a word about stigma and Alzheimer's disease from a Canadian woman. Cathy, who has cared for her husband who has had Alzheimer's disease for the past several years, notes that many people still can't believe that her husband is able to do his daily activities. Kathy states, "My husband is a greeter at our local church. But people ask me all the time, how can he do that?? He has Alzheimer's" (*CTV News,* January 5, 2016. Retrieved from http://www.ctvnews.ca/health/still-here-alzheimer-society-launches-campaign-to-end-disease-stigma-1.2724282).

There have been several types of stigma identified that apply to Alzheimer's disease. **Self-stigma** is a process of internalizing illness stereotypes and formulating prejudice and discrimination against oneself. In a sense, it is buying into the negative thoughts that other people may have about Alzheimer's disease. **Structural stigma** includes the quality of healthcare services and inadequate behaviour of professionals. Interestingly, stigma is not experienced just by the individual who has Alzheimer's disease. **Stigma by association** refers to the emotions and beliefs of those individuals closest to the stigmatized person, including family

BOX 7.4

PERSONAL EXPERIENCES OF STIGMA

"Upon diagnosis [people think] that you have lost your intelligence and you no longer have any of the knowledge you have attained over the years. [People] no longer ask your advice on anything. [They] talk to the person you are with and not you."

"People can over protect you which robs you of your independence much quicker. It should be a gradual process that is ongoing and care should be adjusted to the changes. People avoid conversation once you start showing you are having a word or thought retrieval problem."

"Friends, family are uncomfortable and say they don't know how to behave 'normally' around me anymore—they didn't really give our relationship a chance to move forward."

Source: Alzheimer's Disease International. (2012). *World Alzheimer Report 2012: Overcoming the stigma of dementia.* Retrieved from https://www.alz.co.uk/research/world-report-2012.

members and professionals (Corrigan & Kleinlein, 2005; Fung, Tsang, & Chan, 2010; Fung, Tsang, & Corrigan, 2008). Stigma by association seems to be triggered by attributions related to changes in cognition, behavioural problems, and physical and functional deterioration such as incontinence experienced by the individual with Alzheimer's disease (Werner, Goldstein, & Buchbinder, 2010).

Although stigma has been identified as playing a central role in defining the experience of Alzheimer's disease by Alzheimer's Disease International (2012) and the Alzheimer Society of Canada (2016d), there has been very little empirical research in the area, especially when you look at the abundance of studies pertaining to stigma and mental illness, especially schizophrenia (Brohan, Slade, Clement, & Thornicroft, 2010). However, this is beginning to change. In a review of the literature on stigma in Alzheimer's disease, Werner (2014) found that the amount of research investigating the stigma associated with Alzheimer's disease has increased in recent years. Werner also identified a transition from studies conducted earlier that were more descriptive in nature to more recent studies using more rigorous theoretical and methodological frameworks. Hopefully, the research will provide much-needed answers regarding reduction of the stigma associated with the disease as well as information on how stigma affects the individual with Alzheimer's disease.

7.6 GOOD PRACTICE

Angela K. Troyer, Ph.D.
Baycrest Centre, University of Toronto, Toronto, Ontario

WHERE DID YOU TRAIN?

I completed my undergraduate training at Bethel College in Kansas, and my graduate training at the University of Victoria in British Columbia. I completed a post-doctoral fellowship at the Rotman Research Institute at Baycrest Health Sciences in Toronto, Ontario.

WHERE DO YOU WORK?

Since completing my training, I have worked at Baycrest, an academic health sciences centre with a focus on brain health and aging. I also am cross-appointed in the Department of Psychology at the University of Toronto.

WHAT DO YOU DO?

My first job was as a clinical neuropsychologist, where I developed the Memory and Aging Program and provided neuropsychological evaluations for older adults with cognitive concerns. I currently have an administrative role at Baycrest, where I am responsible for planning, implementing, and evaluating our psychology services to meet the needs of our older-adult clients. I also play a role in ensuring that our psychologists maintain competency and meet legislative and professional standards, and foster a climate of evidence-based practice. I also conduct clinical research focusing on assessment and intervention of memory changes associated with aging.

WHAT DO YOU LIKE ABOUT WORKING WITH OLDER ADULTS?

I find the topic of memory and aging to be incredibly interesting, and am fortunate to have a job where I can continually ask questions and learn. Working with older adults is also personally rewarding. My clients are often very generous in expressing their appreciation for the work we do together, and it is gratifying to leave work at the end of the day knowing I helped someone in one way or another.

DO YOU HAVE ADVICE FOR STUDENTS WHO WANT TO GET INTO THE FIELD?

If you are interested in the field of aging, take a variety of opportunities to learn more about the area. You can do this by taking formal courses, keeping up with current events related to aging, talking with people who work with older adults, working or volunteering at a seniors' centre or hospital, or getting involved in research on aging at your university. These experiences can help you build skills and knowledge, and also can help you decide whether this is the right field for you.

Alyssa Beardy
Villa Caritas Hospital, Geriatric Psychiatry, Edmonton, Alberta

WHERE DID YOU TRAIN?

I graduated from the Registered Psychiatric Nursing Program at MacEwan University in Edmonton Alberta in January 2011.

WHERE DO YOU WORK?

Initially, I was employed at Alberta Hospital Edmonton as an undergraduate nurse in the Geriatric Psychiatry Program and then at Villa Caritas when the program moved to a new building. I work on one of the Acute Geriatric Assessment and Stabilization units.

WHAT DO YOU DO?

I am responsible for the physical care, medication management, and well-being of 7 to 10 patients on the unit. I carry out psychiatric and physical assessments. I work closely with patients to assess and stabilize them as part of an inter-disciplinary team. At our facility, we are responsible for making care plans for each patient, which includes physical, intellectual, emotional, capability, and environmental factors that may affect the well-being of the patient.

WHY DO YOU LIKE WORKING WITH AN OLDER-ADULT POPULATION?

Geriatric psychiatry is a field that I am passionate about because it gives me the opportunity to utilize all my nursing skills to help a population with often complex and diverse needs.

DO YOU HAVE ADVICE FOR STUDENTS WHO WANT TO GET INTO THE FIELD?

My best advice for anyone interested in this field of geriatric psychiatry is that you should make no assumptions about the capabilities of older adults. Unfortunately, there is a misconception that older adults are generally forgetful and frail and this is far from the case. The majority of older adults are managing well. One more piece of advice for future nurses is that developing an ability to help older adults remain independent and maintain a high level of functioning is key.

- The American Psychiatric Association has made some significant changes to its classification of dementia in the *DSM-5*, including the name. Dementia is now referred to as neurocognitive disorder.

- Dementia is an umbrella term that describes a wide range of symptoms associated with a decline in memory or other thinking abilities, with this decline in abilities eventually severe enough to affect an individual's ability to perform everyday activities.

- Alzheimer's disease is the most common form of the progressive dementias. There are two types of Alzheimer's disease: familial and sporadic.

- The two main risk factors for Alzheimer's disease are age and gender.

- The hallmark pathological changes in the brain with Alzheimer's disease are plaques and tangles.

- There are new diagnostic criteria for Alzheimer's disease that include the presence of biomarkers and the formalization of an asymptomatic phase.

- Mild cognitive impairment (MCI) identifies a spectrum of disease that includes impairment in both memory and non-memory cognitive domains. The deficits associated with MCI are not severe enough to interfere with an individual's day-to-day functioning.

- Other common dementias include vascular, fronto-temporal, and Lewy body. Vascular dementia is the second-most-common form of the progressive dementias.

- Parkinson's disease is a chronic, progressive disorder of the nervous system that affects movement. There is no known cause of Parkinson's disease and presently there is no cure. Sometimes dementia occurs with Parkinson's disease.

- Agitation and aggression occur in approximately 20 to 30 percent of individuals who have Alzheimer's disease who live in the community and approximately 40 to 60 percent of individuals with Alzheimer's disease who live in care facilities.

- Acetylcholinesterase inhibitors are used for the treatment of progressive neurocognitive disorders. However, the clinical significance of these improvements is minimal, if at all.

- Informal care accounts for more than 80 percent of the care needed by people with long-term mental or physical conditions. Caregiving can be a joy despite the many challenges that occur.

- Older adults represent the fastest-growing sector of the inmate population. There are ethical considerations to consider with continued incarceration of those individuals who have a dementia.

- In Canada today, driving-related crashes are the leading cause of accidental deaths for individuals 65 years of age and older. These crashes most often have to do with illness, not age. Physicians and families play an important role in identifying drivers with a dementia who are no longer safe to drive.

- Stigma is not just experienced by the individual who has Alzheimer's disease. Several types of stigma have been identified that apply to Alzheimer's disease: self-stigma, structural stigma, and stigma by association.

Key Terms

Acetylcholinesterase Inhibitors (AChEIs)
Drugs used to treat dementia (donepezil, galantine, rivastigmine, and memantine).

Activities of Daily Living (ADLs)
Routine activities of everyday living. There are six ADLs: eating, bathing, dressing, toileting, transferring (walking), and continence.

Amyloid Plaques
The sticky buildup of beta-amyloid protein outside neurons.

Amyloid Precursor Protein (APP)
This protein is found in many tissues and organs, including the brain and spinal cord. Little is known about the function of APP, but it is thought to be key in the development of Alzheimer's disease.

Atrophy
The wasting away or decrease in size of an organ or tissue in the body.

Biomarker(s)
Measurable substance or substances in an organism whose presence is indicative of some phenomenon such as disease, infection, or environmental exposure.

Caregiver Burden
Effects of providing care to an individual (most often a family member). The care commonly is perceived as a chronic stressor, with caregivers often experiencing negative psychological, behavioural, and physiological effects on their daily lives and health.

Cerebral Vascular Accident (CVA)
The sudden death of some brain cells due to lack of oxygen when the blood flow to the brain is impaired by blockage or rupture of an artery to the brain. A CVA also is referred to as a stroke.

Clinical-Pathological
A term used to refer to situations when the observable symptoms of disease are consistent with changes in the brain causing the symptoms.

Compassionate Release
A process by which inmates in criminal justice systems may be eligible for immediate early release on grounds of compelling circumstances that could not reasonably have been foreseen by the court at the time of sentencing (e.g., developing a dementia).

Computerized Tomography Scans
An imaging procedure that uses special x-ray equipment to create detailed pictures, or scans, of areas inside the body.

Dementia Anxiety
An increased fear of developing dementia in caregivers as a result of caring for a loved one who has dementia.

Early Onset-Familial Alzheimer's Disease
An uncommon form of Alzheimer's disease that usually strikes before the age of 65 years of age and is inherited in an autosomal dominant fashion.

Mnemonics
Any learning technique that aids information retention in the human memory.

Multi-sensory Stimulation (MSS)
A therapy that can be used with individuals who have dementia, developmental difficulties, autism, or a brain injury. MSS involves placing the person in a soothing and stimulating environment. These types of environments are specially designed to deliver stimuli to various senses using lighting effects, colour, sounds, music, scents, and so on. Often the walls have a combination of different materials that may be explored using tactile senses. An aide or therapist is in the room with the person to facilitate relaxation.

Neurofibrillary Tangles
These form inside the neuron and are made up of twisted fibres of a protein called tau.

Non-fluent Aphasia
Difficulty communicating orally and with written words.

Positron Emission Tomography Imaging
Positron emission tomography uses small amounts of radioactive materials called radio-tracers, a special camera, and a computer to help evaluate how your brain, other organs, and tissues are functioning.

Primary Progressive Aphasia
A neurological syndrome in which language capabilities become slowly and progressively impaired.

Reminiscent Therapy
Involves the discussion of past activities, events, and experiences with another person or group of people, usually with the aid of tangible prompts such as photographs and other familiar items from the past.

Respite Care
Respite care provides caregivers a temporary rest from caregiving while the person they are caring for continues to receive care in a safe environment, often the home of the care-recipient.

Screening Tools
Tests used to identify individuals who may need further evaluation in a defined area (e.g., cognitive performance), with these tests being easy to administer, short in administration time, validated for the area under investigation, and relatively free of educational, language, and cultural bias.

Secretases
Enzymes that cut pieces off the amyloid precursor protein (APP), which is embedded in the neuron's membrane. Secretases act on the APP to cleave the protein into three fragments.

Self-Stigma
Internalizing the stereotypes about the illness you have.

Small Vessel Disease
Small vessel disease is thought to arise from damage to small arteries, arterioles, capillaries, and small veins in the brain, which often are referred to as white matter lesions.

Sporadic Alzheimer's Disease
The most common form of Alzheimer's disease that happens to people age 65 and older. The ApoE gene has been associated with the development of this type of Alzheimer's disease, but the disease seems to occur because of a combination of genes, lifestyle, and environmental factors.

Stigma by Association
The emotions and beliefs of those individuals closest to the stigmatized person, including family members and professionals.

Structural Stigma
The poor quality of healthcare services and inadequate behaviour of professionals.

Photawa/iStockphoto.com

CHAPTER

08

CANADA'S ETHNIC DIVERSITY

"We are all different, which is great because we are all unique. Without diversity life would be very boring."

Catherine Pulsifer

Not only is the world aging but it also is becoming more culturally diverse with virtually all countries in the world having populations consisting of individuals from different ethnic backgrounds. Canada is no exception to this phenomenon and is, in fact, one of the most ethnically diverse countries in the world. There have been over 200 ethnic origins identified in Canada (Statistics Canada, 2013a). You have learned by now that individuals do not age the same. So, not only are older adults different from each other in terms of how they age, but they also are different from each other in terms of cultural background. How will culture influence our aging population? Unfortunately, we do not know that much about the older-adult immigrant's experience in Canada. However, research is growing in this area and with new Canadian data being available in the next few years, we hopefully will learn more about the aging of immigrants in Canada. What we do know is presented in the following pages.

8.1 CANADA'S DIVERSE CULTURE
LEARNING OBJECTIVES

To understand:
- a few interesting facts about Canada's population
- ethnic diversity in Canada
- where visible minorities live before coming to Canada
- the diversity in languages spoken in Canada
- where the majority of immigrants live in Canada
- how this pattern of immigrant settlement is changing

A WORD ABOUT CANADA

Before you learn about the ethnic diversity in Canada, we thought it would be helpful to give you some information about Canada. The country has a relatively small population considering that it is geographically the second-largest country in the world. In Canada, there are four people per square kilometre. To give you some perspective, there are 145 people per square kilometre in China! Interestingly, despite the low population density of Canada, Toronto is one of the largest cities in North America. In 2016, the number of people in Canada was approximately 35.16 million. In terms of population distribution, approximately 81 percent of the population lives in urban areas. According to the 2011 Canadian Census, there are just under six million people living in rural areas, and this number has been declining steadily since 1851. Canada's North is sparsely populated. As of 2011, only about 107 265 people lived in that part of the country (Statistics Canada, 2016a). Almost 90 percent of the Canadian population lives within 161 kilometres of the U.S. border.

One of Canada's unique characteristics is that it is a bilingual country. According to the 2011 National Household Survey, approximately 22 percent of Canadians reported French as their mother tongue while 58 percent reported English as their mother tongue (Statistics Canada, 2012d). In addition, almost 20 percent of Canadians can have a conversation in both of Canada's official languages. Eight of the 10 provinces are considered anglophone because the primary language spoken in those provinces is English. Most native French speakers in Canada live in Quebec, which is considered a francophone province because French is the official language in that province. About 80 percent of the residents of Quebec are native francophones and 95 percent of the population speaks French as their first or second language. However, the number of Canadians who report French as their mother tongue outside the province of Quebec is growing, with this number now over one million people (Statistics Canada, 2012d). Approximately three-quarters of the people who speak French as a mother tongue outside of Quebec live in New Brunswick or Ontario (Statistics Canada, 2012d). Interestingly, New Brunswick is Canada's only officially *bilingual* province (Office of the Commissioner of Official Languages for New Brunswick, n.d.).

CANADA'S ETHNIC DIVERSITY

We also think it is important that you have a general understanding of the ethnic diversity in Canada to provide you with some context in which to understand the older immigrant population. Therefore, we will start by giving you some general information. Over time, **immigrants** and their children who are born here have shaped the cultural diversity in Canada and, each year, new immigrants add to the nation's ethnic and cultural makeup. According to Statistics Canada (2013c), there were more than 200 ethnic origins reported by those surveyed. Thirteen of these ethnic groups have surpassed the one million mark in terms of membership. As you can see from Figure 8.1, Canada is indeed a culturally diverse country. The most commonly reported ethnic origin was Canadian followed by English, French, Scottish, Irish, and German. However, the length of time an immigrant spends in their host country can influence ethnic identity. In an interesting study, Ng and Northcott (2009–2010) investigated ethnic and national identity in 161 older immigrants from South Asia who resided in Edmonton. These researchers found that older age at immigration and low English-language proficiency were significant predictors of ethnic identity retention. For example, older Asian immigrants who came to Canada in later life tended to retain their ethnic identities, while those older immigrants who came to Canada earlier in life were more likely to have developed a bicultural identity that incorporated both their ethnic and Canadian identities.

Interestingly, patterns of immigration have shifted over time. Historically speaking, the immigration policies of Canada were more favourable to the admission of individuals from European countries. For example, in 1961, 71 percent of immigrants came from Europe—most notably the United Kingdom, Germany, Italy, and the Netherlands. In contrast, in 2011, immigrants from Europe accounted for only 14 percent of newcomers to Canada (Statistics Canada, 2016a). According to Statistics Canada (2016a), over half of recent newcomers to Canada (57 percent) are visible minorities from Asia (i.e., India and the Phillipines) and China.

> What could be some of the challenges faced by Canadians living in such an ethnically diverse country?

FIGURE 8.1

CANADA IS BECOMING INCREASINGLY ETHNICALLY DIVERSE

Jonny White/Alamy Stock Photo

Over the years, there has been considerable variability in the annual number of immigrants received by Canada. For example, in order to populate the Western provinces of Canada, the Canadian government admitted record numbers of immigrants in the early part of the last century. These numbers are presented in Figure 8.2. As you can see, the number of immigrants coming to Canada fell sharply during the Great Depression and World War II, reaching an all-time low of 8000 immigrants in 1942. Since the 2000s, Canada has accepted, on average, approximately 246 000 immigrants per year. Most people tend to migrate when they are relatively young. So it's not surprising that approximately 60 percent of those who came to Canada between 2006 and 2011 were between 25 and 54 years of age (Statistics Canada, 2013c).

In 2011, one in five Canadians were immigrants, also known as "foreign-born" (Ng, Lai, Rudner, & Orpana, 2012). According to demographic projections, by 2031, approximately 30 percent of Canada's population could belong to a **visible minority** group (Statistics Canada, 2016c). Canada has the highest proportion of foreign-born individuals compared to Australia and G8 countries. Japan has the lowest proportion of foreign-born with only 1 percent of its population being born outside of the country (Statistics Canada, 2016a).

You may be interested to know that in 2012, the majority of all immigrants to Canada were admitted under the **economic class** of the Canadian immigration policy. In this category, individuals are accepted into Canada because they have the skills or the financial means to stimulate the Canadian economy, or these individuals can readily fit into the labour market

FIGURE 8.2

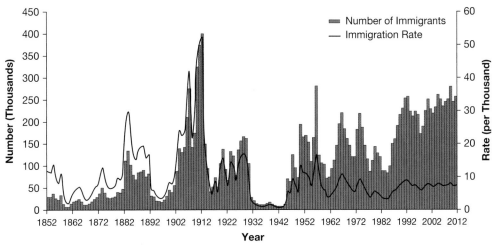

Note: Data available as of October 2013.

Source: Statistics Canada. (2016a). *Canadian demographics at a glance: Second edition* (Catalogue no. 91-003-x). Retrieved from www.statcan.gc.ca/pub/91-003-x/91-003-x2014001-eng.pdf.

because of age, education level, or knowledge of Canada's official languages (Statistics Canada, 2016a). In 2012, almost 32 000 people were admitted in the **humanitarian class**, which, of course, fluctuates based on international events. A recent example would be the large number of Syrian refugees taken in by Canada and other countries because of the Syrian crisis. Immigrants also can be accepted under the **family class** category. In this category, family members living in Canada can sponsor spouses and partners, dependent children, parents, and grandparents. As sponsors, individuals initially had to support their parents or grandparents for 10 years, but this number has recently changed to 20 years. For a spouse or partner, the requirement for support is three years and for children it can be 10 years or less. Under Canadian family law, after a sponsorship ends, the family may still be responsible for financial support for those they have sponsored (Franklin, 2015). It should be pointed out that while immigration is on the increase in Canada, the number of immigrants admitted under the family-class category is declining, and, in particular, there is reluctance by the government to admit parents and grandparents. This is because of the controversial perception that older immigrants are unable to contribute to Canada's economy (Franklin, 2015; VanderPlatt, Ramos, & Yoshida, 2012). More about the economic contributions of older immigrants in a moment.

REFLECTIVE QUESTION

Why do you think Immigration Canada increased the number of sponsorship years of parents and grandparents to 20 years?

LINGUISTIC CHARACTERISTICS OF AN ETHNICALLY DIVERSE CANADIAN POPULATION

As you may have guessed, Canada is a country of tremendous linguistic diversity. There is a growing number of immigrants whose first language is neither English nor French. As you can see from Figure 8.3, among those immigrants whose first language is not French or English, the Philippine-based language Tagalog has the greatest percentage increase as the language spoken most often at home (increasing by 64 percent between 2006 and 2011!). Mandarin has the second-greatest percentage increase as the most common language spoken at home followed by Arabic, Hindi, and Creole (Statistics Canada, 2012e).

Interestingly, almost two million immigrants who report speaking a language other than English or French live in Toronto, which is home to the largest immigrant population. Vancouver

FIGURE 8.3

COMMON LANGUAGES SPOKEN IN CANADIAN HOMES OTHER THAN FRENCH OR ENGLISH

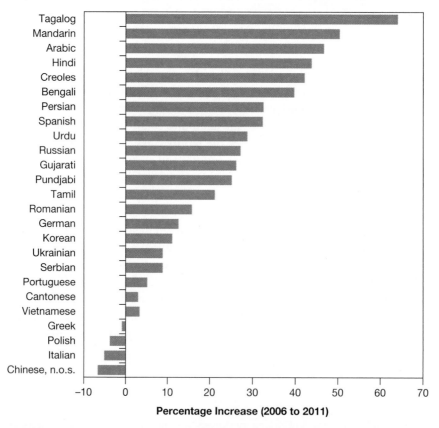

Note: Chinese, n.o.s. refers to persons who reported "Chinese" without specifying further in the question on language spoken most often at home.

Source: Statistics Canada. (2012e). *Linguistic characteristics of Canadians: Language, 2011 Census of Population* (Catalogue no. 98314-x2011001). Retrieved from http://www12.statcan.gc.ca/census-recensement/2011/as-sa/98-314 -x/98-314-x2011001-eng.cfm.

is home to the second-largest immigrant population who speak a language other than English or French at home (Statistics Canada, 2012e). Table 8.1 shows the number of Canadian immigrants who reported speaking one of the top 12 foreign languages most often at home in the six largest census metropolitan areas. From looking at this table, you really can get a good understanding of the linguistic diversity of Canada.

TABLE 8.1

SIZE AND PERCENTAGE OF POPULATION THAT REPORTED SPEAKING ONE OF THE TOP 12 IMMIGRANT LANGUAGES MOST OFTEN AT HOME IN THE SIX LARGEST CENSUS METROPOLITAN AREAS IN CANADA, 2011					
Toronto			**Montreal**		
Language Most Often Spoken	**Number**	**Percent**	**Language Most Often Spoken**	**Number**	**Percent**
Cantonese	156 425	8.8	Arabic	107 910	17.2
Punjabi	142 345	8.0	Spanish	95 020	15.2
Chinese (n.o.s.)	124 960	7.0	Italian	50 500	8.1
Urdu	105 545	5.9	Chinese (n.o.s.)	35 440	5.7
Tamil	102 700	5.7	Creole	34 015	5.4
Tagalog	99 980	5.6	Greek	25 235	4.0
Spanish	94 315	5.3	Romanian	24 725	3.9
Mandarin	91 670	5.1	Vietnamese	22 375	3.6
Italian	81 390	4.6	Russian	20 335	3.2
Persian (Farsi)	69 570	3.9	Portuguese	17 995	2.9
Portuguese	65 810	3.7	Persian (Farsi)	15 530	2.5
Russian	64 700	3.6	Tamil	13 730	2.2
Other immigrant languages	587 590	32.9	Other immigrant languages	163 215	26.1
Total	1 786 995	100.0	Total	626 045	100.0
Vancouver			**Calgary**		
Language Most Often Spoken	**Number**	**Percent**	**Language Most Often Spoken**	**Number**	**Percent**
Punjabi	126 100	17.7	Punjabi	27 435	12.1
Cantonese	113 610	16.0	Tagalog	23 710	10.4
Chinese (n.o.s.)	86 580	12.2	Chinese (n.o.s.)	20 835	9.2
Mandarin	83 825	11.8	Spanish	17 900	7.9
Tagalog	47 640	6.7	Cantonese	16 920	7.4
Korean	38 870	5.5	Urdu	12 320	5.4
Persian (Farsi)	28 970	4.1	Arabic	11 625	5.1
Spanish	22 505	3.2	Vietnamese	10 800	4.7

	Number	Percent		Number	Percent
Hindi	18 355	2.6	Mandarin	9 900	4.4
Vietnamese	18 225	2.6	Korean	6 565	2.9
Russian	11 765	1.7	Russian	5 755	2.5
Japanese	9 920	1.4	Persian (Farsi)	5 495	2.4
Other immigrant languages	105 140	14.8	Other immigrant languages	58 255	25.6
Total	711 515	100.0	Total	227 515	100.0

Edmonton			Ottawa–Gatineau		
Language Most Often Spoken	**Number**	**Percent**	**Language Most Often Spoken**	**Number**	**Percent**
Tagalog	19 645	11.8	Arabic	28 665	20.4
Punjabi	18 165	10.9	Spanish	11 325	8.1
Chinese (n.o.s.)	14 810	8.9	Chinese (n.o.s.)	10 490	7.5
Cantonese	11 260	6.8	Mandarin	6205	4.4
Spanish	10 865	6.5	Somali	5405	3.8
Arabic	9 755	5.9	Persian (Farsi)	5 225	3.7
Vietnamese	6 650	4.0	Vietnamese	5 210	3.7
Mandarin	6 425	3.9	Cantonese	4 790	3.4
Hindi	5 460	3.3	Russian	4 550	3.2
Urdu	5 460	3.3	Italian	4 110	2.9
Polish	5 205	3.1	Tagalog	3 735	2.7
German	3 770	2.3	Portuguese	3 570	2.5
Other immigrant languages	46 680	29.3	Other immigrant languages	47 395	33.7
Total	166 145	100.0	Total	140 675	100.0

Note: *n.o.s. = not otherwise specified

Statistics Canada. (2012e). *Linguistic characteristics of Canadians: Language, 2011 Census of Population* (Catalogue no. 98314-x2011001). Retrieved from http://www12.statcan.gc.ca/census-recensement/2011/as-sa/98-314-x/98-314-x2011001-eng.cfm.

WHERE DO IMMIGRANTS LIVE WHEN THEY COME TO CANADA?

When immigrants come to Canada they tend to settle in urban areas. According to the 2011 Canadian Census, the majority of immigrants chose to settle in Toronto, Montreal, and Vancouver (Statistics Canada, 2013c). However, this has changed somewhat in recent years because of the Provincial Nominee Program (PNP). The PNP allows provincial governments to actively select and nominate immigrants under the economic class to meet the province's need for population growth and economic development (Bonikowska, Hou, & Picot, 2015). As a result, increasing numbers of new immigrants are settling in Winnipeg and the provinces of Alberta and Saskatchewan. However, these increased numbers do not come near to the sheer numbers of immigrants who settle in Vancouver and Toronto. For example, more than 45 percent of Metro Vancouver residents are foreign-born and almost 50 percent of Toronto's population is foreign-born (Statistics Canada, 2016a). In fact, in some large suburban municipalities around Toronto and Vancouver, visible minorities make up a majority of the population. For example, 72 percent of the population of the municipality of Markham, Ontario, consists of visible minorities. Brampton, Ontario, has a visibly minority population that comprises 66 percent of its population. In Richmond, British Columbia, 70 percent of the population consists of visible minorities.

8.2 THE ETHNIC AND CULTURAL DIVERSITY OF OLDER CANADIAN ADULTS

LEARNING OBJECTIVES

To understand:
- how many older adults in Canada are immigrants
- the living arrangements of older-adult immigrants
- some of the reasons people migrate in old age
- the financial health of older-adult immigrants
- the physical and mental health of older immigrants
- some of the problems with the current Canadian literature on immigrant populations

WHAT DO WE KNOW ABOUT OLDER-ADULT IMMIGRANTS?

According to the 2006 Canadian census, nearly 30 percent of older adults who were 65 years of age and older were foreign-born, and just under 10 percent identified themselves as a visible minority (Ng et al., 2012). The majority of the older adults who immigrated to Canada in 2006 were age 65 to 74 and many (60 percent) were from Asia (Statistics Canada, 2008a). Not surprisingly, the geographical location of older immigrants is very similar to the rest of the immigrant population in Canada with the majority of older immigrants living in Toronto, Montreal, and Vancouver.

Although there has been a significant increase in the study of older adults over the last 20 years, there are very few studies that have explored the experience of older-adult immigrants in Canada (Ng et al., 2012). The studies that have been done have focused on those individuals who immigrated to Canada at a young age and grew old in Canada (Ng & Northcott, 2013).

LIVING ARRANGEMENTS OF OLDER-ADULT IMMIGRANTS

More often than not, cultural values influence which family member(s) will provide care for older family members and the context in which that care should take place. Although it appears that Eastern cultures' views of **filial piety** are shifting, there is a good deal of evidence that would suggest that those ethnic groups holding collectivist cultural values (e.g., Chinese, South Asian, and East Indian) are more likely than their Western counterparts (e.g., British, Dutch, and German) to live with family members (Chappell & Kusch, 2007; Kaida, Moyser, & Park, 2009; Lee & Edmonston, 2014; Ng & Northcott, 2013). For example, Ng and Northcott (2013) examined the living arrangements of 161 older South Asian immigrants in Edmonton, Alberta. They found that living with extended family was the most common type of living arrangement. However, several factors influence whether older immigrants live with their families.

REFLECTIVE QUESTION

Can you think of any factors that might influence whether older immigrants from visible minorities live with their families?

In addition to health and functional status, other important factors that influence the living arrangements of older immigrants from ethnic minorities are economic status and level of education. Ng and Northcott (2013) and Lee and Edmonston (2014) found that the probability of older immigrants from visible minorities living alone or with only their spouse increased as income and higher education increased. Lee and Edmonston also found that those older immigrants who had immigrated at a younger age and who lived and worked in Canada long enough to collect benefits from the Canadian Pension Plan or the Quebec Pension Plan and had private retirement income were more likely to reside independently. Those immigrants who arrive when they are older typically live with adult children, as many do not have an income of their own and are not eligible for financial assistance from the government (Da & Garcia, 2015). This can create several challenges, as you will soon learn.

Another factor that influences whether or not older ethnic immigrants live with their children is **cultural identity**. Cultural identity is part of a person's self-conception and self-perception, and this identity is related to nationality, ethnicity, religion, or any kind of social group that has its own distinct culture. For example, Chinese immigrants who identify strongly with Chinese culture and hold the cultural belief of filial piety may perceive that not living with children (usually the oldest adult son) will bring shame and embarrassment to the family, which results in a loss of face (Da & Garcia, 2015). In this way, cultural identity influences living arrangements.

Of note is that the majority of studies investigating living arrangements among older immigrants use only ethnic group membership as a measure of cultural preference and practice. However, Ng and Northcott (2013) chose to do their research a little differently. Rather than using ethnic membership alone to determine cultural preference and practice, they collected data on 161 older South Asians' subjective cultural identity as well as the number and kind of cultural behaviours each participant engaged in to determine cultural preference and practice. These researchers found that subjective cultural identity was a significant predictor of living arrangements. The participants in their study who perceived themselves as more South Asian than Canadian and maintained South Asian cultural traditions tended to live in extended families compared with those who lived independently. Those older adults who lived independently saw themselves equally as South Asian and Canadian or as more Canadian.

An older immigrant's level of **acculturation** to the host country's norms also can influence the living arrangements of older adults from ethnic minorities. For example, Kawakami and Son (2015) investigated older Japanese women's attitudes toward family-based care. These researchers found that those women who immigrated to the United States from Japan at a young age were more accepting of the North American norm of an independent parent–child relationship. The women in the study valued their independence and they preferred to get support and care from friends and formal support systems rather than their children. Canadian researchers also have found that older immigrants who come to Canada at a young age and who have become acculturated adjust their filial expectations and do not expect to live with their children (Lee & Edmonston, 2014; Migliore & Dorazio-Migliore, 2010).

WHY MIGRATE IN OLD AGE?

You might assume immigrants who relocate to a foreign country in old age do so because they need the help and support of family members. Although this makes sense, this is not always the case. As it turns out, many people who immigrate in old age do so to help their own children rather than the other way round. For example, Da and Garcia (2015) found that 21 of the 31 older Chinese participants in their London, Ontario study moved to Canada because their adult children had requested that they come to Canada to help raise their grandchildren. Rather than being cared for, they found themselves cooking, cleaning, gardening, and supervising homework in addition to looking after their grandchildren. In the Lived Experience Box 8.1, you can read some of the study participants' comments.

However, this living arrangement seems to create several challenges. For one, there appears to be a shift in family dynamics. Immigrants who immigrate in old age and who live with their children seem to experience a decline in status among family members. For example, older immigrant males no longer have control over finances or decision making as they no longer are viewed as the head of the household. If caretaking is the primary role of older immigrants, they often are financially dependent on their children. Further, recently arrived older immigrants who live with their sons or daughters might not be able to communicate with their grandchildren who might not be fluent in their first language. Certainly, this would make taking care of grandchildren a challenge. Older immigrants who live with family members might be socially isolated and they might have unmet social and emotional needs (Lin, Bryant, Boldero, & Dow, 2015; Da & Garcia, 2015). This isolation can be exacerbated by the lack of knowledge of the official language of the host country and the necessity of older immigrants to rely on adult children to act as interpreters. Importantly, adult children may not understand what the needs of their parents are. For example, Kilbride (as cited in Rosic, n.d.) interviewed older immigrants in Ontario who had arrived in Canada within the

---

BOX 8.1

OLDER IMMIGRANTS TAKING ON CHILD CARE ROLES

Susan, who is in her early 70s and was a physician in China

"The reason I came to Canada was to take care of my grandsons (twins) because I felt an obligation .... I decided to come over to help temporarily ... but I could not leave them because my daughter needed me desperately to help her care for the babies. Then my daughter found a full-time job, and I extended my visa again and again ....

eventually became a permanent resident" (Da & Garcia, 2015, p. 223).

John, who is in his late 70s (his son sponsored John and his wife to come to Canada to take care of their grandchildren)

"We [John and me and my wife his wife] help our son take care of our grandchildren when they [his son and daughter-in-law] go to work. Every day we also cook the meal, clean the house, and do some gardening" (Da & Garcia, 2015, p. 223).

last 10 years as well as their sponsoring family members. She found that the older immigrants in the study consistently expressed the wish and need to learn English. However, many members of these immigrants' families stated that their family member was not interested in acquiring English, and that he or she lacked the capacity to learn or retain a new language (Rosic, n.d.). Finally, there also is an increased risk for conflict between immigrants who come in their later years and their children. Those immigrants who come to Canada when they are older typically expect the duty of filial piety from their children who now may have acculturated to Western views of independence and who no longer see filial piety as a duty (Lin et al., 2015). So, many immigrants who arrive in Canada in their later years help their children by looking after grandchildren. As a result, their children can be gainfully employed, which contributes to the economic welfare of family members and helps their family make their way in Canadian society (Ng & Northcott, 2013). In this way, they contribute to the Canadian economy. VanderPlatt and her colleagues (2012) confirm this. These researchers looked at data from the 2005 Longitudinal Survey of Immigrants to Canada. They found that two-thirds of older immigrants who were sponsored under the family class of immigration work or are self-employed, engage in homemaking, and/or care for their family.

ARE OLDER-ADULT IMMIGRANTS FINANCIALLY SECURE?

As you may have guessed, the earlier that individuals migrate to the host country, the more likely that they will have economic security as they age. However, although most immigrants come to Canada under the economic class, a lack of recognition of their international qualifications and skills may be a barrier to finding employment in Canada (Jafari, Baharlou, & Mathias, 2010; Jibeen & Khalid, 2010). This can lead to unemployment or working at low-paying jobs for which they are overqualified. This can be a very demeaning experience.

Because the majority of foreign-born older adults came to Canada at a young age and have had time to work in the Canadian labour force (even if not at the profession they are trained in), they are entitled to the Canada Pension Plan. In fact, older immigrants who came to Canada when they were younger show patterns of government support similar to those of Canadian-born older adults (Kaida & Boyd, 2011). In addition, many immigrants who age in the host country may have pensions from employer-paid pension plans.

So, how financially secure are those older immigrants who do not age in Canada but move to Canada in their older years? Researchers have found that older immigrants who come to Canada in their later years have greater economic disadvantages than both those older adults who were born in Canada and those immigrants who came at a young age (Ng et al., 2012). It should be noted that Canada has social security agreements with a number of other countries that offer comparable government pension programs. A **social security agreement** is an international agreement between Canada and another country for the purposes of coordinating the pension programs of the two countries for people who have lived or worked in both countries. The agreements help eligible immigrants to qualify for Old Age Security, Disability, and Survivor benefits offered through the Canadian government (Government of Canada, 2016b). However, unless the country of origin has one of these agreements with Canada, the person who immigrates at an older age is not eligible for government assistance for a period of 20 years. What this means is that the sponsoring family member is obligated to support and cover all the expenses of their family member for that period of time. According to Kaida and Boyd (2011), living with adult children in an extended family is one way to lessen the effects of poverty for older immigrants. But, it is accompanied by many of the challenges just discussed. As you can see, living arrangements for immigrants is a very complex issue.

With increasing numbers of immigrants migrating to Canada and other parts of the world, there has been a growing interest in understanding the prevalence of mental and physical health disorders among immigrants as well as their use of healthcare services in their host country. What we do know from the studies conducted is that the healthy immigrant effect has been consistently found. You know from reading Chapter 5 that immigrants who arrive in Canada are healthier than the general population of Canada. This is due to self-selection and rigorous screening by the host country. However, this effect diminishes over time as immigrants adopt the eating habits and lifestyle of their host county.

Unfortunately, there is very little research on the physical health of visible minorities in Canada regardless of age. Khan, Kobayashi, Lee, and Vang (2015) conducted a review of 99 Canadian studies published between 1978 and 2014. These researchers found that very few studies used nationally representative data to compare visible minorities with white Canadians on specific health conditions or behaviours.

If we look at those older immigrants who recently moved to Canada, the research also is mixed. Some researchers have shown that recently arrived older immigrants do not have a health advantage when compared to Canadian-born older adults (Gee, Kobayashi & Prus, 2004; Newbold & Filice, 2006), while other researchers have found that older immigrants have equal or better self-reported health than those born in Canada (Chow, 2010; Ng et al., 2012). It is not clear what accounts for the difference in these findings but it could be due to the shortcomings of the literature.

Khan and colleagues (2015) have identified several shortcomings in the existing literature on the physical health of immigrants in Canada. For example, studies of visible minorities often fail to discriminate between immigrants who are born in Canada and those that are foreign-born, which confounds the results of studies looking at health outcomes. In addition, there is a tendency by researchers to combine visible minority status into one homogenous group and ignore the cultural diversity within each group. For example, the category could be East Asian but it may include people from the Philippines as well as from India, which are very distinct cultures. A further methodological issue is that the measures used in studies rarely have a clear cross-cultural validation and many studies have very small sample sizes, which makes it difficult, if not impossible, to generalize the findings to the larger population of immigrants.

One of the other difficulties in determining the physical health of younger and older adults from different minorities is that there are differences in how individuals from different cultures define health. In addition, there are cultural differences in the use of medicine (e.g., belief in traditional medicine) and of the healthcare systems. Finally, most studies fail to take into consideration the country of origin. For example, using data from three waves of the 2007 Longitudinal Survey of Immigrants to Canada, Settia, Lynch, Abrahamowicz, Tousignat, and Quesnel-Vallee (2011) found that those women who emigrated from countries with very low levels of gross national income were more likely to report poor health. In addition, both men and women from countries with high infant mortality rates and that were politically unstable also were more likely to report poor health.

Similarly, there is limited information on rates of mental health issues and mental illness for different racial or ethnic groups in Canada. Many of the studies conducted share the shortcomings previously identified in the physical health literature (Hansson, Tuck, Lurie, & McKenzie, 2012).

Researchers have found that immigrants who come to Canada as refugees have more mental health problems than immigrants who enter Canada under the economic or family class categories. Refugees also have more mental health issues than those individuals born in Canada. Systematic reviews of the literature on the mental health of refugee populations confirm that refugees are at a substantially higher risk of developing post-traumatic stress disorder because of their experiences of violence, torture, migration, and exile in their home countries (Fazel, Wheeler, & Danesh, 2005; Lindert, von Ehrenstein, Priebe, Mielck, & Brähler, 2009). In addition, refugees are more vulnerable to the development of psychotic disorders than immigrants who are sponsored by family or who come to Canada under the economic category (Anderson, Cheng, Susser, McKenzie, & Kurdyak, 2015; Durbin, Moineddin, Lin, Steele, & Glazier, 2015; Kirkbride & Hollander, 2015). But, the **incidence rate** of psychotic disorders typically is not found to be elevated in the country the refugee originated from, which suggests that the migratory or post-migration experience of refugees may play a significant role in the development of psychotic disorders. This is likely an understatement!

While there is little research available that addresses the mental health of immigrants from ethnic minorities in general, there is even less research on mental health issues in older immigrants from specific ethnic minorities. Let's look now at a couple of studies that have been done. Moztarzadeh and O'Rourke (2015) interviewed a sample of Iranian men and women (mean age = 66 years) living in metro Vancouver. These researchers found that the participants in general had high levels of depressive symptoms, especially if it was not the participant's choice to leave Iran and immigrate to Canada. There also are data that indicate that the rate of depression among older Chinese immigrants is nearly twice that found in the general population of older Canadian adults (Lai, 2000). However, Chow (2010) found different results in his sample of older Chinese immigrants living in Calgary. The older participants in this study reported good mental health overall. It could be that the amount of social support and level of acculturation account for some of these differences found in the rates of mental health in older-adult immigrants (Kim, Sangalang, & Kihl, 2012)—another area where more research is needed.

Of note is that there are many determinants of both physical and mental health. Gender, income, social support, level of education, and employment are important determinants that can affect a person's physical and mental health. Other determinants of health are an individual's social and physical environment, personal health practices, and use of health services. However, there are social factors that are more specific to refugee and immigrant populations, such as the experience of migration, perceived discrimination, and language difficulties, that also have been associated with an increased risk of mental illness and poor physical health. Beiser (2005) argues that researchers should examine the experiences of specific groups of immigrants and refugees rather than focusing on which ethnic group people belong to. This may help us to have a better understanding of the processes that lead to differences in risks and rates of both physical and mental illness in immigrant populations.

REFLECTIVE QUESTION

What kinds of difficulties do you think immigrants over the age of 65 face when they come to Canada?

CHALLENGES AND BARRIERS TO ACCESSING SERVICES FOR OLDER-ADULT IMMIGRANTS

Older adults from ethnic minorities face unique challenges when it comes to accessing services. Stewart and her colleagues (2011) interviewed older immigrants who arrived in Canada in the last 10 years as well as service providers and policymakers from organizations serving older immigrants. Older immigrants reported that they experienced financial and language difficulties, discrimination and negative attitudes of service providers, family conflicts, and social isolation. Government policies, culturally inappropriate programs, and lack of transportation all were identified as barriers to accessing social and healthcare services. Most importantly, lack of language skills and opportunities to learn English or French were identified as significant barriers to accessing social and health services. In addition, many older immigrants did not know about the availability of services or how to go about finding resources. Of interest, many of these experiences of older immigrants identified above are very similar to those of our non-immigrant older adults. In this same study, the service providers and policymakers reported that the high cost of programs, inadequate financial and human resources, and inadequate training and information about the needs of older immigrants interfered with the provision of appropriate supports. Both service providers and the older immigrants in the study acknowledged that the heavy reliance on family, friends, and interpreters contributes to feelings of powerlessness and the sense of having little control over their lives. Given that Canada will continue to be an ethnically diverse country, it is important to develop strategies that alleviate these many difficulties as well as widen and integrate support services into communities in Canada.

8.3 ABORIGINAL PEOPLES IN CANADA
LEARNING OBJECTIVES

To understand:
- the numbers of Aboriginal peoples who live in Canada
- the language diversity of First Nations people
- the lasting effects of the residential school system
- the problems with the research on Canada's Aboriginal peoples
- the difficulties that are faced by First Nations people
- the unique challenges faced by older Aboriginal peoples

STATISTICS ON ABORIGINAL PEOPLES

Collectively, the term "Aboriginal" refers to the original inhabitants of Canada and their descendants, including Métis, Inuit, and First Nations peoples. According to the 2011 Canadian National Household Survey (NHS), there were almost 1.5 million individuals who self-identified as Aboriginal, representing 4.3 percent of Canada's total population (Statistics Canada, 2013a). Of those 1.5 million surveyed, approximately 60 percent of individuals self-identified as First Nations. Approximately half of First Nations people reported living on reserves, while the other half lived off the reserve with the majority of these individuals residing in urban areas (Statistics Canada, 2008b). Many people who self-identify as First Nations are not registered under Canada's 1876 Indian Act. This Act defines who is considered a Status Indian and thus who is eligible for a range of programs and services offered by federal and provincial agencies. People who identify as First Nations but who are not "registered Indians" are considered non-Status Indians. The Indian Act is a controversial document even though it has been revised over the years. Howard Adler is a registered Indian and a filmmaker based in Ottawa. His film *Status* explores the issues regarding gaining Indian status under the Indian Act. If you are interested in learning more about this controversial topic, please Google the words "Status" and "Howard Adler" to watch his film. Based on the 2011 National Household Survey, there were 213 900 First Nations people who were not registered Indians in Canada, representing 25 percent of the total Aboriginal population (Statistics Canada, 2013a).

LINGUISTIC CHARACTERISTICS OF ABORIGINAL PEOPLES

The Aboriginal population is diverse and comprises many distinct cultural groups and nations. In fact, in the 2011 Canadian National Household Survey, 630 distinct communities were identified as well as approximately 60 different languages, which can be grouped into 12 distinct language families. The language family spoken most often among First Nations is Algonquian (Statistics Canada, 2011d). Algonquian consists of many different languages and, interestingly, five of these languages (Salish, Tsimshian, Wakashan, Kutenai, and Haida) are primarily spoken in British Columbia. In fact, the province of British Columbia is home to over 30 different Aboriginal mother tongues (Statistics Canada, 2011d).

Today's Métis predominantly speak French as well as numerous Aboriginal tongues but English is a strong second language. Close to 70 percent of Inuit speak Inuktitut. However, the number of people reporting Inuktitut as their first language is declining as is the number of people who report speaking an Aboriginal language as a first language (Statistics Canada, 2008b).

THE RESIDENTIAL SCHOOL SYSTEM IN CANADA

During the colonization of North America, serious efforts were made to assimilate the Aboriginal populations into European ways of living and thinking. Of particular significance is the impact that the residential school system had on Aboriginal peoples. Aboriginal children were forcibly taken from their families and sent into the residential schools system. Run by the church, these schools were funded by the Canadian government and were located across Canada. The purpose of these schools was to eliminate parental involvement in the cultural, spiritual, and intellectual growth of their children. Children in the residential school system were not permitted to speak their native language, participate in cultural rituals, or practise their spirituality, and death was not an unusual occurrence (Schiffer, 2016). Those children who did survive returned to their communities having experienced significant trauma. Table 8.2 shows several factors contributing to the negative health and well-being of residential school attendees. As you can see in the last row of the table, confidence intervals are reported. These interval estimates give an indication of how much uncertainty there is in the estimate of the true mean. The narrower the interval, the more precise the estimate.

When these children returned to their communities, they no longer knew their language or their cultural ways. As they grew into young adults, these children often ended up on the margins of society as they no longer fit into their own culture nor did they fit into mainstream culture. Many children of residential school survivors also carry significant trauma with them as the result of the violence and abuse they experienced from their parents at home (Adams & Clarmont, 2016). This experience is called **intergenerational trauma**.

In 2008, it was formally recognized that the consequences of the Indian residential schools policy were profoundly negative and that this policy has had a lasting and damaging impact on

TABLE 8.2

FACTORS CONTRIBUTING TO THE NEGATIVE HEALTH AND WELL-BEING OF RESIDENTIAL SCHOOL ATTENDEES, FIRST NATIONS PEOPLE IN FIRST NATIONS COMMUNITIES, AGED 18 YEARS AND OVER, 2008–2010			
NEGATIVE IMPACT REPORTED	**FIRST NATIONS ADULTS IN FIRST NATIONS COMMUNITIES WHO ATTENDED RESIDENTIAL SCHOOL**	**95% CONFIDENCE INTERVAL**	
	(Percentage)	Lower	Upper
Isolation from family	77.6	73.1	81.5
Verbal or emotional abuse	73.1	68.7	77.1
Separation from community	69.7	65.1	73.9
Harsh discipline	69.3	64.7	73.5
Loss of cultural identity	68.6	64.8	72.2
Physical abuse	66.9	62.2	71.2
Language loss	62.6	58.5	66.6
Loss of traditional religion/spirituality	62.0	57.6	66.1
Bullying	61.3	56.2	66.0
Poor education	44.7	40.3	49.2
Harsh living conditions	44.0	39.5	48.5
Lack of food	42.3	38.1	46.7
Sexual abuse	38.2	34.2	42.4
Lack of proper clothing	37.6	33.7	41.5

Source: © All rights reserved. *A statistical profile on the health of First Nations in Canada: Determinants of health, 2006 to 2010.* Health Canada, 2014. Adapted and reproduced with permission from the Minister of Health, 2017.

Aboriginal culture, heritage, and language. In June of 2008, then–prime minister of Canada, the Right Honourable Stephen Harper, made a statement of apology to former students of Indian residential schools on behalf of the Government of Canada. He organized a team of investigators to gather evidence of the many abuses suffered by Aboriginal peoples and the Truth and Reconciliation Commission of Canada (TRCC) was born. The work of the commission was completed in December 2015. The federal government now is collaborating with Aboriginal communities to implement the recommendations laid out in the findings of the TRCC (Leech-Crier, 2016).

DIFFICULTIES WITH RESEARCH ON ABORIGINAL PEOPLES

Unfortunately, there are limitations in the current research and statistics that are available regarding Aboriginal peoples. Presently, most of the available research and data consider Aboriginal peoples as a homogenous group and fail to take into account differences among First Nations, Inuit, and Métis. There also is a failure to distinguish between urban and rural populations and on- and off-reserve populations. It is difficult to get information on those reserves that are isolated because, in some cases, official birth and death records are not kept (Health Canada, 2014). Also lacking are data that are longitudinal and national in scale, and data that compare the same variables across the same cohort over the same time period. This makes it very hard to completely understand the health and social needs of Aboriginal peoples. In the next section, we discuss what we do know about these needs.

Why do you think the Aboriginal population in Canada is much younger than the rest of the Canadian population on average?

PHYSICAL AND MENTAL HEALTH OF ABORIGINAL PEOPLES

A common history of colonialism and the resulting economic, social, and cultural marginalization has had a significant effect on the health of Aboriginal peoples not only in Canada but also around the world (Gracey & King, 2009; King, Smith, & Gracey, 2009). The Aboriginal populations in Canada have major health problems at a much higher rate than non-Aboriginal populations (Health Council of Canada, 2013). These health issues include high maternal morbidity and mortality, high infant and young child mortality, and high levels of infectious disease. There also are much higher rates of diseases and death associated with cigarette smoking, alcohol, and drugs. In Aboriginal populations, the rates of obesity, diabetes, hypertension, cardiovascular illness, and chronic renal disease are much higher than in the general population. Consider that the incidence of tuberculosis is 26 times higher in the First Nations' population than the non-Aboriginal population (National Collaborating Centre for Aboriginal Health [NCCAH], 2013; Reading & Wien, 2009). There also is a disproportionately high rate of HIV-AIDS when compared to non-Aboriginal populations (NCCAH, 2013; Reading & Wien, 2009).

Similar to physical illness, Aboriginal populations also have a significantly higher rate of mental illness compared to non-Aboriginal populations. Consider that Inuit communities experience suicide that is estimated to be 11 times higher than the rest of the Canadian population. However, the rate of suicide among First Nations youth is far from uniform as suicide rates vary greatly among communities. For example, some First Nations communities experience virtually no suicides while others experience suicide at a rate that is nearly 800 times the national average (Kielland & Simeone, 2014). Recall in 2015 when the First Nations community of Attawapiskat received national attention when as many as 11 youth tried to commit or committed suicide in a very short period of time. Dr. Michael Chandler, who is a professor in the department of psychology at the University of British Columbia, found that those First Nations communities who were able to preserve their language and cultural practices had much lower rates of youth suicide than those communities who were not able to do this (Chandler & Lalonde, 2008; Health Council of Canada, 2013). As part of the TRCC, efforts are being made and more resources are becoming available to help First Nations communities restore their language and culture. There is much work to be done.

Unfortunately, equal access to health services is made difficult by the multiple authorities involved in the delivery of both physical and mental healthcare to Aboriginal populations. Coordination problems have created service gaps in many areas of care including palliative care, detoxification services, and psychiatric care (Kielland & Simeone, 2014). As a result, First Nations people and Inuit, particularly those living off reserve or outside their traditional territories, can face challenges in accessing comprehensive and culturally responsive health services (NCCAH, 2009).

Northern and remote communities face additional challenges. For example, there is a lack of appropriate health infrastructure, there are shortages in healthcare providers, and the cost of healthcare delivery is high (NCCAH, 2009).

In order to deal with these numerous challenges, there have been several Aboriginal models of care developed to address the overall health of Aboriginal families and communities. Most focus on restoring the relationships and cultural practices that historically promoted wellness in Aboriginal cultures. As mentioned earlier in this chapter, this involves reconnection to the land through ceremony as well as spiritual growth, and learning the language of their community (Schiffer, 2016). In addition, a national Hope for Wellness Help Line has been established; this service provides culturally competent crisis intervention counsellors to Inuit and First Nations people (see https://www.canada.ca/en/health-canada/services/first-nations-inuit-health/health-promotion/mental-health-wellness.html). The help line is open 24 hours a day, 7 days a week.

WHAT DO WE KNOW ABOUT OLDER ABORIGINAL PEOPLES?

In 2013, the Health Council of Canada conducted interviews with senior officials from the provincial, territorial, and federal governments as well as senior officials from First Nations, Métis, and Inuit organizations. They also held regional meetings across Canada to speak to Aboriginal older adults and learn about their challenges. This next section briefly summarizes the findings. If you are interested in learning more about older Aboriginal peoples in Canada, you are encouraged to Google "Canada's Most Vulnerable: Improving Health Care for First Nations, Inuit and Métis Seniors."

Compared to the non-Aboriginal Canadian older-adult population, more Aboriginal older adults are in poorer mental and physical health. Like their younger counterparts, many older Aboriginal adults experience emotional and mental health concerns due to the traumatic legacy of residential schools, loss of family members and friends, and poor state of youth and families in their communities. Several participants in the interviews shared stories of personally struggling to cope with the suicides of their grandchildren. They also experience more chronic health conditions and disabilities than non-Aboriginal Canadian older adults. Aboriginal older adults are more likely than younger generations to live in rural and remote communities where the majority of the population is Aboriginal, and where they can be connected to their culture. However, treating complex health issues is a challenge because these reserves are often in remote locations where healthcare resources are scarce. For example, organizing home care services or palliative care is tremendously challenging on reserves and often these services are not offered. Long-term-care facilities lack culturally appropriate care. Participants in the survey reported that if they felt ill or were having trouble managing their daily activities, they were unlikely to report this because of a fear of being taken out of their communities to care centres hundreds of miles away from family and their way of life.

On a more positive note, despite these challenges, many older Aboriginal adults are resilient and serve as role models and primary caregivers for grandchildren. Older Aboriginal adults hold valuable cultural knowledge; passing along cultural beliefs and practices as well as language is key to rebuilding Aboriginal culture (see Figure 8.4). In fact, in a study done by Thompson, Cameron, and Fuller-Thomson (2013), caring for their grandchildren gave Aboriginal older adults an opportunity to rejuvenate cultural traditions. One grandfather described his role as "walking the red road," which entailed a responsibility "to provide wisdom and ... protection" to his grandchildren (Thompson et al., 2013).

The health and wellness of the total community is one of the key components of the Aboriginal view of wellness of the individual (Statistics Canada, 2013a). Because of the recommendations made by the TRCC, federal, provincial, and territorial governments and agencies are

FIGURE 8.4

ABORIGINAL COMMUNITIES WHO RETAIN THEIR LANGUAGE AND CULTURE ARE HEALTHIER THAN THOSE THAT DO NOT

Lanzellotto Antonello/AGF/UIG via Getty Images

collaborating with Aboriginal peoples and communities to develop new health and wellness polices. Just this year, there was a groundbreaking transfer of healthcare to the First Nations Authority in British Columbia. In addition, Aboriginal wellness centres that focus on the whole person are being built in Canada. Some of these wellness centres even offer assisted living and long-term care. If you are interested in learning more, Google "Siksika Health and Wellness Centre, Alberta." The hope is that, in time, the health and well-being and cultural practices of the Aboriginal peoples in Canada will be restored. Attending events such as National Aboriginal Day can help all Canadians learn more about our First Nations, Métis, and Inuit populations.

CULTURAL COMPETENCE

We thought we would end the chapter with a word on cultural competence. It is important that healthcare providers or other service providers have a significant understanding of the Aboriginal or immigrant population they are working with. There are variations in the definition of cultural competence depending on the discipline you are in (e.g., social work, nursing, psychology), but, essentially, it is the possession of the skills and knowledge required to manage cross-cultural relationships effectively. Cultural competence has four major components: awareness, attitude, knowledge, and skills. You can have a great attitude toward and knowledge about other cultures but unless an individual develops the skills necessary to work with different populations, interventions may do more harm than good. Central to developing cultural competency is being aware of your own cultural biases, stereotypes, and prejudices (Pack-Brown, Thomas, & Seymore, 2008). In Canada, there now are several training opportunities and guidelines available to individuals who provide services to the Canadian immigrant and Aboriginal population. The Canadian Psychological Association has compiled a list of resources for those who work with individuals from different cultural backgrounds. This information can be found at https://www.cpa.ca/practitioners/Cultural.

Stacey Mushanski, Rec.T.
Vila Caritas Hospital, Recreational Therapy, Edmonton, Alberta

WHERE DID YOU TRAIN?

I am a graduate of the Saskatchewan Institute of Applied Science and Technology Program in Saskatoon, Saskatchewan. I graduated in 1992.

WHERE DO YOU WORK?

I currently work at Villa Caritas Hospital, which is an acute care facility designed especially for older adults. I started at Alberta Hospital Edmonton in November 1993 where I was first introduced to the field of mental health as a volunteer. In April 1994, a recreation therapist position came up in geriatric psychiatry and I was the successful candidate. I have been working with older adults since 1994 and have never looked back. I worked with the dementia population for 17 years, and these past 6 years I have been working with both dementia patients and those with mood and thought disorders.

WHAT DO YOU DO?

As a recreation therapist, I am responsible for providing both therapeutic and leisure programs to all patients based on their interests and likes and capabilities. I work alongside another recreation therapist. My caseload on average is 75 patients. Our department also has six therapy assistants who are caring and compassionate and love their jobs. Without them, we would not be able to carry out such a great program. Every patient is assessed upon admission and, based on their interests and physical and cognitive abilities, we provide a schedule of programs to attend.

WHY DO YOU LIKE WORKING WITH AN OLDER-ADULT POPULATION?

I have enjoyed working with older adults ever since I can remember. From a very young age, I spent a lot of time volunteering at our local long-term-care centre and thoroughly loved what I was doing and how I was making a difference. During my schooling, all my placements were focused on the older-adult population as I knew that is what my final goal would be. I also enjoy working with older adults as they are all kind and caring and have such wonderful stories to share. They all have a great sense of humour and are appreciative of the work that we do as well.

DO YOU HAVE ADVICE FOR STUDENTS WHO WANT TO GET INTO THE FIELD?

If I had to give any advice to students entering this field, I would have to say that all older adults were once in our shoes. They are all someone's parent or sibling or grandparent. They may have some form of an illness or disability but older adults still have values as people. If students remember that, it will help greatly in developing therapeutic relationships.

Kathryn Stokes, Ph.D.
Baycrest Centre, Toronto, Ontario

WHERE DID YOU TRAIN?

My path to the present was not a straight line. After flirting with English literature as a major, my focus shifted to physiological psychology and psychobiology, although I always maintained an interest in neuropsychology. My Ph.D. was on neural mechanisms involved in memory through a combination program of psychobiology, neuroscience, and clinical psychology at the University of Virginia, and my post-doctoral training focused on hormonal influences on cognition at the University of Western Ontario (now Western University). Over my years of training, my interest in animal models of memory lessened and in human neuropsychology flourished. I began my supervised practice experience at Baycrest and never left.

WHERE DO YOU WORK?

Currently, I work in the area of clinical neuropsychology at Baycrest Centre in Toronto.

WHAT DO YOU DO?

I provide clinical neuropsychological assessment, diagnostic, and feedback/psycho-education services to clients of the Ross Memory Clinic. This clinic services primarily community-dwelling adults experiencing memory or other cognitive changes due to a variety of potential etiologies, including normal aging, mild cognitive impairment, or early dementia syndromes attributable to neurodegenerative and/or cerebrovascular disease, mood/other psychiatric disorders, or other medical problems. Although any adult with potential neurodegenerative disease will be seen, the focus of the clinic is on the older adult.

WHY DO YOU LIKE WORKING WITH AN OLDER-ADULT POPULATION?

Working with older adults has proven to be very rewarding and enriching for me. When I first started at Baycrest, many of my clients were survivors of the camps of World War II. That was a humbling experience, hearing the stories of what these men and women had lived through, how they made new lives from so little, and how they felt almost affronted to have survived so much only to have their minds betray them. There are, as well, many clients who come from fortunate backgrounds, with families, successful businesses or careers, and productive and engaged lives. These individuals also express a sense of betrayal and wonderment at the changes they are experiencing. Many of the people I have met in this position have been truly inspirational in terms of their fortitude, patience, generosity of spirit, and tolerance. They are good models both of successful aging and of coping with adversity. Part of the neuropsychological component of their clinic work-up to me includes an acknowledgement of and appreciation for who these people were and are as individuals in addition to an attempt to determine what process might be affecting them. Although the news is not always good, I feel I have done my job well if I can help people to limit their fears with knowledge and can assist them to feel hope through realizing there is something they can do to address their cognitive concerns.

DO YOU HAVE ADVICE FOR STUDENTS WHO WANT TO GET INTO THE FIELD?

In my career, I have enjoyed being able to specialize as a diagnosis-focused neuropsychologist; in the future, I believe neuropsychologists will need to provide a greater diversity of services. Students who would like to do neuropsychology in the future will find that a solid background in structural and functional neuroanatomy and in research, while essential, is not enough: good psychotherapeutic (particularly in cognitive-behavioural or mindfulness-based approaches) and cognitive rehabilitation skills also will be useful, and the neuropsychologists of the future will likely need to wear many hats.

- Canada has a relatively small population considering it is the second-largest country in the world. In 2016, approximately 35.16 million people lived in Canada.

- There are more than 200 ethnic origins in Canada. Thirteen of these ethnic groups have surpassed the one million mark in terms of membership.

- Immigrants who come to Canada in later life tend to retain their ethnic identities while those older immigrants who came to Canada earlier in life are more likely to have developed a bicultural identity that incorporates both their ethnic and Canadian identities.

- Canada has the highest proportion of foreign-born individuals of the G8 countries and Australia. The majority of older immigrants are admitted to Canada under the family class of the Canadian Immigration policy. Most older adults who immigrate settle in Toronto and Vancouver, which are home to the largest immigrant populations in Canada.

- According to the 2006 Canadian Census, nearly 30 percent of older adults who were 65 years of age and older were foreign-born and just under 10 percent identified themselves as a visible minority.

- The age of individuals at the time they immigrate is the most critical factor affecting their life satisfaction, quality of life, and socio-economic well-being as they age in the host country.

- Most older-adult immigrants who are ethnic minorities live with family members but there are several factors that influence this decision.

- Immigrants who relocate to a foreign country in old age often do so to help their own children rather than looking for help themselves, but this comes with challenges.

- The earlier individuals migrate to the host country, the more likely that they will have economic security as they age. Older immigrants who move in their old age are more economically disadvantaged that those older adults who are born here or who immigrate at an earlier age.

- The needs of older immigrants are very similar to the needs of older adults in general, and they experience many of the same challenges in accessing services as do older adults who are born in Canada. However, language barriers exacerbate these challenges. The high cost of programs, inadequate financial and human resources, and inadequate training and information about the needs of older immigrants interfere with the provision of appropriate supports.

- Algonquian languages are spoken most often among First Nations. The Métis today predominantly speak French and most Inuit speak Inuktitut.

- In 2008, it was formally recognized that the consequences of the Indian Residential School policy were profoundly negative. As such, this policy has had a lasting and damaging impact on Aboriginal culture, heritage, and language.

- Unfortunately, there are limitations in the current research and statistics on the health and social needs of

Aboriginal peoples. This makes it very hard to completely understand these needs for both old and young Aboriginal peoples.

- Compared to the non-Aboriginal Canadian population, more Aboriginal older adults live on low incomes and are in poor mental and physical health. Financial abuse is common, particularly in small communities that have few economic opportunities.

- Aboriginal older adults in Canada also are more likely than younger generations to live in rural and remote communities. Treating complex health issues is a challenge because these reserves often are in remote locations where healthcare resources are scarce.

Key Terms

Acculturation
The modification of an individual or a group by adapting to or borrowing traits from another culture.

Creole Language
A stable natural language developed from a mixture of different languages.

Cultural Competence
The possession of the skills and knowledge required to manage cross-cultural relationships effectively. Cultural competence has four major components: awareness, attitude, knowledge, and skills.

Cultural Identity
The identity or feeling of belonging to a group. It is part of a person's self-conception and self-perception and is related to nationality, ethnicity, religion, social class, generation, locality, or any kind of social group that has its own distinct culture.

Culture
The integrated pattern of human knowledge, belief, and behaviour that is transmitted to succeeding generations.

Economic Class of Immigration
A category under which immigrants are admitted to a county because they have attributes that are thought to be helpful to economic growth.

Ethnicity
A state of belonging to a social group that has a common national or cultural tradition.

Family Class of Immigration
A category under which immigrants are admitted to Canada for the purposes of family reunification.

Filial Piety
In Confucianism, the virtue and primary duty of respect, obedience, and care for one's parents and grandparents.

Humanitarian Class of Immigration
A category under which immigrants are admitted because they have been forced from their country due to war, are in fear of persecution, or are, for example, at risk of torture.

Immigrant
Persons residing in Canada who were born outside of Canada.

Incidence Rate
A measure of the probability of an occurrence of a given medical condition within a specified period of time.

Intergenerational Trauma
The transmission of oppression and its negative consequences across generations.

Social Security Agreement

An international agreement between Canada and another country for the purposes of coordinating the pension programs of the two countries for people who have lived or worked in both countries. This agreement helps eligible immigrants to qualify for Old Age Security, disability, and survivor benefits offered through the Canadian government.

Visible Minority

Visible minorities in Canada are persons who are non-Caucasian in race or non-white in colour and who do not report being Aboriginal.

Mehmet Hilmi Barcin/iStockphoto.com

CHAPTER 09

AGING AND PERSONALITY DEVELOPMENT

CHAPTER OUTLINE

"I have a funny side. I have a soft and sympathetic side. I have a serious side, and a seriously romantic side. I have lots of sides; it's the main course I haven't quite figured out."

Richelle A. Goodrich

What is personality? Is it something that we are born with? Does it change with age? What about culture? or gender? Do either of these factors influence personality? Is there more to us than our dispositional traits? These all are good questions. Since Murray (1938) and Allport (1937) first conceptualized personality as a field of study, personality psychologists have focused on how we differ from each other. As you will learn, there are several ways to understand personality development over the lifespan.

9.1 TRAIT APPROACHES TO UNDERSTANDING PERSONALITY DEVELOPMENT

LEARNING OBJECTIVES

To understand:

- what personality is
- how personality traits are measured
- personality development across adulthood from a trait perspective
- mean-level and rank-order changes in personality
- how personality traits differ cross-culturally
- the theories of personality development
- the relationship between health and illness and personality traits

PERSONALITY DEFINED

As you can see from the quote in the opening of this chapter, individuals can think about themselves in many different ways (see Figure 9.1). Although there is no one definition of personality, it is usually described in terms of traits. Think of traits as an individual's characteristic way of behaving, thinking, and feeling. Notice the word "characteristic." This means an individual's *usual* way of behaving. For example, most of you will know someone who is usually friendly, or shy, or quarrelsome. Personality traits are different from personality states which reflect brief changes

FIGURE 9.1

Elena Ray/Alamy Stock Photo

in an individual's personality in response to an event that is happening inside or outside of the individual (Hooker & McAdams, 2003). For example, a person who usually is calm might be angry and yelling at people in other vehicles during his or her drive home in rush-hour traffic. Identifying and measuring personality traits have received the most research attention in the field of personality psychology (Griffin, Mroczek, & Wesbecher, 2015).

REFLECTIVE QUESTION

As you reflect on the definition of personality, what personality traits do you see in yourself?

HOW ARE PERSONALITY TRAITS MEASURED?

When trying to determine if personality traits change over time, most researchers look at **mean-level change** and **rank-order consistency**. Both approaches measure change at a group level. Mean-level change is measured by comparing mean levels of a personality trait, such as neuroticism, between two or more points in time. For example, a measure of a trait is taken when individuals in a group are at the age of 30 and then again when the same individuals are at the age of 60 (Roberts, Walton, & Viechtbauer, 2006). Rank-order consistency refers to the stability of an individual's rank-order within a certain group over time. For example, when compared to others in the group, do the most neurotic individuals at the first round of data collection remain among the most neurotic individuals in the second round of data collection? This type of question is usually answered by measuring the consistency in which individuals retain their relative order for a trait between two points in time. Rank-order correlations are used to measure the degree to which individuals in the group change rank-order on a particular trait (Roberts et al., 2006). What you will find as you read this chapter is that personality development involves both stability and change.

THE BIG FIVE–FACTOR MODEL OF PERSONALITY

As you might recall from your introductory psychology classes, over the years, many psychologists have tried to identify the basic traits that are central to our personalities. As early as 1950, Raymond Cattell (1950; 1966) began his work on condensing a list of personality traits first identified by Allport (1937). Using **factor analysis**, Cattell made Allport's original list of traits considerably smaller. He reasoned that an individual's personality could be fully understood using the 16 related traits identified through factor analysis. Costa and McCrae also used factor analysis to categorize personality traits (Costa & McCrae, 1992). Their original model included just three factors: neuroticism, extraversion, and openness. However, they revised their original model and argued that most personality traits come from five higher-order factors, which are described in their Five-Factor Model (FFM) of personality, which is sometimes referred to as the "Big Five" (Costa & McCrae, 1992; McCrae & Costa, 1999). The personality traits that stem from the five factors are typically measured using the NEO Personality Inventory or the NEO-PI-Revised. The NEO-PI initially included only the three original factors of neuroticism, extraversion, and openness (hence the name "NEO") (McCrae & Costa, 1987). The factors of agreeableness and conscientiousness were added in 1987 (McCrae & Costa, 1987). Although there still is some disagreement regarding the organization and number of personality traits, the FFM is the most widely accepted trait theory in the field of personality psychology (Griffin et al., 2015). The FFM of personality and the traits that underlie each factor are presented in Table 9.1. As you can see, each of the five factors in the model has many dimensions.

REFLECTIVE QUESTION

Do you see any difficulties that might arise by having a high score on the trait of Agreeableness?

TABLE 9.1

THE FIVE-FACTOR MODEL OF PERSONALITY	
TRAIT	**DESCRIPTION OF DIMENSIONS**
Openness to Experience	Original, imaginative, creative, curious, daring, artistic, independent
Conscientiousness	Careful, reliable, hard-working, ambitious, well-organized, energetic, persevering
Extraversion	Sociable, fun-loving, affectionate, friendly, passionate, active
Agreeableness	Good-natured, soft-hearted, courteous, selfless, easygoing, forgiving
Neuroticism	Fearful, angry, anxious, insecure, moody, jealous, self-conscious

Source: Adapted from McCrae & Costa. (1987). Validation of the five-factor model of personality across instruments and observers. *Journal of Personality and Social Psychology, 52*(1), 81–90.

Based on their early research findings, McCrae and Costa (1999) argued that if there is going to be a change in a personality trait, this change most likely will occur before the individual is 30 years of age and then the trait will remain relatively stable thereafter. This argument led researchers Srivastava, John, Gosling, and Potter (2003) to label this theory the "hard plaster hypothesis." In fact, it was very common to think that personality did not change as you got older. This type of thinking led to clichés such as "you can't teach an old dog new tricks." However, here is some food for thought. Let's consider the baby boom generation for a moment. The observation that personality is set like plaster by the age of 30 might make sense for this generation. Consider that by the age of 30 many baby boomers achieved several major developmental milestones such as having a stable career (many right out of high school), getting married, and starting a family. However, in recent years, researchers have found that the transition to adulthood is taking longer for young people to complete. Young people are living with their parents longer, attaining higher levels of education, and marrying later in life than their baby boom parents did (Marantz Henig & Henig, 2012). Many young adults today do not start careers, get married, or have their first child until their early 30s. Therefore, it could be the case that evaluating personality change in present-day 30-year-olds would likely not show trait stability because of the delayed attainment of milestones in this cohort. Consequently, cohort effects might interfere with the identification of the developmental path of personality (Smits, Dolan, Vorst, Wicherts, & Timmerman, 2011). Something to think about for sure. We don't know about you, but we are really interested in what future research shows us about the developmental pattern of personality.

Let's turn now and look at what current research on mean-level differences and rank-order stability in the Big Five personality dimensions from childhood to old age has to say. As you will learn, both methods contradict the hard plaster hypothesis.

CHANGE AND STABILITY OF PERSONALITY TRAITS ACROSS THE LIFESPAN

MEAN-LEVEL CHANGES

Regarding mean-level changes, whether the data come from cross-sectional or longitudinal research designs, studies have consistently shown that personality traits do continue to change across the lifespan (Allemand, Zimprich, & Martin, 2008; Bleidorn, Kandler, Reimann, Spinath, & Angleitner, 2009; Helson & Kwan, 2000; Lucas & Donnellan, 2009; Mõttus, Johnson, & Deary,

2012; Roberts & DelVecchio, 2000; Soto, John, Gosling, & Potter, 2011; Terracciano, McCrae, Brant, & Costa, 2005). Overall, the research on the Big Five traits indicates a normative pattern of development in which individuals become more agreeable and emotionally stable, more conscientious, and less neurotic with age. Caspi and colleagues (2005) called this the **maturity principle**. Individuals who have this combination of developmental traits tend to be more successful in both their professional and personal lives and they tend to be healthier and live longer (Roberts, Kuncel, Shiner, Caspi, & Goldberg, 2007). For example, Mroczek and Spiro (2007) found that men who had higher levels of the trait neuroticism had much lower survival rates than men who had lower levels of this trait.

The largest study to date investigating mean-level changes of the Big Five personality traits across adulthood was done by Roberts and colleagues (2006). They used 92 studies in their meta-analysis, which included an age range of individuals 10 to 102 years old. A modified version of the FFM was used to categorize the standardized mean differences of personality trait change. They modified the FFM by dividing the trait of extraversion into social dominance (independence and self-confidence) and social vitality (sociability, friendliness, and positive affect). As you can see from Figure 9.2, Roberts and his colleagues (2006) found significant mean-level changes in all trait domains at some point in development. Although most of the mean-level changes occurred between the ages of 20 and 40 and then levelled off, small changes at the mean level for agreeableness, conscientiousness, and openness to experience continued to occur past the age of 40.

Are you wondering what, if any, change you would see if only older adults were included in the sample? Mõttus and colleagues (2012) were curious about this as well. They compared a group of participants 69 to 72 years of age with a group of participants 81 to 87 years of age. The older group showed significantly larger mean-level declines on the traits of extraversion, openness to experience, agreeableness, and conscientiousness than the younger group. Neuroticism increased between the ages of 81 and 87 years but only for women. As Griffin and his colleagues (2015) point out, we might want to rethink the assumption that older adults get stuck in their ways.

REFLECTIVE QUESTIONS

Why do you think that the oldest adults had larger declines on the traits of extraversion, agreeableness, and conscientiousness than the younger older adults?

Is there benefit to this? Why would the oldest adults become more neurotic?

Although there is much evidence to suggest that personality is the most stable during middle-age, researchers are emphasizing the point that some personality change continues throughout life. This viewpoint contradicts McCrae and Costa's 1992 argument that an individual's personality does not change past the age 30. Now, having said that, the changes are not as pronounced as the changes seen in young adulthood but change is still occurring past age 30.

One of the most interesting findings from investigating mean-level changes in personality traits is that it appears that young adulthood, rather than adolescence, is an important phase in the development of an individual's personality across the lifespan. This makes sense if you consider that young adulthood typically is a period where important changes take place in terms of deciding on a career, developing relationships that are more intimate, and, in many cases, taking

FIGURE 9.2

META-ANALYSIS OF SIX BIG FIVE PERSONALITY TRAITS

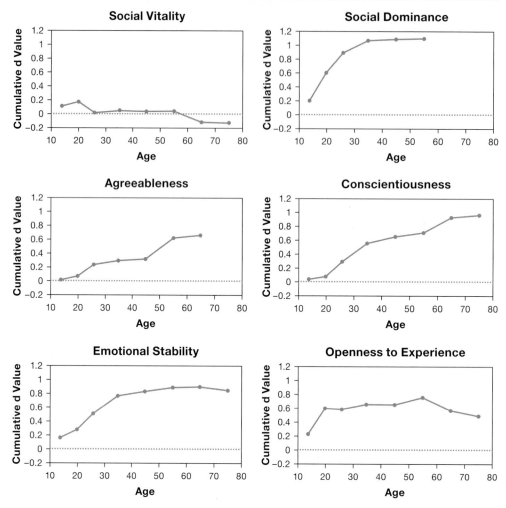

Source: Roberts, B.W., Walton, K.E., & Viechtbauer, W. (2006). Patterns of mean-level change in personality traits across the life course: A meta-analysis of longitudinal studies. *Psychological Bulletin, 132*(1), 1–25. doi:10.1037/0033-2909.132.1.1.

on the role of a parent (Donnellan, Hill, & Roberts, 2015). This is quite different from Erik Erikson's (1959) **stage theory** where he proposed that adolescence is the time where personality changes the most.

RANK-ORDER STABILITY

While there is much evidence that would suggest that there are some mean-level changes in personality traits with age, it also is the case that individuals might retain their relative positions or rank-orders regarding the Big Five personality traits. Roberts and DelVecchio (2000) conducted a meta-analysis of 152 studies in order to examine the rank-order stability of traits from childhood to older adulthood. As you can see from Figure 9.3, it would appear that as we age, rank-order

FIGURE 9.3

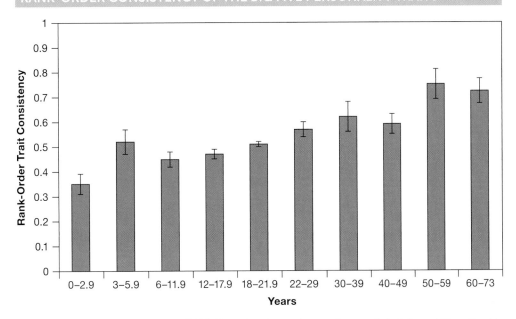

Source: Roberts, B.W., & DelVecchio, W.F. (2000). The rank-order consistency of personality traits from childhood to old age: A quantitative review of longitudinal studies. *Psychology Bulletin, 126*(1), 3–25. doi:10.1037/0033-2909.126.1.3.

change increases in a linear yet step-like fashion where it reaches a peak sometime after age 50. These researchers found the lowest stability coefficients were in studies based on children (averaging 0.40), increased to higher levels among adults aged 18 to 39 (0.55), and reached a plateau of 0.75 for older adults aged 50 to 70 years. However, some rank-order change is occurring because the correlations are not 1.00, which would indicate complete stability.

What about rank-order change in people over the age of 70 years? Unfortunately, there are very few studies that include these oldest cohorts. In a study that did include people over 70 years of age, Specht, Egloff, and Schmukle (2011) found that the traits of extraversion, conscientiousness, and agreeableness showed more rank-order change in the over-75 age group than in the 60- to 70-year-old age group. Much more research is needed in the oldest age groups to help us get a greater understanding of rank-order change in personality and/or development in the later years of life.

As you think about these two types of personality measurements, can you see any problems with measuring personality in this way? You would be correct if you said that measuring personality change using statistical analyses such as means and correlations masks *individual* differences in change (Griffin et al., 2015). For example, the amount of a trait such as openness to experience might increase or decrease in some individuals as they age, and this would counterbalance each person's change, resulting in an absence of mean-level change overall (Roberts et al., 2006). As such, even though it might appear that there are no mean-level changes over time regarding a personality trait in a particular group, there can still be considerable individual differences. Some traits might stay the same in an individual while other traits can change very quickly or slowly over time.

Because of the shortcomings associated with measuring personality change at the group level, researchers have begun investigating personality change at the individual level. This is called **intra-individual change**. Investigating change at this level has become more easily accomplished because of advances in statistical procedures (Mroczek, Almeida, Spiro, & Pafford, 2006). For example, Vaidya, Gray, Haig, Mroczek, and Watson (2008) found individual differences in changes in the trait conscientiousness. Recall that the developmental pattern is an increase in this trait until advanced age. However, these researchers found that in their sample of young adults, some individuals became much more conscientious than others, and other individuals showed a measurable decline in this trait. Other studies have shown some interesting findings as well. Donnellan, Conger, and Burzette (2007) followed 427 adolescents over a period of 10 years, from 17 to 27 years of age. They found that those adolescents who have a tendency to change very little on the Big Five traits over time are usually those individuals who already show high levels of the Big Five traits associated with the maturity principle. In other words, those adolescents that were relatively mature showed fewer personality changes over time. They did not change because the normal developmental pattern of personality change occurred earlier in their lifespan (Griffin et al., 2015). Lönnqvist, Mäkinen, Paunonen, Henriksson, and Verkasalo (2008) followed a sample of young men from the ages of 20 to 35 for 15 years and found similar results. Those who matured at a younger age showed very little change in the Big Five personality traits over the 15 years. Further research on intra-individual change might show us some more interesting results that deviate from the normal developmental pattern shown in the mean-level-change studies.

WHAT ACCOUNTS FOR PERSONALITY CHANGE ACROSS THE LIFESPAN?

At this point, it seems clear that personality trait development as you age involves both change and stability. The question is, why? You likely will not be surprised by the answer. While a discussion of the many proposed theories of personality change is beyond the scope of this chapter, it basically comes down to the same old nature versus nurture argument. The belief that genetics is very important to how your personality develops is known as the **biological essentialist perspective** (McAdams & Olson, 2010). This is the basis of the FFM of personality in which McCrae and Costa (1999) originally argued that personality trait development is governed by genetic factors rather than environmental factors. In a review of studies, Krueger, Johnson, and Kling (2006) found that between 40 percent and 60 percent of the differences in personality traits can be attributed to genetics. However, as you can see from these numbers, genetics is not the whole story.

Another approach to understanding personality change proposes that environmental factors account for changes in personality traits across the lifespan. This approach is known as the **contextualist model** (Bandura, 1999; Zelli & Dodge, 1999). The idea is that one's personality development is influenced by one's interaction with the environment (Roberts et al., 2006). So how does the environment account for both stability and change? Jackson (2011) explains that stability occurs because an individual's personality traits influence the type of life experiences that the individual will seek out. For example, people high on the excitement-seeking facet of extraversion might choose to skydive or race cars. This aspect of personality will remain stable as they age because they will seek out social environments that support the part of them that seeks out excitement. Roberts, Donnellan, and Hill (2013) call this the **correspondence principle**, in which personality stability is influenced by the active choices we make. Griffin et al. (2015) argue that the correspondence principle also can explain the mean-level changes that are observed in personality development. Generally speaking, agreeable adolescents are more likely to become more agreeable adults because they are more likely to find themselves in social situations that reinforce the behaviours, thoughts, and feelings associated with this trait (Griffin et al., 2015).

Finally, there are those researchers who argue that personality development is the result of both genes and the social environment. The **interactional model** considers both the person and the environment in the development of personality (Kogan, 1990; Levinson, 1978). However, the debate continues about how much each of these factors contributes to personality development, and in which way.

GENDER DIFFERENCES AND AGE IN THE BIG FIVE PERSONALITY TRAITS

While it is clear that the Big Five personality traits are found in both genders (Allemand et al., 2008; Bleidorn et al., 2009; Helson & Kwan, 2000; Lucas & Donnellan, 2009; Mõttus et al., 2012; Roberts & DelVecchio, 2000; Soto et al., 2011; Terracciano et al., 2005, McCrae, Brant, & Costa, 2005), it is less clear if these traits change differentially in men and women as they age. For example, Lucas and Donnellan (2009) reported that, in men only, the traits of neuroticism and extraversion were negatively related after age 70, while agreeableness was positively related to extraversion. Looking at a Canadian sample of men and women aged 55 to 85 years, Small, Hertzog, Hultsch, and Dixon (2003) found that, over a six-year period, men increased in the trait neuroticism while women decreased in this same trait. Chapman, Duberstein, Sörensen, and Lyness (2007) examined a sample of 751 men and women aged 65 to 98 (with an average age of 75) and found higher levels of neuroticism and agreeableness among older women than among the older men. However, gender differences among the Big Five traits were absent in Donnellan and Lucas's (2008) sample of 16-to 85-year-olds. In a recent study, Iveniuk, Laumann, Waite, McClintock, and Tiedt (2015) did find gender differences among the Big Five traits. Figure 9.4 shows line graphs that plot the mean factor scores of the Big Five traits by age and gender. Data were obtained from 3337 American participants in the National Social Life, Health, and Aging Project (NSHAP). The first wave of data was collected in 2005 to 2006 and the second wave was collected in 2010 to 2011. In general, women were much more agreeable than men. This gap begins to close in the middle-age category (70–79), and there is no longer a significant difference between men and women on the trait of agreeableness in the oldest-old (80–92). For the other four traits, the widest gap between women and men occurs for those in the middle-age category (70–79) for openness and neuroticism. For the traits of conscientiousness and extraversion, you can see that there are few differences between men and women across all three age groupings, with these differences not statistically significant. It is not clear what accounts for these differences, and more research is needed to understand gender differences over the course of the lifespan among the Big Five personality traits.

CULTURAL DIFFERENCES IN PERSONALITY TRAITS

Whether the Big Five personality traits can be found in other cultures has been of interest to many researchers. As mentioned earlier in this chapter, the five factors that make up the Big Five are measured using the NEO PI-R and the NEO PI self-report questionnaires. In one of the largest studies to date, McCrae and colleagues (2005) looked at 50 different ethnic groups and found that all the Big Five factors were present in most of the ethnic groups examined, but not all. Because of the evidence that there are some cultural differences regarding the presence of the Big Five personality traits and likely language barriers when answering the self-report questionnaires,

FIGURE 9.4

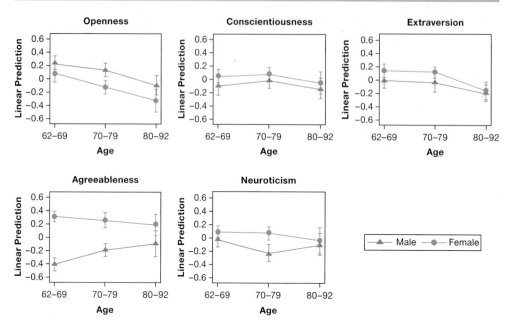

Source: Iveniuk, J., Laumann, E.O., Waite, L.J., McClintock, M.K., & Tiedt, A. (2015). Personality measures in the National Social Life, Health, and Aging Project. *Journals of Gerontology, Series B: Psychological Sciences and Social Sciences, 69*(Suppl. 2), S117-S124. doi:10.1093/geronb/gbu073. Reprinted by permission of Oxford University Press.

other researchers have begun to develop personality measures reflective of the culture being studied. For example, Cheung et al. (1996) developed the Chinese Personality Inventory (CPAI), which consists of very different personality factors than the NEO PI-R or the NEO PI. The four factors that make up the CPAI are dependability, accommodation, interpersonal relatedness, and social potency. Cheung and colleagues (2001) conducted a joint factor analysis on the NEO PI-R and the CPAI and found that the interpersonal-relatedness factor, which includes personality features important to a collectivist culture such as harmony and reciprocity in a relationship, was not related to any of the NEO-PI-R factors. In addition, the NEO-PI-R openness to experience factor was not related to any of the CPAI factors suggesting that, maybe, the openness to experience trait is more important in Western cultures. As such, the findings might reflect cultural differences in the underlying psychological meaning of openness (Cheung et al., 2008; Cheung, van de Vijver, & Leong, 2011). In a joint analysis of the revised version of the CPAI-2 and the MMPI-2, Cheung and colleagues (2008) and Cheung (2009) replicated the finding that the interpersonal-relatedness factor is distinct to Asian cultures.

The development of culturally relevant personality inventories is just beginning, and the research that will be generated in the future will be very informative. Ethnic diversity is growing in many nations in the world and, as a result, it is becoming more and more important to understand each other's viewpoints. How cultural variables influence personality development over the course of one's life will provide a greater understanding of cultural differences.

HEALTH AND PERSONALITY TRAITS

Research has shown that personality traits can influence physical health, longevity, and mortality (Hampson & Friedman, 2008; Weston, Hill, & Jackson, 2015). Interestingly, this is not a new idea. In the late 1950s, cardiologists Meyer Friedman and Ray H. Rosenman presented the concept of the Type A personality to the world (Friedman & Rosenman, 1959). This concept was based on observations of their patients. They found that the patients who had a Type A behaviour pattern (TABP) tended to be work oriented, driven, competitive, hostile, and easily angered. Friedman and Rosenman linked TABP personality to the development of coronary artery disease (CAD). Initially, early research supported a strong association between TABP and CAD, especially if the individual also had high levels of hostility (Suarez, Williams, Khun, Zimmerman, & Schanberg, 1991). In fact, in 1980, TABP was officially regarded as a cardiovascular risk factor (Cooper, Detre, & Weiss, 1981). However, results from more rigorous research conducted in the last 20 years are mixed regarding the relationship between CAD and TABP. In general, a weak to zero correlation between TABP and coronary artery disease has been identified (Myrtek, 2001; Šmigelskas, Žemaitienė, Julkunen, & Kauhanen, 2015). For example, Šmigelskas and colleagues followed a random sample of 2682 middle-aged men from the Kuopio Ischemic Heart Disease Risk Factor Study for over 20 years, and these researchers found that there was no significant relationship between TABP and CAD.

Of the Big Five personality traits, conscientiousness consistently has been found to be the best predictor of mortality with low levels of conscientiousness associated with higher mortality (Friedman, Kern, Hampson, & Duckworth, 2014; Jackson, Connolly, Garrison, Leveille, & Connolly, 2015; Kern & Friedman, 2008). This finding also has been confirmed through **meta-analyses** (Jokela et al., 2013). On the other hand, the relationship between neuroticism and mortality is not well understood with the research results mixed. In other words, some researchers find that high levels of neuroticism are positively associated with mortality (Mroczek, Spiro, & Turiano, 2009; Ploubidis & Grundy, 2009; Terracciano, Löckenhoff, Crum, Bienvenu, & Costa, 2008), whereas other researchers have found a negative association between the two (Weiss & Costa, 2005). Still other researchers have found no relationship at all between neuroticism and mortality (Iwasa et al., 2008). However, a recent study did find a relationship between the risk of developing a disease and having higher levels of the trait neuroticism. Weston and colleagues (2015) wanted to further understand the relationship between the Big Five personality traits and illnesses such as lung disease, stroke, cancer, diabetes, and heart disease. Data were gathered in 2006 and again four years later in 2010 from the Health and Retirement Study, which is a nationwide study of aging American adults. These researchers found that high levels of conscientiousness decreased the probability of diagnoses of stroke, high blood pressure, diabetes, and arthritis. On the other hand, high levels of neuroticism were associated with a higher risk of developing diseases such as lung disease, high blood pressure, and arthritis. Other researchers also have found that lower levels of conscientiousness and higher levels of neuroticism have each been linked to unhealthy behaviours such as alcohol abuse, smoking, physical inactivity, and obesity (Bogg & Roberts, 2004; Kotov, Gamez, Schmidt, & Watson, 2010; Mroczek et al., 2009; Rhodes & Smith, 2006; Turiano, Chapman, Gruenewald, & Mroczek, 2015).

There is now accumulating evidence that personality traits are associated with the development of Alzheimer's disease (Duberstein et al., 2011; Low, Harrison, & Lackersteen, 2013; Terracciano et al., 2013; Terracciano et al., 2014; Wilson, Schneider, Arnold, Bienias, & Bennett, 2007). Terracciano and his colleagues (2014) examined the relationship between the Big Five personality traits and Alzheimer's disease among participants of the Baltimore Longitudinal Study of Aging

FIGURE 9.5

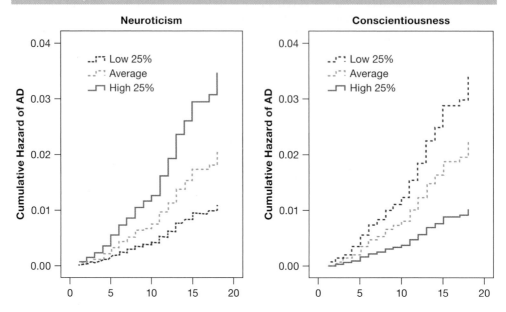

Source: *Alzheimer's & Dementia: The Journal of the Alzheimer's Association* by Alzheimer's Association. Reproduced with permission of ELSEVIER in the format Book via Copyright Clearance Center.

(BLSA). A sample of 1671 participants from the BSLA was followed over a period of 22 years. They found that individuals with scores in the top quartile of neuroticism or in the lowest quartile of conscientiousness had a threefold increased risk of incident Alzheimer's disease. The cumulative hazard of incident Alzheimer's disease is presented in Figure 9.5. What the hazard ratio measure tells us is whether the ratings in the different personality traits are associated with the risk of developing Alzheimer's disease.

As part of the same research discussed above, Terracciano and colleagues (2014) also conducted a meta-analysis of the relationship between the Big Five personality traits and the development of Alzheimer's disease. The results also strongly supported the theory that high levels of neuroticism and low levels of conscientiousness increase the risk of developing Alzheimer's disease. These researchers found this to be a remarkable finding given that the five studies included in the meta-analysis varied regarding the samples used, study designs, and length of follow-up. Terracciano and his colleagues suggest that these results can be explained through the relationship between health-related behaviours and personality. As mentioned previously in this chapter, low levels of conscientiousness and higher levels of neuroticism each have been linked to many unhealthy behaviours such as smoking, obesity, and physical inactivity. Each of these factors also has been associated with the development of Alzheimer's disease. In addition, neuroticism has been linked to the development of depression, which also has been associated with the development of Alzheimer's disease (Barnes & Yaffe, 2011).

In a different study, Terracciano and colleagues (2013) examined the brains of 111 people who were participants in the autopsy program in the BLSA. Participants agreed to regular follow-ups in which clinical and neuropsychological data were collected as well as data from the NEO-PI and the NEO-PI-R personality inventories (recall that these personality inventories measure the Big Five personality traits). They wanted to determine if there was a relationship between the severity of neuritic plaques and the stage of neurofibrillary tangles with the Big Five personality factors. Using the criteria set out by the Consortium to Establish a Registry for Alzheimer's Disease (CERAD) to establish the severity of neuritic plaques as well as the criteria put forth by Braak and Braak (1991; 1998) to measure the severity of neurofibrillary tangles, Terracciano and his colleagues divided the participants into three groups. The control group consisted of participants who had no history of cognitive or behavioural deficits or cerebrovascular disease. When the brains of these participants were evaluated at autopsy, minimal neuritic plaques and tangles were observed. Another group was made up of participants who had a diagnosis of Alzheimer's disease. As was expected, a moderate degree of neuritic plaques and neurofibrillary tangles could be seen in the brains of participants with Alzheimer's disease. The asymptomatic Alzheimer's disease group (ASYMAD) included participants who, like the control group, were cognitively intact and did not have a history of behavioural deficits or cerebrovascular disease. Interestingly, autopsies revealed tangles and plaques in the brains of the ASYMAD group that were similar in severity and stage to the Alzheimer's disease group. What this means is that even though these participants did not show any symptoms of Alzheimer's disease, the brains of the participants were very similar to the group of participants who did have a diagnosis of Alzheimer's disease. These researchers found that none of the five factors of personality were associated with the severity of the neuritic plaques. However, higher scores on neuroticism and lower scores on agreeableness were associated with higher stages of neurofibrillary tangles. As can be seen in Figure 9.6, a high level of conscientiousness was associated with a reduced risk of developing Alzheimer's disease. Specifically, the ASYMAD group scored lower on neuroticism, vulnerability to stress, anxiety, and depression than the control subjects or the group who developed Alzheimer's disease. The ASYMAD group did not differ significantly from controls on the trait of conscientiousness but low scores on this trait were found in the Alzheimer's disease group. The authors concluded that low neuroticism increases resilience while low conscientiousness increases vulnerability to developing Alzheimer's disease.

It is clear from the research discussed above that high levels of the trait neuroticism are associated with poor health outcomes while high levels of the trait conscientiousness are associated with good health outcomes. Interestingly, in the medical community, there is a growing interest in using personality assessment as part of regular practice to identify people who are at risk for developing poor overall health and who exhibit behaviours harmful to their health (Chapman, Roberts, & Duberstein, 2011).

How would you feel if your family physician asked you to do a personality test?

REFLECTIVE QUESTION

FIGURE 9.6

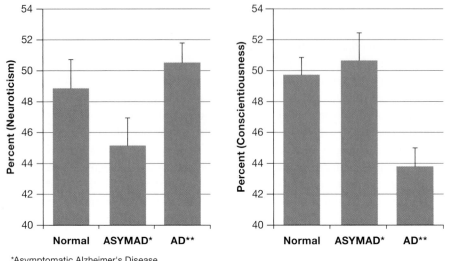

*Asymptomatic Alzheimer's Disease
**Alzheimer's Disease

Source: *Neurobiology of aging* by ELSEVIER INC. Reproduced with permission of ELSEVIER INC. in the format Book via Copyright Clearance Center.

CAN PERSONALITY TRAITS BE CHANGED THROUGH DIRECT INTERVENTION?

As you have learned, personality traits can change over the lifespan. However, can you change personality traits through direct intervention? The few studies that have been done suggest that you can. Jackson, Hill, Payne, Roberts, and Stine-Morrow (2012) conducted a 16-week home-based cognitive-training intervention with male participants ranging in age from 60 to 94 years (average age 73 years). Over the 16 weeks, older adults learned inductive reasoning skills and completed 10 hours a week of crossword and Sudoku puzzles. Results indicated that participants in the intervention condition increased in the trait "openness to experience" compared to the wait-list group. The authors interpreted these results in terms of the saying "use it or lose it." Using it (i.e., using their cognitive abilities) led the participants to view themselves as being more open. In another study, Krasner and colleagues (2009) trained medical students to become more mindful. The results of the mindfulness intervention were that participants had increases in conscientiousness, agreeableness, empathy, and emotional stability. So, it seems that interventions can change personality traits but the question persists, do these changes remain? In the future, studies that use longitudinal research methods will help to answer this question. It is an exciting field of study for sure. Imagine if we could develop interventions that create long-lasting personality changes. This would have the potential to improve not only health outcomes but the general well-being of people as well.

As we wrap up the section on personality traits, you have learned that personality traits can and do change as we age. However, changes in our traits do not seem to capture the whole story of personality development. Let's turn now to look at personality development from the psychodynamic perspective.

9.2 PSYCHODYNAMIC APPROACHES TO UNDERSTANDING PERSONALITY DEVELOPMENT

LEARNING OBJECTIVES

To understand:

- the differences between Freud, Jung, and Erikson's theories of personality development
- the stages of personality development in adulthood
- how generative concerns change across the lifespan and what factors might account for this change
- the limited research on integrity and despair

SIGMUND FREUD

Sigmund Freud gave us a lot to think about when he first described his theory of personality development. He divided the unconscious mind into the id (which demands immediate gratification and operates by the pleasure principle), the ego (which is the decision-making component of personality and operates by the reality principle), and the superego (which is the moral aspect of personality and incorporates social expectations about what is right and wrong) (Freud, 1923). He believed that our behaviour is the outcome of ongoing internal conflict between the id, the ego, and the superego. He also argued that we are driven by unconscious urges that are sexual or aggressive in nature. Because these urges cause us a lot of anxiety, which is distressing, Freud believed that we use various defense mechanisms to help to rid us of the anxiety and guilt that our internal conflict creates. Freud proposed that personality development is complete by adolescence.

CARL JUNG

Carl Jung initially held similar thoughts to Freud about the unconscious mind and the two became good friends. However, Jung came to understand the unconscious mind very differently from Freud and the pair ended their friendship in 1912 with the publication of Jung's revolutionary work *Psychology of the Unconscious* (1912). Jung was the first theorist to argue that the development of personality occurred through adulthood, which was a major break from traditional Freudian thought.

Carl Jung introduced the personality concepts of **extrovert** and **introvert**, and he argued that younger individuals are more extraverted than older adults because of a need to establish a career and find a mate, for example. However, as we get older, Jung argued, we become more introverted because of a need to reflect about our own aging and mortality. He also argued that each of us has a masculine and a feminine side. When we are young, we show only one side of ourselves to others because we often are acting in agreement with gender-specific roles set out by the culture we live in. As we age, though, Jung believed that we become more relaxed and allow the expression of our hidden self, including sex roles. This is not a reversal of sex roles but simply an expression of all aspects of the self. He also was one of the first to say outright that old age has meaning. Please see his quote in Box 9.1.

ERIK ERIKSON

Although Carl Jung was the first to include the period of adulthood in personality development, it was Erik Erikson (1959; 1963; 1982) who provided the first widely accepted theory of personality development over the lifespan. To Erikson, not only did personality continue to

develop over an individual's life but it also did so in an organized, stage-like fashion. His eight-stage theory of psychosocial development is presented in Figure 9.7. Unlike Freud, Erikson emphasized the role that culture and environment play in the development of an individual's personality.

There are three stages in Erikson's theory that involve development in adulthood. The first of the adult stages is *intimacy versus isolation*, which occurs in early adulthood. This is a time when young adults are becoming interested in developing more meaningful friendships and romantic relationships. If an individual is unable to develop these types of relationships, feelings of isolation occur. The next stage is *generativity versus stagnation*. At this point in development, individuals who develop generativity are concerned with giving back to family and community. The focus shifts from developing intimate relationships to concern about the well-being of one's own generation as well as future generations. Mentoring children or younger family members, becoming involved in charitable work, and giving to others in ways that are meaningful all are examples of generativity (see Figure 9.8). Erikson's idea of caring for others was not limited to people you know but to the larger community and the world. Erikson believed that generativity peaks in importance in middle-age and then declines as one

FIGURE 9.7

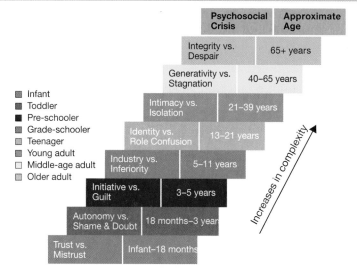

ERIK ERIKSON'S STAGES OF PSYCHOSOCIAL DEVELOPMENT

Psychosocial Crisis	Approximate Age
Integrity vs. Despair	65+ years
Generativity vs. Stagnation	40–65 years
Intimacy vs. Isolation	21–39 years
Identity vs. Role Confusion	13–21 years
Industry vs. Inferiority	5–11 years
Initiative vs. Guilt	3–5 years
Autonomy vs. Shame & Doubt	18 months–3 years
Trust vs. Mistrust	Infant–18 months

- ■ Infant
- ■ Toddler
- ■ Pre-schooler
- ■ Grade-schooler
- ■ Teenager
- ■ Young adult
- □ Middle-age adult
- ■ Older adult

Increases in complexity

Source: Adapted from Erikson (1950; 1959; 1982).

moves into old age. According to Erikson, individuals who do not develop generativity become self-absorbed and stagnate. Persons who stagnate are concerned only about themselves and their own needs and wants.

Ego integrity versus *despair* is the final stage of development in Erikson's theory. This last task involves examining both the good and maybe not so good aspects of your life and trying to find meaning in your life story. Those older adults who can reflect upon their life in a positive way and who can identify accomplishments, accept that there have been mistakes made, and not only recognize but accept that life is drawing to a close will achieve ego integrity. The outcome of this is wisdom. Those older adults who cannot come to terms with the choices they have made or the events that occurred during their life often ruminate over past mistakes and become bitter and resentful. These older adults will view their life as unproductive and meaningless. The outcome of this is despair (Torges, Stewart, & Duncan, 2008).

Erik Erikson's theory makes sense on many levels and it has had a tremendous impact on our understanding of personality development. However, his theory has been criticized because it is difficult to test empirically. Over the years, several researchers have tried to modify or expand on his theory (see Logan, 1986). The psychosocial stage that has been given the most research attention has been the adult stage of generativity versus stagnation. Before we explore that research, let's look at an interesting study done in 2009 by Whitbourne, Sneed, and Sayer. These researchers followed two cohorts of women and men from college age through mid-life. The first cohort consisted of alumni who attended the University of Rochester in 1960 and the second cohort attended in 1970. The purpose of the study was to evaluate each participant's movement through Erikson's psychosocial levels of development. They found that the early psychosocial issues of trust, autonomy, and initiative demonstrated a slow upward direction of growth across both cohorts, but they found that individuals differed in the amount of change over time. Generativity

FIGURE 9.8

vgajic/iStockphoto.com

also was found to have an upward growth. Consistent with previous research discussed in this chapter, this study also supports the idea that personality development continues into older ages. For example, in the study by Whitbourne and colleagues, the struggle of autonomy, trust, and initiative, which are thought to be resolved in childhood, showed continued growth in individuals until they were in their mid-50s. On the other hand, observed increases in ego integrity in early and middle adulthood indicated that later psychosocial issues can become more important at earlier points in life. Whitbourne and her colleagues suggest that thinking about Erikson's theory as a matrix rather than as a ladder is a better way to understand the theory. The psychosocial stages and their associated conflicts that are thought to be resolved at younger ages are continually revised throughout our lives. On the other hand, the conflicts of generativity versus stagnation and integrity versus despair that are thought to occur in the mid to late life stages can occur earlier on in our personality development. In fact, Joan Erikson (1991), who continued to develop her husband, Erik Erikson's, work after he died, thought it would be impossible for each issue to be solved fully at one point in life given the challenges that we all experience throughout our lives. A better way to understand the psychosocial stages might be to consider that each stage is not fixed, and each one must be continually worked on in the context of issues that arise as we age. Let's turn now to look at the research that has been done on the adult stage, generativity versus stagnation.

GENERATIVITY VERSUS STAGNATION: CAN WE BECOME MORE SELFLESS WITH AGE?

McAdams is one researcher who offers insight into Erikson's stage of generativity versus stagnation (see McAdams & de St. Aubin, 1998). He first discussed generativity within his life-story theory of adult identity, which suggests that adults give purpose to their lives by creating and internalizing stories that define themselves. More about this in a moment. McAdams and de St. Aubin (1992) put forth a widely accepted empirically based model of generativity. An adaptation of this model is presented in Figure 9.9.

As you can see, generativity is very complex in this model. It includes seven psychosocial features: desire, demand, concern, belief, commitment, action, and narration. In our adult years, we begin to desire symbolic immortality (a). This, combined with societal expectations (b), produces a conscious concern for the next generation (c). Having a belief in the overall goodness of people (d) acts to motivate generative commitment (e). If all goes as planned, this will produce action (f). All seven features of generativity focus on the overall goal that, ideally, the individual *and* society share the task of providing for the next generation. What this means is that society requires adults to take responsibility for the next generation in their roles as parents, teachers, mentors, leaders, and organizers (McAdams, Hart, & Maruna, 1998). Finally, an individual's

FIGURE 9.9

SEVEN FEATURES OF GENERATIVITY

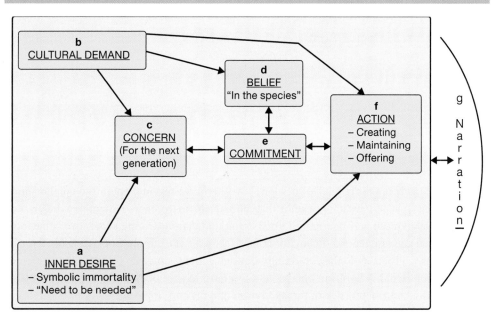

Source: McAdams, D.P., Hart, H.M., & Maruna, S. (1998). The anatomy of generativity. In D.P. McAdams & E. de St. Aubin (Eds.), *Generativity and adult development: How and why we care for the next generation* (pp. 7–43). Washington, DC: American Psychological Association.

unique narration of this process will determine its meaning. McAdams (2001) suggests that different aspects of generativity might take on greater importance at certain times over the life course. For example, young adults might have aspirations to behave in generative ways but might not have the ability to put this desire into action because they do not have the resources to do so. These resources often are obtained in middle adulthood.

McAdams and de St. Aubin (1992) developed the widely used Loyola Generativity Scale (LGS) to assess individual differences in generativity. Empirical research utilizing the LGS reveals that adults with sound generative concerns report more meaningful and satisfactory social relationships and stronger feelings of community attachment. In addition, generative concern has a strong positive relationship with measures of psychological well-being (Gruenewald, Liao, & Seeman, 2012; McAdams & Olson, 2010; Rothrauff & Cooney, 2008). A positive relationship also has been identified between generativity and all the Big Five personality traits except neuroticism. This trait, not surprisingly, has a negative relationship with generativity (Ackerman, Zuroff, & Moskowitz, 2000; de St. Aubin & McAdams, 1995; McAdams et al., 1998). Cross-sectional research has shown that generativity concerns vary with age in that generative concerns are highest in mid-life (Keyes & Ryff, 1998). For example, McAdams, de St. Aubin, and Logan (1993) used three cohorts to investigate changes in generative concerns. The young group included adults aged 22 to 27, the middle-age group included a sample of participants aged 37 to 42, and the older age group consisted of participants 72 to 76 years of age. What they found was that the older age group expressed fewer generative concerns than those in the mid-life age group but not fewer than the younger age group. These results suggest that generative concerns peak in mid-life. Of interest, Keyes and Ryff (1998) found very similar results in their research in this area.

There have been very few longitudinal investigations looking at the development of generativity over the lifespan. An exception is a recent study by Einolf (2014). He used longitudinal data from the 1995 and 2005 waves of the MacArthur Foundation's Mid-life in the United States Study. He found that generative concerns peaked in mid-life and then declined in adults 60 years of age and older.

REFLECTIVE QUESTION

What do you think explains the decline in generative concerns past middle-age?

As you think about the reflective question above, here are a few more points to ponder. Einolf (2014) suggests that perhaps it is not aging that causes changes in generative concerns but, rather, life events. Schoklitsch and Baumann (2012) argue that demonstrating generative behaviours with advanced age can depend on environmental factors. For example, not only must there be opportunities to give back to the community through activities such as volunteering or mentoring young children in school, but older adults also must have opportunities to get to the places where they can contribute. Lack of transportation options and impairments in physical health are important factors that can affect the ability of older adults to contribute to their community. Factors that also can affect generativity in older adults are isolation and ageism. Mühlig-Versen, Bowen, and Staudinger (2012) go a bit further and suggest that it is not enough to just provide opportunities for older adults to participate in society. Opportunities to learn and develop the skills to be successful, while helping in the community, also need to be offered as well as incentives that encourage older adults to learn new skills.

So how can we create opportunities for more older adults to behave in generative ways? Glass and colleagues (2004) created a very interesting conceptual framework called Experience Corps (see Figure 9.10). Essentially, the program recruits, trains, and then deploys many older adults who volunteer their time and experience in underserved elementary schools to improve the lives and academic achievements of children. In turn, older adults remain productive and involved in the community. In Canada, there is an organization called Elder Service Corps which is funded through an organization called Carya. This is a dynamic and forward-thinking program that gives older adults an opportunity to make a difference. It is a 32-week program in Calgary, Alberta, for adults aged 65 and older who are looking to use their life skills and experience in a structured and productive program. Through this training program, the group selects, develops, and implements community projects with support from the Carya team. To watch a video about the experiences of older adults involved in this project, please Google Carya. These programs are very similar to those in various European nations that are creating opportunities for older adults to become involved in the larger community. More of these initiatives are needed. In addition, much more research—in particular, more longitudinal research—is needed to fully determine the path of generativity as we age. We also need much more research to understand generative concerns in the older age groups.

FIGURE 9.10

EXPERIENCE CORPS

This program organizes older adults to go into schools to improve the lives and academic achievements of children.

RGB Ventures/SuperStock/Alamy Stock Photo

Can you think of ways that you can get older adults more involved in your community?

INTEGRITY VERSUS DESPAIR

Before moving on, let's look at some of the research that has investigated Erikson's final stage of development, integrity versus despair. It should be pointed out that it is an older adult's willingness to remember and review the past that most influences his or her success or failure in achieving ego integrity (Torges, Stewart, & Duncan, 2008). However, this is much more than a general reminiscing about the past. Butler (1963; 1974; 2002) and Butler and Lewis (1982) put forth the idea of a process called "life review." Both Erikson (Erikson, Erikson, & Kivnick, 1986) and Butler (1974) talked about a critical cognitive process that occurs during late adulthood, which not only involves remembering and reviewing past events (as would occur with reminiscing), but also involves dealing with the emotional side effects of these events. To both these researchers, the life-review process is important to the final reorganization and integration of personality.

Ingersoll-Dayton and Krause (2005) observed that one method older adults used in the process of life review was to change the standard they used to evaluate the mistakes of the past. This allows individuals to frame their past behaviour as forgivable. In fact, Torges and her colleagues (2008) found that resolving regret in mid-life predicted higher levels of ego integrity in later life. In another study, Hearn and his colleagues (2012) validated a new measure of integrity versus despair. Participants included 97 adults aged 65 years of age and older who responded to the Self-Examination Interview. This measure has four categorizes of integrity, which are presented in Table 9.2.

TABLE 9.2

CATEGORIES OF INTEGRITY IN THE SELF-EXAMINATION INTERVIEW	
CATEGORY	**DESCRIPTION**
Integrated-Integrity	Older adults in this category have achieved integrity and are self-aware. They are not particularly self-critical and are well connected to family, friends, and the community.
Despairing	Although there may be some areas of life satisfaction, older adults are generally unsatisfied with how life turned out. They frequently express failure and regret about the past. This sometimes occurs in the form of sarcasm and self-criticism.
Non-Exploratory	Non-explorers are those older adults who are generally satisfied with their life and have enjoyed family and/or career successes. However, a key characteristic is that they tend to have the same worldview and attitudes in their older years as they learned while growing up. They appear to be closed to further growth and stay in a restricted comfort zone of thoughts, emotions, and attitudes.
Pseudo-Integrated	Older adults who are pseudo-integrated wish to appear successful and present themselves in a very favourable light, either because of a lack of self-awareness or an unwillingness to examine or acknowledge problems.

These researchers believe that the Self-Examination Interview holds promise to not only identify older adults who have not reached the integrated stage of integrity but also to facilitate the development of effective interventions aimed at helping older adults find rewarding and meaningful integration of their past experiences.

9.3 LIFE NARRATIVES
LEARNING OBJECTIVES

To understand:
- the meaning of narrative identity
- the effects of culture on narrative identity

Starting in the 1980s, several psychologists began to develop new theories of personality development that moved away from the stage theories of development (McAdams, 1985; Tomkins, 1987). Dan McAdams, who was introduced in the previous section, was one of these psychologists. He believes that we are much more than an assortment of dispositional traits. He argues that each of us is a storyteller. Central to our identity is a story of where we started, where we have been, where we are going, and who we will become. McAdams (1985) also argues that we all have an internalized and ever-changing story about ourselves, which he calls a **narrative identity**. The aim of this identity is to provide a sense of unity, purpose, and meaning to an individual's life (McAdams & Olson, 2010). However, it is not merely telling your friends a story about the holiday you took last year or what happened last week; it is a story that describes a "meaningful sequence of life events to explain how the person has developed into who he or she is now and may develop into who he or she may be in the future" (McAdams & Olson, 2010, p. 528). In Western societies, it is believed that our narrative identities begin to develop in late adolescence and early adulthood.

A longitudinal study investigating life narratives was conducted by McAdams and colleagues (2006). These researchers asked college-age participants to describe and recall 10 key scenes in their life story. They found that the life narratives of the participants became more complex and rich in themes over the three-year period, which suggested to these researchers that personal growth had occurred in the participants. The research available from cross-sectional studies indicates that middle-aged adults tend to construct more complex and coherent life narratives than do younger adults (Baddeley & Singer, 2007). Pasupathi and Mansour (2006) also found that the life narratives of middle-aged adults were more psychologically sophisticated than the younger adults who participated.

There is very little narrative identity research done that includes older adults in the participant pool. One cross-sectional study that did include older adults was conducted by Singer, Rexhaj, and Baddeley (2007). They compared the self-defining memories of older adults aged 50 to 85 (mean age=65) to the self-defining memories of college-age students 17 to 22 years (mean age=19). When compared to the self-defining memories of the college-age students, older adults' self-defining memories were expressed in a more positive emotional tone and had greater integrative meaning. Having an ability to look back on one's life and experiences in a positive light is consistent with the developmental pattern discussed previously. That is, older adults seem to have lower levels of neuroticism and higher levels of agreeableness as they age (Singer et al., 2007). This finding also is consistent with Erikson's final stage of personality development, which, if successfully achieved, sees older adults come to accept and forgive past mistakes and focus on the positive moments in their lives.

Does culture have an impact on life narratives? Hammack (2008) and McAdams and Olson (2010) suggest that culture can have a most profound effect on life narratives. For example, if you look at your own life narrative, we are sure that you have been influenced by cultural stories handed down from your parents and grandparents about belief systems and about appropriate ways to behave or what goals are important to strive for in life. Narrative identities are created by accepting and personalizing the stories given to you through your culture (McAdams & Olson, 2010).

9.4 MID-LIFE CRISIS—FACT OR FICTION?

LEARNING OBJECTIVES

To understand:

- the meaning of mid-life
- what a mid-life crisis is
- if a mid-life crisis is fact or fiction

WHAT IS MID-LIFE? WHEN DOES MID-LIFE BEGIN?

Identifying mid-life seems pretty straightforward, right? It should be in the middle of your life. Interestingly, though, it is not as well defined as you might think, nor is it very well understood (Lachman, Teshale, & Agrigoroaei, 2015). Many researchers believe that chronological age is not the best marker of middle-age. Freund and Ritter (2009) and Lachman and colleagues (2015) argue that mid-life might be better understood in terms of roles, life experience, and the timing of events in a person's life rather than chronological age. Today, there still remains many misconceptions about middle-age with the most common misconception being the legendary mid-life crisis. We'll turn now to learn about the mid-life crisis.

MID-LIFE CRISIS: RESEARCH AND FINDINGS

In 1965, the Canadian psychologist Elliott Jacques coined the term "mid-life crisis" to describe the turmoil many people feel in middle-age when they realize that they have likely more life behind them than they do in front of them. He based this on a historical analysis of famous

---

BOX 9.2

CASE STUDY: THE STEREOTYPICAL MID-LIFE CRISIS

Stanley is a 44-year-old man. He is balding and has a bit of a paunch. You have known him all his life and you have found him to be a good friend, husband, and father. He is conservative and reliable, and you can count on him for anything. One day, as you are mowing your lawn, you see Stanley pull up to his house and you look up and give a wave but ... something is very different about Stanley. He no longer has a bald spot, he is wearing expensive, colourful clothing, and he is driving a brand-new sports car. Sitting in the passenger seat is a lovely young woman who you have never seen before. Stanley comes over to you with a big smile and says he just stopped by to say goodbye. He has quit his job, has left his wife, and is heading out to Vancouver with Rebecca (the woman in the car) to start a new life. "Best of luck" you say to Stanley as he turns to go back to his car. As he speeds away, you are left scratching your head and wondering ... what happened to Stanley? What else could it be but a mid-life crisis?

artists and a few clinical case studies. The Case Study in Box 9.2 describes the stereotypical scenario for a mid-life crisis. Based on his work with a somewhat larger sample of healthy adults, Levinson (1978; 1986) grounded the mid-life crisis in a developmental framework and identified the time frame in which it occurs as between 40 and 45 years of age. According to Levinson, it is a predictable phase of adult development that usually happens to men. This belief really took hold. Freund and Ritter (2009) found from their Internet survey that 92 percent of respondents reported that they believed in the existence of a mid-life crisis! However, research investigating the mid-life crisis has been criticized on several grounds. For example, earlier studies used clinical samples that provided a very pessimistic view of middle-age. Unstandardized qualitative interview techniques, as well as cross-sectional studies rather than longitudinal studies, were used to gather data (Schaie & Willis, 1968). Another criticism is that the samples were very small, and not representative of the larger population. Data from the MIDUS Study, which is a large and representative sample of individuals, has shown that a crisis in mid-life is not a predictable occurrence with only 10 to 20 percent of people in the study reporting that they had experienced one (Wethington, 2000). Some of the participants surveyed said that their mid-life crisis was associated with getting older. Others said it was associated with getting divorced, the occurrence of health problems, or the loss of employment, which can happen at other times in life, not just in mid-life. It seems that those who do experience a crisis in mid-life have high levels of neuroticism meaning that, if one has a mid-life crisis, it is more likely the result of some underlying pathology rather than aging (Freund & Ritter, 2009; Lachman, 2004; Lachman et al., 2015). Not to say that middle-age does not have its challenges. For example, in what is called the **sandwich generation**, many middle-aged adults are trying to manage all the responsibilities that come with caring for children and aging parents at the same time. Middle-aged adults might be in the middle of paying off a mortgage or two and financing children's post-secondary education. However, it also might be a time when they are enjoying financial freedom and career success, meaningful relationships with family and friends, and giving back to the community (Finke, Huston, & Sharpe, 2006). It also could be a little of both.

There is very little empirical support that would suggest that when you reach middle-age, you should expect a time of extreme stress and turmoil. In fact, adults aged 65 to 85 said they preferred middle-age over any other phase in life (Lachman, Lewkowicz, Marcus, & Peng, 1994; Wethington, 2000). In Freund and Ritter's (2009) study, older adults did not want to be young again and identified middle-age as the age they would like to return to. Now having said that, Freund and Ritter argue that, perhaps, the notion of a mid-life crisis should be retained but with a different understanding of the concept. These researchers believe that maintaining the term "mid-life crisis" would be useful for understanding the complexities of mid-life. They argue that the challenges that occur in middle adulthood arise mainly from life-review and social-comparison processes that are triggered by a particular age. Freund and Ritter suggest that

> due to a strong social expectation that middle adulthood is a time for reviewing one's accomplishments, people are more likely to compare their actual self-image with their ideal self-image as well as with social expectations about what one ought to have achieved by middle adulthood. Moreover, middle adulthood is commonly viewed as the middle of life, the change in time perspective as time until death is likely to highlight the limited remaining time for redirection or correcting one's personal developmental path. Even if this process does not lead to a crisis, it poses a developmental challenge that needs to be mastered. (p. 589)

For these researchers, conceptualizing a mid-life crisis as one that is reflective and corrective, rather than dramatic, would be a more useful way to understand the complexities of middle-age.

9.5 PERSONALITY DISORDERS IN OLDER ADULTS
LEARNING OBJECTIVES

To understand:
- what a personality disorder is and how it interferes with functioning
- the prevalence of personality disorders in adults and older adults
- measurement and classification issues when diagnosing an older adult with a personality disorder
- the relationship between personality disorders and health

WHAT DEFINES A PERSONALITY DISORDER?

A personality disorder (PD) is defined in the *DSM-5* (American Psychiatric Association [APA], 2013) as "an enduring pattern of inner experience and behaviour that deviates markedly from the expectations of the person's culture" (p. 647). Important elements of this general definition are that the pattern of maladaptive behaviour must be inflexible and pervasive across a wide range of social and personal situations. This way of behaving and thinking must cause the person significant distress or impairment in personal and occupational functioning and it must be stable, of long duration, and traceable back to early adolescence or young adulthood. In addition to this general definition, each of the 10 PDs is characterized by specific traits and behaviours. PDs are typically thought of in terms of clusters. Cluster A includes paranoid, schizoid, and schizotypal PDs. Individuals with this type of PD often are observed to be odd or eccentric. Dramatic, emotional, or erratic in behaviour describes individuals with Cluster B traits, which include borderline, antisocial, histrionic, and narcissistic PDs. Finally, individuals in Cluster C are seen as fearful and anxious. PDs found in this cluster are dependent, avoidant, and obsessive-compulsive.

> **REFLECTIVE QUESTION**
>
> Can you see any potential problems with the PD diagnostic criteria of having to trace a PD back to early adolescence or young adulthood?

It's no fun having a PD and, in short, PDs cause a lot of problems for individuals of all ages. People with PDs have major problems in relationships—both personal and work related. Depression and anxiety and other mental health issues are more likely to occur in individuals with a PD than in those individuals without a PD (Balsis, Zweig, & Molinari, 2015; Samuels, 2011). PDs often interfere with the development of a therapeutic relationship between the clinician and the patient, which, in turn, impairs the course of treatment and the treatment outcomes of mental health disorders such as anxiety and depression. As we will see later, PDs also are associated with an increased use of medical services and poor health outcomes (Powers & Oltmanns, 2012; Samuels, 2011).

HOW MANY ADULTS HAVE A PERSONALITY DISORDER?

Samuels (2011) reviewed six studies (conducted 2000–2010) that examined the prevalence of PDs in community-dwelling adults. Three of these studies were based in the United States, one in Australia, one in Norway, and one in Britain. All studies used *DSM-III* (APA, 1980; rev. 1987) and *DSM-IV* (APA, 1994) criteria to establish a diagnosis of PD. Based on the results, Samuels estimated that between 6 and 10 percent of individuals living in the community have a PD. Samuels also found that the prevalence of a particular PD varied across socio-demographic groups. For example, he found the rate of PDs was higher in those who were divorced or who had dropped out of high school. Also, there was considerable variability if one looked at specific PDs. Narcissistic and histrionic PDs were found to be relatively rare, with obsessive-compulsive and avoidant PDs the most common. If you are wondering, the presence of a PD always is higher in clinical samples. For example, the presence of an antisocial PD rises to greater than 70 percent among males with severe alcohol-use disorder and among males in substance abuse clinics and prisons (APA, 2013).

PREVALENCE OF PERSONALITY DISORDERS IN OLDER ADULTS

Based on other sections of this chapter, we bet you already know that we are going to tell you that there is an absence of research regarding PDs among older adults. Greater understanding of how a PD presents itself in an older adult is important for several reasons. First, it offers an opportunity for researchers to understand how PDs affect individuals over their lifespan. In other words, what are the long-term effects of having a PD? Second, features of PDs might be exaggerated by some of the transitions that often are unique to an older adult population such as losing a spouse or moving into a care facility (Oltmanns & Balsis, 2010; Rossi, Van den Broeck, Dierckx, Segal, & van Alphen, 2014). Finally, older adults who have personality disorders might find themselves in a position where they need the help of others due to physical or cognitive limitations. An inability to get along with others will make it challenging for both family members and healthcare workers to provide care. Information about PDs in this population would help to create treatment and support programs for individuals and their families.

The general conclusion from the limited information gathered from cross-sectional research suggests that with age, the prevalence of most PDs declines (Abrams & Bromberg, 2006; Gutiérrez et al., 2012; Reynolds, Pietrzak, El-Gabalawy, Mackenzie, & Sareen, 2015; Samuels et al., 2002; Schuster, Hoertel, Le Strat, Manetti, & Limosin, 2013; Ullrich & Coid, 2009). In these studies, PD diagnoses were found to occur less often or were less severe in older adults. This trend seems to be similar for the oldest age groups as well. For example, in one of the only studies conducted that stratified their sample by age, Canadian researcher Reynolds and her colleagues (2015) found fewer PDs among their sample of individuals over the age of 85 when compared to the other age groups in their study (55 to 64, 65 to 74, and 75 to 84 years of age). The trend of fewer or less severe diagnoses was more prominent in the externalizing Cluster C personalities such as borderline PD and antisocial PD. The few longitudinal studies conducted in this area have found similar results (Lenzenweger, Johnson, & Willett, 2004; Schuster et al., 2013). This had led some researchers to believe that personality disorders burn out in old age. In addition, the impulsivity and erratic behaviours associated with PDs such as antisocial and borderline PDs lead to higher mortality rates among these individuals. In other words, they die before they reach old age (Balsis et al., 2015). But do PDs really decline with age? As it turns out, this is a controversial subject. Let's turn now to look at some of the difficulty in assessing and diagnosing PDs in older adults.

MEASUREMENT AND CLASSIFICATION OF PERSONALITY DISORDERS IN OLDER ADULTS

There are many issues in the classification and assessment of PDs in older adults. Classifications systems such as the *DSM-IV* and the *DSM-5* have not included older adults when developing the diagnostic criteria of PDs. As a result, many PDs in late life might go undetected because the criteria used to assess the presence of a PD were created using younger adults. In fact, one study found that approximately half of the PD criteria might contain measurement bias across younger and older age groups (Balsis, Gleason, Woods, & Oltmanns, 2007). In this same study, Balsis and colleagues also found that 29 percent of the diagnostic criteria for PDs in the *DSM-IV* resulted in under- or over-diagnosis of PDs in older adults. As Balsis and colleagues (2015) point out, some of the criteria that suggest the presence of a PD are not appropriate for an older adult because the reason behind a particular behaviour might be different for an older adult versus a younger adult. For example, one of the diagnostic criteria for schizoid PD is "has little interest in sexual experiences." Some older adults might not be interested in sexual activities but possibly because they do not have a partner or are in poor health, not because of an underlying sexual disinterest. Although the *DSM-5* has introduced an alternative dimensional trait approach for further research on PDs, older adults were not considered in the alternative dimensional approach either (Rossi et al., 2014). Before we can begin to understand personality pathology in later life, we first need to develop measurement instruments that are designed for, or at least include, older adults.

There is a host of criticisms about using the current diagnostic criteria to identify PDs in older adults. Do you remember the reflective question earlier that asked you to think about whether there might be problems with the diagnostic criteria that a PD must be traceable back to early adolescence or young adulthood? How would you determine this? Imagine that you are a healthcare professional and you have an older adult 75 years of age sitting in your office. How would you determine the validity of information regarding PD from early adolescence or young adulthood in older adults with memory problems? What if the person has no family to confirm this information? Could a personality disorder not occur for the first time in later life? Some researchers suggest that introducing the concept of late-onset personality disorder might be very helpful to our understanding of PDs in older adults (Oltmanns & Balsis, 2010; Van Alphen et al., 2012).

But wait—there are still more criticisms of the assessment and measurement of PDs in older adults. Van Alphen and colleagues (2012) and Morgan, Chelminski, Young, Dalrymple, and Zimmerman (2013) suggest that perhaps the features of PDs change with age. If this is the case, then many PDs might go undiagnosed. For example, Morgan and colleagues investigated borderline PD in 46 older (age 45–68) and 97 younger (age 18–25) adults. They found that older adults had significantly different clinical presentations of borderline PD than younger adults. That is, older adults were more likely to report chronic feelings of emptiness and less likely to report self-harm behaviours, impulsivity, and unstable mood as compared to younger adults. Older adults also reported higher levels of social impairment than their younger counterparts. In order to avoid missing borderline PD in an older adult population, these researchers emphasize the importance of assessing less prototypic features of the disorder. You might be wondering how these shortcomings in assessment and classification can be overcome. Researchers have come up with several good ideas.

If you are thinking that we need more longitudinal research to understand the developmental path of PDs over the life course, researchers would agree with you. Another suggestion that has been made is to develop age-neutral personality assessment measures (Balsis et al., 2007; Tackett, Balsis, Oltmanns, & Krueger, 2009). Still other researchers believe we should move away from using only self-report measures to assess PD and include information from informants (Edelstein & Segal, 2011; Oltmanns & Balsis, 2011). This, of course, could apply to personality assessment over the lifespan, not just with older adults. Determining if the prevalence of PDs changes, increases, or fades away across the lifespan is another area in which more research is clearly needed. Let's turn now to our final section in the chapter—the relationship between PDs and health.

THE RELATIONSHIP BETWEEN PERSONALITY DISORDERS AND HEALTH

You have learned now that high levels of the trait neuroticism and low levels of the trait conscientiousness are associated with poor health outcomes. Based on this, you likely will not be surprised to learn that PDs also are associated with poor health outcomes. Recent research has associated PDs with increased healthcare use and decreased health-related quality of life among middle-aged adults (Powers & Oltmanns, 2012). Other researchers have found a relationship between PDs and sleep disturbance, obesity, chronic pain, headaches, and substance use disorders; individuals with PDs are at a higher risk of developing heart disease and stomach disorders (Dixon-Gordon, Whalen, Layden, & Chapman, 2015; Quirk et al., 2015; Trull, Jahng, Tomko, Wood, & Sher, 2010). In one of the only studies that included older adults in their sample, Schuster and colleagues (2013) found that respondents aged 65 and older with PDs had a higher risk of medical conditions such as high blood pressure and, in particular, heart disease. Clearly, PDs are associated with a host of health problems. Given the poor health and well-being associated with PDs, it is important that researchers continue to investigate PDs across the lifespan.

9.6 GOOD PRACTICE

Shreyasi Gollapudi Brodhecker, M.D., F.R.C.P.C.
Villa Caritas Hospital, Geriatric Psychiatry, Edmonton, Alberta

WHERE DID YOU TRAIN?

University of Alberta Psychiatry Program

WHERE DO YOU WORK?

Villa Caritas Hospital

WHAT DO YOU DO?

I'm a geriatric psychiatrist working in a specialized in-patient psychiatric hospital program for older adults who have mental health issues. I also work as a consultant geriatric psychiatrist in the community and run group and individual psychotherapy programs with adult patients. In future, I plan to incorporate group psychotherapy with older adults in the in-patient and community settings into my practice.

WHY DO YOU LIKE WORKING WITH AN OLDER-ADULT POPULATION?

Older adults have unique perspectives on the world, specific stage-of-life concerns, and rich life histories and stories that I feel privileged to hear and learn about. In addition, the complexities of psychiatric assessment and treatment in geriatric psychiatry (given patients' cognitive and medical co-morbidities) make this work rewarding. My work lends itself well to interdisciplinary and holistic perspectives, as well as working with families and public health issues, which I also enjoy being a part of.

DO YOU HAVE ADVICE FOR STUDENTS WHO WANT TO GET INTO THE FIELD?

I would suggest spending time in several different parts of mental health care to better appreciate the unique rewards and challenges of this field. Even within the field of working with older adults, it is helpful to find a specific niche since the scope of in-patient and community work is diverse and will only grow further in the next few decades.

Shauna Kessler, Rec.T.
Kipnes Centre for Veterans, Edmonton, Alberta

WHERE DID YOU TRAIN?

I obtained a Bachelor of Arts in recreation, sport, and tourism specializing in recreation therapy at the University of Alberta, Edmonton, Alberta.

WHERE DO YOU WORK?

I work for CapitalCare at the Kipnes Centre for Veterans. Besides working with older adults who have a mental health diagnosis, I also have experience working with those who have an acquired brain injury, people who require chronic ventilators, and those who have spinal cord injuries.

WHAT DO YOU DO?

I assess residents' recreation and leisure interests and develop individual treatment plans based on their interests, strengths, and experience.

WHY DO YOU LIKE WORKING WITH AN OLDER ADULT POPULATION?

I like working with older adults as I feel it is a way for me to give back to them. They have so much life experience and I enjoy hearing all about it and providing ways to enhance their current lifestyle, even though they are aging. In my career, I enjoy providing opportunities for each one of them to have a leisure interest in which they can find enjoyment, purpose, and a sense of accomplishment.

DO YOU HAVE ADVICE FOR STUDENTS WHO WANT TO GET INTO THE FIELD?

While relying on your professional expertise to provide great care, try to get to know each person individually by listening to them; talk about their past—who they were, what they did—and embrace the knowledge they share with you.

9.7 SUMMARY

- Personality is a very complex area of study. Identifying and measuring personality traits have received the most research attention in the field of personality psychology. Costa and McCrae's Five-Factor Model is the most widely used model to understand trait development.

- From a trait perspective, personality was initially viewed as unchangeable after the age of 30. However, a developmental pattern of trait change has been consistently identified in which individuals become more agreeable and emotionally stable, more conscientious, and less neurotic with age.

- The Big Five personality traits have been found in other cultures but not all cultures. Although this area of research is just beginning, researchers are developing culturally relevant scales to measure personality traits in other cultures.

- High levels of conscientiousness have been associated with good health outcomes, while high levels of neuroticism have been associated with poor health outcomes. Recent research has found a relationship between the development of neuro-cognitive disorders such as Alzheimer's disease and high levels of the trait neuroticism.

- We can change personality traits through direct intervention. What we do not know is whether these changes are long-lasting.

- The mid-life stage of generativity versus stagnation has received the most research attention. In general, adults with sound generative concerns report more meaningful and satisfactory social relationships and stronger feelings of community attachment. Research also has shown that generative concerns peak in middle-age. It might be the case that older adults have less opportunity to act in generative ways.

- As we age, we construct more complex life narratives that are richer in themes and more psychologically sophisticated than younger adults.

- The concept of mid-life is not well understood and researchers suggest that chronological age might not be the best marker of middle-age. Although it seems that many people still believe in the existence of a mid-life crisis, research does not support this idea. Conceptualizing a mid-life crisis as one that is reflective and corrective rather than dramatic might be more useful to understand the complexities of middle-age.

- In general, personality disorders seem to decline or become less severe with age. However, there are many problems with the classification and measurement of personality disorders in old age. First and foremost, developing appropriate diagnostic criteria is needed.

- Not surprisingly, individuals who have a personality disorder have more health problems, including heart disease, and use healthcare services more often than others.

Key Terms

Biological Essentialist Perspective
The belief that genetics is central to personality development.

Contextualist Perspective
The emphasis on the role of the environment in personality development.

Correspondence Principle
Personality stability is influenced by life choices.

Extrovert
An external focus on the world of people and things.

Factor Analysis
A type of statistical procedure that is conducted to identify clusters or groups of related items (called factors) on a test.

Intra-individual Change
Refers to changes that occur at an individual level as opposed to changes that occur at the group level.

Introvert
A preoccupation with one's internal world of feelings, thoughts, and experiences.

Maturity Principle
The notion that individuals become more agreeable and emotionally stable, more conscientious, and less neurotic with age.

Mean-Level Change
A measure that compares mean-levels of a variable across two or more points in time.

Narrative Identity
An internal and ever-changing story about our life.

Sandwich Generation
A generation of people (usually in their 30s or 40s) who care for their aging parents while supporting their own children.

Stage Theory
Description of the distinct phases we experience as we develop. In each phase of development, people display characteristic behaviour patterns and establish certain abilities.

Transactional Model
Personality development is influenced by both genes and the environment.

CHAPTER

10

RELATIONSHIPS

CHAPTER OUTLINE

"Old age is like climbing a mountain. You climb from ledge to ledge. The higher you get the more tired and breathless you become, but your views become more extensive."

Ingmar Bergman

In Canada, and around the world, relationships are becoming increasingly diverse and complex. Although married couples with children are still the predominant family structure, common-law or cohabiting relationships are on the rise as are same-sex marriages. Growing up in stepfamilies is occurring more frequently as well as growing up in one-parent families. So how does aging play into this diversity in relationships? We will explore this question in this chapter.

10.1 RELATIONSHIP STATUS OF CANADIANS
LEARNING OBJECTIVES

To understand:
- the diversity in romantic partnerships
- the diversity among families in Canada
- marriage in Canada
- divorce trends in Canada
- re-partnering in the context of widowhood and divorce
- the benefits and challenges of singlehood
- dating in older adulthood

DIVERSITY IN ROMANTIC PARTNERSHIPS

Although marriage remains one of the most important social institutions in Canada, the marriage rate in Canada is declining and, as a result, the conventional portrait of what a family looks like is changing. For example, in the 1961 Canadian Census, married couples accounted for almost 92 percent of the families surveyed. However, in 2011, this number fell to 67 percent (Statistics Canada, 2012f). According to the Census, there were approximately six million married couples in Canada in 2011. The proportion of married couples in the Census was highest in Prince Edward Island, Ontario, and Alberta (Milan, 2013).

It seems that more and more people are choosing to live common-law or cohabitate. As you can see from Figure 10.1, the number of common-law couples rose considerably from 1961 to 2011. In fact, this is one of the most noteworthy changes in Canadian demographics in the past 20 years (Turcotte & Schellenberg, 2007). Interestingly, according to the 2011 Census, cohabiting always has been proportionally higher in the province of Quebec as well as in the territories. In fact, the proportion of couples in Quebec who are cohabiting (38 percent) is higher than in Sweden and Finland where common-law couples constitute a large share of all couples (Statistics Canada, 2012g). The reasons for this are unclear. Cohabitation also is very common in the United States where approximately 50 to 60 percent of marriages are preceded by cohabitation (Stanley, Amato, Johnson, & Markman, 2006).

FIGURE 10.1

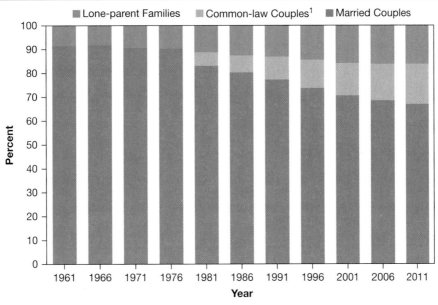

1. Data on common-law couples are not available prior to the 1981 census.

Source: Statistics Canada. (2012f). Fifty years of families in Canada: 1961 to 2011. *Families, households and marital status, 2011 census of population (Catalogue No. 98-312-X2011003).* Retrieved from http://www12.statcan.gc.ca/census-recensement/2011/as-sa/98-312-x/98-312-x2011003_1-eng.pdf.

REFLECTIVE QUESTION

What do you think might account for the high rates of cohabitation in Quebec?

Cohabitating before marriage gives couples an opportunity to learn about each other's quirky habits and work out any kinks in the relationship prior to marriage, right? Well, this is not always the case. Individuals who live together before they get married have a greater risk of a marital breakup than those who do not cohabitate (Rhoades, Stanley, & Markman, 2009). This is referred to as the **cohabitation effect**. Couples, who probably would not have gotten married had they been living apart, slide into marriage because they are already living together and it appears to be the thing to do next. However, Lu, Qian, Cunningham, and Li (2012) found that it was only serial cohabitators (those who have lived in more than one cohabitating relationship) who showed a high cohabitation effect.

Of note is that cohabitation has grown most rapidly among older age groups in recent years. The number of individuals aged 65 to 69 in common-law unions rose 66.5 percent between 2006 and 2011, the fastest pace of all age groups (Milan, Wong, & Vézina, 2014). Interestingly, older cohabitators tend to perceive their relationships as an alternative to marriage while younger people see cohabitation as a prelude to marriage (Sassler, 2010).

What do you think might account for this rise in common-law relationships among older adults?

Although not shown in Figure 10.1, the number of same-sex couples nearly tripled between 2006 and 2011, which reflects the first five-year period since same-sex marriage became legal in Canada (Statistics Canada, 2012g). We will be talking about same-sex couples in relation to older adults later in the chapter.

DIVERSITY IN FAMILIES

As you can see from Figure 10.1, lone-parent families also increased between 1961 and 2011 in Canada. The 2011 Census data also included information on stepfamilies for the first time. **Stepfamilies** accounted for almost 13 percent of families in 2011. Interestingly, more families in Canada were multi-generational in 2011 than in 2006. Most of these multi-generational households consisted of children, their parents, and at least one grandparent (Statistics Canada, 2012g). It should be pointed out that there have been significant changes in the living arrangements of young adults aged 20 to 29. Approximately 42 percent of young adults aged 20 to 29 lived in the parental home in 2011. Consider that in 1981, only 27 percent of young adults aged 24 to 29 lived at home (Statistics Canada, 2012h). Young men are more likely to live at home than young women.

What would be some reasons why young adults are remaining in their parents' home longer?

According to Statistics Canada (2012h), there are several reasons why young adults in their 20s remain in or return to their parents' home. Some of these reasons include a breakup of a relationship, cost of housing, pursuit of higher education, cultural preferences, or difficulty finding employment. Those children who return home after an absence are known as **boomerang kids**.

MARRIAGE IN CANADA

A fairly recent study by Bibby (2009) showed that 90 percent of Canadian adolescents surveyed expected to get married and stay married. Although divorce is becoming more common, it seems that individuals have hope that their own marriages can last! The average age at which both Canadian males and females first marry is increasing. Have a look at Figure 10.2. For young adults aged 25 to 29, the proportion who were never married rose from about one-quarter in 1981 to almost three-quarters in 2011. Even among individuals in their early 30s, the proportion of men and women who were never married increased significantly from 1981 to 2011 (Milan, 2013). One aspect of marriage that appears to be stable is that, on average, men tend to marry women who are younger.

FIGURE 10.2

PROPORTION OF POPULATION AGED 15 AND OVER THAT WAS NEVER MARRIED BY AGE GROUP AND SEX, CANADA, 1981–2011

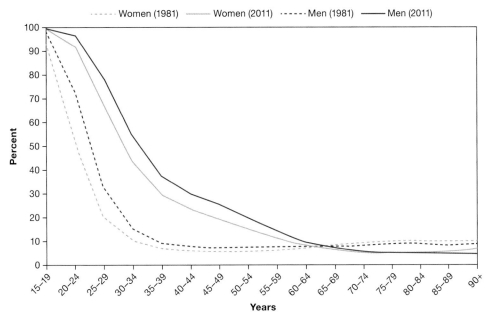

Notes: In 1981, the never married population excludes common-law partners whose legal marital status was 'never married'. Less than 4% of the population aged 15 and over lived common-law in 1981.

Source: Milan, A. (2013). *Marital status: Overview, 2011* (Catalogue no. 91-209-X). Ottawa, ON: Statistics Canada. Retrieved from http://www.statcan.gc.ca/pub/91-209-x/2013001/article/11788-eng.pdf.

Can you see any aspects, good or bad, that can result from marrying at a later age?

REFLECTIVE QUESTION

According to the 2011 Census, more than three-quarters of men 65 years of age and over and close to one-half of women 65 years of age and older lived as married spouses or were cohabitating (Milan et al., 2014). The number of older adults living as a couple has increased significantly since 1981. One of the reasons is the increased life expectancy of men, which allows relationships to endure further into old age. Another possible reason is that in 2011, older-adult couples were increasingly close in age (Milan et al., 2014). Although older women are more likely to be widowed because they live longer, having a partner closer in age may mean that couples are potentially less likely to experience widowhood until later in their adult years. Interestingly, in 2011, the majority of older adults 65 years of age and older had been married only once. The baby boom generation will surely change this statistic (Milan et al., 2014).

So, are long-term marriages different than those marriages that are just starting? It has been widely accepted among researchers that marriage satisfaction follows a U-shaped pattern in which couples report high satisfaction at the beginning of their marriage and then this satisfaction falls as the couple is raising children. Once the children have left home, marital satisfaction is again high. This pattern is found in married couples and those who cohabitate (Kamp Dush, Taylor, & Kroeger, 2008; Hansen, Moum, & Shapiro, 2007). In general, researchers have found that satisfaction among individuals in long-term relationships tends to continue to increase even after retirement. However, marital satisfaction may decrease if one of the partners develops health problems, and this decrease appears to be directly related to the amount of perceived support that is received by each partner (Landis, Peter-Wight, Martin, & Bodenmann, 2013). In fact, Landis and her colleagues found that the perception of a spouse's support is the most important predictor of remaining married.

There also has been a good deal of evidence from meta-analytic studies that older married individuals report higher life satisfaction; better health, longevity (especially for men), and well-being; and greater happiness than those who are not married (Proulx, Helms, & Buehler, 2007; Turcotte & Schellenberg, 2007). Naturally, one would think that that there must be several factors at play that will determine both marital satisfaction and the quality of long-term marriages. We speak from experience when we say that staying married for a long time takes a good deal of effort and perseverance. A good sense of humor also is helpful!

Interestingly, some researchers have found that older couples in long-term marriages describe their partner more positively than do middle-aged married couples. They also show reduced marital conflict when compared to middle-age couples (Henry, Berg, Smith, & Florsheim, 2007; O'Rourke & Cappeliez, 2005). However, other researchers have not found an increase in positivity and a decrease in negativity when comparing interactions between older and younger couples (Smith et al., 2009). Smith and his colleagues argue that most of the findings are cross-sectional in nature, and if we are truly to understand what long-term marriages look like, more data from longitudinal studies are needed.

DIVORCE TRENDS IN CANADA

In 1968, Canada's first unified divorce law was passed. At that time, divorce became easier to obtain but it was not until 1986 when the Divorce Act was revised that married couples could divorce quite easily. In fact, in the year following, the crude rate of divorce was 364 divorces per 100 000 in Canada, which was a record high (Milan, Keown, & Robles Urquijo, 2011). Although the media would have you believe that the majority of marriages end in divorce, this is not true. The difficulty is that divorce rates are very complex to figure out. The people getting divorced in a given year are not the same people who are getting married so it is difficult to compare marriages to divorces to determine the likelihood of divorce occurring. In addition, the divorce rate in any given year includes individuals who are getting a divorce for the second or third time. The rate of divorce in second and third marriages is about 10 percent higher, which inflates the divorce rate for all marriages (Lambert, 2009).

In 2008, the crude divorce rate was 211 divorces per 100 000 population. Since approximately the late 1990s, the number of divorces and the crude divorce rate have been relatively stable, perhaps because more people are living common-law, are reluctant to legally marry, or both. In addition, some marriage breakdowns might not be formalized by a legal divorce if neither spouse wants to marry again (Milan et al., 2011). Although there is much variability in the length of a marriage nationally, the average length is 14 years, which is similar to other regions of the world (Eichler, 2015).

Interestingly, the number of divorces occurring among older adults is rising. This trend is commonly referred to as **grey divorce** and this refers to marital breakups among adults over 50 years of age after approximately 20 years or more of marriage. From 1981 to 2011, the proportion of individuals 65 years of age and older who were divorced or separated rose from 4 percent to 12 percent. Even among the population aged 85 and over, 4 percent were divorced or separated in 2011 compared with 1 percent in 1981 (Milan et al., 2014).

Researchers are not entirely sure what accounts for increased divorce rates and there are likely many contributing factors. For example, the significant increase in women in the labour force and improvements to government sponsored pension programs have been identified as factors contributing to increased divorce rates (Milan et al., 2014). As a result, many women are less economically dependent on their husbands than they have been in the past. The age that people get married also has been identified as a reason for marital breakups with those marrying in their teens and early twenties having more than double the risk of a marital breakup than those individuals who choose to marry in their late twenties and beyond (Milan et al., 2014). The reduction of social and religious sanctions against divorce also are thought to be contributing factors (Eichler, 2015).

But, after living most of one's life with another person, why get a divorce? Researchers think it is because we are living longer. Wu and Schimmele (2007) argue that long-term marriages may not survive because of the changing needs or desires of the partners as they age in the marriage. Wu and Schimmele also suggest that some individuals age 55 or 60 who realize that they could live another 25 years choose to leave unhappy marriages to avoid a drawn-out period of marital problems or life dissatisfaction in their old age. Also, couples get busy raising children and they can grow apart. In addition, once children have left home, there may be no reason to stay married.

Other explanations for divorce are similar for both younger and older couples. For example, marital dissatisfaction often is accompanied by an increase in problematic behaviours such as abuse (emotional and physical), and infidelity or financial troubles (Milan et al., 2011). One study of Canadian couples married for at least 20 years indicated long-term gender inequality or role imbalance in the marriage as well as poor communication were reasons for their marital dissatisfaction and subsequent divorce (Canham, Mahmood, Stott, Sixsmith, & O'Rourke, 2012).

Divorcing in later life can come with a host of challenges. For example, an individual might no longer be as financially secure, especially older women (Vespa, 2012). Divorce also affects an individual's social life in that social networks often become smaller. For example, Connidis (2010) found that divorced older men have the smallest social networks, the weakest ties to their families, and the lowest life satisfaction of any divorced age group.

RE-PARTNERING IN THE CONTEXT OF WIDOWHOOD AND DIVORCE

Much like several other areas in aging research, we don't know that much about union formation and re-partnering in mid and late life (Sassler, 2010). The little we do know about re-partnering at these life stages comes from studies of people who are widowed. We know even less about the re-partnering experiences of individuals who are divorced or separated cohabitors (Brown, Bulanda, & Lee, 2012). Let's begin by examining what the research says about widowhood.

WIDOWHOOD

Older women are more likely to be widowed than older men. Consider that in 2015, there were over one million widowed females and fewer than 300 000 widowed males in Canada (Statistics Canada, 2012f). That is quite a gender difference and what this means is that the likelihood of re-partnering after widowhood is much greater for men (Connidis, 2010).

For many individuals, losing a spouse is an extremely difficult experience. Bereaved individuals have more somatic problems (e.g., pain or fatigue) and lower life satisfaction compared to their married counterparts (Sasson & Umberson, 2014). Spousal loss has other consequences. Often bereavement is accompanied by a significant change in an individual's friendships and social relations in terms of reduced social networks and contacts (Perrig-Chiello, Spahni, Höpflinger, & Carr, 2016). Bereaved men generally show more emotional vulnerability than women. In fact, widowers typically experience higher rates of both loneliness and suicide than widows (Lee & DeMaris, 2007; Stroebe, Schut, & Stroebe, 2007). Carr (2004) suggests that, overall, this is a reflection of men's higher levels of practical and emotional dependence on their spouses, combined with relatively few close emotional ties outside the marriage. Death of a spouse also has been associated with depression, but the literature regarding gender differences is mixed. This could be due to the methodology and the different study populations used in previous studies. In an attempt to determine if there are indeed gender differences in depression following bereavement, Sasson and Umberson (2014) analyzed 14 years of longitudinal data from the *Health and Retirement Study* which began in the United States in 1994. These researchers found no gender difference in depressive symptoms among the widowed in the study. For both men and women, widowhood was associated with an increase in depressive symptoms that diminished over time. However, they found that premature widowhood is associated with poor psychological well-being that does not seem to improve over time. In other words, the consequences of losing a spouse at a younger age are considerable and prolonged for those who remain widowed, whereas those widowed at later ages are more likely to recover, at least in terms of depression.

As you read this you are likely thinking that the research you have just read is really quite negative with regard to widowhood. However, there is research that shows that, in general, older adults cope well with widowhood. Adjusting to life after the death of a spouse is a process that takes time as widowers and widows adjust to their lives without their partners. Even in the oldest-old (85 years and older), Isherwood, King, & Luszcz (2017) found that with the mobilization of social supports, many of the older adults in their study were able to continue to lead socially engaged and meaningful lives.

The phenomenon of re-partnering after widowhood in late life has become more common and accepted in developed and modern individualistic cultures in comparison to more traditional collectivist cultures or developing countries. In collectivist cultures and developing countries, there is a more defined role to widowhood and women often endure significant hardships (Loomba Foundation, 2015). Within cultures located between tradition and modernity, such as Israel, late-life re-partnering is becoming more accepted as a legitimate choice in old age but is not officially recognized (Koren & Eisikovits, 2011).

According to Vespa (2013), the choice to re-partner depends on the perception that the benefits of re-partnering outweigh the benefits of being single. Studies that have been done previously have found that some older individuals choose not to remarry because they prefer the benefits of being single. Some of these perceived benefits are personal and financial independence, preservation of existing social relationships, and avoidance of the burden and personal costs that can accompany caregiving (De Jong Gierveld, 2002; Karlsson & Borell, 2005). In fact, Karlsson and Borell (2005) observed that for older women, widowhood often represents so-called retirement from a caregiver role and becoming a widow reduces their domestic responsibilities. Women often gain a sense of independence and renewed ties with their social network after their bereavement period following the death of their spouse (Vespa, 2013). Because men have a tendency to depend on their wives for social support, the desire to re-partner is higher for widowers than for widows (Brown, Lee, & Bulanda, 2006). However, when widowers have adequate social support, such as friends in the community, their desire to re-partner is not that much different from widows (Schimmele & Wu, 2016).

As you are learning, cohabitating is becoming increasingly popular, especially among older adults. Cohabitation provides the benefits of living with another, but it is a more flexible arrangement than marriage with regard to the pooling of financial resources and division of labour (Brown et al., 2012). Could this be the reason why cohabitation is increasing faster than any other type of living arrangement in the older age groups?

Wu, Schimmele, & Ouellet (2015) wanted to investigate the prevalence of cohabitation after widowhood and compare it to the prevalence of marriage after widowhood. These researchers used data from the *Canada's* 2007 *General Social Survey*, which is a nationally representative sample of Canadians aged 45 and older. They found that the majority of re-partnering after widowhood in Canada occurs within 10 years of this event or not at all. However, the rate of remarriage overall was twice as high as the rate of cohabitation for both widows and widowers. The exception to this was in the province of Quebec where there was a far higher percentage of older adults choosing to cohabitate after widowhood rather than remarry. This makes sense as cohabitation is a more prevalent choice than marriage at any age in that province. Okay, let's think about something for a minute. We know from the 2006 to 2011 data from Statistics Canada that the rate of cohabitation rose the fastest in the older age groups. So why is this not reflected in the results of Wu and colleagues? It is likely because the research of Wu and colleagues is based on data from 2007 and does not capture the rising trend of cohabitation in the more recent Statistics Canada survey. It will be interesting to see what the next round of Statistics Canada data shows.

RE-PARTNERING AFTER UNION DISSOLUTION

The baby boom generation experienced higher rates of divorce and remarriage than any generation before it (Brown & Lin, 2012). As the baby boomers continue to age, we will likely see more changes regarding marital status than are currently being reported. Before we begin, we need to clarify something. "Union dissolution" is the term now used in the literature to describe marital breakups. The term is more encompassing than the term "divorce," and it includes marital breakups and those breakups that occur when cohabitating.

Using data from the *Canada's 2007 General Social Survey*, Schimmele and Wu (2016) found that among people aged 45 and older, the mean age of union dissolution was 59 years for women and 56 years for men. For more than two-thirds of the study population, this event represented the breakup of a first union whether it be a marital union or a cohabiting union. These researchers also found cohort differences in the type of re-partnering after union dissolution. Among those aged 45 to 64, there was a preference for cohabitation over marriage. However, they found a preference for marriage over cohabitation among older adults aged 65 and over. This could reflect more negative attitudes towards cohabitation held by individuals who grew up in the cohort before the baby boomers. Or, it could be again that these data do not capture the trend in increased cohabitation seen in the 2006 to 2011 Statistics Canada data.

Like their widowed female counterparts, the re-partnering after union dissolution was much lower for women than for men. Schimmele and Wu (2016) ask an interesting question. How much of this gender gap in re-partnering is attributable to a smaller pool of available men to re-partner with versus gender differences in the perceived costs and benefits of re-partnering at older ages? Hopefully, future research will explore this question.

LIVING APART TOGETHER

As you have learned, many older women are reluctant to get tangled up with a new partner, perhaps because of the domestic and caregiving workload it tends to involve. But living alone does not necessarily mean being single. A number of older people are opting for Living Apart Together (LAT) relationships. LAT unions are intimate relationships between unmarried partners who live in separate households but identify themselves as part of a couple (Duncan & Phillips, 2010) (see Figure 10.3). Establishing an LAT relationship allows individuals to maintain their own living space, their personal freedom, and pre-existing relationships with family and friends.

This was confirmed in a study by Kobayashi, Funk, & Khan (2016). They examined the various reasons for choosing a LAT relationship among 28 older couples (mean age=59 years) living in Victoria, British Columbia. Participants disclosed that they chose to enter into an LAT relationship because it gave them the opportunity to remain independent, and it protected them from the financial and legal risks associated with living together. An interesting option for sure. However, in 2011 in Canada, this union was rare with 4 percent of those aged 50 to 59 and 2 percent of those aged 60 and older in such a relationship. Young adults, many of whom live with their parents, were much more likely to be part of an LAT couple. For example, among 20- to 24-year-olds, nearly one in three individuals were in an LAT relationship (Turcotte, 2013).

BEING SINGLE THROUGHOUT LIFE

Historically, never-married singles in various cultures have been stigmatized (Band-Winterstein & Manchik-Rimon, 2014). Perceived as a burden to their families due to mental and/or social problems, singles were viewed as cold and less caring than married people or those in intimate relationships (Hertel & Schütz, 2006). Greitemeyer (2008) found that both female and male single individuals were rated as more neurotic, less satisfied with their lives, less sociable, lonelier, and having lower self-esteem than those individuals in partnerships. However, Greitemeyer and other researchers (e.g., Sarkisian & Gerstel, 2016; Simpson, 2016) have not found this to be a true characterization of individuals who are single. Although societal views on singlehood are changing, there is still considerable stigma attached to being single,

FIGURE 10.3

Adam Vilimek

especially in older ages and especially for women. Consider terms such as "spinster" or "old maid." While these terms may be outdated, their stereotypical meaning persists. Interestingly, we can't think of a comparable term for men.

In Canada, the proportion of Canadians aged 65 and over who are single and never married is around 5 percent (Turcotte & Schellenberg, 2007). Again, we do not know very much about the lives and social relationships of single older adults, especially men. But, like their younger counterparts, they often are viewed as lonely and socially disconnected (DePaulo & Morris, 2006).

It appears that how individuals perceive their singlehood (e.g., as a choice or circumstance or as temporary or permanent) can influence their satisfaction with being single, and can influence their overall well-being. For example, singlehood for some individuals is a conscious choice, but for others, becoming single occurs following a chain of life events that are not the result of a conscious choice (Band-Winterstein & Manchik-Rimon, 2014). For example, Timonen and Doyle (2014) interviewed men and women aged 64 to 85 who lived in Ireland. These researchers found that the women and men who had chosen singlehood associated this status with self-fulfillment, independence, and autonomy throughout their life course. In other words, they were happy with their choice to be single. McDill, Hall, and Turell (2006) interviewed single females over 40 years of age living in the United States. They also found that the participants in their study who chose to be single or fully accepted their singlehood were self-satisfied, socially productive, and well-adjusted to their single status. In contrast, older adults who perceived that they had no choice in their singlehood because of caregiving, poverty, family roles, or cultural norms expressed regret and dissatisfaction with their single status.

10.2 RELATIONSHIPS
LEARNING OBJECTIVES

To understand:
- the developmental pattern of friendships
- gay and lesbian relationships among older adults
- the responsibility of the sandwich generation
- intergenerational ties
- the joys and challenges of grandparenting
- elder abuse and its risk factors

DEVELOPMENTAL PATTERN OF FRIENDSHIPS

Research has shown us how friendships change over the lifespan. For example, as young adults, individuals typically have more friends than at any other time during their life (Blieszner & Roberto, 2012). Generally speaking, married individuals have fewer friends than their single counterparts, and as individuals age, their circle of friends becomes smaller still. However, regardless of the size of your friendship circle, friendship is important to both men and women over the life course (Marion, Laursen, Zettergren, & Bergman, 2013). In fact, there is a lot of evidence to suggest that having friends is associated with better physical and mental health (Cable, Bartley, Chandola, & Sacker, 2013; Fiori, Antonucci, & Cortina, 2006). Interestingly, friends seem to be more important than family as a protective factor against poor mental health among older adults. Fiori and her colleagues (2006) found that older adults aged 65 years and older who had no friends but had family had significantly higher depressive symptomatology than did those who had a family network but no friends. These findings suggest that the absence of family in the context of friends is less detrimental than the absence of friends in the context of familial support.

<table>
<tr><td>REFLECTIVE QUESTION</td><td>What do you think could account for friends being more important than family for well-being?</td></tr>
</table>

It was originally thought older adults had fewer friends simply because of the fact that friends die. However, recent research paints an entirely different picture. It appears that having fewer friendships in older age may be due more to the fact that older adults are more selective in their friendships. Conscious of the time they have left to live, older adults seek out meaningful relationships and they have less time for drama. This phenomenon is part of a theory called **socio-emotional selectivity** developed by Carstensen and her colleagues (Carstensen, 2006; Charles & Carstensen, 2010; Reed & Carstensen, 2012). These researchers argue that social contact is motivated by a variety of goals including information seeking, self-concept, and emotional regulation. When information seeking is the goal, which tends to be the goal of young adults, individuals are trying to figure out who they are and their place in the world. Meeting new people and having friends is part of that process. When emotional regulation is the goal, as it is with older adults, they become highly selective in their choice of friends and prefer to hang out with individuals who have similar values and interests. Both of these goals are balanced in mid-life.

Until recently, not only were older adults thought to have fewer relationships, but also these relationships were thought to be less satisfying (Luong, Charles, & Fingerman, 2011). However, recent research has found that older adults generally experience more satisfying and positive relationships than younger adults. Why might this be? Luong and colleagues suggest that because of the awareness of the limited time left to live, older adults become more motivated to have social experiences that are more meaningful.

There is research that suggests that women have more friends and form more intimate relationships than men do (Adams & Ueno, 2006). However, Gillespie, Lever, Frederick, and Royce (2015) found different results in their survey using anonymous data collected via a survey posted on NBCNews.com. The 25 185 respondents were stratified by age and gender. On average, young and middle-aged men and women both reported having approximately the same number of friends they could talk to or call when in trouble. As expected, older adults identified having fewer friends. So, what might account for the finding that men and women had a similar number of friends? Well, the researchers think it might be how they asked the questions about friendship. For example, they stayed away from what they called "female-typical" definitions of friendship that assess only personal disclosure and other intimate talk but neglect to include **instrumental support** as a critical aspect of friendship. These researchers included instrumental support as part of their definition of friendship. Their data challenge previous studies that conclude that women have more friendships than men. Another area where more research is needed.

LGBTQ OLDER ADULTS

Historically, non-heterosexual orientation was understood as a mental illness. In fact, the American Psychiatric Association (APA) listed homosexuality as a sociopathic personality disturbance in 1952, and it was not removed from the *Diagnostic and Statistical Manual of Mental Disorders* until 1973. In Canada, it was not until 2004 that the Supreme Court of Canada declared that an individual could not be discriminated against because of his or her sexual orientation (Egale Canada, 2004). Even though there have been changes in law and social policy that acknowledge the rights and welfare of many LGBTQ individuals, the job of tearing down multiple forms of social and institutional discrimination has been largely left up to individuals and groups of LGBTQ activists (Brotman, Ferrer, Sussman, Ryan, & Richard, 2015). It is notable that for the first time in Canadian history, the Right Honourable Prime Minister Justin Trudeau recently marched in Gay Pride parades in Vancouver and Toronto. In short, legal rights and social policy for the LGBTQ community have come a long way, but there is still more work to do, especially in terms of de-stigmatization. Consider that homosexuality currently is illegal in 75 countries and punishable by death in five (Carroll & Itaborahy, 2015).

Approximately 4 percent of adults aged 65 and over were part of a same-sex couple in 2006 (Milan et al., 2011). However, this number could be much higher because older adults are less likely to disclose their sexual orientation. Approximately 50 percent of same-sex couples in Canada live in Montreal, Toronto, and Vancouver, which makes sense as these three cities are in the provinces that legalized same-sex marriage a couple of years prior to the national legalization of same-sex marriage in 2005 (Milan et al., 2011). It should be noted that although research on LGBTQ and aging has grown in the last decade, the majority of this work addresses only gay men and lesbian women.

In a review of the literature on same-sex couple characteristics, Peplau and Fingerhut (2007) concluded that there are some differences between same-sex couples and heterosexual couples. For example, there is a greater sharing of household chores and child care among same-sex couples. Although this is changing, domestic chores and childcare responsibility often are left up to the female in heterosexual relationships.

We think it's important to remember that many older LGBTQ individuals lived through a time where disclosure of their sexual orientation could result in imprisonment or enforced medical interventions (Barrett, Whyte, Comfort, Lyons, & Crameri, 2015). For example, Alan Turing was a gay man who had a key role in cracking intercepted coded messages from the Germans during World War II. He did his best to hide his sexuality but, eventually, the authorities found out that he was gay and they imprisoned him. Unfortunately, he died in prison. *The Imitation Game* is a movie about his experiences. For more information on Alan Turing, please go to www.turing.org.uk/publications/dnb.html.

While they have lived through social and political transitions of LGBTQ rights and liberations, older LGBTQ individuals today still are less likely than their post-liberation peers to have had their sexual orientation acknowledged or celebrated. They also are less likely to have developed a positive self-esteem and self-image (Brotman et al., 2015; Cronin & King, 2014). In fact, older adult participants in one study reported that sharing their sexual orientation with family frequently resulted in negative responses from family members, which, in turn, eroded the participant's self-esteem, confidence, and trust in other people. In addition, disclosure to an individual's family most often resulted in very limited contact with them from that point forward (Barrett et al., 2015). Because LGBTQ older adults are less likely to have children and less likely to have contact with family than their younger counterparts, they are more likely to rely on partners and friends for support (Croghan, Moone, & Olsen, 2014; Guasp, 2011; McParland & Camic, 2016).

Older LGBTQ individuals often are in poorer health and have higher rates of depression and loneliness than their heterosexual counterparts (Fredriksen-Goldsen et al., 2011). However, they are less likely to seek out help because of fear of discrimination. In fact, all LGBTQ individuals, regardless of age, have reported a range of negative reactions from service providers including rejection, outright hostility, refusal of treatment, and breach of confidentiality (Brotman et al., 2015). Based on these findings, it is not surprising to find that older LGBTQ individuals are not likely to disclose their sexual orientation to healthcare providers or other people for that matter (Jenkins Morales, King, Hiler, Coopwood, & Wayland, 2014). When you think about it, older individuals who are LGTBQ are rarely visible in healthcare institutions, mainstream networks for older adults, and society in general (Brotman et al., 2015).

Many older individuals who are LGBTQ want to remain in their home and community as they age ("aging in place") like many of their heterosexual counterparts. Aging in place often requires the assistance of home-care providers. However, Brotman and colleagues (2015) found that homophobia was problematic among providers of home care. This is important to consider.

Many older adults have had to hide their sexuality from others. Often their own home is the only safe place to express their sexuality. Requiring home-care assistance may result in the loss of the only space where in LGBTQ individuals can be themselves (Brotman et al., 2015).

Most of what we know about the experiences of LGBTQ individuals in long-term-care (LTC) facilities comes from studies done in the United States. However, the few studies done in Canada have found similar results. For example, Brotman and her colleagues (2015) concluded that many older adults who are LGBTQ worry about becoming a resident in LTC facilities for fear of discrimination and violence. Although policies are changing on several fronts with regard to the welfare and rights of all LGBTQ individuals, it seems that action with regard to carrying out these policies is a little further behind. In a recent study in Canada, 31 LTC and retirement facilities in Ontario, Quebec, and British Columbia that were considered to be sensitive to LGBTQ issues were surveyed. Sussman and colleagues (2012) found that only 20 of these facilities had engaged in some types of staff training, only seven had made efforts to connect with the LGBTQ community, and only four had adapted materials that were more inclusive of their LGBTQ residents. Clearly, we are a long way away from implementing many practice recommendations found in the literature regarding the LGBTQ community, and much more work needs to be done. As researchers have pointed out, attitudes of LTC staff and the larger community will need to change before any real implementation of the many recommended policy changes occurs (Brotman et al., 2015; Grigorovich, 2013).

THE SANDWICH GENERATION (CONSIDER THE PANINI)

Much of the focus in the caregiving and aging literature has been on adult children who provide care to their aging parents or parents-in-law. However, more and more people are finding themselves looking after their aging parents as well as children of their own. The term **sandwich generation** was first coined by Miller (1981) to describe these typically middle-aged caregivers who are sandwiched between the demands of caring for their own children and their aging parents. Traditionally, the term referred to middle-aged caregivers who were looking after aging parents and children younger than 18 who were still living at home. But, these days, it also could refer to young adult children who no longer live at home but who rely on their parents financially or to **boomerang children** who left home but have returned to live with their parents. In 2012, 28 percent of Canadians were considered sandwiched with similar trends being found in the United States (Boyczuk & Fletcher, 2016).

Sandwich caregiving is associated with increased rates of depression and decreased well-being. In addition, it has been found that the stress of being sandwiched can cause job burnout and failure to meet obligations at work (Lero, Spinks, Fast, Hilbrecht, & Tremblay, 2012; Pines, Neal, Hammer, & Ickeson, 2011). In fact, addressing the needs of employees providing care for older parents is an emerging concern within the Canadian workplace. Lero and colleagues (2012) found that common consequences of employees providing care for parents included arriving late, leaving early, and unscheduled absenteeism. Of concern is that 58 percent of the organizations he investigated in his study considered providing support for employees with eldercare responsibilities a low priority. This is troublesome as we will likely see more individuals sandwiched in terms of caregiving roles over the next several decades. As Boyczuk and Fletcher (2016) point out, having a better understanding of the root causes of stress for individuals who find themselves sandwiched between care of children and parents can lead to the development of better support services.

Finally, there is the **Panini sandwich**. It is not always the case that children look after their parents. Abramson (2016) would like us to think about the older adults who often are simultaneously pressed between caring for themselves as they age and caring for others. Consider those who are in a lifelong role of caring for a child who is developmentally delayed or who has struggles with mental illness. Abramson calls this the "Panini sandwich." Abramson (2016) argues that it is of utmost importance that we begin to provide supports and interventions to help older adults who are in these roles cope with the numerous strains and stressors and worries that result from being sandwiched between a lifetime of caregiving and their own aging experiences.

INTERGENERATIONAL TIES

Over the past 30 years, relationships among adults and their parents have become stronger (Fingerman, Sechrist, & Birditt, 2013). Research has demonstrated that behavioural indicators of the parent–child relationship such as frequency of contact, co-residence, or exchanges of support have increased especially among young adults and their parents (Fingerman, Cheng, Tighe, & Birditt, & Zarit, 2012). This is demonstrated in the United States Family Exchange Study (FES), which has examined the relationships among baby boomers aged 42 to 60 and their spouses, parents, and multiple grown children since 2008. Most boomers reported frequent contact and exchanges of support with both parents and grown children. Findings indicate that middle-aged

FIGURE 10.4

BABY BOOMERS SPEND MORE TIME WITH THEIR CHILDREN THAN THEIR PARENTS SPENT WITH THEM AND THIS TREND CONTINUES WITH TODAY'S PARENTS

© Spotmatik | Dreamstime.com

baby boomers offered their children emotional support and a listening ear more than once a week, advice at least once a month, and practical and financial assistance anywhere from monthly to several times a year on average (Fingerman, Miller, Birditt, & Zarit, 2009) (see Figure 10.4).

REFLECTIVE QUESTION

Do you seek out a parent, step-parent, or grandparent for advice?

Baby boomers are much more involved with their own children than their parents were with them. Data from the *National Survey of Families and Households* collected in 1988 showed that less than half (46 percent) of parents offered advice to an adult child in the past month and only 31 percent provided practical assistance (Eggebeen, 1992). By contrast, in 2008, 89 percent of parents gave advice to at least one child every month, and almost 70 percent gave practical support (Fingerman, Kim, Tennant, Birditt, & Zarit, 2016).

So, will baby boomers get the care in their older years that many have lavished on their children? This is a very interesting question. Supporting aging parents may be more difficult for the children of baby boomers: Poor economic times have the potential to limit job or career opportunities, which may mean that they are working in jobs that are not stable in the long run or working several jobs. They simply may not have the resources or time to look after aging parents. Another factor that may prove to be significant in determining parental support is that there have been tremendous changes in the structure of families in recent decades. Since the baby boom cohort, there has been a noteworthy increase in divorce and remarriage and an increase in cohabitation. As a consequence, more complex family structures have displaced the traditional nuclear family. Consider stepfamilies for a minute. It is not really clear what role stepchildren should play in providing assistance to their step-parents (Pezzin, Pollak, & Schone, 2013). In fact, recent research has shown that older adults who have only stepchildren for support had worse health outcomes than older adults with biological children. Using data from the *U.S. Health and Retirement Study*, Pezzin and her colleagues (2013) found that older adult mothers with only stepchildren become physically unwell and institutionalized sooner than their counterparts with biological children. Furthermore, disability and institutionalization outcomes for mothers with only stepchildren were significantly worse than those of childless women. Pezzin and her colleagues also found that older men with only stepchildren have shorter longevity relative to their counterparts with only biological children. They also found that the effect of membership in a blended family (i.e., a family of biological and stepchildren) differs by gender. Relative to those with only biological children, mothers in blended families have greater longevity and become disabled later. The researchers suggest that this may be because mothers in blended families strive for equality, thereby investing equally in all children in the household; this results in enhanced relationships among children, which translates into more support in their older years. In contrast, the results of the health outcomes for men in blended families were very similar to those older men with stepchildren in that they had greater rates of institutionalization and reduced longevity. These results raise concerns about the support networks available to older parents in stepfamilies and blended families. This will have implications for public programs that may have to fill in the gap of care resulting from changing family patterns (Pezzin et al., 2013).

Have you thought about how or if you will support your parents as they age?

One final comment on intergenerational relationships. As of late, there has been growing concern about **intergenerational conflict**. This term refers to the potential conflict between older and younger generations as they compete for jobs and resources. One of the key factors driving attention to the possibility of future intergenerational conflict is the aging of the baby boom cohort. The issue of the potential for intergenerational conflict surfaced in Canada during the mid-1990s with the fear that funding for the Canada Pension Plan might run out as the cohort of older adults is living into their 80s and 90s (Foot & Venne, 2005). Population aging further affects intergenerational relationships as it raises fundamental questions about how resources are shared between generations. In the research, at least three major issues are regularly discussed within the context of intergenerational equity: (1) the distribution of resources between children and older adults, including healthcare; (2) the apprehension over large national deficits caused by expansive programs such as Social Security and Medicare in the United States and healthcare and government-sponsored pension plans in Canada; and (3) the fairness of financing Old Age Security programs by younger generations. If the younger generation starts perceiving that the older generation is holding them back in term of accessing resources such as work and public programs, their reactions are likely to be strong (North & Fiske, 2012). However, there is a debate in the literature as to whether or not intergenerational conflict will actually occur.

GRANDPARENTING

According to Statistics Canada, in 2011, there were about seven million grandparents aged 45 and over in private households, representing 57 percent of the population in this age group. However, if you look at Canadians aged 75 and over, 94 percent were grandparents in 2011 (Milan, Laflamme, & Wong, 2015). On average, grandparents have four grandchildren but this will likely decline in the future if fertility rates remain low. In 2011, approximately 4 percent of grandparents lived with their grandchildren with either one or both parents of the grandchildren.

In 2011, the number of Indigenous and immigrant grandparents who lived with their children and grandchildren was much higher for cultural and economic reasons (Milan et al., 2015). Those immigrants who arrived after the age of 60 were even more likely to live with grandchildren as most of them immigrated to Canada for the purpose of family reunification and were a key source of child care. Approximately 12 percent of grandparents lived in a **skip-generation household**, in which the parents of the grandchildren were absent (Milan et al., 2015). In skip-generation households, grandparents look after their grandchildren because the grandchildren's own parents are unable to provide care. Raising grandchildren is not easy and, not surprisingly, it can create a lot of stress as grandparents learn to juggle their needs with those of their grandchildren. It also can create financial stress. However, this type of care situation can create close emotional bonds between grandchildren and their custodial grandparents. Fortunately, the majority of custodial grandparents are able to cope. In addition, most of these grandparents think that raising their grandchildren themselves is better than other alternatives (Hayslip et al., 2013; Thompson, Cameron, & Fuller-Thomson, 2012).

Research has shown that grandparents positively influence their grandchildren's lives in a variety of ways such as contributing to their development in terms of their values, their emotional and spiritual well-being, and their cultural identity (Manssoon, 2014). Grandparents also are seen as dispensers of wisdom, family historians, and someone to play games with and have fun with. In turn, grandchildren contribute positively to their grandparents' well-being and overall life satisfaction (Di Gessa, Glaser, & Tinker, 2014; Manssoon, 2014; Powdthavee, 2011).

The role of grandparents is less defined when the parents of their grandchildren are divorced. Often grandchildren are closest to maternal grandparents and are likely to see more of them than their paternal grandparents after a divorce (Monserud, 2011). Further, former daughters-in-law and sons-in-law can interfere with children seeing grandparents by keeping their former spouse from seeing the children. As you can see, divorce is much more complex than two people splitting up. Did you know that grandparents do not have an automatic right to see their grandchildren? Following a parental divorce, grandparents can go to court and apply for access to see a grandchild. But, access is not automatically granted and this process can be very stressful for both the grandparents and the grandchildren they would like to see.

There are several not-for-profit organizations across Canada of which the purpose is to support grandparents who are denied access to their grandchildren (e.g., Volunteer Grandparent, Canadian Grandparents Rights Association). Another organization in Canada is called Grandparents Requesting Access and Dignity (GRAND). All of these organizations provide support to grandparents who are denied access to their grandchildren, usually because of family court sole-custody decisions or other conflicts that show no fault or unfitness of the grandparents. GRAND has made several lobbying attempts to modify the federal Divorce Act. The goal is to have the Divorce Act modified so that parents cannot interfere with the grandparents' visitation of their grandchildren without a serious reason (Novak, Campbell, & Northcott, 2014).

ELDER ABUSE

Elder abuse is not a new problem and, in fact, the term "granny bashing" first appeared over 30 years ago in the *British Medical Journal* (Baker, 1975). The World Health Organization (2016b) defines elder abuse as "a single, or repeated act, or lack of appropriate action, occurring within any relationship where there is an expectation of trust which causes harm or distress to an older person." However, many key organizations across the world have created their own definition of abuse and neglect of older adults. Let's pause for a moment to think about this last statement. Do you see any difficulties with this? Although the WHO definition is arguably the most widely used, the problem is that despite more than three decades of research and discussion on the issues, there are ongoing challenges concerning the conceptualization and definition of elder abuse. This in turn makes elder abuse hard to detect and even harder to measure.

REFLECTIVE QUESTION

What do think is the most common type of elder abuse?

According to the National Seniors Council of Canada (2007), elder abuse can take numerous forms: financial, physical, emotional or psychological, sexual abuse, and neglect. Depending on how elder abuse is conceptualized, other forms of elder abuse may include systemic and spiritual abuse. The five most common types of elder abuse talked about in the literature are presented in Table 10.1. Of these, financial abuse appears to be the most common (Government of Canada, 2016c).

In Canada, it is estimated that between 4 percent and 10 percent of older adults are abused in some manner (National Seniors Council of Canada, 2007). However, these numbers are thought to be substantially higher because of healthcare professionals' limited knowledge of elder abuse, a lack of protocols to identify abuse, reluctance on behalf of the victims to acknowledge the abuse, and the small number of services available to support older adults in these situations (Hirst et al., 2016). To make matters worse, until recently, there were no clinical guidelines for preventing and addressing abuse and neglect in older adults. In a review of recent literature on elder abuse, Hirst and her Canadian colleagues (2016) also found that there is no solid evidence to support the idea that the practice of screening for elder abuse actually reduces its occurrence.

So, why does elder abuse happen? The short answer is that we don't know for sure. Ageism and a general negative attitude towards older adults, substance abuse on the part of the abuser, mental health problems, caregiver burden, and a cycle of family violence have all been identified as factors contributing to elder abuse in the community (Government of Canada, 2016). According to Edwards (2012), dependency is a characteristic of both the victims and perpetrators of elder abuse. For example, having a cognitive impairment such as a dementia increases

TABLE 10.1

THE MAIN CATEGORIES OF ELDER ABUSE

TYPE OF ABUSE	DESCRIPTION
Physical Abuse	Involves inflicting physical discomfort, pain, or injury. It includes behaviours such as slapping, hitting, punching, beating, burning, and rough handling. Such maltreatment as the inappropriate use of drugs, physical restraints, and force-feeding also are considered physical abuse.
Sexual Abuse	Involves non-consensual sexual contact of any kind with an older adult. Sexual contact with any person incapable of giving consent also is considered sexual abuse.
Emotional Abuse	Involves name calling, yelling, insulting, threatening, imitating, swearing, ignoring, isolating, excluding from meaningful events, and deprivation of rights. Emotional abuse diminishes the identity, dignity, and self-worth of the older person.
Financial Abuse	Involves the misuse of money or property. It includes stealing money or possessions, forging a signature on pension cheques or legal documents, misusing a power of attorney, and forcing or tricking an older adult into selling or giving away his or her property.
Neglect	Involves behaviours on behalf of the caregiver such as abandonment and the denial of food, water, medication, medical treatment, therapy, nursing services, health aids, clothing, and visitors.

Source: Adapted from Government of Canada. (2016c). *Elder abuse: It's time to face the reality*. Retrieved from https://www.canada.ca/en/public-health/services/health-promotion/stop-family-violence/prevention-resource-centre/prevention-resources-older-adults/elder-abuses-time-face-reality.html

dependency on a caregiver which may increase the risk of abuse. In turn, abusers may be dependent on the victim (e.g., financial reliance on the victim) especially if the abuser has a substance abuse problem. Older adults who have greater functional impairment are at more risk of elder abuse, especially for emotional and physical abuse as it is more difficult to defend oneself (Burnes et al., 2015).

Does elder abuse occur cross-culturally? Yes, but Tam and Neysmith (2006) caution researchers in the field of elder abuse "about applying elder abuse categories derived from a Western cultural perspective to understand or account for abuse in other cultures" (Tam & Neysmith, 2006, p. 149). There is very little published literature on the perception of elder abuse among Canadian cultural groups (Ploeg, Lohfeld, & Walsh, 2013). According to Lai, Daoust, and Li (2014), Canadian researchers studying older immigrants and diverse ethno-cultural populations have emphasized that emotional and verbal abuse, particularly being disrespected, is perceived as especially serious in the context of traditional family values and expectations. For example, Chinese women who immigrated to Canada and lived with their adult children saw losing traditionally expected positions of respect within the family as abusive. Ploeg and her colleagues (2013) conducted focus groups with various older minority populations in Canada to determine their understanding of elder abuse. Aboriginal men and women disclosed that the type of abuse they mostly experienced was financial abuse by their adult children in the form of taking their pension or disability cheque or abusing their power of attorney responsibilities. The Aboriginal participants also provided examples of neglect, such as withholding food. Female refugees from Afghanistan and Iran talked mostly about the continuation of culturally sanctioned physical, emotional, and sexual abuse at the hands of their husbands. Interestingly, all groups saw institutionalization (i.e., placing a parent in long-term care (LTC)) as a form of abuse as the participants viewed this as neglect and abandonment by family members. As you can see, individuals from different cultures understand elder abuse differently, and this highlights the fact that we need much more research if we are to fully understand elder abuse cross-culturally (McDonald, 2011).

Using a focus group format, Haukioja (2016) interviewed front line workers from the Inter-Cultural Association of Greater Victoria (ICA), which is a not-for-profit, multicultural services organization for immigrants and refugees, to get their perspective on elder abuse. Although the sample size of four was small, the participants provided insights into elder abuse in the Chinese and East Asian community in Victoria, British Columbia. The participants reported that older immigrant adults will stay with their family members despite experiences of elder abuse. How can this be so? Well, the participants explained that there are several reasons why. For example, many of the older immigrants they work with are very dependent on their family members because of language barriers, financial vulnerability, lack of affordable housing, lack of transportation, and sponsorship policies. In terms of sponsorship policies, older immigrants do not qualify for rent or income subsidies because the family sponsored them to come to Canada. The ICA front line workers reported that many family sponsors use this dependency as a way to exercise control. For example, the ICA workers reported that a number of adult children force older adults to stay home to babysit, clean, and cook, and often use threats such as "If you don't do what I tell you then I send you back home" (Haukioja, 2016, p. 58). The ICA front line workers made an interesting point in terms of resources needed to address the issue of elder abuse. Because of significant language barriers, the participants explained that a visual resource containing concise information would be the most appropriate way to address elder abuse in minority communities. If information is presented visually, the older immigrant would be able to see the images of abuse and relate to them. It was emphasized that resources such as this need to be made available and accessible in several locations, including physician's offices, pharmacies, recreation facilities, places of worship, and the main ferry terminal. Another point made by the participants was that awareness of the issue of elder abuse should be targeted towards the whole family, not just the victim. In this way, the "parents can understand [what elder abuse is] and children can understand that it is a crime" (Haukioja, 2016, p. 61).

Before we move on, you should know that there is a growing concern about the abuse occurring in LTC facilities; both staff-to-resident and resident-to-resident. What is particularly disturbing is that, over the course of a one-year investigation, *W5* (which is an investigative journalism show) uncovered at least 23 521 cases of abuse in LTC facilities in 2013. That number is likely higher due to under-reporting of incidents. For more information on abuse in LTC settings, please read Box 10.1.

McDonald and her colleagues (2015) undertook a scoping review to enhance the understanding of resident-to-resident abuse in LTC homes in Canada. These researchers found that the majority of residents in LTC are over age 80 and tend to be frailer and more dependent on others to provide care than they were a decade ago. As a result, they may be more vulnerable to abuse from staff and other residents. In addition, residents are more likely to exhibit complex behavioural disturbances due to an increase in chronic disability and cognitive impairment that may result in expressions of aggression, which, in turn, can act as a trigger for abusive behaviour from staff.

BOX 10.1

INVESTIGATION OF ABUSE IN LONG-TERM-CARE FACILITIES

In March 2012, *W5* aired a broadcast on abuse in long-term-care facilities in Ontario. Following the broadcast, they received many emails and phone calls from across Canada telling them of similar cases. Looking for national statistics, they discovered none were kept so they decided to compile their own. In the course of their investigation, *W5* obtained the data by filing access-to-information requests with 42 provincial, territorial, and regional health authorities seeking statistical information and incident reports of staff-to-resident abuse for the 2013 calendar year. The documents obtained under the Access to Information (ATI) requests showed 23 521 occurrences of all types of abuse in one year. In 26 of the 38 jurisdictions, the data provided specific information about the type of incident—6494 resident-on-resident altercations. They also uncovered at least 1500 cases of staff-to-resident abuse and neglect in nursing homes across Canada in that time period. And given the culture of under-reporting that is prevalent in the long-term-care sector, the real number is likely higher. One of the immediate outcomes of working with *W5* and analyzing the data collected through ATI requests is that Lynn McDonald, a professor at the University of Toronto's Institute for Life Course and Aging, and her team will continue the research "on our own accord, to dig further into the data and collect more in order to better understand the scope of elder abuse in Canada." For access to the videos *Crisis in Care*, Parts 1 to 3, go to http://www.ctvnews.ca/w5/nursing-home-residents-at-risk-w5-investigation-reveals-startling-national-statistics-1.1149215.

What do you think accounts for the increase in frailty and dependence in current residents of LTC homes since 1981?

McDonald and her colleagues (2015) also identified a number of circumstances that can initiate resident-to-resident abuse. For example, invasion of personal space especially such issues as crowding, TV volume/channel, room temperature, and lighting were noted to have fuelled aggression between residents. In addition, hostile actions such as physical violence, sexual aggression, and theft have been shown to trigger abusive reactions from the resident being targeted. Furthermore, they found that self-reported victimization was associated with a reduction in life satisfaction and a greater risk for depression, anxiety, loneliness, low self-esteem, and overall negative mood. Finally, victims of resident-to-resident abuse were found to be four times more likely to experience neglect from nursing home staff, which may be why the victimization occurred in the first place.

Of note is that LTC facilities in the United States have been criticized because of the lack of guidelines for reporting and documenting abuse (Teresi et al., 2013), and it seems that the same could be said about Canada (McDonald et al., 2015). Currently, police are very rarely involved in abuse cases in LTC, especially in resident-to-resident sexual abuse cases (Ramsey-Klawsnik, Teaster, Mendiondo, Marcum, & Abner, 2008). It seems to be the case that situations involving sexual abuse are difficult to substantiate due to cognitive impairment present in both the victims and the initiators. McDonald and her colleagues highlight that resident-to-resident abuse is a serious societal issue that is under-researched and requires further investigation in order to minimize its occurrence and to develop strategies to appropriately manage its consequences. It often is too easy to forget that LTC facilities are now home for a portion of the older adult population. It should be a given that older adults living in these facilities have an environment that preserves their well-being, safety, and dignity (McDonald et al., 2015). One day it may be you.

10.3 SEXUALITY AMONG OLDER ADULTS
LEARNING OBJECTIVES

To understand:
- sexual patterns in old age
- the ins and outs of online dating for older adults
- the challenges of sexual expression in long-term-care settings
- HIV-AIDS in older adults

SEXUAL PATTERNS IN OLD AGE

One of the pervasive stereotypes of older age is that an individual becomes asexual; that is, they no longer are interested in engaging in sexual activities. Despite much research evidence to the contrary, this stereotype persists. Several large nationally representative research studies conducted in the United States have demonstrated that many older individuals have an interest in sex throughout life (Lindau et al., 2007; Waite, Laumann, Das, & Schumm, 2009), especially if an individual is in good health and has a partner. This is wonderful news if you consider that there is much agreement about the beneficial effects of sexuality for older people, which include pleasure, intimacy, decreased pain sensitivity, increased relaxation, and lower levels of depression (Ni Lochlainn & Kenny, 2013; Syme, 2014). As you may have guessed, women tend to stop having sexual relations earlier than men because of a lack of a partner due to widowhood and a smaller available pool of men. The frequency that individuals have sex declines with age. However, those older adults who remain sexually active report having partnered sex fairly often and these rates remain constant through the ages of 65 to 75 (Waite et al., 2009). Have a look at Table 10.2. You might find it hard to believe, but 54 percent of older adults have sex two to three times a month or more. Notice also the difference in sexual activities by age (e.g., oral sex). Waite and her colleagues explain that this variation in sexual practice could be the result of cohort differences in patterns of sexual behaviour established at younger ages and carried over into old age. For example, the youngest respondents to the *National Social Life, Health and Aging Study* are part of the baby boom cohort who experienced the sexual revolution. The oldest respondents were teenagers during the 1940s, a period of more conservative sexual attitudes and behaviors. On the other hand, these age differences also could be from changes in sexual repertoires due to changes in health and functioning. It would make sense that specific types of sexual activity desired or engaged in may change or need to be adapted in order to accommodate for the physical realities of older bodies (Fileborn, Thorpe, Hawkes, Minichiello, & Pitts, 2015).

Waite and her colleagues (2009) concluded that for partnered women and men, sexual inactivity occurs because of declining physical vigour rather than declining interest in sexual activity. Lindau and her colleagues (2007) also concluded from the data from a nationally representative sample of 3005 older Americans that physical health is more strongly associated with sexual functioning than is age. Lindau suggested that older adults who have medical problems and who are seeking treatment that might affect sexual functioning should be counselled according to health status rather than age. However, these researchers also found that older adults rarely talk about their sexual functioning with their physicians. Some of the reasons given by participants were the negative attitudes of physicians towards sexual expression among older adults and gender and age differences.

Many older adults report feeling more experienced, more relaxed, and more satisfied in their sexual relations in old age than when they were younger (Carpenter & DeLamater, 2012; Novak et al., 2014). Sexual expression among older adults often includes more touching, hugging, and holding hands than younger adults (Hurd Clarke, 2006).

In terms of sexual problems in late life, Lindau and her colleagues (2007) and Waite and her colleagues (2009) reported that the most frequently reported sexual dysfunctions for women were low desire, difficulty with vaginal lubrication, and an inability to have an orgasm. The most frequently reported sexual dysfunctions for men were erectile difficulties. It is good news for many that there are numerous medications available on the market to treat sexual difficulties. It is rare that one can get through an evening of watching television without seeing a commercial for Viagra. Anyway, a quote by Thomas (1982) sums up sexuality in older ages quite nicely and with humour. He compared sexuality in older ages to popcorn: "It is not harmful nor is it essential but it is one of the pleasures of life." By the looks of the literature, it is a pleasure for many throughout their lives.

TABLE 10.2

PREVALENCE OF SELECTED SEXUAL PRACTICES IN PRECEDING YEAR, BY AGE AND GENDER

	WOMEN				MEN			
	PERCENTAGE[a]				PERCENTAGE[a]			
	Age 57–64	Age 65–74	Age 75–85	Trend test[b]	Age 57–64	Age 65–74	Age 75–85	Trend test[b]
Any sex in preceding year								
Full sample	61.6 (2.4)	39.5 (2.4)	16.7 (2.1)	<0.001	83.7 (3.0)	67.0 (2.5)	38.5 (2.5)	<0.001, 0.12** (0.03)
Sub-sample with partners[c]	80.7 (2.4)	62.8 (2.9)	41.4 (4.8)	<0.001	90.5 (2.4)	74.7 (2.3)	47.3 (3.0)	<0.001
Sex frequency in preceding year[d]								
Two/three times a month or more	62.6 (3.6)	65.4 (4.4)	54.1 (6.2)	0.126	67.5 (3.3)	65.4 (3.2)	54.2 (5.0)	0.094
Once/twice a week or more	34.4 (3.6)	30.9 (3.8)	23.6 (6.2)	0.052	39.7 (2.3)	31.2 (2.9)	22.9 (3.6)	0.001
Vaginal sex usually/ always[d]	86.8 (2.3)	85.4 (3.0)	74.4 (6.9)	0.112	91.1 (1.4)	78.5 (2.7)	83.5 (3.4)	<0.001
Foreplay usually/ always[d]	88.8 (1.7)	88.5 (2.4)	88.7 (5.9)	0.959	94.3 (1.2)	90.2 (2.1)	92.2 (2.3)	0.067
Any oral sex[d,e]	52.7 (3.8)	46.5 (4.4)	35.6 (6.2)	0.024	62.2 (3.2)	48.2 (2.6)	28.3 (5.3)	<0.001
Used a condom usually/always[f]	2.1 (0.7)	4.8 (1.8)	2.8 (1.9)	0.262	4.3 (1.1)	3.5 (0.8)	0.8 (0.6)	0.124
Masturbated in preceding year	31.6 (2.6)	21.9 (2.1)	16.4 (2.3)	<0.001	63.4 (3.2)	53.0 (2.5)	27.9 (2.2)	<0.001

Notes: [a] All estimates are weighted to account for differential probabilities of selection and differential non-response. Design-based standard errors are given in parentheses.

[b] p value for a Wald test (using design-based SE) of the age coefficient for logistic regression on age (in years).

[c] Sample restricted to those reporting a spouse, cohabiting, or romantic partner in preceding year.

[d] Asked only of participants reporting any sex in preceding year.

[e] Indicates ever giving or receiving oral sex in preceding year.

[f] Indicates condom use during vaginal sex. Asked only if participant reported any vaginal sex in preceding year.

Source: Waite et al., 2009. Sexuality: Measures of partnerships, practices, attitudes, and problems in the National Social Life, Health, and Aging Study. *Journal of Gerontology, Series B: Psychological Sciences and Social Sciences, 64* Suppl. (1), 56–66. doi:10.1093/geronb/gbp038. Reprinted by permission of Oxford University Press.

SEXUAL EXPRESSION IN LONG-TERM-CARE SETTINGS

Living in LTC facilities poses many significant barriers to sexual activity among the older adults who live there. Lack of privacy and staff attitudes have been identified as major barriers to sexual activity in LTC facilities (Parker, 2006). For older adults in long-term-care settings, intimacy is further complicated by the pervasive stigma about sexuality and commonly held ageist attitudes. Nonetheless, many older adults who live in LTC have expressed a desire for sexual intimacy (Hillman, 2012). However, several studies have shown that staff in LTC tend to view any attempts at sexual intimacy as problematic rather than expressions of love (Cornelison & Doll, 2013; Mahieu, Van Elssen, & Gastmans, 2011). Further, many individuals in LTC have a dementia and sometimes individuals who have a dementia behave in a sexually inappropriate way. This behaviour may include but is not limited to touching intimate body parts of care providers and visitors, masturbating in social areas, disrobing oneself and others, and using sexually suggestive language. Care providers often do not receive adequate training about appropriate sexual expression—never mind the inappropriate sexual expression that may occur by residents—and are therefore not prepared to respond appropriately (Bentrott & Margrett, 2011; Dominguez & Barbagallo, 2016). This lack of training can lead to inconsistent and even punitive responses. In the absence of formal policies and guidelines, care providers often respond to sexual expression in informal and inconsistent ways. To complicate matters, there are no uniform standards that exist to assess sexual consent capacity in older adults in LTC. It is very important to identify those older adults who are able to provide sexual consent and support these individuals who can make their own sexual decisions, while protecting those who may not be able to (Connolly et al., 2012; Hillman, 2012). The legal ramifications of sexual relations between individuals who are cognitively impaired and are not able to consent are significant.

After reviews of the literature on sexual expression in LTC facilities, researchers have concluded that, in general, staff often are not well equipped to cope with sexual relationships between residents in LTC. Further, they found that educational programs often are non-existent or are inadequate (Cornelison & Doll, 2013; Elias & Ryan, 2011). In the words of a Canadian researcher, "We must ensure that we live up to the moral imperative of creating long-term-care environments that are genuinely welcoming and prepare to meet the needs of the of the older adults who present with a range of gender and sexuality identities" (Sokolowski, 2012, p. 4). For sure, there is a lot of work to be done.

DATING: IT IS NOT JUST FOR YOUNG PEOPLE

It is increasingly common for single older adults to be involved in dating relationships (Alterovitz & Mendelsohn, 2009). And why not? In fact, an analysis of widows and widowers ages 65 and older found that 18 months after the death of a spouse, 37 percent of men and 15 percent of women were interested in dating (Carr, 2004).

Older adults are becoming more comfortable with social media. Consider that in the United States, between April 2009 and May 2010, social media use by older adults nearly doubled from 22 percent to 42 percent (Madden, 2010). Currently over half of adults ages 50 to 64 have a social networking profile (Duggan & Brenner, 2013). As result, online dating has become increasingly popular with older adults, with one in four adults ages 50 to 64 reporting that they know someone who met and fell in love online (Smith & Duggan, 2013). In response to this growing market, many dating sites have begun catering specifically to an older adult market. Google "older adults and dating" and you will see what we mean!

Do you hold any prejudices against older adults dating?

According to Fileborn and colleagues (2015), the ways in which older adults enter into or seek out new relationships tend to follow highly gendered patterns. For instance, older men tend to seek younger partners and place an emphasis on attractiveness. In comparison, older women often seek older partners, and value intelligence and socio-economic status over physical qualities. In another study, Alterovitz and Mendelsohn (2009) analyzed 600 personal ads from Yahoo! They found that women remained the choosers (in other words, they decided if a date was to occur) at all ages. It is not clear why this should be the case given the increasing ratio of women to men in later life. Alterovitz and Mendelsohn suggest that the reason for this is that older men are not as selective as women when choosing a person to go on a date with because they are more willing to re-partner than are older women. Given that the baby boomers are getting more comfortable using social media, online dating will surely increase in the older adult population. This is good news given that loneliness and social isolation can be issues for many older adults.

SEXUALLY TRANSMITTED INFECTIONS IN OLDER ADULTS

In Canada and around the world, sexually transmitted infections are rising among older adults (Minichiello, Rahman, Hawkes, & Pitts, 2012). According to the Public Health Agency of Canada (2013b), rates of chlamydia, gonorrhea, and syphilis in Canada have been steadily rising since the late 1990s. While young Canadians have the highest reported rates of sexually transmitted infections, increasing numbers of cases are being reported among middle-aged and older adults. In terms of gender differences, among 40- to 59-year-old Canadians, males accounted for approximately 60 percent of reported chlamydia cases, 88 percent of reported gonorrhea cases, and 93 percent of reported infectious syphilis cases (Fang, Oliver, Jayaraman, & Wong, 2010). If we look at the prevalence rates of HIV-AIDS, this also is increasing in older adults. But, before we begin looking at the number of older adults who are living with HIV/AIDS, let's look at the number of individuals worldwide who have HIV/AIDS. We thought you might be interested in knowing that there are two different types of HIV epidemics. In "concentrated" epidemics, transmission occurs largely in defined vulnerable groups such as sex workers, men who have sex with men, and people who use injection drugs. In "generalized" epidemics, transmission is continued through sexual behaviour in the general population and persists despite effective programs for vulnerable groups. North America has a concentrated epidemic of HIV/AIDs whereas sub-Saharan Africa has a generalized epidemic (Canada's Source for HIV and Hepatitis C Information, n.d.).

According to the United Nations (2016), an estimated 36 million people were living with HIV globally in 2015 and an estimated two million new HIV infections occurred worldwide. This means that approximately 5700 people became infected with HIV every day in 2015. Almost 70 percent of new cases are in sub-Saharan Africa (United Nations, 2016). Approximately 75 500 individuals in Canada were living with HIV in 2014 (Government of Canada, 2015b). This represents a 6 percent increase since 2011. As you can see from Figure 10.5, the largest proportion

FIGURE 10.5

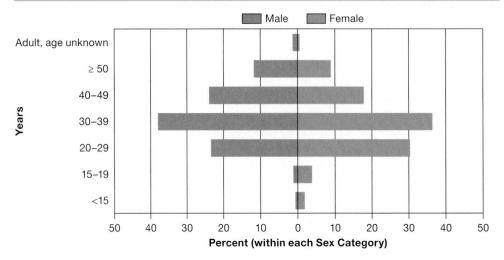

of HIV cases was diagnosed among individuals aged 30 to 39 years of age followed by the 40 to 49 age group. The proportion of HIV cases among those aged 50 and over increased from 15 percent in 2009 to almost 22 percent in 2014. Certain populations in Canada have higher rates of new infections of HIV. For example, Aboriginal peoples have incidence rates of new HIV infections that are 2.7 times higher than people from other ethnicities. Men who have sex with men are in the highest risk group for new HIV infection. Males also have incidence rates much higher than females in Canada (Canada's Source for HIV and Hepatitis C Information, n.d.). Figure 10.6 shows the all-age diagnosis rate of HIV cases (per 100 000 population) by province/territory in 2014.

The U.S. Centers for Disease Control and Prevention estimates that by 2020, older adults will account for 70 percent of all HIV/AIDS cases in the United States (Centers for Disease Control and Prevention, 2017). There are two reasons for this increase in HIV/AIDs in older adults in Canada and the United States: individuals who were diagnosed at a younger age and who are growing old with the disease and individuals who are diagnosed as older adults (Sankar, Nevedal, Neufeld, Berry, & Luborsky, 2011). In spite of the trend of increasing numbers of older adults contracting HIV, they are rarely targeted for HIV/AIDS prevention programs (Altschuler & Katz, 2015). Sexual contact is the main risk factor for new HIV/AIDS cases among older adults.

Researchers are quite certain that we do not have a good understanding of the prevalence of HIV-AIDS in older adults due to under-reporting (Brennan, Emlet, Brennenstuhl, Rueda, & OHTN Cohort Study team and staff, 2013). Because of the widespread belief that older adults are asexual, physicians and other healthcare providers commonly do not address issues of sexuality with older adults. Further, older adults have been overlooked in HIV testing, prevention, and research because of this misconception (Levy, Ding, Lakra, Kosteas, & Niccolai, 2007). To make matters worse, many older adults do not think they are at risk for HIV infection. For these

FIGURE 10.6

National Rate:
5.8 per 100,000

Yukon
8.2

Nunavut
-

Northwest
Territories
-

Newfoundland
and Labrador
1.9

British
Columbia
5.7

Alberta
6.7

Saskatchewan
10.8

Manitoba
6.6

Ontario
6.1

Quebec
5.3

Prince Edward Island
-

Nova Scotia
1.1

New Brunswick
0.4

older adults, HIV is an infection that occurs in younger people (Brennan et al., 2013). Because older adults do not see the risk, they are unlikely to use condoms when having sexual relations (Emanuel, 2014; Schick et al., 2010; Zona et al., 2012). This lack of awareness of the risk of contracting HIV/AIDS among older adults themselves, as well as healthcare professionals, can result in a late diagnosis of HIV/AIDS. The consequences of a late diagnosis are increased morbidity and mortality and reduced responses to HIV treatment (**including antiretroviral therapy**) for older adults (Mugavero, Castellano, Edelman, & Hicks, 2007). Additionally, a late diagnosis may result in an undiagnosed person's continued engagement in unprotected sex, unaware of the infection.

Psaros and her colleagues (2015) interviewed women over 50 to get an understanding of their perspectives of living with HIV. The women described a clear progression of feelings such as shame and disbelief at the time of diagnosis to acceptance and survivorship at the time of the study. The authors believe this resiliency is related to the fact that older adults recognize that their time left on earth already is short and as a result are able to moderate their responses when faced with negative events. These researchers suggest that this is another area where older adults could share their wisdom with younger adults who are dealing with an HIV diagnosis.

Sylvie Belleville, Ph.D.
Université de Montréal and Scientific Director for the Research Centre of the Institut Universitaire de Gériatrie de Montréal, Montreal, Quebec.

WHERE DID YOU TRAIN?

I completed a master's degree in clinical psychology at Université du Québec à Trois-Rivières Quebec and a Ph.D. in cognitive neuroscience at McGill University, Montreal, Quebec.

WHERE DO YOU WORK?

I am now a full professor at the Psychology Department of Université de Montréal and scientific director for the Research Centre of the Institut Universitaire de Gériatrie de Montréal. Early in my career, I worked as a clinical neuropsychologist with an older-adult population. I instantly loved working with this population.

WHAT DO YOU DO?

As a researcher, I am interested in better understanding the cognitive changes associated with aging, dementia, and mild cognitive impairment. I also test and develop non-pharmacological interventions and evaluation tools to be used with older adults by researchers and clinical neuropsychologists. I am highly involved in supervising graduate trainees and in developing ways to transfer my research into clinical practice (for instance: websites, computerized batteries, manualized training programs). Finally, as a scientific director, I develop and support the mission and functioning of a large multidisciplinary research centre comprising more than 50 researchers and 250 students from all disciplines.

WHY DO YOU LIKE WORKING WITH AN OLDER-ADULT POPULATION?

I discovered that older adults are engaging, profound, and interesting. I was impressed by their depth and wisdom. I realized that this was a phase of life characterized by changes and adaptation and that there was a multiplicity of ways to be an older person. Intellectually and as a researcher, I discovered the complexity of the aging process and decided to devote my research career to trying to find answers to the many questions regarding aging.

DO YOU HAVE ADVICE FOR STUDENTS WHO WANT TO GET INTO THE FIELD?

I encourage students to set aside all preconceived ideas about older adults. They will discover how interesting and lively it is to work in that field.

Lynn Burge, R.T. assistant
Villa Caritas Hospital, Geriatric Psychiatry, Edmonton, Alberta

WHERE DID YOU TRAIN?

I attended the Norquest College Recreation Assistant Program, Edmonton, Alberta and got further training through various programs at Alberta Hospital Edmonton.

WHERE DO YOU WORK?

Villa Caritas Hospital

WHAT DO YOU DO?

I help run a variety of programs such as bingo, horticulture, crafting, baking, etc. I try to help older adults with their mental healing and find enjoyment in life again.

WHY DO YOU LIKE WORKING WITH AN OLDER-ADULT POPULATION?

I really enjoy watching older adults get better. Our older patients come into the hospital with lots of issues and to see them leave feeling confident and good about life is very rewarding to me. Many of my patients share personal stories with me and I always listen respectfully.

DO YOU HAVE ADVICE FOR STUDENTS WHO WANT TO GET INTO THE FIELD?

It's very important to keep an open mind. Learn all you can about mental health and the care of older adults. Many of our patients have a mental illness that family or friends are unaware of. It is important to help to decrease the stigma of mental illness by being informed and informative. Be a strong shoulder to lean on and be a caring and listening person.

10.5 SUMMARY

- Relationships are becoming increasingly diverse and complex with married couples with children still the predominant family structure in Canada. Marriage satisfaction follows a U-shaped pattern over the age range. Older long-term married individuals have higher ratings on numerous measures of wellness than those who are not married.

- Cohabitating is becoming increasingly popular, especially among older adults. Living together apart is another option for older adults who do not want to cohabitate or get remarried.

- Over the last 20 years in Canada, divorce rates have been fairly stable. Rates for widowhood have increased over time with many more widowed women than widowed men in the older population.

- Bereavement is very difficult for many although, in general, older adults cope well with time. More widowers re-partner than do widows.

- The view of singlehood is changing and those older adults who choose to remain single are happy with their choice.

- According to the socio-emotional selectivity theory, there is a developmental pattern to friendships. Interestingly, friendships seem to be more important to health and well-being than family in old age.

- Older individuals who are LGBTQ are often in poorer health and have higher rates of depression and loneliness than their same-aged heterosexual counterparts. Much work needs to be done to support and accept the aging LGBTQ community in Canada.

- The sandwich generation consists of those middle-aged caregivers who are sandwiched between the demands of caring for their own children and their aging parents. The term "panini sandwich" refers to older adults who care for themselves as well as others such as a dependent child.

- Baby boomers are much more involved with their own children than their parents were with them. However, the children of baby boomers may not be so involved with their parents (or grandparents).

- There has been growing concern about intergenerational conflict with the aging of the population. However, there is a debate in the literature as to whether this conflict will occur.

- Most grandparents live in separate households although some grandparents live with their grandchildren. This is especially true of Aboriginal and immigrant families for cultural and economic reasons.

- Skip-generation households are those households where grandparents are raising grandchildren in the absence of the middle generation.

- The role of grandparents is less defined when their children are divorced.

- Children most often are closest to maternal grandparents and are likely to see more of them than their paternal grandparents after a divorce.

- Elder abuse is a significant social issue and one that is significantly under-reported. There is growing concern about staff-to-resident and resident-to-resident abuse in LTC facilities. Dementia can exacerbate abuse among residents and between staff and residents.

- Although there is a persistent stereotype that older adults are asexual, this is not the case. Having a reasonably active sex life is associated with good health and well-being.

- More and more older adults are using online dating sites to find friendships and relationships.

- An increasing number of older adults are contracting STIs and HIV. Sexual contact is the main risk factor for acquiring HIV among older Canadians.

Key Terms

Boomerang Kids
Children who return to their parents' home after living on their own.

Cohabitation Effect
Couples who would likely not have gotten married had they been living apart slide into marriage because they already are living together and it appears to be the thing to do next.

Complex Families
A family that includes at least one child of both parents as well as at least one child of one parent only.

Gender Inequality
Unequal treatment or perceptions of individuals based on their gender due to differences in socially constructed gender roles.

Grey Divorce
A term used to describe marriage dissolution among adults over age 50 years after approximately 20 years or more of marriage.

Instrumental Support
Various types of help that friends may provide such as transportation or helping with a housing move.

Intergenerational Conflict
The potential conflict between older and younger generations as they compete for jobs and resources.

Intergenerational Trauma
The transmission of oppression and its negative consequences across generations.

Living Apart Together Relationships
A committed relationship between two people in which separate households are maintained.

Panini Sandwich
Older adults who are caring for themselves and another such as an adult child with a disability.

Sandwich Generation
Individuals who find themselves caring for their aging parents as well as their own children.

Simple Families
A family in which all children are the biological or adopted children of only one married spouse or common-law partner.

Skip-Generation Households
Grandparents living with their grandchildren with no middle generation present.

Socio-emotional Selectivity
A theory that argues that social contact is motivated by a variety of goals including information seeking, self-concept, and emotional regulation.

Stepfamily
A family that is formed on the remarriage of a divorced or widowed person and that includes one or more children.

CHAPTER
11

WORK, RETIREMENT, AND LEISURE

"When you retire, think and act as if you were still working; when you're still working, think and act a bit as if you were already retired."

Author Unknown

Work is an important part of our lives. It makes our lives meaningful and constructive; it provides us with our identity and enhances our self-esteem; it provides inner joy and saves us from dullness and boredom; and it provides us with the financial resources to meet our basic needs. Leisure also is an important part of our lives. In older adults, participation in leisure activities plays a significant role in enhancing quality of life and life satisfaction (Nimrod & Shira, 2016). Let's begin by looking at work patterns in older adults.

11.1 WORK PATTERNS OF OLDER ADULTS
LEARNING OBJECTIVES

To understand:
- the changes in labour force participation in Canada over time
- the labour force participation rates of women over time and to be able to describe the implications of those changes
- the differences in labour force participation rates of older men and women and to be able to describe the implications of those changes
- the type of labour force participation of older workers and the reasons for these participation rates

A HISTORY OF WORK

The cultural **norm** of placing a positive moral value on doing a good job is a relatively recent development in our society. That is, working hard was not the norm for Hebrew, classical, or medieval cultures. Rather, the Greeks, like the Hebrews, regarded work as a curse. For the Romans, work was to be done by slaves, with only two occupations suitable for a free man—agriculture and big business. Physical labour became culturally acceptable for all persons, even the wealthy, during the Protestant Reformation in the 16th century. In 1905, Max Weber coined the term "Protestant work ethic." Key elements of this ethic were diligence, punctuality, deferment of gratification, and primacy of the work domain. Time passed and the attitudes and beliefs that supported hard work became woven into the norms of Western culture. One of the central themes of the work ethic during the pre-industrial times was that an individual could be the master of his own fate through hard work. During the Industrial Age, skill and craftsmanship were replaced by discipline and anonymity. The sense of control over one's destiny was missing in the new workplace, and the emptiness and lack of intellectual stimulation in work threatened the work ethic. By the end of World War II, efforts were made to make people feel important at work. Management used employee awards to enhance the job environment. Box 11.1 highlights some of the efforts that have been made to acknowledge the importance of workers. The Information Age (also known as the Digital Age) began in the 1970s with the introduction of the first personal computer (Knight, 2014). The invention of the World Wide Web followed in 1989, which provided opportunities for greater self-expression by workers, and people began to find more self-fulfillment in their work

LABOUR DAY—ITS HISTORICAL ROOTS

The contribution that working people have made to their respective societies is recognized in many countries worldwide through celebration of an International Worker's Day, which also is known as Labour Day in some places. In Canada, Labour Day is celebrated on the first Monday of September. The origins of Labour Day can be traced back to April 15, 1872, when the Toronto Trades Assembly held the first significant demonstration for workers' rights. Over time, Labour Day evolved as a day to recognize the contribution that many ordinary working people make to their society's way of life (see Figure 11.1). More recently, however, Labour Day is seen as just another statutory holiday and is celebrated by many Canadians across the country as part of a long weekend.

Source: Dawson. (2016). The first Labour Day. *Canada's History.* Retrieved from www.canadashistory.ca/Magazine/Online-Extension/Articles/The-First-Labour-Day.

(Hill, 1996; Stark, 2009). These differences in characteristics and expectations related to work help to explain some of the findings related to older workers that are discussed in this chapter.

CHANGES IN LABOUR FORCE PARTICIPATION IN CANADA

There have been remarkable changes in the labour market since the 1950s. First, the introduction of computer-based technologies has helped to automate workplaces. **Globalization** and the economic emergence of countries such as China and India have reshaped entire industries and increased the volume of international trade. Canadian workers today have more formal education than workers in the 1950s, and the percentage of workers employed in unionized jobs, manufacturing jobs, or jobs covered by employer-sponsored pension plans has fallen (Statistics Canada, 2016d). Let's turn

FIGURE 11.1

LABOUR DAY, WINNIPEG, 1908

Image courtesy of Peel's Prairie Provinces (peel.library.ualberta.ca), a digital initiative of the University of Alberta Libraries.

now and look at the three major changes in **labour force** participation (employment rates) over the past several decades and the significance of these changes in the context of aging.

LABOUR FORCE PARTICIPATION RATES OF WOMEN OVER TIME

One of the most significant changes to the Canadian labour market has been the participation of women. As seen in Figure 11.2, only about one-quarter of females aged 25 to 54 participated in the labour force in 1953 as compared to almost 100 percent of same-aged males during this same period (Statistics Canada, 2016d). However, from 1953 to the early 1990s, the percentage of females participating in the labour force increased steadily to 76 percent in 1990. In contrast, the number of males participating in the labour force stayed about the same during these two time periods. After 1990, the percentage of both men and women aged 25 to 54 in the workforce then began levelling off, reaching 82 percent for this age group of women in 2014 as compared to 91 percent for same-aged men. Why has the labour force participation of women changed so dramatically over the years? One of the main reasons for the influx of women into the labour force during this time was changing social norms regarding gender roles (i.e., that the women stayed home and took care of the children and the home while the men went to work to pursue careers outside the home). The introduction of new technologies (e.g., electrical appliances) that reduced the time needed to perform household chores, fewer children in families, and increased employment opportunities in the service sector also played an important role in the increased participation of women in the labour force (Statistics Canada, 2016d).

The increasing presence of women in the labour market has led to a large rise in the median annual wages and salaries of women. That is, between the mid-1960s and the early 2010s, women's earnings more than doubled, increasing from $15 700 in 1965 to $37 200 in 2010 (calculated in 2014 dollars). This increase can be partially explained by two other labour force trends: a growing share of women working full-time on a full-year basis and an increasing share of women employed in relatively well-paid occupations. For example, while very few, if any, women were employed as financial auditors

FIGURE 11.2

LABOUR FORCE PARTICIPATION RATES OF MEN AND WOMEN AGED 25 TO 54, 1953 TO 2014

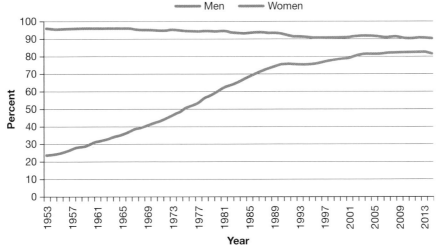

Source: Statistics Canada. (2016d). *The surge of women in the workforce* (Catalogue no. 11-630-X2015009). Ottawa, ON: Author. Retrieved from www.statcan.gc.ca/pub/11-630-x/11-630-x2015009-eng.htm.

WORK, RETIREMENT, AND LEISURE **345**

and accountants in the early 1950s, women aged 25 to 54 accounted for over half (58 percent) of the workforce in this occupational group in 2014 (Statistics Canada, 2016d). These historical differences in labour force participation between men and women have important implications for today's and tomorrow's older adults. Specifically, women have worked at more part-time jobs and have had more career gaps than men, as well as lower salaries and fewer opportunities for job advancements. These differences have important implications for the financial security for women, not only during their working years but also at retirement. Many of today's older women live in poverty due to gaps in career and workforce participation in their younger years. For example, 30 percent of older women in Canada who live on their own today live *below the poverty line*, with older women far more likely to rely on income from Canada's pension plans than their same-aged male counterparts (Canadian Labour Congress, 2015). It also is worth noting the longer life expectancy of women—for which many older women may not have enough money saved to see out their years. The good news is that benefits such as the Canada Pension Plan, Old Age Security, and taxpayer-funded healthcare have helped to push the poverty rate for elderly men and women to one of the lowest in the Western world (McMahon, 2014).

LABOUR FORCE PARTICIPATION RATES OF OLDER ADULTS AND DIFFERENCES IN LABOUR FORCE PARTICIPATION RATES BETWEEN OLDER MEN AND WOMEN

The second significant change to the Canadian labour market in recent years has been the differences in the labour force participation of older adults. Sixty-five has been the common retirement age in many countries worldwide (Van der Heide, Van Rijin, Robroek, Burdof, & Proper, 2013). As you can see from Figure 11.3, the percentage of older adults in Canada who are still working past the age of 65 has increased significantly over the last decade. This trend is not unique to Canada. That is, in many countries (Australia, Austria, Belgium, France, Germany, New Zealand, Russia, Sweden, the United States), labour force participation for both older men and older women has increased in recent years (He, Goodkind, & Kowal, 2016). Why are today's older adults remaining in the workforce? Most often it is because older adults *want* to keep working, particularly professionals with high income and managerial workers (MacEwan, 2012). Declines in some workplace pension coverage, inadequate retirement savings, and changing social norms favouring a later exit from the workforce also are reasons for older adults remaining in the workforce past the traditional retirement age (Hasselhorn & Apt, 2015; Hurd & Rohwedder, 2011; Skugor, Muffels, & Wilthagen, 2012). We'll have more to say on this change in retirement shortly.

FIGURE 11.3

LABOUR FORCE PARTICIPATION OF OLDER ADULTS, 2003–2013

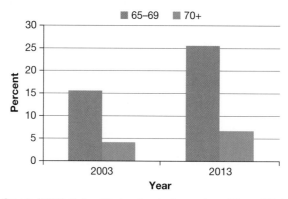

Source: Statistics Canada. (2015f). *National Seniors Day...by the numbers.* Ottawa, ON: Author. Retrieved from http://www.statcan.gc.ca/eng/dai/smr08/2014/smr08_191_2014.

FIGURE 11.4

EMPLOYMENT RATES OF WOMEN AND MEN AGED 65 YEARS AND OVER, CANADA, 1976 TO 2015

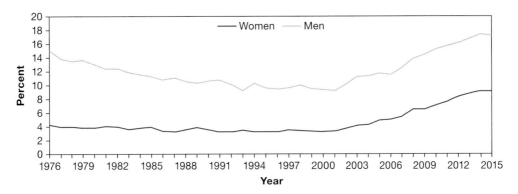

Source: Statistics Canada. (2016e). *Women in Canada: A gender-based statistical report* (Catalogue no. 89-503-X). Ottawa, ON: Author. Retrieved from http://www.statcan.gc.ca/pub/89-503-x/89-503-x2015001-eng.htm.

In addition to the differences in labour force participation over time, it also is interesting to note the differences in **labour force participation rates** between older men and women. As can be seen in Figure 11.4, the labour force participation rate for older men is higher than for older women across all time periods between 1976 and 2015 (Statistics Canada, 2016e). And, as you can see in Figure 11.4, this pattern of labour force participation for older men and women has held relatively steady between 2011 and 2015 (Statistics Canada, 2016e).

TYPE OF LABOUR FORCE PARTICIPATION OF OLDER WORKERS

What do older workers do? The occupations with the highest participation of workers aged 25 to 64 and 65 and older are shown in Table 11.1. As you can see, both younger and older adults are employed in a variety of occupations (Uppal, 2010). With respect to older workers, slightly more than one-quarter of older men and more than one-third of older women are employed in consumer services (e.g., retail salespersons and sales clerks, truck drivers, secretaries, general office clerks), with around 20 percent of older men and women employed in business services (e.g., advertising agencies, accountants). But, the third most common type of work by older men and women differs, with more older men (17.1 percent) employed in primary goods (e.g., farmers and farm managers) and more older women employed in health-related industries (14.8 percent).

If your response to the reflective question was a higher level of education, you are right. In recent decades, more and more young people have been undertaking postsecondary studies to meet the demands of our modern economy (Galarneau, Morissette, & Usalcas, 2013).

There also are differences in part-time work for workers over the age of 65 as compared to younger workers. That is, about 39 percent of workers aged 65 to 69 work part-time compared to just 12 percent of workers aged 25 to 54 (MacEwan, 2012). You might be surprised to learn that the vast majority of older workers work part-time because they choose to! Many of these older retirees return to work by working either part-time or full-time at temporary jobs after leaving their full-time careers (Shultz, 2003), a practice referred to as **bridge employment**. We will discuss this trend of returning to work (or continuing to work) past the age of 65 in more detail in the retirement section of this chapter.

TABLE 11.1

	MEN		WOMEN	
EMPLOYMENT BY INDUSTRY, SENIOR VERSUS PRIME-AGE WORKERS				
	25–64 (%)	**65+ (%)**	**25–64 (%)**	**65+ (%)**
Primary Goods	5.8	17.1	2.3	11.1
Manufacturing	17.7	8.3	8.4	5.2
Construction and Utilities	12.0	8.6	2.2	2.3
Transport	6.6	5.5	2.1	1.8
Consumer Services	25.6	28.8	28.8	36.4
Business Services	16.9	20.6	18.3	17.7
Education	5.0	3.6	11.4	7.6
Health	3.9	4.7	19.9	14.8
Public Administration	6.5	2.8	6.5	3.1

Source: Uppal, S. (2010). Labour market activity among seniors. *Perspectives on Labour and Income, 11*(7). Ottawa, ON: Statistics Canada.

REFLECTIVE QUESTION

What do you think accounts for the differences in the types of employment between younger and older men and women?

IMPACT OF THE AGING OF BABY BOOMERS ON LABOUR FORCE PARTICIPATION

Throughout this book, we have discussed the impact of the aging of the baby boomers on society. These changing demographics have important implications in terms of labour force participation in Canadian society over the next several decades. To determine the effects of changes in the composition of the labour force, demographers calculate what is called an **overall** (or total) **dependency ratio** to gauge the burden that old *and* young people place on the working age population. The overall dependency ratio is expressed as the number of dependents (e.g., 0 to 14 years + 65 and older) for every 100 workers (15–64; see formula below) (Statistics Canada, 2010). In terms of interpretation, a low dependency ratio is desirable because it indicates that there are proportionally more adults of working age who can support the young and older adult populations.

$$\text{Overall dependency ratio} = \frac{\text{Population 0–14 years of age} + 65 \text{ and older}}{\text{Population 15–64 years of age}}$$

REFLECTIVE QUESTIONS

Do the changes in labour force participation in Canada due to the aging of the baby boomers concern you?

If so, what are your concerns?

In looking at the overall dependency ratio for Canada over time (see Figure 11.5), you can see that this ratio started to increase in 2011 (recall that this was the year that the first of the baby boomers turned 65), with the ratio steadily increasing from approximately 45 dependents in 2011 to 46.5 in 2014. You might be wondering why there hasn't been an even *greater* increase in the overall dependency ratio given the aging of the population. The answer can be found by looking at the dependency ratios for *each* of the populations aged 0 to 14 and 65 and older during this same period. It also is evident, in looking at Figure 11.5, that the dependency ratio for the population 0 to 14 years of age steadily *declined* between 1990 and 2014. In contrast, the dependency ratio for the population 65 and older steadily *increased* during the same time period.

In addition to an aging population, various other factors can affect the overall dependency ratio. Some of those factors include immigration and fertility, with low levels of immigrants of working age and fertility rates below the **fertility replacement level** negatively affecting the overall dependency ratio.

What are the implications of a higher overall dependency ratio due to population aging? Two arguments have been made regarding the changing overall dependency ratio. First, a higher percentage of retired people translates into lower tax revenues as most retired people pay lower amounts of income tax. In many developed countries, including Canada, the overall decrease in the population of workers (due in large part to the aging of the baby boomers) is expected to lead to lower growth in output and income and a possible increase in labour shortages (Conference Board of Canada, 2010). This expected change in economic growth due to population aging also is expected to decrease government revenues, which will negatively affect the government's capacity to finance growth in public expenditures (e.g., pension plans, healthcare) at rates as high as in the past (Department of Finance Canada, 2012). At the same time, population aging will put increased pressure on public expenditures, notably for age-related programs such as healthcare (due to the strong association

FIGURE 11.5

AGE DEPENDENCY RATIO (PERCENTAGE OF WORKING-AGE POPULATION) IN CANADA, 2006–2014

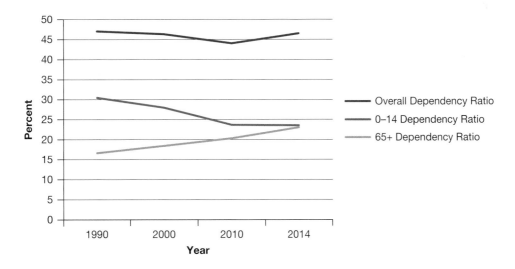

Source: Adapted from Trading Economics. (2017). *Age dependency ratio (% of working-age population) in Canada.* Retrieved from http://www.tradingeconomics.com/canada/age-dependency-ratio-percent-of-working-age-population-wb-data.html.

between age and illness) and benefit programs for older adults such as **Old Age Security pension** (OAS) and **Guaranteed Income Supplement** (GIS) (Department of Finance Canada, 2012).

On the other hand, some changes in social policies could *reduce* governmental costs of an older population. Those changes include later retirement, changes in eligibility criteria for government pensions, and investments of surplus government revenue in income-generating markets (Department of Finance Canada, 2012). For example, government policies that allow for a later retirement (i.e., past the age of 65) would lower the overall dependency ratio by decreasing the number of older non-working Canadians. Changing eligibility for government pensions to an older age would reduce pension costs and encourage older workers to remain in the workforce longer. This, in turn, would increase the number of older people contributing to the pension system *and* reduce the number of years that older adults would draw a pension. Investment of pension plan surpluses in income-generating markets also could help to keep pension plans financially solid. So, it may not be all doom and gloom!

Of interest, the Canadian government has implemented some of the social policy changes described above to address the costs of an older population. For example, the Canadian government

REFLECTIVE QUESTIONS

What are some of the disadvantages of the changes in social policies described above?
What are some of the advantages of the changes in social policies described above?

has taken steps to invest Canada Pension Plan (CPP) surpluses in income-generating markets, with the expectation that this move will keep the CPP **financially solvent** for years to come (Novak, Campbell, & Northcott, 2014). The Canadian government also had intended to increase the age for receiving pension benefits in an attempt to keep more older workers in the workforce, thereby reining in the costs associated with pension payments. That is, in 2012, the Canadian government, under Prime Minister Stephen Harper, announced an increase in the age of eligibility for the OAS pension and the GIS from 65 to 67, beginning in April 2023, with the increase fully phased in by January 2029. However, under the new Liberal government of Prime Minister Justin Trudeau, the eligibility for OAS has been rolled back to age 65 (see https://openparliament.ca/bills/42-1/C-26/).

In contrast, the age of 67 is the new benchmark for retirement in the Netherlands, Denmark, Belgium, France, Germany, and Spain, with the change in policy phased in over time. In the United States, our closest neighbour, the age for receiving full Social Security benefits for both men and women has been increased from age 65 to 66 for people born between 1943 and 1954, and will gradually rise to age 67 for those born in 1960 or later (Allentuck, 2016).

In previous sections of this chapter, we have discussed some of the societal costs of an aging population. But, we would be remiss if we did not point out the benefits. Future older adults will have higher levels of education, better health, and longer life expectancy than older adults of the past. Tomorrow's older adults are likely to remain active during retirement, either through continued employment, volunteering, caring for grandchildren, or travelling. In a recent paper, Kluge , Zagheni, Loichinger, and Vogt (2014) investigated some of the opportunities that aging societies create. The authors used Germany as a case study as Germany today has the second-highest median age (44.3 years) worldwide (topped only by Japan's median age of 44.9 years) and the aging process of Germany will occur at a rapid pace. These researchers identified long-term economic growth due to a larger share of the population with tertiary education; reduced healthcare costs due to an anticipated longer time in good health for the upcoming cohort of older adults; and the need for care for spouses and/or older family members pushed to higher ages. The authors also note that retirement and reduced travel with age may have an overall favourable effect on carbon emissions! Again, having an aging population may not be all doom and gloom.

Are you concerned about population aging?

If so, what aspects of population aging are you most concerned about?

STEREOTYPES OF OLDER WORKERS

As is the case in other areas of our society, negative **stereotypes** about older workers are common. For example, older workers often are assumed to be less productive on the job than younger workers, to be resistant to change, to be more difficult to train, to be less adaptable and flexible, and to have lower future potential (McDaniel, Pesta, & Banks, 2012). In a recent review and meta-analysis, Ng and Feldman (2012) identified six common negative stereotypes about older workers. Those stereotypes are that older workers, compared to younger workers, 1) are poorer performers, 2) are less motivated, 3) are less willing to participate in training and career development, 4) are less trusting, 5) are less healthy, and 6) experience more work–family imbalance. How valid are these stereotypes? When Ng and Feldman (2012) examined the evidence that supports or refutes these stereotypes, their results showed that the only stereotype that was supported by the empirical evidence was that older workers are generally less willing to participate in training and career development. These findings have important implications for combating stereotypes associated with older workers in the real world. Some of the ways that organizations can combat these negative stereotypes include blinding (withholding the candidates' age from decision makers), use of affirmative action practices (actions, policies, and procedures designed to achieve equal employment opportunity), raising conscientiousness about age stereotypes in the workplace, encouraging more frank and open discussions about age stereotypes among employees, and increasing opportunities for younger employees to work alongside older employees (Ng & Feldman, 2012).

There also are positive stereotypes of older workers. These stereotypes are that older workers are more reliable, more loyal, and provide more stability than younger workers (Finkelstein, Burke, & Raju, 1995; Taylor & Walker, 1994). Unfortunately, the research evidence indicates that these positive stereotypes do not seem to translate into positive perceptions of older job applicants. For example, results from a meta-analysis by Bal, Reiss, Rudolph, and Baltes (2011) indicated that although employers perceived older workers as more reliable than younger workers, the ratings of suitability for hiring were more negative for older workers than their younger counterparts. Older persons also are perceived to be more qualified for jobs that demand specialized expertise and less qualified for jobs that are fast-paced and require greater energy (Wanberg, Kanfer, Hamann, & Zhang, 2015). Finally, age stereotypes may be strongest in certain industries that are viewed as preferring young individuals such as retail, hotel and catering, finance, and insurance (Posthuma & Campion, 2009). Have a look at the benefits of why employers should consider including older workers as part of the workforce, as identified by the Federal/Provincial/Territorial Ministers for Seniors (2012) in Table 11.2.

CHALLENGES OF BEING OLD AND UNEMPLOYED

There is evidence that older workers take considerably longer than younger workers to find work once unemployed due, in part, to possible age discrimination (Gunderson, 2003). As well, compared to younger job-seekers, older adults receive fewer job offers, search for work weeks longer, and are less likely to find re-employment after losing a job (Wanberg et al., 2015). For example, in a study of older

TABLE 11.2

- Enabling a successful transfer of your organization's knowledge, skills, and experience to your future leaders, as well as those to areas that require specialized expertise.
- Potentially reducing turnover and costs associated with hiring, training, and orienting new staff, as older workers tend to remain with employers for longer periods, resulting in fewer costs for hiring and training new staff.
- Building on the networks, knowledge, and experience of older workers, thereby adding value to your organization.
- Remaining competitive by attracting and retaining older workers to help address changes in labour force growth.
- Potentially increasing productivity, as older workers tend to have a strong work ethic, work well in team settings, and require minimal supervision.

Source: Federal/Provincial/Territorial Ministers Responsible for Seniors. (2012). *Age-friendly workplaces: Promoting older worker participation*. https://www.canada.ca/content/dam/esdc-edsc/documents/corporate/seniors/forum/promoting.pdf. Employment and Social Development Canada, 2017. Reproduced with the permission of the Minister of Employment and Social Development Canada, 2017.

REFLECTIVE QUESTIONS

Do you have negative stereotypes of older workers? Positive ones?

Has reading this section changed your thinking about older workers?

unemployed Canadians (defined as 55 to 64 years of age), researchers found that the older unemployed individuals were more likely to have been unemployed longer than the younger (aged 20 to 34) unemployed, more likely to receive employment insurance, and more likely to be looking for part-time work even though they often have more work experience than their younger counterparts (Bernard, 2012). In this same study, the older unemployed individuals were more pessimistic about their chances of finding a job in the next three months as compared to the younger unemployed. When asked what would help them most in finding an acceptable job, 25 percent of the older unemployed identified "better health" or "being younger," with only 2 percent of the younger unemployed citing these characteristics as helping them most in finding a job. The older unemployed also were more inclined to accept a wage decrease (10 percent lower than their previous job) than the younger unemployed (Bernard, 2012). Perhaps not surprisingly, the older unemployed were, on average, less educated (Statistics Canada, 2011e) and were less likely to have recently attended school or taken job-related training (Park, 2012).

11.2 RETIREMENT
LEARNING OBJECTIVES

To understand:
- the changing nature of retirement and the implications of these changes
- bridge employment and the factors influencing it
- the importance of financial planning for retirement and the different components of it

Retirement, as a social institution, emerged in modern industrialized societies at the beginning of the 20th century (Macdonald, 2012). In 1889, the German chancellor Otto von Bismarck introduced a pension scheme to appeal to the German working class and combat the power of the Socialist Party in Germany. Somewhat cynically, Bismarck knew that the program would cost little because the average German worker never reached the age of 65, and many of those who did lived only a few years beyond that age. The law was proclaimed on June 26, 1889, with a retirement age of 70. Nearly two decades after his death in 1898, the retirement age was reduced, in 1916, to 65 years of age (Von Herbay, 2014).

THE CHANGING NATURE OF RETIREMENT

Retirement, defined as withdrawal from paid working life (Denton & Spencer, 2009), was once considered a normative life event with 65 years of age the standard age for retirement. However, as you have just learned, retiring today at age 65 is, in general, a thing of the past. Interestingly, men are more likely to retire due to mandatory retirement (Gomez & Gunderson, 2011), with women more likely to retire due to caregiving responsibilities (Humble, 2009).

The decision to retire is one of the most important life-course decisions. There are many factors that influence this decision. Age is negatively correlated with employment, with *fewer* individuals 65 years of age and older employed than those 15 to 64 years of age (Statistics Canada, 2016f). Gender and marital status also affect retirement. For example, women tend to retire at an earlier age than men (Lefebvre, Merrigan, & Michaud, 2011; Turcotte & Schellenberg, 2007). This is partly because couples often decide to retire at the same time and women usually are younger than their spouses (Bélanger, Carrière, & Sabourin, 2016). You might be wondering if there are differences in the timing of retirement for married people compared to others. Generally, having another family member with positive earnings (thus, likely employed) increases the probability of continuing to work (Uppal, 2010). Education also affects retirement with older workers with higher levels of education more likely to delay retirement (Stenberg & Westerlund, 2013; Uppal, 2010). Health is an important aspect of labour market participation, with poor health associated with early exits from the labour market (Park, 2010). In fact, high-intensity caregiving (providing 15 or more hours of care weekly) is associated with full retirement for women and men aged 55 to 69 (Jacobs, Laporte, Van Houtven, & Coyte, 2014). Financial factors play an important role in retirement decisions, with **financial readiness** the most common reason for retirement (Pignal, Arrowsmith, & Ness, 2010). You may be surprised that individuals who enjoy a higher socio-economic status tend to work longer than individuals with lower socio-economic status (Li, Hurd, & Loughran, 2008). One of the reasons for this is that individuals with a higher socio-economic status often work in less physically demanding jobs and might therefore have the ability to remain in the workforce longer (Li et al., 2008). Technological change also has been found to affect retirement. Based on data from the Health and Retirement Study in the United States, Burlon and Vilalta-Bufí (2016) found that the effect of technical change on the probability of early retirement depends on the degree of technical change. That is, when technical change is fast, it will cause more people to retire early, because older workers find it difficult to adapt to the new, more technical job environment. As such, as their skills become more obsolete, they are more likely to retire early. However, once a certain degree of technical change has been reached, the probability of retiring early decreases.

Although retirement often is thought of as a voluntary transition, approximately 20 percent to 30 percent of older workers actually perceive retirement as forced, and mainly a result of health-related issues or organizational restrictions (Hershey & Henkens, 2013; Szinovacz & Davey, 2005; Van Solinge & Henkens, 2007). Finally, being prepared mentally, socially, emotionally, and physically are important factors in the retirement decision. Although most of you reading this are a long way from retirement, you can take the Retirement Readiness Quiz at http://www.pmgsurvey.com/investorsgroup_rr/ig_rr_survey.asp. The questions will help you start thinking about what you need to do to prepare for your retirement—down the road, that is!

BRIDGE EMPLOYMENT

Although retirement at the age of 65 is still the norm in Canada for many people, many Canadians subsequently return to work (Bélanger et al., 2016; Schellenberg, Turcotte, & Ram, 2005). Recall that this pattern of returning to work following retirement is referred to as bridge employment. Why do older adults return to work following retirement? From a theoretical perspective, the Activity Theory of Aging argues that the more active and involved older adults are, the more satisfying their lives will be (Connidis & Willson, 2011; Knapp, 1977). As we noted at the beginning of this chapter, work is meaningful beyond just earning a living, and many adults return to work for the intrinsic benefits. Continuity Theory, which argues that adults adapt to old age by maintaining a degree of consistency with their earlier lives, also helps to explain why older adults return to work following retirement (Atchley, 1989).

How common is bridge employment? In Canada, as in many other countries in the world, bridge employment has become increasingly common. The results from two *Canadian General Social Surveys* (2002 and 2007 cycles) indicate that over one-quarter of recent retirees engaged in bridge employment of some form (Hiscott, 2013). As with traditional retirement, several factors are associated with bridge retirement, which include age, gender, education, family status, health status, and financial circumstances. With respect to age, older retirees (those age 60 and older) are less likely to return to the labour force as compared to younger retirees (those aged 50 to 59) (Cahill, Giandrea, & Quinn, 2011; Schellenberg et al., 2005; Wannell, 2007a). In terms of gender, retired males are more likely to return to work following retirement as compared to their female counterparts (Deschenes & Stone, 2006; Schellenberg et al., 2005; Wannell, 2007a). Education also is positively correlated with the probability of returning to work (Cahill et al., 2006; Lefebvre et al., 2011). The presence and employment status of a spouse also affect bridge employment rates, with retired married individuals more likely to return to work than their non-married counterparts. In general, having a spouse in the labour force increases the likelihood of a retired spouse/partner returning to work, as does having adult children in the home (Kim & Feldman, 2000). Not surprisingly, health status is an important factor in decisions related to bridge employment, with better health status associated with a greater likelihood of returning to work (Cahill et al., 2011; Kerr & Armstrong-Stassen, 2011; Schellenberg et al., 2005; Zhang, Wang, Liu, & Schultz, 2009). Finally, financial circumstances affect decisions related to bridge employment: retirees with debt, those not receiving a pension from their previous work, and those without registered retirement savings plans (RRSPs) or other investments are more likely to return to work (Cahill et al., 2011; Gougeon, 2009; Hebert & Luong, 2008; Morissette & Ostrovsky, 2007; Wannell, 2007a; 2007b).

For a more personal view of why individuals return to work, read Box 11.2. You also can go to the following link and hear from five baby boomers on why they are not ready for retirement: http://www.theglobeandmail.com/globe-investor/retirement/the-boomer-shift -how-canadas-economy-is-headed-for-majorchange/article27159892/.

FINANCIAL PLANNING: CANADA'S THREE-PILLAR PENSION SYSTEM

Canada's retirement system has three pillars—two public and one private. Canada's two public pension programs are the Canada Pension Plan/Quebec Pension Plan and the OAS program. The third pillar consists of personal pensions or investments. Each of these components is discussed in the sections that follow.

COOL JOBS FOR BABY BOOMERS WHO WANT TO WORK IN RETIREMENT

Whether out of necessity or simply to stay active, working in retirement has become the new norm. Yet, making extra money during retirement doesn't necessarily mean toiling away at a mundane job. There are plenty of cool ways to earn some additional cash and boost your savings. These days, retirees are seeking adventure in their encore careers, securing work at national parks, on cruises, with whale-watching tours, and at ski resorts, to name a few. Take Laura Cammarano, 59, who recently retired from her job as a senior engineer at Skyworks Solutions in Woburn, Massachusetts. Almost immediately, she sold her full-time residence in the suburbs of Boston and is now a ski instructor in Vermont in the winter—a job that is more fun than lucrative—and lives in Eastham, Massachusetts, in the summer, on the shores of Cape Cod. In her spare time, she flips houses. And she does nearly all the renovations herself, from framing and installing drywall to tiling and painting. "I had done several projects on my own home over the years," she said, "and I enjoy doing it." To keep her income flowing, she plans to flip one or two houses a year in the Cape Cod area. In mid-June, Cammarano bought her first property, for $300 000. She plans to have the house on the market by September at a list price of $525 000. Minus the cost of materials and some labour she had to contract out, she is hoping to make $80 000. "Not bad for two months' work," she said.

Source: Booth, B. (2016, August 17). "Retirees seek adventure with encore careers," *CNBC*. Retrieved from http://www.thefiscaltimes.com/2016/08/17/Cool-Jobs-Baby-Boomers-Who-Want-Work-Retirement.

THE CANADA PENSION PLAN/QUEBEC PENSION PLAN

The Canada Pension Plan (CPP) operates throughout Canada, except in Quebec, where the Quebec Pension Plan (QPP) provides similar benefits. These two pension plans ensure that all those who contribute are protected, no matter where they live. With very few exceptions, every person over the age of 18 who works in Canada outside of Quebec and earns more than a minimum amount ($3500 per year) must contribute to the CPP. Individuals who have an employer pay half the required contributions and the employer pays the other half. Individuals who are self-employed make the whole contribution themselves (Government of Canada, 2016d). The CPP provides pensions and benefits when contributors retire, become disabled, or die. Individuals who have contributed to the CPP can apply for and receive a full CPP retirement pension at age 65. There also is the option to receive the CPP retirement pension at the age of 60 with a reduced pension or as late as age 70 with an increase in pension benefits. For those individuals who become severely disabled to the extent that they cannot work, they and their children may receive a monthly benefit. When an individual who has contributed to CPP dies, the CPP survivor benefits may be paid to the estate, the surviving spouse or common-law partner, and children. There also is a death benefit associated with the CPP. This benefit provides a one-time payment to the estate of the deceased CPP contributor (Government of Canada, 2016d).

The amount of money that a person receives from the CPP depends on the length of time that the person has contributed and the amount that he/she has contributed. A person can figure out how much they will receive by getting their CPP Statement of Contribution. This document lists all the years that a person is eligible to contribute from age 18 to 65 and how much they have contributed. You can access this document by going to the following website: http://www.canada.ca/en/services/benefits/publicpensions/cpp/statement-contributions.html benefit/amount.html. Importantly, this Statement of Contributions can assist both older and younger individuals in their retirement planning. The maximum CPP/QPP benefit for those who retire at age 65 in 2017 is $1114.97 per month (see http://www.canada.ca/en/services/benefits/publicpensions/cpp/cpp-benefit/amount.html; Government of Canada, 2016d). Recent data indicate that the average amount of CPP payments for new beneficiaries in January of 2016 was $685.11 per month (Government of Canada, 2016d).

In recent years, there has been concern that the CPP will not be there for many Canadians when they retire, with these fears fuelled by the increases in age and lifespan of Canadians. Fortunately, this concern is more of a myth than a reality. In a recent report, the chief actuary of Canada indicated that the CPP is sustainable over a 75-year projection period and that CPP contributions will exceed annual benefits paid until 2023 (CPP Investment Board, 2016). In addition to the CPP, Canada also has the OAS program and the GIS and Allowance program. Let's turn now and look at these programs.

THE OLD AGE SECURITY PROGRAM (OAS) PROGRAM

In addition to the CPP, the other public pension program in Canada is the OAS pension program. Most Canadian adults aged 65 and over receive the monthly OAS pension. The amount of OAS payment is determined by the length of time an individual has lived in Canada after the age of 18. Older adults who have lived in Canada for at least 40 years after age 18 may receive a full basic OAS pension. Older adults who do not meet this requirement may receive a partial pension if they have lived in Canada for at least 10 years after age 18. The maximum annual individual income that a person can earn in order to receive the OAS pension is $119 615, with individuals (regardless of marital status) having an annual income above this amount ineligible to receive OAS (see http://www.canada.ca/en/services/benefits/publicpensions/cpp/old-age-security/payments.html; Government of Canada, 2016e).

What is the process for applying for the OAS pension? In the past, a person had to apply for the OAS pension in order to receive it. However, in April of 2013, the Government of Canada (Service Canada) initiated an automatic enrollment process which allows many older adults to be automatically enrolled to receive their OAS pension, eliminating the need to apply. However, those who have already reached 65 and who wish to start their OAS pension immediately and who are not automatically enrolled need to apply as soon as possible so they do not lose any payments (they may be able to receive a retroactive payment for up to a maximum of 11 months from the date they receive the application). As of July 2013, individuals who are eligible can defer receiving their OAS pension for up to 60 months (five years) after the date they become eligible in exchange for a higher monthly amount. For those who choose to delay receiving their OAS pension, their monthly pension payment will be increased by 0.6 percent for every month of delay, up to a maximum of 36 percent at age 70.

THE GUARANTEED INCOME SUPPLEMENT (GIS)

Individuals who have a low income and are living in Canada are eligible to receive the GIS. The GIS provides a monthly non-taxable benefit to OAS pension recipients, with the monthly payment amount dependent on marital status, receipt of full OAS pension by spouse/common-law partner, and receipt of the GIS by spouse/common-law. One-third of Canadian older adults who receive the OAS pension also receive the GIS. In recent years, the Government of Canada has increased the GIS for the lowest-income older adults by up to $600 annually for single older adults and $840 for couples. This investment of $300 million each year improves the well-being of approximately 680 000 older adults across Canada. It is the highest percentage increase in over 25 years (Government of Canada, 2014c).

IMPACT OF THE OAS AND GIS PROGRAMS

The OAS and GIS, as well as personal pensions or investments, help to ensure that Canadians maintain a basic standard of living in retirement. The CPP and OAS programs provide approximately $76 billion every year in fully indexed retirement income payments (Government of Canada, 2014c). Due in part to the CPP and the OAS programs, the poverty rates for older couples have been reduced from 17.7 percent in 1976 to 2.4 percent in 2011. For individuals who are not married, poverty has been reduced from 55.9 percent to 12.2 percent for single men over 65, and from 68.1 percent to 16.1 percent for single women over 65 (Mackenzie, 2014). How does Canada compare to other developed countries in terms of poverty rates for older adults? As you can see in Figure 11.6, Canada has the third-lowest rate of poverty among older adults, with only the Netherlands and France having lower rates (Conference Board of Canada, 2016). Like Canada, the Netherlands and France offer a universal pension. Note that Australia has the highest rate of poverty in older adults, with nearly 40 percent of Australian older adults living in relative poverty. The high rate of poverty in the older population is due to the relatively low level of the Age Pension, which is an income-support payment program in Australia (Whitehouse, 2009). Canada's challenge going forward is to ensure that the poverty rates of older adults remain some of the lowest in the world and that Canada's social policy continues to be a major success story!

PERSONAL PENSIONS AND INVESTMENTS

In addition to the CPP or QPP, some Canadians have employer-sponsored pension plans as part of their total pay offered by the company. These plans are a valuable means of saving for retirement. Employer pension plans generally are one of two types: defined contribution pension plans or defined benefit pension plans. Defined contribution pension plans establish a set amount that you and your company will contribute to your plan each year, with the amount contributed based on how much you earn. Defined contribution pension plans do not guarantee how much you will receive when you retire. Rather, that amount depends on how well the plan is managed. A defined benefit pension plan promises to pay you a set income when you retire. A formula determines how much you will receive, with this amount often based on your income when you were working and the number of years you

FIGURE 11.6

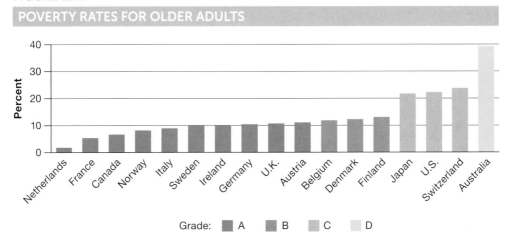

POVERTY RATES FOR OLDER ADULTS

Source: Conference Board of Canada. (2016). *Elderly poverty*. Retrieved from http://www.conferenceboard.ca/hcp/details/society/elderly-poverty.aspx. Reprinted by permission of the Conference Board of Canada.

have worked (see Government of Canada, 2016e). Defined contribution pension plans require that the plan be collapsed by the end of the year that the individual turns 71. At that point, the individual can withdraw the funds and pay tax on the income, transfer the assets to a **registered retirement income fund** (RRIF), or purchase an **annuity** (Government of Canada, 2016d).

In terms of income for older adults, in 2010, over 40 percent of older adults' income was from government sources, with the vast majority coming from CPP/QPP and OAS/GIS. In 2010, the median benefits received were $6800 for CPP/QPP and $6200 for OAS/GIS annually. Each of these sources was received by over 90 percent of the older adult population (Statistics Canada, 2011e). About 30 percent of older adults' income is from private retirement income, with about 59 percent of older adults receiving private pensions (with a median amount of $11 700 annually). People aged 65 years and over also are more likely to have investment income.

Based on results from a recent survey, slightly over one-third of those surveyed expected their primary source of retirement income to be workplace pensions with slightly less than one-third expecting their main source of retirement income to be from RRSPs or registered income funds (RIFs). Thirteen percent of those surveyed expected their main source of income to be government pensions, 10 percent listed other sources, and 12 percent did not know what their primary source of retirement income would be (see Figure 11.7).

Retirement planning will continue to be an important issue for Canadians of all ages given the aging of the population and the ongoing changes in the pension system and pension coverage (Uppal, 2016). Importantly, between 1977 and 2013, the proportion of the overall employed Canadian population covered by registered pension plans (RPPs) declined from 46 percent to 36 percent, mainly due to a drop in the defined benefit plan coverage (Boisclair, Lusardi, & Michaud,

FIGURE 11.7

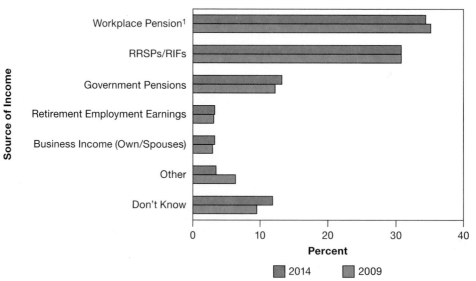

PRIMARY SOURCE OF INCOME ANTICIPATED IN RETIREMENT, 2009 AND 2014

1. Includes OAS/GIS and CPP/QPP.
Note: Includes only labour force participants aged 25 to 64 who reported that they are financially preparing for retirement.
Source: Statistics Canada, Canadian Financial Capability Survey, 2009 and 2014.

Source: Uppal, S. (2016). *Insights on Canadian society: Financial literacy and retirement planning* (Catalogue no. 75-006-X). Ottawa, ON: Statistics Canada.

2014). Research also indicates that some middle-income Canadians are not saving adequately for retirement. It is anticipated that private pension plans and personal savings will play a more important role for retirement income in the future, which means that, increasingly, individuals will need to become more knowledgeable about saving for retirement (Uppal, 2016). Of interest, research indicates that there is a gender gap in financial knowledge particularly among older Canadians, with older men more knowledgeable financially than older females (Drolet, 2016).

To assist Canadians in determining their financial readiness for retirement, the Government of Canada has developed an online tool called the Canadian Retirement Income Calculator. This online tool provides individuals with retirement income information, including CPP retirement and OAS pension benefits. By working through a series of modules, individuals can estimate their retirement incomes from various sources and compare them to their goal income. The Canadian Retirement Income Calculator can be accessed at the following website:https://srv111.services .gc.ca/GeneralInformation/Index.

11.3 LEISURE

LEARNING OBJECTIVES

To understand:
- the importance of leisure activities in later life
- the types of leisure activities in later life
- how different leisure activities benefit older adults differentially
- the differences in the leisure activities between today's and tomorrow's older adults
- that many older adults engage in lifelong learning and to understand why this is important for older adults
- why older adults volunteer
- the benefits of volunteering to older adults and to society

LEISURE ACTIVITIES IN LATER LIFE

According to the Activity Theory of Aging, staying active and socially engaged is very important in old age (Cumming & Henry, 1961; Havighurst, 1961; Adams, Leibbrandt, & Moon, 2011). There are several conceptualizations of the **leisure activities** of older adults. For example, Stobert, Dosman, & Keating (2006) identified two broad types of leisure activities of older adults: passive leisure and active leisure. Passive leisure activities consist of watching television, listening to the radio, or taking a pleasure drive. Active leisure activities include reading, going to movies, playing cards, socializing with friends, and physical recreation. Turcotte and Schellenberg (2007), on the other hand, divide leisure activities into four categories with passive leisure defined the same as Stobert and colleagues and active leisure divided into three separate categories: cognitive leisure, social leisure, and physical leisure. Cognitive leisure is made up of reading books or newspapers, educational activities, attending entertainment events, participating in hobbies, playing cards, and using the computer or the Internet. Social leisure includes socializing with friends and relatives and talking on the phone. Finally, physical leisure includes all physical recreation including exercise, walking, sports, and travel.

In looking at the type of leisure activities of Canadian men and women across different age ranges (see Figures 11.8 and 11.9), you can see that, overall, all age groups (35–44, 45–54, 55–64, 65–74, 75 and over) spend more time in active leisure activities than in passive leisure activities. The exception is men aged 75 and older; the amount of time this group spends in active and passive leisure activities is equal. In a recent study, Szanton and her colleagues (2015) used data from the first wave of the National Health and Aging Trends Study in the United States to understand older adults' favourite activities. The data were collected in 2011 and the sample was 8245 persons age 65 years of age and older. These researchers found that four of the top five favourite activities of older adults were active leisure activities. In fact, contrary to the stereotype that older adults prefer to simply watch TV, the older adults in this study would rather walk, jog, garden, or play sports.

However, other studies have found the opposite trend. For example, Gardner and colleagues (2014) found that older adults spent 60 to 70 percent of their waking time in passive leisure activities. In her review of the literature, Adams and her colleagues (2011) came to the conclusion that differences in the definitions and measurement of leisure activities make it difficult to draw inferences about research in this area. Clearly, more research is needed to determine how older adults spend their time and this is an important question. It is well documented that physical exercise (e.g., brisk walking, aerobic exercise) increases quality of life and is related to improvements in physical, psychological, social, and spiritual **well-being** (Erikson et al., 2011; Gow, Pattie, Whiteman, Whalley, & Deary, 2007; Nimrod & Shira, 2016). We also know that the amount of time spent in sedentary activities is an important risk factor for a number of illnesses common in older adults, such as cardiovascular disease and diabetes. It is no wonder that leisure activities such as physical exercise have emerged as the most important target for lifestyle change among older adults. The *Canadian Physical Activity Guidelines* recommend that adults 65 years of age and older engage in at least 150 minutes of moderate-to-vigorous intensity aerobic physical activity per week in bouts of 10 minutes or more. These same guidelines recommend the addition of muscle and bone strengthening activities at least two days per week for this age group (Canadian Society for Exercise Physiology, 2012). Finally, physical activity guidelines increasingly incorporate recommendations to limit the amount of time spent sedentary.

FIGURE 11.8

HOURS PER DAY SPENT IN ACTIVE AND PASSIVE LEISURE ACTIVITIES BY CANADIAN WOMEN 35 YEARS OF AGE AND OLDER

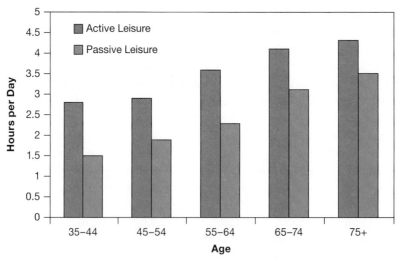

Source: Turcotte, M., & Schellenberg, G. (2007). *A portrait of seniors in Canada 2006* (Catalogue no. 89-519-XIE). Ottawa, ON: Statistics Canada. Retrieved from http://www.statcan.gc.ca/pub/89-519-x/2006001/c-g/4181565-eng.htm.

FIGURE 11.9

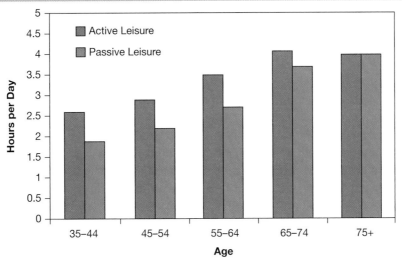

Source: Turcotte, M., & Schellenberg, G. (2007). *A portrait of seniors in Canada 2006* (Catalogue no. 89-519-XIE). Ottawa, ON: Statistics Canada. Retrieved from http://www.statcan.gc.ca/pub/89-519-x/2006001/c-g/4181565-eng.htm.

BARRIERS AND ENABLERS TO ENGAGING IN ACTIVE LEISURE ACTIVITIES

In a number of recent studies on perceived enablers and barriers to physical activity in older adults, identified barriers included health issues, fear of falling, financial costs, feeling too old, lack of knowledge, perceptions that physical activity is inconvenient (e.g., inconvenient hours of operation at exercise facilities), and the living environment not being conducive to physical activity (Ashe, Miller, Eng, & Noreau, 2009; Bethancourt, Rosenberg, Beatty, & Arterburn, 2014; Mathews et al., 2010; Wilcox, Oberrecht, Bopp, Kammermann, & McElmurray, 2005). Enablers to physical activity in older adults included the expectation of health benefits (e.g., improved brain health, mental health, weight management), social support or companionship, and access to physical activity programs or facilities (Jurabe, Turok, & Perez-Stable, 2002; Mathews et al., 2010). The relationship between physical activity and health is complex in that health status may serve as being both a barrier and a motivator to older adults being active (Cohen-Mansfield, Marx, & Guralnik, 2003).

There have been several successful programs developed that are helping to remove barriers to physical activity for older adults and helping older adults to age actively. Some of these initiatives are the World Health Organization's (WHO's) *Global Age-Friendly Cities: A Guide* (WHO, 2007) and *Age-Friendly World: Adding Life to Years* (WHO, 2014e). In Canada, we have the *Age-Friendly Rural and Remote Communities: A Guide* Initiative (Federal/Provincial/Territorial Ministers Responsible for Seniors, 2008) and *Age-Friendly Communities* (Public Health Agency of Canada [PHAC], 2016). Fortunately, many Canadian communities are addressing these barriers by becoming more age-friendly. For example, more attention is being paid to keeping sidewalks in good repair, adding benches in public areas, implementing exercise displays and equipment for adults in city parks, redesigning streets to promote cycling, and providing more information on activities for older adults in accessible formats and venues (Plouffe & Gillis, 2016).

Before we move on, we should look at some research that has investigated the effects of leisure activity on cognitive decline and dementia. Wang, Xu, and Pei (2012) found that engagement in mental leisure activities (e.g., reading, playing games, doing crossword puzzles, discussions) had a protective effect on cognitive decline in older adults, but the effect on the risk of developing a dementia was inconsistent (i.e., while most studies show a protective effect, others do not). In this same study, the researchers found that the effects of engagement in other types of leisure activities (e.g., social, recreational) on reducing the risk of cognitive decline and dementia were also inconsistent. Again, more research is needed before we can for sure determine the effects of leisure activity on cognitive decline.

LEISURE ACTIVITIES: TOMORROW'S OLDER ADULTS

An interesting question is whether the preferences of tomorrow's older adults will be similar to those of today's older adults. Sperazza and Banerjee (2010) examined the differences in expectations of community recreation programs between today's older adults (those born before 1946) and tomorrow's older adults (those born between 1946 and 1964—the baby boomers). All participants were asked to rate their preferences for different programs/activities. These researchers found that baby boomers were significantly more likely to choose aquatics, sports, outdoor programs, and self-improvement programs as compared to today's older adults. There was some commonality between the two groups, with both today's older adults and baby boomers

REFLECTIVE QUESTION

What barriers to leisure activity participation of older adults are there in your community?

indicating that they would be likely to choose leisure programs related to the arts, social recreation, health/wellness, hobbies, and travel/tourism.

These results have important implications for facilities and programs targeting the older population. Specifically, public and private services will have to make changes to their programs and services to meet the changing demands of the baby boomer population. Key programs targeting tomorrow's older adults include more active leisure programs (aquatics, sports, outdoor activities) as well as programs related to arts, culture, and education. The findings are particularly relevant to seniors' centres in our communities. In a recent study on the benefits of social participation on the health and well-being of older adults, Novek, Menec, Tran, and Bell (2013) examined the benefits of senior centres as well as some of the challenges that affect participation. Relevant to our discussion, some of the oldest-old surveyed indicated that the activity preferences of the young-old (older adults in the 55 to 65 age group) were different: One participant in the study said, "The seniors don't play cards anymore. I was brought up playing cards. Times are a changing" (Novek et al., 2013, p. 40). Bingo also is becoming a thing of the past!

REFLECTIVE QUESTION

Why do you think there are more women than men who pursue lifelong learning?

OLDER ADULT LEARNERS

Another way older adults spend their time is in the pursuit of lifelong learning. Livingstone and Raykov (2103) make the distinction between further education (formal learning), which uses a formal curriculum, and **self-directed informal learning**, which does not rely on a teacher or an externally organized curriculum. Not surprisingly, most lifelong learners participate in self-directed informal learning. Interestingly, the title of a course plays a central role in engaging older adults in lifelong learning. The following results are based on information gathered from several focus groups conducted with older adults by the American Council on Education (ACE, 2007). Researchers concluded that programs or courses using terms like "Senior" or "Older Adult", in an attempt to attract older individuals to a particular course, did not appear to increase interest in those courses because the older adults surveyed did not identify themselves as being part of that population. Not surprisingly, the focus group participants also said that they would prefer intergenerational learning to age-segregated learning because the widespread belief among focus group participants was that older and younger students can learn from each other. These older adults see lifelong learning as one avenue for staying active and engaged. For example, one 67-year-old participant summed up the experience of many focus group members when she said, "Going back to school has been a rejuvenating experience for me. … I really enjoy stretching my brain" (ACE, 2007, p. 8).

In Canada, researchers at the University of Manitoba (Sloane-Seale & Kops, 2010) were interested in finding out more about the educational pursuits of those adults aged 55 and over who live in Manitoba. These researchers found that 69 percent of their sample of 321 participants had taken part in educational activities over the past two years and were engaged in activities related to health, computers, leisure, art, and personal development pursuits such as self-development and spirituality. In another study of just under 3000 older adults in Canada, researchers found that both formal and informal lifelong learning was highly associated with healthy lifestyles and a higher perceived quality of life (Wister, Malloy-Weir, Rootman, & Desjardins, 2010). Merriam and Kee (2014) argue that lifelong learning not only reduces dependency on government-funded social services but also enhances community well-being. For example, in Japan, a lifelong learning policy called Knowledge-Recycling-Oriented Society is being promoted "where the outcome of individual learning based on each individual learner's needs is given back to society and contributes to the improvement of the sustainable educational potential of the whole society" (Sawano, 2012, p. 668). Interestingly, more women pursue lifelong learning than do men.

WHAT MOTIVATES OLDER ADULTS TO LEARN?

Researchers have identified several key factors that motivate older adults to seek out lifelong learning. A desire for self-fulfillment, a desire to learn new skills in order to give back to the community (generativity), a desire to remain independent, keeping active and engaged in life, and, finally, social contact have all been identified as factors that influence older adults' pursuit of lifelong learning (Sloane-Seale & Kops, 2010; University of the Third Age[U3A], 2014; Yi-Yin & Sandmann, 2012). In addition, older adults return to school to keep up-to-date in their current career or to learn skills and knowledge to branch into a new career, even during traditional retirement years (ACE, 2007). Perhaps the most important reason is that lifelong learning can contribute value and meaning to an older adult's life (see Box 11.3 and Figure 11.10 for examples of the value of lifelong learning to an older adult).

EDUCATIONAL PROGRAMS FOR OLDER ADULTS

Of note is that there is an organization called the University of the Third Age (U3A), which is a learning cooperative of older people who meet in small groups on university campuses and in each other's homes to share educational, creative, and leisure activities. The aim of the U3A is to promote active learning, research, and community among older adults everywhere. The U3A movement is growing all the time; approximately 50 new U3As are started every year. Most local U3As offer a combination of opportunities to study, create, and socialize, which contribute greatly to members' overall health and well-being (U3A, 2014). According to Formosa (2009), U3As "increase the social integration and harmony of older persons in society as well as make older adults more visible in society" (p. 178). Programs are even offered online. U3A is now offered worldwide and has branches in most provinces in Canada.

You are likely more familiar with the term Elderhostel International, which was founded in 1975 and is a world leader in educational travel for older adults. While Elderhostel is still the parent company to a wide selection of lifelong learning experiences, the name of the company's travel adventures was changed in 2009 to Road Scholar. They have branches in most provinces in Canada as well and offer different types of travel learning adventures for older adults including intergenerational programs for grandparents and grandchildren.

VOLUNTEERING

Volunteer work is important not only to those who volunteer but to our society as a whole. According to the 2011 United Nations' *State of the World's Volunteer Report*, "Volunteerism benefits both society at large and the individual volunteer by strengthening trust, solidarity, and reciprocity among citizens, and by purposefully creating opportunities for participation" (United Nations Volunteers, 2011, p.1). Recent data indicate that 36 percent of older adults in Canada perform volunteer work, with volunteers aged 65 to 74 each contributing about 231 hours a year and adults 75 and older each contributing 196 hours a year in 2013, compared to the national average of 154 hours (Turcotte, 2015). Volunteering is one of the top five social activities for both men and women aged 65 and older (Gilmour, 2012).

Why do older adults volunteer? A growing body of research indicates that there are social, emotional, and even physical health benefits of volunteering. In their research, which included more than 200 volunteers 50 years of age and older, Tang, Choi, and Morrow-Howell (2010) found that volunteers reported significant improvements in their mental health, greater feelings of productivity, increases in social activity, as well as an overall sense that their life had improved. Notably, volunteers were far more likely to enjoy the identified benefits when the

BOX 11.3

ACCORDING TO BERTIE GLADWIN, YOU CAN TEACH AN OLD DOG NEW TRICKS

Bertie Gladwin resides in the United Kingdom. Bertie, who left school at the age of 14 with no interest to pursue further education, graduated in 2012 at the age of 91 with a master's degree with distinction in military service. He reported that his time at university has helped him understand young people and he hopes he showed young people that "old people aren't too bad either." Mr. Gladwin stated, "You are never too old to learn—it's a pleasure to be able to carry on learning through your life; it makes the experience [of living] all the more enjoyable" (retrieved from http://www.dailymail.co.uk/news/article-2147643/Bertie-Gladwin-Britains-oldest-student-graduates-degree-military-intelligence-aged-91.html#ixzz42Kajb81n).

FIGURE 11.10

Rawpixel.com/Shutterstock.com

volunteer organization gave them adequate training, ongoing support, and greater flexibility in choosing activities and schedules. The authors concluded that engagement in meaningful volunteer activities and contribution to others leads to increased psychological well-being of older adults. Other studies have found similar benefits, with volunteering associated with reductions in symptoms of depression, better overall health, fewer functional limitations, and greater longevity (Anderson et al., 2014). It also has been reported that vulnerable older adults (i.e., those with chronic health conditions) might benefit the most from volunteering (Dulin, Gavala, Stephens, Kostick, & McDonald, 2012; Lee, Steinman, & Tan, 2011; McDonnall, 2011; Okun, Rios, Crawford, & Levy, 2011). Although the reasons for this are unclear, it might be that many of the positive outcomes of volunteering in general (e.g., increases in feelings of usefulness, boosts in self-esteem, and increases in social networks) have a greater impact on vulnerable older adults in that they might have more limited opportunities to experience those positive outcomes in their daily lives as compared to non-vulnerable older adults.

The Government of Canada supports a number of programs and initiatives to encourage and recognize the volunteer work of all Canadians including older adults. One of the programs is the New Horizons for Seniors Program (NHSP), which helps older adults benefit from and contribute to the quality of life in their community through social participation and active living. Canada's Volunteer Awards Program, established in 2012, recognizes the significant contributions that volunteers, not-for-profit organizations, and businesses across Canada make to their communities. In 2012, two of the three award recipients in the Community Leadership category were older adults.

Patricia Ebert, Ph.D.
Rockyview Hospital, Calgary, Alberta

WHERE DID YOU TRAIN?

B.Sc. Psychology & Neuroscience, University of Toronto, Ontario.
M.Sc. Institute of Medical Sciences & Program in Neuroscience, University of Toronto
Ph.D. Clinical Neuropsychology, University of Victoria, B.C.

WHERE DO YOU WORK?

I work in the Specialized Seniors Health Clinic at Rockyview Hospital in Calgary, Alberta, which is part of Alberta Health Services.

WHAT DO YOU DO?

I work as a clinical neuropsychologist. Generally, I complete neuropsychological assessments for older adults with suspected cognitive impairment, dementia, and/or neurodegenerative disorders as well as medically complex older adults with suspected cognitive difficulties. Neuropsychological assessments provide comprehensive information about cognitive abilities and help with differential diagnosis of dementia and/or neurodegenerative diseases. After the assessment, I discuss the results with the individual and their family potentially disclosing a diagnosis of dementia or mild cognitive impairment. I then provide individuals and their families support, information, and education on managing the cognitive changes in their daily lives.

WHY DO YOU LIKE WORKING WITH AN OLDER-ADULT POPULATION?

Because it is lifelong learning! In my position, I need to have a good understanding of brain functioning, different types of dementia, different assessment tools, and developmental changes in aging. I also need to stay current on research and clinical developments. Therefore, I am always learning and growing in my knowledge and understanding of aging, neuropsychology, and dementia. In addition, older adults have a wealth of unique experiences and perspectives so I learn a great deal from the people I work with.

Because it is challenging! The clinical cases I am involved with are often clinically complex as older adults often have significant medical co-morbidity and/or mental health concerns in addition to their cognitive concerns. As well, I enjoy working within a team context, which is often needed due to the complexity involved in diagnosing and managing dementia.

DO YOU HAVE ADVICE FOR STUDENTS WHO WANT TO GET INTO THE FIELD?

Examine your own stereotypes and attitudes about older adults as these may affect the working relationship you have with older adults. Be cautious of the language you use when working with older adults. Treat an older adult with respect and dignity no matter the type or severity of cognitive impairment that they may have. Exercise patience. Listen carefully to what older adults are saying. Try not to make assumptions or jump to conclusions about what they are telling you. Older adults may take longer to respond or perform tasks. Work at their pace, not yours.

Be careful about attributing changes in emotional, physical, or cognitive functioning to aging to avoid missing important health or mental health concerns. The diagnosis of dementia or a neurodegenerative disorder is a terminal illness. Be respectful and sensitive when discussing this information. Allow individuals and families to grieve and accept on their own terms.

Doneka Simmons, B.S.W.
Sage Seniors Association, This Full House Program, Edmonton, Alberta

WHERE DID YOU TRAIN?

I did my training at the University of Victoria and graduated in 2016.

WHERE DO YOU WORK?

Sage Seniors Association in Edmonton, Alberta.

WHAT DO YOU DO?

I work as an outreach worker and I am the coordinator of This Full House Program, which is a program for older adults who hoard.

WHY DO YOU LIKE WORKING WITH OLDER ADULTS?

I couldn't imagine working with any other population. I've worked in the field of gerontology for all my adult career, which now spans over 20 years. I am inspired by the trials and triumphs of the older-adult population. Their stories of resilience, hope, and strength give me hope for my future old age. The rewards that come from working with the older-adult population are immeasurable. Each day comes with a special pearl of wisdom that will give you hope in humanity and for the future. I am honoured to work alongside and serve this population and every day I am grateful for the opportunity.

DO YOU HAVE ADVICE FOR STUDENTS WHO WANT TO GET INTO THE FIELD?

Embrace the challenges that come from working with what is sometimes a complex population. Continue to learn and grow and give thanks for the lessons older adults gift you with. You have been blessed.

11.5 SUMMARY

- Many factors contributed to the changes in labour force participation in Canada. One of the most significant changes to the Canadian labour market has been the participation of women.

- The aging of the baby boomers will have important implications in terms of labour force participation in Canadian society over the next several decades.

- Stereotypes about older workers are common. However, many of these stereotypes are not supported by the empirical evidence.

- There also are positive stereotypes of older workers. However, these positive stereotypes do not translate into positive perceptions of older job applicants.

- Retirement as a social institution began in the beginning of the 20th century. Retirement was once considered a normative life event. But, mandatory retirement at age 65 is now the exception in many countries in the world, including Canada.

- Some factors that affect retirement include longer life expectancy, changes in labour laws and pension rules, economic conditions, as well as health status, gender, marital status, and financial status.

- There are now four different retirement situations of older workers: never retired, partially retired, fully retired, and previously retired but returned to work.

- Canada's retirement system has three pillars—two public and one private.

Personal pensions and investments also are important for financial health in retirement.

- Financial literacy is becoming increasingly important for baby boomers and older adults. Research indicates that there is a gender gap in financial knowledge particularly among older men and women.

- Leisure also is an important part of our lives, with leisure activities playing a significant role in successful aging.

- Current *Canadian Physical Activity Guidelines* recommend that adults 65 years of age and older spend at least 150 minutes of moderate- to vigorous-intensity aerobic physical activity per week in bouts of 10 minutes or more. These same guidelines recommend the addition of muscle and bone strengthening activities at least two days per week for adults 65 years of age and older.

- A number of programs help to remove barriers to physical activity for older adults. *Age-Friendly Cities*, a program of the World Health Organization (WHO), and the Canadian *Age-Friendly Rural and Remote Communities* guide are examples of successful programs.

- Another way older adults spend their time is through lifelong learning. A desire for self-fulfillment, generativity, to remain independent, and to keep active and engaged in life have all been identified as factors that influence older adults' pursuit of lifelong learning.

- The leisure activities of tomorrow's older adults will be different from today's older adults. In terms of expectations of community recreation programs, baby boomers are significantly more likely to choose aquatics, sports, outdoor programs, and self-improvement programs as compared to today's older adults. These results have important implications for facilities and programs targeting the older population.

- Older adults make significant contributions to society through volunteering. Volunteering is associated with significant improvements in mental health, greater feelings of productivity, increases in social activity, as well as an overall sense of life satisfaction.

Key Terms

Annuity
A form of insurance or investment entitling the investor to a series of annual sums. Annuities are most commonly used to generate retirement income.

Bona Fide Occupational Requirements
A rule that establishes a requirement that is necessary for proper or efficient performance of a job. In Canada, the bona fide occupational requirement (BFOR) exception is included in virtually all human rights codes.

Bridge Employment
The pattern of returning to work following retirement.

Fertility Replacement Level
Defined as the total fertility rate—the average number of children born per woman—at which a population exactly replaces itself from one generation to the next, without migration. This rate is roughly 2.1 children per woman for most countries, although it may modestly vary with mortality rates.

Financially Solvent
Being able to service the debt and meet its other obligations especially in the long-term.

Further Education
Education that uses a formal curriculum. Programs can range from baccalaureate degrees to adult continuing education offerings.

Globalization
The tendency of businesses, technologies, or philosophies to spread throughout the world, or the process of making this happen. The global economy sometimes is referred to as a globality, characterized as a totally interconnected marketplace, unhampered by time zones or national boundaries.

Guaranteed Income Supplement (GIS)
One of the supplementary benefits payable under the Old Age Security (OAS) Act. The GIS is a monthly non-taxable benefit that is paid to eligible pensioners, in addition to the basic monthly OAS amount.

Labour Force
Refers to the number of persons actually working or willing to work.

Labour Force Participation Rate
The participation rate for a particular group (age, sex, marital status, geographic area, etc.) is the total labour force in that group expressed as a percentage of the population 15 years of age and over in that group.

Leisure Activities
Activities outside of work and household responsibilities. Examples of leisure activities include watching TV, playing sports, and playing cards.

Old Age Security (OAS) Pension
A taxable monthly social security payment available to most Canadians 65 years of age or older with individual income less than a defined amount.

Overall Dependency Ratio
The ratio of the combined youth population (0 to 19 years) and senior population (65 years and older) to the working-age population (20 to 64 years). The dependency ratio is expressed as the number of dependents for every 100 workers.

Norm(s)
Cultural products (including values, customs, and traditions) that represent individuals' basic knowledge of what others do and think that they should do.

Registered Retirement Income Fund (RRIF)
A tax-deferred retirement plan under the Canadian tax law. RRIFs are an extension of RRSPs; that is, RRSPs are used to save for retirement while RRIFs are used to withdraw income during retirement.

Retirement Readiness
Being financially prepared for retirement.

Self-Directed Informal Learning
Learning without direct reliance on a teacher or mentor or organized curriculum.

Stereotypes
A pre-conceived notion or thought that can be adopted about specific types of individuals or certain ways of doing things. These thoughts or beliefs may or may not accurately reflect reality.

Well-Being
A dynamic concept that includes subjective, social, and psychological dimensions as well as health-related behaviours.

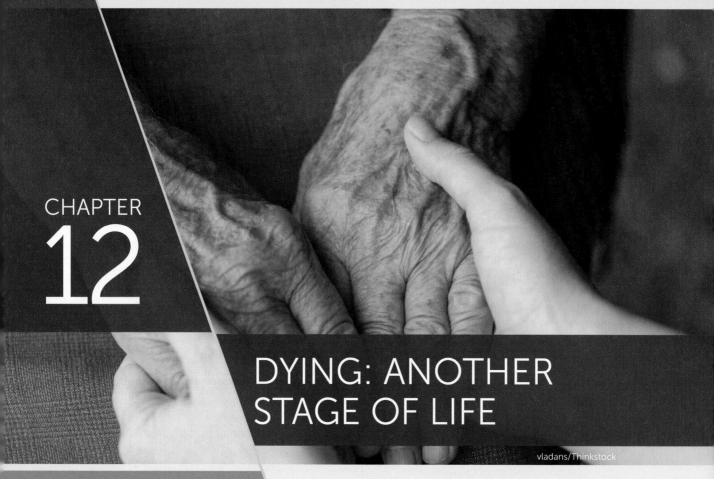

DYING: ANOTHER STAGE OF LIFE

vladans/Thinkstock

CHAPTER OUTLINE

"While I thought that I was learning how to live, I have been learning how to die."

Leonardo da Vinci

The experience of death, as well as attitudes and practices concerning death, have changed considerably in Canada over the past several decades. The introduction of palliative care and end-of-life care has resulted in more openness related to the process of dying, as well as improvements in quality of life for individuals who are dying and for the bereaved. A significant change in Canada is the legalization of medical assistance in dying—Canada's version of physician-assisted suicide. While still controversial, medical assistance in dying gives individuals more control over their own death. Customs regarding beliefs about death, the afterlife, and funeral and burial practices are as diverse as Canada's ethnic makeup. In addition to traditional funerals, celebrations of life are becoming more common as are frank and open conversations of death for individuals of all ages. As you read through this chapter, we hope the information provided helps you to think about the death and dying experience and the choices that you will have to make in your journey of life.

12.1 DEATH AND DYING
LEARNING OBJECTIVES

To understand:
- the changes in the experiences of death and dying over time
- mortality rates in Canada

CHANGES IN THE EXPERIENCE OF DEATH AND DYING OVER TIME

The experiences of death and dying have changed dramatically over the past 120 years. At the time of Confederation until the middle of the 20th century (1950), most people were cared for by family and friends and died at home. Following World War II, the location of both birth and death shifted from home to hospital, with over half of all deaths in Canada taking place in hospitals. Often, this meant that the individual died alone in a foreign environment, away from family and friends (Arnup, 2013).

In the late 1960s, Dr. Elisabeth Kübler-Ross, a Swiss-born American psychiatrist, brought "death into the public eye" (Arnup, 2013, p. 10). In her 1969 book, *On Death and Dying*, Kübler-Ross not only described five stages of dying; she also suggested that death be considered a normal stage of life. The **five stages of death** have since come under criticism. That is, there is no real evidence that there are stages that people go through when coping with death. There also is no evidence that people who are dying go through the stages in the order identified by Kübler-Ross (Metzger, 1980; Schulz & Aderman, 1974). Finally, the research methodology (qualitative interviews) that Kübler-Ross used in the development of the five stages of death has been criticized. That is, although the qualitative interviews provided some valuable insights into the dying process, they were just a starting point. As noted by Kastenbaum (1986), ongoing research using other methods of data collection and different types of patients are needed to validate her original research. Of interest, some of the criticism came from Dr. Kübler-Ross herself! In her 2005 book, *On Grief and Grieving,* Kübler-Ross wrote about her own grief and noted, "I now know that the purpose of my life is more than these stages. I have been married, had kids, then grandkids, written books, and traveled. I have loved and lost, and I am so much more than five stages. And so are you" (Kübler-Ross & Kessler, 2005, p. 216). Despite the criticism, Dr. Kübler-Ross's work has been very influential in changing attitudes, stimulating open discussions, and getting people thinking about death. Before discussing end-of-life care, bereavement, and cultural perspectives on death and dying, let's first review mortality rates in Canada.

MORTALITY RATES IN CANADA

Since the mid-1930s, the number of deaths recorded each year in Canada has followed an upward trend, with the overall number of deaths increasing from about 120 000 per year in 1936 to almost 250 000 deaths in 2011 (Martel, 2013) (see Figure 12.1).

The increase in the number of deaths in Canada since 1936 can be explained by two factors—population growth and the aging of the population. In looking at the trends in mortality rates by age and gender (Figure 12.2), you can see that the age at which the number of deaths in Canada peaked in 2011 was 85 years for males and 89 years for females.

FIGURE 12.1

NUMBER OF DEATHS, CANADA, 1926 TO 2011

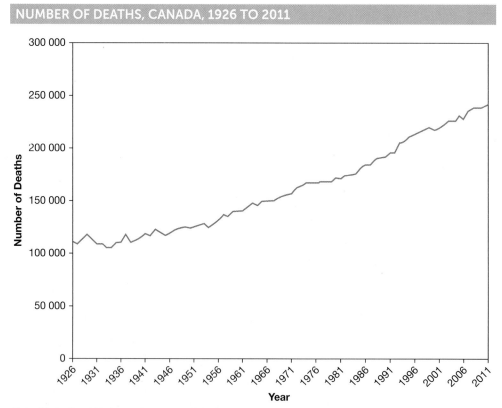

Note: Deaths for which the province or age of death was unknown were prorated using the observed distribution.

Source: Martel, L. (2013). *Mortality: Overview, 2010 and 2011* (Catalogue no. 91-209-X). Ottawa, ON: Statistics Canada. Retrieved from http://www.statcan.gc.ca/pub/91-209-x/2013001/article/11867/fig/fig1-eng.htm.

FIGURE 12.2

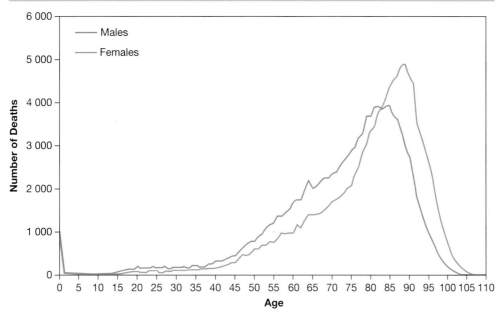

Notes: Deaths for which the province or age of death was unknown were prorated using the observed distribution.

Source: Martel, L. (2013). *Mortality: Overview, 2010 and 2011* (Catalogue no. 91-209-X). Ottawa, ON: Statistics Canada. Retrieved from www.statcan.gc.ca/pub/91-209-x/2013001/article/11867/fig/fig3-eng.htm.

You also can see in Figure 12.3 (on the next page) that the probability of dying over the lifespan varies, with the probability of dying relatively high in the first year of life; it then decreases to reach the lowest levels between ages 1 and 14. The probability of death then steadily increases through the remaining adulthood and "senior" years (Martel, 2013). By age 105 and over, the probability of dying is about 40 percent (two chances out of five in a given year) (Martel, 2013). Let's turn now and look at palliative care and end-of-life care.

12.2 PALLIATIVE CARE AND END-OF-LIFE CARE
LEARNING OBJECTIVES

To understand:

- palliative care and the reasons for the emergence of the palliative care movement in Canada
- end-of-life care and the differences and similarities between palliative care and end-of-life care
- the challenges and benefits of providing palliative care and end-of-life care
- what is meant by a good death and the components of a good death
- medical assistance in dying in Canada, the two options available to Canadians, and the conditions of those options
- end-of-life care issues including advance care planning

What is "palliative care"? The World Health Organization (WHO, 2016c) defines palliative care as an approach that improves quality of life of patients and their families who are facing

FIGURE 12.3

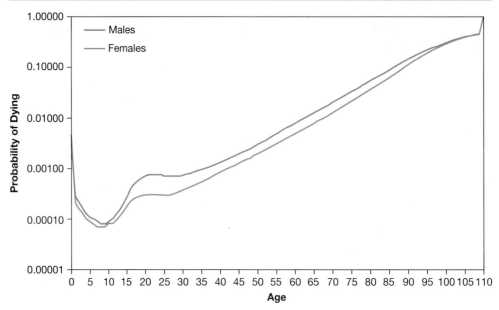

Notes: Deaths for which the province or age of death was unknown were prorated using the observed distribution. The probability of dying at age 110 is equal to 1 and represents the probability for the open age group of 110 and over.

Source: Martel, L. (2013). *Mortality: Overview, 2010 and 2011* (Catalogue no. 91-209-X). Ottawa, ON: Statistics Canada. Retrieved from http://www.statcan.gc.ca/pub/91-209-x/2013001/article/11867/fig/fig1-eng.htm.

the problems associated with life-threatening illnesses. This improvement in quality of life is achieved through "the prevention and relief of suffering by way of early identification and impeccable assessment and treatment of pain and other problems" (e.g., physical, psychosocial, or spiritual) (WHO, 2016c, para. 1).

You also may have heard the term "end-of-life care." What does end-of-life care mean? End-of-life care is defined as care for people who are deemed to be **terminal** or dying in the foreseeable (near) future (Canadian Institute for Health Information [CIHI], 2011c). This definition is similar to the definition of palliative care. However, end-of-life care often is seen as being broader than palliative care in that it provides respite and care in the home. "Hospice care" is another term that is used in the context of end-of-life care. Hospice care is aimed at relieving suffering and improving the quality of life for persons who are living with, or dying from, advanced illness or who are bereaved. Palliative care today is provided across a variety of settings including hospitals, in the home, in long-term-care facilities, and in hospices. As such, the terms palliative care, end-of-life care, and hospice care often are now used interchangeably.

The palliative care movement began in Canada in the 1970s with the first palliative care service established at the Royal Victoria Hospital in Montreal in 1974/1975. The movement was led by Dr. Balfour Mount—the "father of palliative care in North America" (McGill University, 2016). By the mid-1980s, palliative care quickly became a widely accepted societal movement (Canadian Hospice Palliative Care Association, 2016a). Palliative care often is the main focus of care when a cure for the illness is no longer possible. In her influential report on the subject of palliative care—*Raising the Bar: A Roadmap for the Future of Palliative Care in Canada*—Senator

Sharon Carstairs notes that palliative care "is not synonymous with death—it is about life, about the proper care of someone who is alive, someone who still has days, months, or years remaining in their life" (Carstairs, 2010, p. 16). As such, for some individuals, palliative care services also are helpful during the earlier stages of an illness (e.g., for individuals receiving chemotherapy). Families also benefit from palliative care when their family member is dying and after the death of a family member through training and support in areas such as care planning and coordination of care. The types of services provided to individuals receiving palliative care are shown in Table 12.1.

In her 2010 report, Senator Carstairs also indicated that 90 percent of Canadians who die can benefit from palliative care. Yet, only 16 percent to 30 percent of Canadians who die have access to or receive palliative and end-of-life care services (Canadian Hospice Palliative Care Association, 2014). Some of the reasons for not accessing these services include lack of awareness of the services and financial considerations (Canadian Hospice Palliative Care Association, 2014). What percentage of Canadians 65 years of age and older have access to or receive palliative care? Unfortunately, that is a difficult question to answer as there are no national statistics available. There are, however, statistics from the western (British Columbia, Alberta, Saskatchewan, and Manitoba) and eastern (New Brunswick, Newfoundland, Nova Scotia, and Prince Edward Island) Canadian provinces. In Western Canada, the overall percentage of individuals aged 65 and older receiving palliative care in 2006 was 13.5 percent (CIHI, 2007c). In the Atlantic Provinces, the percentage was much higher, with 57.9 percent of individuals 65 and older who died in an acute-care hospital receiving palliative care in 2011 (CIHI, 2011c). The reasons for the differences across the two areas of Canada are unclear—it may be that the two different time periods (2006 vs. 2011) account for a lot of the differences in that palliative care has grown in prominence over the last several years.

Despite the movement toward providing palliative care in settings outside of hospitals, the majority (70 percent) of palliative *and* end-of-life care in Canada still is provided in hospitals with 10 percent to 15 percent of patients admitted to the intensive care unit on their final

TABLE 12.1

PALLIATIVE CARE: WHO DEFINITION OF PALLIATIVE CARE

PALLIATIVE CARE

- Provides relief from pain and other distressing symptoms.
- Affirms life and regards dying as a normal process.
- Intends neither to hasten or postpone death.
- Integrates the psychological and spiritual aspects of patient care.
- Offers a support system to help patients live as actively as possible until death.
- Offers a support system to help the family cope during the patient's illness and in their own bereavement.
- Uses a team approach to address the needs of patients and their families, including bereavement counselling, if indicated.
- Will enhance quality of life, and also may positively influence the course of illness; and
- Is applicable early in the course of illness, in conjunction with other therapies that are intended to prolong life, such as chemotherapy or radiation therapy, and includes those investigations needed to better understand and manage distressing clinical complications.

Source: World Health Organization. (2016c). Reprinted from *WHO definition of palliative care.* http://www.who.int/cancer/palliative/definition/en/ © 2017. Reprinted by permission of the World Health Organization.

hospital admission (CIHI, 2013; Heyland, Lavery, Tranmer, & Shortt, 2000; Heyland, Lavery, Tranmer, Shortt, & Taylor, 2000). However, when asked about their preferences for care, 70 percent of hospitalized patients (primarily 65 years of age and older) indicated that they wanted comfort measures as opposed to life-prolonging treatments such as those that are provided in intensive care units (Fowler & Hammer, 2013). In a recent survey of 2976 Canadian adults, the majority of respondents (more that 87 percent) thought that palliative care should be provided in the patient's setting of choice; that it should involve all care providers, and that it should be available early in the course of a disease. In addition, 93 percent felt that palliative care greatly reduces the stress and burden placed on the family (Canadian Hospice Palliative Care Association, 2014).

REFLECTIVE QUESTIONS

Why do you think most palliative care takes place in a hospital setting?
What can be done to change this?

In many instances, members of a palliative care team provide palliative care, with members of the team determined by the needs of the patient and his or her family. Often, the team includes nurses with specialized palliative care skills, the patient's family physician, a physician specialized in palliative care, a social worker, a spiritual counsellor, and a pharmacist. Volunteers also play an important role in palliative care by providing companionship, relief for the caregiver, and transportation. When required, either by the person or the family, others may be added to the team (e.g., nutritionists, physiotherapists, occupational therapists, and home support workers) (Canadian Hospice Palliative Care Association, 2016b). For more information about the evolution of palliative care, we encourage you to read about Helen Hays in Box 12.1.

An important component of palliative care is financial support for those who take a leave of absence from paid work to care for a terminally ill family member. The Compassionate Care Benefits, introduced in Canada in 2004, are Employment Insurance benefits paid to people who have to be away from work temporarily to provide care or support to a family member who is gravely ill and who has a significant risk of death within six months. Individuals also can receive compassionate care benefits when caring for a non-family member who is gravely ill and who considers this individual a family member (e.g., a close friend or neighbour). In 2016, the basic benefit rate was 55 percent of the applicant's average insurable earnings, up to a yearly maximum insurable amount of $50 800. This means that, in 2016, an applicant could receive a maximum payment of $537 per week (Government of Canada, 2016f). Despite the importance of this program, the uptake has been low—in the first five months of 2016, only 220 individuals across Canada were receiving Compassionate Care Benefits. Reasons for the low uptake include lack of knowledge about the program, the complex application process, eligibility requirements, and low compensation rates (Statistics Canada, 2016g).

What is being done to improve palliative care in Canada? In Canada, there are two national initiatives related to end-of-life care—The Quality End-of-Life Care Coalition (QELCC) and Pallium Canada. Both initiatives focus on improving the quality of palliative and hospice care for Canadians. The QELCC is a group of over 36 national organizations that advocates for quality end-of-life/hospice palliative care in Canada. Pallium Canada was created to improve the quality of hospice and palliative care services through the development and dissemination

BOX 12.1

HONOURING HELEN HAYS—A LEADER IN PALLIATIVE CARE IN ALBERTA

Doctors are honoured for healing the sick and wounded, but doctors who provide care for those who cannot be healed deserve special regard. Dr. Helen Hays has devoted her life to treating terminally ill patients, conducting research on treatment of chronic pain, and pioneering new approaches to end-of-life care. From early childhood, Helen wanted to be a doctor, just like her father. But, in the 1950s, females were most often trained not as physicians so she chose training in nursing, graduating in 1954 from St. George's Hospital in London. However, soon after, she began completing her requirements for a Bachelor of Medicine degree! Following immigration to Canada, and several decades later, she fulfilled her dream of becoming a doctor by graduating from the University of Alberta's Faculty of Medicine and Dentistry in 1971. Her interest in palliative care was spurred by a young mother dying of leukemia. Palliative care was a relatively new discipline at the time, and most doctors had little to no training in this area. Dr. Hays took it upon herself to learn more about complicated pain management and ways to enhance quality of life for terminally ill patients. In 1982, she was recruited to lead the first Palliative Care Unit at Edmonton General Hospital, the first of its kind in the region. In addition to training herself in this new area of medicine, she started a program of forums and workshops to train the province's doctors about pain management and palliative care. Six years later, Dr. Hays became Medical Director of Palliative Care Services at Edmonton's Misericordia Hospital, where she championed the involvement of doctors and nurses, as well as social workers, chaplains and therapeutic specialists. This interdisciplinary approach to end-of-life care, which is now in common use, is her legacy. In 1994, Dr. Hays and Marion Boyd, both a nurse and friend, founded Edmonton's Pilgrims Hospice. Pilgrim's Hospice continues to this day – offering practical and emotional support for people with terminal illness and their families through outpatient programs and services. Dr. Hays is a member of the Order of Canada and was inducted into the Alberta Order of Excellence in 2008. Her other recognitions include Edmontonian of the Century, the Queen's Golden Jubilee Medal and a Lifetime Achievement Award from the Canadian Pain Society.

Sources: University of Alberta Alumni Association. (2013, December). Helen Hays. *Winter 2013 New Trail: The Impact Issue*, pp. 42–43, https://www.ualberta.ca/newtrail/winter2013/features/helen-hays; The Alberta Order of Excellence, https://www.lieutenantgovernor.ab.ca/Aoe/health/helen-hays/index.html; and http://chronicpaincanada.com/about_cpac/helen_hays_award.

of peer-reviewed education, resources, and clinical decision-making tools for health and pastoral-care workers. Learning Essential Approaches to Palliative Care (LEAP) courses also are available for carers (family members, friends), educators, and leaders of organizations "who strive for the best of care" (Pallium Canada, 2016, para. 2). Topics include taking ownership, decision making, pain management, essential conversations, last days and hours, and grief and bereavement. Examples of some of the resources that Pallium Canada has developed for healthcare professionals and carers are provided in Figure 12.4. The Pallium Palliative Pocketbook is a practical one-stop resource for healthcare professionals. This downloadable app provides access to information such as essential conversation tips, national resources, as well as clinical

FIGURE 12.4

Courtesy of Pallium Canada

decision-support tools for healthcare professionals and a framework to input provincial and local resources. In addition to these national initiatives, all 17 medical schools in Canada educate medical students in palliative care, and family physicians and specialists can take a one-year accredited program in Palliative Medicine.

A GOOD DEATH

How individuals want to die and where they want to die are concepts related to what is referred to as a "good death." What is a good death? Interestingly, the answer is not as simple as one might think. In essence, the answer to the question depends on who you ask! In a recent systematic review of the literature on defining a good death, Meier, Gallegos, Montross-Thomas, Depp, Irwin, and Jeste (2016) found that patients, families, and healthcare professionals identified 11 core themes as being important components of a good death (see Table 12.2 for core themes and sub-themes). The three core themes identified by the majority (60 percent and higher) of the three groups were preference for the dying process, pain-free status, and emotional well-being. Although all three groups rated these three core themes as being important for a good death, the percentage ratings for the importance of the themes differed across the groups. For example, quality of life was identified as being important for a good death by 70 percent of family members. In contrast, only 35 percent of patients rated quality of life as being important for a good death. Surprisingly, one of the other core themes (a relationship with healthcare professionals) was rated as being important for a good death by only 40 percent of family members, 39 percent of healthcare professionals, and 20 percent of patients.

How well does Canada do in terms of providing a good death? We can answer that question by looking at Canada's placing on the international ranking of end-of-life care. This international ranking rates countries on a **quality of death index**, with quality of life for those approaching end of life measured by characteristics such as having a national palliative care

TABLE 12.2

CORE THEMES AND SUB-THEMES OF A GOOD DEATH AS IDENTIFIED BY PATIENTS, FAMILIES, AND HEALTHCARE PROFESSIONALS

CORE THEMES	SUB-THEMES
Preference of the dying process	Death scene (how, who, where, and when) Dying during sleep Preparation for death (e.g., advance directives, funeral arrangements)
Pain-free status	Not suffering Pain and symptom management
Emotional well-being	Emotional support Psychological comfort Chance to discuss meaning of death
Life completion	Saying goodbye Life well lived Acceptance of death
Treatment preferences	Not prolonging life Belief that all available treatments were used Control over treatment Euthanasia/Physician-assisted suicide Living as usual
Dignity	Respect as an individual Independence
Family	Family support Family acceptance of death Family is prepared for death Not to be a burden to family
Quality of life	Living as usual Maintaining hope, pleasure, and gratitude Life is worth living
Relationship with healthcare professional	Trust/Support/Comfort from physician/nurse Physician comfortable with death/dying Discuss spiritual beliefs/fears with physician
Religiosity/Spirituality	Religious/Spiritual comfort Faith Meet with clergy
Other	Recognition of culture Physical touch Being with pets Healthcare costs

Source: Meier, E.A., Gallegos, J.V., Montross-Thomas, L.P., Depp, C.A., Irwin, S.A., & Jeste, D.V. (2016). Defining a good death (successful dying): Literature review and a call for research and public dialogue. *The American Journal of Geriatric Psychiatry, 24*(4), 261–271. doi: 10.1016/j.jagp.2016.01.135. AMERICAN JOURNAL OF GERIATRIC PSYCHIATRY by AMERICAN ASSOCIATION FOR GERIATRIC PSYCHIATRY; AMERICAN PSYCHIATRIC PRESS. Reproduced with permission of AMERICAN PSYCHIATRIC PUBLISHING, INC. in the format Book via Copyright Clearance Center.

policy framework in place, the amount of public spending on healthcare services, the availability of palliative care training resources and subsidies to reduce the financial burden of palliative care on patients, the provision of **opioid analgesics**, and the promotion of palliative

What do you think are the most important attributes of a good death?

care through public awareness campaigns. Countries are scored on 20 indicators based on the five categories, with scores ranging from 0 to 100. Where does Canada rank in terms of overall quality of death scores? Based on Quality of Index scores from countries around the world, Canada ranked relatively well, scoring 11th out of the 80 countries surveyed, with a score of 77.8 (see Figure 12.5).

As mentioned at the beginning of this section, the majority of end-of-life care in Canada is provided in hospitals. Have you ever wondered what physicians' attitudes are to end-of-life care and how death affects physicians who are caring for patients receiving end-of-life care? Unfortunately, research in this area is relatively sparse. Redinbaugh and colleagues (2003) assessed physicians' experiences in providing care to dying patients, their emotional reactions to their patients' deaths, and their use of coping and social resources to manage their emotions. The majority (74 percent) of the 188 physicians in the study reported satisfying experiences in caring for a dying patient, with many physicians indicating a moderate emotional impact from a patient's death. However, longer durations of providing care were consistently associated with stronger emotional reactions by the physicians. In terms of grief, female physicians reported more symptoms of grief than their male counterparts. In a recent Canadian study, Whitehead (2014) explored physicians' experiences in dealing with patient death. The results of in-depth interviews with 10 physicians revealed that physicians can experience very strong and lasting emotional reactions to some patient deaths, including intense feelings of professional responsibility (e.g., Had they done everything they could have, or should have, for the patient?). One of the important findings from this study was that physicians who had been trained in palliative care felt less of a need to do something for the patient. Rather, they focused on simply being present "knowing that some suffering you can't change, and that you'll be there with them in it" (Whitehead, 2014, p. 273).

What are other healthcare professionals' attitudes toward death? In a recent review of 15 studies on nurses' attitudes toward death that involved nurses from a broad range of countries, Peters and colleagues (2013) identified three major themes related to death: 1) level of **death anxiety**; 2) death anxiety and attitudes toward caring for the dying; and 3) the need for education on death. Of interest, the age of the nurses and length of work experience were the best predictors of death anxiety, with older nurses and nurses who had more work experience having less anxiety about death. The researchers also found that nurses with specific palliative care education did not have a fear of death and had less difficulty in talking about death and dying. These results support the need for training and support to help healthcare professionals in dealing with end-of-life care.

What are your attitudes toward death? Two commonly used scales to measure death anxiety are the Death Anxiety Scale (DAS) (Templer, 1970) and the Collett-Lester Fear of Death Scale—an original and revised versions (Collett & Lester, 1969, 2010; Lester, 1990; Lester & Abdel-Khalek, 2010). The 2010 Collett-Lester Fear of Death Scale has a number of subscales, which include Your Own Death, Your Own Dying, The Death of Others, and the Dying of Others.

FIGURE 12.5

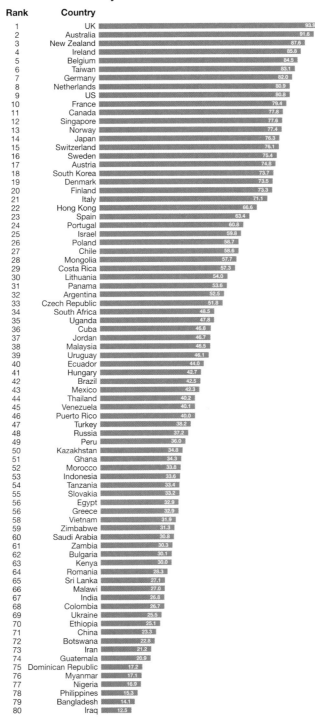

2015 Quality of Death Index—Overall Scores

Rank	Country	Score
1	UK	93.9
2	Australia	91.6
3	New Zealand	87.6
4	Ireland	85.8
5	Belgium	84.5
6	Taiwan	83.1
7	Germany	82.0
8	Netherlands	80.9
9	US	80.8
10	France	79.4
11	Canada	77.8
12	Singapore	77.6
13	Norway	77.4
14	Japan	76.3
15	Switzerland	76.1
16	Sweden	75.4
17	Austria	74.8
18	South Korea	73.7
19	Denmark	73.5
20	Finland	73.3
21	Italy	71.1
22	Hong Kong	66.6
23	Spain	63.4
24	Portugal	60.8
25	Israel	59.8
26	Poland	58.7
27	Chile	58.6
28	Mongolia	57.7
29	Costa Rica	57.3
30	Lithuania	54.0
31	Panama	53.6
32	Argentina	52.5
33	Czech Republic	51.8
34	South Africa	48.5
35	Uganda	47.8
36	Cuba	46.8
37	Jordan	46.7
38	Malaysia	46.5
39	Uruguay	46.1
40	Ecuador	44.0
41	Hungary	42.7
42	Brazil	42.5
43	Mexico	42.3
44	Thailand	40.2
45	Venezuela	40.1
46	Puerto Rico	40.0
47	Turkey	38.2
48	Russia	37.2
49	Peru	36.0
50	Kazakhstan	34.8
51	Ghana	34.3
52	Morocco	33.8
53	Indonesia	33.6
54	Tanzania	33.4
55	Slovakia	33.2
56	Egypt	32.9
56	Greece	32.9
58	Vietnam	31.9
59	Zimbabwe	31.3
60	Saudi Arabia	30.8
61	Zambia	30.3
62	Bulgaria	30.1
63	Kenya	30.0
64	Romania	28.3
65	Sri Lanka	27.1
66	Malawi	27.0
67	India	26.8
68	Colombia	26.7
69	Ukraine	25.5
70	Ethiopia	25.1
71	China	23.3
72	Botswana	22.8
73	Iran	21.2
74	Guatemala	20.9
75	Dominican Republic	17.2
76	Myanmar	17.1
77	Nigeria	16.9
78	Philippines	15.3
79	Bangladesh	14.1
80	Iraq	12.5

Source: The Economist Intelligent Unit. (2015). *The 2015 Quality of Death Index: Ranking palliative care across the world.* Retrieved from https://www.eiuperspectives.economist.com/healthcare/2015-quality-death-index. © Reproduced by permission of The Economist Intelligence Unit.

Do you see dying as a part of living?

PHYSICIAN-ASSISTED SUICIDE/MEDICAL ASSISTANCE IN DYING

You most likely are aware that the federal government recently passed legislation that allows eligible adults in Canada to request **physician-assisted suicide** or "physician-assisted death." In Canada, this is referred to as **medical assistance in dying**. Before discussing this new legislation, let's first clarify the terminology and then look at the history of physician-assisted suicide around the world. One of the things you will notice right away is that different jurisdictions use different terminology (e.g., physician-assisted suicide, euthanasia, medical assistance in dying). Throughout this section, we have defined each of the different terms, and have stayed true to using the term that each of the jurisdictions use. **Voluntary euthanasia** refers to the practice where a physician or nurse practitioner directly administers a substance (e.g., injection of a drug) that causes death. In some jurisdictions, this often is referred to as voluntary active euthanasia. **Non-voluntary euthanasia**, or passive euthanasia, on the other hand, is when someone lets the person die either by withdrawing treatment (e.g., switching off a life-support machine) or withholding treatment (e.g., stopping fluids and/or food intake) to intentionally end a patient's life. This type of euthanasia often takes places toward the very end of a person's life (Emanuel, Onwuteaka-Philipsen, Urwin, & Cohen, 2016). The term **medically assisted suicide** is where a physician or nurse practitioner gives or prescribes a drug that is *self-administered* to cause death. In some jurisdictions, this is referred to as to as physician-assisted suicide or physician-assisted death.

In 1942, Switzerland became the first country in the world to allow physician-assisted suicide but not voluntary **euthanasia**, which is forbidden. Switzerland also allows non-citizens to seek physician-assisted suicide in the country and several Canadians have done so over the years (see Box 12.2). In April of 2002, the Netherlands became the first country to legalize voluntary euthanasia and physician-assisted suicide. However, the country's courts have permitted these actions since 1984. Other jurisdictions that allow for physician-assisted suicide and/or voluntary euthanasia worldwide are Belgium, Columbia, and Luxembourg.

Oregon was the first state in the United States to pass a law allowing physician-assisted suicide. On October 27, 1997, Oregon enacted the Death with Dignity Act (DWDA). The DWDA allows terminally ill Oregonians to end their lives through the voluntary self-administration of lethal medications, expressly prescribed by a physician for that purpose. Although the law was challenged in subsequent years, it was upheld by the U.S. Supreme Court in 2006. Since introducing physician-assisted suicide, the number of people in Oregon for whom DWDA prescriptions were written have totalled 1545 (1998–2015), and 991 (64 percent) of those who have had prescriptions written have died from ingesting the medications prescribed under the DWDA during this same time period (see Figure 12.6). The majority of patients who have died from ingesting the DWDA medications have been 65 years of age and older, with the number of males and females almost equal. The majority of deceased patients had been enrolled in end-of-life care and the majority died at home. Most deceased patients had malignant neoplasms (cancer) as their underlying illness. The three primary end-of-life concerns of the DWDA patients were being less able to engage

FIGURE 12.6

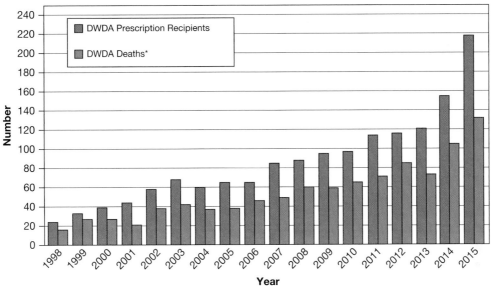

*As of January 27, 2016

Source: Oregon Public Health Division. (2016). *Oregon Death with Dignity Act: 2015 data summary.* Retrieved from https://public.health.oregon.gov/ProviderPartnerResources/EvaluationResearch/DeathwithDignityAct/Pages/index.aspx.

in activities making life enjoyable, losing autonomy, and the loss of dignity (Oregon Public Health Division, 2016). Physician-assisted suicide, excluding euthanasia, is legal in four other states in the United States: Washington, Montana, Vermont, and California.

In terms of Canadian history, in February 2015, the Supreme Court of Canada passed legislation that allows eligible adults in Canada to request medical assistance in dying (or what other countries refer to as physician-assisted suicide or physician-assisted death). That is, the Supreme Court ruled in **Carter v. Canada (Attorney General) (2015)** that parts of the *Criminal Code of Canada* that prohibited medical assistance in dying were in violation of some sections of the *Canadian Charter of Rights and Freedoms* and that these sections needed to be changed. The Supreme Court of Canada gave the government until June 6, 2016, to create a new law. In response, the government introduced **Bill C-14**, which allows eligible adults to request medical assistance in dying. Bill C-14 was passed in the House of Commons June 16, 2016 (Government of Canada, 2016g). (See Box 12.2 and Figures 12.7 and 12.8 for the cases of Sue Rodriguez and Kay Carter, which led to the creation of Bill C-14.) In addition to making medical assistance in dying a non-criminal offense (when it is provided according to the conditions and safeguards in the law), Bill C-14 also specifies eligibility criteria and the safeguards that must be respected before medical assistance in dying may be provided to a person. Those criteria include the requirement that medical assistance in dying would be legally permitted only in a medical context; that medical professionals other than physicians could provide medical assistance in dying, specifically nurse practitioners; and that medical assistance in dying be limited to those individuals whose natural death is "reasonably foreseeable." The provisions of Bill C-14 also mean that Canadians suffering from non-terminal medical conditions

BOX 12.2

ASSISTED DYING CASES IN CANADA
SUE RODRIGUEZ

Sue Rodriguez, a 42-year-old mother who was born in Winnipeg, Manitoba, grew up in Ontario, and later lived in British Columbia, was diagnosed with amyotrophic lateral sclerosis (ALS, or Lou Gehrig's disease) in 1992 at the age of 42. In 1993, she found out that she would not live more than a year, and made it known that she wished to have a physician assist her in terminating her life at a time of her choosing. However, section 241(b) of the *Criminal Code of Canada* made assisted suicide illegal in Canada. She applied to the Supreme Court of British Columbia for an order declaring section 241(b) invalid under the *Canadian Charter of Rights and Freedoms*. In *Rodriguez v. British Columbia (Attorney General)* (1993), the Supreme Court of British Columbia dismissed her application and the British Columbia Court of Appeal affirmed that ruling. She then appealed to the Supreme Court of Canada, and argued that section 241(b) violated section 7 (the right to "life, liberty, and security of the person"), section 12 (protection against "cruel and unusual punishment"), and section 15(1) (equality) of the *Canadian Charter of Rights and Freedoms*. The Supreme Court of Canada, in a 5–4 decision, dismissed the appeal and ruled that section 241(b) of the *Canadian Charter of Rights and Freedoms* was constitutional. In 1994, Ms. Rodriguez decided to take her own life with the help of an anonymous physician. Twenty-two years later, the Supreme Court's ruling in *Rodriguez v. British Columbia (Attorney General)* (1993) was overturned in *Carter v. Canada (Attorney General)* (2015).

CARTER V. CANADA (ATTORNEY GENERAL) (2015)

This case represented a challenge to the *Rodriguez v. British Columbia (Attorney General)* (1993) ruling, with the challenge coming from four plaintiffs—Gloria Taylor, Dr. William Shoichet, Lee Carter, and Hollis Johnson. In 2009, Gloria Taylor was diagnosed with ALS (Lou Gehrig's disease). A month after her diagnosis, she was told that she would likely be paralyzed within six months and die within a year. In 2012, along with the British Columbia Civil Liberties Association, Ms. Taylor decided to challenge the prohibition on assisted suicide. Ms. Taylor was joined in her claim by three other individual plaintiffs—Dr. William Shoichet, a physician willing to perform assisted suicide in appropriate cases if the law was changed, and Lee Carter and Hollis Johnson, the daughter and son-in-law of Kay Carter. Kay Carter was an 89-year-old resident of a North Vancouver nursing home and mother of seven who suffered from a terminal condition called spinal stenosis. The condition confined her to a wheelchair, unable to feed herself or go to the bathroom without assistance and suffering from chronic pain. In 2010, Mrs. Carter travelled with family to an assisted suicide clinic in Zurich, Switzerland. Her daughter and son-in-law travelled with her despite knowing that they could be prosecuted.

In *Carter v. Canada (Attorney General)* (2015), the plaintiffs argued that the prohibition against assisted suicide in *Rodriguez v. Canada (Attorney General)* (1993) was contrary to the *Canadian Charter of Rights and Freedoms*. On February 6, 2015, the Supreme Court of Canada released its decision regarding physician-assisted dying in *Carter v. Canada (Attorney General)* (2015). This decision declared that sections 241(b) and 14 of the *Criminal Code of Canada*, which prohibit a physician's assistance in terminating life, infringe upon the right to life, liberty, and security of the person for individuals who want access to physician-assisted death. And, as you now know, the Government introduced a new law (Bill C-14) that allows eligible adults to request medical assistance in dying, with this new law passed June 16, 2016 (Cartagena, 2016).

cannot seek medical assistance to end their lives. Of interest, when Bill C-14 was sent by the **Lower House** (the House of Commons) to the **Upper House** (the Senate), the Senate amended the Bill to include those who are not terminally ill. However, the Lower House rejected that amendment, and Bill C-14 was accepted and received **Royal Assent** June 17, 2016. You can learn more about the history of medical assistance in dying and understand the impact of this legislation on those who are wishing to end their life through two case histories in Box 12.2. With the passage of Bill C-14, medical assistance in dying can occur two ways in Canada. An individual may request that a physician or nurse practitioner administer a substance that causes an individual's death or a request can be made in which a physician or nurse practitioner prescribes a substance for an individual to self-administer to cause their own death.

There are eligibility criteria for medical assistance in dying and individuals must meet all of the following conditions: 1) be eligible for health services funded by the federal government or a province or territory (as such, visitors to Canada generally are not eligible);

FIGURE 12.7

SUE RODRIGUEZ

In 1993, the Supreme Court turned down Sue Rodriguez's request to be euthanized.

THE CANADIAN PRESS/Chuck Stoody

DYING: ANOTHER STAGE OF LIFE **385**

2) be at least 18 years old and mentally competent (i.e., capable of making healthcare decisions for oneself); 3) have a **grievous and irremediable medical condition**; 4) make a request for medical assistance in dying that is not the result of outside pressure and influence; and 5) give informed consent to receive medical assistance in dying (meaning that the individual has consented to medical assistance in dying after being given all the information needed to make the decision).

How does an individual go about initiating a request for medical assistance in dying? The process of requesting the service, and how and where the services are provided, is determined at the provincial and territorial levels. That is, each of the provinces and territories must follow this new criminal law but they can develop their own related laws or rules such as the specific forms to fill out, the special medical training needed to provide medical assistance in dying, and how information and data on this service are collected. More information on medical assistance in dying can be found at the Government of Canada website (http://www.healthycanadians .gc.ca/health-system-systeme-sante/services/end-life-care-soins-fin-vie/medical-assistance -dying-aide-medicale-mourir-eng.php#a6).

You might be wondering what public attitudes are toward euthanasia and physician-assisted suicide. In a review of the literature on public and physician attitudes to euthanasia and physician-assisted suicide, Emanuel and colleagues (2016) found that how the question is

FIGURE 12.8

KAY CARTER

Hollis Johnson, left, and his wife, Lee Carter, leave the B.C. Court of Appeal.

THE CANADIAN PRESS/Darryl Dyck

asked makes a difference in the level of public support. That is, if the information is presented in terms of not prolonging life (positive framing) or in terms of ending life (negative framing), support for both passive and active euthanasia was higher when the situation was framed positively (Gamliel, 2013). Support also varies depending on patient age (higher support for patients 65 and older), their medical diagnosis (higher support for patients who are terminally ill with an illness such as a cancer), and symptoms (higher support for those who are in pain) (Emanuel et al., 2016; Gamliel, 2013). Overall, results from public opinion surveys in the United States indicate that support for voluntary euthanasia and physician-assisted suicide increased from 37 percent in 1947 to a peak of 75 percent in 2005, with a decline to 64 percent in 2012 (Emanuel et al., 2016). In Western Europe, there has been an increase in support for voluntary euthanasia and physician-assisted suicide but decreasing support in central and Eastern Europe. In Canada, a recent telephone survey of 2271 randomly selected adults indicated that 72 percent approved of physician-assisted suicide, 16 percent disapproved, and 12 percent "didn't know" (Forum Research Inc., 2016). Of interest, the approval rating was about the same across the age range, with ratings ranging from 63 percent (adults 65 and older) to 70 to 82 percent for those between the ages of 18 and 64. Approval ratings also were about the same for females and males at around 72 percent. Income also was a factor with respondents with higher incomes more likely to indicate approval as compared to those with lower incomes. Finally, approval ratings across the country ranged from a high in Quebec (80 percent) to a low of 61 percent in Manitoba and Saskatchewan.

Why do you think factors such as income or place of residence affect approval ratings on physician-assisted suicide?

The wish to die is not confined to individuals with grievous and irremediable medical conditions. A movement that began in the Netherlands in 2009 has as its goal the legalization of assistance in dying for older individuals who consider their life complete. In a 2012 study, Buiting and colleagues studied older adults' attitudes toward an end-of-life pill (which also is referred to as **Drion's pill**). Three samples aged 64 years or older from the Longitudinal Ageing Study Amsterdam were studied. Respondents (n=1284 [2001]; n=1303 [2005]; and n=1245 [2008]) were asked whether they could imagine requesting their physician to end their life (euthanasia), or imagine asking for a pill to end their life if they became tired of living in the absence of a severe disease. The percentage of respondents with a positive attitude toward both euthanasia and an end-of-life pill increased over time. For voluntary euthanasia, the percentage by year was as follows: 58 percent (2001), 64 percent (2005), and 70 percent (2008). For an end-of-life pill, the percentage by year was 31 percent (2001), 33 percent (2005), and 45 percent (2008).

In a review of the literature on the experiences and motivations underlying wishes to die in older people who are tired of living, Van Wijingaarden, Leget, and Goossensen (2014) found that the age-related losses in control due to physical declines in areas such as mobility, vision, hearing, speaking, and cognition; loss of connectedness to public life; and feelings that life has no meaning anymore were associated with a wish to die. These, as well

BOX 12.3

ONE OF MANY

Evelyn was born on the 27th of March, 1896. She died on the 7th of April, 2000. One hundred and four years old. A woman of two millennia and two World Wars. The last twenty years of her life she longed for death. And certainly not in silence. She talked about it with her children and her doctor. But any further than talking and longing it didn't get. Evelyn just wouldn't get ill so she was obliged to live. She suffered more from this, more than she could have suffered from an illness, her daughter Lenny says. For a number of people old age is a blessing; for others a disaster. The well-known saying that "getting old is not an art but being old is" does therefore not apply. The story of Evelyn says it all, it doesn't matter how old someone is but how [she/]he is old.... Daughter Lenny tells about her mother a story of love, death, and old age...."Her life waned and she became more and more dependent on others. She suffered badly from it. She knew that a human being doesn't have eternal life and the ripe old age limits the range. But knowing is one thing, to experience it is another. How much she has suffered under this experience has been underestimated by many. During this period arose the longing for death, not sporadically but persistently."

Source: Adapted from Beekman, W. (2011). Completed life of the elderly. In *The self-chosen death of the elderly* (pp. 14–20). Naarden, NL:Society for Old Age Rational Society.

REFLECTIVE QUESTION

Should Bill C-14 be amended to include those who are not terminally ill?

as personal characteristics (e.g., strong-willed, stubborn, introverted) appear to play a role in the wish to die of older people who are tired of living (see Box 12.3 for a case history of a 104-year-old woman who "longed for death").

The wish to die is not unique to older people who are tired of living. In a Canadian video produced by the Canadian Partnership Against Cancer organization, Dr. Donald Low, a Canadian microbiologist noted for his role in battling the SARS outbreak of 2003 and who was diagnosed with a brain tumour in 2013, makes a plea to those who are opposed to physician-assisted suicide. In the video, Dr. Low says, "I know I'm going to die; what worries me is how I'm going to die" (see http://www.cbc.ca/news/canada/toronto/sars-doctor-donald-low-s-posthumous-plea-for-assisted-suicide-1.1866332). In this video, Dr. Low verbalizes what many who are in the process of dying are thinking. At one point or another, all of us are likely to be with family or friends who are facing the end of life. The film *Hold Me* touches on a number of themes in the exploration of "physician-assisted suicide." You can watch the trailer at http://www.youtube.com/watch?v=ftkHTCg1S6U. There are a lot of very poignant stories about individuals who want control over the end of their life.

ADVANCE DIRECTIVES AND WILLS

Advance directives are directions given by a competent individual concerning what and/or how and/or by whom decisions should be made in the event that, at some time in the future, the individual becomes incompetent to make certain decisions (Health Law Institute, n.d.). In Canada, there are two types of advance directives—personal directives/living wills and powers of attorney. A personal directive is a legal document that gives authority to a person (referred to as an "agent") to make non-financial decisions on behalf of another person. These decisions can be related to health and medical treatment and/or about housing transitions (e.g., being placed in a long-term-care facility). Personal directives are like wills but are designed to take effect when the person making the personal directive loses the mental capacity to make certain personal decisions themselves. There is no legal requirement for an individual to make a personal directive. However, individuals with a personal directive have greater control over personal matters in their future and can specify not only who they want to make decisions on their behalf but also who will determine their capacity, who is to be notified that the personal directive has come into effect, and who can gain personal information about the maker of the personal directive. To be valid, a personal directive must be in writing, dated, and signed in the presence of one witness. A personal directive can be done at any time and we encourage you (and your family members) to do so. Having an advance directive in place at any age is valuable as it minimizes or eliminates the stress on family members when they know that they are following the wishes of their relative.

In some provinces in Canada (Alberta and British Columbia), an individual can choose to register their personal directive with the provincial registry (see http://www.humanservices.alberta.ca/guardianship-trusteeship/register-a-personal-directive.html). In many instances, the personal directive is held by a legal entity (the lawyer/law firm that holds the individual's will). Power of attorney is a legal document that gives an individual the power to make financial decisions on someone else's behalf. Any competent adult or financial institution can be appointed power of attorney. As with personal directives, power of attorney must be in writing, dated, signed by the person in the presence of a witness, and signed by the witness in the presence of the person making the power of attorney. Because each province/territory in Canada regulates advance directives differently, advance directives vary depending on where the person lives in Canada. The legislative documents related to advance directives in each province/territory are provided in Table 12.3.

TABLE 12.3

LEGISLATIVE DOCUMENTS RELATED TO ADVANCE DIRECTIVES IN EACH PROVINCE/TERRITORY	
PROVINCE/TERRITORY*	**LEGISLATION**
Alberta	Personal Directives Act, RSA 2000, c P-6 Personal Directives Regulation, Alta Reg 99/2008 Personal Directives (Ministerial) Regulation, Alta Reg 26/1998
British Columbia	Health Care (Consent) and Care Facility (Admission) Act, RSBC 1996, c 181 Health Care Consent Regulation, BC Reg 20/2000 Representation Agreement Act, RSBC 1996, c 405 Representation Agreement Regulation, BC Reg 199/2001 Adult Guardianship Act, RSBC 1996, c 6 Patients Property Act, RSBC 1996, c 349

PROVINCE/TERRITORY*	LEGISLATION
Manitoba	The Health Care Directives Act, CCSM c H 27
New Brunswick	Infirm Persons Act, RSNB 1973, c I-8
Newfoundland and Labrador	Advance Health Care Directives Act, SNL 1995, c A-4.1
Northwest Territories Personal	Directives Act, SNWT 2005 c 16
Nova Scotia	Personal Directives Act, SNS 2008, c 8 Personal Directives Regulations, NS Reg 31/2010
Ontario	Health Care Consent Act, SO 1996, c 2 Sch A Evaluators, O Reg 104/96 Substitute Decisions Act, 1992, SO 1992, c 30 Capacity Assessment, O Reg 460/05
Prince Edward Island	Consent to Treatment and Health Care Directives Act RSPEI 1988, c C-17.2 General Regulations PEI Reg EC356/00
Quebec	Civil Code of Québec, CQLR c C-1991 Public Curator Act, RSQ c C-81 Regulation respecting the application of the Public Curator Act, chapter C-81 r.1
Saskatchewan	The Health Care Directives and Substitute Health Care Decision Makers Act SS 1997, c H-0.001 The Health Care Directives and Substitute Health Care Decision Makers Regulations RRS c H-0.001 Reg 1
Yukon	Care Consent Act SY, 2003, c 21, Sch B

*Note: Nunavut is in the initial stages of an initiative related to palliative care and advance care directives.

Source: Health Law Institute. (n.d.). *Advance directives.* Retrieved from http://eol.law.dal.ca/?page_id=231.

The recent Supreme Court decision on medical assistance in dying has stimulated broader discussions on end-of-life care, including the types of interventions that individuals want at the end of their lives. In a recent study that examined how often advance directives were given in 982 long-term-care facilities in Canada between 2009 and 2010 and between 2011 and 2012, the CIHI found that three-quarters of long-term-care residents have a **do-not-resuscitate** (DNR) directive with fewer residents having a do-not-hospitalize (DNH) directive. For the DNR directive, only about one in 2500 residents received resuscitation despite having a DNR order indicating that these directives appear to be followed well. With respect to the DNH directive, it too appears to be followed well with one in 14 residents with a DNH directive admitted to hospital, primarily due to injuries from falls and infections. Individuals most likely to be admitted to hospital despite a DNH directive were younger (> 90 years of age), more independent, and more stable in terms of their health status (CIHI, 2016).

At this point, you might be wondering what the difference is between a will and an advance directive. Advance directives (living wills and powers of attorney) are documents that deal with decisions about an individual's non-financial and financial matters while the person is alive. A will, on the other hand, is a written legal document that establishes how an individual's property and assets will be divided when the individual dies. There are formal requirements that need to be met in order for a will to be valid. As with advance directives, the legal requirements related to wills are determined on a provincial/territorial basis. What happens if an individual dies without a will? Many people incorrectly assume that if they were to die without a will, their estate would simply pass to their spouse. However, this would happen only for assets that were held jointly with right of survivorship with the spouse (except in Quebec). In Canada, if an individual dies without a will, they are considered to have died "intestate." This means that the individual's provincial government, and not the individual, decides how the assets will be divided. Each province and territory has intestacy rules that define the estate's beneficiaries and how much each beneficiary is to receive. Usually, it means that the legal spouse and biological and adopted children end up with the assets of the estate. However, **intestacy rules** do not take into account any intentions the deceased may have had for distributing his/her assets. Even worse—intestacy can result in additional legal costs for the beneficiaries (RBC Insurance, 2016). See Table 12.4 for an overview of personal directives, enduring power of attorney, general power of attorney, and wills.

Advance care planning (i.e., having advance directives) is associated with better patient experiences (Biola, Sloane, Williams, Daaleman, & Zimmerman, 2010) and lower costs for the health system (Ouslander et al., 2011). To increase awareness of the importance of advance care planning, April 16th has been designated as the Advance Care Planning Day in Canada, with the same day designated as the National Healthcare Decisions Day in the United States. To assist in the promotion of difficult conversations related to end-of-life care, there even are care planning cookies! These edible cookies with a message inside are designed to stimulate conversations on living well and dying well.

TABLE 12.4

WHEN TO USE PERSONAL DIRECTIVES, ENDURING POWER OF ATTORNEY, GENERAL POWER OF ATTORNEY, AND WILLS.	
DOCUMENT	**WHEN TO USE**
Personal Directive	Use for making non-financial decisions when a person becomes incapable of doing so for himself.
Enduring Power of Attorney	Similar to general power of attorney. Refers to when a person appoints someone else to act on their behalf with regard to their financial matters.
General Power of Attorney	Use for making financial decisions when a person becomes incapable of doing so for herself.
Will	Use for deciding what happens to a person's property after he or she dies.

REFLECTIVE QUESTION

Have you thought about who you might appoint as your power of attorney?

12.3 BEREAVEMENT

BEREAVEMENT, GRIEF, AND SUPPORT

Bereavement refers to a period of **mourning** following the loss of a loved one or a close friend through death. Because death is more common in the older age groups, bereavement is disproportionately experienced by older adults. **Grief** is a natural response to the loss of someone or something that is very dear to a person. For example, the death of a family member, the death of a pet, or the loss of a job may lead to grief. Common elements of grief are yearning, longing, sorrow, and thoughts and memories of the person or thing that died, with the quality and intensity of these thoughts and feelings decreasing in intensity with time (Bonanno, Moskowitz, Papa, & Folkman, 2005; Shear, 2015).

Bereaved older adults may seek support from healthcare professionals, religious and /or spiritual leaders, or family and friends. Others may seek out support from community-based programs on bereavement. Despite the availability of these programs, there has been little research to date on utilization or the helpfulness of the services that are provided. Bergman, Haley, and Small (2011) examined the use of bereavement services by 224 caregivers caring for individuals with dementia. They found that one in three of the caregivers used bereavement services, such as support groups, counselling, and psychotropic medication, in almost similar proportions to help them adjust to their loss. Not surprisingly, caregivers with depressive symptoms, anxiety, or complicated grief were more likely to use bereavement services.

COMPLICATED GRIEF

Sooner or later, most of us will experience the loss of someone that we love. Research shows that the passage of time helps most people recover from the loss of a loved one, or something that was very dear to the person (PDQ® Supportive and Palliative Care Editorial Board, 2014). However, about 10 to 12 percent of bereaved individuals experience a syndrome of grief that does not resolve naturally and persists for an indefinite period with varying degrees of incapacitation. This has been labelled **complicated or prolonged grief** disorder and this type of grief can have adverse long-term health effects (Prigerson et al., 2009). How does complicated or prolonged grief differ from normal grief? According to Prigerson, Vanderwerker, and Maciejewski (2008), the normal bereavement process is not as persistent or intense as complicated or prolonged grief, nor is it as disabling or life-altering, and it is not experienced as a severe threat by the bereaved individual. Conversely, individuals experiencing complicated or prolonged grief become incapacitated by grief and are focused on the loss to the exclusion of other interests and concerns. There is rumination about the death and longing for reunion with the deceased, as well as an inability to accept the loss, an inability to feel pleasure, bitterness, difficulty trusting others, and a feeling of being stuck in the grieving process. Individuals experiencing complicated or prolonged grief often report loss of self-worth and sense of self, feel emotionally disconnected from others, and do not wish to move on from bereavement. Some feel that moving on represents a betrayal of the deceased. These experiences associated with the bereavement process are present every day, cause distress or functional impairment, and persist for more than six months after bereavement (Prigerson et al., 1996). Although not previously identified in the *Diagnostic and Statistical Manual of Mental Disorders (DSM)* (American Psychiatric Association[APA], 2000), persistent complex bereavement disorder (PCBD) has been catalogued separately for further discussion and evaluation in the most recent *DSM-5* (APA, 2013).

BOX 12.4

STRATEGIES THAT CAN HELP IN THE PROCESS OF GRIEVING

- **Talk about the death of your loved one**. Talk with friends and colleagues in order to understand what happened and remember your friend or family member. Denying the death is an easy way to isolate yourself, and will frustrate your support system in the process.
- **Accept your feelings**. People experience all kinds of emotions after the death of someone close. Sadness, anger, frustration, and even exhaustion are all normal.
- **Take care of yourself and your family**. Eating well, exercising, and getting plenty of rest help us get through each day and move forward.
- **Reach out and help others dealing with the loss**. Helping others has the added benefit of making you feel better as well. Sharing stories of the deceased can help everyone cope.
- **Remember and celebrate the lives of your loved ones**. Possibilities include donating to a favourite charity of the deceased, framing photos of fun times, passing on a family name to a baby, or planting a garden in memory. What you choose is up to you, as long as it allows you to honour that unique relationship in a way that feels right to you. If you feel stuck or overwhelmed by your emotions, it may be helpful to talk with a licensed psychologist or other mental health professional who can help you cope with your feelings and find ways to get back on track.

Source: American Psychological Association. (2016). *Grief: Coping with the loss of your loved one.* Washington, D.C. http://www.apa.org/helpcenter/grief.aspx. Copyright © 2016 American Psychological Association. Reproduced with permission.

What factors are associated with the development of complicated or prolonged grief? First-degree relationship to the deceased, a poorly functioning marriage or insecure attachment style prior to widowhood, emotional dependency on the deceased, lack of preparation for the death, and in-hospital death of the loved one all can contribute to the development of complicated or prolonged grief (Ott, Lueger, Kelber & Prigerson, 2007; Waldoph & Kutner, 2013). Strategies that can help in the process of grieving are provided in Box 12.4.

12.4 CULTURAL PERSPECTIVES ON DEATH AND DYING

LEARNING OBJECTIVE

- To understand cultural perspectives on death and dying

CULTURAL DIVERSITY IN BELIEFS ABOUT DEATH

Canada is a multicultural country; as a result, there are many different cultural and religious beliefs including those surrounding death and dying. What are some of the different religious beliefs at the time of death? First, let's look at the statistics on the different faiths in Canada. Based on data from the 2011 National Household Survey, the largest faith in Canada was **Christianity**, with about two-thirds of Canada's population (67.3 percent) reporting that they were affiliated with a Christian religion. Roman Catholics were the largest Christian religious group, with 38.7 percent of Canada's population as a whole identifying themselves as Roman Catholic. Consistent with Canada's changing immigration patterns, there were growing proportions of the population who reported religious affiliations other than Christian. These religions included Muslim, Hindu, Sikh, and Buddhist. Approximately one-quarter of Canada's population (23.9 percent) had no religious affiliation, up from 16.5 percent a decade earlier (Statistics Canada, 2013d). The beliefs and funeral and burial practices of Aboriginal, Buddhist, Catholic, Christian, Hindu, Jewish, Muslim, and Sikh religions are outlined in Table 12.5.

CHANGES IN FUNERAL PRACTICES IN CANADA

As noted in the section above, funeral practices consist of customary observances for the dead and arrangements made for disposition of the body (*The Canadian Encyclopedia*, 2016). You also have learned that funeral services differ according to religious and cultural practices. For Christians, the

TABLE 12.5

BELIEFS AND FUNERAL AND BURIAL PRACTICES OF COMMON RELIGIONS IN CANADA

RELIGION	BELIEFS	FUNERAL	BURIAL
Aboriginal	Upon death, the original mother (Mother Earth) reclaims the physical form and the original father (the Creator) takes the spirits to return them to their place of origin. Believe that the spirit lives forever.	Funeral rites determined by the family, clan, and nation according to the duties that the deceased occupied in life. Funeral ceremonies may be conducted in the sacred lodge with the funeral rites conducted by elders and spiritual leaders associated with the tradition.	Burial customs vary widely from tribe to tribe.
Buddhist	Believe in rebirth (believe that when they die, they will be reborn again).	Funeral traditions vary because there are so many different types of Buddhism.	May be either cremated or buried depending on tradition. There may be speeches and chants on the impermanence of life.
Catholic	Believe in an afterlife. Believe in repentances for sins, with repentence required to enter into the full glory of Heaven.	Funeral rite called the Order of Christian Funerals. Prayer service (Vigil of the Deceased) held the night before the funeral with the Requiem Mass held the day of the funeral.	Rite of Committal celebrated at the grave or place where the body has been entombed.
Hindu	Believe that when a person dies their soul merely moves from one body to the next on its path to Nirvana (Heaven).	Deceased is bathed and dressed in white traditional clothing. If a woman dies before her husband, she will be dressed in red.	The body is cremated because it is believed that burning of the body releases the spirit. The flames represent Brahma (the Creator).

RELIGION	BELIEFS	FUNERAL	BURIAL
Jewish	Beliefs vary depending on whether the Jewish person is Orthodox, Reform, or Conservative. Jewish people believe that when they die they will go to Heaven to be with God. Death is seen as a part of life.	Jewish people may be cremated or embalmed. The body is wrapped in a white shroud.	The burial takes place as soon as possible after the death. Pallbearers carry the casket to the grave, and a family member will throw a handful of earth into the casket with the body. Jewish law stipulates that each grave must have a tombstone to remember the deceased.
Muslim (Islamic)	There are two types of Muslims—Shi'ite and Sunni. Customs and beliefs are slightly different for each. Muslims believe that there will be a day of judgment by Allah (God), and on judgment day, they will go to either Heaven or Hell.	The funeral takes place at the graveside and involves prayer and readings from the Koran.	Cremation is not permitted in Islam. Burial is in a graveyard. The body is buried with the face turned to the right to face Mecca. No women are allowed at the graveyard.
Sikh	Believe in reincarnation but also believe in an afterlife where the soul meets God.	Friends and family drive in a procession to the crematorium, with the funeral taking place as soon as possible. Death is not seen as a sad occasion but an act of God. Crying is forbidden.	Cremation is the norm although only small children and babies will be buried. The ashes are spread in running water and are traditionally sent to India.

Source: Connectability (n.d.). *Different cultural beliefs at time of death*. Retrieved from: http://connectability
.ca/2014/09/11/different-cultural-beliefs-at-time-of-death/; Loddon Mallei Regional Palliative Care Consortium.
(2011). *An outline of different cultural beliefs at the time of death*. Castlemaine, AUS: Author.

norm is to have the funeral service at the church with the body present. For some of the Christian faiths, the church is the only sanctified location where a mass may be held. However in many religious communities, the church is regarded as the proper place for funerals, no matter what the denomination. Interestingly, a more recent trend, which has increased significantly in the last two decades, is a shift to a memorial service. Unlike a funeral service, a memorial service honours the deceased person through a celebration of her/his accomplishments, with the service consisting of music and poetry reflecting the tastes of the deceased, as well as anecdotes of their life. Often, a memorial service is devoid of any religious reference and an urn containing the ashes of the deceased, rather than the casket, is present. Whatever it is called—A Celebration of Life, a Fabulous Farewell, or the Last Hurrah—the key is to celebrate the life that was lived.

The trend toward cremation, rather than interment in the ground, is becoming increasingly common in Canada. Another recent trend in some parts of the world including Canada is a green burial. Also referred to as a natural burial, a green burial is the act of returning a body as naturally as possible to the earth. Rather than being embalmed or cremated, the body is instead buried in a simple casket or shroud in a protected green space. In Canada, there currently are four sites for natural (green) burials—the Royal Oak Burial Park in Victoria, British Columbia;

Union Cemetery in Cobourg, Ontario; Meadowvale Cemetery in Brampton, Ontario; and Duffin Meadows Cemetery in Pickering, Ontario, with more in the planning stages (Natural Burial Association, 2013). You can watch an award-winning documentary on green burials, entitled *A Will for the Woods*; retrieved from http://www.naturalburialassoc.ca/wp-content/uploads/2013/05/willforthewoods_flat.jpg (see Figure 12.9).

REFLECTIVE QUESTIONS

What do you think of green burials?

Is this something you or your family members would choose?

FIGURE 12.9

A WILL FOR THE WOODS: A LAST ACT, A GIFT TO THE PLANET

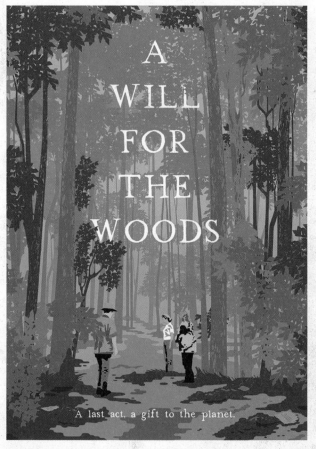

Reprinted with permission.

Ashli Watt, Ph.D.
Rockyview Hospital, Calgary, Alberta

WHERE DID YOU TRAIN?

I completed my undergraduate training at Brandon University, Brandon, Manitoba and my graduate training at the University of Calgary, Calgary, Alberta, Clinical Psychology Program.

WHERE DO YOU WORK?

I work at the Specialized Seniors Health Neuropsychology Clinic at the Rockyview General Hospital in Calgary, Alberta. This clinic sees patients referred by the Specialized Seniors Health Clinic. Primarily these are outpatient referrals, but we also serve geriatric rehabilitation in-patient units at the hospital. Patients present with medically complex issues and/or cognitive impairment. Referral questions typically involve differential diagnosis of potential neurodegenerative disorders, discrimination between mild cognitive impairment and dementia, assessing mood, and recommendations for management and intervention.

WHAT DO YOU DO?

I work as a geriatric neuropsychologist.

WHY DO YOU LIKE WORKING WITH AN OLDER-ADULT POPULATION?.

I was raised in a small rural community and had a great deal of contact with older adults at various community events. I was able to form a number of friendships with these individuals and it became apparent how important interpersonal relationships were in a person's life. My first real summer job was working as a recreation assistant at a long-term-care facility.

I enjoyed spending one-on-one time with the residents. Just listening to their stories and trying to truly understand their needs had a significant and positive affect on their mood. This experience changed my career aspirations. I continue to find it rewarding to listen to and understand an older person's experience. Conducting neuropsychological assessments with an older-adult population is particularly challenging and keeps me on my toes. These adults typically present with a long history of medical and psychosocial issues. The diagnostic issues are often very complex. I enjoy when I can offer clarity as to why people are struggling more in their daily lives. I also enjoy providing practical solutions that may make their lives easier.

DO YOU HAVE ADVICE FOR STUDENTS WHO WANT TO GET INTO THE FIELD?

I think that as a geriatric neuropsychologist it is important to be interested in the brain but to be more interested in the person. The focus should always be on helping rather than simply diagnosing the patient. In addition, in this field one needs to be comfortable with not always having the answer. What we know about dementia changes every day. One needs to be aware of what one knows and does not know.

Karen Chipman, Ph.D.
Nova Scotia Health Authority, Halifax, Nova Scotia
Adjunct, Department of Psychology and Neuroscience, Dalhousie University, Halifax, Nova Scotia
Assistant Professor, Department of Psychiatry, Dalhousie University, Halifax, Nova Scotia

WHERE DID YOU TRAIN?

I completed a Bachelor of Psychology (Honours) degree at the University of Prince Edward Island, followed by a Master of Arts degree and a Doctor of Philosophy degree in clinical neuropsychology at Western University London, Ontario. I also completed a one-year predoctoral internship in clinical neuropsychology at Baycrest Centre for Geriatric Care Toronto, Ontario, where I received specialized training in geriatric neuropsychological assessment and the differential diagnosis of dementia.

WHERE DO YOU WORK?

I am a staff neuropsychologist in the Mental Health and Addictions Program for the Nova Scotia Health Authority. My clinical service is in a psychiatric hospital in Dartmouth, Nova Scotia.

WHAT DO YOU DO?

An important aspect of my work is to provide neuropsychological assessment services to older adults in the mental health program who are showing early signs of cognitive decline in keeping with the possibility of mild cognitive impairment (MCI) or dementia. My role is to use the assessment information to address questions about differential diagnosis and treatment planning. I identify individualized cognitive (e.g., memory) strategies and aids to help improve daily functioning. I also provide psychoeducation to clients and their families, caregivers, and other healthcare workers to help them understand and cope with the cognitive changes that are occurring. In addition, I co-facilitate a 10-week memory-training group for individuals who have been diagnosed with MCI as part of a research project, whereby participants learn to use practical strategies to help them cope with everyday memory challenges.

WHY DO YOU LIKE WORKING WITH AN OLDER-ADULT POPULATION?

I find it very rewarding to work with an aging population for a number of reasons. I especially enjoy the unique challenges involved in clinically evaluating older adults and making diagnostic determinations in the context of varied and complex biopsychosocial factors. I also feel that I am making a difference when I can assist the care team by addressing the causes for an individual's cognitive (e.g., memory) problems and contribute information that can hopefully lead to an early and accurate diagnosis. It is particularly gratifying to know that I can play a role in reducing the worries of my clients and their families, and that I also can give them practical suggestions to help improve their cognitive well-being and independence. Working with older adults has further taught me a great deal about resilience in aging, and I have much respect for the life experiences that my clients have shared with me over the years.

DO YOU HAVE ADVICE FOR STUDENTS WHO WANT TO GET INTO THE FIELD?

A career in this field involves a lifelong learning process, so it is important to be passionate about working with an older-adult population. I would encourage students to research the registration requirements in their province so that they can tailor their learning and training experiences in a graduate program that will move them closer to their goal of specializing in geriatric psychology. There also is much to be gained from the knowledge and expertise of mentors who are already working in the field. It will take time for students to build on their own knowledge and skill base, but if they choose this path, I'm certain that it will lead them to a very fulfilling and meaningful career!

- The experiences of death and dying have changed dramatically over the past 120 years. Today, over half of all deaths in Canada now take place in hospitals.

- Palliative care, end-of-life care, and hospice care are all terms used to describe care for people who are deemed to be terminal or dying in the foreseeable (near) future.

- Although 90 percent of Canadians who die can benefit from palliative care, only 16 to 30 percent of Canadians who die have access to or receive palliative and end-of-life care services.

- How individuals want to die and where they want to die are concepts related to what is referred to as a "good death."

- Switzerland was the first country in the world to allow physician-assisted suicide, and Oregon was the first state in the United States to pass a law allowing physician-assisted suicide.

- The Canadian federal government passed legislation on June 16, 2016, that allows eligible adults in Canada to request medical assistance in dying.

- There now are two types of medical assistance in dying available to Canadians: voluntary and medically assisted.

- Advance directives are directions given by a competent individual concerning what, how, and/or by whom decisions should be made in the event that, at some time in the future, the individual becomes incompetent to make certain decisions.

- Bereavement refers to a period of mourning following the loss of a relative or a close friend through death. Grief is a natural response to the loss of someone or something that is very dear to a person.

- Complicated or prolonged grief disorder occurs when grief does not resolve naturally and persists for an indefinite period. Beliefs about death vary across different cultures.

- The trend toward cremation, rather than interment in the ground, is becoming increasingly common in Canada. Green burials also are becoming more popular.

Key Terms

Bereaved
Refers to an individual who is experiencing grief and mourning following the loss of someone or something that is very dear to them.

Bill C-14
Legislation passed in June 2016 amending the *Criminal Code of Canada* and other related Acts, limiting the right to medical assistance in dying to those whose natural death is "reasonably foreseeable."

Carter v. Canada (Attorney General) (2015)
A landmark Supreme Court of Canada decision where the prohibition of assisted suicide was challenged as contrary to the *Canadian Charter of Rights and Freedoms*. In a unanimous decision on February 6, 2015, the Court struck down the provision in the *Criminal Code of Canada*, thereby giving Canadian adults who are mentally competent and suffering intolerably and enduringly the right to a doctor's help in dying.

Christianity
The religion based on the person and teachings of Jesus of Nazareth, or its beliefs and practices.

Complicated or Prolonged Grief
Grief that does not resolve naturally and persists for an indefinite period with varying degrees of incapacitation

Death Anxiety
The persistent fear of one's own mortality with this fear consisting of a feeling of dread, apprehension, or anxiety.

Do-Not-Resuscitate Order
A do-not-resuscitate order, or DNR order, is a medical order written by a doctor and based on previous consultation with/directive from the patient. It instructs healthcare providers not to do cardiopulmonary resuscitation (CPR) if a patient's breathing stops or if the patient's heart stops beating.

Drion's Pill
Huib Drion, then-vice-president of the Dutch Supreme Court, put forward the idea of having an easily available suicide pill for older adults who wanted to end their lives. This suicide pill came to be known as the Drion Pill or Drion's Pill.

Euthanasia
A process that involves a deliberate action with the express intention of ending a life to relieve intractable (persistent, unstoppable) suffering. The action may be either non-voluntary or voluntary.

Five Stages of Death
A model of death developed by Elisabeth Kübler-Ross, consisting of five stages of dying that people experience when faced with their own impending death: denial, anger, bargaining, depression, and acceptance. While the stages are listed in order, they do not necessarily occur in the same sequence with every individual and more than one stage may be present at the same time.

Grief
A natural response to the loss of a loved one or someone or something very dear to a person.

Grievous and Irremediable Medical Condition
One criteria for medical assistance in dying; an individual must have a serious illness, disease, disability; be in an advanced state of decline that cannot be reversed; be suffering unbearably from the illness, disease, disability, or state of decline; and be at a point where natural death is foreseeable.

Intestacy Rules
When a person dies without leaving a valid will, their property (the estate) must be shared out according to certain rules. Each province has intestacy rules that define an estate's beneficiaries and how much each is to receive.

Lower House
Also known as the House of Commons—a component of the Parliament of Canada, along with the Senate and the Monarch (represented by the governor general).

Medical Assistance in Dying
Legislation that allows eligible adults in Canada to request physician-assisted suicide or physician-assisted death. There are two types of medical assistance in dying available to Canadians—voluntary euthanasia and medically assisted suicide.

Medically Assisted Suicide
When a physician or nurse practitioner gives or prescribes a drug that is *self-administered* to cause death. In some jurisdictions, this is referred to as physician-assisted suicide or physician-assisted death.

Mourning
The cultural and/or public display of grief through one's behaviour. It is the process through which the resolution of grief may be accomplished.

Non-Voluntary Euthanasia
When a physician or someone else administers a medication such as a sedative or a neuromuscular relaxant or other intervention to intentionally end the life of a non-competent patient who could not give informed consent (e.g., an adult with Alzheimer's disease or other condition that compromises decision-making capacity); also called "passive euthanasia."

Opioid Analgesics
Pain relievers, also known as narcotic analgesics, that act on the central nervous system.

Physician-Assisted Suicide
When the physician provides medication or a prescription to a patient as per the patient's explicit request, with the understanding that the patient intends to use the medication to end his or her life. This often is referred to as physician-assisted death.

Quality of Death Index
A measure of the quality of palliative care in 80 countries using 20 quantitative and qualitative indicators across five categories: the palliative and healthcare environment, human resources, the affordability of care, the quality of care, and the level of community engagement.

Royal Assent
The Canadian Constitution Act of 1867 states that the approval of the Crown, signified by Royal Assent, is required for any bill to become law after passage by both the Senate and the House of Commons.

Terminal
Predicted to lead to death, especially slowly; incurable.

Upper House
Also known as the Senate—a component of the Parliament of Canada, along with the House of Commons and the Monarch (represented by the governor general).

Voluntary Euthanasia
When a physician or someone else administers a medication such as a sedative or a neuromuscular relaxant or other intervention to intentionally end a mentally competent patient's life, with this intervention done at the individual's request. This often is referred to as voluntary active euthanasia.

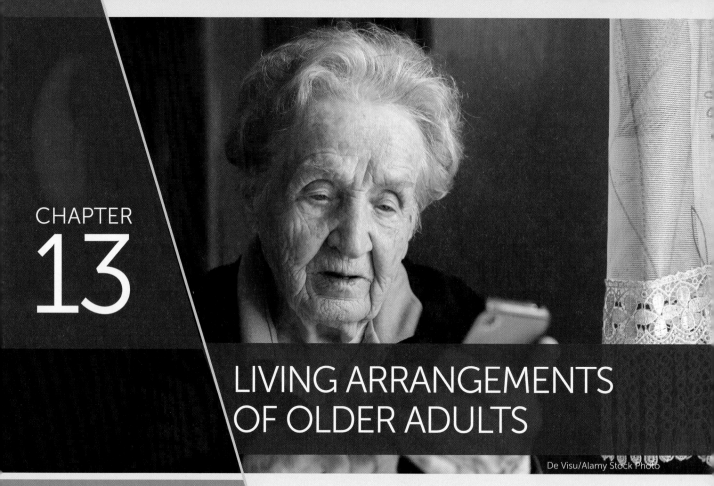

De Visu/Alamy Stock Photo

LIVING ARRANGEMENTS OF OLDER ADULTS

"Though no one can go back and make a brand new start, anyone can start from now and make a brand new ending."

Carl Bard

In this chapter, we discuss the living arrangements of older adults. Living arrangements refer to the type of **household** an individual lives in. As you read through the first section of this chapter, you will become more familiar with the current living arrangements of older Canadian adults as well as the many types of housing options available. Older adults prefer to age in place, and with the help of advancements in technology, older adults are more able to do this. However, some older adults are not able to age in place and will move to more supportive living arrangements. The good news is that there is now more variability in living arrangements for older adults. We hope that after you read this chapter, you will understand that the majority of older adults are not in nursing homes and are functioning well. We also hope that you will be able to discuss some of the new living arrangements with your parents or grandparents.

13.1 LIVING ARRANGEMENTS OF OLDER ADULTS

LEARNING OBJECTIVES

- To understand the current living arrangements of older adults in Canada
- To be able to describe the types of housing options available for older adults in Canada
- To understand policies and programs that facilitate home ownership for older adults

CURRENT LIVING ARRANGEMENTS OF OLDER ADULTS

At the turn of the 20th century, an older adult could expect to live and die in their own home and community, with support from family, friends, and neighbours as needed (Cassel & Demel, 2001). Today, contrary to the common stereotype that older adults live out their lives in nursing homes or in other "seniors only" housing, most older adults today continue to live at home and wish to age in place, staying in their communities as they grow older (Government of Canada, 2014c). The term "living arrangements" refers to the type of household an individual lives in. A household is defined as a person or group of persons who occupy the same dwelling and do not have a usual place of residence elsewhere in Canada (Statistics Canada, 2015g). This dwelling may be either a **private dwelling** (e.g., private house) or a **collective dwelling** (e.g., residence for senior citizens, nursing home, chronic-care facility). The type of household that an older adult needs is based on a number of factors. Those factors include health status, age, marital status, income, and functional abilities. Older adults in poor health, those in the upper age ranges, as well as those older adults who are single or have low incomes often are in need of more **supportive housing**. Now that you have an overview of the type of living arrangements of older adults, let's turn and examine in more detail where older adults live in Canada.

In 2011, there were nearly five million individuals aged 65 and over in Canada (Statistics Canada, 2012i). Of these older adults, you will be surprised to learn that the vast majority (92 percent) lived in private households or dwellings, with the remaining 8 percent living in collective dwellings. Of those older adults living in collective dwellings, you can see that some

FIGURE 13.1

LIVING ARRANGEMENTS OF SENIORS

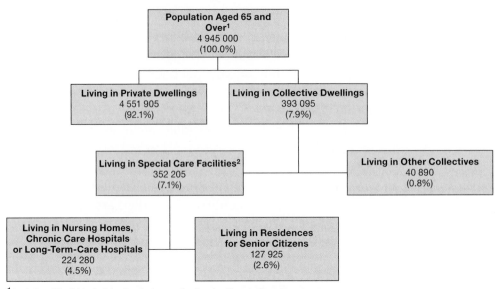

[1] Includes all individuals living in private or collective dwellings in Canada.
[2] Nursing homes, chronic care, long-term-care hospitals, and residences for senior citizens.

Source: Statistics Canada. (2012i). *Living arrangements of seniors. Families, households and marital status. Structural type of dwelling and collectives, 2011 Census of Population* (Catalogue no. 98-312-X2011003). Ottawa, ON: Author. Retrieved from www12.statcan.gc.ca/census-recensement/2011/as-sa/98-312-x/98-312-x2011003_4-eng.pdf.

lived in special-care facilities or in other collectives (e.g., rehabilitation hospitals, group homes). Those living in special-care facilities lived in either nursing homes, chronic-care, long-term-care hospitals, or residences for senior citizens (see Figure 13.1). We'll discuss each of these types of living arrangements shortly, including the advantages and disadvantages of each.

FACTORS AFFECTING THE LIVING ARRANGEMENTS OF OLDER ADULTS

A number of factors affect the living arrangements of older adults. Those factors include marital status, age, and sex. In 2011, most adults 65 years of age and older lived as a couple, either as a married spouse or as a common-law partner (Statistics Canada, 2012i). For example, in 2011, the majority of older adults (approximately 56.0 percent overall) lived as a couple, with seven out of ten (72.1 percent) older men and approximately four in ten (43.8 percent) older women living as a couple (Statistics Canada, 2012i). However, as depicted in the population pyramid in Figure 13.2, the number of older adults living as a couple decreases with age. Only one in ten centenarian men lived as part of a couple in 2011, while less than one in 100 centenarian women lived as part of a couple in this same time period (Statistics Canada, 2012i). You also can see from Figure 13.2 that both age and sex affect *where* older adults live. That is, the probability of living in a collective dwelling increases with age, with a greater number of older females living in collective dwellings than older males across the age ranges. The primary reason for this is that females live, on average, longer than their male counterparts. As such, older females are more likely to be widowed. The combination of increasing age and being widowed often serves as triggers for older women having to move into a collective dwelling. However, results from this same study indicated that over

FIGURE 13.2

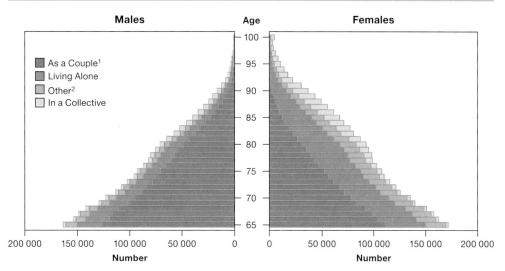

[1] Refers to married spouses and common-law partners.

[2] "Other" includes seniors who are lone parents, living with other relatives or non-relatives, or adult children living with their parent(s).

Source: Statistics Canada. (2012i). *Living arrangements of seniors. Families, households and marital status. Structural type of dwelling and collectives, 2011 Census of Population* (Catalogue no. 98-312-X2011003). Ottawa, ON: Author. Retrieved from http://www12.statcan.gc.ca/census-recensement/2011/as-sa/98-312-x/98-312-x2011003_4-eng.pdf.

one-half of adults 90 years of age and over lived in private households in 2011. And, among centenarians—people aged 100 and over—about one-third lived in private households in 2011 while two-thirds lived in collective dwellings. For men aged 100 and over, close to half lived in private households as did about one-third of women in this age group. Of interest, the overall proportions of housing arrangements of older adults are relatively unchanged from 2001 when 92.6 percent of the older-adult population lived in private households and 7.4 percent lived in collective dwellings such as nursing homes or residences for older adults (Statistics Canada, 2012i).

The percentage of older adults who live alone also changes with age and by gender. As shown in Figure 13.3, the percentage of older women living alone starts increasing at about age 55, with the percentage increasing sharply for older women between the ages of 70 and 85, followed by a decline. The trend for older men is quite different, with the percentage of men aged 65 to 85 and older living alone increasing somewhat but not nearly as much as that of same-aged older women. This gender difference is due to the lower life expectancies of men and the tendency for women to form unions with spouses or partners who are older than themselves. As a result, older women are more likely than older men to be widowed, and then subsequently live alone. Another interesting trend is the more dramatic decline in the percentage of older women who lived alone between 2001 and 2011 as compared to their same-aged male counterparts. This difference may be due partly to the fact that life expectancy for men has increased at a faster rate than for women in recent years. As a result, proportionally more older women have remained in couples until older ages (Statistics Canada, 2012i).

For many older adults, the presence of one or more illnesses and/or disabilities triggers a change in living arrangements. And, because of the strong association between age and illness, the percentage of the population aged 65 and over living in long-term-care facilities (also referred to as

FIGURE 13.3

PERCENTAGE OF THE POPULATION AGED 15 AND OVER LIVING ALONE BY AGE GROUP, CANADA, 2001 AND 2011

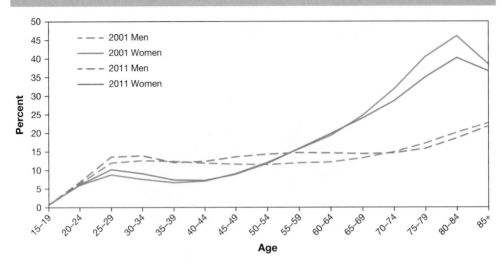

Source: Statistics Canada. (2012i). *Living arrangements of seniors. Families, households and marital status. Structural type of dwelling and collectives, 2011 Census of Population* (Catalogue no. 98-312-X2011003). Ottawa, ON: Author. Retrieved from http://www12.statcan.gc.ca/census-recensement/2011/as-sa/98-312-x/98-312-x2011003_4-eng.pdf.

special-care facilities) increases with age. As can be seen in Figure 13.4, in 2011, less than 5 percent of the Canadian population 65 to 70 years of age lived in long-term-care facilities (e.g., nursing homes, **chronic-care** or **long-term-care hospitals**, and **residences for senior citizens**). More evidence that most older adults do not live in long-term-care facilities! Although this number rises to almost 30 percent for adults 85 years of age and older, the majority of older adults are still not living in long-term-care facilities. Note that a higher percentage of women than men this age are living in long-term-care facilities. We will discuss long-term-care facilities in more detail later.

HOME OWNERSHIP

Home ownership is one of the most significant investments that individuals make, and this investment often results in the building of wealth over a lifetime (Hou, 2010). In Canada, home ownership rises quickly with age up to approximately age 40 and then climbs at a slower pace, until reaching a plateau at about age 65. Home ownership rates change very little between the ages of 65 and 74, and then start to decline from age 75 onwards (Hou, 2010). Notably, the majority of Canadians 65 years of age and older continue to own their homes for more than 10 years after the age of 65 (Hou, 2010). Of interest, recent statistics indicate that the **equity** that older adults have in their principal residence represents the second most significant share of overall **household wealth** (Lafrance & LaRochelle-Côté, 2012), with the primary source of income coming from employer-sponsored registered pension plans (e.g., RPPs/RIPs), public pension plans (e.g., Canada Pension Plan/Quebec Pension Plan, Old Age Security/Government Income Supplement), and private pension plans (Registered Retirement Savings Plans). As such, many older adults are able to maintain the standard of living that they had before retirement, including living in their own home. As you now know, older unattached individuals (and especially older females) are particularly disadvantaged in terms of

FIGURE 13.4

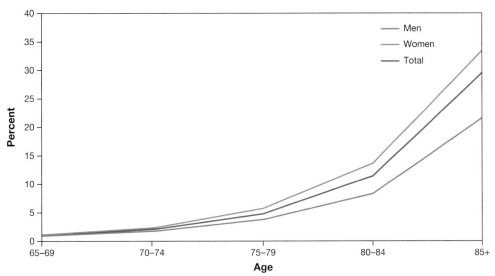

Source: Statistics Canada. (2012i). *Living arrangements of seniors. Families, households and marital status. Structural type of dwelling and collectives, 2011 Census of Population* (Catalogue no. 98-312-X2011003). Ottawa, ON: Author. Retrieved from http://www12.statcan.gc.ca/census-recensement/2011/as-sa/98-312-x/98-312-x2011003_4-eng.pdf.

living arrangements. These results have important implications when it comes to providing supportive living for this segment of the population. More about this later!

> What are your expectations about owning your own home?

REFLECTIVE QUESTION

PROGRAMS THAT FACILITATE HOME OWNERSHIP FOR OLDER ADULTS

There are a number of federal and provincial programs that can facilitate new or ongoing home ownership for older adults. A snapshot of these programs is provided in the following subsections.

HOME BUYER'S PLAN

The Home Buyer's Plan is a program that allows an individual to withdraw up to $25 000 in a calendar year from their Registered Retirement Savings Plans (RRSPs) to buy or build a qualifying home for themselves or for a related person with a disability (Government of Canada, 2017a). As such, this program may enable an older adult or an older couple to continue to live in the community by building a home that would accommodate their disability. However, there are conditions associated with this program. For example, the individual applying to the Home Buyer's Plan must be a first-time home buyer (i.e., the applicant must not have not occupied a home that she or her current spouse owned in the previous four years). However, individuals can qualify as first-time home buyers if they have a disability or they are helping a related person with a disability buy or build a qualifying home. More detailed information can be found at www.cra-arc.gc.ca/hbp.

HOME MAINTENANCE PROGRAMS

Canada Mortgage and Housing Corporation's (CMHC's) Programs and Financial Assistance offers financial assistance for new affordable housing; to upgrade existing housing that may be in need of renovations or accessibility modifications; and provide rent subsidies for individuals and families in need (CMHC, 2017a).

RESIDENTIAL REHABILITATION ASSISTANCE PROGRAM (RRAP) SECONDARY/ GARDEN SUITE ON-RESERVE

The federal government's RRAP provides financial assistance to First Nations owning residential properties for the creation of a self-contained secondary or garden suite. Households who will occupy the newly created self-contained unit must have an income at or below an established income threshold (see CMHC, 2017b).

VETERANS INDEPENDENCE PROGRAM

The Veterans Independence Program (VIP) helps veterans with war injuries and/or disabilities remain independent and self-sufficient in their home and community (Government of Canada, 2017b). Funds are available for home adaptations to modify areas such as bathrooms, kitchens, and doorways so that the individual can more easily carry out basic activities of daily living. Examples of eligible modifications are ramps, handrails, chair lifts, bath lifts, height adjustments to countertops, and cues for doorbells/fire alarms. Funding is based on eligibility and an occupational therapist's assessment.

INVESTMENT IN AFFORDABLE HOUSING PROGRAM

The CMHC also has allocated approximately $240 million toward new and existing affordable housing through the Investment in Affordable Housing (IAH) program (see CMHC, 2017c). The IAH program gives individual provincial and territorial governments in Canada the flexibility to provide affordable housing programs that meet community housing needs. Under the IAH program, provinces and territories match the CMHC's investment and report to their citizens on how they are using the funding to improve access to affordable housing. Adults aged 65 and older are one of the target groups for this program.

REVERSE MORTGAGES

For some older adults, the cost of owning and maintaining a home can be prohibitive. For a number of older adults, the house can be **liquidated** for retirement income (e.g., income for everyday costs of living, travel, other needs) (Financial Consumer Agency of Canada, 2015; Thomas, 2005) or for paying for care. One means of liquidating the house is through a reverse mortgage. You may have seen advertisements on television about a CHIP (Canadian Home Income Plan) reverse mortgage. **Reverse mortgages** are loans that allow homeowners 55 years of age and older to borrow against the equity in their home, which is the portion of the home's value that is debt-free, in exchange for offering the home as **collateral**. The amount of money that is available to the homeowner is based on the appraised value of the house, the age and gender of the homeowners, marital status, property type, and location.

Although reverse mortgages have been available in the United States for many years, they have only been available in Canada since 1986. The advantages and disadvantages of reverse mortgages are shown in Table 13.1.

Who might benefit from a reverse mortgage? Reverse mortgages were originally designed for lower-income older adults, and it appears that this segment of the older population who is house-rich and cash-poor can benefit from a reverse mortgage. The Financial Consumer Agency of Canada has developed a tip sheet on Understanding Reverse Mortgages (see www.fcac-acfc .gc.ca/eng/resources/publications/mortgages/Pages/Understa-Comprend.aspx).

What are some alternatives to a reverse mortgage? Options include **refinancing an existing mortgage**, taking out a **home-equity loan**, taking out a home-equity line of credit, and selling the home and/or **downsizing**. Each of these alternatives has benefits and risks, and, as with many other financial transactions, careful consideration of the advantages, disadvantages, and risks in the context of an individual's overall financial plan is needed.

What housing options, resources, and programs are available in your community to help older adults meet their current and future housing needs?

TABLE 13.1

ADVANTAGES AND DISADVANTAGES OF REVERSE MORTGAGES

ADVANTAGES	DISADVANTAGES
You can convert some of the equity of your home into cash for income, home repairs, or emergencies.	Since you are not making any payments, your equity will steadily **decrease** for as long as you have the reverse mortgage.
You will continue to be the owner of your home.	As long as you are the owner of your home, you will remain responsible for all repairs and taxes.
The money that you get from your reverse mortgage is not taxable.	Reverse mortgages are relatively expensive and this includes a higher interest rate for reverse mortgages than for a traditional mortgage or line of credit.
Most reverse mortgages don't require you to make any payments on the principal for as long as you live in your home.	When you and your spouse die or sell the home, all loans must be repaid in full with interest. This includes any fees or charges that have accumulated.
This income does not affect the Old-Age Security (OAS) or Guaranteed Income Supplement (GIS) benefits that you may be receiving.	The costs associated with a reverse mortgage are usually quite high. They can include, but are not limited to, the following: • a higher interest rate than for a traditional mortgage or line of credit; • a home appraisal fee, an application fee, or closing fees; • a repayment penalty for selling your house or moving out within three years of obtaining a reverse mortgage; and legal fees.

Source: Financial Consumer Agency of Canada. (2015). *Understanding reverse mortgages*. Retrieved from www.fcac-acfc.gc.ca/eng/resources/publications/mortgages/Pages/Understa-Comprend.aspx.

13.2 AGING IN PLACE

LEARNING OBJECTIVES

To understand:

- aging in place
- the home adaptations that facilitate aging in place
- the role of technology to support aging in place
- the characteristics and advantages of age-friendly communities

WHAT IS AGING IN PLACE?

The concept of "aging in place" is a relatively new term in gerontology, and has numerous meanings (Pastalan, 1990). The early definition of aging in place referred to older individuals growing old in their own homes with an emphasis on modification of the home environment to compensate for the limitations and disabilities that can occur with the aging process (Pynoos, 1993). However, the term has evolved over time, with aging in place defined as "remaining living in the community, with some level of independence, rather than in residential care" (Davey, Nana, de Joux, & Arcus, 2004, p. 133), "the ability to live in one's own home and community safely, independently, and comfortably, regardless of age, income, or ability level" (Centers for Disease Control and Prevention, 2013, para. 4), and "having the health and social supports and services you need to live safely and independently in your home or your community for as long as you wish and are able" (Federal/Provincial/Territorial Ministers Responsible for Seniors, 2012, p. 2). More recently, aging in place has evolved and related terms include **age-friendly cities** (World Health Organization [WHO], 2007), **age-friendly cities and communities** (WHO, 2008), and an **age-friendly world** (WHO, 2016d).

The concept of aging in place is related to early work conducted by Lawton (1982), which emphasized the role of the interaction between personal competence and the physical home environment in older people's well-being. The interaction between personal competence and environment is reflected in what is called **competence–environmental press**. The competence–environmental press approach is a good example of a theory that incorporates the biological and psychological abilities of the individual (physical and functional health, cognitive and affective functioning, quality of life, and sense of efficacy or mastery) with the individual's home environment, their neighbourhood environment, and their social environment. Fundamental to the approach is the interaction between the person and the environment. Optimal fit occurs when an individual's abilities are consistent with the demands of their environment.

In addition to Lawton's work, Baltes and Baltes' (1990) presented a useful framework for explaining successful adaptation to aging. This model argues that at all stages of human development, individuals manage their lives successfully through three processes—**selection**, **optimization**, and **compensation**—with these processes helping individuals to maximize gains and minimize losses over time. For example, an older woman who relocates to a smaller apartment following the death of her spouse because she can no longer maintain the house engages in the process of selection. In addition, her choice of a small apartment, rather than a more protective setting such as a seniors' lodge, reflects the process of optimization in that it allows her to live more independently. And, her decision to have housekeeping services once a month for the heavier housecleaning reflects the process of compensation.

Both personal and environmental resources contribute to aging well (Wahl, Iwarsson, & Oswald, 2012). For example, individuals' attachment to their place or places over time, their perceived control of their physical environment, the relationship between the demands of their physical environment and their functional abilities (including their use of compensatory strategies to deal with declines in functional abilities) all play an important role in an older person's ability to remain independent for as long as possible as well as help them maintain their identity and well-being (Wahl & Oswald, 2010). There also is consensus that although the physical environment has the potential to impose significant constraints in late life, it also may enhance opportunities for aging well. Housing figures prominently in the lives of older adults, who tend to prefer to age in place (Frank, 2002). Results from recent surveys support these claims. In a 2013 Ipsos Reid survey of 2159 Canadian adults aged 50 and over, approximately 91 percent indicated that "staying in their home or in their neighbourhood close to family and friends" was very/somewhat appealing and that they wished to live independently as long as possible. Similar results have been reported by the AARP (American Association of Retired Persons), with 90 percent of Americans over the age of 65 wanting to stay in their home for as long as possible, and with 80 percent believing that their current residence is where they will always live (National Conference of State Legislatures & AARP Public Policy Institute, 2011). It also is noteworthy that the majority (>80 percent) of respondents in the 2013 Ipsos Reid survey rated "staying in their home and paying for home care" as very/somewhat appealing. Few respondents (<25 percent) found "living with family" very/somewhat appealing and even fewer (<15 percent) found receiving care in a long-term-care facility as very/somewhat appealing. Interestingly, the results from this survey were similar irrespective of whether respondents were retired or not retired. In this same Ipsos Reid survey, a change in health was the most common reason given for retired Canadians to move out of their home, with 66 percent of respondents indicating that this was the trigger that forced a change in residence.

HOME ADAPTATIONS THAT FACILITATE AGING IN PLACE

In 2005, almost two-thirds of older adults in Canada were considered to be in good functional health (Statistics Canada, 2006a). Despite these positive findings, some older adults do experience limitations in functional abilities because of long-term health conditions. These changes make aging in place difficult due to impairment in their Activities of Daily Living (ADLs) and Instrumental Activities of Daily Living (IADLs). Fortunately, there are a number of adaptations that can be made to the home that can not only enhance independence but also help to prevent accidents in the home. These housing adaptations can take many forms including improvements in lighting; installation of handrails, grab bars, and/or ramps; installation of reachable cupboards, storage, and door handles; and elimination of carpets and throw rugs to prevent falls. The CMHC has developed a *Maintaining Senior's Independence through Home Adaptations: A Self-Assessment Guide* (CMHC, 2012a) to assist older adults identify and implement minor home adaptations that can help them to remain in their homes.

How many older adults take advantage of these home adaptations? Surprisingly, there has not been a lot of research in this area (Gitlin, 2003), with this research falling under the field of **environmental gerontology**. In a 2009 study, Stark and colleagues implemented home modifications in a sample of 80 older community-dwelling adults (average age of 82), with the modifications based on a preliminary needs assessment. Modifications included installation of adaptive equipment (tub bench), architectural modifications (ramps), and major home renovations (roll-on shower). Training also was provided in the use of compensatory supports and strategies. The interventions had an overall positive effect on performance of daily activities, with the participants reporting satisfaction immediately post-intervention.

An important component of this study was the investigation of the importance of the role of personal **autonomy** to older adults in decisions about independent living. For example, in an earlier study, Steinfeld and Shea (2001) examined the types of barriers that older adults with functional impairments (e.g., visual impairments, use of a wheelchair, semi-ambulant, dementia) face. In the study, participants were provided with a free home assessment with recommendations for interventions through home modifications or other related services. Participants who were either renters or homeowners were then randomly split into two groups: the first group received only the free home assessment (i.e., the control group), and the second group received additional technical assistance and referral services to help implement any of the recommended services (i.e., the experimental group). The researchers then followed up with an interview 18 months later to identify which recommendations had been implemented. An interesting finding was that the individuals in the experimental group implemented twice as many recommendations as the control group, which suggests that availability of technical assistance and knowledge of referral services are needed to enact change. Results from follow-up interviews also indicated that *perceived lack of control* over the circumstances was given as the reason for inaction, with this reason given irrespective of whether the participant was a renter or homeowner. Why is this finding so important? There now is a substantial body of research that shows that *active participation* in one's own well-being hinges in part on the belief that one is capable of having some control over one's own successful functioning within one's particular environment (Mallers, Claver, & Lares, 2013). However, stereotypes of older adults abound including beliefs that they have declining capacities and are incapable of making responsible decisions. It becomes even more serious when older adults buy into these aging stereotypes.

Other factors that can affect the implementation or use of home adaptations by older adults are stigmatization and stereotypes. That is, home adaptations may be viewed negatively in that they symbolize a loss of function and abilities (Aplin, de Jonge, & Gustafsson, 2014; Gitlin, 1995). The adoption of home adaptations also may be perceived as reinforcement of one of the negative stereotypes of aging, which depict later life as a time of ill health, dependency, and poor physical and mental functioning (Diongi, 2015). Let's turn now and look at the role of technology to support aging in place.

ROLE OF TECHNOLOGY TO SUPPORT AGING IN PLACE

An older adult's ability to age in place has a number of benefits including the ability to maintain contact with family and friends, as well as continuing to be engaged in their community. Aging in place also can help to reduce societal costs associated with the provision of healthcare services and long-term-care. Assistive technologies such as hearing aids and assistive listening devices (amplified telephones, personal voice amplifiers, alerting systems, remote control speaker phones), vision aids (glasses, magnifiers, large-print telephones and clocks, remote control speakerphones, mobility lights), and communication (choice board, communication placemat, request cards) and mobility aids (canes, walkers, wheelchairs) allow an older adult to age in place. **Smart environments** also can facilitate an older adult's ability to age in place (Chan, Campo, Esteve, & Fourniols, 2009). Specifically, smart homes can enhance in-home safety of older adults and monitor health conditions through the use of technology, thereby enhancing an older adult's independence and quality of life. Examples of smart homes include the Place Lab (MIT) and the Gator Tech Home Smart House for the Elderly in Florida. In the 2500 square foot Gator Tech single-family home, researchers test technologies to help older people who are living alone. For example, their experiments have included a smart mirror that gives reminders to take medication, a smart closet that suggests clothing based on the weather, and a smart bathtub that regulates water temperature to prevent scalding. A smart toilet also will inform an outside service centre when toilet paper needs refilling. In the kitchen, a smart microwave uses radio-frequency identification to determine what a person wants to eat. It also plays a video of how to open the food item and will alert the resident on a display when the food is ready to eat (see http://techable .world/the-future-of-elder-care-robots-smart-homes-and-other-aging-in-place-technologies/). In addition to the smart home features just mentioned, there are now robot companions and talking pets that make it easier for older adults to live at home (see Figure 13.5).

How effective are these smart homes at enabling aging in place? There is a growing body of literature on the effectiveness of and acceptance of smart technology by older adults. For example, in a clinical trial using smart technology, 113 older adults living alone in their own homes were randomized to treatment ($n = 46$) and control ($n = 67$) groups in order to determine the effect of smart technology on functional abilities (Tomita, Mann, Stanton, Tomita, & Sundar, 2007). All participants were at least 60 years of age, were cognitively intact, and had difficulties in ADLs or IADLs. Results indicated that although the groups were equivalent in function at the beginning of the trial, there were significant differences in mobility, cognition, and IADL function between the two groups at the end of the trial, with older adults using the technology having significantly better mobility.

In Canada, research is being conducted at the Toronto Rehabilitation Institute on smart technology and its application to older adults. Mihailidis and colleagues are developing and testing cognitive assistive technologies such as robot companions, intuitive devices such as sensor systems that detect falls, and intelligent homes. One of their experiments involves a mobile robotic in a simulated home lab. Equipped with a video screen face and wheels for feet, ED the robot gives voice prompts to assist people with dementia on how to make tea and wash their hands (see link to video at http://globalnews.ca/news/2648777/

FIGURE 13.5

GERIJOY ROBOT COMPANION

Source: Courtesy of care.coach.corporation

how-a-robot-could-help-your-family-member-with-dementia-and-aging/). The development of technologies related to the needs of older adults has fostered the emergence of what is called **geron-technology** (also called "gerotechnology"). We bet you didn't know that gerontechnology has captured the attention of start-up companies, venture capital investors, and high-tech corporations, including those in Silicon Valley! There's Seniorly, a two-year-old San Francisco-based start-up that provides a free online platform to make navigating the confusing world of assisted-living facilities as easy as booking an Airbnb. San Bruno-based CareLinx and San Francisco-based Honor let users summon caregivers on demand via online platforms or mobile apps, paying the caregivers a set rate for hours or months of care. And both Lyft and Uber have launched programs to shuttle older adults to doctors' appointments and other errands even if they don't have smartphones—a service also provided by independent start-ups like GoGoGrandparent (see www.mercurynews.com/2016/09/29/on-demand-style-services-for-seniors/).

How accepting are older adults of this smart technology? This is another important area of research today! For example, Charness and colleagues are studying factors affecting the adoption of new technologies (e.g., the Internet, smartphones, healthcare technology in the home) that can improve quality of life and extend functional independence (Charness & Best, 2009; Charness, Best, & Evans, 2016). There is a considerable amount of research indicating that older adults are open to the use of smart technology if doing so would improve their safety, independence, and quality of life and allow them to stay in their own homes longer (Demiris, Hensel, Skubic, & Rantz, 2008; Demiris, Oliver, Dickey, Skubic, & Rantz, 2008; Jacelon & Hanson, 2012; Johnson, Davenport, & Mann, 2007; Tomita et al., 2007). Older adults also have indicated that smart technology is more likely to be well received if it is not too costly, not intrusive, reliable, and user-friendly. On the other hand, older adults have expressed concerns about privacy and who has access to their information (Jacelon & Hanson, 2012). Older adults who are most likely to benefit from smart technology are those who are cognitively impaired (e.g., Alzheimer's disease, dementia), those who need help with IADLs or ADLs, and those living in rural or remote communities with limited access to health services. Interventions that support aging in place go beyond the personal home. Let's turn now and look at the characteristics of the community that can help older adults age in place.

REFLECTIVE QUESTION

What can be done to increase awareness and use of smart technology in the older-adult population?

CHARACTERISTICS OF AN AGE-FRIENDLY COMMUNITY

What does an age-friendly community look like? In communities that are age-friendly, the policies, the services, and the structures related to the physical and **social environment** are designed to help older adults "age actively" (Public Health Agency of Canada, 2011b). In other words, in an age-friendly community, the community is set up to help old adults live safely, enjoy good health, and stay involved. The characteristics of an age-friendly community are provided in Table 13.2.

How can a community become more age-friendly? In the **ecological model of aging**, Lawton and Nahemow (1973) argue that human behaviour and well-being are seen as being strongly related to the environment where the individual lives as well as to the individual's capabilities. Consistent with this model, the physical features of the neighbourhood (e.g., mix of residential development,

TABLE 13.2

What Does an Age-Friendly Community Look Like?

In an age-friendly community:

- outdoor areas and public buildings are pleasant, safe, and accessible*
- housing is affordable, safe, and well designed for seniors
- roads and walkways are accessible and kept in good shape
- public transportation is affordable and accessible neighbourhoods are safe
- relationships are respectful
- health and community support services are available
- opportunities for seniors to be socially active exist
- seniors can take part in volunteer, political, and employment positions; and
- information is easy to find and easy to understand.

* Easy to get to and can be used by everyone.

shops, community and recreation facilities, parks and open space), neighbourhood characteristics and amenities (e.g., pedestrian infrastructure that is well maintained, an adequate number of benches, the presence of street lights), low traffic volume and flow, adequate public transportation (e.g., adequate transit routes, physical design of bus stops), and enjoyable scenery all can play a role in supporting the mobility of older residents in their neighbourhood (Cauwenberg et al., 2011; Grant, Edwards, Sveistrup, Andrew, & Egan, 2010a; 2010b; Michael, Gold, Perrin, & Hillier, 2011; Rosenberg, Huang, Simonovich, & Belza, 2013; Rosso, Grubesic, Auchincloss, Tabb, & Michael, 2013). Perceived safety and trust among neighbours also are associated with increased engagement in physical activity (Yen & Anderson, 2012), increases in psychological well-being (Greenfield & Reyes, 2015), improvements in self-rated health (Norstrand & Chan, 2014), and decreases in functional impairments (Keysor et al., 2010). Neighbourhood characteristics such as noise, safety/crime, cleanliness, lighting, and availability of public transportation have been associated with health and functioning of older adults (Rosso et al., 2013; Yen, Michael, & Perdue, 2009). Importantly, older adults also are more vulnerable to the influence of their residential environment as they tend to travel less often outside their own neighbourhoods. Declines in physical and/or mental health, smaller social networks, and loss of social support also can reduce an older individual's ability to cope with neighbourhood environments that are not age-friendly (Rosso, Auchincloss, & Michael, 2011; Rosso et al., 2013).

Meeting the mobility needs of older adults is critical to their being able to age in place. Although most older adults are licensed to drive, licensing rates do decline with age due to the presence of one or more illnesses. In Canada, almost 80 percent of adults 65 to 74 years of age hold a valid driver's licence. However, this decreases to less than 20 percent for those aged 90 and older (Turcotte, 2012). Older women are in double jeopardy when it comes to transportation mobility in that they are not only more likely to be non-drivers but also are more likely to be widowed than their same-aged male counterparts (with their husbands most often in charge of driving). What this means is that, overall, as one gets older, the probability of having to rely on other forms of transportation (i.e., being driven by someone else, relying on public transportation) increases significantly. Although public transportation often is seen as the solution to maintaining mobility when driving is no longer an option, factors leading to not driving in older adults also serve as barriers to using conventional forms of public transportation. Those barriers include long walks to bus stops, long wait times (and often without any benches available), difficulty getting on and off buses, difficulty transporting parcels such as groceries, and concerns about personal safety (Peck, 2010). In Canada, our long winters present additional challenges. Given these barriers, it is not surprising that only 6 percent of older adults use conventional forms of public transportation (e.g., buses and Light Rail Transit) as a means of getting where they want to go, with public transit often becoming "the mode of last resort" (Alsnih & Hensher, 2003, p. 10). In a recent telephone survey of 2296 adults aged 45 to 64, adults 65 years of age and older, and persons with disabilities (PWD) 18 years of age and older, Dobbs and Pidborochynski (2016) found that older adults and PWD in communities throughout the Alberta Capital Region had unmet transportation needs. *Non-driving* adults 65 and older had more than a four-fold increase in unmet transportation needs as compared to *drivers* aged 65 and older, and PWD had more than double the unmet transportation needs as compared to *non-drivers* aged 65 and older.

What can be done to help older adults in meeting their mobility needs? Implementation of alternative forms of transportation outside of conventional forms of transportation (e.g., public transportation, private vehicle) is a viable and responsive solution. In a national and international scan to identify unique and/or promising **alternative transportation for seniors** (ATS) models and innovative solutions, Dobbs, Lee, and Song (2011) identified 178 ATS service providers in Australia, Canada, the United Kingdom, and the United States meeting study criteria. Most of the providers were not-for-profit (e.g., community-based programs provided by seniors' centres, Handi-Van societies) with the remainder being for-profit (e.g., Driving Miss Daisy). Not surprisingly, there is a greater diversity of ATS service provider models in urban settings versus rural settings. Low population densities (e.g., small towns, villages, and hamlets) and large geographical areas present challenges in providing ATS service provision in rural areas. Yet, older adults in rural areas have more unmet needs than their urban counterparts because of the deficiencies of alternative forms of transportation in rural areas. These results highlight the importance of implementing ATS service provision in rural Canada that is both responsive and sustainable.

What are the implications of lack of transportation for older adults? Not having a ride means that many older adults are unable to get to their medical appointments, shop for groceries, or attend social and spiritual activities in their communities. Use of ride-scheduling software is a new trend in providing ATS service. This ride-scheduling software has many benefits (e.g., rides can be scheduled online, drivers' and riders' locations can be monitored, cost of rides can be calculated, etc.). You might be surprised to know that Lyft and Uber now see the over-65 age group as an important segment of their service population (see www.smithsonianmag.com/innovation/lyft-uber-want-to-give-old-folks-ride-180961688/).

ADVANTAGES OF AN AGE-FRIENDLY COMMUNITY

Currently, there is a limited amount of research on the impact that age-friendly communities have on older adults. However, research on how the social and physical characteristics of a neighbourhood influence the health and well-being of older adults is growing in quality and quantity (Beard et al., 2009; Beard & Petitot, 2010; Freedman, Grafova, Schoeni, & Rogowski, 2008; Lager, Van Hoven, & Huigen, 2016; Norstrand & Chan, 2014; Rosso et al., 2011; Yen et al., 2009). There are a number of valuable resources to assist communities in becoming age-friendly. One of those resources is the *WHO Global Age-Friendly Cities: A Guide* (see Figure 13.6). Another valuable resource is the *Age-Friendly Communities in Canada: Community Implementation Guide* (Public Health Agency of Canada, 2012). There also is a guide to assist rural and remote communities to become more age-friendly (Federal/Provincial/Territorial Ministers Responsible

FIGURE 13.6

Reprinted from World Health Organization. (2007). *Global age-friendly cities: a guide,* http://www.who.int/ageing/publications/Global_agy_friendly_cities_Guide_English.pdf. Reprinted by permission.

for Seniors, 2008). In Canada, all 10 provinces are promoting age-friendly initiatives. To learn more about what is being done in each of these provinces, go to www.phac-aspc.gc.ca/seniors -aines/afc-caa-eng.php#sec2.

How age-friendly is your community?

13.3 HOUSING TRANSITIONS

LEARNING OBJECTIVES

To understand:
- the different housing options for older adults
- the availability and cost of supportive housing in Canada
- new models of care for older adults

Although most older adults prefer to remain living in their own homes, living arrangements do change for a significant number of older adults. For those needing to make a transition, there are several housing options available that cater to a wide range of needs and personal preferences of older adults.

HOUSING OPTIONS FOR OLDER ADULTS

In Canada, housing matters are primarily within the jurisdiction of provincial and territorial governments. All provinces and territories, as well as many municipalities, provide housing information to older adults, often via information lines or counselling specialists. In addition, several federal government departments and agencies (e.g., CMHC, Veterans Affairs Canada, and Health Canada) have programs and information on housing that can be of great value to older adults and their children.

CMHC has developed a continuum of housing options that includes the range of housing types and services that older adults need in order for them to age in place. Those housing options consist of mainstream housing, independent living accommodation, assisted-living facilities, and long-term-care accommodation (CMHC, 2012b). Mainstream housing includes the housing that older adults have occupied their working lives as well as housing for older adults who down-size to condominiums or rental apartments. Independent living accommodation is designed to accommodate older adults in need of minimal assistance with their daily living activities. Adult lifestyle communities, which often combine accommodation with recreational facilities and ame-nities, are a form of independent living accommodation. Independent living accommodation can be in the form of rental or **freehold**. Assisted-living accommodation is intended for older adults who require more personalized levels of service (e.g., from meal preparation and house-keeping to bathing, dressing, and taking medications). This type of accommodation typically consists of rental units within an apartment building/complex that also is a retirement residence. Assisted-living accommodation also includes a range of supportive housing options that includes on- or off-site delivery of personal-care services and/or recreational activities that are available to residents of the facility as well as to older adults living in the surrounding neighbourhood or community. The last type of accommodation for older adults is long-term-care accommodation. Long-term-care accommodation includes nursing homes, continuing-care facilities, and long-term-care facilities or hospitals. Long-term-care accommodation is designed for individuals who can no longer live independently and who require 24-hour care and supervision.

INDEPENDENT LIVING OPTIONS

SINGLE-FAMILY HOMES

In 2011, slightly more than 50 percent of older adults in Canada lived in single-detached homes, but this percentage decreases with age (see Table 13.3). You also can see in Table 13.3 that the proportion of older adults living in apartments, other than duplexes, increases with age.

INDEPENDENT LIVING COMMUNITIES

Other names for independent living communities are 55+ communities, active adult communities, adult lifestyle communities, life-lease communities, retirement communities, retirement homes, seniors' apartments, and seniors' housing. Independent living communities are designed for healthy, active older adults who do not need assistance with ADLs such as grooming, personal care, and eating. Typical independent living features include apartment-style one- or two-bedroom units in a community setting; convenient location to retail shops and recreational activities; community features such as gardens, pools, golf courses, hair salons, and fitness centres; and options for housekeeping, meals, laundry, and transportation. These communities are typically private pay. Depending on the location, community, and amenity options, costs can range from $1400 to $3500 per month (A Place for Mom, 2016).

Another independent living option for older adults is a garden suite. A "garden suite," which also is called a granny flat, a coach or carriage house, or a Fonzie suite, is a self-contained dwelling unit without a basement. It is installed in the rear or side of a yard of a lot within an existing

TABLE 13.3

STRUCTURE TYPE BY AGE OF PRIMARY HOUSEHOLD MAINTAINER, CANADA, 2011*			
DWELLING TYPE	**55 TO 64 (PERCENTAGE)**	**65 TO 74 (PERCENTAGE)**	**75+ YEARS (PERCENTAGE)**
Single-detached	62	59	52
Semi-detached	5	4	4
Apartment (5+ storeys)	7	10	15
Apartment (< 5 storeys)	14	16	19
Apartment (duplex)	5	5	4
Row house	5	5	5

*Include all households, regardless of tenure.

Source: Canada Mortgage and Housing Corporation. (2012b). *Housing for older Canadians.: The definitive guide to the over-55 market*. Retrieved from www.cmhc-schl.gc.ca/odpub/pdf/67514.pdf.; and Statistics Canada (2011f). *National Household Survey*.

FIGURE 13.7

Courtesy of the Canadian Mortgage and Housing Corporation.

permanent single-family home. Garden suites are usually intended for individuals or couples over the age of 65, with the people living in the permanent dwelling (usually family members) providing support, companionship, and security to the occupants of the garden suite. In addition to being an affordable solution for taking care of family members, granny suites provide a healthy and supportive living environment that can enable individuals to continue to live independently longer (CMHC, 2014). Garden suites must meet the National Building Code of Canada requirements, and they are typically governed by municipal planning or zoning regulations. If new, the cost of a garden suite can range from between $45 000 and $85 000 (Cleverley, 2014). A picture of a traditional garden suite is shown in Figure 13.7. Recently, shipping container homes have been introduced into Canada. As the name suggests, these homes are made out of shipping containers (see Figure 13.8). The units range from $99 000 Canadian for a studio to $147 000 for a two-bedroom suite.

ADULT DAY PROGRAMS

Adult day programs are an important component of community-based care services for frail older adults in Canada and the United States. Adult day programs consist of daycare in a service facility with a focus on assessment and treatment. The Comprehensive Home Option of Integrated Care for the Elderly (CHOICE) is modelled after the Program for All-inclusive Care (PACE) in the United States. The CHOICE program in Edmonton, Alberta, was developed in 1996 and was the first program of its kind in Canada. CHOICE is a comprehensive community-based model of coordinated care that helps to support older people who are experiencing multiple ongoing health problems. The goals of the program are to allow clients to remain living independently in

FIGURE 13.8

ChompooSuppa/Shutterstock.com

their own homes longer and to reduce their use of emergency room and in-patient services. The program offers recreational activities, physiotherapy, occupational therapy, and social work, as well as 24-hour on-call services and a 10-bed treatment centre that is used for management of acute illnesses and for respite. In a recent study that looked at whether the CHOICE programs in Edmonton reduced the use of emergency room (ER) visits and in-patient services, Samuel and colleagues (2015) found that the average number of ER visits, hospital admissions, and falls decreased significantly in the year following CHOICE enrollment compared to the year before they enrolled in the program.

HOME CARE

Many older adults with illnesses that impair their ability to function independently wish to remain in their homes for as long as possible. Home care, which consists of assistance with personal care, medical care, transportation, home maintenance, and/or financial management, can help individuals with long-term health conditions to live at home with independence and dignity. All Canadian provinces and territories provide home care services. In 2012, 2.2 million Canadians (8 percent) 15 years of age and older received home care (Turcotte, 2014). Older adults were by far the most likely to receive home care, with 10 percent of those 65 to 74, 21 percent of those 75 to 84, and 45 percent of those aged 85 and older receiving home care (Turcotte, 2014). You might be wondering how many older adults are falling through the cracks. The good news is that even though older adults are more likely than others to receive home care, they are less likely to have unmet needs when it comes to receiving home care (Busque & Légaré, 2012; Turcotte, 2014). Why might this be? Older adults are more likely to have a regular physician, who would likely ensure their patients receive home care as needed. In addition, many home care services are primarily intended for older adults. Finally, more older adults are living in institutions than those under age 65 and, as such, are not included in general surveys on unmet home care needs. In terms of benefits, home care is less expensive than **residential care**. In terms of cost, private home-care service can cost from $12 to $90 per hour for personal care or nursing care (Canadian Life and Health Insurance Association, 2015). It often is assumed that older adults are happier living at home than in residential care. However, the evidence for this is scarce. In a study by Canadian researchers, Chappel and colleagues (2004) found that ratings on life satisfaction were similar between older adults receiving home care and those receiving residential care. However, research from Japan shows that, in terms of quality of life, the life satisfaction of older adults living in a residential care home was significantly higher than that of their counterparts living in the community (Ho et al., 2003; Wolff, 2012). It may be that age makes a difference: Rodriguez-Blazquez et al. (2012) found that older adults who are younger are happier at home, while adults over 78 years of age are happier in residential care. It appears that the amount of support needed increases with age, with residential care facilities more able to provide a higher level of support.

REFLECTIVE QUESTION

Why do you think that older adults living in residential care facilities rate their satisfaction with life higher than older adults receiving home care?

ASSISTED-LIVING FACILITIES

Assisted-living facilities are a type of housing that provides hospitality services and personal assistance, in addition to housing, to older adults who can live independently but require some assistance with ADLs. Hospitality services typically include some or all meals, housekeeping, laundry, and social and recreational opportunities. Personal assistance can include assistance with eating, dressing, bathing, grooming, mobility, and medications, and 24-hour emergency service. Other names for assisted-living facilities in Canada are personal-care homes, special-care homes, supportive living facilities, community care facilities, and enriched living. On the continuum of care for older adults, assisted-living facilities fall between home care and long-term-care.

Assisted-living facilities come in all shapes and sizes. They can be towering apartment buildings in urban centres, sprawling complexes in the suburbs, or smaller, more intimate complexes with a relatively small number of residents. Assisted-living facilities have fewer regulatory requirements than licensed nursing homes but there is considerable variability in the requirements across provinces and territories. Assisted-living facilities can be run by for-profit or not-for-profit organizations, with some assisted-living facilities having both publicly funded and non-publicly funded units. Some assisted-living facilities charge a fee for each service on an a la carte basis, allowing residents to pay only for services they use. In addition to these charges, entrance fees and deposits also may be required. Costs of assisted living can range from $1500 to $5000 per month, depending on location of the community, amenity options, and whether medical or health services are needed (A Place for Mom, 2016).

In many instances, assisted living is a care option that is an intermediate step between living at home and living in long-term-care. What triggers a move from assisted living to long-term-care? In a recent study, Maxwell and colleagues (2013) looked at the factors that were predictive of nursing home placement from assisted-living facilities in Canada. They found that older age (75 to 84 years), the presence of cognitive and/or functional impairment, recent falls and hospitalizations/emergency room visits, incontinence, little involvement in activities, and having poor social relations all were factors that were predictive of nursing home placement (i.e., placement in a long-term-care facility).

LONG-TERM-CARE FACILITIES

Before discussing long-term-care facilities, it is important to first discuss what long-term-care is and the goals of long-term-care. Long-term-care is for individuals (most often adults 65 years of age and older) with chronic and (often) irreversible illness or disability. The goal of long-term-care is not to cure but to improve the quality of a person's remaining life. In general, long-term-care is provided in facilities such as **nursing homes**, **continuing-care facilities**, and

BOX 13.1

ACCOMMODATING BABY BOOMERS

Going forward, a number of changes will be needed to assistive living facilities to meet the needs of the baby boomers. When building a new facility or remodelling or expanding an existing facility, consideration of private rooms will be necessary. Boomers will want autonomy, and they will prefer to live the remainder of their years in a meaningful way where they control what and when they eat, when they go to bed and get up, and what activities are best suited to their interests. Personal choice will be more important to the next generation of residents, making them more likely than the current population to demand flexible scheduling options. They will appreciate access to transportation should they wish to leave a facility for outings such as physician appointments, shopping, or meeting friends. They will want to reside in a place that complements their lifestyles, with comfortable living and the ability to obtain good medical care for physical issues. Facilities also will need to address communication needs. The expectation will be for Internet access to help residents keep in touch with family, friends, and social networks as well as the rest of the world. Activities also will need to change to meet baby boomers' expectations. Adding space for activities will be important as will hiring fitness trainers to help prevent injuries and creating exercise rooms with appropriate equipment as well as contracting with specialized eldercare yoga and tai chi instructors. Replacing a large activity room with smaller rooms that could become destinations for residents will be attractive to boomers. A library, for instance, is a potential destination for all residents, which could offer listening stations for music, computers for education and recreation, books, and magazines. Educational sessions could be readily provided there for small groups of residents. Other considerations for rooms or areas include an outdoor patio for barbecues and social gatherings, as well as activities centred around hobbies and interests such as photography, poker, bridge, and dance classes.

Source: Siberski, J., & Siberski, C. (2015).

long-term-care facilities or hospitals. Long-term-care is not included under the Canada Health Act, which means that it is not available to all Canadians on a universal basis nor is it a publicly insured service. That is, contrary to common belief, the cost of long-term-care is not fully paid by the government. In the 2012 publication entitled *A Guide to Long-Term-Care Insurance*, accommodation in long-term-care facilities typically costs from $900 to more than $5000 per month, based on the type of room and the level of government funding available (Canadian Life and Health Insurance Association, 2015).

What is quality of life like in long-term-care facilities? In a large-scale study, Kehyayan, Hirdes, Tyas, and Stolee (2016) looked at the ratings on quality of life from 928 residents in long-term-care facilities from six Canadian provinces. The results showed that residents did rate some aspects of their life as positive, such as having privacy during visits (76.9 percent) and staff being honest with them (73.6 percent). Although two-thirds of residents liked the food and enjoyed mealtimes, less than half reported that they were able to get their favourite foods. With respect to decision-making autonomy about daily aspects of life, three-quarters reported positively about having control over when to go to bed and when to get up. However, only about one-third reported positively about being able to have a bath or shower as often as they wanted. In terms of being treated with respect, almost 90 percent indicated that they were treated with respect. In terms of personal relationships, less than half reported positively about having another resident in the facility as their close friend. The lowest reported quality of life measure was related to affection or romance, with only 21 percent reporting positively in this area. These results indicate that, despite the implementation of the **person-centred-care approach** in long-term-care facilities in recent years, there is still a gap between philosophies of care and the way that care is delivered. In another recent Canadian study, Williams, Hadjistavropoulos, Ghandehari, Yao, and Lix (2015) found that although staff members in long-term care support the person-centred-care approach, implementation and maintenance of the approach was proving too difficult. Unfortunately, there are data to support this finding. After a review of data from 3717 women in British Columbia who were living with dementia, Cloutier and Penning (2017) came to the conclusion that there has not been substantial progress in the provision of person- and family-centred care in LTC facilities. In the end, the person requiring care and their family members get lost in a cracked and broken system (Cloutier & Penning, 2017).

REFLECTIVE QUESTION

What do you think long-term-care facilities can do to improve the care of older adults living in residential care facilities?

What is the waiting time to get into long-term-care facilities? On any given day, about 5 percent of patients in acute hospital beds across Canada are waiting to move. One in five of them wait more than a month, with most of these patients aged 65 or older. Patients with dementia or receiving palliative care are among those most likely to wait. These long wait times not only have negative consequences for older adults but also result in increased costs to the healthcare system (Canadian Institute for Health Information, 2012).

The quality of care provided to older adults in long-term-care will become increasingly significant over the next 30 years. First, although the proportion of individuals aged 65 and older living in institutions has remained stable since 1981 (Ramage-Morin, 2006), the actual number living in healthcare institutions increased from 173 000 to more than 263 000 residents in 2005 (Ramage-Morin, 2006). Despite the many aging in place initiatives in Canada, we can expect that there will continue to be a substantial number of older adults needing institutional care (Ramage-Morin, 2006). Assuming the same level of institutional care is maintained, Trottier, Martel, Houle, Berthelot, and Légaré (2000) projected that over a half a million (565 000) Canadians will require long-term-care by 2031. As such, the quality of care, including the prevention of abuse and neglect of residents, will become increasingly significant (McDonald et al., 2012).

AVAILABILITY OF SUPPORTIVE HOUSING IN CANADA

In 2015, there were 224 342 spaces in seniors' housing residences in Canada, with the vast majority designated as "standard" spaces (defined as being occupied by a resident paying market rent and who does not receive heavy care (defined as 1.5 hours of care per day). Overall, the availability of these standard spaces decreased from 8.7 percent in 2014 to 8.1 percent in 2015 (see Figure 13.9) (CMHC, 2015). But, when looking at the individual provinces, you can see that vacancy rates decreased between 2014 and 2015 in six of the provinces, and increased in the remaining four provinces.

FIGURE 13.9

VACANCY RATES OF STANDARD SPACES, CANADA AND PROVINCES, 2014 AND 2015

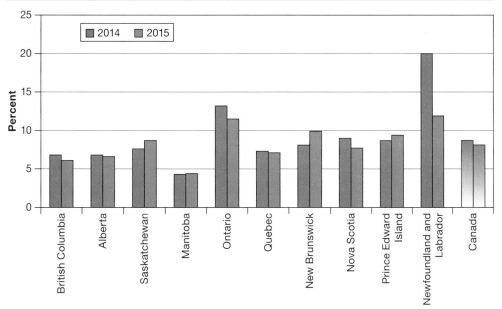

Source: Canada Mortgage and Housing Corporation. (2015). *Seniors housing report Canada highlights.* https://www
.cmhc-schl.gc.ca/odpub/esub/65991/65991_2015_A01.pdf. Reprinted by permission of the Canadian Mortgage and
Housing Corporation.

LONG-TERM-CARE INSURANCE

Under the Canada Health Act, all residents of Canada have reasonable access to medically necessary hospital and physician services. Extended services, such as long-term-care, are not and never have been insured under the Canada Health Act (Government of Canada, 2004). Rather, provincial and territorial legislation governs long-term-care, with the range of services and cost of those services differing across jurisdictions. Long-term-care insurance (LTCI) is a form of insurance intended to pay for expenses due to some form of disability. The care involved can be delivered either at home to maintain a level of independence or in a facility. In general, LTCI will cover the cost of home care, assisted living, adult daycare, respite care, hospice care, and care provided in nursing home and Alzheimer's disease care facilities. LTCI, which was introduced in the 1980s in the United States, is relatively new to Canada. Only a few insurance companies sell LTCI policies in Canada. There are three types of LTCI policies—reimbursement policies, indemnity policies, and income policies. The cost of LTCI policies are based on a number of factors including your age, your health status (most policies are on an accept or reject basis for those with pre-existing conditions, with some policies accepting pre-existing conditions for a premium surcharge), and type of coverage. For more information, see The Council on Aging of Ottawa (2008) at www.cupfa.org/wp-content/uploads/.../6N-Long_Term_Care_Insurance_Oct2008.pdf.

NEW MODELS OF CARE FOR OLDER ADULTS

In 2012, the WHO called on countries to invest in health and social systems to improve care and services for people with dementia and their caregivers in the report *Dementia: A Public Health Priority*. The Netherlands has been a frontrunner in developing national plans to care for the estimated 250 000 living with dementia in the country. The **green-care farm**, which provides 24-hour nursing home care for people with dementia, is one such new care environment. Green-care farms come in different forms, and are referred to by a variety of terms, such as social farming, multifunctional agriculture, and farming for health (Hassink & Van Dijk, 2006). These farms, which combine agricultural activities with care services, enable older adults to live independently and to participate in society for as long as possible. Green-care farms are developing in many areas of the world. Countries that are leading this initiative are Norway, the Netherlands, France, and Italy, with more than 3000 green care farms combined. Other jurisdictions with fewer green-care farms (<500) are Belgium, Austria, the United Kingdom, Germany, and Ireland (De Boer et al., 2015) (see Figure 13.10). You can watch a video on green-care farms at https://vimeo.com/109903443.

The Hogewey dementia village is another example of this new type of care environment for individuals with dementia. This village, which is located about 20 kilometres outside of Amsterdam, consists of 160 residents. The village is complete with shops, restaurants, and even a movie theatre, and has 23 residential units, each shared by six to eight residents. Around-the-clock care is provided by 240 villagers who are actually trained geriatric nurses and caregivers dressed in street clothes. The staff takes care of everything from cooking meals and planning activities to assisting with bathing and personal care and administering medications. In addition to the villagers, the individuals staffing the various village so-called businesses are trained in dementia care (Dementia Village Advisors, n.d.). You can see what this new type of care environment looks like by going to http://hogeweyk.dementiavillage.com/en.

FIGURE 13.10

GREEN-CARE FARMS

YuriyS/iStockphoto.com

Canada's version of Hogewey is located in Penetanguishene, Ontario. The memory care unit at Lakeridge Seniors Residence, named after Dr. Sandra Black, a dementia researcher at Toronto's Sunnybrook Health Sciences Centre, is designed in the style of decades past. It was purposefully designed in this way to make dementia patients feel comfortable in surroundings similar to the time in which they grew up. Like Hogewey, this new model of care emphasizes individualized care, builds on residents' personal strengths, and supports the overall well-being of residents. The most important element is providing a high quality of life, and this model values autonomy, individualization, and preservation of the individual's sense of identity and personhood. Another recent innovation in care environments for older adults is the integration of preschools and nursing homes/long-term-care facilities (see Box 13.2).

An important area of future research is the impact of these different care environments on the daily lives of residents, the quality of care provided, and the experiences of caregivers compared with other nursing home-care environments. Importantly a longitudinal study has recently been done (from April 2014 to December 2015) by De Boer and colleagues on green-care farms. In a recently published study with results based on a large number (n = 16, 840) of "ecological momentary assessments," De Boer and colleagues (2017) found that, when compared with residents of traditional nursing homes, residents of green care farms participated more often in domestic activities and outdoor/nature-related activities, and less often engaged in passive/purposeless activities, with these differences all statistically significant. Furthermore, residents of green care farms had significantly more active engagement and more social interaction, and came outside significantly more often than residents of traditional nursing homes. As noted by the authors, these results indicate that green care farms provide an attractive homelike setting for older adults, with activities that have a positive influence on the residents engagement and social interaction.

REFLECTIVE QUESTIONS

Have you thought about the time when your parents may need to go into a long-term-care facility?

If so, what do you think would be most important to them in selecting a facility?

What would be most important to you?

Edouard St-Pierre, Ph.D.

Seniors Community Health Programs, Thunder Bay, Ontario.

WHERE DID YOU TRAIN?

I completed my M.A. in experimental psychology with a specialization in gerontology at Lakehead University, Thunder Bay, Ontario, followed by a Ph.D. in clinical psychology at Lakehead University. I graduated in 2006.

WHERE DO YOU WORK?

I have worked for the Seniors Community Mental Health Programs of St. Joseph's Care Group in Thunder Bay, Ontario, since 2006.

WHAT DO YOU DO?

I complete cognitive, personality, and mental health assessments of older adults and facilitate individual and group therapy with older adults. The majority of my work is cognitive assessment for the differential diagnosis of neurocognitive disorders.

WHY DO YOU LIKE WORKING WITH AN OLDER-ADULT POPULATION?

Relative to other populations I have worked with, I find that older adults are more appreciative of the services they receive, and they have a sincere desire to make positive changes in their lives.

DO YOU HAVE ADVICE FOR STUDENTS WHO WANT TO GET INTO THE FIELD?

Try to enjoy the clients; listen to them and learn from them. They possess a great deal of wisdom. Allow them to reminisce and teach you something and you will have an instant and strong rapport with them, as they will view their contact with you as reciprocal and feel less ashamed about needing help.

Liza Stelmach, Ph.D.

Care West Day Hospital, Calgary, Alberta

WHERE DID YOU TRAIN?

I completed my Ph.D. in clinical psychology at the University of Calgary, Calgary, Alberta.

WHERE DO YOU WORK?

For more than 10 years, I have been working as a geriatric psychologist in an outpatient rehabilitation program for older adults at the Care West Day Hospital.

WHAT DO YOU DO?

One of the greatest benefits of my work environment is being part of a multidisciplinary team. Within this team, I take on several roles, including conducting individualized psychotherapy, leading pain management groups, providing psychoeducation on topics related to emotional well-being and cognition, conducting cognitive assessments, consulting with team members on clients' mental health and cognition, and case management.

WHY DO YOU LIKE WORKING WITH AN OLDER-ADULT POPULATION?

The complexity of the older-adult population is a main reason I continue to find my career interesting, challenging, and rewarding. One cannot look at mental health or cognition in isolation in older adults. Therefore, as a geriatric psychologist, I see first-hand the significant impact that improved mood can have physically, cognitively, and socially, which has led to an extremely rewarding career. However, the clients themselves are what I enjoy most. I have found that older adults have years of experience and wisdom to draw upon to cope with current issues; they dedicate their time to psychotherapy work, and they are extremely appreciative of the services that are provided.

DO YOU HAVE ADVICE FOR STUDENTS WHO WANT TO GET INTO THE FIELD?

When I was a student wanting to pursue a career in geriatric psychology, a few occurrences helped to shape me into the psychologist I am today. First, I gained experience by volunteering with older adults with emotional and cognitive difficulties early on in my university career. Second, while volunteering I started to challenge some of my assumptions about older adults, which greatly impacted how I relate to my clients today. Finally, I gained exposure to and in turn respect for the services other disciplines can provide older adults, and today I use this knowledge to the benefit of my clients.

13.5 SUMMARY

- Contrary to the common stereotype that older adults live out their lives in nursing homes or in other "seniors only" housing, the majority of older adults today continue to live at home and wish to age in place, staying in their communities as they grow older.

- The type of household that an older adult needs is based on a number of factors such as health status, age, marital status, income, and functional abilities.

- For many older adults, the presence of one or more illnesses and/or disabilities triggers a change in living arrangements. Income also affects living arrangements.

- There are a number of federal and provincial programs that can facilitate new or ongoing home ownership for older adults. For some older adults, the cost of owning and maintaining a home can be prohibitive. Several options are available to help older adults stay in their own home. Each of these alternatives has benefits and risks.

- Aging in place, which is defined broadly as the ability to live in one's own home and community safely, independently, and comfortably, regardless of age, income, or ability level, is a relatively new term in gerontology. The vast majority of Canadian older adults want to age in their own homes.

- The concept of aging in place is related to early work conducted by Lawton (1982). The concept emphasizes the role of the interaction between personal competence and the physical home environment in older people's well-being.

- Adaptations can be made to the home that can help older adults age in place.

- Smart environments can help some older adults remain in their homes longer. Having these smart technologies in the home is associated with significantly better outcomes in mobility, cognition, and IADL functioning.

- Communities that are age-friendly have policies, services, and the physical and social characteristics designed to help older adults age actively.

- Although the majority of older adults are licensed to drive, licensing rates do decline with age due to the presence of one or more illnesses. There are many barriers to older adults using public transportation.

- Many alternative transportation options for older adults are available through not-for-profit organizations. However, not all communities have these types of services, especially those in rural areas.

- There are many housing options for older adults and many enable older adults to continue to live independently longer.

- Home-care services can help older adults remain in their own homes longer. Assisted-living facilities are a type of housing that provides housing, hospitality services, and personal assistance to older adults who can live

independently but require some assistance with ADLs.

- Long-term-care facilities include nursing homes, continuing-care facilities, and long-term-care facilities or hospitals. In general, ratings on quality of life in long-term-care facilities are positive. However, there are a number of aspects of long-term-care that are not rated positively.

- Quality of care, including the prevention of abuse and neglect of residents, is an important consideration for older adults living in healthcare institutions.

- The availability of supportive living spaces in Canada is a concern as this availability has been decreasing in all provinces and territories in Canada. Long-term-care insurance (LTCI) is a form of insurance intended to pay for expenses as a result of some form of disability. The cost of LTCI policies is based on factors such as age, health status, and type of coverage.

- New models of care for older adults are emerging in jurisdictions around the world. The green-care farm and Hogeway are two examples of these new models of care, with demonstrated positive outcomes.

- As demonstrated by recent results, the impact of these care environments on the daily lives of residents, the quality of their care, and the experiences of caregivers compared with other nursing home-care environments is an exciting area of research.

Key Terms

Age-Friendly City
A city that optimizes opportunities for health, participation, and security to enhance quality of life as people age.

Age-Friendly Community
A community where the policies, services, and structures related to the physical and social environment are designed to help older adults age actively. In other words, the community is set up to help older adults live safely, enjoy good health, and stay involved.

Age-Friendly World
A place that enables people of all ages to actively participate in community activities; that treats everyone with respect, regardless of their age; that makes it easy to stay connected to those around you and those you love; that helps people stay healthy and active even at the oldest ages; and that helps those who can no longer look after themselves to live with dignity and enjoyment.

Alternative Transportation for Seniors
Transportation provided to adults 65 years of age and older outside of the public transportation system.

Autonomy
The ability of individuals to make their own decisions without being controlled by anyone else.

Chronic-Care and Long-Term-Care Hospitals
Establishments that provide continuous medical, nursing, and professional health-care supervision for long-term patients who are dependent in all activities of daily living and are unable to perform most or all personal-care tasks.

Collateral
A property or other assets that a borrower offers a lender to secure a loan. If the borrower stops making the promised loan payment(s), the lender can seize the collateral to recoup its losses.

Collective Dwelling
A dwelling used for commercial, institutional, or communal purposes.

Compensation
One of the three processes in Baltes and Baltes' *Model of Successful Aging* to help individuals manage their lives; for example, older adults can maintain a given level of functioning in the face of loss and decline by investing in compensatory means such as hiring a housekeeper to provide assistance with heavier housecleaning.

Competence–Environmental Press
Model of stress and adaption where adaptive functions depend on the interaction between external demands and an individual's competence to meet demands.

Continuing-Care Facilities
Hospitals with continuing-care beds, commonly known as extended, auxiliary, chronic, or complex-care beds, as well as residential care facilities, commonly known as nursing homes, personal-care homes, or long-term-care facilities.

Downsizing
Moving from current dwelling to another dwelling, with a decrease in the number of rooms, size of dwelling, and/or value of dwelling.

Ecological Model of Aging
A model of aging that stresses the importance of the balance between environmental demands and the individual's capabilities.

Environmental Gerontology
A field of gerontology that seeks to describe and explain the relationship between older people and their socio-spatial surroundings.

Equity
The value of a piece of property (such as a house) after any debts (e.g., the remaining mortgage, if any) have been subtracted.

Freehold
Where the property is owned for an unlimited period.

Gerontechnology
An interdisciplinary field that links existing and developing technologies to the aspirations and needs of aging and aged adults.

Green-Care Farm
A new model of care for older adults that combines agricultural activities with care services. These farms enable older adults to live independently and to participate in society for as long as possible.

Home-Equity Loan
A loan that is a single lump sum payment based on the equity in your home.

Household
A person or group of persons who occupy the same dwelling and who do not have a usual place of residence elsewhere in Canada.

Household Wealth
The total value of real estate holdings and other non-housing sources of financial wealth such as savings accumulated in investment funds and retirement savings plans, minus outstanding debt.

Liquidated
The process of selling a property, business, or other assets, particularly to pay off a debt.

Long-Term-Care Facility
A facility that provides a range of healthcare services, from periodic assistance to regular nursing care, for elderly residents.

Nursing Homes
A type of long-term-care accommodation that provides housing, support, and direct care to frail seniors who are unable to function independently.

Optimization
One of the three processes in Baltes and Baltes' *Model of Successful Aging* to help individuals manage their lives; for example, older adults can acquire new skills to help manage their limitations due to aging.

Person-Centred-Care Approach
An approach that aims to see the person as an individual, rather than focusing on the person's illness or on abilities that he or she may have lost.

Private Dwelling
A separate set of living quarters with a private entrance either from outside the building or from a common hall, lobby, vestibule, or stairway inside the building.

Refinancing an Existing Mortgage
Renegotiating the terms of one's mortgage to lower monthly payments and free up some cash.

Residences for Senior Citizens

Residences that provide support services (such as meals, housekeeping, medication supervision, and assistance in bathing) and supervision for residents 65 years of age and older who are independent in most activities of daily living.

Residential Care

Residential care facilities can include lodges, assisted living, supportive housing, and long-term-care homes. Other terms across Canada are nursing and personal-care homes.

Reverse Mortgages

A mortgage where the lender advances a lump sum to the borrower or provides a set amount of money each month.

Selection

One of the three processes in Baltes and Baltes' *Model of Successful Aging* that refers to an individual focusing attention on fewer, more important goals; for example, some older adults may choose to downsize to a smaller house to help manage their physical limitations.

Smart Environments

A residence equipped with technology that allows monitoring of its inhabitants and/or encourages independence and the maintenance of good health.

Social Environment

The immediate physical surroundings, social relationships, and sociocultural context or milieu in which people live and interact.

Supportive Housing

A type of housing that helps individuals in their daily living through the provision of a physical environment that is safe, secure, enabling, and home-like. Assisted living is a type of supportive housing.

GLOSSARY

Abstainers Individuals who drank fewer than two drinks in the previous year.

Accommodation The ability of the lens of the eye to change focus from distant to near objects (and vice versa).

Acculturation The modification of an individual or a group by adapting to or borrowing traits from another culture.

Acetylcholinesterase Inhibitors (AChEIs) Drugs used to treat dementia (donepezil, galantine, rivastigmine, and memantine).

Actinic Keratosis An actinic keratosis is a rough, scaly patch on the skin that develops as a result of years of exposure to the sun. It is most commonly found on the face, lips, ears, back of the hands, forearms, scalp, or neck. A small percentage of actinic keratosis lesions can become cancerous.

Activities of Daily Living (ADLs) Routine activities of everyday living. There are six ADLs: eating, bathing, dressing, toileting, transferring (walking), and continence.

Acute Diseases Diseases characterized by a relatively sudden onset of symptoms that are usually severe.

Acute Requiring serious attention or action.

Adaptive Immune System The adaptive immune system, which is more complex than the innate immune system, includes the thymus, spleen, tonsils, bone marrow, circulatory system, and lymphatic system.

Age Changes Changes in an individual due to the aging process.

Age Differences Differences between age groups due to differences in experiences and not due to the aging process.

Age Effect(s) Differences, such as biological, psychological, or sociocultural changes, as the consequences of growing older.

Age-Friendly City A city that optimizes opportunities for health, participation, and security to enhance quality of life as people age.

Age-Friendly Community A community where the policies, services, and structures related to the physical and social environment are designed to help older adults age actively. In other words, the community is set up to help older adults live safely, enjoy good health, and stay involved.

Age-Friendly World A place that enables people of all ages to actively participate in community activities; that treats everyone with respect, regardless of their age; that makes it easy to stay connected to those around you and those you love; that helps people stay healthy and active even at the oldest ages; and that helps those who can no longer look after themselves to live with dignity and enjoyment.

Ageism A form of discrimination against older adults based on age alone.

Agency A philosophical term referring to the capacity for human beings to make choices.

Age-Related Macular Degeneration (AMD) A chronic eye disease that causes vision loss in the centre of an individual's field of vision. There are two types of AMD—wet and dry macular degeneration.

Age-Standardized A statistical technique used to allow populations to be compared when the age profiles of the populations are quite different.

Alternative Transportation for Seniors Transportation provided to adults 65 years of age and older outside of the public transportation system.

Amyloid Plaques The sticky buildup of beta-amyloid protein outside neurons.

Amyloid Precursor Protein (APP) This protein is found in many tissues and organs, including the brain and spinal cord. Little is known about the function of APP, but it is thought to be key in the development of Alzheimer's disease.

Analogue Hearing Aid A form of hearing aid. With analogue hearing aids, sound is processed as an electrical signal by a microphone. Analogue sound is like making a photocopy—the sound is registered and you get an overall picture. But the actual processing is like re-copying a photocopy—it can only be done to a certain extent because it causes a deterioration of the original imprint.

Androgenetic Alopecia A common type of hair loss in men, with a typical pattern of receding hairline and hair thinning on the crown of the head. It commonly is known as male pattern baldness.

Annuity A form of insurance or investment entitling the investor to a series of annual sums. Annuities are most commonly used to generate retirement income.

Anonymity Refers to either not collecting identifying information from research participants (e.g., name, address, email address, etc.) or not linking individual responses with participants' identities.

Anosmia Loss of the sense of smell.

Antipsychotic Medication Used to treat psychotic illness. Antipsychotic medications are generally divided into two categories. First-generation antipsychotics are called typical and second-generation antipsychotics are called atypical. The main difference between the two types is that the first-generation drugs block dopamine and the second-generation drugs block dopamine and also affect serotonin levels.

Arteriosclerosis Thickening and hardening of the walls of the arteries, occurring typically in old age.

Atrophy The wasting away or decrease in size of an organ or tissue in the body.

Attention The cognitive process of selectively concentrating on one aspect of the environment while ignoring other things.

Attrition Occurs in research when participants who have been recruited for a study drop out. Attrition threatens the internal validity of a study.

Authenticated Proof of age by birth certificate.

Autonomy The ability of individuals to make their own decisions without being controlled by anyone else.

Average Longevity A statistical measure that refers to the age at which half of the individuals born in a given year will have died.

Baby Boom A sudden rise in the number of births observed from year to year.

Baby Boomers People born in the postwar baby boom (1946–1965).

Basal Cell Carcinoma A type of skin cancer that begins in the basal cells—a type of cell within the skin that produces new skin cells as old ones die off. Most basal cell carcinomas are thought to be caused by long-term exposure to ultraviolet (UV) radiation from sunlight. Basal cell carcinomas are the least dangerous of skin cancers in that they rarely metastasize (spread) or become life-threatening. However, they should be treated.

Bereaved Refers to an individual who is experiencing grief and mourning following the loss of someone or something that is very dear to them.

Bilateralization A term that refers to evidence that in older brains, activations for cognitive tasks spread out to both hemispheres of the prefrontal cortex, whereas in the young, activations are typically confined to a single hemisphere.

Bill C-14 Legislation passed in June 2016 amending the *Criminal Code of Canada* and other related Acts, limiting the right to medical assistance in dying to those whose natural death is "reasonably foreseeable."

Biological Age A description of a person's development based on the aging of various physical systems.

Biological Essentialist Perspective The belief that genetics is central to personality development.

Biomarker(s) Measurable substance or substances in an organism whose presence is indicative of some phenomenon such as disease, infection, or environmental exposure.

Blister Packs A special method of packing medications, where each dose of medication is placed in a small plastic bubble and backed by a sheet of foil. Medications are organized by day, usually for up to a week at a time. This method of packaging medications allows the patient to see which doses of medication(s) he or she has taken. Blister packages are prepared by a pharmacist.

Body Mass Index (BMI) BMI is a simple calculation using a person's height and weight. The formula is BMI = kg/m2 where kg is a person's weight in kilograms and m2 is their height in metres squared.

Bona Fide Occupational Requirements A rule that establishes a requirement that is necessary for proper or efficient performance of a job. In Canada, the bona fide occupational requirement (BFOR) exception is included in virtually all human rights codes.

Boomerang Kids Children who return to their parents' home after living on their own.

Bridge Employment The pattern of returning to work following retirement.

Caloric Restriction A strategy to increase longevity by reducing calories, without malnutrition.

Canada Health Act Legislation adopted in 1984 that specifies conditions required by provinces and territories to receive funding for healthcare.

Cognitive Capacity The total cognitive resources available at any given time.

Caregiver Burden Effects of providing care to an individual (most often a family member). The care commonly is perceived as a chronic stressor, with caregivers often experiencing negative psychological, behavioural, and physiological effects on their daily lives and health.

Carotenoids Plant pigments responsible for bright red, yellow, and orange hues in many fruits and vegetables. Dietary carotenoids are thought to provide health benefits by decreasing the risk of disease, particularly certain cancers and eye disease.

Carter v. Canada (Attorney General) (2015) A landmark Supreme Court of Canada decision where the prohibition of assisted suicide was challenged as contrary to the *Canadian Charter of Rights and Freedoms*. In a unanimous decision on February 6, 2015, the Court struck down the provision in the *Criminal Code of Canada*, thereby giving Canadian adults who are mentally competent and suffering intolerably and enduringly the right to a doctor's help in dying.

Cataract A clouding of the crystalline lens of the eye.

Cellular Theories of Aging Theories of aging that propose that human aging is the result of cellular aging, whereby an increasing proportion of cells reach senescence, a terminal stage at which cells will cease to divide.

Centenarian An individual who lives to be 100 to 110 years.

Central Executive A part of the working memory model, proposed by Baddeley (2000), that controls and coordinates the three other components of working memory.

Cerebral Vascular Accident (CVA) The sudden death of some brain cells due to lack of oxygen when the blood flow to the brain is impaired by blockage or rupture of an artery to the brain. A CVA also is referred to as a stroke.

Christianity The religion based on the person and teachings of Jesus of Nazareth, or its beliefs and practices.

Chronic-Care and Long-Term-Care Hospitals Establishments that provide continuous medical, nursing, and professional healthcare supervision for long-term patients who are dependent in all activities of daily living and are unable to perform most or all personal-care tasks.

Chronic Diseases Diseases that persist over a long period. The symptoms of chronic diseases are sometimes less severe than those of the acute phase of the same disease.

Chronological Age The number of years a person has lived.

Circumlocutions A roundabout or indirect way of speaking; the use of more words than necessary to express an idea.

Classic Aging Pattern The developmental trend in which crystallized intelligence increases with age while fluid intelligence declines with age.

Clinical-Pathological When the observable symptoms of disease are consistent with changes in the brain causing the symptoms.

Coercion Threat of harm or punishment for failure to participate in research. Coercion exists if individuals do not feel they can refuse to participate in research, if refusal causes a perceived substantial loss to the individual, or if individuals believe that participation is not truly voluntary.

Cognitive Domains Cognitive domains include attention, memory, perception, language, problem solving, and creativity.

Cognitive Epidemiology A field of research that investigates the relationship between intelligence and health.

Cognitive Reserve The idea that certain factors help to maintain cognitive functioning in the risk of accumulating brain pathology. These characteristics are thought to be high education level, complex work, and engaging in stimulating leisure and social activities.

Cohabitation Effect Couples who would likely not have gotten married had they been living apart slide into marriage because they already are living together and it appears to be the thing to do next.

Cohort Effect(s) The effect that having been born in a certain time, region, or period, or having experienced the same life experience (in the same time period) has on the development or perceptions of a particular group. These perceptions, characteristics, or effects are unique to the group in question.

Cohort-Sequential Design A research design consisting of two or more cross-sectional studies done at two different time periods.

Cohort(s) Refers to an aggregate (group/groups) of individuals within a given population who experience the same event within the same time interval.

Collagen A fibrous protein that provides strength and elasticity to skin, bones, cartilage, and connective tissue.

Collateral A property or other assets that a borrower offers a lender to secure a loan. If the borrower stops making the promised loan payment(s), the lender can seize the collateral to recoup its losses.

Collective Dwelling A dwelling used for commercial, institutional, or communal purposes.

Commission Errors Errors that result from doing something wrong (e.g., pressing a button twice instead of once on a psychological task).

Co-morbidity Co-occurrence of multiple chronic or acute diseases and medical conditions in an individual.

Compassionate Release A process by which inmates in criminal justice systems may be eligible for immediate early release on grounds of compelling circumstances that could not reasonably have been foreseen by the court at the time of sentencing (e.g., developing a dementia).

Compensation One of the three processes in Baltes and Baltes's *Model of Successful Aging* to help individuals manage their lives; for example, older adults can maintain a given level of functioning in the face of loss and decline by investing in compensatory means such as hiring a housekeeper to provide assistance with heavier housecleaning.

Compensation In older adults, activations for cognitive tasks spread out to both hemispheres of the prefrontal cortex, whereas in the young, they are typically confined to a single hemisphere.

Compensation-Related Utilization of Neural Circuit Hypothesis (CRUNCH) A model that explains that older brains will work harder to search for available resources to use in a particular cognitive task.

Competence–Environmental Press Model of stress and adaption where adaptive functions depend on the interaction between external demands and an individual's competence to meet demands.

Complex Families A family that includes at least one child of both parents as well as at least one child of one parent only.

Complicated or Prolonged Grief Grief that does not resolve naturally and persists for an indefinite period with varying degrees of incapacitation

Compression of Morbidity Hypothesis that proposes that the average age that one becomes disabled for the first time is postponed, therefore decreasing the time between onset of disease and death.

Computerized Tomography A neuroimaging technique that creates detailed images of internal organs, bones, soft tissue, and blood vessels.

Computerized Tomography Scans An imaging procedure that uses special x-ray equipment to create detailed pictures, or scans, of areas inside the body.

Conductive Hearing Loss Hearing loss that occurs when sound is not conducted efficiently through the outer ear canal to the ear drum and the tiny bones (ossicles) in the middle ear.

Confidentiality Refers to the protection of participant information and/or responses collected in research studies, with this information available only to the investigator(s) or members of the research team. The easiest way to protect participants is through the collection and use of anonymous or anonymized data.

Confucianism A system of philosophical and ethical teachings founded by Confucius.

Congenital Existing at or dating from birth.

Contextualist Perspective The emphasis on the role of the environment in personality development.

Continuing-Care Facilities Hospitals with continuing-care beds, commonly known as extended, auxiliary, chronic, or complex-care beds, as well as residential care facilities, commonly known as nursing homes, personal-care homes, or long-term-care facilities.

Coping The actions people use to decrease stress. These can be positive actions such as running or deep breathing or negative actions such as drinking too much alcohol or spending too much money.

Coronary Artery Disease A disease of the coronary arteries—the major blood vessels that supply your heart with blood, oxygen, and nutrients. The presence of cholesterol-containing deposits (plaque) in the arteries and inflammation usually are to blame for coronary artery disease.

Correspondence Principle Personality stability is influenced by life choices.

Creole Language A stable natural language developed from a mixture of different languages.

Cross-Sectional Design A research design where individuals of different ages are compared at a single point in time.

Cross-Sequential Design A research design that combines a cross-sectional and a longitudinal design.

Crystallized Intelligence An individual's accumulated skills, knowledge, and life experiences.

Cultural Competence The possession of the skills and knowledge required to manage cross-cultural relationships effectively. Cultural competence has four major components: awareness, attitude, knowledge, and skills.

Cultural Identity The identity or feeling of belonging to a group. It is part of a person's self-conception and self-perception and is related to nationality, ethnicity, religion, social class, generation, locality, or any kind of social group that has its own distinct culture.

Culture The integrated pattern of human knowledge, belief, and behaviour that is transmitted to succeeding generations.

Cutaneous Aging Aging of the skin.

Dark Adaptation The ability of the pupil to adjust to changes in the amount of available light through reflex pupil dilation and activation of rod cells in preference to the cone cells.

Death Anxiety The persistent fear of one's own mortality with this fear consisting of a feeling of dread, apprehension, or anxiety.

Dementia Anxiety An increased fear of developing dementia in caregivers as a result of caring for a loved one who has dementia.

Dermis The inner layer of the skin that lies below the epidermis.

Determinism A philosophical term that presumes that all events are completely determined by previously existing causes.

Diffusion Tensor Imaging A neuroimaging technique that uses the diffusion of water molecules to determine the health of the white matter in the brain.

Disability An umbrella term, covering impairments, activity limitations, and participation restrictions. An *impairment* is a problem in a body function or structure; an *activity limitation* is a difficulty encountered by an individual in executing a task or action; while a *participation restriction* is a problem experienced by an individual in involvement in life situations.

Do-Not-Resuscitate Order A do-not-resuscitate order, or DNR order, is a medical order written by a doctor and based on previous consultation with/directive from the patient. It instructs healthcare providers not to do cardiopulmonary resuscitation (CPR) if a patient's breathing stops or if the patient's heart stops beating.

Downsizing Moving from current dwelling to another dwelling, with a decrease in the number of rooms, size of dwelling, and/or value of dwelling.

Drion's Pill Huib Drion, then-vice-president of the Dutch Supreme Court, put forward the idea of having an easily available suicide pill for older adults people who wanted to end their lives. This suicide pill came to be known as the Drion Pill or Drion's Pill.

Dynamic Equilibrium Hypothesis that proposes that postponement of death is accompanied by delays in disability so that the relative time in poor health remains the same.

Early Onset-Familial Alzheimer's Disease An uncommon form of Alzheimer's disease that usually strikes before the age of 65 years of age and is inherited in an autosomal dominant fashion.

Echoic Memory A component of sensory memory that is specific to retaining auditory information.

E-Codes Documentation of cessation of treatment or care by hospital administration that is connected to deliberate self-harm is identified by the presence of an external cause of injury or poisoning code, an E-code, according to the *International Classification of Diseases* (*ICD-10*) system.

Ecological Model of Aging A model of aging that stresses the importance of the balance between environmental demands and the individual's capabilities.

Economic Class of Immigration A category under which immigrants are admitted to a county because they have attributes that are thought to be helpful to economic growth.

Elaborative Rehearsal A type of rehearsal, as defined by Craik and Lockhart (1972) in relation to their levels of processing theory, that involves linking new information to information that already is in long-term memory to assist in retention of that information.

Encoding The initial process of getting information into the memory system for storage and later retrieval.

Environmental Gerontology A field of gerontology that seeks to describe and explain the relationship between older people and their socio-spatial surroundings.

Epidemiological Relating to the study of the causes and effects of health conditions and diseases in defined populations.

Epidermis The outer layer of the skin.

Episodic Buffer A part of the working memory model, proposed by Baddeley (2000), that holds information from the phonological loop and the visuospatial sketchpad, as well as information from long-term memory.

Episodic Memory The part of long-term memory that is responsible for storing personally experienced events or episodes.

Equity The value of a piece of property (such as a house) after any debts (e.g., the remaining mortgage, if any) have been subtracted.

Error Theories of Aging Theories that argue that aging is due to environmental insults that result in progressive damage to living organisms. The wear and tear theory and free radical theory are two examples of error theories of aging.

Established Immigrants An individual who has been a permanent resident of Canada for more than 10 years.

Ethnicity A state of belonging to a social group that has a common national or cultural tradition.

Euthanasia A process that involves a deliberate action with the express intention of ending a life to relieve intractable (persistent, unstoppable) suffering. The action may be either non-voluntary or voluntary.

Executive Functions A set of cognitive processes (attention, inhibitory control, working memory, problem solving, reasoning, and planning) that are necessary for the cognitive control of behaviour.

Expansion of Morbidity Hypothesis that proposes people will live longer in poor health.

External Validity The extent to which results of a study can be generalized to other people (population validity), to other settings (ecological validity), or over time (historical validity).

Extrinsic Aging Aging due to external factors such as exercise, diet, exposure to sunlight, and smoking.

Extrovert An external focus on the world of people and things.

Factor Analysis A type of statistical procedure that is conducted to identify clusters or groups of related items (called factors) on a test.

Family Class of Immigration A category under which immigrants are admitted to Canada for the purposes of family reunification.

Fertility Replacement Level Defined as the total fertility rate—the average number of children born per woman—at which a population exactly replaces itself from one generation to the next, without migration. This rate is roughly 2.1 children per woman for most countries, although it may modestly vary with mortality rates.

Filial Piety In Confucian philosophy, filial piety is a virtue of respect for one's parents, elders, and ancestors.

Financially Solvent Being able to service the debt and meet its other obligations especially in the long-term.

First Age One of the four ages of life, with this age described as from youth to the early 20s.

Five Stages of Death A model of death developed by Elisabeth Kübler-Ross, consisting of five stages of dying that people experience when faced with their own impending death: denial, anger, bargaining, depression, and acceptance. While the stages are listed in order, they do not necessarily occur in the same sequence with every individual and more than one stage may be present at the same time.

Fluid Intelligence Those intellectual abilities needed for problem solving in novel situations.

Forgetting Curve A term, based on research by Ebbinghaus, that is used to describe the rapid loss of information after it is learned and the role of rehearsal in retaining information.

Fourth Age One of the four ages of life, with this age described as older than 75 years of age.

Freehold Where the property is owned for an unlimited period.

Free Radical Theory of Aging A theory that argues that organisms age because cells accumulate free radical damage over time. Free radicals, which are formed naturally in the body, are highly reactive and have the potential to cause damage to cells.

Functional Age A measure of how well an individual can function in his or her environment. This measure takes into account biological, psychological, and social age, as well as the environment.

Functional Magnetic Resonance A neuroimaging technique that measures brain activity by detecting changes associated with blood flow.

Functional Neuroimaging A neuroimaging technique that provides information about brain activity rather than brain structure.

Further Education Education that uses a formal curriculum. Programs can range from baccalaureate degrees to adult continuing education offerings.

G7 Countries Canada, France, Germany, Italy, Japan, the United Kingdom, and the United States. The European Union also is represented within the G7. These countries are the seven major advanced economies as reported by the International Monetary Fund.

G8 Countries Refers to the group of eight highly industrialized nations—Canada, France, Germany, Italy, Japan, the United Kingdom, the United States, and Russia—that hold an annual meeting to foster consensus on global issues like economic growth and crisis management, global security, energy, and terrorism.

Gender Inequality Unequal treatment or perceptions of individuals based on their gender due to differences in socially constructed gender roles.

Generalizable The extension of research findings and conclusions from a study conducted on a sample population to the population at large or to other settings.

General Wisdom The body of ideas or explanations generally accepted as true by the public or by experts in a field.

Gerontechnology An interdisciplinary field that links existing and developing technologies to the aspirations and needs of aging and aged adults.

Gerontology Gerontology, from the Greek words for "old man" and "study of," was coined by Ilya Ilyich Mechnikov in 1903. It is the study of the biological, psychological, and sociological aspects of aging.

Glaucoma A group of eye conditions that damage the optic nerve. This damage often is the result of an abnormally high pressure in the eye.

Glial Cells Cells in the brain that provide support and protection for neurons in the central and peripheral nervous systems.

Globalization The tendency of businesses, technologies, or philosophies to spread throughout the world, or the process of making this happen. The global economy sometimes is referred to as a globality, characterized as a totally interconnected marketplace, unhampered by time zones or national boundaries.

Green-Care Farm A new model of care for older adults that combines agricultural activities with care services. These farms enable older adults to live independently and to participate in society for as long as possible.

Grey Divorce A term used to describe marriage dissolution among adults over age 50 years after approximately 20 years or more of marriage.

Grey Matter Composed of neuronal cell bodies and unmyelinated axons, grey matter serves to process information in the brain. Structures within the grey matter process signals generated in the sensory organs or other areas of the grey matter.

Grief A natural response to the loss of a loved one or someone or something very dear to a person.

Grievous and Irremediable Medical Condition One criteria for medical assistance in dying; an individual must have a serious illness, disease, disability; be in an advanced state of decline that cannot be reversed; be suffering unbearably from the illness, disease, disability, or state of decline; and be at a point where natural death is foreseeable.

Gross Domestic Product (GDP) The value of all the goods and services produced in a country within a time period, usually calculated annually.

Guaranteed Income Supplement (GIS) One of the supplementary benefits payable under the Old Age Security (OAS) Act. The GIS is a monthly non-taxable benefit that is paid to eligible pensioners, in addition to the basic monthly OAS amount.

Hayflick Limit Theory A theory that argues that the human cell is limited in the number of times it can divide. The argument is that human cells divide approximately 50 times, after which they stop dividing and die.

Health A state of complete physical, mental, and social well-being and not merely the absence of disease or infirmity (WHO, 1948).

Healthy Immigrant Effect Foreign-born individuals tend to live longer and are in better health than those who are native-born; also known as the foreign-born health advantage.

Heart Failure A common condition that develops after the heart has become damaged (e.g., a heart attack) or weakened by other medical conditions such as high blood pressure that is undiagnosed or untreated for a long period of time.

Hemispheric Asymmetry Reduction (HAROLD) A theory that claims that the higher level of bilateral activations in the prefrontal cortex of aging brains demonstrate a compensatory strategy for numerous cognitive tasks.

Home-Equity Loan A loan that is a single lump sum payment based on the equity in your home.

Hormone Replacement Therapy (HRT) Therapy that involves treating symptoms of menopause with estrogen and progesterone.

Household A person or group of persons who occupy the same dwelling and who do not have a usual place of residence elsewhere in Canada.

Household Wealth The total value of real estate holdings and other non-housing sources of financial wealth such as savings accumulated in investment funds and retirement savings plans, minus outstanding debt.

Humanitarian Class of Immigration A category under which immigrants are admitted because they have been forced from their country due to war, are in fear of persecution, or are, for example, at risk of torture.

Hypertension High blood pressure, which is defined by a systolic blood pressure greater than 140 mmHg (millimetres of mercury) and a diastolic blood pressure greater than 90 mmHg.

Hypodermis The hypodermis lies between the dermis and underlying tissues and organs.

Iconic Memory A type of sensory memory for visual information that fades very rapidly.

Immigrant Persons residing in Canada who were born outside of Canada.

Immigrant seniors Refers to individuals 65 years of age and older and who were not born in Canada and/or did not have Canadian citizenship at birth.

Immunological Memory The ability of the immune system to respond more rapidly and effectively to a pathogen that has been encountered previously.

Incidence Rate A measure of the probability of an occurrence of a given medical condition within a specified period of time.

Independent Variable The variable that is manipulated in a research study.

Information-Processing Model A model of memory proposed by Atkinson and Shiffrin (1968). Based on a computer metaphor, the model is hypothesized to have three main storage compartments (sensory, short-term, and long-term memory) that hold information at different points during the processing of information.

Informed Consent Indication of agreement by an individual to become a participant in a research project.

Innate Immune System The immune system that is present at birth and includes our skin, the cough reflex, mucous membranes, and stomach acid.

Insight An understanding of the motivations behind one's thoughts or behaviour.

Insomnia A sleep disorder characterized by difficulty in getting to sleep or in staying asleep.

Instrumental Activities of Daily Living (IADLs) Complex everyday tasks such as shopping, banking, taking medication, and preparing meals.

Instrumental Support Various types of help that friends may provide such as transportation or helping with a housing move.

Insulin A hormone that is important for metabolism and utilization of energy from the ingested nutrients—especially glucose.

Intelligence Quotient A single score derived from a set of standardized tests developed to measure cognitive abilities in relation to one's age group.

Intergenerational Conflict The potential conflict between older and younger generations as they compete for jobs and resources.

Intergenerational Trauma The transmission of oppression and its negative consequences across generations.

Internal Validity Effects observed in the research study are due to the manipulation of the independent variable and not due to extraneous or confounding variables.

Intestacy Rules When a person dies without leaving a valid will, their property (the estate) must be shared out according to certain rules. Each province has intestacy rules that define an estate's beneficiaries and how much each is to receive.

Intra-individual Change Refers to changes that occur at an individual level as opposed to changes that occur at the group level.

Intraocular Pressure Fluid pressure inside the eye.

Intrinsic Aging A form of aging that takes place over the years and occurs irrespective of extrinsic factors; the gradual irreversible changes in structure and function of an organism.

Introvert A preoccupation with one's internal world of feelings, thoughts, and experiences.

Labour Force Participation Rate The participation rate for a particular group (age, sex, marital status, geographic area, etc.) is the total labour force in that group expressed as a percentage of the population 15 years of age and over in that group.

Labour Force Refers to the number of persons actually working or willing to work.

Larynx Also known as the voicebox, the larynx is a hollow, tubular organ connected to the top of the windpipe (trachea); air passes through the larynx on its way to the lungs. The larynx also produces vocal sounds and prevents the passage of food and other foreign particles into the lower respiratory tract.

Left-Branching Sentences A sentence in which subordinate elements of the sentence appear before the main meaning of the sentence (e.g., sweating in the noon heat, the man cut down the tree).

Leisure Activities Activities outside of work and household responsibilities. Examples of leisure activities include watching TV, playing sports, and playing cards.

Levels of Processing Theory A theory, proposed by Craik and Lockhart in 1972, that hypothesizes that the depth of memory processing affects memory function. The authors argued that deep processing leads to longer-lasting memories whereas shallow processing leads to memories that decay easily.

Liquidated The process of selling a property, business, or other assets, particularly to pay off a debt.

Living Apart Together Relationships A committed relationship between two people in which separate households are maintained.

Longitudinal Design A research design where data are collected from the same participants over time (often several years).

Long-Term-Care Facility A facility that provides a range of healthcare services, from periodic assistance to regular nursing care, for elderly residents.

Lower House Also known as the House of Commons—a component of the Parliament of

Canada, along with the Senate and the Monarch (represented by the governor general).

Magnetic Resonance Imaging A neuro-imaging technique that uses a magnetic field and pulses of radio wave energy to make pictures of organs and structures inside the body. MRI also may show problems that cannot be seen with other imaging methods such as CT scans.

Maintenance Rehearsal A type of rehearsal, as defined by Craik and Lockhart (1972) in relation to their levels of processing theory, that involves repeating information over and over again in a short period of time to assist in retention of that information.

Maturation Effect(s) Changes that can occur in a participant due to normal development processes as a function of time. These effects can threaten the internal validity of the study.

Maturity Principle The notion that individuals become more agreeable and emotionally stable, more conscientious, and less neurotic with age.

Maximum Longevity The oldest age one can possibly live.

Mean-Level Change A measure that compares mean-levels of a variable across two or more points in time.

Medicaid The second type of public health insurance in the United States; provides coverage for certain economically disadvantaged groups (e.g., older adults, blind, people with disabilities, or members of families with dependent children). Medicaid is jointly financed by the federal and state governments and is administered by each state.

Medical Assistance in Dying Legislation that allows eligible adults in Canada to request physician-assisted suicide or physician-assisted death. There are two types of medical assistance in dying available to Canadians—voluntary euthanasia and medically assisted suicide.

Medically Assisted Suicide When a physician or nurse practitioner gives or prescribes a drug that is *self-administered* to cause death. In some jurisdictions, this is referred to as physician-assisted suicide or physician-assisted death.

Medicare A national public health insurance program for aged and disabled individuals in the United States that is administered by the federal government. There are different components of Medicare (Part A and Part B), with each component providing coverage for different services and each has a different funding stream.

Medigap An extra health insurance that Americans can buy from a private company to pay healthcare costs not covered by Original Medicare, such as co-payments, deductibles, and healthcare for travelling outside the United States. Medigap policies do not cover long-term care, such as stays in a nursing facility, dental care, or vision care.

Mediterranean Diet A diet found in Mediterranean countries such as Greece that emphasizes consumption of fruits, vegetables, nuts, grains, olive oil (as opposed to butter), and grilled or steamed chicken and seafood (as opposed to red meat), plus a glass or two of red wine.

Melanin A natural substance produced by hair follicles that gives colour to hair, skin, and eyes.

Melanoma The most serious type of skin cancer. It develops in the cells that produce melanin. Exposure to ultraviolet (UV) radiation from sunlight or from tanning lights or beds increases the risk of developing melanoma.

Meta-analysis A systematic method that takes data from several independent studies and integrates those data using statistical analysis.

Minimum Data Set A standardized assessment instrument developed for long-term care settings that includes demographic information, medical diagnoses, as well as social and emotional functioning.

Mnemonics Any learning technique that aids information retention in the human memory.

Motivational Interviewing A technique in which the interviewer becomes a helper in the change process and expresses acceptance of her/his client.

Mourning The cultural and/or public display of grief through one's behaviour. It is the process through which the resolution of grief may be accomplished.

Multi-compartment Compliance Aids Containers that have different compartments with the medications organized by time of day (e.g., morning, noon, afternoon, and bedtime), usually for up to a week at a time. Typically, MCAs are filled by the individual.

Multi-sensory Stimulation (MSS) A therapy that can be used with individuals who have dementia, developmental difficulties, autism, or a brain injury. MSS involves placing the person in a soothing and stimulating environment. These types of environments are specially designed to deliver stimuli to various senses using lighting effects, colour, sounds, music, scents, and so on. Often the walls have a combination of different materials that may be explored using tactile senses. An aide or therapist is in the room with the person to facilitate relaxation.

Myelin An insulating layer that forms around nerves, including those in the brain and spinal cord. It is made up of protein and fatty substances. Myelin allows electrical impulses to transmit quickly and efficiently along the nerve cells.

Myelination The process of coating the axon of each neuron with a fatty coating called myelin, which protects the neuron and helps it conduct signals more efficiently.

Narrative Identity An internal and ever-changing story about our life.

Near Infrared Spectroscopic Imaging A neuroimaging technique that allows functional imaging of brain activity (or activation) through monitoring of blood oxygenation and blood volume in the prefrontal cortex.

Negative Self-Stereotyping When an older adult believes the negative stereotypes associated with aging and integrates these concepts into his or her self-concept.

Neurofibrillary Tangles These form inside the neuron and are made up of twisted fibres of a protein called tau.

Neuroimaging An umbrella term that refers to a variety of methods and technologies for investigating the brain in both humans and animals.

Neurotransmitters A chemical substance, released at the end of a nerve fibre following the arrival of a nerve impulse, that diffuses across the synapse, resulting in the transfer of the impulse to another nerve or muscle fibre, or some other structure.

Non-fluent Aphasia Difficulty communicating orally and with written words.

Non-normative Influences Random, unexpected events that are unique to an individual. Winning the lottery would be an example of a non-normative event.

Non-voluntary Euthanasia When a physician or someone else administers a medication such as a sedative or a neuromuscular relaxant or other intervention to intentionally end the life of a non-competent patient who could not give informed consent (e.g., an adult with Alzheimer's disease or other condition that compromises decision-making capacity); also called "passive euthanasia."

Normative Age-Graded Influences Normal age-related changes that most people experience. Puberty and menopause are examples of normative age-graded influences.

Normative History-Graded Influences Influences that are experienced by most people in a specific area or culture at the same time. These tend to be large in scale like the recent war in Syria or the terrorist attacks in Belgium in 2016.

Normosmic A normal sense of smell.

Norm(s) Cultural products (including values, customs, and traditions) that represent individuals' basic knowledge of what others do and think that they should do.

Nosocomial Infections Also known as a hospital-acquired infections (HAIs), nosocomial infections are infections that are acquired in a hospital or other health care facility.

Nursing Homes A type of long-term-care accommodation that provides housing, support, and direct care to frail seniors who are unable to function independently.

ObamaCare A law in the United States enacted in 2012 that aims to reform the

American healthcare system by providing affordable healthcare to more Americans; also known as the Affordable Care Act.

Obesity Body mass index greater than or equal to 30.

Obsessive-Compulsive Disorder (OCD) An anxiety disorder characterized by uncontrollable, unwanted thoughts and repetitive, ritualized behaviours that an individuals with OCD often recognize that their obsessive thoughts and compulsive behaviours are irrational but these thoughts and behaviours are very difficult to resist.

OECD Countries The Organization for Economic Cooperation and Development (OECD) countries are a group of 20 countries that collaborate information to promote policies that aim to improve the social well-being of the global population.

Old Age Security (OAS) Pension A taxable monthly social security payment available to most Canadians 65 years of age or older with individual income less than a defined amount.

Omission Errors Failure to identify the target letter in a distractor task.

Opioid Analgesics Pain relievers, also known as narcotic analgesics, that act on the central nervous system.

Optimization One of the three processes in Baltes and Baltes' *Model of Successful Aging* to help individuals manage their lives; for example, older adults can acquire new skills to help manage their limitations due to aging.

Oral Hypoglycemic Agents Drugs used in the treatment of diabetes mellitus. These drugs are taken orally and are used to lower glucose levels in the blood.

Osteoarthritis A type of arthritis that occurs when the protective cartilage on the ends of the bones wears down over time. It is the most common form of arthritis, affecting millions of people worldwide.

Osteoporosis A disease characterized by low bone mass and deterioration of bone tissue.

Over-Accommodation Relying on negative stereotypes of older adults to guide communication.

Overall Dependency Ratio The ratio of the combined youth population (0 to 19 years) and senior population (65 years and older) to the working-age population (20 to 64 years). The dependency ratio is expressed as the number of dependents for every 100 workers.

Panini Sandwich Older adults who are caring for themselves and another such as an adult child with a disability.

ParticipACTION A national nonprofit organization whose mission is to help Canadians sit less and move more. ParticipACTION, which was originally established in 1971, was re-established in 2007 with a goal of making physical activity a vital part of everyday life in Canada.

Performance-Based Assessment Assessing an individual's ability to perform ADLs and IADLs.

Peripheral Vascular Diseases Diseases of the blood vessels (arteries and veins) located outside the heart and brain.

Personal Wisdom Knowledge that is gained through experience.

Person-Centred-Care Approach An approach that aims to see the person as an individual, rather than focusing on the person's illness or on abilities that he or she may have lost.

Pessaries A plastic device inserted into the vagina that may help prevent urine leakage by supporting the neck of the bladder.

Pharmacodynamics The study of the effects of drugs and the mechanism of their action.

Pharmacokinetics The study of the absorption, distribution, metabolism, and excretion of drugs.

Pharmacotherapy Treatment of disease with medication.

Phonological Loop A part of the working memory model, proposed by Baddeley (2000), that stores and rehearses speech-based information, and deals with spoken and written material.

Physician-Assisted Suicide When the physician provides medication or a prescription to a patient as per the patient's explicit request, with the understanding that the patient intends to use the medication to end his or her life. This often is referred to as physician-assisted death.

Polypharmacy The simultaneous use of multiple medications by one patient.

Positron Emission Tomography Imaging Positron emission tomography uses small amounts of radioactive materials called radiotracers, a special camera, and a computer to help evaluate how your brain, other organs, and tissues are functioning.

PPP Public healthcare expenditure per person.

Practice Effects Outcomes that can occur when participants are tested more than once on the same measure of interest.

Premorbid Functioning How a person was functioning before the onset of physical or emotional illness.

Presbycusis An age-related hearing loss characterized by a gradual and progressive inability to hear, particularly high-frequency sounds.

Presbyopia The gradual loss of the ability to focus actively on nearby objects (e.g., loss of near vision).

Presbyphonia Changes associated with the aging voice.

Prevalence A statistical concept referring to the number of cases of a disease that are present in a particular population at a given time.

Primary Aging The gradual and inevitable process of bodily deterioration that takes place throughout life.

Primary Memory A former description of memory used to define memory that is retained for only a very short period of time. It has since been referred to as short-term memory in the dual store model of memory.

Primary Progressive Aphasia A neurological syndrome in which language capabilities become slowly and progressively impaired.

Private Dwelling A separate set of living quarters with a private entrance either from outside the building or from a common hall, lobby, vestibule, or stairway inside the building.

Programmed Theories of Aging Theories that argue that aging is genetically programmed to occur with time, and this process of deterioration eventually leads to death.

Proprioception The ability to sense stimuli arising within the body regarding position, motion, and equilibrium.

Proxy/Proxies A person/persons authorized to act on behalf of someone else.

Psychological Age An attempt to understand development by how an individual thinks, reasons, and acts independent of chronological age.

Psychometric Approach The branch of psychology that deals with the design, administration, and interpretation of quantitative tests for the measurement of psychological variables such as intelligence, aptitude, and personality traits.

Psychotropic Medications used in the treatment of mental illness that have an effect on thinking, feeling, and behaviours.

Quality of Death Index A measure of the quality of palliative care in 80 countries using 20 quantitative and qualitative indicators across five categories: the palliative and healthcare environment, human resources, the affordability of care, the quality of care, and the level of community engagement.

Recent Immigrants Individuals who have been a permanent resident of Canada for less than 10 years.

Refinancing an Existing Mortgage Renegotiating the terms of one's mortgage to lower monthly payments and free up some cash.

Registered Retirement Income Fund (RRIF) A tax-deferred retirement plan under the Canadian tax law. RRIFs are an extension of RRSPs; that is, RRSPs are used to save for retirement while RRIFs are used to withdraw income during retirement.

Rehearsal The process of continuously repeating to-be-remembered information. This method is effective in maintaining information over a short period of time.

Reminiscent Therapy Involves the discussion of past activities, events, and experiences with another person or group of people, usually with the aid of tangible prompts such as photographs and other familiar items from the past.

Residences for Senior Citizens Residences that provide support services (such as meals, housekeeping, medication supervision, and assistance in bathing) and supervision for residents 65 years of age and older who are independent in most activities of daily living.

Residential Care Residential care facilities can include lodges, assisted living, supportive housing, and long-term-care homes. Other terms across Canada are nursing and personal-care homes.

Respite Care Respite care provides caregivers a temporary rest from caregiving while the person they are caring for continues to receive care in a safe environment, often the home of the care-recipient.

Response Time The time that passes between the introduction of a stimulus and the reaction by the individual (subject) to that stimulus.

Retinoids A class of chemical compounds that are forms of vitamin A or are chemically related to it. Retinoids minimize the appearance of wrinkles, bolster the thickness and elasticity of the skin, slow the breakdown of collagen, and lighten brown spots caused by sun exposure.

Retirement Readiness Being financially prepared for retirement.

Retrieval Refers to the ability to get information out of the memory system when needed.

Reverse Mortgages A mortgage where the lender advances a lump sum to the borrower or provides a set amount of money each month.

Rheumatoid Arthritis A chronic inflammatory disorder that typically affects the small joints in hands and feet. Unlike the wear-and-tear damage of osteoarthritis, rheumatoid arthritis affects the lining of the joints, causing a painful swelling that can eventually result in bone erosion and joint deformity.

Royal Assent The Canadian Constitution Act of 1867 states that the approval of the Crown, signified by Royal Assent, is required for any bill to become law after passage by both the Senate and the House of Commons.

Sandwich Generation A generation of people (usually in their 30s or 40s) who care for their aging parents while supporting their own children.

Scaffolding Theory of Cognitive Aging (STAC) According to this theory, performance on various tasks of cognition is maintained due to the continuous engagement of compensatory scaffolding by the brain.

Screening Tools Tests used to identify individuals who may need further evaluation in a defined area (e.g., cognitive performance), with these tests being easy to administer, short in administration time, validated for the area under investigation, and relatively free of educational, language, and cultural bias.

Second Age One of the four ages of life, with this age described as from the early 20s through the 40s.

Secondary Aging The physical or cognitive changes that are related to lifestyle, disease, or injury and are not part of the normal aging process

Secondary Memory The vast body of knowledge stored over a lifetime.

Secretases Enzymes that cut pieces off the amyloid precursor protein (APP), which is embedded in the neuron's membrane. Secretases act on the APP to cleave the protein into three fragments.

Selection One of the three processes in Baltes and Baltes' *Model of Successful Aging* that refers to an individual focusing attention on fewer, more important goals; for example, some older adults may choose to downsize to a smaller house to help manage their physical limitations.

Self-Directed Informal Learning Learning without direct reliance on a teacher or mentor or organized curriculum.

Self-Stigma Internalizing the stereotypes about the illness you have.

Semantic Memory The part of long-term memory that is responsible for storing information about the world (e.g., the names of colours, the sounds of letters, capitals of countries in the world, and other basic facts).

Sensorineural Hearing Loss Hearing loss that occurs as a result of damage to the inner ear (cochlea) or the nerve pathways from the inner ear to the brain. Sensorineural hearing loss is progressive and irreversible and is the most common type of permanent hearing loss.

Sequential Design A type of research design that involves a combination of longitudinal and cross-sectional designs and that follows several cohorts of different ages over time.

Signal Intensity A measure of areas of abnormal tissue in the brain. When the brain is injured a scar will form over the injury. During MRI scanning, this scarring will give off a high signal that differentiates it from normal (unscarred) tissue.

Simple Families A family in which all children are the biological or adopted children of only one married spouse or common-law partner.

Single Photo Emission Computerized Tomography A nuclear neuroimaging technique that uses gamma rays.

Skip-Generation Households Grandparents living with their grandchildren with no middle generation present.

Small Vessel Disease Small vessel disease is thought to arise from damage to small arteries, arterioles, capillaries, and small veins in the brain, which often are referred to as white matter lesions.

Smart Environments A residence equipped with technology that allows monitoring of its inhabitants and/or encourages independence and the maintenance of good health.

Social Age A measure of how well a person's behaviour fits with the norms or expectations that society has for a person of a particular age.

Social Environment The immediate physical surroundings, social relationships, and sociocultural context or milieu in which people live and interact.

Social Security Agreement An international agreement between Canada and another country for the purposes of coordinating the pension programs of the two countries for people who have lived or worked in both countries. This agreement helps eligible immigrants to qualify for Old Age Security, disability, and survivor benefits offered through the Canadian government.

Socio-emotional Selectivity A theory that argues that social contact is motivated by a variety of goals including information seeking, self-concept, and emotional regulation.

Sporadic Alzheimer's Disease The most common form of Alzheimer's disease that happens to people age 65 and older. The ApoE gene has been associated with the development of this type of Alzheimer's disease, but the disease seems to occur because of a combination of genes, lifestyle, and environmental factors.

Squamous Cell Carcinoma A common form of skin cancer that develops in the thin, flat squamous cells that make up the outer layer of the skin. If not adequately treated at an early stage, squamous cell carcinoma can become life-threatening.

Stage Theory Description of the distinct phases we experience as we develop. In each phase of development, people display characteristic behaviour patterns and establish certain abilities.

Stepfamily A family that is formed on the remarriage of a divorced or widowed person and that includes one or more children.

Stereotyped Threat Fear of being judged in accordance with a negative stereotype of the group you belong to.

Stereotypes A pre-conceived notion or thought that can be adopted about specific types of individuals or certain ways of doing things. These thoughts or beliefs may or may not accurately reflect reality.

Stigma by Association The emotions and beliefs of those individuals closest to the stigmatized person, including family members and professionals.

Storage The ability to retain information in the memory system over time.

Stroke A medical condition that occurs when the blood supply to a part of the brain is interrupted or severely reduced, depriving the brain tissue of oxygen and nutrients. Because brain cells begin to die within minutes, a stroke is a medical emergency.

Structural Neuroimaging A neuroimaging technique that provides detailed images of the brain's anatomical structure at a certain point in time.

Structural Stigma The poor quality of healthcare services and inadequate behaviour of professionals.

Substance Abuse The habitual misuse of alcohol or drugs.

Substance Dependence An adaptive state that develops from repeated misuse of alcohol or drugs, which results in withdrawal upon cessation of drug or alcohol use.

Sub-syndromal Depressive Symptoms A term that is used when an individual has some depressive symptoms but not enough to meet the criteria for a diagnosis of a major depressive episode.

Supercentenarian Individuals who live over 110 years.

Supportive Housing A type of housing that helps individuals in their daily living through the provision of a physical environment that is safe, secure, enabling, and home-like. Assisted living is a type of supportive housing.

Tactile Memory Memory that is collected through feeling or touching something. It also is known as haptic memory.

Taste buds Sensory organs that are found on the tongue and allow us to experience tastes that are sweet, salty, sour, bitter, and umami.

Terminal Drop A rapid decline in cognitive functioning just prior to death.

Terminal Predicted to lead to death, especially slowly; incurable.

Terror Management Theory A theory that proposes a basic psychological conflict that results from having a desire to live but realizing that death is inevitable. This conflict produces terror, and is believed to be unique to human beings. It explains why people engage in certain behaviours to reduce this conflict.

Tertiary Aging The rapid decrease in cognitive and functional ability in the years prior to death.

Third Age One of the four ages of life, with this age described as from roughly 50 to 75 years of age.

Time of Measurement Effect(s) Differences due to cultural, historical, environmental, or other events at the time that the data are collected.

Time-Sequential Design A research design that compares two or more cross-sectional samples at two or more times of measurement.

Tip-of-the-Tongue Phenomena Refers to the experience of being unable to produce a name or a word despite the experience of feeling confident of one's knowledge of the name or word.

Transactional Model Personality development is influenced by both genes and the environment.

Under-Accommodation Failure to consider how normal age-related changes affect speaking and listening.

Undue Influence Can occur when participants are recruited to participate in research by those who have some form of control over them. This influence may cause the participant to act otherwise than by their own free will or without adequate attention to the consequences.

UPPAC Mnemonic for the five principles that the Canadian healthcare system is based on: Universality, Portability, Public administration, Accessibility, and Comprehensiveness.

Upper House Also known as the Senate—a component of the Parliament of Canada, along with the House of Commons and the Monarch (represented by the governor general).

Vaccination Involves the injection of a killed microbe in order to stimulate the immune system against the microbe, thereby preventing disease. Vaccination (also called immunization) against viral diseases involves injection of a virus that has been weakened or killed. Vaccination against bacterial diseases generally involves using only a small portion of the dead bacteria to stimulate the formation of antibodies against the whole bacteria.

Valvular Heart Disease A type of heart disease that occurs when one or more of the four valves (tricuspid, pulmonary, mitral, and aortic) of the heart do not work correctly.

Variable In research, a variable is any attribute, characteristic, or phenomenon that can be controlled or changed. There are three types of variables in research: the independent variable, the dependent variable, and the control variable, also known as the constant variable.

Visible Minority Visible minorities in Canada are persons who are non-Caucasian in race or non-white in colour and who do not report being Aboriginal.

Visuospatial Sketchpad A part of the working memory model, proposed by Baddeley (2000), that stores and manipulates visual and spatial information.

Voluntary Euthanasia When a physician or someone else administers a medication such as a sedative or a neuromuscular relaxant or other intervention to intentionally end a mentally competent patient's life, with this intervention done at the individual's request. This often is referred to as voluntary active euthanasia.

Wear and Tear Theory A theory that argues that the effects of aging are caused by damage done to cells and body systems over time. Essentially, the body systems "wear out" due to use, and, once they wear out, these body systems can no longer function correctly.

Well-Being A dynamic concept that includes subjective, social, and psychological dimensions as well as health-related behaviours.

White Matter Composed of bundles of axons that connect various grey matter areas of the brain to each other and carry nerve impulses between neurons.

Working Memory Model A model of working memory proposed by Baddeley and Hitch (1974) and revised by Baddeley in 2000. It is a model that has replaced what used to be called short-term memory. Working memory is conceptualized as consisting of a central executive, a phonological loop, a visuospatial sketchpad, and an episodic buffer. All the components play an important part in the temporary storage of information.

REFERENCES

A Place for Mom. (2016). *Guide to seniors housing in Canada.* Retrieved from www.aplaceformom.com/canada/canada-seniors-housing-guide

Abrams, R.C., & Bromberg, C.E. (2006). Personality disorders in the elderly: A flagging field of inquiry. *International Journal of Geriatric Psychiatry, 21*(11), 1013–1017. doi:10.1002/gps.1614

Abramson, T.A. (2016). Older adults: The "Panini sandwich" generation. *Clinical Gerontologist, 38*(4), 251–267. doi:10.1080/07317115.2015.1032466

Ackerman, S., Zuroff, D.C., & Moskowitz, D.S. (2000). Generativity in midlife and young adults: Links to agency, communion, and subjective well-being. *The International Journal of Aging and Human Development, 50*(1), 17–41. doi:10.2190/9F51-LR6T-JHRJ-2QW6

Adams, K.B., Leibbrandt, S., & Moon, H. (2011). A critical review of the literature on social and leisure activity and wellbeing in later life. *Ageing and Society, 31*(4), 683–712. doi:10.1017/S0144686X10001091

Adams, R.G., & Ueno, K. (2006). Middle aged and older adult men's friendships. In V.H. Beford & B. Formaniuk Turner (Eds.), *Men in relationships: A new look from a life course perspective* (pp. 103–124). New York, NY: Springer.

Adams, W., & Clarmont, W. (2016). Intergenerational trauma and indigenous healing. *Visions, 11*(4), 7–9. Retrieved from http://www.heretohelp.bc.ca/visions/indigenous-people-vol11/intergenerational-trauma-and-indigenous-healing

Aday, R. (2003). *Aging prisoners: Crisis in American corrections.* Westport, CT: Praeger Publishers.

Aichele, S., Rabbit, P., & Ghisletta, P. (2015). Life span decrements in fluid intelligence and processing speed predict mortality risk. *Psychology and Aging, 30*(3), 598–612. http://dx.doi.org/10.1037/pag0000035

Albert, M.S., DeKosky, S.T., Dickson, D., Dubois, B., Feldman, H.H., Fox, N.C., … Phelps, C.H. (2011). The diagnosis of mild cognitive impairment due to Alzheimer's disease: Recommendations from the National Institute on Aging-Alzheimer's Association workgroups on diagnostic guidelines for Alzheimer's disease. *Alzheimer's & Dementia, 7*(3), 270–279. doi:10.1016/j.jalz.2011.03.008

Alberta Caregivers Association. (2014). *About caregivers.* Retrieved from www.albertacaregivers.org/caregivers/

Alberta Order of Excellence, The. (2008). https://www.lieutenantgovernor.ab.ca/Aoe/health/helen-hays/index.html

Alberts, N.M., Hadjistavropoulos, H.D., Pugh, N.E., & Jones, S.L. (2011). Dementia anxiety among older adult caregivers: An exploratory study of older adult caregivers in Canada. *International Psychogeriatrics, 23*(6), 880–886. doi:10.1017/S1041610211000299

Allemand, A., Steiner, M., & Hill, P.L. (2013). Effects of a forgiveness intervention for older adults. *Journal of Counseling Psychology 60*(2), 279–286. doi:10.1037/a0031839

Allemand, M., Zimprich, D., & Martin, M. (2008). Long-term correlated change in personality traits in old age. *Psychology and Aging, 23*(3), 545–557. doi:10.1037/a0013239

Allentuck, A. (2016, March 17). Taking OAS eligibility to age 65 makes Canada the odd one out when it comes to global pensions. *Financial Post.* Retrieved from http://business.financialpost.com/personal-finance/retirement/taking-oas-eligibility-back-to-age-65-makes-canada-the-odd-one-out-when-it-comes-to-global-pensions

Allport, G.W. (1937). *Personality: A psychological interpretation.* New York, NY: Holt, Rinehart & Winston.

Almeida, D.M., Draper, B., Pirkis, J., Snowdon, J., Lautenschlager, N.T., Byrne, G., … Pfaff, J. (2012). Anxiety, depression and comorbid anxiety and depression: Risk factors and outcomes over two years. *International Psychogeriatrics, 24*(10), 1622–1632. doi:10.1017/S1041611021200107X

Almeida, D.M., Piazza, J.R. Stawski R.S., & Klein, L.C. (2011). The speedometer of life: Stress, health, and aging. In K.W. Schaie & S.L. Willis (Eds.), *The handbook of the psychology of aging* (7th ed., pp.

191–206). New York, NY: Elsevier. doi:10.1016/B978-0-12-380882-0.00012-7

Altmann, A., Tian, L., Henderson, V.W., & Greicius, M.D. (2014). Sex modifies the APOE-related risk of developing Alzheimer disease. *Annals of Neurology, 75*(4), 563–573. doi:10.1002/ana.24135

Alterovitz, S.S., & Mendelsohn, G.A. (2009). Partner preferences across the lifespan: Online dating by older adults. *Psychology and Aging, 24*(2), 513–517. doi:10.1037/a0015897

Altschuler, J., & Katz, A. (2015). "Of course it's relevant!": A focus group study of older adults' perceived importance of HIV/AIDS prevention education. *Qualitative Social Work, 14*(5), 687–701. doi:10.1177/1473325014566667

Alsnih, R., & Hensher, D.A. (2003). The mobility and accessibility expectations of seniors in an aging population. *Transportation Research Part A, 37*(10), 903–916. doi:10.1016/S0965-8564(03)00073-9

Alzheimer Society of Canada. (2014a). *Understanding genetics and Alzheimer's disease.* Toronto, ON: Author. Retrieved from www.alzheimer.ca/~/media/Files/national/Research/understanding_genetics_e.pdf

Alzheimer Society of Canada. (2014b). *Risk factors.* Toronto, ON: Author. Retrieved from www.alzheimer.ca/en/About-dementia/Alzheimer-s-disease/Risk-factors

Alzheimer Society of Canada. (2014c). *Mild cognitive impairment.* Toronto, ON: Author. Retrieved from www.alzheimer.ca/~/media/Files/national/Other-dementias/other_dementias_MCI_e.pdf

Alzheimer Society of Canada. (2015). *Other dementias: Vascular dementia.* Toronto, ON: Author. Retrieved from www.alzheimer.ca/~/media/Files/national/Other-dementias/other_dementias_Vascular_e.pdf

Alzheimer Society of Canada. (2016a). *Latest information and statistics.* Toronto, ON: Author. Retrieved from http://www.alzheimer.ca/en/Get-involved/Advocacy/Latest-info-stats

Alzheimer Society of Canada. (2016b). *Prevalence and monetary cost of dementia in Canada.* Toronto, ON: Author. Retrieved from www.alzheimer.ca/~/media/Files/national/Statistics/prevalence_summary_e.pdf

Alzheimer Society of Canada. (2016c). *Alzheimer's disease and other dementias.* Retrieved from www.alzheimer.ca/~/media/Files/.../Other-dementias

Alzheimer Society of Canada. (2016d). *Stigma.* Retrieved from www.alzheimer.ca/en/About-dementia/What-is-dementia/Stigma

Alzheimer's Association. (2016a). 2016 Alzheimer's disease facts and figures. *Alzheimer's & Dementia, 12*(4), 459–509. doi:10.1016/j.jalz.2016.03.001

Alzheimer's Association. (2016b). *Alzheimer brain tangles.* Retrieved from www.alz.org/braintour/tangles.asp

Alzheimer's Disease International. (2012). *World Alzheimer Report 2012: Overcoming the stigma of dementia.* Retrieved from https://www.alz.co.uk/research/world-report-2012

Alzheimer's Disease International. (2015). *Women and dementia. A global research review.* Retrieved from https://www.alz.co.uk/women-and-dementia

American Civil Liberties Union. (2012). *At America's expense: The mass incarceration of the elderly.* New York, NY: Author. Retrieved from www.aclu.org/files/assets/elderlyprisonreport_20120613_1.pdf

American Council on Education (ACE). (2007). *Framing new terrain: Older adults and higher education.* Washington, DC: Author. Retrieved from http://plus50.aacc.nche.edu/documents/older_adults_and_higher_education.pdf.

American Geriatric Society. (2003). *Screening recommendation: Clinical guidelines for alcohol use disorders in older adults.* Retrieved from www.americangeriatrics.org/products/positionpapers/alcohol.shtml

American Psychiatric Association. (1980). *Diagnostic and statistical manual of mental disorders* (3rd ed.). Washington, D.C.: Author.

American Psychiatric Association. (1987). *Diagnostic and statistical manual of mental disorders* (3rd ed., rev.). Washington, DC: Author.

American Psychiatric Association. (1994). *Diagnostic and statistical manual of mental disorders* (4th ed.). Washington, D.C.: Author.

American Psychiatric Association. (2000). *Diagnostic and statistical manual of mental disorders* (4th ed., rev.). Washington, DC: Author.

American Psychiatric Association. (2013). *Diagnostic and statistical manual of mental disorders* (5th ed.). Arlington, VA: Author.

American Psychiatric Association. (2014). Guidelines for psychological practice with older adults. *American Psychologist, 69*(1), 34–65. doi:10.1037/a003506

American Psychological Association. (2016). *Grief: Coping with the loss of your loved one.* Washington, DC: APA Press. Retrieved from www.apa.org/helpcenter/grief.aspx

American Society of Plastic Surgeons. (2017a). *New statistics reflect the changing nature of plastic surgery. American Society of Plastic Surgeons.* Retrieved from /

www.plasticsurgery.org/news/press-releases/new
-statistics-reflect-the-changing-face-of-plastic-
surgery

American Society of Plastic Surgeons. (2017b). *More than $16 billion spent in cosmetic plastic surgery.* Retrieved from www.plasticsurgery.org/news/press -releases/more-than-16-billion-spent-on-cosmetic -plastic-surgery

Anand, A., & MacLullich, A.M.J. (2013). Delirium in hospitalized older adults. *Medicine, 41*(1), 39–42. doi:10.1016/j.mpmed.2012.10.011

Anand, A., & MacLullich, A.M.J. (2017). Delirium in hospitalized older adults. *Medicine, 45*(1), 46–50. doi:10.1016/j.mpmed.2016.10.006

Anderson, K.K., Cheng, J., Susser, E., McKenzie, K.J., & Kurdyak, P. (2015). Incidence of psychotic disorders among first generation immigrants and refugees in Ontario. *CMAJ, 187*(9), 279–286. doi:10.1503/cmaj.141420

Anderson, N.D., Damianakis, T., Kroger, E., Wagner, L.M., Dawson, D.R., Binns, M.A., … The Bravo Team. (2014). The benefits associated with volunteering among seniors: A critical review and recommendations for future research. *Psychological Bulletin, 140*(6), 1505–1533. doi:10.1037/a0037610

Anderson, N.D., Murphy, K.J., & Troyer, A.K. (2012). *Living with mild cognitive impairment: A guide to maximizing brain health and reducing risk of dementia.* New York, NY: Oxford University Press.

Andreescu, C., & Varon, D. (2015). New research on anxiety disorders in the elderly and an update on evidence-based treatments. *Current Psychiatric Reports,* 1–7. doi:10.1007/s11920-015-0595-8

Andrews, G.J., Campbell, L., Denton, M., & McGilton, K.S. (2009). Gerontology in Canada: History, challenges, research. *Ageing International, 34,* 136–153. doi:10.1007/s12126-009-9042-7

Aplin, T., de Jonge, D., & Gustafsson, L. (2014). Understanding home modifications impact on clients and their family's experience of home: A qualitative study. *Australian Occupational Therapy Journal, 62*(12), 123–131. doi:10.1111/1440-1630.12156

Ardekani, B.A., Convit, A., & Bachman, A.H. (2016). Analysis of the MIRIAD data shows sex differences in hippocampal atrophy progression. *Journal of Alzheimer's Disease, 50*(3), 847–857. doi:10.3233.JAD-150780

Ardelt, M. (2003). Empirical assessment of a three-dimensional wisdom scale. *Research on Aging, 25*(3), 275–324. doi:10.1177/0164027503025003004

Ardelt, M. (2008). Self-development through selflessness. The paradoxical process of growing wiser. In H.A. Wayment & J.J. Bauer (Eds.), *Transcending self-interest: Psychological explorations of the quiet ego* (pp. 221–223). Washington, DC: American Psychological Association.

Ardelt, M. (2010). Age, experience, and the beginning of wisdom. In D. Dannefer & C. Phillipson (Eds.), *The SAGE handbook of social gerontology* (pp. 306–316). Thousand Oaks, CA: Sage Publications.

Ardelt, M. (2011). Wisdom, age, and wellbeing. In K.W. Schaie & S.L. Willis (Eds.), *Handbook of the psychology of aging* (7th ed., pp. 279–291). Amsterdam, NI: Elsevier. doi:10.1016/B978-0-12-380882-0.00018-8

Ardelt, M. (2015). Disentangling the relations between wisdom and different types of well-being in old age: Findings from a short-term longitudinal study. *Journal of Happiness Studies, 17*(5), 1–22. doi:10.1007/s10902-015-9680-2

Arias, E. (2015). United States life tables, 2011. *National Vital Statistics Reports, 64*(11), 1–62.

Armanios, M. (2013). Telomeres and age-related disease: How telomere biology informs clinical paradigms. *Journal of Clinical Investigation, 123*(3), 996–1002. doi:10.1172/JCI66370

Armstrong, L., Wuthrich, V.M., Knight, A., & Joiner, R. (2014). Worry and depression in the old and young: Differences and mediating factors. *Behavior Change, 31* (4), 279–289. doi.org/10.1017/bec.2014.21

Arndt, S., Clayton, R., & Schultz, S. (2011). Trends in substance abuse treatment 1998–2008: Increasing older adult first-time admissions for illicit drugs. *American Journal of Geriatric Psychiatry, 19*(8), 704–711. doi:10.1097/JGP.0b013e31820d942b

Arnup, K. (2013). *Death, dying and Canadian families.* Ottawa, ON: The Vanier Institute of the Family.

Asbell, P.A., Dualan, I., Mindel, J., Brocks, D., Ahmad, M., & Epstein, S. (2005). Age-related cataract. *The Lancet, 365*(9459), 599–609. doi:10.1016/ S0140-6736(05)17911-2

Ashe, C.A., Miller, W.C., Eng, J.J., & Noreau, L. (2009). Older adults, chronic disease and leisure-time physical activity. *Gerontology, 55*(1), 64–72. doi:10.1159/000141518

Atchley, R.C. (1989). A continuity theory of normal aging. *The Gerontologist, 29*(2), 183–190. doi:10.1093/ geront/29.2.183

Atkinson, R.C., & Shiffrin, R.M. (1968). Human memory: A proposed system and its control processes. In K.W. Spence & J.T. Spence (Eds.), *The psychology* of learning and motivation: Advances in research and theory (Vol. 2, pp. 89–195). New York, NY: Academic Press. doi:10.1016/S0079-7421(08)60422-3

Atkinson, R.M., Turner, J.A., Kofoed, L.L., & Tolson, R.L. (1985). Early versus late alcoholism in older persons: Preliminary findings. Alcoholism, Clinical and Experimental Research, 9, 513–515. doi:10.1111/j.1530-0277.1985.tbo5594.x

Au, J., Sheehan, E., Tsai, N., Duncan, G.J., Buschkuehl, M., & Jaeggi, S.M. (2015). Improving fluid intelligence with training on working memory: A meta-analysis. Psychonomic Bulletin and Review, 22(2), 366–377. doi:10.3758/s13423-014-0699-x

Ayers, C.R., Namji, S., Mayes, T.L., & Dozier, M.E. (2015). Hoarding disorder in older adulthood. American Journal of Geriatric Psychiatry, 23(4), 416–422. doi:10.1016/j.jagp.2014.05.009

Ayers, C.R., Saxena, S., Golshan, S. & Wetherell, J.L. (2010). Age at onset and clinical features of late life compulsive hoarding. International Journal of Geriatric Psychiatry, 25(2), 142–149. doi:10.1002/gps.2310

Ayers, C.R., Scheisher, D., Liu, L., & Wetherell, J.L. (2012). Functional impairment in geriatric hoarding patients. Journal of Obsessive-Compulsive and Related Disorders, 1(4), 263–266. doi.org/10.1016/j.jocrd.2012.07.002

Ayers, C.R., Wetherell, J.L., Golshan, S., & Saxena, S. (2011). Cognitive-behavioral therapy for geriatric compulsive hoarding. Behavior Research and Therapy, 49(10), 689–694. doi:10.1016/j.brat.2011.07.002

Babatunde, O.T., Outlaw, K.R., Forbes, B., & Gay, T. (2014). Revisiting Baby Boomers and alcohol use: Emerging trends. Journal of Human Behavior in the Social Environment, 24, 597–611. doi:10.1080/10911359.2014.914830

Baddeley, A.D. (1986). Working memory. Oxford, UK: Oxford University Press.

Baddeley, A.D. (2000). The episodic buffer: A new component of working memory? Trends in Cognitive Sciences, 4(11), 417–423. doi:10.1016/S1364-6613(00)01538-2

Baddeley, A.D. (2006). Working memory: An overview. In S. Pickering (Ed.), Working memory and education. (pp. 1–31). New York, NY: Academic Press.

Baddeley, A.D. (2010). Working memory. Current Biology, 20(4), R136-R140. doi:10.1016/j.cub.2009.12.014

Baddeley, A.D., & Hitch, G. (1974). Working memory. In G.A. Bower (Ed.), The psychology of learning and motivation: Advances in research and theory (Vol. 8, pp. 47–89). New York, NY: Academic Press.

Baddeley, J., & Singer, J.A. (2007). Charting the life story's path: Narrative identity across the lifespan. In J. Clandinin (Ed.), Handbook of narrative inquiry: Mapping a methodology (pp. 177–202). New York, NY: SAGE Publications. doi:10.413/9781452226552.n7

Baker, A.A. (1975). Granny battering. Modern Geriatrics, 5(8) 20–24. Retrieved from https://www.ncbi.nlm.nih.gov/pmc/articles/PMC1674523/pdf/brmedj01463-0050b.pdf

Bal, A.C., Reiss, A.E., Rudolph, C.W., & Baltes, B.B. (2011). Examining positive and negative perceptions of older workers: A meta-analysis. The Journals of Gerontology, Series B: Psychological Sciences and Social Sciences, 66(6), 687–698. doi:10.1093/geronb/gbr056

Balazs, A. (2014). Advertising and marketing. In C.L. Harrington, D.D. Bielby, & A.R. Bardo (Eds.), Aging, media, and culture (pp. 25–36). Lanham, MD: Lexington Books.

Ball, K., Berch, D.B., Helmers, K.F., Jobe, J.B., Leveck, M.D., Marsiske, M., … Willis, S.L., for the ACTIVE study group (2006). Effects of cognitive training interventions with older adults. A randomized clinical trial. Journal of the American Medical Association, 288(18), 2271–2281. doi:10.1001/jama.288.18.2271

Ballard, C., Corbett, A., Chitramohan, R., & Aarsland, D. (2009). Management of agitation and aggression associated with Alzheimer's disease: Controversies and possible solutions. Current Opinion in Psychiatry, 22(6), 532–540. doi:10.1097/YCO.0b013e32833111f9

Balsis, S., Gleason, M.E.J., Woods, C.M., & Oltmanns, T.F. (2007). An item response theory analysis of DSM-IV personality disorder criteria across younger and older age groups. Psychology and Aging, 22(1), 171–185. doi:10.1037/0882-7974.22.1.171

Balsis, S., Zweig, R.A., & Molinari, V. (2015). Personality disorders in late life. In P.A. Lichtenberg & B.T. Mast (Eds.), APA handbook of clinical geropsychology (Vol. 2, pp. 79–93). Washington, DC: American Psychological Association.

Baltes, P.B. (1987). Theoretical propositions of lifespan developmental psychology: On the dynamics between growth and decline. Developmental Psychology, 23(5), 611–626. Retrieved from http://library.mpib-berlin.mpg.de/ft/pb/PB_Theoretical_1987.pdf

Baltes, P.B., & Baltes, M.M. (1990). Psychological perspectives on successful aging: The model of selective optimization with compensation. In P.B. Baltes & M.M. Baltes (Eds.), Successful aging: Perspectives from the behavioral sciences (pp. 1–34). Cambridge, UK: Cambridge University Press.

Baltes, P.B. & Smith, J. (2004). Lifespan psychology: From developmental contextualism to developmental biocultural co-constructivism. *Research in Human Development*, *1*(3), 123–144. doi:10.1207/s15427617rhd0103_1

Band-Winterstein, T., & Manchik-Rimon, C. (2014). The experience of being an old never-married single: A life course perspective. *The International Journal of Aging & Human Development*, *78*(4), 379–401. doi:10.2190/AG.78.4.d

Bandura, A. (1999). *Social cognitive theory of personality*. In L.A. Pervin & O.P. John (Eds.), *Handbook of personality: Theory and research* (2nd ed., pp. 154–196). New York, NY: Guilford Press.

Bangen, K.J., Meeks, T.W., & Jeste, D.V. (2013). Defining and assessing wisdom: A review of the literature. *The American Journal of Geriatric Psychiatry*, *21*(12), 1254–1266. doi:10.1016/j.jagp.2012.11.020

Barak, B. (2009). Age identity: A cross-cultural global approach. *International Journal of Behavioral Development*, *33*(1), 2–11. doi:10.1177/0165025408099485

Barak, B., & Schiffman, L.G. (1981). Cognitive age: A non chronological age variable. In K.B. Monroe (Ed.), *Advances in consumer research* (Vol. *8*, pp. 602–606). Ann Arbor, MI: Association for Consumer Research.

Barnes, C., & Mercer, G. (2003). *Disability*. Cambridge, UK: Polity Press.

Barnes, D.E., & Yaffe, K. (2011). The projected effect of risk factor reduction in Alzheimer's disease prevalence. *The Lancet. Neurology*, *10*(9), 819–828. doi:10.1016/S1474-4422(11)70072-2

Barrett, C., Whyte, C., Comfort, J., Lyons, A., & Crameri, P. (2015). Social connection, relationships, and older lesbian and gay people. *Sexual and Relationship Therapy*, *30*(1), 131–142. doi:10.1080/14681994.2014.963983

Batty, G.D., Deary, I.J., Benzeval, M., & Der, G. (2008). Does IQ predict cardiovascular disease mortality as strongly as established risk factors? Comparison of effect estimates using the West of Scotland twenty-07 Cohort Study. *European Journal of Cardiovascular Prevention and Rehabilitation*, *17*(1), 24–27. doi:10.1097/HJR.0b013e328321311b

Batty, G.D., Deary, I.J., & Gottfredson, L.S. (2007). Premorbid (early life) IQ and later mortality risk: Systematic review. *Annals of Epidemiology*, *17*(4), 278–288. doi:10.1016/j.annepidem.2006.07.010

Batelaan, N.M., Ten Have, M., Van Balkom, A.J., Tuithof, M., & De Graaf, R. (2014). Anxiety disorders and onset of cardiovascular disease: The differential impact of panic phobias and worry. *Journal of Anxiety Disorders*, *28*(2), 252–258. doi:10.1016/j.anxdis.2013.12.003

Baumgart, M., Snyder, H.M., Carillo, M.C., Fazio, S., Kim, H., & Johns, H. (2015). Summary of the evidence of modifiable risk factors for cognitive decline and dementia: A population-based perspective. *Alzheimer's & Dementia*, *11*(6), 718–726. doi:10.1016/j.alz.2015.05.016

Bauman, N. (2015). The hearing aids of yesteryear: A brief history of hearing aids from then to now. *Canadian Audiologist*, *2*(4). Retrieved from http://canadianaudiologist.ca/the-hearing-aids-of-yesteryear/

Baum, S., & Titone, D. (2014). Moving toward a neuroplasticity view of bilingualism, executive control, and aging. *Applied Psycholinguistics*, *35*(5), 857–894. doi:10.1017/S0142716414000174

Bayliss, E.A., Edwards, A.E, Steiner, J.F., & Main, D.S. (2008). Processes of care desired by elderly patients with multimorbidities. *Family Practice*, *25*(4), 287–293. doi:10.1093/fampra/cmn040

Beach, T.G., Monsell, S.E., Phillips, L.E., & Kukull, W. (2012). Accuracy of the clinical diagnosis of Alzheimer disease at National Institute on Aging Alzheimer's Disease Centers, 2005–2010. *Journal of Neuropathology & Experimental Neurology*, *71*(4), 266–273. doi:10.1097/NEN.0b013e31824b211b

Beard, J.R., Blaney, S., Cerda, M., Frye, V., Lovasi, G.S., Ompad, D., … Vlahov, D. (2009). Neighborhood characteristics and disability in older adults. *The Journals of Gerontology, Series B: Psychological Sciences & Social Sciences*, *64*(2), 252–257. doi:10.1093/geronb/gbn018

Beard, J.R., & Petitot, C. (2010). Ageing and urbanization: Can cities be designed to foster active ageing? *Public Health Reviews*, *32*(2), 427–450. doi:10.1136/medethics-2011-100066. Epub January 12, 2012.

Beason-Held, L.L., Kraut, M.A., & Resnick, S.M. (2008a). Longitudinal changes in aging brain function. *Neurobiology of Aging*, *29*(4), 483–496. doi:10.1016/j.neurobiolaging.2006.10.031

Beason-Held, L.L., Kraut, M.A., & Resnick, S.M. (2008b). Temporal patterns of longitudinal change in aging brain function. *Neurobiology of Aging*, *29*(4), 497–513. doi:10.1016/j.neurobiolaging.2006.11.011

Beaujot, R., & McQuillan, K., (1982). *Growth and dualism: The demographic development of Canadian Society*. Toronto, ON: University of Toronto Press. doi:10.1353/can.1983.0089

Beck, A.T. (1967). *Depression: Causes and treatment*. Philadelphia, PA: University of Pennsylvania Press.

Beck, A.T., Steer, R.A., & Brown, G.K. (1996). *BDI-II Manual*. San Antonio, TX: Psychological Corporation.

Beekman, W. (2011). Completed life of the elderly. In *The self-chosen death of the elderly* (pp. 14–20). Naarden, NL: Society for Old Age Rational Society.

Beiser, M. (2005). The health of immigrants and refugees in Canada. *Canadian Journal of Public Health*, *96* (Suppl. 2), S30-S44. Retrieved from www.researchgate.net /profile/Morton_Beiser2/publication/7680586_The _health_of_immigrants_and_refugees_in_Canada /links/0c9605302642ed12f8000000.pdf

Bélanger, A., Carrière, Y., & Sabourin, P. (2016). Understanding employment participation of older workers: The Canadian perspective. *Canadian Public Policy*, *42*(1), 94–109. doi:10.3138/cpp.2015-042

Ben-David, B.M., & Schneider, B.A. (2010). A sensory origin for color-word Stroop effects in aging: Simulating age-related changes in color-vision mimics age-related changes in Stroop. *Aging, Neuropsychology, and Cognition*, *17*(6), 730–746. doi: 10.1080/13825585.2010.510553

Bennett, D.A., Schneider, J.A., Arvanitakis, Z., Kelly, J.F., Aggarwal, N.T., Shah, R.C., & Wilson, R.S. (2006). Neuropathology of older persons without cognitive impairment from two community-based studies. *Neurology*, *66*(12), 1837–1844. doi:10.1212/01.wnl.0000219668.47116.e6

Bennett, S., & Thomas, A.J. (2014). Depression and dementia: Cause, consequence or coincidence? *Maturitas*, *79*(2), 184–190. doi:10.1016/j.maturitas.2014.05.009

Bennett, T., & Gaines, J. (2010). Believing what you hear: The impact of ageing stereotypes upon the old. *Educational Gerontology*, *36*, 435–455. doi:10.1080/0360127/0903212336

Bentrott, M., & Margrett, J. (2011). Taking a person-centered approach to understanding sexual expression among long-term care residents: Theoretical perspectives and research challenges. *Ageing International*, *36*(3), 401–417. doi:10.1007/s12126-011-9110-7

Bergfeld, W.F. (1997). The aging skin. *International Journal of Fertility and Women's Medicine*, *42*(2), 57–66. Retrieved from www.unboundmedicine.com/ medline/journal/International_journal_of_fertility _and_women's_medicine

Berglund, E., Lytsy, P., & Westerling, R. (2015). Health and wellbeing in informal caregivers and non-caregivers: A comparative cross-sectional study of the Swedish general population. *Health and Quality of Life Outcomes*, *13*(109). doi:10.1186/s12955-015-0309-2

Bergman, E.J., Haley, W.E., & Small, B.J. (2011). Who uses bereavement services? An examination of service use by bereaved dementia caregivers. *Aging & Mental Health*, *15*(4), 531–540. doi:10.1088/13607863.2010.543661

Bergsma, A., & Ardelt, M. (2012). Self-reported wisdom and happiness: An empirical investigation. *Journal of Happiness Studies*, *13*(3), 481–499. doi:10.1007/s10902-011-9275-5

Bernard, A. (2012). *The job search of the older unemployed* (Component of Statistics Canada Catalogue no. 75-001-X). Ottawa, ON: Statistics Canada.

Bethancourt, H.J., Rosenberg, D.E., Beatty, T., & Arterburn, D.E. (2014). Barriers to and facilitators of physical activity program use among older adults. *Clinical Medicine & Research*, *12*(1–2), 10–20. doi:10.3121/cmr.2013.1171

Bherer, L., Erickson, K.I., & Liu-Ambrose, T. (2013). A review of the effects of physical activity and exercise on cognitive and brain functions in older adults. *Journal of Aging Research, 2013*, 8 pages. doi:10.1155/2013/657508

Bialystok, E., Craik, F.I.M., & Freedman, M. (2007). Bilingualism as a protection against the onset of symptoms of dementia. *Neuropsychologia*, *45*(2), 459–464. doi:10.1016/j.neuropsychologia.2006.10.009

Bibby, R.W. (2009). *The emerging millennials: How Canada's newest generation is responding to change and choice*. Lethbridge, AB: Project Canada Books.

Biola, H., Sloane, P.D., Williams, C.S., Daaleman, T.P., & Zimmerman, S. (2010). Preferences versus practice: Life-sustaining treatments in last months of life in long-term care. *Journal of the American Medical Directors Association*, *11*(1), 42–51. doi10.106/ j.jamda.2009.07.005

Blackburn, R., & Bradshaw, T. (2014). Music therapy for service users with dementia: A critical review of the literature. *Journal of Psychiatric and Mental Health Nursing*, *21*(10), 879–888. doi:10.1111/jpm.12165

Bleidorn, W., Kandler, C., Reimann, R., Spinath, F.M., & Angleitner, A. (2009). Patterns and sources of adult personality development: Growth curve analyses of the NEO PI-R scales in a longitudinal twin study. *Journal of Personality and Social Psychology*, *97*(1), 142–155. doi:10.1037/a0015434

Blieszner, R., & Roberto, K.A. (2012). Partners and friends in adulthood. In S.K. Whitbourne & M.J. Sliwinski (Eds.), *The Wiley-Blackwell handbook of adulthood and aging* (pp. 381–398). Oxford, UK: Wiley-Blackwell.

Blow, F.C., & Barry, K.L. (2012). Alcohol and substance misuse in older adults. *Current Psychiatry Reports*, *14*(4), 310–319. doi:10.1007/s11920-012-0292-9

Blow, F.C. & Barry, K.L. (2014). Substance misuse and abuse in older adults: What do we need to know to help? Generations, *Journal of the American Society on Aging*, *38*(3), 53–67. Retrieved from https://experts.umich.edu/en/publications/substance-misuse-and-abuse-in-older-adults-what-do-we-need-to-kno

Boduroglu, A., Yoon, C., Luo, T., & Park, C.D. (2006). Stereotypes about young and old adults: A comparison of Chinese and American Cultures. *Gerontology*, *52*(5), 324–333. doi:10.1159/000094614

Boisclair, D., Lusardi, A., & Michaud, P.C. (2014). *Financial literacy and retirement planning in Canada* (NBER Working Paper No. 20297). Cambridge, MA: The National Bureau of Economic Research.

Bogg, T., & Roberts, B.W. (2004). Conscientiousness and health-related behaviors: A meta-analysis of the leading behavioral contributors to mortality. *Psychological Bulletin*, *130*(6), 887–919. doi:10.1037/0033-2909.130.6.887

Bonanno, G.A., Moskowitz, J.T., Papa, A., & Folkman, S. (2005). Resilience to loss in bereaved spouses, bereaved parents, and bereaved gay men. *Journal of Personality and Social Psychology*, *88*(5), 827–843.

Bondy, S.C. (2016). Low levels of aluminum can lead to behavioral and morphological changes associated with Alzheimer's disease and age-related neurodegeneration. *Neurotoxicology*, *52*, 222–229. doi:10.1016/j.neuro.2015.12.002

Bonikowska, A., Hou, F., & Picot, G. (2015). *Changes in the regional distribution of new immigrants to Canada* (Catalogue no. 11F0019M - No. 366). Ottawa, ON: Statistics Canada. Retrieved from www.statcan.gc.ca/pub/11f0019m/11f0019m2015366-eng.htm.

Booth, B. (2016, August 17). "Retirees seek adventure with encore careers," CNBC. Retrieved from http://www.cnbc.com/2016/08/12/retirees-seek-adventure-with-encore-careers.html

Bopp, K.L., & Verhaeghen, P. (2005). Aging and verbal memory span: A meta-analysis. *Journals of Psychological Sciences and Social Science, Series B*, *60*(5), 223–233. doi:10.1093/geronb/60.5.P223

Bottiggi Dassel, K., Ewan, H., Car, D., Manning, L., Leach, C., & Fitzgerald, K. (2014). What can I do with a doctoral degree in gerontology? Expanding your options. *Journal of Gerontology and Geriatrics Education*, *35*(3), 277–284. doi:10.1080/02701960.2013.870901.

Bower, E.S., & Loebach-Wetherell, J. (2015). Late life anxiety disorders. In P.A. Lichtenberg & B.T. Mast (Eds.), *APA handbook of clinical geropsychiatry: Assessment and treatment of issues of later life*,

(Vol. 2, pp. 49–70). Washington, DC: American Psychiatric Association.

Bowles, R.P., Grimme, K.J., & McArdle, J.J. (2005). A structural factor analysis of vocabulary knowledge and relations to age. *The Journals of Gerontology, Series B: Psychological Sciences and Social Sciences*, *60*(5), 234–241. doi:10.1093/geronb/60.5.P234

Bowling, A., & Dieppe, P. (2005). What is successful aging and who should define it? *British Medical Journal*, *331*(7531), 24–31. doi:10.1136/bmj.331.7531.1548

Boyce, J.M., & Shone, G.R. (2006). Effects of ageing on smell and taste. *Postgraduate Medical Journal*, *82*(966), 239–241. doi:10.1136/pgmj.2005.039453

Boyczuk, A.M., & Fletcher, P.C. (2016). The ebbs and flows: Stresses of sandwich generation caregivers. *Journal of Adult Development*, *23*(1), 51–61. doi:10.1007/s10804-015-9221-6

Braak, H., & Braak, E. (1991). Neuropathological stageing of Alzheimer-related changes. *Acta Neuropathologica*, *82*(4), 239–259. Retrieved from http://info-centre.jenage.de/assets/pdfs/library/braak_braak_ACTA_NEUROPATHOL_1991.pdf

Braak, H., & Braak, E. (1998). Evolution of neuronal changes in the course of Alzheimer's disease. *Journal of Neural Transmission: Supplementa*, *53*, 127–140. Retrieved from http://link.springer.com/chapter/10.1007/2F978-3-7091-6467-9_11

Bradford, A., Kunik, M.E., Schulz, P., Williams, S.P., & Singh, H. (2009). Missed and delayed diagnosis of dementia in primary care: Prevalence and contributing factors. *Alzheimer's Disease and Associated Disorders*, *23*(4), 306–314. doi:10.1097/WAD.0b013e3181a6bebc

Brakoulias, V., & Milicevic, D. (2015). Assessment and treatment of hoarding disorder. *Australasian Psychiatry*, *23*(4), 358–360. doi:10.1177/1039856215587235

Braver, T.S., & West, R. (2008). Working memory, executive control, and aging. In F.I.M. Craik & T.A. Salthouse (Eds.), *The handbook of aging and cognition* (3rd ed., pp. 311–372). New York, NY: Psychology Press.

Brennan, D.J., Emlet, C.A., Brennenstuhl, S., Rueda, S., & OHTN Cohort Study team and staff. (2013). Socio-demographic profile of older adults with HIV/AIDS: Gender and sexual orientation differences. *Canadian Journal on Aging*, *32*(1), 31–43. doi:10.1017/S0714980813000068

Brenes, G.A., Guralnik, J.M., Williamson, J.D., Fried, L.P., Simpson, C., Simonsick, E.M., & Penninx, B. (2005). The influence of anxiety on the progression of disability. *Journal of the American Geriatric Society, 53*, 34–39. doi:10.1111/j.1532-5415.2005.53007.x

Brier, M.R., Gordon, B., Friedrichsen, K., McCarthy, J., Stern, A., Christensen, J., … Ances, B.M. (2016). Tau and Aβ imaging, CSF measures, and cognition in Alzheimer's disease. *Science Translational Medicine, 8*(338), 338ra66.doi:10.1126/scitranslmed.aaf2362

Brinker, J.K., Roberts, P., & Radnidge, B. (2014). The Game of Late Life: A novel education activity for the psychology of ageing. *Educational Gerontology, 40*, 90–101. doi:10.1080/15412002.2013.795038

Brohan, E., Slade, M., Clement, S., & Thornicroft, G. (2010). Experiences of mental illness stigma, prejudice and discrimination: A review of measures. *BMC Health Services Research, 10*, 80. doi:10.1186/1472-6963-10-80

Brooks, J.O., Goodenough, R.R., Crisler, M.C., Klein, N.D., Alley, R.L., Koon, B.L., … Willis, R.F. (2010). Simulator sickness during driving simulation studies. *Accident Analysis and Prevention 42*(3), 788–796. doi:10.1016/j.aap.2009.04.013

Brotman, S., Ferrer, I., Sussman, T., Ryan, B., & Richard, B. (2015). Access and equity in the design and delivery of health and social care to LGBTQ older adults: A Canadian perspective. In N.A. Orel & C.A. Fruhauf (Eds.), *The lives of LGBT older adults: Understanding challenges and resilience* (pp. 111–140). Washington, DC: The American Psychological Association.

Brown, L.B., & Ott, B.R. (2004). Driving and dementia: A review of the literature. *Journal of Geriatric Psychiatry and Neurology, 17*(4), 232–240. doi:10.1177/0891988704269825

Brown, S.L., Bulanda, J.R., & Lee, G.R. (2012). Transitions into and out of cohabitation in later life. *Journal of Marriage and the Family, 74*(4), 774–793. doi:10.1111/j.1741-3737.2012.00994.x

Brown, S.L., Lee, G.R., & Bulanda, J. (2006). Cohabitation among older adults: A national portrait. *The Journals of Gerontology, Series B: Psychological Sciences and Social Sciences, 61*(2), S71-S79. doi:10.1093/geronb/61.2.S71

Brown, S.L., & Lin, I.-F. (2012). The gray divorce revolution: Rising divorce among middleaged and older adults, 1990–2010. *The Journals of Gerontology, Series B: Psychological Sciences and Social Sciences, 67*(6), 731–741. doi:10.1093/geronb/gbs089

Brunelle, S., Cole, M.G., & Elie, M. (2011). Risk factors for the late-onset psychosis: A systematic review of cohort studies. *International Journal of Geriatric Psychiatry, 27*, 240–252. doi:10.1002/gps.2702

Brugman, G.M. (2006). *Wisdom and aging.* Amsterdam, NI: Elsevier.

Bryant, C., Jackson, H., & Ames, D. (2008). The prevalence of anxiety disorders in older adults: Methodological issues and a review of the literature. *Journal of Affective Disorders, 109*(3), 233–250. doi:10.1016/j.jad.2007.11.008

Büchtemann, D., Luppa, M., Bramesfeld, A., & Reidel-Heller, S. (2012). Incidence of late-life depression: A systematic review. *Journal of Affective Disorders, 142*(1-3), 172–179. doi:10.1016/j.jad.2012.05.010

Buiting, H.M., Deeg, D.J.H., Knol, D.L., Ziegelmann, J.P., Pasman, H.R.W., Widdershoven, G.A.M., & Onwuteaka-Philipsen, B.D. (2012). Older people's attitudes toward euthanasia and an end-of-life pill in The Netherlands: 2001–2009. *Journal of Medical Ethics, 38*(5), 267–273. doi:10.1136/medethics-2011-100066

Burke, D.M., & Laver, G.D. (1990). Aging and word retrieval: Selective age differences in language. In E.A. Lovlace (Ed.), *Aging and cognition: Mental processes, self-awareness, and interventions,* (pp. 281–300). New York, NY: North Holland.

Burke, D.M., MacKay, D.G., Worthley, J.S., & Wade, E. (1991). On the tip of the tongue: What causes word finding failures in older and young adults. *Journal of Memory and Language, 30*(5), 542–579. https://doi.org/10.1016/0749-596X(91)90026-G

Burke, D.M., & Shafto, M.A. (2004). Aging and language production. *Current Directions in Psychological Science, 13*(1), 21–24. doi:10.1111/j.0963-7214.2004.01301006.x

Burlon, L., & Vilalta-Bufí, M. (2016). A new look at technical progress and early retirement. *IZA Journal of Labor Policy, 5*(5), 1–39. doi:10.1186/s40173-016-0058-9

Burnes, D., Pillemer, K., Caccamise, P.L., Mason, A., Henderson, C.R., Jr., Berman, J., … Lachs, M.S. (2015). Prevalence and risk factors for elder abuse and neglect in the community: A population-based study. *Journal of the American Geriatrics Society, 63*(9), 1906–1912. doi:10.1111/jgs.13601

Business Wire. (2016). Alopecia market analysis by treatment (oral, topical, injectable), by gender (men, women) and segment forecasts to 2024. Retrieved from www.businesswire.com/news/home/20160628006016/en/Alopecia-Market-Worth-USD-11.8-Billion-2024

Busque, M.A., & Légaré, J. (2012). Unmet needs for home services among Canadian seniors. *Canadian Journal on Aging, 31*(3), 271–283. doi:10.1017/S0714980812000189

Butler, R. (1969). Ageism: Another form of bigotry. *The Gerontologist*, *9*(3), 243–246. doi:10.1093/geront/9.4_Part_1.243

Butler, R.N. (1963). The life review: An interpretation of reminiscence in old age. *Psychiatry*, *26*, 65–76. doi:10.1007/978-3-662-38534-0_20

Butler, R.N. (1974). Successful aging and the role of the life review. *Journal of the American Geriatrics Society*, *22*(12), 529–535. doi:10.1111/j.1532-5415.1974.tb04823.x

Butler, R.N. (2002). Life review. *In Encyclopedia on aging*. Retrieved from http://www.encyclopedia.com/topic/Life_Review.aspx

Butler, R.N., & Lewis, M.I. (1982). Aging and mental health: *Positive psychosocial approaches*. St. Louis, MI: C.V. Mosby Company.

Butt, P., Beirness, D., Gliksman, L., Paradis, C., & Stockwell, T. (2011). *Alcohol and health in Canada: A summary of evidence and guidelines for low-risk drinking*. Ottawa, ON: Canadian Centre on Substance Use and Addiction. Retrieved from www.ccsa.ca/Resource%20Library/2011-Summary-of-Evidence-and-Guidelines-for-Low-Risk%20Drinking-en.pdf

Byers, A.L., Yaffe, K., Covinsky, K.E., Freidman, M.B., & Bruce, M.L. (2010). High occurrence of mood and anxiety disorders among older adults. The National Comorbidity Survey Replication. *Archives of General Psychiatry*, *67*(5), 489–496. doi:10.1001/archgenpsychiatry.2010.35

Cabeza, R., Andersen, N.D., Locantore, J.K., & MacIntosh, A.R. (2002). Aging gracefully: Compensatory brain activity in high performing older adults. *NeuroImage*, *17*(3), 1394–1402. https://doi.org/10.1006/nimg.2002.1280

Cabeza, R., Daselaar, S.M., Dolcos, F., Prince, S.E., Budde, M., & Nyberg, L. (2004). Task-independent and task-specific age effects on brain activity during working memory, visual attention and episodic retrieval. *Cerebral Cortex*, *14*(4), 364–375. doi:10.1093/cercor/bhg133

Cable, N., Bartley, M., Chandola, T., & Sacker, A. (2013). Friends are equally important to men and women, but family matters more for men's well-being. *Journal of Epidemiology &Community Health*, *67*(2), 166–171. doi:10.1136/jech-2012-201113

Cahill, K.E., Giandrea, M.D., & Quinn, J.F. (2011). Reentering the labor force after retirement. *Monthly Labor Review*, *134*(6), 34–42.

Cairney, J., Corna, L.M., & Streiner, D.L. (2010). Mental health care use in late life: Results from a national survey of Canadians. *The Canadian Journal of Psychiatry*, *55*(3), 157–164. doi:10.1177/070674371005500307

Callahan, D. (1987). *Setting limits: Medical goals in an aging society with "a response to my critics"*. New York, NY: Simon and Schuster.

Calleja-Agius, J., & Brincat, M. (2012). The effect of menopause on the skin and other connective tissues. *Gynecological Endocrinology*, *28*(4), 273–277. doi:10.3109/09513590.2011.613970

Canada's Source for HIV and Hepatitis C Information. (n.d). *HIV in Canada: A primer for service providers*. Retrieved from www.catie.ca/en/hiv-canada/1

Canada Mortgage and Housing Corporation (CMHC). (2012a). *Maintaining seniors' independence: A guide to home adaptations*. Ottawa, ON: Author.

Canada Mortgage and Housing Corporation (CMHC). (2012b). *Housing for older Canadians. The definitive guide to the over-55 market. Volume 1: Understanding the market*. Retrieved from www.cmhc-schl.gc.ca/odpub/pdf/67514.pdf

Canada Mortgage and Housing Corporation (CMHC). (2014). *About your house: Garden suites*. Retrieved from www.cmhc-schl.gc.ca/odpub/pdf/65009.pdf

Canada Mortgage and Housing Corporation (CMHC). (2015). *Seniors housing report: Canada highlights*. Ottawa, ON: Author. Retrieved from www.cmhcschl.gc.ca/odpub/esub/65991/65991_2015_A01.pdf

Canada Mortgage and Housing Corporation (CMHC). (2017a). *Programs and financial assistance*. Retrieved from www.cmhc-schl.gc.ca/en/inpr/afhoce/fuafho/

Canada Mortgage and Housing Corporation (CMHC). (2017b). *Residential Rehabilitation Assistance Program for Persons with Disabilities (RRAP-D) On-Reserve*. Retrieved from https://www.cmhc-schl.gc.ca/en/first-nation/financial-assistance/renovation-programs/residential-rehabilitation-assistance-program-persons-disabilities-on-reserve.cfm

Canada Mortgage and Housing Corporation (CMHC). (2017c). *Investment in affordable housing*. Retrieved from www.cmhc-schl.gc.ca/en/inpr/afhoce/fuafho/

Canadian Cancer Society. (2012). *Skin cancer*. Retrieved from www.cancer.ca/~/media/cancer.ca/CW/publications/Reduce%20your%20risk%20skin%20cancer/Skin-RYR-2012-EN.pdf

Canadian Centre for Addiction and Mental Health. (2006). *Responding to older adults with substance use, mental health, and gambling challenges: A guide for workers and volunteers The CAHM Health Aging Project*. Toronto, ON: Author. Retrieved from www.camh.ca/en/education/about/camh_publications/Pages/healthy_aging.aspx

Canadian Centre on Substance Use and Addiction. (2017). Canada's low-risk alcohol drinking guidelines. http://www.ccsa.ca/Resource%20Library/2012-Canada-Low-Risk-Alcohol-Drinking-Guidelines-Brochure-en.pdf. Reprinted by permission of the Canadian Centre on Substance Use and Addiction

Canadian Coalition for Seniors' Mental Health. (2006). National Guidelines for Seniors' Mental Health: The assessment of suicide risk and prevention of suicide. Retrieved from http://ccsmh.ca/wp-content/uploads/2016/03/final-supplement.pdf

Canadian Continence Foundation, The. (2014). *Incontinence: The Canadian perspective.* Peterborough, ON: Author.

Canadian Diabetes Association. (2013). Canadian Diabetes Association clinical practice guidelines for the prevention and management of diabetes in Canada. *Canadian Journal of Diabetes, 37*(Suppl. 1) S1–S227. Retrieved from http://guidelines.diabetes.ca/app_themes/cdacpg/resources/cpg_2013_full_en.pdf

Canadian Encyclopedia, The. (2016). *Funeral practices.* Retrieved from www.thecanadianencyclopedia.ca/en/article/funeral-practices/

Canadian Hospice Palliative Care Association. (2014). *Fact sheet: Hospice palliative care in Canada.* Retrieved from www.chpca.net/media/330558/Fact_Sheet_HPC_in_Canada%20Spring%202014%20Final.pdf

Canadian Hospice Palliative Care Association. (2016a). *History.* Retrieved from www.chpca.net/about-us/history.aspx

Canadian Hospice Palliative Care Association. (2016b). *Who provides palliative care?* Retrieved from www.chpca.net/family-caregivers/faqs.aspx

Canadian Institute for Health Information (CIHI). (2007). *Health care use at the end of life in Western Canada.* Ottawa, ON: Author.

Canadian Institute for Health Information (CIHI). (2011a). *Health care in Canada, 2011: A focus on seniors and aging.* Ottawa, ON: Author.

Canadian Institute for Health Information (CIHI). (2011b). *Seniors and the health care system: What is the impact of multiple chronic conditions?* Ottawa, ON: Author.

Canadian Institute for Health Information (CIHI). (2011c). *Health care use at the end of life in Atlantic Canada.* Ottawa, ON: Author.

Canadian Institute for Health Information (CIHI). (2012). *Health care in Canada: A focus on wait times.* Ottawa, ON: Author.

Canadian Institute for Health Information (CIHI). (2013). *End-of-life hospital care for cancer patients.* Ottawa, ON: Author.

Canadian Institute for Health Information (CIHI). (2015). *Worsened depressive mood in long-term care.* Retrieved from http://indicatorlibrary.cihi.ca/display/HSPIL/Worsened+Depressive+Mood+in+Long-Term+Care

Canadian Institute for Health Information (CIHI). (2016). *A snapshot of advance directives in long-term care: How often is "do not" done?* Ottawa, ON: Author.

Canadian Labour Congress. (2015). *Did you know senior women are twice as likely to live in poverty as men?* Retrieved from http://canadianlabour.ca/issues-research/did-you-know-senior-women-are-twice-likely-live-poverty-men

Canadian Life and Health Insurance Association. (2015). *A guide to long-term care insurance.* Toronto, ON: Author.

Canadian Medical Protective Services. (2015). *Fitness to drive: When do physicians have a duty to report?* Retrieved from www.cmpa-acpm.ca/-/fitness-to-drive-when-do-physicians-have-a-duty-to-report

Canadian Public Health Association. (n.d.). *Food fortification with vitamins and minerals.* Retrieved from www.cpha.ca/en/programs/history/achievements/09-shf/fortification.aspx

Canadian Society for Exercise Physiology. (2012). *Canadian physical activity guidelines/Canadian sedentary behavior guidelines.* Ottawa, ON: Author.

Canadian Veterinary Medical Association. (2017). *Hoarding.* Retrieved from https://www.canadianveterinarians.net/policy-advocacy/recognizing-abuse-hoarding

Canevelli, M., Quarata, F., Remiddi, F., Lucchini, F., Lacorte, E., Vanacore, E., … Cesari, M. (2017). Sex and gender differences in the treatment of Alzheimer's disease: A systematic review of randomized controlled trials. *Pharmacological Research, 115,* 218–223. doi:10.1016/j.phrs.2016.11.035

Canham, S.L. Mahmood, A., Stott, A., Sixsmith, J., & O'Rourke, N. (2012). Till divorce do us part: Marriage dissolution in later life. *Journal of Divorce & Remarriage, 55*(8), 591–612. doi:10.1080/10502556.2014.959097

Caputo, F., Vignoli, T., Leggio, I., Addolorato, G., Zoli, G., & Bernardi, M. (2012). Alcohol use disorders in the elderly: A brief overview from epidemiology to treatment options. *Experimental Gerontology, 47*(6), 411–416. doi:10.1016/j.exger.2012.03.019

Carbonneau, H., Caron, C., & Desrosiers, J. (2010). Development of conceptual framework of positive aspects of caregiving in dementia. *Dementia, 9*(3), 327–353. doi:10.1177/1471301210375316

Carpenter, B.D., Xiong, C., Porensky, E.K., Lee, M.M., Brown, P.J., Coats, M., … Morris, J.C (2008). Reaction to a dementia diagnosis in individuals with Alzheimer's disease and mild cognitive impairment. *Journal of the American Geriatrics Society, 56*(3), 405–412. doi:10.1111/j.1532-5415.2007.01600.x

Carpenter, L., & DeLamater, J. (2012). Sexualities from midlife to later life. In L. Carpenter & J. DeLamater (Eds.), *Intersections: Sex for life: From virginity to Viagra, how sexuality changes throughout our lives* (pp. 217–235). New York, NY: New York Press.

Caron, J., Fleury, M.J., Perrault, M., Crocker, A., Tremblay, J., Tousignant, M., Kestens, Y., Cargo, M., & Daniel, M. (2012). Prevalence of psychological distress and mental disorders, and use of mental health services in the epidemiological catchment area of Montreal South-West. *Biomed Central Psychiatry, 12*, 183–194. doi:10.1186/1471-244X-12-183

Carr, D. (2004). The desire to date and remarry among older widows and widowers. *Journal of Marriage and the Family, 66*(4), 1051–1068. doi:10.1111/j.0022-2445.2004.00078.x

Carr, D.B., & Ott, B.R. (2010). The older adult driver with cognitive impairment: "It's a very frustrating life". *JAMA, 303*(16), 1632–1641. doi:10.1001/jama.2010.481

Carrieré, Y., Martel, L., Légaré, J., & Picard, J-F. (2016). *The contribution of immigration to the size and ethno-cultural diversity of future cohorts of seniors.* Statistics Canada, Catalogue no. 75-006-X ISSN 2291-0840.

Carroll, A., & Itaborahy, L.P. (2015). *State sponsored homophobia 2015: A world survey of laws, criminalization, protection, and recognition of same-sex love.* Geneva, CH: ILGA. Retrieved from http://old.ilga.org/Statehomophobia/ILGA_State_Sponsored_Homophobia_2015.pdf

Carroll, J.B. (1993). *Human cognitive abilities: A survey of factor analytic studies.* New York, NY: Cambridge University Press. Retrieved from http://steinhardtapps.es.its.nyu.edu/create/courses/2174/reading/Carroll_1.pdf

Carson, J., Muir, M., Clark, S., Wakely, E., & Chander, A. (2010). Piloting a gratitude intervention in a community mental health team. *Groupwork, 20*(3), 73–87. doi:10.1921/095182410X576868

Carstairs, S. (2010). *Raising the bar: A roadmap for the future of palliative care in Canada.* Ottawa, ON: The Senate of Canada.

Carstensen, L.L. (1992). Social and emotional patterns in adulthood: Support for socio-emotional selectivity theory. *Psychology and Aging, 7*(3), 331–338. http://doi.apa.org/record/1993-01043-001?doi=1

Carstensen, L.L. (2006). The influence of a sense of time on human development. *Science, 312*(5782), 1913–1915. doi:10.1126/science.1127488

Carstensen, L.L., Fung, H.H., & Charles, S.T. (2003). Socioemotional selectivity theory and the regulation of emotion in the second half of life. *Motivation and Emotion, 27*(2), 103–123. doi:10.1023/A:1024569803230

Carstensen, L.L., Isaacowitz, D.M., & Charles, S.T. (1999). Taking time seriously: A theory of socio-emotional selectivity. *American Psychologist, 54*(3), 165–181. doi.org/10.1037/0003-066X.55.3.343.a

Cartagena, R.C. (2016). The Supreme Court of Canada decision: Physician-assisted death. *Health Bulletin.* Retrieved from: www.fasken.com/physician-assisted-death/

Carter v. Canada (Attorney General). 2015 SCC5, 1 S.C.R 331 (2015). Retrieved from https://scc-csc.lexum.com/scc-csc/scc-csc/en/item/14637/index.do

Caspi, A., Roberts, B.W., & Shiner, R.L. (2005). Personality development: Stability and change. *Annual Review of Psychology, 56*(1), 453–484. doi:10.1146/annurev.psych.55.090902.141913

Cash, T.F., Price, V.H., & Savin, R.C. (1993). Psychological effects of androgenetic alopecia on women: Comparisons with balding men and with female control subjects. *Journal of the American Academy of Dermatology, 29*(4), 568–575. PMID: 8408792

Cassel, C.K., & Demel, B. (2001). Remembering death: Public policy in the USA. *Journal of the Royal Society of Medicine, 94*(9), 433–466. Retrieved from www.ncbi.nlm.nih.gov/pmc/articles/PMC1282180/

Cassilhas, R.C., Viana, V.A.R., Grassmann, V., Santos, R.T., Tufik, S., & Mello, M.T. (2007). The impact of resistance exercise on the cognitive function of the elderly. *Medicine and Science in Sports and Exercise, 39*(8), 1401–1407. doi:10.1249/mss.0b013e318060111f

Castle, S.C. (2000). Clinical relevance of age-related immune dysfunction. *Clinical Infectious Diseases, 31*(2), 578–585. doi:10.1086/313947

Cattell, R.B. (1950). *Personality: A systematic, theoretical, and factual study* (1st ed.). New York, NY: McGraw-Hill. doi:10.1037/10773-000

Cattell, R.B. (1963). Theory of fluid and crystallized intelligence: A critical experiment. *Journal of Educational Psychology, 54,* 1–22. doi:10.1037/h0046743

Cattell, R.B. (1966). *The scientific analysis of personality.* Baltimore, MD: PenguinBooks, Inc.

Cauwenberg, J.V., De Bourdeaudhuij, I., De Meester, F., Van Dyck, D., Salmon, J., Clarys, B., & Deforche, B. (2011). Relationship between the physical environment and physical activity in older adults: A systematic review. *Health & Place, 17*(2), 458–469. doi:10.1016/j.healthplace.2010.11.010

Cavanaugh, J.C., & Whitbourne, S.K. (2003). *Gerontology: An interdisciplinary perspective.* New York, NY: Oxford Press.

CBC News. (2013, October 24). Canadian boomers want to stay in their homes as they age. (2013). *CBCNews/Business.* Retrieved from www.cbc.ca/news/business/canadian-boomers-want-to-stay-in-their-homes-as-they-age-1.2224171

Centers for Disease Control and Prevention. (2013). *Health places terminology.* Retrieved from www.cdc.gov/healthyplaces/terminology.htm

Centers for Disease Control and Prevention. (2017). HIV among people aged 50 and older. Retrieved from www.cdc.gov/hiv/group/age/olderamericans/

Cernin, P.A., Lysack, C., & Lichtenberg, P.A. (2011). A comparison of self-rated and objectively measured successful aging concepts in an urban sample of African American older adults. *Clinical Gerontologist, 34*(2), 89–102. doi:10.1080/07317115.2011.539525

Chan, M., Campo, E., Esteve, D., & Fourniols, J.Y. (2009). Smart homes—current features and future perspectives. *Maturitas, 64*(2), 90–97. doi:10.1016/j.maturitas.2009.07.014

Chandler, M., & Lalonde, C.E. (2008). Cultural continuity as a moderator of suicidal risk among Canada's First Nations. In L. Kirmayer & G. Valaskakis (Eds.), *Healing traditions: The mental health of Aboriginals in Canada* (pp. 221–248). Vancouver, BC: University of British Columbia Press.

Chapman, B.P., Duberstein, P.R., Sörensen, S., & Lyness, J.M. (2007). Gender differences in Five Factor Model personality traits in an elderly cohort: Extension of robust and surprising findings to an older generation. *Personality and Individual Differences, 43*(6), 1594–1603. doi:10.1016/j.paid.2007.04.028

Chapman, B.P., Roberts, B.W., & Duberstein, P. (2011). Personality and longevity: Knowns, unknowns, and implications for public health and personalized medicine. *Journal of Aging Research, 2011*(1), 1–24. doi:10.4061/2011/759170

Chappell, N.L., Dlitt, B.H., Hollander, M.J., Miller, J.A., & McWilliam, C. (2004). Comparative costs of home care and residential care. *The Gerontologist, 44*(3), 389–400. doi:10.1093/geront/44.3.389

Chappell, N.L., & Kusch, K. (2007). The gendered nature of filial piety: A study among Chinese Canadians. *Journal of Cross-Cultural Gerontology, 22*(1), 29–45. doi:10.1007/s10823-006-9011-5

Chaplin, R, Farquharson, L., Clapp, M., & Crawford, M. (2015). Comparison of access, outcomes and experiences of older adults and working age adults in psychological therapy. *International Journal of Geriatric Psychiatry, 30,* 178–184. doi:10.1002/gps.4122

Charles, S.T., & Carstensen, L.L. (2010). Social and emotional aging. *Annual Review of Psychology, 61,* 383–409. doi:10.1146/annurev.psych.093008.100448

Charness, N., & Best, R. (2009). Aging and information technology use potential and barriers. *Aging and Information Technology, 18*(5), 253–258.

Charness, N., Best, R., & Evans, J. (2016). Supportive home health care technology for older adults: Attitudes and implementation. *Gerontechnology, 15*(4), 233–242. doi:10.4017/gt.2016.15.4.006.00

Chasteen, A.L., Pichora-Fuller, M.K., Dupuis, K., Smith, S., & Singh, G. (2015). Do negative views of aging influence memory and auditory performance through self-perceived abilities? *Psychology and Aging, 30*(4), 881–93. doi:10.1037/a0039723

Chertkow, H., Whitehead, V., Phillips, N., Wolfson, C., Atherton, J., & Bergman, H. (2010). Multilingualism (but not always bilingualism) delays onset of Alzheimer disease: Evidence from a bilingual community. *Alzheimer Disease & Associated Disorders, 24*(2), 118–125. doi:10.1097/wad.0b013e3181ca1221

Cheung, F.M. (2009, July). Factor congruence of the CPAI-2 in Asian and American samples. In F.M. Cheung, & M.P. Born (Co-chairs), *From the east to the west: Generalizability of the Cross Cultural Personality Assessment Inventory (CPAI) in Western contexts.* Symposium conducted at the 11th European Congress of Psychology, Oslo, NO.

Cheung, F.M., Cheung, S., & Zhang, J. (2001). Convergent validity of the Chinese Personality Assessment Inventory and the Minnesota Multiphasic Personality Inventory-2: Preliminary findings from a normative sample. *Journal of Personality Assessment, 82*(1), 92–103. doi:10.1207/s15327752jpa8201_14

Cheung, F.M., Cheung, S.F., Zhang, J., Leung, K., Leong, F., & Yeh, K.H. (2008). Relevance of openness as a personality dimension in Chinese culture: Aspects of its cultural relevance. *Journal of Cross-Cultural Psychology*, *39*(1), 81–108. doi:10.1177/002202210731196

Cheung, F.M., Leung, K., Fan, R.M., Song, W.Z., Zhang, J.X., & Zhang, J. (1996). Development of the Chinese Personality Assessment Inventory. *Journal of Cross-Cultural Psychology*, *27*(2), 181–199. doi:10.1177/0022022196272003

Cheung, F.M., Leung, K., Zhang, J.K., Sun, H.A., Gan, Y.Q., Song, W.Z., & Xie, D. (1996). The case of the Chinese personality assessment inventory. In M.H. Bond (Ed.), *The Oxford handbook of Chinese psychology* (pp. 295–308). New York, NY: Oxford University Press.

Cheung, F.M., Leung, K., Zhang, J.X., Sun, H.F., Gan, Song, W.Z., & Xie, D. (2001). Indigenous Chinese personality constructs: Is the Five-Factor Model complete? *Journal of Cross-Cultural Psychology*, *32*(4), 407–433. doi:10.1177/0022022101032004003

Cheung, F.M., Van de Vijver, F.J.R., & Leong, F.T.L. (2011). Toward a new approach to the study of personality in culture. *The American Psychologist*, *66*(7), 593–603. doi:10.1037/a0022389

Ching, S., Thoma, A., McCabe, R.E., & Antony, M.M. (2003). Measuring outcomes in aesthetic surgery: A comprehensive review of the literature. *Plastic Reconstructive Surgery*, *111*(1), 468–480. doi:10.1097/01.PRS.000003604167101.48

Chiu, H.F.K., & Brodaty, H. (2013). For debate: Is the very early diagnosis of AD using the new criteria beneficial for patients? Arguments against the biomarker-driven diagnosis of Alzheimer's disease. *International Psychogeriatrics*, *25*(2), 177–181. doi:10.1017/S1041610212002104

Chlebowski, R.T., Hendrix, S.L., Langer, R.D., Stefanick, M.L., Gass, M., Lane, D., … McTiernan, A. (2003). Influence of estrogen plus progestin on breast cancer and mammography in healthy postmenopausal women: The women's health randomized trial. *Journal of the American Medical Association*, *289*(24), 3243–3C253. doi:10.1001/jama.289.24.3243

Choi, N.G., DiNitto, D.M., & Marti, C.N. (2015). Alcohol and other substance use, mental health treatment use, and perceived unmet treatment need: Comparison between Baby Boomers and older adults. *The American Journal on Addiction*, *24*(4), 299–307. doi:10.1111/ajad.12225

Chorn Dunham, C.C., & Casadonte, D. (2009). Children's attitudes and classroom interaction in an intergenerational program. *Educational Gerontology*, *35*(5), 453–464. doi:10.1080/03601270802605473

Chou, K-L. (2009). Age of onset of generalized anxiety disorder in older adults. *American Journal of Geriatric Psychiatry*, *17*(6), 455–464. doi.org/10.1097/JGP.0b013e31818f3a93

Chow, H.P.H. (2010). Growing old in Canada: Physical and psychological well-being among elderly Chinese immigrants. *Ethnicity & Health*, *15*(1), 61–72. doi:10.1080/13557850903418810

Christen, W.G., Liu, S., Glynn, R.J., Gaziano, J.M., & Buring, J.E. (2008). Dietary carotenoids, vitamins C and E, and risk of cataract in women: A prospective study. *Archives of Ophthalmology*, *126*(1), 102–109. doi:10.1001/archopht.126.1.102

Chronic Pain Association of Canada. (2007). Dr. Helen Hays Award. http://chronicpaincanada.com/about_cpac/helen_hays_award

Chung, C., & Lin, Z. (2012). A cross cultural examination of the positivity effect in memory: United States vs. China. *The International Journal of Aging and Human Development*, *75*, 31–44. doi:10.2190/AG.75.1.d

Chung, K.W., Kim, D.H., Park, M.H., Choi, Y.J., Kim, N.D., Lee, J., … Chung, H.Y. (2013). Recent advances in caloric restriction and aging. *Experimental Gerontology*, *48*(10), 1049–1053. doi:10.1016/j.exger.2012.11.007

Chung, S., & Park, S-J. (2008). Successful ageing among low-income older people in South Korea. *Ageing and Society*, *28*(8), 1061–1074. doi:10.1017/S0144686X08007393

Ciorba, A., Bianchini, C., Pelucchi, S., & Pastore, A. (2012). The impact of hearing loss on the quality of life of elderly adults. *Journal of Clinical Interventions in Aging*, *7*, 159–163. doi:10.2147/CIA.S26059

Cipriani, G., Lucetti, C., Carlesi, C., Danti, S., & Nuti, A. (2015). Depression and dementia: A review. *European Geriatric Medicine*, *6*(5), 479–486. doi:10.1016/j.eurger.2015.07.010

Cipriani, G., Vedovello, M., Nuti, A., & Di Fiorino, M. (2011). Aggressive behavior in patients with dementia: Correlates and management. *Geriatrics & Gerontology International*, *11*(4), 408–413. doi:10.1111/j.1447-0594.2011.00730.x

Cleverley, B. (2014, May 3). No rush to build garden suites in Victoria. *Times Colonist*. Retrieved

from www.timescolonist.com/news/local/
no-rush-to-build-garden-suites-in-victoria-1.1020472

Cloutier, D.S., & Penning, M.J. (2017). Janus at the crossroads: Perspectives on long-term care trajectories for older women with dementia in a Canadian context. *The Gerontologist*, 57(1), 68–81. doi:10.1093/geront/gnw158

CNIB. (2015a). *Fast facts about vision loss*. Retrieved from www.cnib.ca/en/about/media/vision-loss/pages/default.aspx

CNIB. (2015b). *Cataracts: A leading cause of vision loss*. Retrieved from www.cnib.ca/en/your-eyes/eye-conditions/cataracts/pages/default.aspx

Cohen, C.I., Pathak, R., Ramirez, P.M., & Vahia, I. (2009). Outcome among community dwelling older adults with schizohprenia: Results using five conceptual models. *Community Mental Health Journal*, *45*, 151–156. doi:10.1007/s10597-008-9161-8

Cohen-Mansfield, J., & Billig, N. (1986). Agitated behaviors in the elderly: A conceptual review. *Journal of the American Geriatrics Society 34*(10), 711–721 doi:10.1111/j1532-5415.1986.tb04302.x

Cohen-Mansfield, J., Marx, M.S., & Guralnik, J.M. (2003). Motivators and barriers to exercise in an older community-dwelling population. *Journal of Aging and Physical Activity*, *11*(2), 242–253.

Collard, R.M., Boter, H., Schoevers, R.A., & Oude Voshaar, R.C. (2012). Prevalence of frailty in community-dwelling older persons: A systematic review. *Journal of the American Geriatrics Society*, *60*(8), 1487–1492. doi:10.1111/j.1532-5415.2012.04054.x

Collett, L., & Lester, D. (1969, 2010). The fear of death and the fear of dying. *Journal of Psychology*, *72*, 179–181.

Colliver, J.D., Compton, W.M., Gfroerer, J.C., & Condon, T. (2006). Projecting drug use among aging baby boomers in 2020. *Annals of Epidemiology*, *16*(4), 257–265. doi:10.1016/j.annepidem.2005.08.003

Concordia University. (n.d.). *Healthy eating: A practical guide*. Retrieved from www.concordia.ca/.../Healthy%20Eating%20A%20Practical%20G

Conference Board of Canada. (2010). *Retirement of baby boomers to slow Canada's long-term economic growth*. Retrieved from www.conferenceboard.ca/press/newsrelease/10-04-28/retirement_of_baby_boomers_to_slow_canada_s_long-term_economic_growth.aspx

Conference Board of Canada. (2015). *Provincial and territorial ranking: Suicides*. Retrieved from www.conferenceboard.ca/hcp/provincial/health/suicide.aspx

Conference Board of Canada. (2016). *Elderly poverty*. Retrieved from www.conferenceboard.ca/hcp/details/society/elderly-poverty.aspx

Conn, D., Gibson, M., & McCabe, D. (2014). *2014 CCSMH guideline update - The assessment and treatment of mental health issues in long term care homes (Focus on mood and behaviour symptoms)*. Toronto, ON: Canadian Coalition for Seniors' Mental Health (CCSMH). www.csma.ca

Conn, D.K., Malach, F., Wilson, K.J., Buchanan, D., Gibson, M.C., Grek, A., ... Tourigny-Rivard, M-F. (2006). National guidelines for seniors' mental health: Introduction and project background. *The Canadian Journal of Geriatrics*, *9*(2), 535–571. Retrieved from http://ccsmh.ca/wp-content/uploads/2016/03/final-supplement.pdf

Connectability. (n.d.). Different cultural beliefs at time of death. Retrieved from http://connectability.ca/2014/09/11/different-cultural-beliefs-at-time-of-death/

Connidis, I.A. (2010). *Family ties and aging* (2nd ed.). Los Angeles, CA: Pine Forge Press.

Connidis, I.A., & Willson, A.E. (2011). Aging. In W.E. Hewitt, J. White, & J.J. Teevan (Eds.), *Introduction to sociology: A Canadian focus* (10th ed.) (pp. 204–225). Toronto, ON: Pearson Canada.

Connolly, M.-T., Breckman, R., Callahan, J., Lachs, M., Ramsey-Klawsnik, H., & Solomon, J. (2012). The sexual revolution's last frontier: How silence about sex undermines health, well-being, and safety in old age. *Generations - Journal of the American Society on Aging 36*(3), 43–52. Retrieved from www.asaging.org/blog/sexual-revolutions-last-frontier

Connor, L.T. (2001). Memory in old age: Patterns of decline and preservation. *Seminars in Speech and Language*, *22*(2), 119–128. doi:10.1055/s-2001-13936

Cook, T.M., & Wang, J.L. (2010). Descriptive epidemiology of stigma against depression in a general population in Alberta. *BMC Psychiatry*, *10*, 1–11. doi:10.1186/1471-244X-10-29

Cooper, T., Detre, T., & Weiss, S.M. (1981). Coronary-prone behavior and coronary heart disease: A critical review. The review panel on coronary prone behavior and coronary heart disease. *Circulation*, *63*(6), 1199–1215. doi:10.1161/01.CIR.63.6.1199

Cornelison, L.J., & Doll, G.M. (2013). Management of sexual expression in long-term care: Ombudsmen's perspective. *The Gerontologist*, *53*(5), 780–789. doi:10.1093/geront/gns162

Correctional Investigator Canada, The. (2012). *Annual report of the Office of the Correctional Investigator 2011–2012*. Ottawa, ON: Author. Retrieved from www.oci-bec.gc.ca/cnt/rpt/pdf/annrpt/annrpt20112012-eng.pdf

Correctional Investigator Canada, The. (2015). *Annual report of the Office of the Correctional Investigator 2014–2015*. Ottawa, ON: Author. Retrieved from www.oci-bec.gc.ca/cnt/rpt/pdf/annrpt/annrpt20142015-eng.pdf

Correctional Investigator Canada, The. (2016). *Annual report of the Office of the Correctional Investigator 2015–2016.* Retrieved from www.oci-bec.gc.ca/cnt/rpt/annrpt/annrpt20152016-eng.aspx

Corrigan, P.W., & Kleinlein, P. (2005). The impact of mental illness stigma. In P.W. Corrigan (Ed.), *On the stigma of mental illness: Practical strategies* (pp. 11–44). Washington, DC: American Psychological Association.

Costa, P.T. Jr., & McCrae, R.R. (1992). *Revised NEO Personality Inventory (NEO-PI-R) and NEO Five-Factor Inventory (NEO-FFI) professional manual.* Odessa, FL: Psychological Assessment Resources, Inc.

Cotelli, M., Manenti, R., & Zanetti, O. (2012). Reminiscence therapy in dementia: A review. *Maturitas, 72*(3), 203–205. doi:10.1016/j.maturitas.2012.04.008

Coudin, G., & Alexopoulos, T. (2010). 'Help me! I'm old!' How negative stereotypes create dependency among older adults. *Aging and Mental Health, 14*(5), 516–523. doi:10.1080/13607861003713182

Coulson, I., Harper, L., Galenza, S., Bratt, S., & Haase, M. (2015, February). *Living well in the fourth age: Opportunities for eudemonia for people living in continuing care centers. The pursuit of spirituality through the development of eudemonia.* Paper presented at Covenant Health's Research Day, Misericordia Hospital, Edmonton, AB.

Council of Aging of Ottawa, The. (2008). *Long term care insurance in Canada: What it is and do I need it?* Ottawa, ON: Author. Retrieved from www.cupfa.org/wp-content/uploads/.../6N-Long_Term_Care_Insurance_Oct2008.pdf

CPP Investment Board. (2016). *Sustainability of the CPP.* Retrieved from www.cppib.com/en/our-performance/cpp-sustainability.html

Crabb, R., & Hunsley, J. (2006). Utilization of mental health care services among older adults with depression. *Journal of Clinical Psychology, 62*(3), 299–312. doi:10.1002/jclp.20231

Craik, F.I.M. (1986). A functional account of age differences in memory. In F. Klix & H. Hagendrof (Eds.), *Human memory and cognitive capabilities: Mechanisms and performances* (pp. 409–422). Amsterdam, NI: Elsevier.

Craik, F.I.M., & Byrd, M. (1982). Aging and cognitive deficits: The role of attentional resources. In F.I.M. Craik & S. Trehub (Eds.), *Aging and cognitive processes* (pp. 191–211). New York, NY: Plenum Press.

Craik, F.I.M., & Lockhart, R.S. (1972). Levels of processing: A framework for memory research. *Journal of Verbal Learning and Verbal Behavior, 11*(6), 671–684. doi:10.1016/S0022-5371(72)80001-X

Crane, J.D., Macneil, L.G., & Tarnopolsky, M.A. (2013). Long-term aerobic exercise is associated with greater muscle strength throughout the life span. *The Journals of Gerontology A: Biological Sciences and Medical Sciences, 68*(6), 631–638. doi:10.1093/gerona/gls237

Cranswick, K., & Dosman, D. (2008). *Eldercare: What we know today* (Component of Statistics Catalogue no. 11–008-X – no. 862008002). Ottawa, ON: Statistics Canada.

Crawley, E., & Sparks, R. (2005). Hidden injuries? Researching the experiences of older men in English prisons. *The Howard Journal of Criminal Justice, 44*(4), 345–356. doi:10.1111/j.1468-2311.2005.00380.x

Croghan, C.F., Moone, R.P., & Olsen, A.M. (2014). Friends, family, and caregiving among midlife and older lesbian, gay, bisexual and transgender adults. *Journal of Homosexuality, 61*(1), 79–102. doi:10.1080/00918369.2013.835238

Cronin, A., & King, A. (2014). Only connect? Older lesbian, gay and bi-sexual (LGB) adults and social capital. *Ageing and Society, 34*(2), 258–279. doi:10.1017/S0144686x12000955

Crosson, B., Ford, A., McGregor, K.M., Meinzer, M., Cheshkov, S., L., Xiufeng., … Briggs, R.W. (2010). Functional imaging and related techniques: An introduction for rehabilitation researchers. *Journal of Research Rehabilitation and Development, 47*(2), 1–33. doi:10.1682/JRRD.2010.02.0017

CTV News. (2016, January 5). *Still here: Alzheimer Society launches campaign to end disease stigma.* Retrieved from www.ctvnews.ca/health/still-here-alzheimer-society-launches-campaign-to-end-disease-stigma-1.2724282

Cuijpers, P., Karyotaki, E., Pot, A.M., Park, M., & Reynolds, C.F. III. (2014b). Managing depression in older age: Psychological interventions. *Maturitas, 79*(2), 160–169. doi:10.1016/j.maturitas.2014.05.027

Cuijpers, P., Vogelzangs, N., Twisk, J., Kleiboer, A., Li, J., & Pennix, B. (2014a). Comprehensive meta-analysis of excess mortality in depression in the general community versus patients with specific illnesses. *American Journal of Psychiatry, 171*(4), 454–562. doi:10.1176/appa-ajp.2013.13030325

Cumming, E., & Henry, W.E. (1961). *Growing old: The process of disengagement.* New York, NY: Basic Books, Inc.

Cummings, S.M, Bride, B., & Rawlins-Shaw, A.M. (2006). Alcohol abuse treatment for older adults: A review of recent empirical evidence. *Journal of Evidenced Based Social Work, 3*(1), 79–99. doi:10.1300/J39vo3nol_05

Cunningham, S.A., Ruben, J.D., & Narayan, K.M. (2008). Health of foreign born people in the United States: A review. *Health and Place, 14*(4), 623–635. doi.10.1016/j.healthplace.2007.12.002

Cuthbert, B.N., & Insel, T.R. (2013). Toward the future of psychiatric diagnosis: The seven pillars of RDoC. *BMC Medicine, 11*, 126. doi:10.1186/1741-7015-11-126

Da, W-W., D., & Garcia, A. (2015). Later life migration: Sociocultural adaptation and changes in quality of life at settlement among recent older Chinese immigrants in Canada. *Activities, Adaption, & Aging, 39*(3), 214–242. doi:10.1080/01924788.2015.1063330

Dalton, D.S., Cruickshanks, K.J., Klein, B.E., Klein, R., Wiley, T.L., & Nondahl, D.M. (2003). The impact of hearing loss on quality of life in older adults. *The Gerontologist, 43*(5), 661–668. doi:10.1093/geront/43.5.661

Daneman, M., & Carpenter, P.A. (1980). Individual differences in working memory and reading. *Journal of Verbal Learning and Verbal Behavior, 19*, 450–466. doi:10.1016/S0022-5371(80)90312-6

Daniels, N. (2013). Global aging and the allocation of health care across the life span. *The American Journal of Bioethics 13*(8), 1–2. doi:10.1080/15265161.2013.807187

Davey, J., Nana, G., de Joux, V., & Arcus, M. (2004). *Accommodation options for older people in Aotearoa/New Zealand.* Wellington, NZ: NZ Institute for Research on Ageing/Business & Economic Research Ltd, for Centre for Housing Research Aotearoa/New Zealand.

Davis, A., McMahon, C.M., Pichora-Fuller, M.K., Russ, S., Lin, F., Olusanya, B.O., … Tremblay, K.L. (2016). Aging and hearing health: The life-course approach. *The Gerontologist, 56*(S2), S256-S267. doi:10.1093/geront/gnw033

Davies, M. (2011). The reintegration of elderly prisoners: An exploration of services provided in England and Wales. *Internet Journal of Criminology.* Retrieved from http://www.book.y-lib.info/17-political/243617-1-the-reintegration-elderly-prisoners-exploration-services-provided-engl.php

Dawson, J. (2016). The first Labour Day. Canada's History. Retrieved from www.canadashistory.ca/Magazine/Online-Extension/Articles/The-First-Labour-Day

De Boer, B., Hamers, J.P.H., Beerens, H.C., Zwakhalen, S.M.G., Tan, F.E.S., & Verbeek, H. (2015). Living at the farm, innovative nursing home care for people with dementia— study protocol of an observational longitudinal study. *BMC Geriatrics,* 15(144). doi:10.1186/s12877-015-0141-x

De Boer, B., Hamers, J.P.H., Zwakhalen, S.M.G., Tan, F.E.S., Beerens, H.C., & Verbeek, H. (2017). Green care farms as innovative nursing homes, promoting activities and social interaction for people with dementia. *JAMDA, 18*, 40–46. doi:10.1016/j.jamda.2016.10.013

De Boer, M.E., Hertogh, C.M., Dröes, R., Riphagen, I.I., Jonker, C., & Eefsting, J.A. (2007). Suffering from dementia—the patient's perspective: A review of the literature. *International Psychogeriatrics, 19*(6), 1021–1039. doi:10.1017/S1041610207005765

De Jong Gierveld, J. (2002). The dilemma of repartnering: Considerations of older men and women entering new intimate relationships in later life. *Ageing International, 27*(4), 61–78. doi:10.1007/s12126-002-1015-z

De St. Aubin, E., & McAdams, D.P. (1995). The relations of generative concern and generative action to personality traits, satisfaction/happiness with life, and ego development. *Journal of Adult Development, 2*(2), 99–112. doi:10.1007/BF02251258

Deary, I.J., Weiss, A., & Batty, G.D. (2010). Intelligence and personality as predictors of illness and death: How researchers in differential psychology and chronic disease epidemiology are collaborating to understand and address health inequalities. *Psychological Science in the Public Interest, 11*(2), 53–79. doi:10.1177/1529100610387081

Decady, Y., & Greenberg, L. (2014). *Health at a glance: Ninety years of change in life expectancy* (Catalogue no. 82–624-X). Ottawa, ON: Statistics Canada.

Deifenbach, G.M., DiMauro, J., Frost R.O, Steketee, G., & Tolin, D.F. (2013). Characteristics of hoarding in older adults. *American Journal of Geriatric Psychiatry, 21*(10), 1043–1047. doi:10.1016/j.jagp.2013.01.028

Dementia Village Advisors. (n.d.). *Dementia villages.* Retrieved from http://dementiavillage.com/

Demiris, G., Hensel, B.K., Skubic, M., & Rantz, M. (2008). Senior residents' perceived need and preferences for "smart home" sensor technologies. *International Journal of Technology Assessment in Health Care*, 24(1), 120–124. doi:10.1017/S0266462307080154

Demiris, G., Oliver, D.P., Dickey, G., Skubic, M., & Rantz, M. (2008). Findings from a participatory evaluation of smart home application for older adults. *Technology and Health Care: Official Journal of the European Society for Engineering and Medicine*, 16(2), 111–118.

Dennerstein, L., Dudley, E.C., Hopper, J.L., Guthrie, J.R., & Burger, H.G. (2000). A prospective population-based study of menopausal symptoms. *Obstetrics and Gynecology*, 96(3), 351–358. doi:10.1016/S0029-7844(00)00930-3

Denton, F.T., & Spencer, B.G. (2009). What is retirement? A review and assessment of alternative concepts and measures. *Canadian Journal on Aging*, 28(1), 63–76. doi:10.1017/S0714980809090047

Department of Finance Canada. (2012). *Economic and fiscal implications of Canada's aging population* (Catalogue no. F2-217/2012E-PDF). Ottawa, ON: Author. Retrieved from https://www.fin.gc.ca/pub/eficap-rebvpc/eficap-rebvpc-eng.pdf

Department of Finance Canada. (2017). *Economic and fiscal implications of Canada's aging population.* Retrieved from https://www.fin.gc.ca/pub/eficap-rebvpc/report-rapport-eng.asp

DePaulo, B.M., & Morris, W.L. (2006). The unrecognized stereotyping and discrimination against singles. *Current Direction in Psychological Science*, 15(5), 251–254. doi:10.1111/j.1467-8721.2006.00446.x

Deschenes, N., & Stone, L.O. (2006). The probability of reaching the state of retirement—a longitudinal analysis of variations between men and women. In L.O. Stone (Ed.), *New frontiers of research on retirement* (Catalogue no. 75-511-XIE) (pp. 219–246). Ottawa, ON: Statistics Canada.

Desjardins, M. (2015). General review: Vascular correlates of aging in the brain: Evidence from imaging data. *IRBM*, 36(3), 158–165. doi:10.1016/j.irbm.2015.01.016

DeSalvo, K.B., Fan, V.S., McDonell, M.B., & Fihn, S.D. (2005). Predicting mortality and healthcare utilization with a single question. *Health Services Research*, 40(4), 1234–1246. doi:10.1111/j.1475-6773.2005.00404.x

Devanand, D.P., Lee, S., Manly, J., Andrews, H., Schupf, N., Masurkar, A., … Doty, R.L. (2015). Olfactory identification deficits and increased mortality in the community. *Annals of Neurology*, 78(3), 401–411. doi:10.1002/ana.24447

Di Castelnuovo, A., Costanzo, S., Bagnardi, V., Donati, M.B., Iacoviello, L., & De Gaetano, G. (2006). Alcohol dosing and total mortality in men and women. An updated meta-analysis of 34 prospective studies. *Archives of International Medicine*, 166(22), 2437–2445. doi:10.1001/archinte.166.22.2437

Di Gessa, G., Glaser, K., & Tinker, A. (2016). The health impact of intensive and nonintensive grandchild care in Europe: New evidence from SHARE. *Journals of Gerontology, Series B, Psychological Sciences and Social Sciences*, 71(5), 867–879. doi:10.1093/geronb/gbv055

Diaez, B.S., Nunes, P.V., Machado-Vieira, R., & Forlenza, O.V. (2011). Current pharmacological approaches and perspectives in the treatment of geriatric mood disorders. *Current Opinion in Psychiatry*, 24(6), 473–477. doi:10.1097/YCO.0b013e32834bb9bd

Dinapoli, E.A., LaRocca, M., & Scogin, F. (2015). Cognitive behavior therapy and behavioral activation for late-life depression. In P. Areán (Ed.), *Treatment of late-life depression, anxiety, trauma, and substance abuse.* (pp. 49–70). Washington, DC: American Psychological Association. doi.org/10.1037/14524-003

Dinse, H.R., Tegenthoff, M., Heinisch, C., & Kalisch, T. (2009). Ageing and touch. In B. Goldstein (Ed.), *The Sage encyclopedia of perception* (pp. 21–24). London, UK: Sage.

Diongi, R.A. (2015). Stereotypes of aging: Their effects on the health of older adults. *Journal of Geriatrics*, 2015, 1–9. doi:10.1155/2015/954027

Dixon-Gordon, K.L., Whalen, D.J., Layden, B.K., & Chapman, A.L. (2015). A systematic review of personality disorder and health outcomes. *Canadian Psychology*, 56(2), 168–190. doi:10.1037/cap0000024

Dobbs, A.R., Heller, R.B., & Schopflocher, D. (1998). A comparative approach to identify unsafe older drivers. *Accident Analysis and Prevention*, 30(3), 363–370. doi:10.1016/S0001-4575(97)00110-3

Dobbs, B., Harper, L., & Wood, A. (2009). Transitioning from driving to driving cessation: The role of specialized driving cessation support groups for individuals with dementia. *Topics in Geriatric Rehabilitation*, 25(1), 73–86. doi:10.1097/01.TGR.0000346058.32801.95

Dobbs, B., & Pidborochynski, T. (2016). *Capital Region transportation needs assessment of seniors and persons with disability. 2016 Final Report.* Edmonton, AB: The DR Group.

Dobbs, B., Pidborochynski, T., & Rehani, M. (2016). *Transportation Toolkit for the implementation of alternate transportation for seniors in Alberta.* Edmonton, AB: The DR Group.

Dobbs, B.M., Lee, V., & Song, J. (2011). *Seniors' alternate transportation: A national and international scan of existing models and identification of unique models and innovative solutions. Report for the Federal, Provincial, and Territorial Ministers of Seniors.* Edmonton, AB: The DR Group.

Dobbs, B.M., & Schopflocher, D. (2010). The introduction of a new screening tool for the identification of cognitively impaired medically at-risk drivers: The SIMARD a modification of the DemTect. *Journal of Primary Care and Community Health, 1*(2), 119–127. doi:10.1177/2150131910369156

Donnellan, M.B., Conger, R.D., & Burzette, R.G. (2007). Personality development from late adolescence to young adulthood: Differential stability, normative maturity, and evidence for the maturity-stability hypothesis. *Journal of Personality, 75*(2), 237–263. doi:10.1111/j.1467-6494.2007.00438.x

Donnellan, M.B., Hill, P.L., & Roberts, B.W. (2015). Personality development across the life span: Current findings and future directions. In M. Mikulincer & P.R. Shaver (Eds.), *APA Handbook of personality and social psychology* (Vol. *4*, pp. 107–126). Washington, DC: American Psychological Association.

Donnellan, M.B., & Lucas, R.E. (2008). Age differences in the Big Five across the life span: Evidence from two national samples. *Psychology and Aging, 23*(3), 558–566. doi:10.1037/a0012897

Dominguez, L.J., & Barbagallo, M. (2016). Ageing and sexuality. *European Geriatric Medicine, 7*(6), 512–518. doi:10.1016/j.eurger.2016.05.013

Doty, R.L., & Kamath, V. (2014). The influences of age on olfaction: A review. *Frontiers in Psychology, 5*(20), 1–20. doi:10.3389/psyq.2014.00020

Drolet, M. (2016). *Gender differences in the financial knowledge of Canadians.* (Catalogue no. 75-006-X) (pp. 1–13). Ottawa, ON: Statistics Canada.

Du, Y., Buchsbaum, B.R., Grady, C.L., & Alain, C. (2016). Increased activity in frontal motor cortex compensates impaired speech perception in older adults. *Nature Communications, 7*, 1–12. doi:10.1038/ncomms12241

Duberstein, P.R., Chapman, B.P., Tindle, H.A., Sink, K.M., Bamonti, P., Robbins, J., …Franks, P. (2011) Personality and risk for Alzheimer's disease in adults 72 years of age and older: A 6-year follow up. *Psychology and Aging, 26*(2), 351–362. doi:10.1037/a0021377

Dubois, B., Feldman, H.H., Jacova, C., Cummings, J., Dekosky, S.T., Barberger-Gateau, P., … Scheltens, P. (2010). Revising the definition of Alzheimer's disease: A new lexicon. *The Lancet Neurology, 9*(11), 1118–1127. doi:10.1016/S1474-4422(10)70223-4

Dubois, B., Feldman, H.H., Jacova, C., Dekosky, S.T., Barberger-Gateau, P., Cummings, J., …Scheltens, P. (2007). Research criteria for the diagnosis of Alzheimer's disease: Revising the NINCDS-ADRDA criteria. *The Lancet Neurology, 6*(8), 734–746. doi:10.1016/S1474-4422(07)70178-3

Duckworth, A.L., Steen, T.A., & Seligman, M.E.P. (2005). Positive psychology in clinical practice. *Annual Review of Clinical Psychology, 1*, 629–651. doi:10.1146/annurev.clinpsy.1.102803.144154

Duggan, M., & Brenner, J. (2013). *The demographics of social media users*—2012. Washington, DC: Pew Research Center. Retrieved from www.pewinternet.org/~/media//Files/Reports/2013/PIP_SocialMediaUsers.pdf

Dulin, P.L., Gavala, J., Stephens, C., Kostick, M., & McDonald, J. (2012). Volunteering predicts happiness among older Maori and non-Maori in the New Zealand Health, Work, and Retirement Longitudinal Study. *Aging & Mental Health, 16*(5), 617–624. doi:10.1080/13607863.2011.641518

Duncan, H.D., Phillips, N.A., Nicoladis, E., & Montanari, S. (2016). The contribution of bilingualism to cognitive reserve in health aging and dementia. In E. Nicoladis & S. Montanari (Eds.), *Bilingualism across the lifespan: Factors moderating language proficiency* (pp. 305–322). Washington, DC: American Psychological Association.

Duncan, S., & Phillips, M. (2010). People who live apart together (LAT) - How different are they? *The Sociological Review, 58*(1), 112–134. doi:10.1111/j.1467-954X.2009.01874.x

Durbin, A., Moineddin, R., Lin, E., Steele, L.S., & Glazier, R.H. (2015). Mental health service use by recent immigrants from different world regions and by non-immigrants in Ontario Canada: A cross sectional study. *Biomed Central, 15*, 1–15. doi:10.1186/s12913-015-0995-9

Ebbinghaus, H. (1885). *Über das gedchtnis. Untersuchungen zur experimentellen psychologie*. Leipzig, Ger: Duncker & Humblot.

Ebbinghaus, H. (1913). *Memory. A contribution to experimental psychology*. New York, NY: Teachers College, Columbia University.

Economist Intelligence Unit, The. (2015). *The 2015 Quality of Death Index: Ranking palliative care across the world*. London, UK: Author.

Edelstein B.A., Bamonti, P.M., Gregg, J.J., & Gerolimatos, L.A. (2015). Depression in late life. In P.A. Lichtenberg and B.T. Mast (Eds.), *APA handbook of clinical geropsychology: Assessment, treatment, and issues of later life*, (Vol. 2, pp. 2–47). Washington, DC: American Psychological Association.

Edelstein, B.A., & Segal, D.L. (2011). Assessment of emotional and personality disorders in older adults. In K. W. Schaie & S.L. Willis (Eds.), *Handbook of the psychology of aging* (7th ed., pp. 325–337). London, UK: Academic Press. doi:10.1016/B978-0-12-380882-0.00021-8

Edwards, C.J., Creaser, J.I., Caird, J.K., Lamsdale, A.M., & Chisholm, S.L. (2003). Older and younger driver performance at complex intersections: Implications for using perception-response time and driving simulation. *Proceedings of the Second International Driving Symposium on Human Factors in Driver Assessment, Training, and Vehicle Design*, Park City, UT, 33–38.

Edwards, P. (2012). *Elder abuse in Canada: A gender-based analysis*. Public Health Agency of Canada. Ottawa, ON: Public Health Agency of Canada. Retrieved from http://publications.gc.ca/collections/collection_2012/aspc-phac/HP10-21-2012-eng.pdf

Edwards, P., & Mawani, A. (2006). *Healthy aging in Canada: A new vision, a vital investment*. A discussion brief prepared for the Healthy Aging and Wellness Working Group of the Federal/Provincial/Territorial (F/P/T) Committee of Officials (Seniors). Retrieved from www.phac-aspc.gc.ca/seniors-aines/publications/public/healthysante/vision/vision-bref/index-eng. php

Egale Canada. (2004). *Outlaws and inlaws: Your guide to LBGT rights, same sex relationships and Canadian law*. Ottawa, ON: Author.

Eggebeen, D.J. (1992). Family structure and intergenerational exchanges. *Research on Aging, 14*(4), 427–447. doi:10.1177/0164027592144001

Eichler, M. (2015). Divorce in Canada. In *The Canadian Encyclopedia*. Retrieved from http://www.thecanadianencyclopedia.ca/en/article/divorce-in-canada/

Einolf, C.J. (2014). Stability and change in generative concern: Evidence from a longitudinal study. *Journal of Research in Personality, 51*, 54–61. doi:10.1016/j.jrp.2014.04.003

El-Gabalawy, R., Mackenzie, C.S., Shooshtari, S., & Sareen, J. (2011). Comorbid physical health conditions and anxiety disorders: A population-based exploration of prevalence and health outcomes among older adults. *General Hospital Psychiatry, 33*(6), 556–564. doi:10.1016/j.genhosppsyc.2011.07.005

El Ghissassi, F., Baan, R., Straif, K., Grosse, Y., Secretan, B., Bouvard, V., … Cogliano, V. (2009). A review of human carcinogens—Part D. Radiation. *The Lancet Oncology, 10*(8), 751–752. doi:10.1016/S1470-2045(09)70213-X

Elias, J., & Ryan, A. (2011). A review and commentary on the factors that influence expressions of sexuality by older people in care homes. *Journal of Clinical Nursing, 20*(11–12), 1668–1676. doi:10.1111/j.1365-2702.2010.03409.x

Emanuel, E.J. (2014, January 18). Sex and the single senior. *The New York Times*. Retrieved from https://www.nytimes.com/2014/01/19/opinion/sunday/emanuel-sex-and-the-single-senior.html

Emanuel, E.J., Onwuteaka-Philipsen, B. D., Urwin, J.W., & Cohen, J. (2016). Attitudes and practices of euthanasia and physician-assisted suicide in the United States, Canada, and Europe. *JAMA: The Journal of the American Medical Association, 316*(1), 79–90. doi:10.1001/jama.2016.8499

Erikson, E.H. (1950). Growth and crisis of the healthy personality. In M.J.E. Senn (ed.), *Symposium on the healthy personality* (pp. 91–146). New York, NY: Josiah Macy Jr., Foundation.

Erikson, E.H. (1959). *Identity and the life cycle*. New York, NY: International University Press.

Erikson, E.H. (1963). *Childhood and society*. New York, NY: Norton.

Erikson, E.H. (1982). *The life cycle completed: A review*. New York, NY: Norton.

Erikson, E.H., Erikson, J.M., & Kivnick, H.Q. (1986). *Vital involvement in old age*. New York, NY: Norton.

Erikson, J.M. (1991). *Wisdom and the senses: The way of creativity*. New York, NY: Norton.

Erikson, K., Voss, M., Prakash, R., Basak, C., Szabo, A., Chaddock, L., … Kramer, A. (2011). Exercise training increases size of hippocampus and improves memory. *Proceedings of the National Academy of Sciences, 108*(7), 3017–3022. doi:10.1073/pnas.1015950108

Erten-Lyons, D., Sherbakov, L.O., Piccinin, A.M., Hofer, S.M., Dodge, H.H., Quinn, J.F., … Kaye, J.A. (2012). Review of selected databases of longitudinal studies. *Alzheimer's & Dementia*, 8(6), 584–589. doi:10.1016/j.jalz.2011.09.232

Etezadi, S., & Pushkar, D. (2013). Why are wise people happier? An explanatory model of wisdom and emotional well-being in older adults. *Journal of Happiness Studies* 14(3), 929–950. doi:10.1007/s10902-012-9362-2

Eurostat European Commission. (2011). *Active ageing and solidarity between generations: A statistical portrait of the European Union edition* (ISSN 1830–7906). Luxembourg, BE: Publications Office of the European Union.

Exley, C. (2014). What is the risk of aluminum as a neurotoxin? *Expert Review of Neurotherapeutics*, 14(6), 589–591. doi:10.1586/14737175.2014.915745

Fair, C.D., & Delaplane, E. (2015). "It is good to spend times with older adults. You can teach them, they can teach you": Second grade students reflect on intergenerational service learning. *Early Childhood Education Journal*, 43(1), 19–26. doi:10.1007/s10643-014-0634-9

Fadul, J.A. (2017). *Encyclopedia of theory & practice in psychotherapy & counseling.* Toronto, ON: Lulu Press.

Fang, L., Oliver, A. Jayaraman, G.C., & Wong, T. (2010). Trends in age disparities between younger and middle-age adults among reported rates of chlamydia, gonorrhea, and infectious syphilis infections in Canada: Findings from 1997 to 2007. *Sexually Transmitted Diseases: Journal of the American Sexually Transmitted Diseases Association*, 37(1), 18–25. doi:10.1097/QLQ.0b013e3181b617dc

Farage, M.A., Miller, K.W., Zouboulis, C.C., Piérard, G.E., & Maibach, H.I. (2012) Gender differences in skin aging and the changing profile of the sex hormones with age. *Journal of Steroids and Hormonale Science*, 3:109. doi:10.4172/2157-7536.1000109

Farkas, K.J. (2006). Alcohol abuse in late life. In S.L. Straussner (Ed.), *Clinical work with substance abusers* (pp. 330–346). New York, NY: Guilford Press.

Fazel, M., Wheeler, J., & Danesh, J. (2005). Prevalence of serious mental disorder in 7000 refugees resettled in western countries: A systematic review. *The Lancet*, (365), 1309–1314. doi:1016/S0140-6736(05)61027-6

Feder, K., Michaud, D., Ramage-Morin, P., McNamee, J., & Beauregard, Y. (2015). Prevalence of hearing loss among Canadians aged 20 to 79: Audiometric results from the 2012/2013 Canadian Health Measures Survey. *Health Reports*, 26(7), 18–25. Retrieved from www.statcan.gc.ca/pub/82-003-x/2015007/article/14206-eng.pdf

Federal/Provincial/Territorial Ministers Responsible for Seniors. (2008). *Age-friendly rural and remote communities: A guide.* Retrieved from www.phac-aspc.gc.ca/seniors-aines/alt-formats/pdf/.../age...rural/AFRRC_en.pdf

Federal/Provincial/Territorial Ministers Responsible for Seniors. (2012). *Age-friendly workplaces: Promoting older worker participation.* Gatineau, QC: Employment and Social Development Canada.

Federal/Provincial/Territorial Ministers Responsible for Seniors. (2012). *Thinking about aging in place.* Ottawa, ON: Government of Canada.

Federal Trade Commission. (2016, January 5). *Lumosity to Pay $2 Million to Settle FTC Deceptive Advertising Charges for Its "Brain Training" Program.* Retrieved from www.ftc.gov/news-events/press-releases/2016/01/lumosity-pay-2-million-settle-ftc-deceptive-advertising-charges

Felson, D.T., & Neogi, T. (2004). Osteoarthritis: Is it a disease of cartilage or of bone? *Arthritis and Rheumatism*, 50(2), 341–344. doi:10.1002/art.20051

Feng, C-Y., Chu, H., Chen, C-H., Chang, Y-S., Chang, Y-S., Chen, T-H., … & Cou, K-R. (2011). The effect of cognitive behavioral group therapy for depression: A meta-analysis 2000–2010. *Worldviews on Evidence-Based Nursing*, 2–16. doi:10.1111/j.1741-6787.2011.00229.x

Fernández-Ballesteros, R., Bustillos, A., & Huici, C. (2015). Positive perception of aging and performance in a memory task: Compensating for stereotype threat? *Experimental Aging Research* 41(4), 410–425. doi:10.1080/0361073X.2015.1053757

Fields, R.D. (2010). Changes in the brains white matter. *Science*, 330(6005), 768–769. doi:10.1126/science.1199139

Fileborn, B., Thorpe, R., Hawkes, G., Minichiello, V., & Pitts, M. (2015). Sex and the (older) single girl: Experiences of sex and dating in later life. *Journal of Aging Studies*, 33, 67–75. doi:10.1016/j.jaging.2015.02.002

Financial Consumer Agency of Canada. (2015). *Understanding reverse mortgages.* Ottawa, ON: Government of Canada. Retrieved from www.fcac-acfc.gc.ca/eng/resources/publications/mortgages/Pages/Understa-Comprend.aspx

Findsen, B., & Formosa, M. (2011). *Lifelong learning in later life.* Rotterdam, NL: Sense Publishers.

Finke, M.S., Huston, S.J., & Sharpe, D.L. (2006). Balance sheets of early boomers: Are they different from pre-boomers? *Journal of Family and Economic Issues*, 27(3), 542–561. doi:10.1007/s10834-006-9026-7

Finkel, D., Reynolds, C.A., McArdle, J.J. Gatz, M., & Pederson, N.L. (2007). Latent growth curve analysis of accelerating decline in cognitive abilities in late adulthood. *Developmental Psychology*, 39(3), 535–550. doi:10.1037/0012-1649.39.3.535

Fingerman, K.., Cheng, Y.-P, Tighe, L., Birditt, K.S., & Zarit, S. (2012). Relationships between young adults and their parents. In B.A. Brown, S.L. Landale, N. Manning, & S.M. McHale (Eds.), *Early adulthood in a family context* (pp. 59–85). Berlin, DE: Springer.

Fingerman, K., Miller, L., Birditt, K., & Zarit, S. (2009) Giving to the good and the needy: Parental support of grown children. *Journal of Marriage and the Family*, 71(5), 1220–1233. doi:10.1111/j.1741-3737.2009.00665.x

Fingerman, K.L., Kim, K., Tennant, P.S., Birditt, K.S., & Zarit, S.H. (2016). Intergenerational support in a daily context. *The Gerontologist*, 56(5), 896–908. doi:10.1093/geront/gnv035

Fingerman, K.L., Sechrist, J., & Birditt, K. (2013). Changing views on intergenerational ties. *Gerontology*, 59(1), 64–70. doi:10.1159/000342211

Finkelstein, L.M., Burke, M.J., & Raju, M.S. (1995). Age discrimination in simulated employment contexts: An integrative analysis. *Journal of Applied Psychology*, 80(6), 652–663. doi:10.1037/0021-9010.80.6.652

Fiori, K.L., Antonucci, T.C., & Cortina, K.S. (2006). Social network typologies and mental health among older adults. *The Journals of Gerontology, Series B: Psychological Sciences and Social Sciences*, 61B(1), P25–P32. doi:10.1093/geronb/61.1.P25

Fiske, A., Wetherell, J.L., & Gatz, M. (2009), Depression in older adults. *Annual Review of Clinical Psychology*, 5, 363–389. doi:10.1146/annurev.clinpsy.032408.153621

Flaherty, D.K. (2011). The vaccine-autism connection: A public health crisis caused by unethical medical practices and fraudulent science. *The Annals of Pharmacotherapy*, 45(10), 1302–1304. doi:10.1345/aph.1Q318

Folstein, M.F., Folstein, S.E., & McHugh, P.R. (1975). "Mini-mental state." A practical method for grading the cognitive state of patients for the clinician. *Journal of Psychiatric Research*, 12(3), 189–198. doi.org/10.1016/0022-3956(75)90026-6

Fontana, L., Meyer, T. E., Klein, S., & Holloszy, J. O. (2004). Long-term calorie restriction is highly effective in reducing the risk for atherosclerosis in humans. *Proceedings of the National Academy of Sciences of the United States of America*, 101(17), 6659–6663. doi:10.1073/pnas.0308291101

Foot, D.K., & Venne, R.A. (2005). Awakening to the intergenerational equity debate in Canada. *Journal of Canadian Studies*, 39(1), 5–21. doi:10.3138/jcs.39.1.5

Formosa, M. (2009). Renewing universities of the third age: Challenges and visions for the future. *Recerca, Revista, De Pensament lAnalisi*, 9, 171–196. Retrieved from www.um.edu.mt/library/oar//handle/123456789/1203

Forum Research Inc. (2016). *Canadians favour advance consent in assisted dying*. Toronto, ON: Author.

Fowler, R., & Hammer, M. (2013). End-of-life care in Canada. *Clinical & Investigative Medicine*, 36(3), E127-E132.

Frank, J.B. (2002). *The paradox of aging in place in assisted living*. London, UK: Bergin & Garvey.

Franklin, D. (2015). *The parent and grandparent sponsorship reforms: The consequence of a neoliberal shift* (RCIS Working Paper Series, No. 2015/5). Toronto, ON: Ryerson Centre for Immigration and Settlement. Retrieved from www.ryerson.ca/rcis/publications/rcisworkingpapers/

Fraser, K.C., Meltzer, J.A., & Rudzicz, F. (2016). Linguistic features identify Alzheimer's disease in narrative speech. *Journal of Alzheimer's Disease*, 49(2), 407–422. doi:10.3233/JAD.150520

Fredriksen-Goldsen, K. I., Kim, H.-J., Emlet, C.A., Muraco, A., Erosheva, E.A., Hoy-Ellis, C.P., … Petry, H. (2011). *The aging and health report: Disparities and resilience among lesbian, gay, bisexual and transgendered old adults*. Seattle, WA: Institute for Multigenerational Health.

Freedman, V.A., Grafova, I.B., Schoeni, R.F., & Rogowski, J. (2008). Neighborhoods and disability in later life. *Social Sciences & Medicine*, 66(11), 2253–2267. doi:10.1016/j.socscimed.2008.01.013

Freud, S. (1923). *Das Ich und das Es*. Vienna, AT: Internationaler Psycho-analytischer Verlag.

Freund, A.M., & Ritter, J.O. (2009). Midlife crisis: A debate. *Gerontology*, 55(5), 582–591. doi:10.1159/000227322

Frey, W.H. (2010). Baby Boomers and the new demographics of America's seniors. *Generations, Journal of the American Society on Aging*, 34(3), 28–37. Retrieved from /www.frey-demographer.org/reports/R-2010-1_Gens_34_3_p_28_37.pdf

Friedman, H.S., Kern, M.L., Hampson, S.E., & Duckworth, A.L. (2014). A new life-span approach to conscientiousness and health: Combining the pieces of the causal puzzle. *Developmental Psychology*, *50*(12), 1377–1389. doi:10.1037/a0030373

Friedman, M., & Rosenman, R.H. (1959). Association of specific overt behavior pattern with blood and cardiovascular findings: Blood cholesterol level, blood clotting time, incidence of arcus senilis, and clinical coronary artery disease. *Journal of the American Medical Association*, *169*(12), 1286–1296. doi:10.1001/jama.1959.03000290012005

Fries, F. (1980). The compression of morbidity: Near or far? *The Milbank Quarterly*, *67*(2), 208–232. www.jstor.org/stable/3350138

Fritze, F., Ehrt, U., Hortobagyi, T., Ballard, C., & Aarsland, D. (2011). Depressive symptoms in Alzheimer's disease and Lewy body dementia: A one-year follow up study. *Dementia and Geriatric Cognitive Disorders*, *32*(2), 143–149. doi:10.1159/000332016

Frost, R.O., & Gross, R.C. (1993). *The hoarding of possessions. Behavior Research and Therapy*, *31*(4), 367–381. doi.org/10.1016/0005-7967(93)90094-B

Frost, R.O., & Hartl, T.L. (1996). A cognitive-behavioral model of compulsive hoarding. *Behavior Research and Therapy*, *34*(4), 341–350. doi.org/10.1016/0005-7967(95)00071-2

Frost, R.O., & Muller, A. (2014). Acquisition of possessions in hoarding disorder. In R. O. Frost & G. Steketee (Eds.), *The Oxford Handbook of Hoarding and Acquiring*, (pp. 86–99). New York, NY: Oxford University Press.

Frost, R.O., Patronek, G., Arluke, A., & Steketee, G. (2015). The hoarding of animals: An update. *Psychiatric Times*, *32*(4). Retrieved from www.psychiatrictimes.com/addiction/hoarding-animals-update

Frost, R.O., Tolin, D.F., Steketee, G., Fitch, K.E., & Selbo-Bruns, A. (2009). Excessive acquisition in hoarding. *Journal of Anxiety Disorders*, *23*(5), 632–639. doi:10.1016/j.janxdis.2009.01.013

Fullana, M.A., Vilagut, G., Rojas-Farreras, S., Mataix-Cols, D., de Graaf, R., Demyttenaere, K., … & ESEMeD/MHEDEA 2000 investigators. (2010). Obsessive-compulsive symptom dimensions in the general population: Results from an epidemiological study in six European countries. *Journal of Affective Disorders* *124*(3), 291–299. doi:10.1016/j.jad.2009.11.020

Fung, K.M., Tsang, H.W., & Chan, F. (2010). Self-stigma, stages of change and psychosocial treatment adherence among Chinese people with schizophrenia: A path analysis. *Social Psychiatry and Psychiatric Epidemiology*, *45*(5), 561–568. doi:10.1007/s00127-009-0098

Fung, K.M., Tsang, H.W., & Corrigan, P.W. (2008). Self-stigma of people with schizophrenia as predictor of their adherence to psychosocial treatment. *Psychiatric Rehabilitation Journal*, *32*(2), 95–104. doi:10.2975/32.2.2008.95.104

Galarneau, D., Morissette, R., & Usalcas, J. (2013). *Insights on Canadian society: What has changed for young people in Canada* (Catalogue no. 75–006-X). Ottawa, ON: Statistics Canada.

Galderisi, S., Heinz, A., Kastrup, M., Beezhold, J., & Sartorius, N. (2015). Towards a new definition of mental health. *World Psychiatry*, *14*(2), 231–233. doi:10.1002/wps.20231

Gallagher, D., & Herrmann, N. (2014). Antiepileptic drugs for the treatment of agitation and aggression in dementia: Do they have a place in therapy? *Drugs*, *74*(15), 1747–1755. doi:10.1007/s40265-014-0293-6

Gamliel, E. (2013). To end life or not to prolong life: The effect of message framing on attitudes toward euthanasia. *Journal of Health Psychology*, *18*(5), 693–703. doi:10.1177/1359105312455078

Gan, D.C., & Sinclair, R.D. (2005). Prevalence of male and female pattern hair loss in Maryborough. *The Journal of Investigative Dermatology*, *10*(3), 184–189. doi:10.1111/j.1087-0024.2005.10102.x

García-Alberca, J.M., Cruz, B., Lara, J.P., Garrido, V., Lara, A., Gris, E., & Gonzalez-Herero, V. (2013). The experience of caregiving: The influence of coping strategies on behavioral and psychological symptoms in patients with Alzheimer's disease. *Aging & Mental Health*, *17*(5), 615–622. doi:10.1080/13607863.2013.765833

Gardner, B., Iliffe, S., Fox, K.R., Jefferis, B.J., & Hamer, M. (2014). Sociodemographic, behavioural and health factors associated with changes in older adults' TV viewing over 2 years. *International Journal of Behavioral Nutrition and Physical Activity*, *11*(102). doi:10.1186/s12966-014-0102-3

Gardner, H. (1983). *Frames of mind: The theory of multiple intelligences*. New York, NY: Basic Books.

Garefalakis, M., & Hickey, M. (2008). Role of androgens, progestins, and tibolone in the treatment of menopausal symptoms: A review of the clinical evidence. *Clinical Interventions in Aging*, *3*(1), 1–8. doi:10.2147/CIA.S1043

Gareri, P., Castagna, A., Francomano, D., Cerminara, G., & De Fazio, P. (2014). Erectile dysfunction in the elderly: An old widespread issue with novel treatment perspectives. *International Journal of Endocrinology, 2014*(10), 1–15. doi:http://dx.doi .org/10.1155/2014/878670

Garnham, B. (2013). Designing "older" rather than denying ageing: Problematizing anti-ageing discourse in relation to cosmetic surgery undertaken by older people. *Journal of Aging Studies, 27*(1), 38–46. doi:10.1016/j.jaging.2012.11.001

Garriguet, D. (2006). *Nutrition: Findings from the Canadian Community Health Survey: Overview of Canadians' eating habits* 2004. Retrieved from http:// publications.gc.ca/Collection/Statcan/82-620-M/82- 620-MIE2006002.pdf

Gee, E.M., Kobayashi, K.M., & Prus, S.G. (2004). Examining the healthy immigrant effect in mid-to- late life: Findings from the Canadian Community Health Survey. *Canadian Journal on Aging, 23*(Suppl. 1), 61–69. Retrieved from http//:socserv.mcmaster.ca/ sedap/p/sedap98.pdf

Gee, E.M.T., Kobayashi, K.M., & Prus, S.G. (2004). Examining the healthy immigrant effect in mid-to later life: Findings from the Canadian Community Health Survey. *Canadian Journal on Aging,* 23(Suppl. 1), S61–S69. PMID:15660311

Genoe, M.R., & Whyte, C. (2015). Confronting ageism through therapeutic recreation practice. *Leisure/Loisir, 39*(2), 235–252. doi:10.1080/14927713.2015.1086583

Gerontological Society of America. (2012). *Communicating with older adults: An evidence- based review of what really works.* Washington, DC: Author. Retrieved from www.geron.org/publications/ communicating-with-older-adults

Gerontologist (2012). Special issue: The baby boomers. [Editorial]. *The Gerontologist, 52*(2), 149– 152. doi:10.1093/geron/gns038

Gerschman, R. (1981). Historical introduction to the "free radical theory" of oxygen toxicity. In D.L. Gilbert (Ed.), *Oxygen and living processes: An interdisciplinary approach* (pp. 44–46). New York, NY: Springer.

Gerstorf, D., Ram, N., Hoppmann, C., Willis, S.L., & Schaie, K.W. (2011). Cohort differences in cognitive aging and terminal decline in the Seattle Longitudinal Study. *Developmental Psychology, 47*(4), 1026–1041. doi:10.1037/a0023426

Gilbert, C.N., & Ricketts, K.G. (2008). Children's attitudes toward older adults and aging: A synthesis of research. *Educational Gerontology, 34*(7), 570–586. doi:10.1080/03601270801900420

Gillespie, B.J., Lever, J., Frederick, D., & Royce, T. (2015). Close adult friendships, gender, and the life

cycle. *Journal of Social and Personal Relationships, 32*(6), 709–736. doi:10.1177/0265407514546977

Gilmour, H. (2012). Social participation and the health and well-being of Canadian seniors. *Health Reports, 23*(4), 23–32. (Catalogue no. 82–003- X). Ottawa, ON: Statistics Canada. Retrieved from www.statcan.gc.ca/pub/82-003-x/2012004/ article/11720-eng.pdf

Giorgio, A., Santelli, L., Tomassini, V., Bosnell, R., De Stephano, N., & Johansen-Berg, H. (2010). Age- related changes in grey and white matter structure throughout adulthood. *NeuroImage, 53*(3), 943–951. doi:10.1016/j.neuroimage.2010.03.004

Gitlin, L.N. (1995). Why older people accept or reject assistive technology. *Generations,* 19(1), 41–46.

Gitlin, L.N. (2003). Conducting research on home environments: Lessons learned and new directions. *The Gerontologist, 43*(5), 628–637.

Glass, T.A., Freedman, M., Carlson, M.C., Hill, J., Frick, K.D., Ialongo, N., ...Fried, L.P. McGillS. (2004). Experience corps: Design of an intergenerational program to boost social capital and promote the health of an aging society. *Journal of Urban Health, 81*(1), 94–105. doi:10.1093/jurban/jth096

Glisky, E.L. (2007). Changes in cognitive function in human aging. In D.R. Riddle (Ed.), *Brain aging: Models, methods, and mechanisms* (pp. 1–15). Boca Raton, FL: CRC Press.

Godfrey, M., Surr, C., Boyle, G., Townsend, G., & Brooker, D. (2005). *Prevention and service provision: Mental health problems in later life: A final report.* Retrieved from http://eprints.worc.ac.uk/2860/

Godlee, F., Smith, J., & Marcovitch, H. (2011). Wakefield's article linking MMR vaccine and autism was fraudulent. *BMJ,* 342, c7452. doi:10.1136/bmj. c7452

Gomez, R., & Gunderson, M. (2011). For whom the retirement bell tolls: Accounting for changes in the expected age of retirement and the incidence of mandatory retirement in Canada. *Canadian Public Policy, 37*(4), 513–530. Retrieved from http://dx.doi .org/10.3138/cpp.37.4.513

Gonçalves, C.G., Mota, P.H., & Marques, J.M. (2009). Noise and age: Influence on the hearing of individuals with ages between 50–70 years. *Pró-fono: Revista de Atualização, Cientifica, 21*(1), 57–62.

Gonçalves, D.C., & Byrne, G.J. (2012). Interventions for generalized anxiety disorder in older adults: Systematic review and meta-analysis. *Journal of Anxiety Disorders, 26*(1), 1–11. doi:10.1016/ j.janxdis.2011.08.010

Gonçalves, D.C., & Byrne, G.J. (2013). Who worries most? Worry prevalence and patterns across the lifespan. *International Journal of Geriatric Psychiatry, 28*(1), 41–49. doi:10.1002/gps.3788

Gonçalves, D.C., Pachana, N.A., & Byrne, G.J. (2011). Prevalence and correlates of generalized anxiety disorder among older adults in the Australian National Survey of Mental Health and Well-Being. *Journal of Affective Disorders, 132*(1-2), 223–230. doi:10.1016/j.jad2011.02.023

Gooneratne, N.S., & Vitiello, M.V. (2014). Sleep in older adults: Normative changes, sleep disorders, and treatment options. *Clinics in Geriatric Medicine, 30*(3), 591–627. doi:10.1016/j.cger.2014.04.007

Gougeon, P. (2009). Shifting pensions. *Perspective on Labour and Income, 10*(5), 16–23.

Gould, C.E., Coulson, M.C., & Howard, R.J. (2012). Efficacy of cognitive behavioral therapy for anxiety disorder in older people: A meta-analysis and meta-regression of randomized control trials. *Journal of the American Geriatrics Society, 60*(2), 218–229. doi:10.1111/j.1532-5415.2011.03824.x

Gould, C.E., Edelstein, B.A., & Gerolimatos, I.A. (2012). Assessment of older adults. In S.K. Whitbourne & Martin J. Sliwinski (Eds.), *The Wiley-Blackwell handbook of adulthood and aging* (pp. 331–354). Hoboken, NJ: Wiley-Blackwell.

Goulding, M.R., Rogers, M.E., & Smith, S.M. (2003). Public health and aging: Trends in aging—United State and worldwide. *Morbidity and Mortality Weekly Report, 52*(6), 101–106. doi:10.1001/jama.289.11.1371

Government of Canada. (2004). *The Canada Health Act overview and options.* Ottawa, ON. Retrieved from www.lop.parl.gc.ca/content/lop/researchpublications/944-e.htm

Government of Canada. (2014a). *The consent process: The Inter-Agency Advisory Panel TCPS 2 —Chapter 3.* Retrieved from www.pre.ethics.gc.ca/eng/policy-politique/initiatives/tcps2-eptc2/chapter3-chapitre3/

Government of Canada. (2014b). *Tri-Council Policy Statement: Ethical conduct for research involving humans.* Ottawa, ON: Canadian Institutes of Health Research, Natural Sciences and Engineering Council of Canada, Social Sciences and Humanities Research Council of Canada.

Government of Canada. (2014c). *Action for seniors report.* Retrieved from https://www.canada.ca/en/employment-social-development/programs/seniors-action-report.html

Government of Canada. (2015a). *Seniors: Active, engaged, informed.* Ottawa, ON: Author. Retrieved from www.seniors.gc.ca/eng/pie/saei/index.shtml

Government of Canada. (2015b). *HIV and AIDS in Canada: Surveillance report to December 31, 2014.* Ottawa, ON: Author. Retrieved from http://healthycanadians.gc.ca/publications/diseases-conditions-maladies-affections/hiv-aids-surveillance-2014-vih-sida/index-eng.php

Government of Canada (2016a). *The Chief Public Health Officer's report on the state of public health in Canada 2015: Resources on alcohol.* Retrieved from www.canada.ca/en/public-health/services/publications/chief-public-health-officer-reports-state-public-health-canada/2015-resources-alcohol.html

Government of Canada. (2016b). *International social security agreements.* Retrieved from www.esdc.gc.ca/en/reports/pension/agreements.page

Government of Canada. (2016c). *Elder abuse: It's time to face the reality.* Retrieved from https://www.canada.ca/en/public-health/services/health-promotion/stop-family-violence/prevention-resource-centre/prevention-resources-older-adults/elder-abuses-time-face-reality.html

Government of Canada. (2016d). *Canada Pension Plan: How much can you receive.* Retrieved from www.canada.ca/en/services/benefits/publicpensions/cpp/cpp-benefit/amount.html

Government of Canada. (2016e). *Old Age Security payment amounts.* Retrieved from https://www.canada.ca/en/services/benefits/publicpensions/cpp/old-age-security/payments.html

Government of Canada. (2016f). *Employment insurance compassionate care benefits.* Ottawa, ON: Author. Retrieved from www.esdc.gc.ca/en/reports/ei/compassionate_care.page#h2.1

Government of Canada. (2016g). *Medical assistance in dying.* Ottawa, ON: Author. Retrieved from www.healthycanadians.gc.ca/health-system-systeme-sante/services/end-life-care-soins-fin-vie/medical-assistance-dying-aide-medicale-mourir-eng.php

Government of Canada. (2017a). *What is the Home Buyers' Plan (HBP)?* Retrieved from http://www.cra-arc.gc.ca/hbp/

Government of Canada. (2017b) *Veterans Independence Program.* Retrieved from http://www.veterans.gc.ca/eng/services/health/veterans-independence-program/

Gow, A.J., Pattie, A., Whiteman, M.C., Whalley, L.J., & Deary, I J. (2007). Social support and successful aging. *Journal of Individual Differences, 28*(3), 103–115. doi:10.1027/1614-0001.28.3.103

Grady, C. (2012). The cognitive neuroscience of ageing. *Nature Review/Neuroscience, 13*(7), 491–505. doi:10.1038/nrn3256

Grady, D. (2006). Management of menopausal symptoms. *The New England Journal of Medicine, 355*(22), 2338–2347. doi:10.1056/NEJMcp054015

Gracey, M., & King, M. (2009). Indigenous health part 1: Determinants and disease patterns. *The Lancet, 374*(9683), 65–75. doi:10.1016/S0140-6736(09)60914-4

Granholm, E., McQuaid, J.R., McClure, F.S., Link, P.C., Perivoliotis, D., Gottlieb, J.D., Patterson, T.L., & Jeste, D.V. (2007). Randomized controlled trial of cognitive behavioral social skills training for older people with schizophrenia: 12-month follow-up. *The Journal of Clinical Psychiatry, 68*(5), 730–737. Retrieved from www.psychiatrist.com/jcp/Pages/home.aspx

Grant, T.L., Edwards, N., Sveistrup, H., Andrew, C., & Egan, M. (2010a). Inequitable walking conditions among older people: Examining the interrelationship of neighbourhood socio-economic status and urban form using a comparative case study. *BMC Public Health, 10*(677). doi:10.1186/1471-2458-10-677

Grant, T.L., Edwards, N., Sveistrup, H., Andrew, C., & Egan, M. (2010b). Neighborhood walkability: Older people's perspective from four neighborhoods in Ottawa, Canada. *Journal of Aging and Physical Activity, 18*(3), 293–312.

Gravel, R., & Béland, Y. (2005). The Canadian Community Health Survey: Health and Well-being. *Canadian Journal of Psychiatry, 50*, 573–579. doi:10.1177/070674370505001002

Greenfield, E.A., & Reyes, L. (2015). Age-friendly community initiatives: Conceptual issues and key questions for an emerging paradigm. *The Gerontologist, 55*(2), 191–198. doi:10.1093/geront/gnv005

Gregory, N.D., Chandran, S., Lurie, D., & Sataloff, R.T. (2012). Voice disorders in the elderly. *Journal of Voice, 26*(2), 254–258. doi:10.1016/j.jvoice.2010.10.024

Greitemeyer, T. (2008). Stereotypes of singles: Are singles what we think? *European Journal of Social Psychology, 39*(3), 368–383. doi:10.1002/ejsp.542

Griffin, P.W., Mroczek, D.K., & Wesbecher, K. (2015). Personality development across the lifespan: Theory, research and application. In P.A. Lichtenberg & B.T. Mast (Eds.), *APA handbook of clinical geropsychology. Volume 1: History and status of the field and perspectives on aging* (pp. 217–234). Washington, DC: American Psychological Association.

Griffith, L., Raina, P., Wu, H., Zhu, B., & Stathokostas, L. (2010). Population attributable risk for functional disability associated with chronic conditions in Canadian older adults. *Age and Ageing, 39*(6), 738–745. doi:10.1093/ageing/afq105

Grigorovich, A. (2013). Long-term care for older lesbian and bisexual women: An analysis of current research and policy. *Social Work in Public Health, 27*(6), 596–606. doi:10.1080/19371918.2011.593468

Gross, A., Parisi, J.M., Spira, A.P., Kueider, A.M., Ko, J.Y., Saczynski, J.S., … Rebok, G.W. (2012). Memory training interventions with older adults: A meta-analysis. *Aging and Mental Health, 16*(6), 722–734. doi:10.1080/13607863.2012.667783

Grotz, C., Seron, X., Van Wissen, M., & Adam, S. (2017). How should proxies of cognitive reserve be evaluated in a population of healthy older adults? *International Psychogeriatrics, 29*(1), 123–136. doi:10.1017/s1041610216001745

Gruenberg, E.M. (1977). The failure of success. *The Milbank Quarterly, 55*(1), 3–24. doi:10.1111/j.1468-0009.2005.00400.x

Gruenewald, T.L., Liao, D.H., & Seeman, T.E. (2012). Contributing to others, contributing to oneself: Perceptions of generativity and health in later life. *The Journals of Gerontology, Series B: Psychological Sciences and Social Sciences, 67*(6), 660–665. doi:10.1093/geronb/gbs034

Guasp, A. (2011). *Lesbian, gay and bisexual people in late life*. London, UK: Stonewall.

Guberman, N., Lavoie, J-P., Blein, L., & Olazabal, I. (2012). Baby boom caregivers: Care in the age of individualization. *The Gerontologist, 52*(2), 210–218. doi.org/10.1093/geront/gnr140

Gum, A.M., Hirsch, A., Dautovich, N.D., Ferrante, S., & Schonfeld, L. (2014). Six-month utilization of psychotherapy by older adults with depressive symptoms. *Community Mental Health Journal 50*(7), 759–764. doi:10.1007/s10597-014-9704-0

Gum, A.M., King-Kallimanis, B., & Kohn, R. (2009). Prevalence of mood, anxiety, and substance-abuse disorders for older Americans in the National Comorbidity Survey-Replication. *The American Journal of Geriatric Psychiatry, 17*(9), 769–781. doi:10.1097/JGP.0b013e3181ad4f5a.

Gunderson, M. (2003). Age discrimination and employment in Canada. *Contemporary Economic Policy, 21*(3), 318–329. doi:10.1093/cep/byg013

Gupta, S., & Warner, J. (2008). Alcohol-related dementia: A 21st-century epidemic? *The British Journal of Psychiatry, 193*(5), 351–353. doi:10.1192/bjp.pb.108.051425

Gutiérrez, F., Gemma, V., Maria, J., Baillés, E., Ferraz, L., Gárriz, M., & Caseras, X. (2012). Personality disorder features through the life course. *Journal of Personality Disorders, 26*(5), 763–774. doi:10.1521/pedi.2012.26.5.763

Hakoyama, M., & MaloneBeach, E.E. (2014). Young adults' perceptions of closeness with their grandparents and attitudes towards aging. *The International Journal of Aging and Society, 3*(4), 53–56. Retrieved from http://cgpublisher.com/product.pub.212/prod.108

Hall, E.M. (1980). *Canada's national-provincial health program for the 1980's: 'A commitment for renewal'.* Ottawa, ON: Department of National Health and Welfare.

Han, B., Gfroerer, J.C., Colliver, J.D., & Penne, M.A. (2009). Substance use disorder among older adults in the United States in 2020. *Addiction, 104*(1), 88–96. doi:10.1111/j.1360-0443.2008.02411.x

Hammack, P.L. (2008). Narratives and the cultural psychology of identity. *Personality and Social Psychology Review, 12*(3), 222–247. doi:10.1177/1088868308316892

Hampson, S.E., & Friedman, H.S. (2008). Personality and health: A lifespan perspective. In O. P. John, R. Robins, & L. Pervin (Eds.), *The handbook of personality: Theory and research* (3rd ed., pp. 770–794). New York, NY: Guilford Press.

Hansen, T., Moum, T., & Shapiro, A. (2007). Relational and individual well-being among cohabitators and married individuals in midlife: Recent trends form Norway. *Journal of Family Issues, 28*(7), 910–933. doi:10.1177/0192513X07299610

Hansson, E.K., Tuck, A., Lurie, S., & McKenzie, K. (2012). Rates of mental illness and suicidality in immigrant, refugee, ethnocultural, and racialized groups in Canada: A review of the literature. *Canadian Journal of Psychiatry, 57*(2), 111–121. doi:10.1177/070674371205700208

Harada, C.N., Natelson-Love, M.C., & Triebel, K. (2013). Normal cognitive aging. *Clinical Geriatric Medicine, 29*(4), 737–752. doi:10.1016/j.cger.2013.07.002

Harding C.M. (2003). Changes in schizophrenia across time: Paradoxes, patterns and predictors. In C.I. Cohen (Ed.), *Schizophrenia in late life,* (pp. 19–42). Washington, DC: American Psychiatric Publishing.

Harkin, J., & Huber, J. (2004). *Eternal youths: How the baby boomers are having their time again.* London, UK: Demos Publishing.

Harman, D. (1956). Aging: A theory based on free radical and radiation chemistry. *Journal of Gerontology, 11*(3), 298–300. doi:10.1093/geronj/11.3.298

Harper, C. (2009). The neuropathology of alcohol-related brain damage. *Alcohol and Alcoholism, 44*(2), 136–140. doi:10.1093/alcalc/agn102

Harper, K., & Armelagos, G. (2010). The changing disease-scape in the Third Epidemiological Transition. *International Journal of Environmental Research and Public Health, 7*(2), 675–697. doi:10.3390/ijerph7020675

Harrington, T. (2000). *About deafness.* Retrieved from http://libguides.gallaudet.edu/content.php?pid=352126&sid=2881882

Hartford, The. (2015). *At the crossroads: Family conversations about Alzheimer's disease, dementia, and driving.,* Hartford CT: The Hartford Financial Services Group, Inc.

Hartl, T.L., Duffany, S.R., Allen, G.J., Steketee, G., & Frost, R.O. (2005). Relationships among compulsive hoarding, trauma, and attention deficit hyperactivity disorder. *Behavior Research and Therapy, 43*(2), 269–276. doi:10.1016/j.brat.2004.02.002

Harvey, P.D. (2005). Clinical features and course of schizophrenia in late life. In P.D. Harvey (Ed.), *Schizophrenia in late life: Aging effects on symptoms and course of illness.* Washington, DC: American Psychiatric Association.

Hasher, L., & Zacks, R.T. (1988). Working memory, comprehension, and aging: A review and a new view. In G.H. Bower (Ed.), *The psychology of learning and motivation* (pp. 193–225). New York, NY: Academic Press.

Hasselhorn, H.M., & Apt, W. (2015). *Understanding employment participation of older workers: Creating a knowledge base for future labour market challenges.* Berlin, DE: Federal Ministry of Labour and Social Affairs and Federal Institute for Occupational Safety and Health.

Hassink, J., & Van Dijk, M. (2006). Farming for health across Europe: Comparison between countries, and recommendations for a research and policy agenda. In J. Hassink & M. Van Dijk (Eds.), *Farming for health: Green-care farming across Europe and the United States of America* (Volume 13, pp. 345–357). Dordrecht, Netherlands: Springer.

Haukioja, H. (2016). Exploring the nature of elder abuse in ethno-cultural minority groups: A community based participatory research study. *The Arbutus Review, 7*(1), 51–67. doi:10.18357/tar71201615681

Havighurst, R.J. (1961). Successful aging. *The Gerontologist, 1*(1), 8–13. doi:10.1093/geront/1.1.8

Hay Health Care Consulting Group, The. (2001, March). The Berger Population Health Monitor. Survey #22.

Hayflick, L. (1996). *How and why we age.* New York, NY: Ballantine Books.

Hayslip, Jr. B., Davis, S.R., Neumann, C.S., Goodman, C., Smith, G.C., Maiden, R.J., & Carr, G.F. (2013). The role of resilience in mediating stressor-outcome relationships among grandparents raising their grandchildren. In B.J. Hayslip & G.C. Smith (Eds.), *Resilient grandparent caregivers: A strengths-based perspective* (pp. 48–69). New York, NY: Routledge/Taylor & Francis Group.

He, W., Goodkind, D., & Kowal, P. (2016). *An aging world: 2015 International Population Reports.* Washington, DC: U.S. Government Publishing Office.

Health Canada. (2012a). *Vitamin D and calcium: Updated dietary reference intakes.* Ottawa, ON: Author. Retrieved from www.hc-sc.gc.ca/fn-an/nutrition/vitamin/vita-d-eng.php

Health Canada. (2012b). *Canadian alcohol and drug use monitoring survey.* Retrieved from https://www.canada.ca/en/health-canada/services/health-concerns/drug-prevention-treatment/drug-alcohol-use-statistics/canadian-alcohol-drug-use-monitoring-survey-summary-results-2012.html

Health Canada. (2014). *A statistical profile on the health of First Nations in Canada. Determinants of health, 2006–2010.* Retrieved from http://publications.gc.ca/collections/collection_2014/sc-hc/H34-193-1-2014-eng.pdf

Health Council of Canada. (2013). *Canada's most vulnerable. Improving health care of First Nation, Metis, and Inuit Seniors.* Toronto, ON: Author. Retrieved from www.metisnation.org/media/422632/senior_ab_report_2013_en_final.pdf

Healthy Aging and Wellness Working Group of the Federal/Provincial/Territorial Committee of Officials (Seniors). (2006). *Healthy aging in Canada: A new vision, a vital investment from evidence to action.* Ottawa, ON: The Alder Group.

Hearn, S., Saulnier, G., Strayer, J., Glenham, M., Koopman, R., & Marcia, J.E. (2012). Between integrity and despair: Toward construct validation of Erikson's eighth stage. *Journal of Adult Development, 19*(1), 1–20. doi:10.1007/s10804-011-9126-y

Heart and Stroke Foundation. (2015). *Getting to the heart of the matter.* Retrieved from www.heartandstroke.com/atf/cf/%7B99452d8b-e7f1-4bd6-a57d-b136ce6c95bf%7D/HSF-2015-HEART-MONTH-REPORT-V2.PDF

Hebert, B.-P., & Luong, M. (2008). Bridge employment. *Perspectives on Labour and Income, 9*(11), 5–12.

Heisel, M.J., Grek., A., Moore, S., Jackson, F., Vincent G., Malach, F.W., & Mokry, J. (2006). National guidelines for seniors' mental health: The assessment of suicide and risk prevention. *Canadian Journal of Geriatrics, 9,* 65–70. Retrieved from http://ccsmh.ca/wp-content/uploads/2016/03/final-supplement.pdf

Heisel, M.J, Talbot, N.L., King, D.A., Tu, X.M., & Duberstein, P.R. (2015). Adapting interpersonal psychotherapy for older adults at risk for suicide. *American Journal of Geriatric Psychiatry, 23*(1), 87–98. doi:10.1016/j.jagp.2014.03.010

Helson, R., & Kwan, V.S.Y. (2000). Personality development in adulthood. The broad picture and processes in one longitudinal study. In S.E. Hamson (Ed.), *Advances in personality psychology.* (Vol. 1, pp. 77–106). New York, NY: Routledge.

Henry, N.J., Berg, C.A., Smith, T.W., & Florsheim, P. (2007). Positive and negative characteristics of marital interaction and their association with marital satisfaction in middle-aged and older couples. *Psychology and Aging, 22*(3), 428–441. doi:10.1037/0882-7974.22.3.428

Herman, R.E., & Williams, K.N. (2009). Elderspeak influence on resistiveness to care. Focus on behavioral events. *American Journal of Alzheimer's Disease and Related Disorders, 24*(5), 417–423. doi:10.1177/1533317509341949

Hershey, D., & Henkens, K. (2013). Impact of different types of retirement transitions on perceived satisfaction with life. The Gerontologist, *54*(2), 232–244. doi:10.1093/geront/gnt006

Herskind, A.M., McGue, M., Holm, N.V. Sorensen, T.I., Harvald, B., & Vaupel, J.W. (1996). The heritability of human longevity: A population-based study of 2872 Danish twin pairs born 1870–1900. *Human Genetics, 97*(3), 319–323. doi:10.1007/BF02185763

Hertel, J., & Schütz, A. (2006). Singles: Maladjusted or stigmatized? In D. Chadee & J. Young (Eds.), *Current themes in social psychology* (pp. 255–270). Kingston, JM: University of the West Indies.

Hester, R.L., Kinsella, G.J., & Ong, B. (2004). Effect of age on forward and backward span tasks. *Journal of the International Neuropsychological Society, 10*(4), 475–481. doi:http://dx.doi.org/10.1017/S1355617704104037

Heyland, D.K., Lavery, J.V., Tranmer, J.E., & Shortt, S.E. (2000). The final days: An analysis of the dying experience in Ontario. *Annals of the Royal College of Physicians and Surgeons of Canada, 33*(6), 356–361.

Heyland, D.K., Lavery, J.V., Tranmer, J.E., Shortt, S.E., & Taylor, S.J. (2000). Dying in Canada: Is it an institutionalized, technologically supported experience? *Journal of Palliative Care, 16*(Suppl.), S10-S16.

Hildreth, C.J., Burke, A.E., & Glass, R.M. (2009). Cataracts fact sheet. *Journal of the American Medical Association, 301*(19), 2060. doi:10.1001/jama.301/19.2060

Hill, R.B. (1996). Historical context of the work ethic. Retrieved from http://rhill.coe.uga.edu/workethic/hist.htm

Hill, R.D., & Smith, D.J. (2015). Positive aging: At the crossroads of positive psychology and geriatric medicine. In P.A. Lichtenberg & B.T. Must (Eds.), *APA handbook of clinical geropsychology: History and status of the field and perspectives in aging,* (Vol. 1, pp. 301–329). Washington, DC: American Psychological Association. doi:10.1037/14458-013

Hillman, J. (2012). *Sexuality and aging: Clinical perspectives.* New York, NY: Springer.

Hirst, S.P., Penney, T., McNeill, S., Boscart, V.M., Podnieks, E., & Sinha, S.K. (2016). Best-practice guideline on the prevention of abuse and neglect of older adults. *Canadian Journal on Aging, 35*(2), 242–260. doi:10.1017/S0714980816000209

Hiscott, R.D. (2013). Determinants of post-retirement employment: Canadian evidence. *The Canadian Journal of Career Development, 12*(2), 59–71.

Hjelmborg, J., Iachine, I., Skytthe, A., Vaupel, J.W., McGue, M., …Christensen, K. (2006). Genetic influence on human lifespan and longevity. *Human Genetics, 119*(3), 312–321. doi:10.1007/s00439-006-0144-y

Ho, H.C.Y., Yeung, D.Y., & Kwok, S.Y.C.L (2014). Development and evaluation of the positive psychology intervention for older adults. *The Journal of Positive Psychology, 9*(3), 187–197. doi:10.1080/17439760.2014.888577

Ho, K.H., Matsubayashi, K., Wada, T., Kimura, M., Yano, S., Otsuka, K., … Saijoh, K. (2003). What determines the life satisfaction of the elderly? Comparative study of residential care home and community in Japan. *Geriatrics and Gerontology International, 3*(2), 79–85. doi: 10.1046/j.1444-1586.2003.00067

Hof, P.R., & Mobbs, C.V. (2009). *Handbook of the neuroscience of aging* (1st ed.). London, UK: Academic Press.

Hoffman, B. (2012). *Health care for some: Rights and rationing in the United States since 1930.* Chicago, IL: University of Chicago Press.

Honigman, R., & Castle, D.J. (2006). Aging and cosmetic enhancement. *Clinical Interventions in Aging, 1*(2), 115–119.

Hong, Y.J., Jang, E.H., Hwang, J., Roh, J.H., & Lee, J.H. (2015). The efficacy of cognitive intervention programs for mild cognitive impairment: A systematic review. *Current Alzheimer Research, 12*(6), 527–542. doi:10.2174/1567205012666150530201636

Hooker, K., & McAdams, D.P. (2003). Personality reconsidered: A new agenda for aging research. *The Journals of Gerontology, Series B: Psychological Sciences and Social Sciences, 58*(6), 269–304. doi:10.1093/geronb/58.6.P296

Hoover, D.R., Siegel, M., Lucas, J., Kalay, E., Gaboda, D., Devanand, D.P., & Crystal, S. (2010). Depression in the first year of stay for elderly long term nursing home residents in the USA. *International Psychogeriatrics, 22,* 1161–1171. doi:10.1017/S1041610210000578

Horn, J.L., & Cattell, R.B. (1966). Refinement and test of the theory of fluid and crystallized intelligence. *Journal of Educational Psychology, 57*(5), 253–270. doi:10.1037/h0023816

Horn, J.L., & Cattell, R.B. (1967). Age differences in fluid and crystallized intelligence. *Acta Psychologica, 26*(2), 107–129. doi:10.1016/0001-6918(67)90011-X

Horton, S., Baker, S., Côté, J., & Deakin, J.M. (2008). Understanding seniors' perceptions and stereotypes of aging. *Educational Gerontology, 34*(11), 997–1017. doi.org/10.1080/03601270802042198

Hou, F. (2010). *Homeownership over the life course of Canadians: Evidence from Canadian censuses of population* (Catalogue no. 11F0019M – No. 325). Ottawa, ON: Statistics Canada.

Howard, R., & Jeste, D.V. (2011). Late onset schizophrenia. In D.R. Weinberger & P.J. Harrison (Eds.), *Schizophrenia,* (pp. 47–61). Hoboken, NJ: Wiley Blackwell.

Hubbard, B.A., Unger, J.G., & Rohrich, R.J. (2014). Reversal of skin aging with topical retinoids. *Plastic and Reconstructive Surgery, 133*(4), 481e-490e. doi:10.1097/PRS.0000000000000043

Huber, M., Knottnerus, H.M., Green, J.A., Van der Horst, L., Jadad, H., Kromhout, A.R., & Smid, D. (2011). How should we define health? *British Medical Journal, 343,* d4163. doi:https://doi.org/10.1136/bmj.d4163

Huh, J.T., Weaver, C.M., Martin, J.L., Caskey, N.H., O'Riley, A., & Kramer, B.J. (2012). Effects of a late life suicide risk-assessment training on multi-discipline healthcare providers. *Journal of the American Geriatric Society, 60,* 775–778. doi:10.1111/j.1532-5415.2011.03843.x

Humble, A.M. (2009). *Retirement processes and outcomes of individuals who retire to give care.*

Halifax, NS: Atlantic Research Centre for Family-Work Issues.

Hummel, K.L. (2012). An examination of the social acceptability of elderspeak by college students and community dwelling older adults. *Theses, Dissertations, and Other Capstone Projects.* Retrieved from http://cornerstone.lib.mnsu.edu/cgi/viewcontent.cgi?article=1027&context=etds

Hummert, M.L. (2011). Age stereotypes and aging. In K.W. Schaie & S. L. Willis (Eds.), *The handbook of the psychology of aging* (7th ed.) (pp. 249–262). London, UK: Academic Press.

Hurd Clarke, L. (2006). Older women and sexuality: Experiences in marital relationships across the life course. *Canadian Journal on Aging, 25*(2), 129–140. doi:10.1353/cja.2006.0034

Hurd Clarke, L. & Griffin, M. (2008). Visible and invisible ageing: Beauty work as a response to ageism. *Ageing and Society, 28*(5), 653–674. doi:10.1017/S0144686X07007003

Hurd Clarke, L., Repta, R., & Griffin, M. (2007). Non-surgical cosmetic procedures: Older women's perceptions and experiences. *Journal of Women & Aging, 19*(3–4), 69–87. doi:10.1300/J074v19n03_06

Hurd, M., & Rohwedder, S. (2011). Trends in labor force participation: How much is due to changes in pensions? *Journal of Population Ageing, 4*(1–2), 811–96. doi:10.1007/s12062-011-9042-8

Idler, E.L., & Kasl, S.V. (1995). Self-rating of health: Do they also predict change in functional ability? *The Journal of Gerontology, Series B: Psychological Sciences & Social Sciences, 50* (6), S344–S353. doi:10.1093/geronb/50B.6.S344

Iervolino, A.C., Perroud, N., Fullana, M.A., Guipponi, M., Cherkas, L., Collier, D.A., & Mataix-Cols, D. (2009). Prevalence and heritability of compulsive hoarding: A twin study. *The American Journal of Psychiatry, 166*(10), 1156–1161. doi:10.1176/appi.ajp.2009.08121789

Iglewicz, A., Meeks, T.W., & Jeste, D.V. (2011). New wine in old bottle: Late-life psychosis. *The Psychiatric Clinics of North America, 34*(2), 295–318. doi:10.1016/j.psc.2011.02.008

Ingersoll-Dayton, B., & Krause, N. (2005). Self-forgiveness: A component of mental health in later life. *Research on Aging, 27*(3), 267–289. doi:10.1177/0164027504274122S

Insurance Institute of Highway Safety. (2015). *Older drivers.* Retrieved from www.iihs.org/iihs/topics/t/older-drivers/fatalityfacts/older-people/2015

International Advisory Group for the Revision of *ICD-10 Mental and Behavioural Disorder.* (2011). A conceptual framework for the revision of the *ICD-10 classification of mental and behavioural disorders. World Psychiatry, 10*(2), 86–92. Retrieved from www.ncbi.nlm.nih.gov/pmc/articles/PMC3104876/

International Federation on Ageing and Revera Inc. (2012). *The Revera report on ageism: A look at gender differences.* Retrieved from http://ageismore.reveraliving.net/research

International Federation on Ageing and Revera Inc. (2014). *The Revera report on ageism.* Retrieved from www.reveraliving.com/revera/files/b2/b20be7d4-4d3b-4442-9597-28473f13b061.pdf

International Federation on Ageing. (2015). *The Revera report on ageism: Independence and choice as we age.* Retrieved from www.geismore.com/report-independence-and-choice

Ipsos Reid. (2013). *2013 RBC retirement myths and realities poll: Most appealing living arrangements for boomers.* Retrieved from www.rbc.com/newsroom/pdf/1024-13-myths-poll.pdf

Isaac, M., Elias, B., Katz, L.Y., Belik, S.L., Deane, F.P., Enns, M.W., & Sareen, J. (2009). Gatekeeper training as a preventative intervention for suicide: A systematic review. *Canadian Journal of Psychiatry, 54*(4), 260-268. doi:10.1177/070674370905400407

Isherwood, L.M., King, D.S., & Luszcz, M.A. (2017). Widowhood in the fourth age: Support exchange, relationships and social participation. *Ageing & Society, 37*(1), 188–212. doi:10.1017/S0144686X15001166

Islam, F., Khanlou, N., & Tamim, H. (2014). South Asian populations in Canada: Migration and mental health. *BMC Psychiatry, 14*, 154. doi:10.1186/1471-244X-14-154

Iveniuk, J., Laumann, E.O., Waite, L.J., McClintock, M.K., & Tiedt, A. (2015). Personality measures in the National Social Life, Health, and Aging Project. *The Journals of Gerontology, Series B: Psychological Sciences and Social Sciences, 69*(Suppl. 2), S117–S124. doi:10.1093/geronb/gbu073

Iwasa, H., Masui, Y., Gondo, Y., Inagaki, H., Kawaai, C., & Suzuki, T. (2008). Personality and all-cause mortality among older adults dwelling in a Japanese community: A five year population-based prospective cohort study. *The American Journal of Geriatric Psychiatry, 16*(5), 399–405. doi:10.1097/JGP.0b013e3181662ac9

Jacelon, C., & Hanson, A. (2012). Older adults' participation in the development of smart environments: An integrated review of the literature. *Geriatric Nursing*, 34(2), 116–121. doi:10.1016/j.gerinurse.2012.11.001

Jack, C.R. Jr., Albert, M.S., Knopman, D.S., McKhann, G.M., Sperling, R.A., Carillo, M.C., … Phelps, C.H. (2011). Introduction to the recommendations from the National Institute on Aging-Alzheimer's Association workgroups on diagnostic guidelines for Alzheimer's disease. *Alzheimer's & Dementia*, 7(3), 257–262. doi:10.1016/j.jalz.2011.03.004

Jackson, J.J. (2011). The effects of educational experiences in personality trait development. *Dissertation Abstracts International: Section B. Sciences and Engineering*, 73(5), 3309. Retrieved from http://hdl.handle.net/2142/26149

Jackson, J.J., Connolly, J.J., Garrison, S.M., Leveille, M.M., & Connolly, S.M. (2015). Your friends know how long you will live: A 75-year study of peer-rated personality traits. *Psychological Science*, 26(3), 335–340. doi:10.1177/0956797614561800

Jackson, J.J., Hill, P.L., Payne, B.R., Roberts, B.W., & Stine-Morrow, E.A. (2012). Can an old dog learn (and want to experience) new tricks? Cognitive training increases openness to experience in older adults. *Psychology and Aging*, 27(2), 286–292. doi:10.1037/a0025918

Jacobs, J.C., Laporte, A., Van Houtven, C.H. & Coyte, P.C. (2014). Caregiving intensity and retirement status in Canada. *Social Science and Medicine*, 102, 74–82. doi:10.1016/j.socscimed.2013.11.051

Jacques, E. (1965). Death and the middle life crisis. *The International Journal of Psychoanalysis*, 46(4), 502–214. Retrieved from http://onlinelibrary.wiley.com/journal/10.1111/(ISSN)1745-8315

Jafari, S., Baharlou, S., & Mathias, R. (2010). Knowledge of determinants of mental health among Iranian immigrants of BC, Canada: "A qualitative study". *Journal of Immigrant and Minority Health*, 12(1), 100–106. doi:10.1007/s10903-008-9130-x

James, L., Jacobs, J. & Roodenburg, J. (2015). Adoption of the Cattell-Horn-Carroll Model of Cognitive Abilities by Australian psychologists: Adoption of CHC by Australian psychologists. *Australian Psychologist*, 50(3), 169–247. doi:10.1111/ap.12110

James, O.G., Doraiswamy, P.M., & Borges-Neto, S. (2015). PET imaging of tau pathology in Alzheimer's disease and tauopathies. *Frontiers in Neurology*, 6(38), 1–9. doi:10.3389/fneur.2015.00038

James, W. (1890). *Principles of psychology* (Vol. 1). New York, NY: Holt.

Jansen, T. (2016, January 20). The preschool inside a nursing home. *The Atlantic*. Retrieved from www.theatlantic.com/education/archive/2016/01/the-preschool-inside-a-nursing-home/424827

Jenkins Morales, M., King, M.D., Hiler, H., Coopwood, M.S., & Wayland S. (2014). The greater St. Louis LGBT health and human services needs assessment: An examination of the silent and Baby Boom generation. *Journal of Homosexuality*, 61(1), 103–128. doi:10.1080/00918369.2013.835239

Jeste, D.V., Ardelt, M., Blazer, D., Kraemer, H.C., Valliant, G., & Meeks, T.W. (2010). Expert consensus on characteristics of wisdom: A delphi method study. *Gerontologist*, 50(5), 668–680. doi:10.1093/geront/gnq022

Jeste, D.V., & Oswald, A.J. (2014). Individual and societal wisdom: Explaining the paradox of human aging and high well-being. *Psychiatry: Interpersonal and Biological processes*, 77(4), 317–330. doi:10.1521/psyc.2014.77.4.317

Jeste, D.V., & Vahia, I. (2008). Comparison of the conceptualization of wisdom in ancient Indian literature with modern views: Focus on the Bhagavad Gita. *Psychiatry*, 71(3), 197–209. doi:10.152/psyc.20008/71.3.197

Jibeen, T., & Khalid, R. (2010). Predictors of psychological well-being of Pakistani immigrants in Toronto, Canada. *International Journal of Intercultural Relations*, 34(5), 452–464. doi:10.1016/j.ijintrel.2010.04.010

Jokela, M., Batty, G. D., Nyberg, S.T., Virtanen,M., Nabi, H., Sing-Manoux, A., & Kivimäki, M. (2013). Personality and all-cause mortality: Individual-participant meta-analysis of 3,947 deaths in 76,150 adults. *American Journal of Epidemiology*, 178(5), 667–675. doi:10.1093/aje/kwt170

Juraska, J.M., & Lowry, N.C. (2012). Neuroanatomical changes associated with cognitive aging. *Current Topics in Behavioral Neurosciences*, 10, 137–162. doi:10.1007/7854_2011_137

Jette, A.M. (2006). Toward a common language for function, disability and health. *Physical Therapy*, 86(5), 726–734. doi:10.1093/ptj/86.5.726

Johnson, J.L., Davenport, R., & Mann, W.C. (2007). Consumer feedback on smart home applications. *Topics in Geriatric Rehabilitation*, 23(1), 60–72.

Johnson, K.A., Schultz, A., Betensky, R.A., Becker, J.A., Sepulcre, J., Rentz, D., … Sperling, R. (2016). Tau positron emission tomographic imaging in aging and early Alzheimer disease. *Annals of Neurology*, 79(1), 110–119. doi:10.1002/ana.24546

Jones, D.M., Song, X., & Rockwood, K. (2004). Operationalizing a Frailty Index from a standardized comprehensive geriatric assessment. *Journal of the American Geriatric Society*, 52(11), 1929–1933. doi:10.1111/j.1532-5415.2004.52521.x

Jones, S.L., Hadjistavropoulos, H.D., & Soucy, J.N. (2016). A randomized controlled trial of guided internet-delivered cognitive behaviour therapy for older adults with generalized anxiety. *Journal of Anxiety Disorders*, 37, 1–9. doi:10.1016/j.janxdis.2015.10.006

Jung, C.G. (1912). *The psychology of the unconscious*. Mineola, NY: Dover Publications Inc.

Jurabe, T., Turok, X.P., & Perez-Stable, E.J. (2002). Perceived benefits and barriers to physical activity among older Latino women. *Western Journal of Nursing Research*, 24(8), 868–886. doi:10.1177/019394502237699

Juurlink, D.N., Herrmann, N., Szalai, J.P., Kopp, A., & Redelmeier, D.A. (2004). Medical illness and the risk of suicide in the elderly. *Archives of Internal Medicine*, 164(11), 1179–1184. doi:10.1001/archinte.164.11.1179

Kaida, L., & Boyd, M. (2011). Poverty variations among the elderly: The roles of income security policies and family co-residence. *Canadian Journal on Aging*, 30(1), 83–100. doi:10.1017/S0714980810000814

Kaida, L., Moyser, M., & Park, S.Y. (2009). Cultural preferences and economic constraints: The living arrangement of elderly Canadians. *Canadian Journal on Aging*, 28(4), 303–313. doi:10.1017/S0714980809990146

Kales, H.C., Kim, H.M., Zivin, K., Valenstein, M., Seyfried, L.S., Chiang, C., … Blow, F.C. (2012). Risk of mortality among individual antipsychotics in patients with dementia. *The American Journal of Psychiatry*, 169(1), 71–79. doi:10.1176/appi.ajp.2011.11030347

Kallio, E. (2011). Integrative thinking is the key: An evaluation of current research in the development of adult thinking. *Theory and Psychology*, 21(6), 785–801. doi:10/1177/0959354310388344

Kamp Dush, C.M., Taylor, M.G., & Kroeger, R.A. (2008). Marital happiness and psychological well-being across the life course. *Family Relations*, 57(2), 211–226. doi:10.1111/j.1741-3729.2008.00495.x

Kaplan, M.S., Huguet, N. Feeny, D., McFarland, B.H., Caetano, R., Bernier, J., … Ross, N. (2012). Alcohol use patterns and trajectories of health-related quality of life in middle-aged and older adults: A 14-year population-based study. *Journal of Studies on Alcohol and Drugs*, 73(4), 581–590. doi:http://dx.doi.org/10.15288/jsad.2012.73.581

Kaplan, M.S., Huguet, N. Feeny, D., McFarland, B.H., Caetano, R., Bernier, J., … Ross, N. (2014). The association between alcohol use and long-term care placement among older Canadians: A 14-year population based study. *Addictive Behaviors*, 39(1), 219–224. doi:10.1016/j.addbeh.2013.09.031

Karel, M.J., Gatz, M., & Smyer, M.A. (2012). Aging and mental health in the decade ahead: What psychologists need to know. *American Psychologist*, 67(3), 184–198. doi:10.1037/a0025393

Karel, M.J, Molinari, V., Emery-Tiburcio, E.E., & Knight, B.G. (2015). Pikes Peak conference and competency-based training in professional geropsychology. In P.A. Lichtenberg & B.T. Mast (Eds.), *APA handbook of clinical geropsychology: History and status of the field and perspectives on aging*, (Vol. 1., pp 19–43). Washington, DC: American Psychiatric Association.

Karg, K., Burmeister, M., Shedden, K., & Sen, S. (2011). The serotonin transporter promoter variant (5-HTTLPR) stress, and depression meta-analysis revisited: Evidence of genetic moderation. *Archives of General Psychiatry*, 68, 444–454. doi:10.1001/archgenpsychiatry.2010.189

Karlsson, S.G., & Borell, K. (2005). A home of their own: Women's boundary work in LAT-relationships. *Journal of Aging Studies*, 19(1), 73–84. doi:10.1016/j.jaging.2004.03.008

Kastenbaum, R. (1986). *Death, society, and human experience* (3rd ed.). Columbus, OH: Charles E. Merrill.

Katz, S. (1983). Assessing self-maintenance: Activities of daily living, mobility and instrumental activities of daily living. *Journal of the American Geriatrics Society*, 31(12), 721–727. doi:10.1111/j.1532-5415.1983.tb03391.x

Katz, S., Ford, A.B., Moskowitz, R.W., Jackson, B.A., & Jaffe, M.W. (1963). Studies of illness in the aged. The index of ADL: A standardized measure of biological and psychosocial function. *JAMA*, 185(12), 914–919. doi:10.1001/jama.1963.03060120024016

Kausler, D.H., Kausler, B.C., & Krupsaw, J.A. (2007). *The essential guide to aging in the twenty-first century: Mind, body, and behavior*. St. Louis, MO: University of Missouri Press.

Kawakami, A., & Son, J. (2015). "I don't want to be a burden": Japanese immigrant acculturation and their attitudes toward non-family-based elder care. *Ageing International*, 40(3), 262–276. doi:10.1007/s12126-015-9220-8

Keast, R.S.J., & Costanzo, A. (2015). Is fat the sixth taste primary? Evidence and implications. *Flavour*, *4*(5). doi:10.1186/2044-7248-4-5

Kehyayan, V., Hirdes, J.P., Tyas, S.L., & Stolee, P. (2016). Predictors of long-term care facility residents' self-reported quality of life with individual and facility characteristics in Canada. *Journal of Aging and Health*, *28*(3), 503–529. doi:10.1177/0898264315594138

Kemper, S. (2015). Language production in late life. In A. Gerstenberg & A. Voeste (Eds.), *Language development: The lifespan* (pp. 59–76). Amsterdam, NI: John Benjamins Publishing. doi:10.1075/impact.37

Kennedy, S., McDonald, J.T., & Biddle, N. (2007). *The healthy immigrant effect and immigrant selection: Evidence from four countries* (SEDAP Research Paper No. *164*). Hamilton, ON: McMaster University.

Kerr, G., & Armstrong-Stassen, M. (2011). The bridge to retirement: Older workers' engagement in post-career entrepreneurship and wage-and-salary employment. *Journal of Entrepreneurship*, *20*(1), 55–76. doi:10.1177/097135561002000103

Kern, M.L., & Friedman, H.S. (2008). Do conscientious individuals live longer? A quantitative review. *Health Psychology*, *27*(5), 505–512. doi:10.1037/0278-6133.27.5.505

Kessler, R.C., Birnbaum, H., Bromet, E., Hwang, I., Sampson, N., & Shahly, V. (2010a). Age differences in major depression: Results from the National Comorbidity Survey Replication (NCS-R). *Psychological Medicine*, *40*(2), 225–237. doi:10.1017/S0033291709990213

Kessler, R.C., Birnbaum, H.G., Shahlu, V., Bromet, E., Hwang, I., McLaughlin, K.A., … Stein, D.J. (2010b). Age differences in the prevalence and co-morbidity of DSM-IV major depressive episodes: Results from the WHO World Mental Health Survey initiative. *Depression and Anxiety*, *27*(4), 351–364. doi:10.1002/da.20634

Keyes, C.L.M., & Ryff, C.D. (1998). Generativity in adult lives: Social Structural Contours and quality of life consequences. In D.P. McAdams & E. de St. Aubin (Eds.),*Generativity and adult development: How and why we care for the next generation* (pp. 227–263). Washington, DC: American Psychological Association.

Keysor, J.J., Jette, A.M., LaValley, M.P., Lewis, C.E., Torner, J., & Nevitt, C. (2010). Community environmental factors are associated with disability in older adults with functional limitations: The MOST study. *The Journals of Gerontology, Series A: Biological Sciences & Medical Sciences*, 65(4), 393–398. doi:10.1093/geronal/glp182

Khan, M., Kobayashi, K., Lee, S.M., & Vang, Z. (2015). (IN)Visible Minorities in Canadian Health Data and Research, *3*(1), Article 5. Retrieved from http://ir.lib.uwo.ca/pclc/vol3/iss1/5.

Kielland, N., & Simeone, T. (2014). *Current issues in mental health in Canada: The mental health of First Nations and Inuit communities* (Publication no. 2014–02-E). Ottawa, ON: Library of Parliament: Legal and Social Affairs Division. Retrieved from www.lop.parl.gc.ca/content/lop/ResearchPublications/2014-02-e.htm

Kiernan, J., & Rajakumar, R. (2013). *Barr's the human nervous system: An anatomical viewpoint* (10th ed.). New York, NY: Lippincott, William, & Williams.

Kim, B.J., Sangalang, C.C., & Kihl, T. (2012). Effects of acculturation and social network support on depression among elderly Korean immigrants. *AgingMental Health*, *16*(6), 787–794. doi:10.1080/13607863.2012.660622

Kim, S., & Feldman, D.C. (2000). Working in retirement: The antecedents of bridge employment and its consequences for quality of life in retirement. *Academy of Management Journal*, *43*(6), 1195–1210. doi:10.2307/15556345

Kilgour, A.H., Starr, J.M., & Whalley, L.J. (2010). Associations between childhood intelligence (IQ), adult morbidity, and mortality. *Maturitas*, *65*(2), 98–105. doi:10.1016/j.maturitas.2009.09.021

King, J., Yourman, L., Ahalt, C., Eng, C., Knight, S.J., Perez-Stable, E.J., & Smith A. (2012). Quality of life in late life disability: "I don't feel bitter because I am in a wheelchair." *Journal of the American Geriatric Society*, *60*(3), 569–576. doi:10.1111/j.1532-5415.2011.03844.x

King, M., Smith, A., & Gracey, M. (2009). Indigenous health part 2: The underlying causes of the health gap. *Lancet*, *374*(9683), 76–85. doi:10.1016/S0140-6736(09)60827-8

King, P.M., & Strohm Kitchener, K. (2002). The reflective judgment model: Twenty years of research on epistemic cognition. In B.K. Hofer & P.R. Pintrich (Eds.), *Personal epistemology: The psychology of beliefs about knowledge and knowing* (pp. 37–61). Mahway, NJ: Lawrence Erlbaum Associates Inc., Publishers.

Kinney, J. (2011). *Loosening the grip: A handbook of alcohol information.* (10th ed.). Boston, MA: McGraw Hill.

Kinsella, G.J., Ames, D., Storey, E., Ong, B., Pike, K.E., Saling, M.M., … Rand, E. (2016). Strategies for improving memory: A randomized trial of memory groups for older people, including those with mild cognitive impairment. *Journal of Alzheimer's Disease*, *49*(1), 31–43. doi:10.3233/JAD-150378

Kiosses, D.N., & Alexopoulos, G.S. (2014). Problem-solving therapy in the elderly. *Current Treatment Options in Psychiatry*, *1*(1), 15–26. doi:10.1007/s40501-103-0003-0

Kiosses, D.N., Leon, A.C., & Areán, P.A. (2011). Psychosocial interventions for late-life major depression: Evidence-based treatments, predictors of treatment outcomes, and moderators of treatment effects. *Psychiatric Clinics of North America*, *34*, 377–401. doi:10.1007/s40501-013-0003-0

Kirkbride, J.B., & Hollander, A. (2015). Migration and risk of psychosis in the Canadian context. *Canadian Medical Association Journal*, *187*(9), 637–638. doi:10.1503/cmaj.150494

Kluge, F., Zagheni, E., Loichinger, E., & Vogt, T. (2014). The advantages of demographic change after the wave: Fewer and older, but healthier, greener, and more productive? *PLOS One*, *9*(9), e108501. doi:10.1371/journal.pone.0108501

Knapp, M.R.J. (1977). The Activity Theory of Aging: An examination in the English context. *The Gerontologist*, *17*(6), 553–559.

Knight, D. (2014). *Personal computer history: The first 25 years*. Retrieved from http://lowendmac.com/2014/personal-computer-history-the-first-25-years/

Knight, J., & Nigam, Y. (2008). Exploring the anatomy and physiology of ageing. Part 5: The nervous system. *Nursing Times*, *104*(35), 18–19. Retrieved from www.nursingtimes.net/story.aspx?storycode=1811796

Kobayashi, K.M., Funk, L., & Khan, M.M. (2016). Constructing a sense of commitment in "Living Apart Together" (LAT) relationships: Interpretive agency and individualization. *Current Sociology*. doi:10.1177/0011392116653237

Kochkin, S., & Rogin, C. (2000). Quantifying the obvious: The impact of hearing instruments on quality of life. *The Hearing Review*, *7*, 6–34. Retrieved from www.hearingreview.com/buyers-guide/listing/hearing-journal-the/

Kogan, N. (1990). Personality and aging. In J.E. Birren & K.W. Schaie (Eds.), *Handbook of the psychology of aging* (3rd ed., pp. 330–346). San Diego, CA: Academic Press

Kong, E.-H., & Park, M. (2015). Effects of music therapy on agitation in dementia: Systematic review and meta-analysis. *Korean Journal of Adult Nursing*, *27*(1), 106–116. doi:10.7475/kjan.2015.27.1.106

Koren, C., & Eisikovits, Z. (2011). Life beyond the planned script: Accounts and secrecy of older persons living in second couplehood in old age in a society in transition. *Journal of Social and Personal Relationships*, *28*(1), 44–63. doi:10.1177/0265407510385430

Kotov, R., Gamez, W., Schmidt, F., & Watson, D. (2010). Linking "big" personality traits to anxiety, depressive, and substance abuse disorders: A meta-analysis. *Psychological Bulletin*, *136*(5), 768–821. doi:10.1037/a0020327

Kramer, M. (1980). The rising pandemic of mental disorders and associated chronic diseases and disabilities. *Acta Psychiatrica Scandinavia*, *62*(S285), 382–397.doi:10.1111/j.1600-0447.1980.tb07714.x

Krasner, M.S., Epstein, R.M., Beckman, H., Suchman, A.L., Chapman, B., Mooney, C.J., & Quill, T.E. (2009). Association of an educational program in mindful communication with burnout, empathy, and attitudes among primary care physicians. *JAMA*, *302*(12), 1284–1293. doi:10.1011/jama.2009.1384

Krendl, A.C., Ambady, N., & Kensinger, E.A. (2015). The dissociable effects of stereotyped threat on older adults' memory encoding and retrieval. *Journal of Applied Research on Memory and Cognition*, *4*(2), 105–109. doi:10.1016/j.jarmac.2015.02.001

Kroll, J.F., Bobb, S.C., Misra, M., & Guo, T. (2008). Language selection in bilingual speech: Evidence for inhibitory processes. *Acta psychologica*, *128*(3), 416–430. http://doi.org/ 10.1016/j.actpsy.2008.02.001

Kroll, J.F., Van Hell, J.G., Tokowicz, N., & Green, D.W. (2010). The Revised Hierarchical Model: A critical review and assessment. *Bilingualism: Language and Cognition*, *13*(3), 373–381. https://doi.org/1017/S136672891000009X

Krueger, R.F., Johnson, W., & Kling, K.C. (2006). Behavior genetics and personality development. In D.K. Mroczek & T.D. Little (Eds.), *Handbook of personality development* (pp. 81–108).Mahwah, NJ: Lawrence Erlbaum Associates, Inc.

Kruse A., and Schmitt, E. (2006). A multi-dimensional scale for the measurement of agreement and age stereotypes and the salience of age in social interaction. *Ageing and Society*, *26*, 393–411. doi:10.1017/S0144686X06004703

Kuerbis, A., & Sacco, P. (2012). The impact of retirement on the drinking patterns of older adults: A review. *Addictive Behavior*, *37*(5), 587–595. doi:10.1016/j.addbeh.2012.01.022

Kuerbis, A., Sacco, P., Blazer, D.G., & Moore, A.A. (2014). Substance abuse among older adults. *Clinical Geriatric Medicine*, *30*(3), 629–654. doi:10.1016/j.cger.2014.04.008

Kübler-Ross, E. (1969). *On death and dying*. New York, NY: The Macmillan Company.

Kübler-Ross, E., & Kessler, D. (2005). *On grief and grieving: Finding the meaning of grieving through the five stages of loss*. New York, NY: Scribner–Division of Simon and Schuster.

Kuluski, K., Williams, A.P., Laporte, A., & Berta, W. (2012). The role of community-based care capacity in shaping risk of long-term care facility placement. *Healthcare Policy, 8*(1), 92–105. doi:10.12927/hcpol.2012.23023

Kurz, A., Kurz, C., Ellis, K., & Lautenschlager, N.T. (2014). What is frontotemporal dementia? *Maturitas, 79*(2), 216–219. doi:10.1016/j.maturitas.2014.07.001

Labbé, M., Nikolitch, K., Penheiro, R., Segal, M., Looper, K.J., Herrmann, N., … Rej, S. (2016). Mindfulness-based cognitive behavioral therapy in the treatment of late-life anxiety and depression–a pilot study (Letter to the editor). *Canadian Geriatrics Journal, 19*(3). doi:10.5770/cgi.19.215

Laborde-Lahoz, P., El-Gabalawy, R., Kinley, J., Kirwin, P.D., Sareen, J., & Pietrzak, R.H. (2015). Subsyndromal depression among older adults in the USA: Prevalence, comorbidity, and risk for new-onset psychiatric disorders in late life. *International Journal of Geriatric Psychiatry, 30*, 677–685. doi:10.1002/gps.4204

Lachman, M.E. (2004). Development in midlife. *Annual Review of Psychology, 55*, 305–331. doi:10.1146/annurev.psych.55.090902.141521

Lachman, M.E., Lewkowicz, C., Marcus, A., & Peng, Y. (1994). Images of midlife development among young, middle-aged, and older adults. *Journal of Adult Development, 1*(4), 201–211. doi:10.1007/BF02277581

Lachman, M.E., Teshale, S., & Agrigoroaei, S. (2015). Midlife as a pivotal period in the life course: Balancing growth and decline at the crossroads of youth and old age. *International Journal of Behavioral Development, 39*(1), 20–31. doi:10.1177/0165025414533223

Lafrance, A., & LaRochelle-Côté, S. (2012). *The evolution of wealth over the life cycle* (Catalogue no. 75-001-X). Ottawa, ON: Statistics Canada.

Lagacé, M, Charmarkeh, H., & Grandena, F. (2012). Cultural perceptions of aging: The perspective of Somali Canadians in Ottawa. *Journal of Cross Cultural Gerontology, 27*, 409–424. doi:10.1007/s10823-012-9180-3

Lager, D., Van Hoven, B., & Huigen, P.P. (2016). Rhythms, ageing and neighbourhoods. *Environment and Planning A, 48*(8), 1565–1580. doi:10.1177/0308518X16643962

Lai, D.W.L. (2000). Depression among the elderly Chinese in Canada. *Canadian Journal on Aging, 19*(3), 409–429. doi:10.1017/S0714980800015063

Lai, D.W.L. (2010). *Health status and social determinants of health of immigrant seniors in Canada*. [PowerPoint slides]. Retrieved from http://canada.metropolis.net/mediacentre/daniel_lai_6dec2010_PHAC_e.pptx

Lai, D.W., Daoust, G.D., & Li, L. (2014). Understanding elder abuse and neglect in older Chinese immigrants in Canada. *The Journal of Adult Protection, 16*(5), 322–334. doi:10.1108/JAP-03-2014-0006

Lambert, A.-M. (2009). *Divorce: Facts, causes, and consequences* (3rd ed.). Ottawa, ON: The Vanier Institute of the Family.

Landis, M., Peter-Wight, M., Martin, M., & Bodenmann, G. (2013). Dyadic coping and marital satisfaction of older spouses in long-term marriage. *Geropsych: The Journal of Gerontopsychology and Geriatric Psychiatry, 26*(1), 39–47. doi:10.1024/1662-9647/a000077

Langa, K.M., & Levine, D.A. (2014). The diagnosis and management of mild cognitive impairment: A clinical review. *JAMA, 312*(23), 2551–2561. doi:10.1001/jama.2014.13806

Langton, A.K., Sherratt, M.J., Griffiths, C.E., & Watson, R.E. (2010). A new wrinkle on old skin: The role of elastic fibres in skin ageing. *International Journal of Cosmetic Science, 32*(5), 330–339. doi:10.1111/j.1468-2494.2010.00574.x

Lawrence, D., Hancock, K.J., & Kisely, S. (2013). The gap in life expectancy from preventable physical illness in psychiatric patients in Western Australia: Retrospective analysis of population based registers. *BMJ, 346*, f2539. doi:10.1136/bmj.f2539

Lawton, M.P. (1982). Competence, environmental press, and the adaptation of older people. In M.P. Lawton, P.G. Windley, & T.O. Byerts (Eds.), *Aging and the environment* (pp. 33–59). New York, NY: Springer.

Lawton, M.P., & Brody, E.M. (1969). Assessment of older people: Self-maintaining and instrumental activities of daily living. *The Gerontologist, 9*(3), 179–186. doi:10.1093/geront/9.3_Part_1.179

Lawton, M.P., & Nahemow, L. (1973). Ecology and the aging process. In C. Eisdorfer & M.P. Lawton (Eds.), *Psychology of adult development and aging* (pp. 619–674). Washington, DC: American Psychological Association.

Lazarus, R., & Folkman, S. (1984). *Stress, appraisal and coping*. New York, NY: Springer.

Le Roux, H., Gatz, M., & Wetherell, J.L. (2005). Age at onset of generalized anxiety disorders in older adults. *The American Journal of Geriatric Psychiatry*, *13*(1), 23–30. doi:10.1097/00019442-200501000-00005

Le, T. (2008). Age differences in spirituality, mystic experiences and wisdom. *Ageing and Society*, *28*(3), 383–411. doi:10.1017/S0144686X0700685X

Lee, G.R., & Demaris, A. (2007). Widowhood, gender, and depression: A longitudinal analysis. *Research on Aging*, *29*(1), 56–72. doi:10.1177/0164027506294098

Lee, S.J., Steinman, M.A., & Tan, E.J. (2011). Volunteering, driving status, and mortality in U.S. retirees. *Journal of the American Geriatric Society*, *59*(2), 274–280. doi:10.1111/j.1532-5414.2010.03265.x.

Lee, S.M., & Edmonston, B. (2014). Residential independence of elderly immigrants in Canada. *Canadian Journal on Aging*, *33*(4), 359–377. doi:10.1017/S0714980814000324

Leech-Crier, N.D. (2016). Vision quests and questioning vision. *Visions*, *11*(4), 12–14. Retrieved from www.heretohelp.bc.ca/visions

Lefebvre, P., Merrigan, P., & Michaud, P.-C. (2011). *The recent evolution of retirement patterns in Canada* (IZA DP No. 5979). Montreal, QC: McMaster University.

Lehert, P., Villaseca, E., Hogervorst, E., Maki, P.M., & Henderson, V.W. (2015). Individual modifiable risk factors to ameliorate cognitive aging: A systematic review and meta-analysis. *Climacteric*, *18*(5), 678–689. doi:10.3109/13697137.2015.1078106

Lemieux, A. (2012). Post formal thought in gerontagogy or beyond Piaget. *Journal of Behavior and Brain Science*, *2*(3), 399–406. doi:10.4236/jbbs.2012.23046

Lenze, E.J., Rollman, R.L., Shear, M.K., Dew, M.A., Pollock, B.G., Ciliberti, C., … Reynoylds, C.F. (2009). Escitalopram for older adults with generalized anxiety disorder: A randomized control trial. *Journal of the American Medical Association*, *301*(3), 2950303. doi:10.1001/jama.2008.977

Lenzenweger, M.F., Johnson, M.D., & Willett, J.B. (2004). Individual growth curve analysis illuminates stability and change in personality disorder features: The Longitudinal Study of Personality Disorders. *Archives of General Psychiatry*, *61*(10), 1015–1024. doi:10.1011/archpsyc.61.10.1015

Lero, D.S., Spinks, N., Fast, J., Hilbrecht, M., & Tremblay, D.-G. (2012). *The availability, accessibility and effectiveness of workplace supports for Canadian caregivers*. Edmonton, AB: University of Alberta, Research on Aging, Policies and Practices.

Lester, D. (1990). The Collett-Lester fear of death scale: The original version and a revision. *Death Studies*, *14*(5), 451–468, doi:10.1080/07481189008252385

Lester, D., & Abdel-Khalek, A. (2010). *Death Studies*, *27*(1), 81–85. doi:org/10.1080/07481180302873

Levinson, D.J. (1978). *The seasons of a man's life*. New York, NY: Ballentine.

Levinson, D.J. (1986). A conception of adult development. *American Psychologist*, *41*(1), 3–13. doi:10.1037/0003-066X.41.1.3

Levy, B.R., Chung, P.H., Bedford, T., & Navrazhina, K. (2014). Facebook as a site for negative age stereotypes. *The Gerontologist*, *54*(2), 172–176. doi:10.1093/geront/gns194

Levy, B.R., Chung, P.H., & Canavan, M. (2011). Impact of explanatory style and age stereotypes on health across the life span. In K. Fingerman, C. Berg, & T. Anntonucci (Eds.), *Handbook of life-span development* (pp. 437–456). New York, NY: Springer.

Levy, B.R., Ding, L., Lakra, D., Kosteas, J., & Niccolai, L. (2007). Older persons' exclusion from sexually transmitted disease risk-reduction clinical trials. *Sexually Transmitted Diseases: Journal of the American Sexually Transmitted Diseases Association*, *34*(8), 541–544. doi:10.1097/01.olq.0000253342.75908.05

Levy, B.R., Zonderman, A.B., Slade, M.B., & Ferrucci, L. (2012). Memory shaped by age stereotypes over time. *The Journals of Gerontology, Series B: Psychological Sciences and Social Sciences*, *67*, 432–436. doi:10.1093/geronb/gbr120

Li, X., Hurd, M., & Loughran, D.S. (2008). *The characteristics of social security beneficiaries who claim benefits at the early entitlement age* (AARP Public Policy Institute Research Report No. 2008–19). Washington, DC: AARP.

Life and Death Matters. (2016). *Advance Care Planning Day—speak up!* Retrieved from http://lifeanddeathmatters.ca/advance-care-planning-day-speak/

Light, L.L. (2012). Dual-process theories of memory in old age, an update. In Naveh-Benjamin, M., & Ohta, N. (Eds.), *Memory and aging: Current issues and future directions*. New York: Psychology Press. Retrieved from

Lin, F.R., Metter, E.J., O'Brien, R.J., Resnick, S.M., Zonderman, A.B., & Ferrucci, L. (2011). Hearing loss and incident dementia. *Archives of Neurology*, *68*(2), 214–220. doi:10.1001/archneurol.2010.362

Lin, F.R., Thorpe, R., Gordon-Salant, S., & Ferrucci, L. (2011). Hearing loss prevalence and risk factors among older adults in the United States. *The Journals of Gerontology Series A: Biological Sciences and Medical Sciences*, *66A*(5), 582–590. doi:10.1093%2Fgerona%2Fglr002

Lin, F.R., Yaffe, K., Xia, J., Xue, Q.L., Harris, T.B., Purchase-Helzner, E., … Simonsick, E.M. (2013). Hearing loss and cognitive decline in older adults. *JAMA Internal Medicine*, *173*(4), 292–299. doi:10.1001/jamainternmed.2013

Lin, J., Epel, E., & Blackburn, E. (2012). Telomeres and lifestyle factors: Roles in cellular aging. *Mutation Research-Fundamental and Molecular Mechanisms of Mutagenesis*, *730*(1-2), 85–89. doi:10.1016/j.mrfm-mm.2011.08.003

Lin, X., Bryant, C., Boldero, J., & Dow, B. (2015). Older Chinese immigrant's relationships with their children: A literature review from a solidarity-conflict perspective. *The Gerontologist*, *55*(6), 990–1005. doi:10.1093/geront/gnu004

Lindau, S.T., Schumm, L.P., Laumann, E.O., Levinson, W., O' Muircheartaigh, C.A., & Waite, L.J. (2007). A study of sexuality and health among older adults in the United States. *The New England Journal of Medicine*, *357*(8), 762–774. doi:10.1056/NEJMoa067423

Lindemann, B., Ogiwara, Y., & Ninomiya, Y. (2002). The discovery of umami. *Chemical Senses*, *27*(9), 843–844. doi:10.1093/chemse/27.9.84

Lindert, J., Von Ehrenstein, O.S., Priebe, S., Mielck, A., & Brähler, E. (2009). Depression and anxiety in labor migrants and refugees—A systematic review and meta-analysis. *Social Science and Medicine*, *69*(2), 246–257. doi:10.1016/j.socscimed.2009.04.032

Lindstrom, R.L., MacRae, S.M., Pepose, J.S., & Hoopes, P.C., Sr. (2013). Corneal inlays for presbyopia correction. *Current Opinion in Ophthalmology*, *24*(4), 281–287. doi:10.1097/ICU.0b013e328362293e

Liu, C.-C., Kanekiyo, T., Xu, H., & Bu, G. (2013). Apolipoprotein E and Alzheimer's disease: Risk, mechanisms, and therapy. *Nature Reviews Neurology*, *9*(2), 106–118. doi:10.1038/nrneurol.2012.263

Livingston, G., Kelly, L., Lewis-Holmes, E., Baio, G., Morris, S., Patel, N., … Cooper, C. (2014). A systematic review of the clinical effectiveness and cost-effectiveness of sensory, psychological, and behavioural interventions for managing agitation in older adults with dementia. *Health Technology Assessment*, *18*(39), 1–226. doi:10.3310/hta18390

Livingstone, D.W., & Raykov, M. (2013). *Adult learning trends in Canada. Basic findings of the WALL 1998, 2004, and 2010 surveys*. Toronto, ON: Centre for the Study of Education and Work. Retrieved from www.wallnetwork.ca/Adult-Learning-Trends-in-Canada-2013.pdf

Ljungquist, B., Berg, S., Lanke, J., McClearn, G.E., & Pedersen, N.L. (1998). The effect of genetic factors for longevity: A comparison of identical and fraternal twins in the Swedish twin registry. *The Journals of Gerontology, Series A, Biological Sciences and Medical Sciences*, *53*(6), M441–M446. doi:10.1093/gerona/53a.6.m441

Löckenhoff, C.E., De Fruyt, F., Terracciano, A., McCrae, R.R., De Bolle, M., Costa, P.T. Jr, … & Yik, M. (2009). Perceptions of aging across 26 cultures and their culture-level associates. *Psychology and Aging*, *24*(4), 941–954. doi:10.1037/a0016901

Loddon Mallei Regional Palliative Care Consortium. (2011). *An outline of different cultural beliefs at the time of death*. Castlemaine, AUS: Author.

Logan, R.D. (1986). A reconceptualization of Erikson's theory: The repetition of existential and instrumental themes. *Human Development*, *29*(3), 125–136. doi:10.1159/000273036

Lönnqvist, J.-E., Mäkinen, S., Paunonen, S., Henriksson, M., & Verkasalo, M. (2008). Psychosocial functioning in young men predicts their personality stability over 15 years. *Journal of Research in Personality*, *42*(3), 599–621. doi:10.1016/j.jrp.2007.08.006

Loomba Foundation. (2015). *The global widows report: A global overview of deprivation faced by widows and their children*. Retrieved from http://theloombafoundation.org/wp-content/uploads/2015/07/Loomba-Foundation-Global-Widows-FULL-Report-2015-V2.2.pdf

Lou, Q., Liu, S., Huo, Y.R., Liu, M., Liu, S., & Ji, J. (2015). Comprehensive analysis of patient and caregiver predictors for caregiver burden, anxiety and depression in Alzheimer's disease. *Journal of Clinical Nursing*, *24*(17–18), 2668–2678. doi:10.1111/jocn.12870

Low, L.F., Harrison, F., & Lackersteen, S.M. (2013). Does personality affect risk for dementia? A systematic review and meta-analysis. *The American Journal of Geriatric Psychiatry*, *21*(8), 713–728. doi:10.1016/j.jagp.2012.08.004

Lu, B., Qian, Z., Cunningham, A., & Li, C.-L. (2012). Estimating the effect of premarital cohabitation on timing of marital disruption: Using propensity score matching in event history analysis. *Sociological Methods and Research*, *41*(3), 440–446. doi:10.1177/0049124112452395

Lucas, R.E., & Donnellan, M.B. (2009). Age differences in personality: Evidence from a nationally representative Australian sample. *Developmental Psychology*, *45*(5), 1353–1363. doi:10.1037/a0013914

Luo, B., Zhou, K., Jin, E.J., Newman, A., & Liang, J. (2013). Ageism among college students: A comparative study between U.S. and China. *Journal of Cross Cultural Gerontology*, *28*(1), 49–63. doi:10.1007/s10823-013-9186-5

Luong, G., Charles, S.T., & Fingerman, K.L. (2011). Better with age: Social relationships across adulthood. *Journal of Social and Personal Relationships*, *28*(1), 9–23. doi:10.1177/0265407510391362

Luoma, J.B., Martin, C.E., & Pearson, J.L. (2002). Contact with mental health and primary care providers before suicide: A review of the evidence. *The American Journal of Psychiatry*, *159*(6), 909–916. doi:10.1176/appi.ajp.159.6.909

Lupien, S., Sindi, S., & Wan, N. (2012). *When we test, do we stress? Guidelines for Health Professionals and Scientists Working with Older Adults.* Centre for Studies on Human Stress. Montreal, QC: Centre for Studies on Human Stress. Retrieved from www.humanstress.ca/documents/pdf/KT/KT_document_EN.pdf

Lustig, C., Shah, P., Seidler, R., & Reuter-Lorenz, P. (2009). Aging, training and the brain: A review and future directions. *Neuropsychological Review*, *19*(4), 504–522. doi:10.1007/s11065-009-9119-9

Lyketsos, C.G., Carrillo, M.C., Ryan, J.M., Khachaturian, P., P., Trzepacz, Amatniek, L., … Miller, D.S. (2011). Neuropsychiatric symptoms in Alzheimer's disease. *Alzheimer's & Dementia*, *7*(5), 532–539. doi:10.1016/j.jalz.2011.05.2410

MacCourt, P., Wilson, K., & Tourigny-Rivard, M. (2011). *Guidelines for comprehensive mental health services for older adults in Canada.* Mental Health Commission of Canada. Calgary, AB: Mental Health Commission of Canada. Retrieved from https://www.mentalhealthcommission.ca/sites/default/files/mhcc_seniors_guidelines_1.pdf

MacDonald, L. (2012). *The evolution of retirement as systematic ageism* (SEDAP Research Paper No. 292). Hamilton, ON: McMaster University.

MacEwan, A. (2012). *Working after age 65. What is at stake?* Ottawa, ON: Canadian Centre for Policy Alternatives. Retrieved from www.policyalternatives.ca/publications/reports/working-after-age-65

Mackenzie, C.S., Reynolds, K., Chou, K-L., Pagura, J., & Sareen, J. (2011). Prevalence and correlates of generalized anxiety disorder in a national sample of older adults. *American Journal of Geriatric Psychiatry*, *19*(4), 305–315. doi:10.1097/JGP.0b013e318202bc62

Mackenzie, C.S., Scott, T., Mather, A., & Sareen, J. (2008). Older adults' help-seeking attitudes and treatment beliefs concerning mental health problems. *American Journal of Geriatric Psychiatry*, *16*(12), 1010–1019. doi:10.1097/JGP.0b013e31818cd3be

Mackenzie, H. (2014). *Risky business: Canada's retirement income system.* Ottawa, ON: Canadian Centre for Policy Alternatives. Retrieved from www.policyalternatives.ca/sites/default/files/uploads/publications/National%20Office/2014/03/Risky_Business.pdf

Mackenzie, P. (2012). Normal changes of ageing. *InnovAiT*, *5*(10), 605–613. doi:10.9310/innovait/ins009

Madden, M. (2010). *Older adults and social media.* Washington, DC: Pew Research Center. Retrieved from http://www.pewinternet.org/2010/08/27/older-adults-and-social-media/

Madore, O. (1992). *The Canadian and American health care systems.* Ottawa, ON: Parliamentary Research Branch, Library of Parliament. Retrieved from http://publications.gc.ca/Collection-R/LoPBdP/BP/bp300-e.htm

Maenner, M.J., Greenberg, J.S., & Mailick, M.R. (2015). Association between low scores and early mortality in men and women: Evidence for a population-based cohort study. *American Journal on Intellectual and Developmental Disabilities*, *120*(3), 244–257. doi:10.1352/1944-7558-120.3.244

Mahieu, L., Van Elssen, K., & Gastmans, C.(2011). Nurses' perceptions of sexuality in institutionalized elderly: A literature review. *International Journal of Nursing Studies*, *48*(9), 1140–1154. doi:10.1016/j.ijnurstu.2011.05.013

Makarenko, J. (2010). *Canada's health care system: An overview of public and private participation.* Retrieved from http://mapleleafweb.com/features/canada-s-health-care-system-overview-public-and-private-participation

Makrantonaki, E., Bekou, V., & Zouboulis, C.C. (2012). Genetics and skin aging. *Dermato-Endocrinology*, *4*(3), 280–284. doi:10.4161/derm.22372

Mallers, M.H., Claver, M., & Lares, L.A. (2013). Perceived control in the lives of older adults: The influence of Langer and Rodin's work on gerontological theory, policy, and practice. *The Gerontologist*, *54*(1), 67–74. doi:10.1093/geront/gnt051

Mani, T.M., Bedwell, J.S., & Miller, L.S. (2005). Age-related decrements in performance on a brief continuous performance test. *Archives of Clinical Neuropsychology, 20*(5), 575–586. doi:10.1016/j.acn.2004.12.008

Manson, J.E., Hsia, J., Johnson, K.C., Rossouw, J.E., Assaf, A.R., Lasser, N.L., … Cushman, M. (2003). Estrogen plus progestin and the risk of coronary heart disease. *The New England Journal of Medicine, 349*(6), 523–534. doi:10.1056/NEJMoa030808

Manssoon, D.H. (2014). Grandparents' expressed affection for their grandchildren: Examining grandparents' own physiological health. *Communication Research Reports, 31*(4), 329–338. doi:10.1080/08824096.2014.963218

Manton, K.G. (1982). Changing concepts of morbidity and mortality in the elderly population. *The Millbank Memorial Fund Quarterly Health and Society,60*(2), 183–244.

Manton, K.G. & Stallard, E. (1981). Methods for evaluating the heterogeneity of aging processes in human populations using vital statistics data: Explaining the black/white mortality crossover by a model of mortality selection. *Human Biology, 53*, 47–67.

Manwell, L.A., Barbic, S.P., Roberts, K., Durisko, Z., Lee, C., Ware, E., & McKenzie, K. (2015). What is mental health? Evidence towards a new definition from a mixed methods multidisciplinary international survey. *BMJ Open, 5*(6), e007079. doi:10.1136/bmjopen-2014-007079

Marantz Henig, R., & Henig, S. (2012). Twentysomething. Why do young adults seem stuck? New York, NY: Hudson Street Press

Marion, D., Laursen, B., Zettergren, P., & Bergman, L.R. (2013). Predicting life satisfaction during middle adulthood from peer relationships during mid-adolescence. *Journal of Youth and Adolescence, 42*(8), 1299–1307. doi:10.1007/s10964-013-9969-6

Martel, L. (2013). *Mortality: Overview, 2010 and 2011.* (Catalogue no. 91–209-X). Ottawa, ON: Statistics Canada.

Martens, A., Goldenberg, J.L., & Greenberg, J. (2005). A terror management perspective on ageism. *Journal of Social Issues, 61*(2), 223–239. doi:10.1111/j.1540-4560.2005.00403.x

Martens, E.J., de Jonge, P., Na, B., Cohen, B.E., Lett, H., & Whooley, M.A. (2010). Scared to death? Generalized anxiety disorder and cardiovascular events in patients with stable coronary artery disease: The Heart and Soul Study. *Archives of General Psychiatry, 67*(7), 750–758. doi:10.1001/archgenpsychiatry.2010.74.

Martin, K.A., & Barbieri, R.L. (2015). Treatment of menopausal symptoms with hormone therapy. *UpTo-Date.* Retrieved from www.uptodate.com/contents/treatment-of-menopausal-symptoms-with-hormone-therapy

Martinson, M., & Berridge, C. (2015). Successful aging and its discontents: A systematic review of the social gerontology literature. *The Gerontologist, 55*(1), 58–69. doi:10.1093/geront/gnu037

Martyn, C.N., Coggon, D.N., Inskip, H., Lacey, R.F., & Young, W.F. (1997). Aluminum concentrations in drinking water and risk of Alzheimer's disease. *Epidemiology, 8*(3), 281–286. Retrieved from http://www.jstor.org/stable/3702254

Maschi, T., Kwak, J., Ko, E., & Morrissey, M.B. (2012). Forget me not: Dementia in Prison. *The Gerontologist, 52*(4), 441–451. doi:10.1093/geront/gnr131

Mataix-Cols, D. (2014). Hoarding disorder. *The New England Journal of Medicine, 370*(21), 2023–2030. doi:10.1056/NEJMcp1313051

Mataix-Cols, D., Frost, R.O., Pertusa, A., Clarke, L-A., Saxena, S., Leckman, J.F. … Wilhelm, S. (2010). Hoarding disorder: A new diagnosis for DSM-V? *Depression and Anxiety, 27*(6), 556-572. doi:10.1002/da.20693

Mathews, A.E., Laditka, S.B., Laditka, J.N., Wilcox, S., Corwin, S.J., Liu, R., … Logsdon, R.G. (2010). Older adults' perceived physical activity enablers and barriers: A multicultural perspective. *Journal of Aging and Physical Activity, 18*(2), 119–140.

Matthews, F.E., Arthur, A., Barnes, L.E., Bond, J., Jagger, C., Robinson, L., & Brayne, C. (2013). A two-decade comparison of prevalence of dementia in individuals aged 65 years and older from three geographical areas of England: Results of the Cognitive Function and Ageing Study I and II. *The Lancet, 382*(9902), 1405–1412. doi:10.1016/S0140-6736(13)61570-6

Mavaddat, N., Parker, R.A., Sanderson, S., Mant, J., & Kinmonth, A.L. (2014). Relationship of self-rated health with fatal and non-fatal outcomes in cardiovascular disease: A systematic review and meta-analysis. *PLoS ONE, 9*(7), e103509. doi:10.1371/journal.pone.0103509

Maxwell, C.J., Soo, A., Hogan, D.B., Wodchis, W.P., Gilbart, E., Amuah, J., … Strain, L.A. (2013). Predictors of nursing home placement from assisted living facilities in Canada. *Canadian Journal on Aging, 32*(4), 333–348. doi:10.1017/S0714980813000469

McCann, R.M., Cargile, A.C., Giles, H., & Bui, C.T. (2004). Communication ambivalence towards elders: Data from North Vietnam, South Vietnam, and the USA. *Journal of Cross-Cultural Gerontology,*

19, 275–297. Retrieved from doi:10.1023/
B:JCCG.0000044685.45304.ca

McAdams, D.P. (1985). *Power, intimacy, and the life story: Personological inquiries intoidentity*. New York, NY: Guilford Press.

McAdams, D.P. (2001). Generativity in midlife. In M.E. Lachmann (Ed.), *Handbook of midlife development* (pp. 395–443). New York, NY: Wiley and Sons.

McAdams, D.P., Bauer, J.J., Sakaeda, A., Anyidoho, N.A., Machado, M.A., Magrino-Failla, K.,…Pals, J. (2006). Continuity and change in the life story: A longitudinal study of autobiographical memories in emerging adulthood. *Journal of Personality*, *74*(5), 1371–1400. doi:10.1111/j.1467-6494.2006.00412.x

McAdams, D.P., & De St. Aubin, E. (1992). A theory of generativity and its assessment through self-report, behavioral acts, and narrative themes in autobiography. *Journal of Personality and Social Psychology*, *62*(6), 1003–1015. doi:10.1037/0022-3514.62.6.1003

McAdams, D.P., & De St. Aubin, E. (Eds.). (1998). *Generativity and adult development: How and why we care for the next generation*. Washington, DC: American Psychology Association.

McAdams, D.P., De St. Aubin, E., & Logan, R.L. (1993). Generativity among young, midlife and older adults. *Psychology and Aging*, *8*(2), 221–230. doi:10.1037/0882-7974.8.2.221

McAdams, D.P., Hart, H.M., & Maruna, S. (1998). The anatomy of generativity. In D.P. McAdams & E. de St. Aubin (Eds.), *Generativity and adult development: How and why we care for the next generation* (pp. 7–43). Washington, DC: AmericanPsychological Association. doi:10.1037/10288-001

McAdams, D.P., & Olson, B.D. (2010). Personality development: Continuity and change over the life course. *Annual Review of Psychology*, *61*, 517–542. doi:10.1146/annurev.psych.093008.100507

McCay, C.M., Crowell, M.F., & Maynard, L.A. (1935). The effect of retarded growth upon the length of life span and upon the ultimate body size. *Journal of Nutrition*, *10*, 63–79. Retrieved from http://jn.nutrition.org/content/10/1/63.full.pdf

McCormack, A., & Fortnum, H. (2013). Why do people fitted with hearing aids not wear them? *International Journal of Audiology*, *52*(5), 360–368. doi:10.3109%2F14992027.2013.769066

McCrae, R.R., & Costa, P.T. Jr. (1987). Validation of the five-factor model of personality across instruments and observers. *Journal of Personality and Social Psychology*, *52*(1), 81–90. doi:10.1037/0022-3514.52.1.81

McCrae, R.R., & Costa, P.T. Jr., (1999). A five-factor theory of personality. In L.A. Pervin & O.P. John (Eds.), *Handbook of personality theory and research* (Vol. 2, pp. 139–153). New York, NY: Guilford Press.

McCrae, R.R., Terracciano, A., & Personality Profiles of Cultures Project. (2005). Personality profiles of cultures: Aggregate personality traits. *Journal of Personality and Social Psychology*, *89*(3), 407–425. doi:10.1037/0022-3514.89.3.407

McDaniel, M.A., Pesta, B.J., & Banks, G.C. (2012). Job performance and the aging worker. In W.C. Borman & J.W. Hedge (Eds.), *The Oxford handbook of work and aging* (pp. 280–297). New York, NY: Oxford University Press. doi:10.1093/oxfordhb/9780195385052.013.0100

McDill, T., Hall, S.K., & Turell, S.C. (2006). Aging and creating families: Never married heterosexual women over forty. *Journal of Women & Aging*, *18*(3), 37–50. doi:10.1300/J074v18n03_04

McDonald, L. (2011). Elder abuse and neglect in Canada: The glass is still half full. *Canadian Journal on Aging*, *30*(3), 437–465. doi:10.1017/S0714980811000286

McDonald, L., Beaulieu, M., Biggs, S., Göergen, T., Goldlist, B., Hirst, S., … Willison, K.D. (2012). *Defining and measuring elder abuse and neglect. Synthesis of preparatory work required to measure the prevalence of abuse and neglect of older adults in Canada* (DMEA Synthesis Paper). Ottawa, ON: National Initiative for the Care of the Elderly.

McDonald, L., Sheppard, C., Hitzig, S.L., Spalter, T., Mather, A., & Mukhis, J.S. (2015). Resident-to-resident abuse: A scoping review. *Canadian Journal on Aging*, *34*(2), 215–236. doi.org/10.1017/S0714980815000094

McDonnall, M.C. (2011). The effect of productive activities on depressive symptoms among older adults with dual sensory loss. *Research on Aging*, *33*(3), 234–255. doi:10.1177/0164027511399106

McGill University. (2016). *Whole person care. Balfour M. Mount, MD.* Montreal, QC: Author. Retrieved from www.mcgill.ca/wholepersoncare/people/balmount

McGrew, K.S. (2009). CHC theory and the human cognitive abilities project: Standing on the shoulders of the giants of psychometric intelligence research. *Intelligence*, *37*(1), 1–10. doi:1016/j.intell.2008.08.004

McGue, M., Vaupel, J.W., Holm, N., & Harvald, B. (1993). Longevity is moderately heritable in a sample of Danish twins born 1870–1880. *Journal of Gerontology*, *48*(6), B237–B244. doi:10.1093/geronj/48.6.B237

McKhann, G.M., Drachman, D., Folstein, M., Katzman, R., Price, D., & Stadlan, E.M. (1984).

Clinical diagnosis of Alzheimer's disease: Report of the NINCDS-ADRDA Work Group under the auspices of the Department of the Health and Human Services Task Force on Alzheimer's Disease. *Neurology, 34*(7), 939–944. doi:10.1212/WNL.34.7.939

McKhann, G.M., Knopman, D.S., Chertkow, H., Hyman, B.T., Jack, C.R. Jr., Kawas, C.H., … Phelps, C.H. (2011). The diagnosis of dementia due to Alzheimer's disease: Recommendations from the National Institute on Aging-Alzheimer's Association workgroups on diagnostic guidelines for Alzheimer's disease. *Alzheimer's & Dementia, 7*(3), 263–269. doi:10.1016/j.jalz.2011.03.005

McLaughlin, S.J., Connell, C.M., Heeringa, S.G., Li, W., & Roberts, J.S. (2010). Successful aging in the United States: Prevalence estimates from a national sample of older adults. *The Journals of Gerontology, Series B: Psychological Sciences & Social Sciences, 65B*(2), 216–226. doi:10.1093/geronb/ghp101

McMahon, T. (2014). Seniors and the generation spending gap. *Macleans*. Retrieved from www.macleans.ca/society/life/seniors-and-the-generation-spending-gap/

McParland, J., & Camic, P.M. (2016). Psychosocial factors and ageing in older lesbian, gay and bisexual people: A systematic review of the literature. *Journal of Clinical Nursing*, 25(23-24),1-23. doi:10.1111/jocn.13251

Meeks, T.W., Vahia, I.V., Lavretsky, H., Kulkarni G., & Jeste, D.V. (2011). A tune in "a minor" can "b major": A review of epidemiology, illness course, and public health implications of subthreshold depression in older adults. *Journal of Affective Disorders, 129*(1-3), 125–142. doi:10.1016/j.jad.2010.09.015

Meier, E.A., Gallegos, J.V., Montross-Thomas, L.P., Depp, C.A., Irwin, S.A., & Jeste, D.V. (2016). Defining a good death (successful dying): Literature review and a call for research and public dialogue. *The American Journal of Geriatric Psychiatry, 24*(4), 261–271. doi:10.1016/j.jagp.2016.01.135

Meléndez, J.C., Mayordomo, T., Sancho, P., & Tomás, J.M. (2012). Coping strategies: Gender differences and development throughout life span. *The Spanish Journal of Psychology, 15*(3), 1089–1098. doi:10.5209/rev_SJOP.2012.v15.n3.39399

Mendelson, M. (2002). *Canadians' thoughts on their health care system: Preserving the Canadian model through innovation*. Ottawa, ON: Commission on the Future Health Care in Canada, Health Canada.

Mener, D.J., Betz, J., Genther, D.J., Chen, D., & Lin, F.R. (2013). Hearing loss and depression in older adults. *Journal of the American Geriatrics Society, 61*(9), 1627–1629. doi:10.1111/jgs.12429

Meng, X., & D'Arcy, C. (2014). Successful aging in Canada: Prevalence and predictors from a population-based sample of older adults. *Gerontology, 60*(1), 65–72. doi:10.1159/000354538

Mental Health Commission of Canada. (2012). *Changing directions, changing lives: The mental health strategy for Canada*. Retrieved from http://strategy.mentalhealthcommission.ca/pdf/strategy-images-en.pdf

Mental Health Commission of Canada. (2013). *Making the case for investing in mental health in Canada*. Retrieved from http://www.mentalhealthcommission.ca/English/system/files/private/document/Investing_in_Mental_Health_FINAL_Version_ENG.pdf

Mental Health Commission of Canada. (2015). *Informing the future: Mental health indicators for Canada*. Retrieved from https://www.mentalhealthcommission.ca/sites/default/files/Informing%252520the%252520Future%252520%252520Mental%252520Health%252520Indicators%252520for%252520Canada_0.pdf

Mental Health Commission of Canada. (2016). *Advancing the mental health strategy for Canada: A framework for action (2017–2022)*. Retrieved from www.mentalhealthcommission.ca/sites/default/files/2016-08/advancing_the_mental_health_strategy_for_canada_a_framework_for_action.pdf).

Merriam, S.B., & Kee, Y. (2014). Promoting community wellbeing: The case for lifelong learning for older adults. *Adult Education Quarterly, 64*(2), 128–144. doi:10.1177/0741713613513633

Metzger, A.M. (1980). A Q-Methodological study of the Kübler-Ross Stage Theory. *Omega: The Journal of Death and Dying, 10*(4), 291–301.

Meyer, P.S., Johnson, D.P., Parks, A., Iwanski, C., & Penn, D.L. (2012). Positive living: A pilot study of group positive psychotherapy for people with schizophrenia. *The Journal of Positive Psychology, 7*(3), 239–248. doi:10.1080/17439760.2012.677467

Meyer, T.E., Kovács, S.J., Ehsani, A.A., Klein, S., Holloszy, J.O., & Fontana, L. (2006). Long-term caloric restriction ameliorates the decline is diastolic function in humans. *Journal of the American College of Cardiology, 47*(2), 398–402. doi.org/10.1016/j.jacc.2005.08.069

Michael, Y.L., Gold, R., Perrin, N.A., & Hillier, T.A. (2011). Built environment and lower extremity physical performance: Prospective findings from the study of osteoporotic fractures in women. *Journal of Aging and Health, 23*(8), 1246–1262. doi:10.1177/0898264311412597

Mick, P., & Pichora-Fuller, M.K. (2016). Is hearing loss associated with poorer health in older adults who might benefit from hearing screening? *Ear & Hearing, 37*(3), e194-e201. doi:10.1097/AUD.0000000000000267

Mielke, M.M., Vemuri, P., & Rocca, W.A. (2014). Clinical epidemiology of Alzheimer's disease: Assessing sex and gender differences. *Clinical Epidemiology, 6*(1), 37–48. doi:10.2147/CLEP.S37929

Migliore, S., & Dorazio-Migliore, M. (2010). "La buona vecchiaia": Aging and well-being among Italian Canadians. In J.E. Graham & P.H. Stephenson (Eds.), *Contesting aging and loss* (pp. 63–84).Toronto, ON: University of Toronto.

Milan, A. (2013). *Marital status: Overview, 2011* (Catalogue no. 91–209-X). Ottawa, ON: Statistics Canada Retrieved from www.statcan.gc.ca/pub/91-209-x/2013001/article/11788-eng.pdf

Milan, A., Keown, L.-A., & Robles Urquijo, C. (2011). *Families, Living arrangements, and unpaid work. Women in Canada: A gender based statistical report* (Catalogue no. 89–503-x).

Milan, A., Laflamme, N., & Wong, I. (2015). *Diversity of grandparents living with their grandchildren* (Catalogue no. 75–006-X). Ottawa, ON: Statistics Canada. Retrieved from www.statcan.gc.ca/pub/75-006-x/2015001/article/14154-eng.pdf

Milan, A., Vézina, M., & Wells, C. (2007). *Family portrait: Continuity and change in Canadian families and households in 2006.* Statistics Canada. Catalogue no. 97–55-XIE. Ottawa, ON: Minister of Industry. Retrieved from www12.statcan.ca/census-recensement/2006/as-sa/97-553/index-eng.cfm

Milan, A., Wong, I., & Vézina, M. (2014). *Emerging trends in living arrangements and conjugal unions for current and future seniors* (Catalogue no. 75–006-X). Ottawa, ON: Statistics Canada. Retrieved from www.statcan.gc.ca/pub/75-006-x/2014001/article/11904-eng.pdf

Miller, D.A. (1981). The 'sandwich' generation: Adult children of the aging. *Social Work, 26*(5), 419–423. doi:10.1093/sw/26.5.419

Miller, M., Gravel, D., Mulvey, M., Taylor, G., Boyd, D., Simon, A., … Kelly, S. (2010). Health care–associated *Clostridium difficile* infection in Canada: Patient age and infecting strain type are highly predictive of severe outcome and mortality. *Clinical Infectious Diseases, 50*(2), 194–201. doi:10.1086/649213

Milner, B., Corkin, S., & Teuber, H.L., (1968). Further analysis of the hippocampal amnesic syndrome: 14-year follow-up study of H.M. *Neuropsychologia, 6*(3), 215–234. doi:10.1016/0028-3932(68)90021-3

Minaker, K.L. (2011). Common clinical sequelae of aging. In L. Goldman & A.I. Schafer (Eds.), *Goldman's Cecil Medicine* (24th ed., pp. 104–109). Philadelphia, PA: Elsevier Saunders.

Minichiello, V., Rahman, S., Hawkes, G., & Pitts, M. (2012). STI epidemiology in the global older population: Emerging challenges. *Perspectives in Public Health, 132*(4), 178–181. doi:10.1177/1757913912445688

Mitnitski, A.B., Mogilner, A.J., & Rockwood, K. (2001). Accumulation of deficits as a proxy measure of aging. *The Scientific World Journal, 1*, 323–336. doi:10.1100/tsw.2001.58

Miyagi, S., Iwama, N., Kawabata, T., & Haseqawa, K. (2003). Longevity and diet in Okinawa, Japan: the past, present and future. *Asia Pacific Journal of Public Health, 15*(1-Suppl), S3-S9. doi:10.1177/101053950301500S03

Mock, S.E., & Eibach, R.P. (2011). Aging attitudes moderates the effect of subjective age on psychological well-being: Evidence from a 10-year longitudinal study. *Psychology and Aging, 26*(4), 979–986. doi:10.1037/a0023877

Mohlman, L., Sirota, K.G., Papp, L.A., Staples, A.M., King, A., & Gorenstein, E.E. (2012). Clinical interviewing with older adults. *Cognitive and Behavioral Practice, 19*(1), 89–100. https://doi.org/10.1016/j.cbpra.2010.10.001

Mojet, J. (2004). *Change in taste with age.* Retrieved from www.napavalley.edu/people/gvierra/Documents/Sensory_Evaluation_of_Wine/TastePerception_with_Age.pdf

Molin, P., & Rockwood, K. (2016). The new criteria for Alzheimer's disease - Implications for geriatricians. *Canadian Geriatrics Journal, 19*(2), 66–73. doi:10.5770/cgj.19.207

Moll, A. (2013). *Losing track of time. Dementia and the ageing prison population: Treatment challenges and examples of good practice.* London, UK: Mental Health Foundation. Retrieved from https://www.mentalhealth.org.uk/publications/losing-track-time

Monserud, M.A. (2011). Changes in grandchildren's adult role statuses and their relationships with grandparents. *Journal of Family Issues, 32*(4), 425–451. doi:10.1177/0192513X10384466

Montepare, J. M. (2009). Subjective Age: Toward a guiding lifespan framework. *International Journal of Behavioral Development 33*(1), 42–46. doi:10.1177/0165025408095551

Montross, L.P., Depp, C., Daly, J., Reichstadt, L., Golshan, S., Moore, D., & Jeste, D.V. (2006). Correlates of self-rated successful aging among community dwelling older adults. *The American Journal of Geriatric Psychiatry*, *14*(1), 43–51. doi:10.1097/01.JGP.0000192489.43179.31

Morcom, A.M., & Friston, K.J. (2012). Decoding episodic memory in ageing: A Bayesian analysis of activity patterns in predicting memory. *Neuroimage*, *59*(2), 1772–1782. doi:10.1016.j.neuroimage.2011.08.071

Morgan, D.G., Walls-Ingram, S., Cammer, A., O'Connell, M.E., Crossley, M., Dal Bello-Haas, V., … Stewart, N. (2014). Informal caregivers' hopes and expectations of a referral to a memory clinic. *Social Science & Medicine*, *102*, 111–118. doi:10.1016/j.socscimed.2013.11.023

Morgan, T.A.Chelminski, I., Young, D., Dalrymple, K., & Zimmerman, M. (2013). Differences between older and younger adults with borderline personality disorder on clinical presentation and impairment. *Journal of Psychiatric Research*, *47*(10), 1507–1513. doi:10.1016/j.jpsychires.2013.06.009

Morell, C.M. (2003). Empowerment and long-living women: Return to the rejected body. *Journal of Aging Studies*, *17*(1), 69–85. doi:10.1016/S0890-4065(02)00091-9

Moriconi, P.A., Nadeau, L., & Demers, A. (2012). Drinking habits of older Canadians: A comparison of the 1994 and 2004 national surveys. *Canadian Journal on Aging*, *31*(4), 379–393. doi:10.1017.S0714980812000347

Morin, C.M., LeBlanc, M., Belanger, L., Ivers, H., Merette, C., & Savard, J. (2011). Prevalence of insomnia and its treatment in Canada. *Canadian Journal of Psychiatry*, *56*(9), 540–548. Retrieved from http://publications.cpa-apc.org/browse/sections/0

Morissette, R., & Ostrovsky, Y. (2007). Pensions and retirement savings of families. *Perspective on Labour and Income*, *8*(11), 5–18.

Mosier, K.E., Vasiliadis, H.M., Lepnurn, M., Puchala, C., Pekrul, C., & Tempier, R. (2010). Prevalence of mental disorders and service utilization in seniors: Results from the Canadian Community health Survey cycle 1.2. *International Journal of Geriatric Psychiatry*, *25*(10), 960–967. doi:10.1002/gps.2434

Mõttus, R., Johnson, W., & Deary, I.J. (2012). Personality traits in old age: Measurement and rank-order stability and some mean level change. *Psychology and Aging*, *27*(1), 243–249. doi:10.1037/a0023690

Mountney-Lessard, E. (2014, February 19). Orma celebrates 111th birthday Wednesday. *The Intelligencer*. Retrieved from www.intelligencer.ca/2014/02/18/orma-celebrates-111th-birthday-wednesday

Moustgaard, H., Joutsenniemi, K., Sihvo, S., & Martikainen, P. (2013). Alcohol-related deaths and social factors in depression mortality: A register-based follow-up of depressed in-patients and anti-depressant users in Finland. *Journal of Affective Disorders*, *148*(2-3), 278–285. doi:10/1016/j.jad.2012.12.008

Mouton, C.P., Bazaldua, O.V., Pierce, B., & Espino, D.V. (2001). Common infections in older adults. *American Family Physician*, *63*(2), 257–268. Retrieved from www.aafp.org/journals/afp.html

Moztarzadeh, A., & O'Rourke, N. (2015). Psychological and sociocultural adaptation: Acculturation, depressive symptoms, and life satisfaction among older Iranian immigrants in Canada. *Clinical Gerontologist*, *38*(2), 114–130. doi:10.1080/07317115.2014.990601

Mroczek, D.K., Almeida, D.M., Spiro, A., & Pafford, C. (2006). Modeling intraindividual stability and change in personality. In D.K. Mroczek & T.D. Little (Eds.), *Handbook of personality development* (pp.163-180). Mahwah, NJ: Lawrence Erlbaum Associates, Inc.

Mroczek, D.K., & Spiro, A. (2007). Personality change influences mortality in older men. *Psychological Science*, *18*(5), 371–376. doi:10.1111/j.1467-9280.2007.01907.x

Mroczek, D.K., Spiro, A., & Turiano, N. (2009). Do health behaviors explain the effect of neuroticism on mortality? Longitudinal findings from the VA Normative Aging Study. *Journal of Research in Personality*, *43*(4), 653–659. doi:10.1016/j.jrp.2009.03.016

Mühlig-Versen, A., Bowen, C.E., & Staudinger, U.M. (2012). Personality plasticity in later adulthood: Contextual and personal resources are needed to increase openness to new experiences. *Psychology and Aging*, *27*(4), 855866. doi:10.1037/a0029357

Mugavero, M.J., Castellano, C., Edelman, D., & Hicks, C. (2007). Late diagnosis of HIV infection: The role of age and sex. *The American Journal of Medicine*, *120*(4), 370–373. doi:10.1016/j.amjmed.2006.05.050

Mukamal, K.J., Chung H., Jenny, N.S., Kuller, L.H., Longstreth, Jr., W.T., Mittleman, M.A., … Siscovick, D.S. (2006). Alcohol consumption and risk of coronary heart disease in older adults: The Cardiovascular Health Study. *Journal of* the *American Geriatric Society, 54*(1), 30–37. doi:10.111/j.1532-5415.2005.00561.x

Munkyong, P., Meydani, S., & Wu, D. (2012). The role of nutrition in enhancing immunity in aging. *Aging and Disease, 3*(1), 91–129. Retrieved from www.aginganddisease.org/EN/Y2012/V3/I1/91

Murray, H.A. (1938). *Explorations in personality*. New York NY: Oxford University Press.

Myrtek, M. (2001). Meta-analyses of prospective studies on coronary heart disease, Type A personality, and hostility. *International Journal of Cardiology, 79*(2–3), 245–251. doi:10.1016/S0167-5273(01)00441-7

Nasreddine, Z.S., Phillips, N.A., Bédirian, V., Charbonneau, S., Whitehead, V., Collin, I., … Chertkow, H. (2005). The Montreal Cognitive Assessment, MoCA: A brief screening tool for mild cognitive impairment. *Journal of the American Geriatrics Society, 53*(4), 695–699. doi.org/10.1111/j.1532-5415.2005.53221.x

Nathanson, J.N. (2009). Animal hoarding: Slipping into the darkness of comorbid animal and self-neglect. *Journal of Elder Abuse and Neglect, 21*(4), 307–324. doi:10.1080/08946560903004839.

Natural Burial Association. (2013). *Natural burials*. Retrieved from www.naturalburialassoc.ca/how-it-works/

National Collaborating Centre for Aboriginal Health. (2009). *Access to health services as a social determinant of First Nations, Inuit and Métis health*. Retrieved from http://www.nccah-ccnsa.ca/docs/fact%20sheets/social%20determinates/Access%20to%20Health%20Services_Eng%202010.pdf

National Collaborating Centre for Aboriginal Health. (2013). *Overview of Aboriginal health in Canada*. Retrieved from www.nccah-censa/Publications/Attachements/101/aboriginal_health_webpdf

National Conference of State Legislatures & AARP Public Policy Institute. (2011). *Aging in place: A state of livability policies and practices*. Washington, DC: AARP Public Policy Institute.

National Eye Institute. (2015). *Facts about age-related macular degeneration*. Retrieved from https://nei.nih.gov/health/maculardegen/armd_facts

National Human Genome Research Institute. (2014). *All about the human genome project (HGP)*. Retrieved from www.genome.gov/10001772

National Institute of Allergy and Infectious Diseases. (2013). *Overview of the immune system*. Retrieved

from www.niaid.nih.gov/topics/immunesystem/Pages/overview.aspx

National Institute of Diabetes and Digestive and Kidney Diseases. (2015). *Your digestive system and how it works*. Retrieved from www.niddk.nih.gov/health-information/health-topics/Anatomy/your-digestive-system/Pages/anatomy.aspx

National Institute on Aging. (2003). *Alzheimer's disease: Unraveling the mystery*. Retrieved from www.bu.edu/alzresearch/files/pdf/ADEARUnravelingtheMystery12-033.pdf

National Institute on Deafness and Other Communicative Disorders. (2014). *Taste disorders*. Retrieved from www.nidcd.nih.gov/health/smelltaste/pages/taste.aspx

National Institutes of Health. (2014). *Vitamin D. Fact sheet for health professionals*. Retrieved from https://ods.od.nih.gov/factsheets/VitaminD-HealthProfessional/

National Seniors Council of Canada. (2007). *Report of the National Seniors Council on Elder Abuse*. Ottawa, ON: Government of Canada. Retrieved from https://www.canada.ca/content/dam/nsc-cna/documents/pdf/policy-and-program-development/publications-reports/2007/elder-abuse-report/elder-abuse-report-en.pdf

Neikrug, A.B., & Ancoli-Israel, S. (2010). Sleep disorders in the older adult—a mini-review. *Gerontology, 56*(2), 181–189. doi:10.1159%2F000236900

Nelson, H.D., Haney, E., Humphrey, L., Miller, J., Nedrow, A., Nicolaidis, C., … Nygren, P. (2005). *Management of menopause-related symptoms* (AHRQ Publication No. 05-E016-2). Rockville, MD: Agency for Healthcare Research and Quality. Retrieved from http://archive.ahrq.gov/downloads/pub/evidence/pdf/menopause/menopaus.pdf

Nelson, T.D. (2011). Ageism: The strange case of prejudice against the older you. In R.L. Wiener & S. L. Willborn (Eds.), *Disability and aging discrimination: perspectives in law and psychology* (pp. 37–47), New York, NY: Springer. doi:10.1007/978-1-4419-6293-5_2

Neufeld, E., Freeman, S., Joling, K., & Hirdes, J.P. (2014). "When the golden years are blue": Changes in depressive symptoms over time among older adults newly admitted to long term care facilities. *Clinical Gerontologist, 37*(3), 298–315. doi:10.1080/07317115.2014.885919

Neufeld, E. Hirdes, J.P., Perlman, C.M., & Rabinowitz, T. (2015). Risk and protective factors associated with intentional self-harm among older community-residing home care clients in Ontario, Canada. *International Journal of Geriatric Psychiatry*, *30*(10), 1032–1040. doi:10.1002.gps.4259

Newbold, K.B. (2006). Chronic condition and the healthy immigrant effect: Evidence from Canadian immigrants. *Journal of Ethnic and Migration Studies*, *32*(5), 765–784. doi:10.1080/13691830600704149

Newbold, K.B., & Filice, J.K. (2006). Health status of older immigrants to Canada. *Canadian Journal on Aging*, *25*(3), 305–319. doi:10.1353/cja.2007.2009

Newman, A. (2010). An overview of the design, implementation, and analyses of longitudinal studies on aging. *Journal of the American Geriatrics Society*, *58*(Suppl 2), S287-S291. doi:10.1111/j.1532-5415.2010.02916.x

Newman, A.B., & Brach, J.S. (2001). Gender gap in longevity and disability in older persons. *Epidemiologic Reviews*, *23*(2), 342–350. doi:10.1093/oxfordjournals.epirev.a000810

Newman, D.L., Fisher, L.M., Ohmen, J., Parody, R., Fong, C.T., Frisina, S.T., … Friedman, R.A. (2012). *GRM7* variants associated with age-related hearing loss based on auditory perception, *Hearing Research*, *294*(0), 125–132. doi:10.1016/j.heares.2012.08.016

Ng, C.F., & Northcott, H.C. (2009-2010). The ethnic and national identity of South Asian immigrant seniors living in Edmonton, Canada. *Canadian Ethnic Studies*, *41–42*(3–1), 131–156. doi:10.1353/ces.2010.0049

Ng, C.F., & Northcott, H. (2013). Living arrangements of South Asian immigrant seniors in Edmonton, Canada: An assessment of the economic, cultural, health, and availability of kin explanations. *Journal of Housing for the Elderly*, *27*(1-2), 1–27. doi:10.1080/02763893.2011.649827

Ng, E., Lai, W.L., Rudner, A.T., & Orpana, H. (2012). *What do we know about immigrant seniors aging in Canada? A demographic, socio-economic, and health profile*. CERIS Working Papers 88–90. CERIS: Ontario Metropolis Centre.

Ng, S.H. (2002). Will families support their elders? Answers from across cultures. In T.D. Nelson (Ed.), *Ageism: Stereotyping and prejudice against older persons* (pp. 295–309). Cambridge, MA: MIT Press.

Ng, T.W.H., & Feldman, D.C. (2012). Evaluating six common stereotypes about older workers with meta-analytical data. *Personnel Psychology*, *65*(4), 821–858. doi:10.1111/peps.12003

Ni Lochlainn, M., & Kenny, R.A. (2013). Sexual activity and aging. *Journal of the American Medical Directors Association*, *14*(8), 562–572. doi:10.1016/j.jamda.2013.01.022

Nimrod, G., & Shira, A. (2016). The paradox of leisure in later life. *The Journals of Gerontology, Series B: Psychological Sciences and Social Sciences*, *71*(1), 106–111. doi:10.1093/geronb/gbu143

Nippold, M.A., Cramond, P.M., & Hayward-Mayhew, C. (2014). Spoken language production in adults: Examining age-related differences in syntactic complexity. *Clinical Linguistics & Phonetics*, *28*(3), 195–207. doi:10.3109/02699206.2013.841292

Noack, H., Lövdén, M., & Schmiedek, F. (2014). On the validity and generality of transfer effects in cognitive training research. *Psychological Research*, *78*(6), 773–789. doi:10.1007/s00426-014-0564-6

Norstrand, J., & Chan, K.T. (2014). The relationship between health and community across aging cohorts. *Journal of Aging Research*, 2014, 1–10. doi:10.1155/2014/626097

North, M.S., & Fiske, S.T. (2012). An inconvenienced youth? Ageism and its potential intergenerational roots. *Psychological Bulletin*, *138*(5), 982–977. doi:10.1037/a0027843

North, M.S., & Fisk, S.T. (2015). Modern attitudes toward older adults in the aging world: A cross cultural meta-analysis. *Psychological Bulletin*, *141*(5), 993–1021. doi:10.1037/a0039469

Novak, M., Campbell, L., & Northcott, H. (2014). *Ageing and society: Canadian perspectives* (7th ed.). Toronto, ON: Nelson Education Ltd.

Novek, S., Menec, V., Tran, T., & Bell, S. (2013). *Exploring the impacts of senior centres on older adults*. Winnipeg, MB: Centre on Aging, University of Manitoba.

Nunney, J.M., & Raynor, T. (2001). How are multi-compartment compliance aids used on primary care? *The Pharmaceutical Journal*, *267*, 784–789.

Nyberg, L., Lövdén, M., Riklund, K., Lindenberger, U., & Bäckman, L. (2012). Memory aging and brain maintenance. *Trends in Cognitive Sciences*, *16*(5), 292–306. doi:10.1016/jtics.2012.04.005

O'Brien, J.T. (2013). For debate: Is the very early diagnosis of AD using the new criteria beneficial for patients? Introduction. *International Psychogeriatrics*, *25*(2), 174–175. doi:10.1017/S1041610212001652

OECD.Stat. (2016). *Total expenditure on health care OECD countries*. Retrieved from http://stats.oecd.org/Index.aspx#

Office of the Commissioner of Official Languages for New Brunswick. (n.d.). http://officiallanguages.nb.ca/

Offsay, J. (2007). Treatment of alcohol-related problems in the elderly. *Annals of Long Term Care*, *15*(7), 39–44. Retrieved from www.annalsoflongtermcare.com/home

Ohayon, M.M., Carskadon, M.A., Guilleminault, C., & Vitiello, M.V. (2004). Meta-analysis of quantitative sleep parameters from childhood to old age in healthy individuals: Developing normative sleep values across the human life span. *Sleep*, *27*(7), 1255–1273. Retrieved from www.journalsleep.org

Okun, M.A., Rios, R., Crawford, A.V., & Levy, R. (2011). Does the relationship between volunteering and well-being vary with health and age? *International Journal of Aging and Human Development*, *72*(3), 265–287. doi:10.2190/AG.72.3.f

Oltmanns, T.F., & Balsis, S. (2010). Assessment of personality disorders in older adults. In P.A. Lichtenberg (Ed.), *Handbook of assessment in clinical gerontology* (2nd ed., pp. 101–121). New York, NY: Elselvier.

Oltmanns, T.F., & Balsis, S. (2011). Personality disorders in later life: Questions about the measurement, course, and impact of disorders. *Annual Review of Clinical Psychology*, *7*, 321–349. doi:10.1146/annurev-clinpsy-090310-120435

Omidvar, S., Jafari, Z., Tahaei, A.A., & Salehi, M. (2013). Comparison of auditory temporal resolution between monolingual Persian and bilingual Turkish-Persian individuals. *International Journal of Audiology*, *52*(4), 236–241. doi:10.3109/14992027.2012.744106

Omran, A.R. (2005). The epidemiological transition: A theory of the epidemiology of population change. *The Milbank Quarterly*, *83*(4), 731–757. doi:10.1111/j.1468-0009.2005.00398.x

Ontario Human Rights Commission. (2016). *Ageism and age discrimination*. Retrieved from www.ohrc .on.ca/en/ageism-and-age-discrimination-fact-sheet

Onyike, C.U., & Diehl-Schmid, J. (2013). The epidemiology of frontotemporal dementia. *International Review of Psychiatry*, *25*(2), 130–137. doi:10.3109/09540261.2013.776523

Opdebeek, C., Martyr, A., & Clare, L. (2016). Cognitive reserve and cognitive function in health older people: A meta-analysis. *Aging, Neuropsychology, and Cognition*, *23*(1), 40–60. doi:10.1080/13825585.2105.1041450

Oregon Public Health Division. (2016). *Oregon Death with Dignity Act: 2015 data summary*. Salem, OR: Oregon Health Authority.

O'Rourke, N., & Cappeliez, P. (2005). Marital satisfaction and self-deception: Reconstruction of relationship histories among older adults. *Social Behavior and Personality: An International Journal*, *33*(3), 273–282. doi:10.2224/sbp.2005.33.3.273

Ott, B.R., & Daiello, L.A. (2010). How does dementia affect driving in older patients? *Aging Health*, *6*(1), 77–85. doi:10.2217/ahe.09.83

Ott, B.R., Heindel, W.C., Papandonatos, G.D., Festa, E.K., Davis, J.D., Daiello, L.A., & Morris, J.C. (2008). A longitudinal study of drivers with Alzheimer disease. *Neurology*, *70*(14), 1171–1178. doi:10.1212/01.wnl.0000294469.27156.30

Ott, C.H., Lueger, R.J., Kelber, S.T., & Prigerson, H.G. (2007). Spousal bereavement in older adults: Common, resilient and chronic grief with defining characteristics. *The Journal of Nervous and Mental Disease*, *195*(4), 332–341. doi:10.1097/01.nmd.0000243890.93992.1e

Otte, S. & Steketee, G. (2011). Psychiatric issues in hoarding: Strategies for diagnosing and treating symptoms of hoarding. *Psychiatric Times*, *28*(8), 9–13. Retrieved from www.psychiatrictimes.com

Ouslander, J.G., Lamb, G., Tappen, R., Herndon, L., Diaz, S., Roos, B.A., … Bonner, A. (2011). Interventions to reduce hospitalizations from nursing homes: Evaluation of the INTERACT II Collaborative Quality Improvement Project. *Journal of the American Geriatrics Society*, *59*(4), 745–753. doi:10.1111/j.1532-5415.2011.03333

Ouwehand, C., de Ridder, D.T.D., & Bensing, J.M. (2007). A review of successful aging models: Proposing proactive coping as an important additional strategy. *Clinical Psychology Review*, *27*(8), 873–884. doi:10.1016/j.cpr.2006.11.003

Pachana, N.A., Liddle, J., Peel, N.M., Juang, C., & Knight, B.G. (2015). Can we do better? Researchers' experience with ethical review boards on projects with a late life focus. *Journal of Alzheimer's Disease*, *43*(3), 701–707. doi:10.3233/JAD-141956

Pack-Brown, S.P., Thomas, T.L., & Seymour, J.M. (2008). Infusing professional ethics into counsellor education programs: A multi-cultural/social justice perspective. *Journal of Counseling and Development*, *86*(3), 296–302. doi:10.1002/j.1556-6678.2008.tb00512.x

Pallium Canada. (2016). *LEAP learning essential approaches to palliative care*. Retrieved from http://pallium.ca/professional-development/leap-2/

Palmer, M., & Harley, D. (2012). Models and measurements in disability: An international review. *Health Policy and Planning, 27*(5), 357–364. doi:10.1093/heapol/czro47

Palmore, E.B. (2004). Research note: Ageism in Canada and the United States. *Journal of Cross-Cultural Gerontology, 19*(1), 41–46. doi:10.1023.B:JCCG.0000015098.62691.ab

Panpalli Ates, M., Karaman, Y., Guntekin, S., & Ergun, M.A. (2016). Analysis of genetics and risk factors of Alzheimer's disease. *Neuroscience, 325*, 124–131. doi:10.1016/j.neuroscience.2016.03.051

Park, D.C., & Reuter-Lorenz, P. (2009). The adaptive brain: Aging and neurocognitive scaffolding. *Annual Review of Psychology, 60*, 173–196. doi:10.1146/annurev.psych.59.103006.093656

Park, J. (2010). *Health factors and early retirement among older workers* (Component of Statistics Catalogue no. 75–001-X). Ottawa, ON: Statistics Canada.

Park, J. (2012). *Job-related training of older workers* (Component of Statistics Catalogue no. 75–001-X). Ottawa, ON: Statistics Canada.

Parker, S. (2006). What barriers to sexual expression are experienced by older people in 24-hour care facilities? *Reviews in Clinical Gerontology, 16*(4), 275–279. doi:10.1017/S0959259807002274

Parsey, C.M., & Schmitter-Edgecombe, M. (2013). Applications of technology in neuropsychological assessment. *The Clinical Neuropsychologist, 27*(8), 1328–1361. doi:10.1080/13854046.2013.834971

Pastalan, L.A. (1990). *Aging in place: The role of housing and social supports.* Birmingham, NY: The Haworth Press, Inc.

Pasupathi, M., & Mansour, E. (2006). Adult age differences in autobiographical reasoning in narratives. *Developmental Psychology, 42*(5), 798–808. doi:10.1037/0012-1649.42.5.798

Patronek, G.J. (2006). *Animal hoarding: Its roots and recognition.* Veterinary Medicine, August 1, 2006. Retrieved from http://veterinarymedicine.dvm360.com/animal-hoarding-its-roots-and-recognition?id=&sk=&date=&pageID=6

Patten, S.B., Williams, J.V.A., Lavorato, D.H., Wang, J.L., McDonald, K., & Bulloch, A.G.M. (2015). Descriptive epidemiology of major depressive disorder in Canada in 2012. *Canadian Journal of Psychiatry, 60*(1), 23–30. doi:10.1177/070674371506000106

Patterson, T.L., Mausbach, B.T., McKibbin, C., Goldman, S., Bucardo, J., & Jeste, D.V. (2006). Functional Adaptation Skills Training (FAST): A randomized trial of a psychosocial intervention for middle-aged and older patients with chronic psychotic disorders. *Schizophrenia Research, 86*(1-3), 291–299. doi:10.1016/j.schres.2006.05.017

PDQ® Supportive and Palliative Care Editorial Board. (2014). *PDQ grief, bereavement, and coping with loss.* Bethesda, MD: National Cancer Institute. Updated October 8, 2014. Available at www.cancer.gov/about-cancer/advanced-cancer/caregivers/planning/bereavement-hp-pdq. Accessed January 10, 2017. [PMID: 26389487].

Peacock, S., Forbes, D., Markle-Reid, M., Hawranik, P., Morgan, D., Jansen, L., … Henderson, S.R. (2010). The positive aspects of the caregiving journey with dementia: A strengths- based perspective to reveal opportunities. *Journal of Applied Gerontology, 29*(5), 640–659. doi:10.1177/0733464809341471

Pearson, C., Janz, T., & Ali, J. (2013). *Mental health and substance use disorders in Canada* (Catalogue no. 82–624-X). Ottawa, ON: Statistics Canada Retrieved from www.statcan.gc.ca/pub/82-624-x/2013001/article/11855-eng.pdf

Peck, M.D. (2010). *Barriers to using fixed-route public transit for older adults* (MTI Report No. 09–16). Sacramento, CA: California Department of Transportation.

Peng, X.D., Huang, C.Q., Chen, L.J., & Lu, Z.C. (2009). Cognitive behavioural therapy and reminiscence techniques for treatment of depression in the elderly: A systematic review. *Journal of International Medical Research, 37*(4), 975–982. doi:10.1177/147323000903711401

Penn, L., White, M., Lindström, J., den Boer, A.T., Blaak, E., Eriksson, J., … Tuomilehto, J. (2013). Importance of weight loss maintenance and risk and risk prediction in the prevention of Type 2 diabetes: Analysis of European Diabetes Prevention Study RCT. *PLoS ONE, 8*(2), e57143. doi:10.1371/journal.pone.0057143

Penning, M.J., & Wu, Z. (2016). Caregiver stress and mental health: Impact of caregiving relationship and gender. *The Gerontologist, 56*(6,), 1102–1113. doi.org/10.1093/geront/gnv038

Penzel, F. (2014). Hoarding in history. In R.O. Frost & G. Steketee (Eds.), *The Oxford Handbook of Hoarding and Acquiring* (pp. 6–16). New York, NY: Oxford University Press.

Pepin, R., Segal, D.L., & Coolidge, F.L. (2009). Intrinsic and extrinsic barriers to mental health care among community-dwelling younger and older adults. *Aging and Mental Health, 13*, 769–777. doi:10.1080/13607860902918231

Peplau, L.A., & Fingerhut, A.W. (2007). The close relationships of lesbians and gay men. *Annual Review of Psychology, 58*, 405–424. doi:0.1146/annurev. psych.58.110405.085701

Perkins, M., Howard, V.J., Wadley, V.G., Crowe, M., Safford, M.M., Haley, W.E., … Roth, D.L. (2013). Caregiving strain and all-cause mortality: Evidence from the REGARDS Study. *The Journals of Gerontology, Series B: Psychological Sciences and Social Sciences, 68*(4), 504–512. doi:10.1093/geronb/gbs084

Perneczky, R., Tene, O., Attems, J., Giannakopoulos, P., Ikram, M.A., Federico, A., … Middleton, L.T. (2016). Is the time ripe for new diagnostic criteria of cognitive impairment due to cerebrovascular disease? Consensus report of the International Congress on Vascular Dementia working group. *BMC Medicine, 14*, 162. doi:10.1186/s12916-016-0719-y

Perrig-Chiello, P., Spahni, S., Höpflinger, F., & Carr, D. (2016). Cohort and gender differences in psychosocial adjustment to later-life widowhood. *The Journals of Gerontology, Series B: Psychological Sciences and Social Sciences*, 71(4), 765–774. doi:10.1093/geronb/gbv004

Persson, N., Ghisletta, P., Dahle, C.L., Bender, A.R., Yang, Y., Yuan, P., . . . Raz, N. (2016). Regional brain shrinkage and change in cognitive performance over two years: The bidirectional influences of the brain and cognitive reserve factors. *NeuroImage, 126*, 15–26. doi:10.1016/jneuroimage.2015.11.028

Peters, L., Cant, R., Payne, S., O'Connor, M, McDermott, F., Hood, K., … Shimoinaba, K. (2013). How death anxiety impacts nurses' caring for patients at the end of life: A review of literature. *The Open Nursing Journal, 7*, 14–21. doi:10.2174/1874434601307010014

Peters, R. (2006). Aging and the brain. *Postgraduate Medical Journal, 82*(964), 84–88. doi:10.1136/pgmj.2005.036665

Pezzin, L.E., Pollak, R.A., & Schone, B.S. (2013). Complex families and late-life outcomes among elderly persons: Disability, institutionalization, and longevity. *Journal of Marriage and the Family, 75*(5), 1084–1097. doi:10.1111/jomf.12062

Pichora-Fuller, M.K., & Singh, G. (2006). Effects of age on auditory and cognitive processing: Implications for hearing aid fitting and audiologic rehabilitation. *Trends in Amplification, 10*(1) 29–59.

Pietrowsky, R., & Mikutta, J. (2012). Effects of positive psychology interventions with depressed patients: A randomized control study. *Psychology, 3*(12), 1067–1073. doi:10.4236/psych.2012.312158

Pignal, J., Arrowsmith, S., & Ness, A. (2010). *First results for the Survey of Older Workers, 2008*. Ottawa, ON: Statistics Canada.

Pines, A.M., Neal, M.B., Hammer, L.B. & Icekson, T. (2011). Job burnout and couple burnout in dual-earner couples in the sandwiched generation. *Social Psychology Quarterly, 74*(4), 361–368. doi:10.1177/0190272511422452

Pinquart, M., Duberstein, P.R., & Lyness, J.M. (2007). Effects of psychotherapy and other behavioral interventions on clinically depressed older adults. *Aging and Mental Health, 11*(6), 645–657. doi:10.1080/13607860701529635.

Pinto, J.M., Wroblewski, K.E., Kern, D.W., Schumm, P., & McClintock, M.K. (2014). Olfactory dysfunction predicts 5-year mortality in older adults. *PLoS One, 9*(10), e107541. doi:10.137/journal.pone.0107541

Platt, A., Sloan, F.A., & Costanzo, P. (2010). Alcohol-consumption trajectories and associated characteristics among adults older than age 50. *Journal of Studies on Alcohol and Drugs, 71*(2), 169–179. doi:http://dx.doi.org/10.15288/jsad.2010.71.169

Ploeg, J., Lohfeld, L., & Walsh, C.A. (2013). What is "Elder Abuse"? Voices from the margin: The views of underrepresented Canadian older adults. *Journal of Elder Abuse & Neglect, 25*(5), 396–424. doi:10.1080/08946566.2013.780956

Ploubidis, G.B., & Grundy, E. (2009). Personality and all cause mortality: Evidence for indirect links. *Personality and Individual Differences, 47*(3), 203–208. doi:10.1016/j.paid.2009.02.022

Plouffe, L., & Gillis, M. (2016). *Age friendly communities are key to a sustainable health plan for aging Canadians*. Retrieved from www.demandaplan.ca/age_friendly_communities_are_key_to_a_sustainable_health_plan_for_aging_canadians

Poon, L.W. (1985). Differences in human memory with aging: Nature, causes, and clinical implications. In J. E. Birren & K.W. Schaie (Eds.), *Handbook of the psychology of aging* (2nd ed. pp. 427–462). New York, NY: Van Nostrand Reinhold.

Poresnsky, E.K., Dew, M.A., Karp, J.F., Skidmore, E., Rollman, B.L., Shear, M.K., & Lenze, E. J. (2009). The burden of late-life anxiety disorder: Effects on disability, health-related quality of life, and healthcare utilization.

American Journal of Geriatric Psychiatry, 17(6), 473–482. Retrieved from http://www.ajgponline.org

Posthuma, R.A., & Campion, M.A. (2009). Age stereotypes in the workplace: Common stereotypes, moderators, and future research directions. *Journal of Management, 35*(1), 158–188. doi:10.1177/0149206308318617

Powdthavee, N. (2011). *Life satisfaction and grandparenthood: Evidence from a national survey* (IZA DP No. 5869). Bonn, DE: Institute for the Study of Labor (IZA).

Powers, A.D., & Oltmanns, T.F. (2012). Personality disorders and physical health: A longitudinal examination of physical functioning, healthcare utilization, and health-related behaviors in middle-aged adults. *Journal of Personality Disorders, 26*(4), 524–538. doi:10.1521/pedi.2012.26.4.524

Prigerson, H.G., Bierhals, A.J., Kasi, S.V., Reynolds, C.F., Shear, M.K., Newsom, J.T. & Jacobs, S. (1996). Complicated grief as a disorder distinct from bereavement-related depression and anxiety: A replication study. *American Journal of Psychiatry, 153*(11), 1484–1486.

Prigerson, H.G., Horowitz, M.J., Jacobs, S.C., Parkes, C.M., Aslan, M., Goodkin, K., … Marwit, S.J. (2009). Prolonged grief disorder: Psychometric validation of criteria proposed for DSM-V and ICD-11. *PLoS Medicine, 6*(8): e100121.

Prigerson, H.G., Vanderwerker, L.C. & Maciejewski, P.K. (2008). A case for the inclusion of prolonged grief disorder in *DSM-5*. In M.S. Stroebe, R.O. Hansson, & H. Schut (Eds.), *Handbook of bereavement research and practice: Advances in theory and intervention* (pp. 165–186). Washington, DC: American Psychological Association.

Prince, M., Comas-Herrera, A., Knapp, M., Guerchet, M., & Karagiannidou, M. (2016). *World Alzheimer report 2016: Improving healthcare for people living with dementia. Coverage, quality and costs now and in the future.* London, UK: Alzheimer's Disease International. Retrieved from http://eprints.lse.ac.uk/67858/

PRNewswire. (2015). *Antiaging products and services: The global market.* Retrieved from www.prnewswire.com/news-releases/antiaging-products-and-services-the-global-market-220249801.html

Proulx, C.M., Helms, H.M., & Buehler, C. (2007). Marital quality and personal well-being: A meta-analysis. *Journal of Marriage and the Family, 69*(3), 576–593. doi:10.1111/j.1741-3737.2007.00393.x

Pruchno, R. (2012). Not your mother's old age: Baby boomers at age 65. *Gerontologist, 52*(2), 149–152. doi:10/1093/geront/gns038

Psaros, C., Barinas, J., Robbins, G.K., Bedoya, C.A., Park, E. R., & Safren, S.A. (2015). Reflections on living with HIV over time: Exploring the perspective of HIV-infected women over 50. *Aging & Mental Health, 19*(2), 121–128. doi:10.1080/13607863.2014.917608

Public Health Agency of Canada. (2006). *The human face of mental health and mental illness in Canada.* Ottawa, ON: Minister of Public Works and Government Services.

Public Health Agency of Canada. (2009). *Tracking heart disease and stroke in Canada.* Ottawa, ON: Author. Retrieved from www.phac-aspc.gc.ca/publicat/2009/cvd-avc/pdf/cvd-avs-2009-eng.pdf

Public Health Agency of Canada. (2010a). *Chapter 3: The health and well-being of Canadian seniors.* Ottawa, ON: Author. Retrieved from www.phac-aspc.gc.ca/cphorsphc-respcacsp/2010/fr-rc/cphorsphc-respcacsp-06-eng.php

Public Health Agency of Canada. (2010b). *Arthritis facts & myths.* Retrieved from www.phac-aspc.gc.ca/cd-mc/arthritis-arthrite/myths-mythes-eng.php

Public Health Agency of Canada. (2010c). *Fast facts from the 2009 Canadian Community Health Survey—osteoporosis rapid response.* Ottawa, ON: Author. Retrieved from www.phac-aspc.gc.ca/cd-mc/osteoporosis-osteoporose/

Public Health Agency of Canada. (2010d). *The Chief Public Health Officer's report on the state of public health in Canada in 2010. Chapter 3: The health and well-being of Canadian older adults.* Ottawa, ON: Author.

Public Health Agency of Canada. (2011a). *Diabetes in Canada: Facts and figures from a public health perspective.* Ottawa, ON: Author. Retrieved from www.phac-aspc.gc.ca/cd-mc/publications/diabetes-sdiabete/facts-figures-faits-chiffres-2011/index-eng.php

Public Health Agency of Canada. (2011b). *On the road to age-friendly communities.* Ottawa, ON: Author. Retrieved from www.phac-aspc.gc.ca/seniors-aines/publications/public/afc-caa/comm-coll/index-eng.php

Public Health Agency of Canada. (2012). *Age-friendly communities in Canada: Community Implementation Guide.* Halifax, NS: Nova Scotia Centre on Aging, Mount Saint Vincent University.

Public Health Agency of Canada. (2013a). *What makes Canadians healthy or unhealthy?* Ottawa, ON. Retrieved from http://www.phac-aspc.gc.ca/ph-sp/determinants/determinants-eng.php

Public Health Agency of Canada. (2013b). *The Chief Public Health Officer's report on the state of public health in Canada, 2013: Infectious disease - the never-ending threat.* Ottawa, ON: Author.

Public Health Agency of Canada. (2014a). *The chief public health officer's report on the state of public health in Canada in 2014.* Ottawa, ON: Author. Retrieved from www.phac-aspc.gc.ca/cphorsphc-respcacsp/2014/chang-eng.php. Ottawa, ON: Author.

Public Health Agency of Canada. (2014b). *Vaccine coverage amongst adult Canadians: Results from the 2012 adult National Immunization Coverage (aNIC) survey.* Ottawa, ON: Author. Retrieved from www.phac-aspc.gc.ca/im/nics-enva/vcac-cvac-eng.php

Public Health Agency of Canada. (2014c). *Senior's falls in Canada: Second report.* Ottawa, ON: Author. Retrieved from http://www.phac-aspc.gc.ca/seniors-aines/publications/public/injury-blessure/seniors_falls-chutes_aines/assets/pdf/seniors_falls-chutes_aines-eng.pdf

Public Health Agency of Canada. (2015). *Report from the Canadian Chronic Disease System: Mood and anxiety disorders in Canada.* Ottawa, ON: Public Health Agency of Canada.

Public Health Agency of Canada. (2016). *Age-friendly communities.* Ottawa, ON: Author. Retrieved from www.phac-aspc.gc.ca/seniors-aines/afc-caa-eng.php

Purcell, B., Heisel, M.J., Speice, J., Franus, N., Conwell, Y., & Duberstein, P.R. (2012). Family connectedness moderates the association between living alone and suicidal ideation in a clinical sample of older adults. *American Journal of Geriatric Psychiatry*, *20*(8), 717–723. doi:10.1097/JGP.0b013e31822ccd79

Puryear-Keita, G. (2014). Speaking up against ageism. *Monitor on Psychology*, *45*(5), 61. Retrieved from www.apa.org/monitor/2014/05/itpi.aspx

Pynoos, J. (1993). Strategies for home modification and repair. In J. Callahan (Ed.), *Aging in place* (pp. 29–38). Amityvillle, NY: Baywood.

Qiu, C., von Strauss, E., Bäckman, L., Winblad, B., & Fratiglioni, L. (2013). Twenty-year changes in dementia occurrence suggest decreasing incidence in central Stockholm, Sweden. *Neurology*, *80*(20), 1888–1894. doi:10.1212/WNL.0b013e318292a2f9

Quirk, S.E., El-Gabalawy, R., Brennan, S.L., Bolton, J.M., Sareen, J., Berk, M., … Williams, L.J. (2015). Personality disorders and physical comorbidities in adults from the United States: Data from the National Epidemiologic Survey on Alcohol and Related Conditions. *Social Psychiatry and Psychiatric Epidemiology*, *50*(5), 807–820. doi:10.1007/s00127-014-0974-1

Rabaglia, C.D., & Salthouse, T.A. (2011). Natural and constrained language production as a function of age and cognitive abilities. *Language and Cognitive Processes*, *26*(10), 1505–1531. doi:10.1080/01690965.2010.507489

Ramage-Morin, P.L. (2006). Successful aging in health care institutions. How healthy are Canadians. *Health Reports*, *16*(Suppl.), 47–56.

Ramage-Morin, P.L. (2009). Medication use among senior Canadians. *Health Reports* (Component of Statistics Canada Catalogue no. 82–003-X), *20*(1), 1–9.

Ramage-Morin, P.L., & Garriguet, D. (2013). Nutritional risk among older Canadians. *Health Reports*, *24*(3), 3–13. Retrieved from www.sfu.ca/uploads/page/21/STATSCAN_2013_nutrition_and_older_adults.

Ramage-Morin, P.L., & Gilmour, H. (2013). *Urinary continence and loneliness in Canadian seniors* (Catalogue no. 82–003-X). Ottawa, ON: Statistics Canada. Retrieved from www.statcan.gc.ca/access_acces/alternative_alternatif .action?l=eng&loc=11872-eng.pdf

Ramsey-Klawsnik, H., Teaster, P.B., Mendiondo, M.S., Marcum, J.L., & Abner, E.L. (2008). Sexual predators who target elders: Findings from the first national study of sexual abuse in care facilities. *Journal of Elder Abuse & Neglect*, *20*(4), 353–376. doi:10.1080/08946560802359375

Rand, D., Weiss, P.L., & Katz, N. (2009). Training multitasking in a virtual supermarket: A novel intervention after stroke, *American Journal of Occupational Therapy*, *63*(5), 535–542. doi:10.5014/ajot.63.5.535

Ravindran, R., Vashist, P., Gupta, S., Young, I., Maraini, G., Camparini, M., … Fletcher, A. (2011). Inverse association of vitamin C with cataract in older people. *Ophthalmology*, *118*(10), 1958–1965. doi:10.1016/j.ophtha.2011/03/016

Raz, N., & Kennedy, K.M. (2009). A systems approach to age-related change: Neuroanatomic changes, their modifiers, and cognitive correlates. In W. Jagust & M. D'Esposito (Eds.), *Imaging and the brain* (pp. 43–70). New York, NY: Oxford University Press.

RBC Insurance. (2016). *Know the consequences of dying without a will*. Retrieved from www.rbcinsurance.com/insuranceneeds/insurancewill/dying-without-will.html

Reading, C.l., & Wien, F. (2009). *Health inequalities and social determinants of Aboriginal peoples' health*. Prince George, BC: National Collaborating Centre for Aboriginal Health. Retrieved from www.sac-conference.ca/wp-content/uploads/2016/04/Fred-Wien-Social-Determinants-of-Health-Among-Aboriginal-Populations-in-Canada-Handout-21.pdf

Reason, B., Terner, M., McKeag, A.M., Tipper, B., & Webster, G. (2012). The impact of polypharmacy on the health of Canadian seniors. *Family practice, 29*(4), 427–432. doi:10.1093/fampra/cmr124

Rebok, G.W., Ball, K., Guey, L.T., Jones, R.N., Kim, H.Y., King J.W., … Willis, S.L. (2014). Ten-year effects of the Advanced Cognitive Training for Independent and Vital Elderly cognitive training trial on cognition and everyday functioning in older adults. *Journal of the American Geriatrics Society, 62*(1), 16–24. doi:10.1111/jgs.12607

Redick T.S., Broadway, J.M., Meier, M.E., Kuriakose, P.S., Unsworth, N., Kane, M.J., & Engle, R.W. (2012). Measuring working memory capacity with automated complex span tasks. *European Journal of Psychological Assessment, 28*, 164–171. doi:10.1027/1015-5759/a000123.

Redinbaugh, E.M., Sullivan, A.M., Block, S.D., Gadmer, N.M., Lakoma, M., Mitchell, A.M., … Arnold, R.M. (2003). Doctors' emotional reactions to recent death of a patient: Cross sectional study of hospital doctors. *BMJ, 327*(7408), 185.

Redzanowski, U., & Glück, J. (2013). Who knows who is wise? Self and peer ratings of wisdom. *The Journals of Gerontology, Series B: Psychological Science and Social Sciences, 68*(3), 391–394. doi:10.1093/geronb/gbs079

Reed, A.E., & Carstensen, L.L. (2012). The theory behind the age-related positivity effect. *Frontiers in Psychology, 3, 339*. doi:10.3389/fpsyg.2012.00339

Reichstadt, J., Depp, C.A., Plainkas, L.A., & Jeste, D.V. (2007). Building blocks of successful aging: A focus group study of older adults perceived contributors to successful aging. *The American Journal of Geriatric Psychiatry, 13*(53), 194–201. doi:10.1097/JGP.0b013e318030255f

Reichstadt, J., Sengupta, G., & Depp, C.A., Palinkas, L.A., & Jeste, D.V. (2010). Older adults' perspectives on successful aging: Qualitative interviews. *The American Journal of Geriatric Psychiatry, 18*(7), 567–575. doi:10.1097/jgp.0b013e3181e040bb

Rieker, P.P., & Bird, C.E. (2005). Rethinking gender differences in health: Why we need to integrate social and biological perspectives. *The Journals of Gerontology, Series B: Psychological Sciences and Social Sciences, 60*(Special Issue 2), S40-S47. doi:10.1093/geronb/60.Special_Issue_2.S40

Reijnders, J., Van Heugten, C., & Van Boxtel, M. (2012). Cognitive interventions in healthy older adults and people with mild cognitive impairment: A systematic review. *Ageing Research Reviews, 12*(1), 263–275. doi:10.1016/j.arr.2012.07.003

Reinhardt, M.M., & Cohen, C.I. (2015). Late-life psychosis: Diagnosis and treatment. *Current Psychiatry Reports, 17*(1), 1–13. doi:10.1007/s11920-014-0542-0

Reitan, R.M. (1958). Validity of the Trail Making Test as an indicator of organic brain damage. *Perceptual and Motor Skills, 9*(g), 271–276. doi:10.2466/PMS.8.7.271-276

Repovš, G., & Baddeley, A. (2006). The multi-component model of working memory: Explorations in experimental cognitive psychology. *Neuroscience, 139*(1), 5–21. doi:10.1016/j.neuroscience.2005.12.061

Reuter-Lorenz, P.A., & Cappell, K.A. (2008). Neurocognitive aging and the compensation hypothesis. *Current Directions in Psychological Science, 17*(3), 177–182. doi:10.1111/j.1467-8721.2008.00570.x

Reuter-Lorenz, P.A., & Park, D.C. (2010). Human neuroscience and the aging mind. A new look at old problems. *The Journals of Gerontology, Series B: Psychological Sciences and Social Sciences, 65*(4), 405–415. doi:10.1093/geronb/gbq035

Reuter-Lorenz, P.A., & Park, D.C. (2014). How does it STAC up? Revisiting the scaffolding theory of aging and cognition. *Neuropsychology Review, 24*(3), 355–370. doi:10.1007/s11065-014-9270-9

Reynolds, K., Pietrzak, R.H., El-Gabalawy, R., Mackenzie, C.S., & Sareen, J. (2015). Prevalence of psychiatric disorders in U.S. older adults: Findings from a nationally representative survey. *World Psychiatry, 14*(1), 74–81. doi:10.1002/wps.20193

Rhoades, G.K., Stanley, S.M., & Markman, H.J. (2009). The pre-engagement cohabitation effect: A replication and extension of previous findings. *Journal of Family Psychology, 23*(1), 107–111. doi:10.1037/a0014358

Rhodes, A.E., Links, P.S., Streiner, D.L., Dawe, I., Cass, D., & Janes, S. (2002). Do hospital E-codes consistently capture suicidal behaviour? *Chronic*

Diseases in Canada. 23(4), 139–145. Retrieved from www.ncbi.nlm.nih.gov/pubmed/12517321

Rhodes, R.E., & Smith, N.E. (2006). Personality correlates of physical activity: A review and meta-analysis. *British Journal of Sports Medicine, 40*(3), 958965. doi:10.1136/bjsm.2006.028860

Ridic, G., Gleason, S., & Ridic, O. (2012). Comparisons of health care systems in the United States, Germany and Canada. *Materia Socio-Medica, 24*(2), 112–120. doi:10.5455/msm.2012.24.112-120

Ridley, N.J., Draper, B., & Withall, A. (2013). Alcohol-related dementia: An update of the evidence. *Alzheimer's Research & Therapy, 5*(1), 3. doi:10.1186/alzrt157

Rincon, F., & Wright, C.B. (2014). Current pathophysiological concepts in cerebral small vessel disease. *Frontiers in Aging Neuroscience, 6*(24). doi:10.3389/fnagi.2014.00024

Rippon, I., & Steptoe, A. (2015). Feeling old vs being old. *JAMA Internal Medicine, 175*(2), 307–309. doi:10.1001/jamainternmed.2014.6580

Ritchie, L.J., & Tuokko, H. (2010). Patterns of cognitive decline, conversion rates, and predictive validity for 3 models of MCI. *American Journal of Alzheimer's Disease and other Dementias, 25*(7), 592–603. doi:10.1177/1533317510382286

Roberts, B.W., & DelVecchio, W.F. (2000). The rank-order consistency of personality traits from childhood to old age: A quantitative review of longitudinal studies. *Psychological Bulletin, 126*(1), 3–25. doi:10.1037/0033-2909.126.1.3

Roberts, B.W., Donnellan, M.B., & Hill, P.L. (2013). Personality trait development in adulthood. In H. Tennen, J. Suls, & I.B. Weiner (Eds.), *Handbook of psychology, Volume 5: Personality and social psychology* (2nd ed., pp. 183–196). Hoboken, NJ: John Wiley &Sons.

Roberts, B.W., Kuncel, N.R., Shiner, R.N., Caspi, A., & Goldberg, L.R. (2007). The power of personality: The comparative validity of personality traits, socioeconomic status, and cognitive ability for predicting important life outcomes. *Perspectives on Psychological Science, 2*(4), 313–345. doi:10.1111/j.1745-6916.2007.00047.x

Roberts, B.W., Walton, K.E., & Viechtbauer, W. (2006). Patterns of mean-level change in personality traits across the life course: A meta-analysis of longitudinal studies. *Psychological Bulletin, 132*(1), 1–25. doi:10.1037/0033-2909.132.1.1

Roberts, R., & Knopman, D.S. (2013). Classification and epidemiology of MCI. *Clinics inGeriatric Medicine, 29*(4), 753–722. doi:10.1016/j.cger.2013.07.003

Rochon, P.A., Grunier, A., Wu, W., Gill, S., Bronskill, S.E., Seitz, D.P., … Anderson, G.M. (2014). Demographic characteristics and healthcare use of centenarians: A population-based cohort study. *Journal of the American Geriatrics Society, 62*(1), 86–93. doi:10.1111/jgs.12613.

Rodriguez v. British Columbia (Attorney General), 3 S.C.R. 519 (1993).

Rodriguez, C., Herman, D., Alcon, J., Chen, S., Tannen, A., Essock, S., & Simpson, H.B. (2012). Prevalence of hoarding disorder in individuals at potential risk of eviction in New York City: A pilot study. *Journal of Nervous and Mental Disease, 200*(1), 91–94. doi:10.1097/NMD.0b013e31823f678b

Rodriguez-Blazquez, C., Forjaz, M.J., Prieto-Flores, M.E., Rojo-Perez, F., Fernandez-Mayoralas, G., Martinez-Martin, P., & Spanish Research Group on Quality of Life and Ageing. (2012). Health status and well-being of older adults living in the community and in residential care settings: Are differences influenced by age? *Aging & Mental Health, 16*(7), 884–891. doi:10.1080/13607863.2012.684664

Roenker, D.L., Cissell, G.M., Ball, K.K., Wadley, V.G., & Edwards, J.D. (2003). Speed-of-processing and driving simulator training result in improved driving performance. *Human Factors, 45*(2), 218–233. doi:10.1518/hfes.45.2.218.27241

Roest, M.A., Zuidersma, M., & De Jonge, P. (2012). Myocardial infarction and generalised anxiety disorder: 10-year follow-up. *The British Journal of Psychiatry, 200*, 38–46. doi:10.1192/bjp.bp.111.103549

Ronksley, P.E., Brein, S.E., Turner, B.J., Mukamal, K.J., & Ghali, W.A. (2011). Association of alcohol consumption with select cardiovascular disease outcomes: A systematic review and meta-analysis. *British Medical Journal, 324*, 1–13. doi:10.1136/bmj.d671

Ropacki, S.A., & Jeste, D.V. (2005). Epidemiology of and risk factors for psychosis of Alzheimer's disease: A review of 55 studies published from 1990–2003. *American Journal of Psychiatry, 162*(11), 2022–2030. doi.org/10.1176/appi.ajp.162.11.2022

Rosebud, R., & Knopman, D.S., (2013). Classification and epidemiology of MCI. *Clinical Geriatric Medicine, 29*(4), 1–19.doi:10.1016/j.cger.2013.07.003

Rosenberg, D.E., Huang, D.L., Simonovich, S.D., & Belza, B. (2013). Outdoor built environment barriers and facilitators to activity among midlife and older adults with mobility disabilities. *The Gerontologist, 53*(2), 268–279. doi:10.1093/geront/gns119

Rosic, I. (n.d.). Family: Speaking with immigrant seniors. *Canadian Newcomer*. Retrieved from www.cnmag.ca/issue-42/1107-speaking-with-immigrant-seniors

Rosnick, C.B., Wetherell, J.L., White, K.S., & Andreescu, C., & Lenze, E.J. (2016). Cogntive-Behavioral Therapy augmentation of SSRI reduces cortical levels in older adults with generalized anxiety disorder: A randomized clinical trial. *Journal of Consulting and Clinical Psychology*, *84*(4), 345–352. doi:10.1037/a0040113.

Rossi, G., Van den Broeck, J., Dierckx, E., Segal, D.L., & van Alphen, S.P.J. (2014). Personality assessment among older adults: The value of personality questionnaires unraveled. *Aging & Mental Health*, *18*(8), 936–940. doi:10.1080/13607863.2014.924089

Rosso, A.L., Auchincloss, A.H., & Michael, Y.L. (2011). The urban built environment and mobility in older adults: A comprehensive review. *Journal of Aging Research*, 2011, 1–10. doi:10.4061/2011/816106

Rosso, A.L., Grubesic, T.H., Auchincloss, A.H., Tabb, L.P., & Michael, Y.L. (2013). Neighborhoods amenities and mobility in older adults. *American Journal of Epidemiology*, 178(5), 761–769. doi:10.1093/aje/kwt032

Rotermann, M., Sanmartin, C., Hennessy, D., & Arthur, M. (2014). *Prescription medication use by Canadians aged 6 to 79* (Component of Statistics Canada Catalogue no. 82–003-X Health Reports). Ottawa, ON. Retrieved from www.statcan.gc.ca/pub/82-003-x/2014006/article/14032-eng.pdf

Rothrauff, T., & Cooney, T.M. (2008). The role of generativity in psychological well-being: Does it differ for childless adults and parents? *Journal of Adult Development*, *15*(3), 148–159. doi:10.1007/s10804-008-9046-7

Rowe, J.W., & Khan, R.L. (1997). Successful aging. *The Gerontologist*, *37*(4), 433–440. doi:10.1093/geron/37.4.433

Rozanova, J., Northcott, H.C., & McDaniel, S.A. (2006). Seniors and portrayals of intra-generational and inter-generational inequality in the Globe and Mail journals. *Canadian Journal on Aging*, *25*(4), 373–386. doi:10.1353/cja.2007.0024

Ruzzoli M., Pirulli, C., Brignani, D., Maioli, C., & Miniussi. C. (2012). Sensory memory during physiological aging indexed by mismatch negativity (MMN). *Neurobiology of Aging*, *33*(3), 625.e21–30. doi:10.1016/j.neurobiolaging.2011.03.021

Ryan, E.B., Giles, H., Bartolucci, G., & Henwood, K. (1986). Psycholinguistics and social psychological components of communication by and with the elderly. *Language and Communication*, *6*, 1–24. https://doi.org/10.1016/0271-5309(86)90002-9

Ryan, E.B., Hummert, M.L., & Boich, L.H. (1995). Communication predicaments of aging: Patronizing behavior toward older adults. *Journal of Language and Social Psychology, Special Issue: Approaches to Natural Language Texts*, *14*(1-2), 144–166. doi:10.1177/0261927X95141008

Ryff, C.D. (1989). Beyond Ponce de Leon and life satisfaction: New directions in the quest of successful aging. *International Journal of Behavioral Development*, *12*(1), 35–55.

Rypma, B., Eldreth, D.A., & Rebbechi, D. (2007). Age-related differences in activation-performance relations in delayed-response tasks: A multiple component analysis. *Cortex*, *43*(1), 65–76. doi:10.1016/S0010-9452(08)70446-5

Salthouse, T.A. (1995). Processing capacity and its role on the relations between age and memory. In F.E. Weinert & W. Schneider (Eds.), *Memory performance and competencies: Issues in growth and development* (pp. 111–125). Hillsdale, NJ: Erlbaum.

Salthouse, T.A. (1996). The processing-speed theory of adult differences in cognition. *Psychological Review*, *103*(3), 403–428. doi:10.1037/0033-295X.103.3.403

Salthouse, T.A. (2010). *Major issues in cognitive aging*. New York, NY: Oxford University Press.

Salthouse, T.A. (2011). Neuroanatomical substrates of age-related cognitive decline. *Psychological Bulletin*, *137*(5), 753–784. doi:10.1037/a0023262

Samuel, S., Mu, L., McKay, R., Dobbs, B., & Babenko, O. (2015, April). *CHOICE 15 years later: An evaluation of the CHOICE Program*. Final report submitted to the Good Samaritan Society, Edmonton, AB, Canada.

Samuels, J. (2011). Personality disorders: Epidemiology and public health issues. *International Review of Psychiatry*, *23*(3), 223–233. doi:10.3109/09540261.2011.588200

Samuels, J.F., Bienvenu, O.J., Gradosa, M.A., Cullena, B., Riddlea, M.A., Liang, K.Y., Eaton, W.W., & Nestadt, G. (2008). Prevalence and correlates of hoarding behavior in a community-based sample. *Behaviour Research and Therapy*, *46*(7), 836-844. doi:10.1016/j.brat.2008.04.004

Samuels, J., Eaton, W.W., Bienvenu, O.J., Brown, C.H., Costa, P.T. Jr., & Nestadt, G. (2002). Prevalence and correlates of personality disorders in a community sample. *The British Journal of Psychiatry*, *180*(6), 536–542. doi:10.1192/bjp.180.6.536

Sankar, A., Nevedal, A., Neufeld, S., Berry, R., & Luborsky, M. (2011). What do we know about older adults and HIV? A review of the social and behavioral literature. *AIDS Care*, *23*(10), 1187–1207. doi:10.1080/09540121.2011.564115

Sareen, J., Cox, B.J., Afifi, T.O., Yu, B.N., & Stein, M.B. (2005). Mental health service use in a nationally representative Canadian Survey. *Canadian Journal of Psychiatry*, *50*(12), 753–761. doi:10.1177/070674370505001204

Sargent-Cox, K., & Anstey, K.J. (2015). The relationship between age-stereotypes and health locus of control across adult age-groups. *Psychology and Health*, *30*(6), 652–670. doi:10.1080/08870446.2014.974603

Sarkisian, N., & Gerstel, N. (2016). Does singlehood isolate or integrate? Examining the link between marital status and ties to kin, friends and neighbors. *Journal of Social and Personal Relationships*, *33*(3), 361–384. doi:10.1177/0265407515597564

Sassler, S. (2010). Partnering across the life course: Sex, relationships, and mate selection. *Journal of Marriage and the Family*, *72*(3), 557–575. doi:10.1111/j.1741-3737.2010.00718.x

Sasson, I., & Umberson, D.J. (2014). Widowhood and depression: New light on gender differences, selection, and psychological adjustment. *The Journals of Gerontology, Series B: Psychological Sciences and Social Sciences*, *69*(1), 135–145. doi:10.1093/geronb/gbt058

Satre, D.D., & Leibowitz, A. (2015). Brief alcohol and drug interventions and motivational interviewing for older adults. In A.P. Areán (Ed.), *Treatment of late life depression, anxiety, trauma and substance abuse*, (pp. 163–180). Washington, DC: American Psychological Association. doi.org/10.1037/14524-008

Sawano, Y. (2012). Lifelong learning to revitalized community: Case studies of citizens' learning initiative in Japan. In D.N. Aspin, J. Chapman, K. Evans, & R. Bagnall (Eds.), *Second international handbook of lifelong learning* (part 2, pp. 665–678). New York, NY: Springer.

Schaefer, D.O., & Wertheimer, A. (2010). The right to withdraw from research. *Kennedy Institute of Ethics Journal*, *20*(4), 329–352.

Schaie, K.W. (2013). *Developmental influences on adult intelligence* (2nd ed.). New York, NY: Oxford University Press.

Schaie, K.W., & Caskie, G.I.L. (2005). Methodological issues in aging research. In D.M. Teti (Ed.), *Handbook of research methods in developmental psychology* (pp. 21–69). Cambridge, UK: Blackwell.

Schaie, K.W., & Willis, S.L. (1968). *Adult development and aging*, (2nd ed.). Boston, MA: Little Brown and Co.

Schaie, K.W., & Willis, S.L. (2010). The Seattle longitudinal study of adult cognitive development. *ISSBD BULL*, *57*(1), 24–29. PMC3607395

Scheidt, R.J. (2017). The defense of my aging self: A report from the field. *Gerontologist*, *57*(1), 110–115. doi:10.1093/geront/gnw082

Schellenberg, G., Turcotte, M., & Ram, B. (2005). Post-retirement employment. *Perspectives on Labour and Income*, *6*(9), 14–17.

Schick, V., Herbenick, D., Reece, M., Sanders, S.A., Dodge, B., Middlestadt, S.E. & Fortenberry, J.D. (2010). Sexual behaviors, condom use, and sexual health of Americans over 50: Implications for sexual health promotion for older adults. *The Journal of Sexual Medicine*, *7*(Suppl. 5), 315–329. doi:10.1111/j.1743-6109.2010.02013.x

Schiffer, J.J. (2016). Why Aboriginal peoples can't just "get over it". Understanding and addressing intergenerational trauma. *Visions*, *11*(4), 10–14. Retrieved from www.heretohelp.bc.ca/visions

Schimmele, C.M., & Wu, Z. (2016). Repartnering after union dissolution in later life. *Journal of Marriage and the Family*, *78*(4), 1013–1031. doi:10.1111/jomf.12315

Schneider, W.J., & McGrew, K.S. (2012). The Cattell-Horn-Carroll Model of Intelligence. In D. Flanagan & P. Harrison (Eds.), *Contemporary intellectual assessment: Theories, tests, and issues* (3rd ed., pp. 99–144). New York, NY: Guilford.

Schoenmakers, B., Buntinx, F., & Delepeleire, J. (2010). Factors determining the impact of care-giving on caregivers of elderly patients with dementia: A systematic literature review. *Maturitas*, *66*(2), 191–200. doi:10.1016/j.maturitas.2010.02.009

Schoklitsch, A., & Baumann, U. (2012). Generativity and aging: A promising future research topic? *Journal of Aging Studies*, *26*(3), 262–272. doi:10.1016/j.jaging.2012.01.002

Schonfield, L., King-Kallimanis, K.L., Duchene, D.M., Etheridge, R.L., Herrera, J.R., Barry, K.L., & Lynn, N. (2010). Screening and brief intervention for substance misuse among older adults: The Florida BRITE Project. *The American Journal of Public Health*, *100*(1), 108–114. doi:10.2105/AJPH.2008.149534

Schulz, R., & Aderman, D. (1974). Clinical research and the stages of dying. *Omega: The Journal of Death and Dying*, *5*(2), 137–143. doi:10.2190/HYRB-7VQK-VU9Y-7L5D

Schuster, J.-P., Hoertel, N., Le Strat, Y., Manetti, A., & Limosin, F. (2013). Personality disorders in older adults: Findings from the national epidemiologic survey on alcohol and related conditions. *The American Journal of Geriatric Psychiatry*, *21*(8), 757–768. doi:10.1016/j.jagp.2013.01.055

Schwartz, W.B., & Aaron, H.J. (1984). Rationing hospital care. Lessons from Britain. *The New England Journal of Medicine*, *310*(1), 52–56.

Scott, T., Mackenzie, C.S., Chipperfield, J.G., & Sareen, J. (2010). Mental health service use among Canadian older adults with anxiety disorders and clinically significant anxiety symptoms. *Aging and Mental Health*, *14*(7), 790–800. doi:10.1080/13607861003713273

Scully, C. (2012). *The changing landscape of Canadian health care: The rise of non-core services and the need for an expanded federal role* (Major research paper, API 6999). Ottawa, ON: University of Ottawa. Retrieved from www.ruor.uottawa.ca/bitstream/10393/23863/1/SCULLY%2c%20Catherine%2020125.pdf

Seligman, M.E., & Csikszentmihalyi, M. (2000). Positive psychology: An introduction. *American Psychologist*, *55*(1), 5–14. doi:10/1037/0003-066x.55.1.5

Seltman, R.E., & Matthews, B.E. (2012). Frontotemporal lobar degeneration: Epidemiology, pathology, diagnosis and management. *CNS Drugs*, *26*(10), 841–870. doi:10.2165/11640070-000000000-00000

Seniormark. (2013). Survey shows what boomers like to be called: Their names! Retrieved from http://ireport.cnn.com/docs/DOC-1066224

Sepulveda, E., Franco, J.G., Trzepacz, P.T., Gaviria, A.M., Viñuelas, E., Palma, J., … Vilella, E. (2015). Performance of the Delirium Rating Scale-Revised-98 against different delirium diagnostic criteria in a population with a high prevalence of dementia. *Psychosomatics*, *56*(5), 530–541. doi:10.1016/j.psym.2015.03.005

Serrano-Aguilar, P.G., Lopez-Bastida, J., & Yanes-Lopez, V. (2006). Impact on health-related quality of life and perceived burden of informal caregivers of individuals with Alzheimer's disease. *Neuroepidemiology*, *27*(3), 136–142. doi.org/10.1159/000095760

Settia, M.S., Lynch, J., Abrahamowicz, M., Tousignant, T., & Quesnel-Vallee, A. (2011). Self-rated health in Canadian immigrants: Analysis of the longitudinal survey of immigrants to Canada. *Health and Place*, *17*(2), 658–670. doi:10.1016/j.healthplace.2011.01.006

Shah, A., Scogin, F., & Floyd, M. (2012). Evidence-based psychological treatments for geriatric depression. In F. Scogin & A. Shaw (Eds.), *Making evidenced-based psychological treatments work with older adults*, (pp. 87–130). Washington, DC: American Psychological Association.

Sharashenidze, N., Schacht, J., & Kevanishvili, Z. (2007). Age-related hearing loss: Gender differences. *Georgian Medical News*, *144*, 14–18.

Shea, Y.F., Chu, L.W., Chan, A.O., Ha, J., Li, Y., & Song, Y.Q. (2016). A systematic review of familial Alzheimer's disease: Differences in presentation of clinical features among three mutated genes and potential ethnic differences. *Journal of the Formosan Medical Association*, *115*(2), 67–75. doi:10.1016/j.jfma.2015.08-004

Shear, M.K. (2015). Clinical practice. Complicated grief. *New England Journal of Medicine*, *372*(2), 153–160. doi:10.1056/NEJMcp1315618

Sheets, D.J., & Gallagher, E.M. (2013). Aging in Canada: State of the art and science. *Gerontologist*, *53*(1), 1–8. doi:10.1093/geront/gns150

Shepherd, S., Depp, C.A., Harris, G., Halpain, M., Palinkas, L.A., & Jeste, D.V. (2012). Perspectives on schizophrenia over the lifespan: A qualitative study. *Schizophrenia Bulletin*, *38*(2), 295–303. doi:10.1093/schbul/sbq075

Sheridan Centre for Elder Research and Revera Inc. (2016). *Revera Report on Ageism: Independence and choice as we age*. Retrieved from http://www.ageismore.com/research/rever-a report-on-ageism-independence-and-choice-a

Shi, F., Liu, B., Zhou, Y., Yu, C., & Jiang T. (2009). Hippocampal volume and asymmetry in mild cognitive impairment and Alzheimer's disease: Meta-analyses of MRI studies. *Hippocampus*, *19*(11), 1055–1064. doi:10.1002/hipo.20573

Shields, M. (2008). Community belonging and self-perceived health. *Health Reports*, *19*(2), 1–10.

Shultz, K.S. (2003). Bridge employment: Work after retirement. In G.A. Adams & T.A. Beehr (Eds.), *Retirement: Reasons, processes, and results* (pp. 214–241). New York, NY: Springer Publishing Company.

Siberski, J., & Siberski, C. (2015). Boomers in nursing homes: Ready or not, here they come. *Today's Geriatric Medicine*, *8*(5), 18.

Simon, S.S., Cordás, T.A., & Bottino, M.C. (2014). Cognitive behavioral therapies in older adults with depression and cognitive deficits: A systematic review. *International Journal of Geriatric Psychiatry*, *30*, 223–233. doi:10.1002/gps.4239

Simpson, R. (2016). Singleness and self-identity: The significance of partnership status in the narratives of never-married women. *Journal of Social and Personal Relationships*, *33*(3), 385–400. doi:10.1177/02654075515611884

Sinforiani, E., Citterio, A., Zucchella, C., Bono, G., Corbetta, S., Merlo, P., & Mauri, M. (2010). Impact of gender differences on the outcome of Alzheimer's disease. *Dementia and Geriatric Cognitive Disorders*, *30*(2), 147–154. doi:10.1159/000318842

Sinha, M. (2013). *Spotlight on Canadians: Results from the General Social Survey. Portrait of caregivers, 2012* (Catalogue no. 89–652-X - No.001). Ottawa, ON: Statistics Canada. Retrieved from http://www.statcan .gc.ca/pub/89-652-x/89-652-x2013001-eng.htm

Sinha, N., Firbank, M., & O'Brien, J.T. (2012). Biomarkers in dementia with Lewy bodies: A review. *International Journal of Geriatric Psychiatry*, *27*(5), 443–453. doi:10.1002/gps.2749

Singer, J.A., Rexhaj, B., & Baddeley, J. (2007). Older, wiser, and happier? Comparing older adults' and college students' self-defining memories. *Memory*, *15*(8), 886–898. doi:10.1080/09658210701754351

Skugor, D., Muffels, R., & Wilthagen, T. (2012). *Labour law, social norms and the early retirement decision: An empirical study* (Discussion Paper No. 11/2012-046). Tilburg, NL: Network for Studies on Pensions, Aging and Retirement.

Sloane-Seale, A., & Kops, B. (2010). Older adults' participation in education and successful aging: Implications for university continuing education in Canada. *Canadian Journal of University Continuing Education*, *36*(1), 1–29. Retrieved from https:// ejournals.library.ualberta.ca/index.php/cjuce-rcepu/ article/view/8493/6858

Small, B.J., Hertzog, C., Hultsch, D.F., & Dixon, R.A. (2003). Stability and change in adult personality over 6 years: Findings from the Victoria Longitudinal Study. *The Journals of Gerontology, Series B: Psychological Sciences and Social Sciences*, *58*(3), P166–P176. doi:10.1093/geronb/58.3.P166

Šmigelskas, K., Žemaitienė, N., Julkunen, J., & Kauhanen, J. (2015). Type A behavior pattern is not a predictor of premature mortality. *International Journal of Behavioral Medicine*, *22*(2), 161–169. doi:10.1007/s12529-014-9435-1

Smith, A., & Duggan, M. (2013). *Online dating and relationships*. Washington, DC: Pew Research Center. Retrieved from http://www.pewinternet. org/2013/10/21/online-dating-relationships/

Smith, R. (2008). *Richard Smith: The end of diseae and the beginning of health* (BMJ Group Blogs). Retrieved from http://blogs.bmj.com/ bmj/2008/07/08/richard-smith-the-end-of-disease -and-the-beginning-of-health/

Smith, T.W., Berg, C.A., Florsheim, P., Uchino, B.N., Pearce, G., Hawkins, M., … Olsen-Cerny, C. (2009). Conflict and collaboration in middle-aged and older couples:1: Age differences in agency and communion during marital interaction. *Psychology and Aging*, *24*(2), 259–273. doi:10.1037/a0015609

Smits, I.A., Dolan, C.V., Vorst, H.C., Wicherts, J.M. & Timmerman, M.E. (2011). Cohort differences in big five personality factors over a period of 25 years. *Journal of Personality and Social Psychology*, *100*(6), 1124–1138. doi:10.1037/a0022874

Snowdon, A., Schnarr, K., Hussein, A., & Alessi, C. (2012). *Measuring what matters: The cost vs. values of health care*. London, ON: International Centre for Health Innovation, Richard Ivey School of Business.

Snowdon, D.A. (1997). Aging and Alzheimer's disease: Lessons from the Nun's Study. *The Gerontologist*, *37*(2), 150–156. doi:10.1093/ geront/37.2.150

Snowdon, J. (2010). Review: Depression in nursing homes. *International Psychogeriatrics*, *22*(7), 1143–1148. doi.org/10.1017/S1041610210001602

Snyder, H.M., Corriveau, R.A., Craft, S., Faber, J.E., Greenberg, S.M., Knopman, D., … Carrillo, M.C. (2015). Vascular contributions to cognitive impairment and dementia including Alzheimer's disease. *Alzheimer's & Dementia*, *11*(6), 710–717. doi:10.1016/j.jalz.2014.10.008

Sokolowski, M. (2012). Sex, dementia, and the nursing home: Ethical issues and reflections. *Journal of Ethics in Mental Health*, *7*, 1–5. Retrieved from www.jemh.ca/issues/v7/documents/JEMH _Vol7SexDementiaandtheNursingHome.pdf

Solomon, H., Man, J.W., & Jackson, G. (2003). Erectile dysfunction and the cardiovascular patient: Endothelial dysfunction is the common denominator. *Heart*, *89*(3), 251–254. Retrieved from http://heart.bmj.com

Sommers, B.D., Gunja, M.Z., Finegold, K., & Musco, T. (2015). Changes in self-reported insurance coverage, access to care, and health under the Affordable Care Act. *JAMA*, *314*(4), 366–374. doi:10.1001/jama.2015.8421

Soto, C.J., John, O.P., Gosling, S.D., & Potter, J. (2011). Age differences in personality traits from 10 to 65: Big five domains and facets in a large cross-sectional study. *Journal of Personality and Social Psychology*, *100*(2), 330–348. doi:10.1037/a0021717

Spearman, C. (1904). "General Intelligence": Objectively determined and measured. *American Journal of Psychology, 15*(2), 201–292. doi:10.2307/1412107

Specht, J., Egloff, B., & Schmukle, S.C., (2011). Stability and change across the life course: The impact of age and major life events on mean-level and rank-order stability of the Big Five. *Journal of Personality and Social Psychology, 101*(4), 862–882. doi:10.1037/a0024950

Sperazza, L.J., & Banerjee, P. (2010). Baby boomers and seniors: Understanding their leisure values enhances programs. *Activities, Adaptation & Aging, 34*(3), 196–215. doi:10.1080/01924788.2010.501484

Sperling, G. (1960). The information available in brief visual presentations. *Psychological Monographs: General and Applied, 74*(11 Whole No. 48), 1–29. Retrieved from http://www.cogsci.uci.edu/~whipl/staff/sperling/PDFs/Sperling_PsychMonogr_1960.pdf

Squire, L.R. (2009). The legacy of patient H.M. for neuroscience. *Neuron, 61*(1), 6–9. doi:10.1016/j.neuron.2008.12.023

Srivastava, S., John, O.P., Gosling, S.D., & Potter, J. (2003). Development of personality in early and middle adulthood: Set like plaster or persistent change. *Journal of Personality and Social Psychology, 84*(5), 1041–1053. doi:10.1037/0022-3514.84.5.1041

Standing Senate Committee on Social Affairs, Science and Technology. (2016). *Dementia in Canada: A national strategy for dementia-friendly communities.* Ottawa, ON: Senate of Canada Retrieved from www.alzheimer.ca/~/media/Files/national/Advocacy/SOCI_6thReport_DementiaInCanada-WEB_e.pdf

Stanley, M.L., Simpson, S.L., Dagenbach, D., Lyday, R.G., Burdette, J.H., & Laurienti, P.J. (2015). Changes in brain network efficiency and working memory performance in aging. *PLOS ONE, 10*(4), 1–17. doi:10.1371/journal.pone.0123950

Stanley, S.M., Amato, P.P., Johnson, C.A., & Markman, H.J. (2006). Premarital education, marital quality, and marital stability. Findings from a large, random, household survey. *Journal of Family Psychology, 20*(1), 117–126. doi:10.1037/0893-3200.20.1.117

Staples, L.G., Fogliati, V.J., Dear, B.F., Nielssen, O., & Titov, N. (2016). Internet-delivered treatment for older adults with anxiety and depression: Implementation of the Wellbeing Plus Course in routine clinical care and comparison with research trial outcomes. *British Journal of Psychiatry Open, 2*(5) 307–313. doi:10.1192/bjpo.bp.116.003400

Stark, S. (2009). *A brief history of work.* Retrieved from www.slideshare.net/stevenstark/a-brief-history-of-work

Stark, S., Landsbaum, A., Palmer, J., Somerville, E.K., & Morris, J.C. (2009). Client-centered home modifications improve daily activity performance of older adults. *Canadian Journal of Occupational Therapy, 76*(Spec. No.), 235–245.

Statistics Canada. (2006a). *CANSIM Table 105–0213 functional health status, by age group and sex, household population aged 12 years and over, Canada, 2005.* Retrieved from www.statcan.gc.ca/pub/82-221-x/2006001/t/4063696-eng.htm

Statistics Canada. (2006b). *2006 census of the population* (Catalogue no. 97–562-X-CB2006010). Ottawa, ON: Author. Retrieved from www12.statcan.gc.ca/census-recensement/2006/index-eng.cfm

Statistics Canada. (2008a). *Immigrant status and place of birth (38), sex (3) and age groups (10) for the population of Canada, provinces, territories, census metropolitan areas and census agglomerations, 2006 census: 20% sample data* (Catalogue no. 97–557-X2006013). Ottawa, ON: Author. Retrieved from wwwl2.statcan.gc.ca/english/census06/data/topic

Statistics Canada. (2008b). *Aboriginal peoples in Canada in 2006: Inuit, Métis and First Nations, 2006 census.* Ottawa, ON: Author. Retrieved from www12.statcan.ca/census-recensement/2006/as-sa/97-558/pdf/97-558-XIE2006001.pdf

Statistics Canada. (2009). *Health at a glance. Suicide rates: An overview* (Catalogue no. 82–624-X). Ottawa, ON: Statistics Canada. . Retrieved from www.statcan.gc.ca/pub/82-624-x/2012001/article/11696-eng.htm

Statistics Canada. (2010). *Population projections for Canada, provinces and territories 2009 to 2036* (Catalogue no. 91–520-X). Ottawa, ON: Author Ottawa, ON: Author.

Statistics Canada. (2011a). *Centenarians in Canada: Age and sex, 2011 Census* (Catalogue no. 98-311-X2011003). Ottawa, ON: Author.

Statistics Canada. (2011b). *Aboriginal peoples in Canada: First nations people, Métis and Inui* (Catalogue no. 99–011-X2011001). Ottawa, ON: Author.

Statistics Canada. (2011c). *Perceived health, 2011.* Retrieved from www.statcan.gc.ca/pub/82-625-x/2012001/article/11665-eng.htm

Statistics Canada. (2011d). *Aboriginal languages in Canada. Language, 2011 census of population* (Catalogue no. 98-314-X2011003). Ottawa, ON: Author. Retrieved from www12.statcan.gc.ca/census-recensement/2011/as-sa/98-314-x/98-314-x2011003_3-eng.pdf

Statistics Canada. (2011e). *2006 Census data products* (Catalogue no. 97-560-XCB2006007). Ottawa, ON: Author Ottawa, ON: Author.

Statistics Canada. (2011f). *National Household Survey (NHS) profile*. Retrieved from:http://www12.statcan.gc.ca/nhs-enm/2011/dp-pd/prof/index.cfm?Lang=E.

Statistics Canada. (2012a). *Generations in Canada: Age and sex, 2011 Census* (Catalogue no. 98-311-X2011003). Ottawa, On: Author. Retrieved from http://www12.statcan.gc.ca/census-recensement/2011/as-sa/98-311-x/98-311-x2011003_2-eng.pdf

Statistics Canada. (2012b). *Leading causes of death in Canada* (Catalogue no. 84-215-X). Ottawa, ON: Author. Retrieved from www5.statcan.gc.ca/olc-cel/olc.action?objId=84-215-X&objType=2&lang=en&limit=0

Statistics Canada. (2012c). *Canada year book 2012: Seniors* (Catalogue no. 11-402-X). Ottawa, ON: Author.

Statistics Canada. (2012d). *French and the Francophonie in Canada* (Catalogue no. 98–314-X2011003). Ottawa, ON: Author. Retrieved from www.12.statcan.gc.ca/censusrecensement/2011/as-sa/98-314-x/98-314-x2011003_1-eng.cfm

Statistics Canada. (2012e). *Linguistic characteristics of Canadians: Language, 2011 Census of population* (Catalogue no. 98314-X2011001). Ottawa, ON: Author. Retrieved from www12.statcan.gc.ca/census-recensement/2011/as-sa/98-314-x/98-314-x2011001-eng.cfm

Statistics Canada. (2012f). *Fifty years of families in Canada: 1961 to 2011. Families, households and marital status, 2011 census of population* (Catalogue no. 98–312-X2011003). Ottawa, ON: Author. Retrieved from www12.statcan.gc.ca/census-recensement/2011/as-sa/98-312-x/98-312-x2011003_1-eng.pdf

Statistics Canada. (*2012g*). *Portraits of families and living arrangements in Canada. Families, households and marital status, 2011 census of population* (Catalogue no. 98-312-X201001). Ottawa, ON: Author. Retrieved from www12.statcan.gc.ca/census-recensement/2011/as-sa/98-312-x/98-312-x2011001-eng.pdf

Statistics Canada. (2012h). *Living arrangements of young adults aged 20 to 29. Families, households and marital status, 2011 census of population* (Catalogue no. 98-312-X2011003). Ottawa, ON: Author. Retrieved from www12.statcan.gc.ca/census-recensement/2011/as-sa/98-312-x/98-312-x2011003_3-eng.pdf

Statistics Canada. (2012i). *Living arrangements of seniors. Families, households and marital status. Structural type of dwelling and collectives, 2011 Census of Population* (Catalogue no. 98-312-X2011003). Ottawa, ON: Author. Retrieved from www12.statcan.gc.ca/census-recensement/2011/as-sa/98-312-x/98-312-x2011003_4-eng.pdf

Statistics Canada. (2013a). *Aboriginal peoples in Canada: First Nations people Métis and Inuit, National Household Survey, 2011*. (Catalogue no. 99-011-X2011001). Ottawa, ON: Author. Retrieved on July 4, 2016, from www12.statcan.gc.ca/nhs-enm/2011/as-sa/99-011-x/99-011-x2011001-eng.pdf

Statistics Canada. (2013b). *Disability in Canada: Initial findings from the Canadian Survey* (Catalogue no. 89-654-X – No 002). Ottawa, ON: Statistics Canada.

Statistics Canada. (2013c). *Immigration and ethnocultural diversity in Canada* (Catalogue no. 99-010-X2011001). Ottawa, ON: Author. Retrieved from www12.statcan.gc.ca/nhs-enm/2011/as-sa/99-010-x/99-010-x2011001-eng.pdf

Statistics Canada. (2013d). *2011 National Household Survey: Immigration, place of birth, citizenship, ethnic origin, visible minorities, language and religion* (Catalogue no. 11-001-X). Ottawa, ON: Author. Retrieved from www.statcan.gc.ca/daily-quotidien/130508/dq130508b-eng.htm

Statistics Canada. (2014). *Annual demographic estimates: Canada, provinces and territories* (Catalogue no. 91-215-x). Ottawa, ON: Author.

Statistics Canada. (2015a). *Canada's population estimates: Age and sex, July 1, 2015*. Retrieved from www.statcan.gc.ca/daily-quotidien/150929/dq150929b-eng.htm

Statistics Canada. (2015b). *Hearing loss of Canadians, 2012 and 2013* (Catalogue no. 86-625-X). Ottawa, ON: Author. Retrieved from www.statcan.gc.ca/pub/82-625-x/2015001/article/14156-eng.htm

Statistics Canada. (2015c). *Number of centenarians by sex, Canada, 2011 to 2061*. Ottawa, ON: Author. Retrieved from http://www12.statcan.gc.ca/census-recensement/2011/as-sa/98-311-x/2011003/fig/fig3_1-1-eng.cfm

Statistics Canada. (2015d). *Health fact sheets: The 10 leading causes of death, 2012* (Catalogue no. 82–625-X). Ottawa, ON: Statistics Canada. Retrieved from www.statcan.gc.ca/pub/82-625-x/2015001/article/14296-eng.htm

Statistics Canada. (2015e). *Canadian tobacco, alcohol and drugs survey: Summary of results for 2013*. Retrieved from http://healthycanadians.gc.ca/science-research-sciences-recherches/data-donnees/ctads-ectad/summary-sommaire-2013-eng.php

Statistics Canada. (2015f). *Adult correctional statistics in Canada, 2013/2014* (Catalogue no. 85-002-x). Ottawa, ON: Author. Retrieved from http://www.statcan.gc.ca/pub/85-002-x/2015001/article/14163-eng.htm

Statistics Canada. (2015g). *Household*. Retrieved from www.statcan.gc.ca/eng/concepts/definitions/house

Statistics Canada. (2015h). *National Seniors Day… by the numbers*. Ottawa, ON: Author. Retrieved from www .statcan.gc.ca/eng/dai/smr08/2014/smr08_191_2014

Statistics Canada. (2016a). *Canadian demographics at a glance: Second edition*. (Catalogue no. 91–003-X). Retrieved from www.statcan.gc.ca/pub/91-003-x/91 -003-x2014001-eng.pdf

Statistics Canada. (2016b). *Fertility: Fewer children, older moms*. Retrieved from www.statcan.gc.ca/ pub/11-630-x/11-630-x2014002-eng.htm

Statistics Canada. (2016c). *Annual demographic estimates: Canada, provinces and territories* (Catalogue no. 91–215-X). Ottawa, ON: Author.

Statistics Canada. (2016d). *The surge of women in the workforce*. (Catalogue no. 11-630-X2015009). Ottawa, ON: Author. Retrieved from www.statcan.gc.ca/pub/ 11-630-x/11-630-x2015009-eng.htm

Statistics Canada. (2016e). *Women in Canada: A gender-based statistical report* (Catalogue no. 89-503-X). Ottawa, ON: Author. Retrieved from http://www.statcan.gc.ca/pub/89-503-x/89-503 -x2015001-eng.htm

Statistics Canada. (2016f). *Labour force characteristics by age and sex*. Retrieved from www.statcan.gc.ca/ tables-tableaux/sum-som/l01/cst01/labor20a-eng.htm

Statistics Canada. (2016g). *Table 276–0020—Employment Insurance program (EI), beneficiaries by province, type of income benefits, sex and age, monthly (persons)* (CANISM). Ottawa, ON: Author. Retrieved from www5 .statcan.gc.ca/cansim/a26?lang=eng&id=2760020#F3

Staudinger, U.M., Dorner, J., & Mickler, C. (2005). Wisdom and personality. In R.J. Sterberg & J. Jordan (Eds.), *A handbook of wisdom, psychological perspectives* (pp. 191–219). New York, NY: Cambridge.

Staudinger, U.M., & Glück, J. (2011). Psychological wisdom research: Commonalities and differences in a growing field. *Annual Review of Psychology*, *62*(1), 215–241. doi:10.1146/annurev.psych.121208.131659

Stefanick, M.L. (2005). Estrogens and progestins: Background and history, trends in use, and guidelines and regimens approved by the US Food and Drug Administration. *The American Journal of Medicine*, *118*(Suppl. 12B), 64–73. doi:10.1016/ j.amjmed.2005.09.059

Steinfeld, E., & Shea, S.M. (2001). Fair housing: Toward universal design in multifamily housing. In W.F.E. Preiser & E. Ostroff (Eds.), *Universal design handbook* (pp. 35.1-35.13). New York, NY: McGraw-Hill.

Steinhorn, L. (2007). *The greater generation: In defense of the baby boom legacy*. New York, NY: Saint Martin's Griffin.

Steketee, G., & Frost, R.O. (2006). *Compulsive hoarding and acquiring: Therapist guide (Treatments that work)*. New York, NY: Oxford University Press.

Steketee, G., & Frost, R.O. (2014). Phenomenology of hoarding. In R.O. Frost & G. Steketee (Eds.), *The oxford handbook of hoarding and acquiring*, (pp. 19–32). New York, NY: Oxford University Press.

Stenberg, A., & Westerlund, O. (2013). Education and retirement: Does university education at mid-age extend working life? *IZA Journal of European Labor Studies*, *2*, 16. doi:10.1186/2193-9012-2-16

Stephan, Y., Demulier, V., & Terracciano, A. (2012). Personality, self-rated health, and subjective age in a life-span sample: The moderating role of chronological age. *Psychology and Aging*, *27*(4), 875–880. doi:10.1037/a0028301

Stern, Y. (2002). What is cognitive reserve? Theory and research application of the reserve concept. *Journal of the International Neuropsychological Society*, *8*(3), 448–460. doi:10.1017.S1355617701020240

Sternberg, R., Sternberg, K., & Mio, J. (2012). Attention and consciousness. *Cognitive psychology* (6th ed., pp. 135–184). Belmont, CA: Wadsworth.

Sterns, A., Lax, G., Sed, C., Keohane, P., & Sterns, R.S. (2008). The Growing wave of older prisoners: A national survey of older prisoner health, mental health, and programming. *English Today*, *70*(4), 70–76. Retrieved from https://www.researchgate.net/ publication/236121499_The_Growing_Wave _of_Older_Prisoners_A_National_Survey_of_Older _Prisoner_Health_Mental_Health_and _Programming

Stewart, M., Shizha, E., Makwarimba, E., Spitzer, D., Khalema, E.N., & Nsaliwa, C. (2011). Challenges and barriers to services for immigrant seniors in Canada: "You are among others but you feel alone." *International Journal of Migration, Health and Social Care*, *7*(1), 16–32. doi:10.1108/17479891111176278

Stobert, S., Dosman, D., & Keating, N. (2006). *General Social Survey on time use: Cycle 19. Aging well: Time use patterns of older Canadians* (Catalogue no. 89–622-XIE).Ottawa, ON: Statistics Canada.

Stone, K., Papadopoulos, I., & Kelly, D. (2012). Establishing hospice care for prison populations: An integrative review assessing the UK and USA perspective. *Palliative Medicine*, *26*(8), 969–978. doi:10.1177/0269216311424219

Stone, S. (2003). Disability, dependence, and old age: Problematic constructions. *Canadian Journal on Aging*, *22*(1), 59–67. doi:10.1017/SO714980800003731

Stowe, D., & Cooney, T.M. (2015). Examining Rowe and Kahn's concept of successful aging: Importance of taking a life course perspective. *The Gerontologist*, *55*(1), 43–50. doi:10.1093/geront/gnu055

Strazzullo, P., D'Elia, L., Kandala, N.B., & Cappuccio, F.P. (2009). Salt intake, stroke, and cardiovascular disease: Meta-analysis of prospective studies. *BMJ (Clinical Research)*, *339*, b4567. doi:10.1136/mbj.b4567

Streiner, D.L., Cairney, J., & Veldhuizen, S. (2006). The epidemiology of psychological problems in the elderly. *Canadian Journal of Psychiatry*, *51*(3), 185–191. doi:10.1177/070674370605100309

Stroebe, M., Schut, H., & Stroebe, W. (2007). Health outcomes of bereavement. *The Lancet*, *370*(9603), 1960–1973. doi:10.1016/S0140-6736(07)61816-9

Strohm Kitchener, K., King, P.M., & DeLuca, S. (2006). Development of reflective judgement in adulthood. In C. Hoare (Ed.), *Handbook of adult development and learning* (pp. 73–98). New York, NY: Oxford University Press.

Suarez, E.C., Williams, R.B., Jr., Khun, C.M., Zimmerman, E.H., & Schanberg, S.M. (1991). Biobehavioral basis of coronary-prone behavior in middle-aged men. Part II:Serum cholesterol, the Type A behavior pattern, and hostility as interactive modulators of physiological reactivity. *Psychosomatic Medicine*, *53*(5), 528–537. Retrieved from http://journals.lww.com/psychosomaticmedicine/pages/default.aspx

Substance Abuse and Mental Health Services Administration. (2013). Results from the 2012 National Survey on Drug Use and Health: Summary of National Findings. NSDUH Series H-46, HHS Publication No. (SMA):13-4795. Rockville, MD.

Surwillo, W.W., & Quilter, R.E. (1964). Vigilance, age, and response-time. *The American Journal of Psychology*, *77*, 614–620. doi:10.2307/1420772

Sussman, T., Brotman, S., Chamberland, L., Daley, A., Dumas, J., MacDonnell, J., … Ryan, B. (2012). *Developing a program of research to identify and address the health and social service needs of lesbian, gay, bisexual, and transgendered (LGBT) older adults who reside in long-term care homes*. CIHR Planning Meeting, Montreal, QC.

Swami, V., Chamorro-Premuzic, T., Bridges, S., & Furnham, A. (2009). Acceptance of cosmetic surgery: Personality and individual difference predictors. *Body Image*, *6*(1), 7–13. doi:10.1016/j.bodyim.2008.09.004

Swanson, J.G., Kaczorowski, J., Skelly, J., & Finkelstein, M. (2005). Urinary incontinence: Common problem among women over 45. *Canadian Family Physician*, *51*, 84–85.

Syme, M.L. (2014). The evolving concept of older adult sexual behavior and its benefits. *Generations - Journal of the American Society on Aging*, *38*(1), 35–41.

Szanton, S.L., Walker, R.K., Roberts, L., Thorpe R.J., Jr, Wolff, J., Agree, E., … Seplaki, C. (2015). Older adults' favorite activities are resoundingly active: Findings from the NHATS study. *Geriatric Nursing*, *36*(2), 131–135. doi:10.1016/j.gerinurse.2014.12.008

Szinovacz , M.E., & Davey, A. (2005). Retirement and marital decision making: Effects on retirement satisfaction. *Journal of Marriage and Family*, *67*(2), 387–398. doi:10.1111/j.0022-2445.2005.00123.x

Tabak, N., & Shemesh-Kigli, R. (2006) Sexuality and Alzheimer's disease: Can the two go together? *Nursing Forum*, *41*(4), 158–166. doi:10.1111/j.1744-6198.2006.00054.x

Tackett, J.L., Balsis, S., Oltmanns, T.F., & Krueger, R.F. (2009). A unifying perspective on personality pathology across the life span: Developmental considerations for the fifth edition of the diagnostic and statistical manual of mental disorders. *Development and Psychopathology*, *21*(3), 687–713. doi:10.1017/S095457940900039X

Tam, S., & Neysmith, S. (2006). Disrespect and isolation: Elder abuse in Chinese communities. *Canadian Journal on Aging*, *25*(2), 141–151. doi:10.1353/cja.2006.0043

Tampi, R.R., Tampi, D.J., Chandran, S., Ghori, A., & Durning, M. (2015). Mild cognitive impairment: A comprehensive review. *Healthy Aging Research*, *4*(39), 1–11. doi:10.12715/har.2015.4.39.

Tan, P.P., Zhang, N., & Fan, L. (2004). Students' attitude toward the elderly in the people's Republic of China. *Educational Gerontology*, *30*(4), 305–314. doi:10.1080/03601270490278830

Tang, F., Choi, E.H., & Morrow-Howell, N. (2010). Organizational support and volunteering benefits for older adults. *The Gerontologist*, *50*(5), 603–612. doi:10.1093/geront/gnq020

Tate, R.B., Lah, L., & Cuddy, T.E. (2003). Definition of successful aging by elderly Canadian males: The Manitoba Follow-up Study. *The Gerontologist*, *43*(5), 735–744.doi:https://doi.org/10.1093/geront/43.5.735

Tay, J., Luscombe-Marsh, N., Thompson, C., Noakes, M., Buckley, J., Wittert, G., … Brinkworth, G. (2014). A very low-carbohydrate, low-saturated fat diet for Type

2 diabetes management: A randomized trial. *Diabetes Care, 37*(11), 2909–2918. doi:10.2337/dc14-0845

Taylor, A. (2011). Older adult, older person, senior, elderly, or elder: A few thoughts on the language we use to reference aging. *British Columbia Law Institute.* Retrieved from www.bcli.org/older-adult-older-person

Taylor, M.G., & Quesnel-Vallée, A. (2017). The structural burden of caregiving: Shared challenges in the United States and Canada. *The Gerontologist, 57*(1), 19–25. doi.org/10.1093/geront/gnw102

Taylor, P., & Walker, A. (1994). The ageing workforce: Employers' attitudes towards older people. *Work, Employment and Society, 8*(4), 569–591. doi:10.1177/095001709484005

Templer, D.J. (1970). The construction and validation of a Death Anxiety Scale. *Journal of General Psychology, 82*(2nd half), 165–177. doi:10.1080/00221 309.1970.9920634

Terracciano, A., Iacono, D., O'Brien, R.J., Troncoso, J.C., An, Y., Sutin, A.R., …Resnick, S.M. (2013). Personality and resilience to Alzheimer's disease neuropathology: A prospective autopsy study. *Neurobiology of Aging, 34*(4), 1045–1050. doi:10.1016/ j.neurobiolaging.2012.08.008

Terracciano, A., Löckenhoff, C.E., Crum, R.M., Bienvenu, O.J., & Costa, P.T. Jr. (2008). Five-Factor Model personality profiles of drug users. *BMC Psychiatry, 8*(22). doi:10.1186/1471-244X-8-22

Terracciano, A., McCrae, R.R., Brant, L.J., & Costa, P.T. Jr. (2005). Hierarchical linear modeling analyses of the NEO-PI-R scales in the Baltimore Longitudinal Study of Aging. *Psychology and Aging, 20*(3), 493–506. doi:10/1037/0882-7974.20.3.493

Terracciano, A., Sutin, A.R., An, Y., O'Brien, R.J., Ferrucci, L., Zonderman, A.B., & Resnick, S.M. (2014). Personality and risk of Alzheimer's disease: New data and meta-analysis. *Alzheimer's & Dementia,10*(2), 179–186. doi:10.1016/j.jalz.2013.03.002

Teresi, J.A., Ramirez, M., Ellis, J., Silver, S., Boratgis, G., Kong, J., … Lachs, M.S. (2013). A staff intervention targeting resident-to-resident elder mistreatment (R-REM) in long-term care increased staff knowledge, recognition and reporting: Results from a cluster randomized trial. *International Journal of Nursing Studies, 50*(5), 644–656. doi:10.1016/j. ijnurstu.2012.10.010

Tergesen, A. (2014, November 30). Why everything you think about aging may be wrong. *The Wall Street Journal.* Retrieved from www.wsj.com/articles/ why-everything-you-think-about-aging-may-be -wrong-1417408057

Theocharopoulou, F., Cocks, N., Pring, T., & Dipper, L.T. (2015). TOT phenomena: Gesture production in young and older adults. *Psychology and Aging, 30*(2), 245–252. doi:10.1037/a0038913

Therrien, Z., & Hunsley, J. (2012). Assessment of anxiety in older adults: A systematic review of commonly used measures. *Aging and Mental Health, 16*(1), 1–16. doi:10.1080/13607863.2011.602960

Thiel, C.M., Studte, S., Hildebrandt, H., Huster, R., & Weerda, R. (2014). When a loved one feels unfamiliar: A case study on the neural basis of Capgras delusion. *Cortex, 52*, 75–87. doi.org/10.1016/ j.cortex.2013.11.011

Thomas, D. (2005). *Socio-demographic factors in the current housing market* (Catalogue no. 11–010). Ottawa, ON: Statistics Canada.

Thomas, L.E. (1982). Sexuality and aging: Essential vitamin or popcorn? *The Gerontologist, 22*(3), 240–243.

Thompson, G.E., Cameron, R.E., & Fuller-Thomson, E. (2012). Achieving balance on the Red Road: First Nations grandparents speak. *Transitions, 3.* Retrieved from www.frp.ca/index.cfm?fuseaction=document .viewDocument&documentid =1168&documentFormatId=2037

Thompson, G.E., Cameron, R.E., & Fuller-Thomson, E. (2013). Walking the red road: The role of First Nations grandparents in promoting cultural well-being. *International Journal of Aging & Human Development, 76*(1), 55–78. doi:10.2190/AG.76.1.c

Thurstone, L.L. (1938). *Primary mental abilities.* Chicago, IL: University of Chicago Press.

Timonen, V., & Doyle, M. (2014). Life-long singlehood: Intersections of the past and present. *Ageing & Society, 34*(10), 1749–1770. doi:10.1017/ S0144686X13000500

Timpano, K.R., Keough, M.E., Traeger, L., & Schmidt, N.B. (2011). General life stress and hoarding: Examining the role of emotional tolerance. *International Journal of Cognitive Therapy, 4*, 263–279. doi:10.1521/ijct.2011.4.3.263

Tjepkema, M. (2005). Insomnia. *Health reports, 17*(1), 1–25. Statistics Canada, Catalogue no. 82–003.

Tolin, D.F., Frost, R.O., Steketee, G., & Fitch, K. (2008). Family burden of compulsive hoarding: Results of an internet survey. *Behaviour Research and Therapy, 46*(3), 434–443. doi:10.1016/j. brat.2007.12.008

Tolin, D.F., Meunier, S.A., Frost, R.O., & Steketee, G. (2010). The course of compulsive hoarding and its relationship to life events. *Depression and Anxiety*, *27*(9), 829–838. doi:10.1002/da.20684

Tombaugh, T.N. (2004). Trail Making Test A and B: Normative data stratified by age and education. *Archives of Clinical Neuropsychology*, *19*(2), 203–214. doi:10.1016/S0887-6177(03)00039-8

Tomita, M., Mann, W., Stanton, K., Tomita, A., & Sundar, V. (2007). Use of currently available smart home technology by frail elders: Process and outcomes. *Topics in Geriatric Rehabilitation*, 21(3), 24–34.

Tomkins, S.S. (1987). Script theory. In J. Aronoff, A.I. Rabin, & R.A. Zucker (Eds.), *The emergence of personality* (pp. 147–216). New York, NY: Springer Publishing Company.

Tomljenovic, L. (2011). Aluminum and Alzheimer's disease: After a century of controversy, is there a plausible link? *Journal of Alzheimer's Disease*, *23*(4), 567–598. doi:10.3233/JAD-2010-101494

Torges, C.M., Stewart, A.J., & Duncan, L.E. (2008). Achieving ego integrity: Personality development in late midlife. *Journal of Research in Personality*, *42*(4), 1004–1019. doi:10.1016/j.jrp.2008.02.006

Tow, A., Holtzer, R., Wang, C., Sharan, A., Kim, S.J., Gladstein, A., … Verghese, J. (2016). Cognitive reserve in postoperative delirium in older adults. *Journal of the American Geriatrics Society*, *64*(6), 1341–1346. doi:10.1111/jgs.14130

Trading Economics. (2017). Age dependency ratio (% of working-age population) in Canada. Retrieved from http://www.tradingeconomics.com/canada/age -dependency-ratio-percent-of-working-age-population -wb-data.html.

Transport Canada. (2014). *Canadian motor vehicle traffic collision statistics 2012*. Ottawa, ON: Author. Retrieved from https://www.tc.gc.ca/media/ documents/roadsafety/cmvtcs2012_eng.pdf

Trevisan, L.A. (2008). Baby boomers and substance abuse: An emerging issue. *Psychiatric Times*, *25*(8), 35–36. Retrieved from www .psychiatrictimes.com/geriatric-psychiatry/ baby-boomers-and-substance-abuse.

Trevisan, L.A. (2014). Elderly alcohol use disorders: Epidemiology, Screening, and Assessment issues. *Psychiatric Times*, *31*(5), 37. Retrieved from www .psychiatrictimes.com/alcohol-abuse/elderly -alcohol-use-disorders-epidemiology-screening-and -assessment-issues

Tricco, A.C., Soobiah, C., Berliner, S., Ho, J.M., Ng, C.H., Ashoor, H.M., … Straus, S.E. (2013). Efficacy and safety of cognitive enhancers for patients with mild cognitive impairment: A systematic review

and meta-analysis. *CMAJ*, *185*(16), 1393–1401. doi:10.1503/cmaj.130451

Trottier, H., Martel, L., Houle, C., Berthelot, J.M., & Légaré, J. (2000). Living at home or in an institution: What makes the difference for seniors? *Health Reports* (Component of Statistics Canada Catalogue no. 82–003), 11(4), 55–68..

Trovato F., & Odynak, D. (2011). Sex differences in life expectancy in Canada: Immigrant and native-born populations. *Journal of Biosocial Sciences*, *43*, 353–367. doi:10.1017/S0021932011000010

Trull, T., Jahng, S., Tomko, R.L., Wood, P.K., & Sher, K.J. (2010). Revised NESARC personality disorder diagnoses: Gender, prevalence, and comorbidity with substance dependence disorders. *Journal of Personality Disorders*, *24*(4), 412–426. doi:10.1521/ pedi.2010.24.4.412

Tully, P.J., Cosh, S.M., & Baune, B. T. (2013). A review of the effects of worry and generalized anxiety disorder upon cardiovascular health and coronary heart disease. *Psychology, Health and Medicine*, *18*(6), 627–644. doi:10.1080/13548506.2012.749355

Turcotte, M. (2012). *Profile of seniors' transportation habits* (Catalogue no. 11–008-X). Ottawa, ON: Statistics Canada.

Turcotte, M. (2013). *Family caregiving: What are the consequences?* (Catalogue no. 75–006-X). Ottawa, ON: Statistics Canada. Retrieved from http://www.statcan .gc.ca/pub/75-006-x/2013001/article/11858-eng.htm

Turcotte, M. (2013). *Living apart together* Statistics Canada. Catalogue no. 75–006-x. Retrieved from www.statcan.gc.ca/pub/75-006-x/2013001/ article/11771-eng.pdf

Turcotte, M. (2014). *Canadians with unmet home care needs* (Catalogue no. 75–006-X). Ottawa, ON: Statistics Canada.

Turcotte, M. (2015). *Volunteering and charitable giving in Canada* (Catalogue no. 89–652-X2015001). Ottawa, ON: Statistics Canada.

Turcotte M., & Schellenberg, G. (2007). *A portrait of seniors in Canada 2006*. (Catalogue no. 89–519-XIE). Ottawa, ON: Statistics Canada. Retrieved from http://www.statcan.gc.ca/pub/89-519-x/89-519 -x2006001-eng.htm

Turiano, N.A., Chapman, B.P., Gruenewald, T.L., & Mroczek, D.K. (2015). Personality and the leading behavioral contributors of mortality. *Health Psychology, 34*(1), 51–60. doi:10.1037/hea0000038

Turner, A., & Findlay, L. (2012). *Informal caregiving for seniors* (Component of Statistics

Canada Catalogue no. 82–003-X). Ottawa, ON: Statistics Canada. Retrieved from http://www.statcan.gc.ca/pub/82-003-x/2012003/article/11694-eng.htm

Twells, L.K., Gregory, D.M., Reddigan, J., & Midodzi, W.K. (2014). Current and predicted prevalence of obesity in Canada: A trend analysis. *CMAJ Open*, *2*(1), E18–E26. doi:10.9778/cmajo.20130016

Tyrer, P. (2014). A comparison of DSM and ICD classifications of mental disorder. Advances in Psychiatric Treatment, 20(4), 280–285. doi:10.1192/apt.bp.113.011296

Ullrich, S., & Coid, J., (2009). The age distribution of self-reported personality disorder traits in a household population. *Journal of Personality Disorders*, *23*(2), 187–200. doi:10.1521/pedi.2009.23.2.187

United Nations. (2016). *AIDS by the numbers*. Retrieved from http://www.unaids.org/en/resources/documents/2016/AIDS-by-the-number

United Nations, Department of Economic and Social Affairs, Population Division. (2013). *World population ageing 2013*, (ST/SEA/SER.A/348). New York, NY: United Nations.

United Nations, Department of Economic and Social Affairs, Population Division. (2015a). *World population ageing 2015*. New York, NY: United Nations.

United Nations, Department of Economic and Social Affairs, Population Division. (2015b). *World population prospects: The 2015 revision*. Retrieved from https://esa.un.org/unpd/wpp/publications/files/key_findings_wpp_2015pdf.

United Nations Volunteers. (2011). *State of the world's volunteerism report: Universal values for global well-being*. UK: United Nations Volunteers.

United States Environmental Protection Agency. (2015). *Health effects of UV radiation*. Retrieved from www2.epa.gov/sunwise/health-effects-uv-radiation

University of Alberta Alumni Association. (2013, December). Helen Hays. *Winter 2013 New Trail: The Impact Issue*, pp. 42–43. Retrieved from www.ualberta.ca/newtrail/winter2013/features/helen-hays

University of Ottawa. (2014). *The 1984 Canada Health Act*. Ottawa, ON: Author. Retrieved from www.med.uottawa.ca/sim/data/Canada_Health_Act.htm

University of the Third Age. (2014). *The 3UA story*. Retrieved from www.u3a.org.uk/useful-weblinks/111-worldwide-lifelong-learning-links/117-canada.html

Unger, W.P., Unger, R.H., & Wesley, C.K. (2013). Androgenetic alopecia. In M. Webwohl, W.

Heymann, J. Berth-Jones, & I. Coulson (Eds.), *Treatment of skin disease: Comprehensive therapeutic strategie*s (4th ed., pp. 36–38). Toronto, ON: Elsevier.

Uppal, S. (2010). Labour market activity among seniors. *Perspectives on Labour and Income*, *11*(7), 5–18. (Statistics Canada Catalogue no. 75–001-XIE). Ottawa, ON: Statistics Canada. Retrieved from www.statcan.gc.ca/pub/75-001-x/2010107/pdf/11296-eng.pdf

Uppal, S. (2016). *Insights on Canadian society financial literacy and retirement planning* (Catalogue no. 75–006-X). Ottawa, ON: Statistics Canada.

U.S. Department of Health & Human Services. (2015). *Key features of the Affordable Care Act (Data file)*. Retrieved from www.hhs.gov/healthcare/facts/timeline/index.html

U.S. Department of Health and Human Services. (2015). *Types of hearing aids*. Retrieved from www.fda.gov/MedicalDevices/ProductsandMedical Procedures/HomeHealthandConsumer/Consumer Products/HearingAids/ucm181470.htm

Vaidya, J.G., Gray, E.K., Haig, J.R., Mroczek, D.K., & Watson, D. (2008). Differential stability and individual growth trajectories of Big Five and affective traits during young adulthood. *Journal of Personality*, *76*(2), 267–304. doi:10.1111/j.1467-6494.2007.00486.x

Vaillant, G.E. (2002). *Aging well: Surprising guideposts to a happier life from the Landmark Study of Adult Development*. Boston, MA: Little, Brown, and Company.

Valkanona, V., & Ebmeier, K.P. (2013). Vascular risk factors and depression in later life: A systematic review and meta-analysis. *Biological Psychiatry*, *73*(5), 406–413. doi:10.1016/j.biopsych.2012.10.028

Valls-Pedret, C., Sla-Vila, A., Serra-Mir, M., Corella, D., de la Torre, R., Gonzalez, M.A., … Ros, E. (2015). Mediterranean diet and age-related cognitive decline: A randomized clinical trial. *JAMA Internal Medicine*, *175*(7), 1094–1103. doi:10.1001/jamainternmed.2015.1668

Van Alphen, S.P.J., Bolwerk, N., Videler, A.C., Tummers, J.H.A., van Royen, R.J.J., Barendse, H.P.J.,…Rosowsky, E. (2012). Age-related aspects and clinical implications of diagnosis and treatment of personality disorders in older adults. *Clinical Gerontologist*, *35*(1), 27–41. doi:10.1080/07317115.2 011.628368

Van der Heide, I., Van Rijin, R.M., Robroek, J.W., Burdof, A., & Proper, K.I. (2013). Is retirement good for your health? A systematic review of longitudinal studies. *BMC Public Health*, *13*(1), 1180. doi:10.1186/1471-2458-13-1180

Van der Mussele, S., Bekelaar, K., Le Bastard, N., Vermeiren, Y., Saerens, J., Somers, N., … Engelborghs, S. (2013). Prevalence and associated behavioral symptoms of depression in mild cognitive impairment and dementia due to Alzheimer's disease. *International Journal of Geriatric Psychiatry*, *28*(9), 947–958. doi:10.1002/gps3909

Van der Mussele, S., Le Bastard, N., Saerens, J., Somers, N., Mariën, P., Goeman, J., … Engelborghs, S. (2015). Agitation-associated behavioral symptoms in mild cognitive impairment and Alzheimer's dementia. *Aging & Mental Health*, *19*(3), 247–257. doi :10.1080/13607863.2014.924900

VanderPlatt, M., Ramos, H., & Yoshida, Y. (2012). A preliminary investigation of the contributions of sponsored parents and grandparents in Canada. *Canadian Journal of Ethnic Studies*, *44*(3), 79–96. Retrieved from https://crdcn.org/a-preliminary-investigation-contributions-sponsored-parents-and-grandparents-canada

Van Solinge, H., & Henkens, K. (2007). Involuntary retirement: The role of restrictive circumstances, timing, and social embeddedness. *The Journals of Gerontology, Series B: Psychological Sciences and Social Sciences*, *62*(5), S295–S303. doi:10.1093/geronb/62.5S295

Van Wijingaarden, E., Leget, C., & Goossensen, A. (2014). Experiences and motivations underlying wishes to die in older people who are tired of living: A research area in its infancy. *Omega (Westport)*, *69*(2), 191–216. doi:10.219/OM.69.2.f

Varothai, S., & Bergfeld, W.F. (2014). Androgenetic alopecia: An evidence-based treatment update. *American Journal of Clinical Dermatology*, *15*(3), 217–230. doi:10.1007/s40257-014-0077-5

Vary, J.C., Jr. (2015). Selected disorders of skin appendages—acne, alopecia, hyperhidrosis. *The Medical Clinics of North America*, *99*(6), 1195–1211. doi:10.1016/j.mcna.2015.07.003

Verbrugge, L.M., & Jette, A.M. (1994). The disablement process. *Social Science and Medicine*, *38*(1), 1–14. doi.org/10.1016/0277-9536(94)90294-1

Verhaeghen, P., & Cerella, J. (2002). Aging, executive control, and attention: A review of meta-analyses. *Neuroscience and Biobehavioural Reviews*. *26*(7), 849–857. https://doi.org/10.1016/S0149-7634(02)00071-4

Verhaeghen, P., Steitz, D.W., Sliwinski, M.J., & Cerella, J. (2003). Aging and dual-task performance: A meta-analysis. *Psychology and Aging*, *18*(3), 443–460. doi:10.1037/0882-7974.18.3.443

Vespa, J. (2012). Unit formation in later life: Economic determinants of cohabitation and remarriage among older adults. *Demography, 49*(3), 1103–1125. doi:10.1007/s13524-012-0102-3.

Vespa, J. (2013). Relationship transitions among older cohabitors: The role of health, wealth and family ties. *Journal of Marriage and the Family, 75*(4), 933–949. doi:10.1111/jomf.12040

Viña, J., & Lloret, A. (2010). Why women have more Alzheimer's disease than men: Gender and mitochondrial toxicity of amyloid-beta peptide. *Journal of Alzheimer's Disease, 20*(Suppl. 2), S527-S533. doi:10.3233/JAD-2010-100501

Virk, S.A., & Eslick, G.D. (2015). Aluminum levels in brain, serum, and cerebrospinal fluid are higher in Alzheimer's disease cases than in controls: A series of meta-analyses. *Journal of Alzheimer's Disease, 47*(3), 629–638. doi:10.3233/JAD-150193

Vitaliano, P.P., Zhang, J., & Scanlan, J.M. (2003). Is caregiving hazardous to one's physical health? A meta-analysis. *Psychological Bulletin, 129*(6), 946–972. doi:10.1037/0033-2909.129.6.946

Von Herbay, A. (2014). Otto Von Bismarck is not the origin of old age at 65. *The Gerontologist, 54*(1), 5. doi:10.1093/geront/gnt111

Von Känel, R., Mausbach, B.T., Patterson, T.L., Dimsdale, J.E., Aschbacher, K., Mills, P.J., … Grant, I. (2008). Increased Framingham Coronary Heart Disease Risk Score in dementia caregivers relative to non-caregiving controls. *Gerontology, 54*(3), 131–137. Retrieved from doi:10.1159/000113649

Wahl, H-W., Iwarsson, S., & Oswald, F. (2012). Aging well and the environment: Toward an integrative model and research agenda for the future. *The Gerontologist, 52*(3), 306–316. doi:10.1093/geront/gnr154

Wahl, H-W., & Oswald, F. (2010). Environmental perspectives on aging. In D. Dannefer & C. Phillipson (Eds.), *The SAGE handbook of social gerontology* (pp. 111–124). London, UK: Sage.

Waite, L.J., Laumann, E.O., Das, A., & Schumm, L.P. (2009). Sexuality: Measures of partnerships, practices, attitudes, and problems in the National Social Life, Health, and Aging Study. *The Journals of Gerontology, Series B: Psychological Sciences and Social Sciences, 64*(Suppl. 1), 56–66. doi:10.1093/geronb/gbp038

Wakefield, A.J., Murch, S.H., Anthony, A., Linnell, J., Casson, D.M., Malik, M., ... Walker-Smith, J.A., et al. (1998). RETRACTED: Ileal-lymphoid-nodular hyperplasia, non-specific colitis, and pervasive developmental disorder in children. *The Lancet, 351*(9103), 637–641. doi:10.1016/S0140-6736(05)78424-5

Waldoph, D., & Kutner, J.S. (2013). What is prolonged grief and how can its likelihood be reduced? In N.E.

Goldestein & R.S. Morrison (Eds.), *Evidence-based practice of palliative medicine*. Philadelphia, PA: Elsevier Sander.

Walling, A.D., & Dickson, G.M. (2012). Hearing loss in older adults. *American Family Physician*, 85(12), 1150–1156.

Wanberg, C.R., Kanfer, R., Hamann, D.J., & Zhang, Z. (2015). Age and reemployment success after job loss: An integrative model and meta-analysis. *Psychological Bulletin*, 142(4), 400–426. doi:10.1037.bul0000019

Wang, C.C., Kosinski, C.J., Schwartzberg, J.G., & Shanklin, A.V. (2003). Physician's guide to assessing and counseling older drivers. Washington, DC: National Highway Traffic Safety Administration.

Wang, H.-X., Xu, W., & Pei, J.-J. (2012). Leisure activities, cognition and dementia. *Biochima et Biophysica Acta*, 1822(3), 482–491. doi:10.1016/j.bbadis.2011.09.002

Wang, L.Y., Borisovskaya, A., Maxwell, A.L., & Pascualy, M. (2014). Common psychiatric problems in cognitively impaired older patients: Causes and management. *Clinics in Geriatric Medicine*, 30(3), 443–467. doi:10.1016/j.cger.2014.04.002

Wang, P.S., Lane, M., Olfson, M., Pincus, H.A., Wells, K.B., & Kessler, R.C. (2005). Twelve-month use of mental health services in the United States: Results from the National Comorbidity Survey Replication. *Archives of General Psychiatry*, 62(6), 629–640. doi:10.1001/archpsyc.62.6.629

Wang, Y.P., & Andrade, L.H. (2013). Epidemiology of alcohol and drug use in the elderly. *Current Opinion in Psychiatry*, 26(4), 343–348. doi:10.1097/YCO.0b013e328360eafd

Wang, Z., Wei, X., Yang, J., Suo, J., Chen, J., Liu, X., & Zhao, X. (2016). Chronic exposure to aluminum and risk of Alzheimer's disease: A meta-analysis. *Neuroscience Letters*, 610, 200–206. doi:10.1016/j.neulet.2015.11.014

Wannamethee, S., Thomas, M., Whincup, P., & Sattar, N. (2009). Associations between dietary fiber and inflammation, hepatic function, and risk of Type 2 diabetes in older men: Potential mechanisms for the benefits of fiber on diabetes risk. *Diabetes Care*, 32(10), 1823–1825. doi:10.2337/dc09-0477

Wannell, T. (2007a). Young pensioners. *Perspectives on Labour and Income*, 8(2), 5–14.

Wannell, T. (2007b). Young pensioners. *Perspectives on Labour and Income*, 8(2), 12–19.

Wardlaw, J.M., Valdes-Hernandez, M.V., & Munoz-Maniega, S. (2015). What are white matter hypertensities made of? Relevance to vascular cognitive impairment. *Journal of the American Heart Association*, 4(6), 1–19. doi.org/10.1161/JAHA.114.001140

Watson, J.D. (2012). Sarcopenia in older adults. *Current Opinion in Rheumatology, 24*(6), 623–627. doi:10.1097/BOR.0b013e32835d59b

Weber, M. (1905). *The Protestant Ethic and the Spirit of Capitalism*. New York: NY: Charles Scribner's Sons (the first English translation was published by Unwin Hyman, London & Boston, 1930.

Wechsler, D. (1939). *The measurement of adult intelligence*. Baltimore, MD: Williams & Williams.

Wechsler, D. (2008). *Wechsler adult intelligence scale—fourth edition (WAIS-IV)*. PsychCorp.

Weinert, B.T., & Timiras, P.S. (2003). Invited review: Theories of aging. *Journal of Applied Physiology, 95*(4), 1706–1716. doi:10.1152/japplphysiol.00288.2003

Weiss, A., & Costa, P.T. Jr. (2005). Domain and facet personality predictors of all-cause mortality among Medicare patients aged 65 to 100. *Psychosomatic Medicine, 67*(5), 724–733. doi:10.1097/01.psy.0000181272.58103.18

Weismann, A. (1882). *Über die Dauer des Lebens: ein Vortrag*. Germany: Jena G. Fischer, Werner, P. (2014). Stigma and Alzheimer's disease: A systematic review of evidence, theory, and methods. In P.W. Corrigan (Ed.), *The stigma of disease and disability: Understanding causes and overcoming injustices* (pp. 233–244). Washington, DC: American Psychological Association.

Werner, P. (2014). Stigma and Alzheimer's disease: A systematic review of evidence, theory, and methods. In P.W. Corrigan (Ed.), The stigma of disease and disability: Understanding 331 causes and overcoming injustices (pp. 233–244). Washington, DC: American Psychological Association.

Werner, P., Goldstein, D., & Buchbinder, E. (2010). Subjective experience of family stigma as reported by children of Alzheimer's disease patients. *Qualitative Health Research, 20*(2), 159–169. doi:10.1177/1049732309358330

Weston, S.J., Hill, P.L., & Jackson, J.J. (2015). Personality traits predict the onset of disease. *Social Psychological and Personality Science, 6*(3), 309–317. doi:10.1177/1948550614553248

Wetherell, J.L., & Gatz, M. (2005). The Beck Anxiety Inventory in older adults with generalized anxiety disorder. *Journal of Psychopathology and Behavioral Assessment, 27*(2), 17–24. doi:10.1007/s10862-005-3261-3

Wethington, E. (2000). Expecting stress: Americans and the "midlife crisis." *Motivation and Emotion, 24*(2), 85–103. doi:10.1023/A:1005611230993

Wetzels, R.B., Zuidema, S.U., de Jonghe, J.F.M., Verhey, F.R., & Koopmans, R.T. (2010). Determinants of quality of life in nursing home residents with dementia. *Dementia and Geriatric Cognitive Disorders, 29*(3), 189–197. doi:10.1159/000280437

Whalley, L.J., Staff, R.T., Fox, H.C., & Murray, A.D. (2016). Cerebral correlates of cognitive reserve. *Psychiatric Research: Neuroimaging, 247*, 65–70. https://dx.doi.org/10.1016/j.pscychresns.2015.10.012

Wheaton M.G., & Van Meter, A. (2014). Comorbidity hoarding disorder. *The Oxford Handbook of Hoarding and Acquiring* (pp. 75–85). New York, NY: Oxford University Press.

Whitbourne, S.E., Culgin, S., & Cassidy, E. (1995). Evaluation of infantilizing intonation and content of speech directed at the aged. *International Journal of Aging and Development, 41*(2), 109–116. doi.10.2190/J9XE-2GB6-H49G-MR7V

Whitbourne, S.K., Sneed, J.R., & Sayer, A. (2009). Psychosocial development from college through midlife: A 34-year sequential study. *Developmental Psychology, 45*(5), 1328–1340. doi:10.1037/a0016550

Whitehead, P.R. (2014). The lived experience of physicians dealing with patient death. *BMJ Supportive & Palliative Care, 4*(3), 217–276. doi:10.1136/bmjspcare-2012-000326

Whitehouse, E. (2009). *Australia highlights from OECD pensions at a glance 2009*. Retrieved from www.oecd.org/els/pensionsystems/43071222.pdf

Whitfield, K.Y., Daniels, J.S., Flesaker, K., & Simmons, D. (2012). Older adults with hoarding behaviour aging in place: Looking to a collaborative community-based planning approach for solutions. *Journal of Aging Research, 2012,* Article ID 205425, 8 pages. doi:10.1155/2012/205425

Whitney, C.R. (1995, February 22). In France, a citizen turns 120. *The New York Times*. Retrieved from www.nytimes.com/1995/02/22/world/in-france-a-citizen-turns-120.html

Wickremaratchi, M.M., & Llewelyn, J.G. (2006). Effects of ageing on touch. *Postgraduate Medical Journal, 82*(967), 301–304. doi:10.1136/pgmj.2005.039651

Wilcox, S., Oberrecht, L., Bopp, M., Kammermann, S.K., & McElmurray, C.T. (2005). A qualitative study of exercise in older African American and White women in rural South Carolina: Perceptions, barriers, and motivations. *Journal of Women & Aging, 17*(1–2), 37–53. doi:10.1300/J074v17n01_04

Wild, S., Roglic, S., Green, A., Sicree, R., & King, H. (2004). Global prevalence of diabetes. Estimates for the year 2000 and projections for 2030. *Diabetes Care, 27*(5), 1047–1053. doi:10.2337/diacare.27.5.1047

Willcox, B.J., & Willcox, D.C. (2014). Caloric restriction, CR mimetics, and healthy aging in Okinawa: Controversies and clinical implications. *Current Opinion in Clinical Nutrition and Metabolic Care, 17*(1), 51–58. doi:10.1097/MCO.0000000000000019

Willcox, D.C., Willcox, B.J., Yasura, S., Ashitomi, I. & Suzuki, M. (2012), Gender gap in healthspan and life expectancy in Okinawa: health behaviours. *Asian Journal of Gerontology and Geriatrics, 7*(1), 49–58.

Williams, B.A., Baillargeon, J.G., Lindquist, K., Walter, L.C., Covinsky, K.E., Whitson, H.E., & Stienman, M.A. (2010). Medication prescribing practices for older prisoners in the Texas prison system. *American Journal of Public Health, 100*(4), 756–761. doi:10.2105/AJPH.2008.154591

Williams, J., Hadjistavropoulos, T., Ghandehari, O., Yao, X., & Lix, L. (2015). An evaluation of a person-centred care programme for long-term care facilities. *Ageing and Society, 35*(3), 457–488. doi:http://dx.doi.org/10.1017/S0144686X13000743

Williams, K.N., Herman, R., Gajewski, B., & Wilson, K. (2009). Elderspeak communication: Impact on dementia care. *American Journal of Alzheimer's Disease and Related disorders, 24*(1), 11–20. doi:10.1177/1533317508318472

Willis, S.L., & Boron, J.B. (2008). The association of personality with cognition and risk of cognitive impairment. In S.M. Hifer & D.F. Alwin (Eds.), *Handbook of cognitive aging: Interdisciplinary perspectives* (pp. 647–660). Grenich, CT: Sage.

Willis, S.L., Tennstedt, S.L., Marsiske, M., Ball, K., Elias, J., Koepke, K.M., … Wright, E. (2006). Long-term effects of cognitive training on everyday functional outcomes in older adults. *Journal of the American Medical Association, 296*(23), 2805–2814. doi:10.1001/jama.296.23.2805

Wilson, J.S., & Barboza, S. (2010). The looming challenge of dementia in corrections. *Correct Care, 24*(2), 12–14 Retrieved from http://www.ncchc.org/filebin/images/Website_PDFs/24-2.pdf

Wilson, R.S., Schneider, J.A., Arnold, S.E., Bienias, J.L., & Bennett, D.A. (2007). Conscientiousness and the incidence of Alzheimer disease and mild cognitive impairment. *Archives of General Psychiatry, 64*(10), 1204–1212. doi:10.1001/archpsyc.64.10.1204

Winslow, B.T., Onysko, M.K., Stob, C.M., & Hazlewood, K.A. (2011). Treatment of Alzheimer disease. *American Family Physician, 83*(12), 1403–1412. Retrieved from http://www.aafp.org/afp/2011/0615/p1403.html

Wister, A.W., Malloy-Weir, L.J., Rootman I., & Desjardins, P. (2010). Lifelong educational practices and resources in enabling health literacy among older adults. *Journal of Aging and Health, 22*(6), 827–854. doi:10.1177/0898264310363502

Wolff, F.C. (2012). Well-being of elderly people living in nursing homes: The benefits of making friends. *Kyklos, 66*(1), 153–171.

Wong, S.L., Gilmour, H., & Ramage-Morin, P.L. (2014). *Parkinson's disease: Prevalence, diagnosis and impact* (Catalogue no. 82–003-X). Ottawa, ON: Statistics Canada. Retrieved from http://www.statcan.gc.ca/pub/82-003-x/2014011/article/14112-eng.htm

Wood, D. (2011, July 18). Right-to-die: Heading towards Sue Rodriguez 2. *The Tyee.* Retrieved from http://thetyee.ca/News/2011/07/18/SueRodriguez2/

Woodhead, E.L., Emery, E.E., Pachana, N.A., Scott, T.L., Konnert, C.A., & Edestein, B.A. (2013). *Graduate student's geropsychology training opportunities and perceived competence in working with older adults.* Unpublished manuscript.

Wooten, J.M. & Galavais, J. (2005). Polypharmacy: Keeping the elderly safe. *Modern Medicine Network.* Retrieved from www.modernmedicine.com/content/polypharmacy-keeping-elderly-safe.

World Health Organization. (1948). *Preamble to the Constitution of the World Health Organization as adopted by the International Health Conference,* New York, June 19–22, 1946.

World Health Organization. (1980). *International classification of impairments, disabilities, and handicaps.* Geneva, CH: Author.

World Health Organization. (1986). *Ottawa Charter for Health Promotion.* Ottawa, ON: Author.

World Health Organization. (1997). *Measuring quality of life.* Geneva, CH: Author.

World Health Organization. (2002). *Towards a common language for disability, functioning and health, ICF.* Geneva, CH: Author.

World Health Organization. (2003). *Sun protection: A primary teaching resource.* Geneva: Author.

World Health Organization. (2004). *Promoting mental health: Concepts, emerging evidence, practice summary report* Geneva, CH: A Report of the World Health Organization, Department of Mental Health and Substance Abuse in collaboration with the Victorian Health Promotion Foundation and The University of Melbourne. Retrieved from www.who.int/mental_health/evidence/en/promoting_mhh.pdf

World Health Organization. (2005). *Promoting mental health: Concepts, emerging evidence, practice.* Retrieved from www.who.int/mental_health/evidence/MH_Promotion_Book.pdf

World Health Organization. (2007). *Global age-friendly cities: A guide.* Geneva, SUI: Author. Retrieved from www.who.int/ageing/age_friendly_cities_guide/en/

World Health Organization. (2008). *Ageing and life course. Age-friendly cities and communities.* Geneva, SUI: Author. Retrieved from www.who.int/ageing/projects/age-friendly-cities-communities/en/

World Health Organization. (2010, reprinted 2011). *Global status report on noncommunicable diseases 2010.* Geneva, CH: Author. Retrieved from http://whqlibdoc.who.int/publications/2011/9789240686458_eng.pdf?ua=1

World Health Organization. (2012a). *WHO global estimates on prevalence of hearing loss. Mortality and burden of diseases and prevention of blindness and deafness.* Geneva, SUI: Author. Retrieved from www.who.int/pbd/deafness/WHO_GE_HL.pdf

World Health Organization. (2012b). *Dementia: A public health priority.* Geneva, SUI: Author. Retrieved from www.who.int/mental_health/publications/dementia_report_2012/en/

World Health Organization (2013). *Mental health action plan.* Retrieved from http://apps.who.int/iris/bitstream/10665/89966/1/9789241506021_eng.pdf?ua=1

World Health Organization. (2014a). *World health statistics 2014.* Geneva, CH: Author. Retrieved from www.who.int/mediacentre/news/releases/2014/world-health-statistics-2014/en/

World Health Organization (2014b). *Mental health atlas.* Retrieved from http://apps.who.int/iris/bitstream/10665/178879/1/9789241565011_eng.pdf?ua=1

World Health Organization. (2014c). *Mental health: Strengthening our response.* Retrieved from www.who.int/mediacentre/factsheets/fs220/en/

World Health Organization. (2014d). *Preventing suicide: A global imperative.* Retrieved from http://apps.who.int/iris/bitstream/10665/131056/1/9789241564779_eng.pdf?ua

World Health Organization. (2014e). *Age-friendly world: Adding life to years.* Geneva, SUI: Author. Retrieved from https://extranet.who.int/agefriendlyworld/who-network/

World Health Organization. (2015a). *World report on ageing and health.* Geneva, CH: Author. Retrieved from www.who.int/ageing/events/world-reprot-2015-launch/en/

World Health Organization. (2015b). *The determinants of health.* Retrieved from www.who.int/hia/evidence/doh/en/

World Health Organization. (2015c). *Fact sheet no 311: Obesity and overweight.* Retrieved from www.who.int/mediacentre/factsheets/fs311/en/

World Health Organization. (2015d). *Management of substance abuse: Alcohol.* Retrieved from www.who.int/substance_abuse/facts/alcohol/en/

World Health Organization. (2016a). *Global life expectancy, both sexes, 2015.* Retrieved from http://gamapserver.who.int/mapLibrary/Files/Maps/Global_LifeExpectancy_bothsexes_2015.png.

World Health Organization. (2016b). *Elder abuse fact sheet.* Retrieved from www.who.int/mediacentre/factsheets/fs357/en/

World Health Organization. (2016c). *WHO definition of palliative care.* Geneva, SUI: Author. Retrieved from www.who.int/cancer/palliative/definition/en/

World Health Organization. (2016d). *Ageing and life-course. Towards an age-friendly world.* Geneva, SUI: Author. Retrieved from www.who.int/ageing/age-friendly-world/en/

World Heart Federation. (2015). *Cardiovascular risk factors.* Retrieved from www.world-heart-federation.org/cardiovascular-health/cardiovascular-disease-risk-factors/

Wu, L., & Zhao, L. (2016). ApoE2 and Alzheimer's disease: Time to take a closer look. *Neural Regeneration Research, 11*(3), 412–413. doi:10.4103/1673-5374.179044

Wu, Z., & Schimmele, C.M. (2007). Uncoupling in late life. *Generations, 31*(3), 41–46.

Wu, Z., C.M. Schimmele, & Ouellet, N. (2015). Repartnering after widowhood. *The Journals of Gerontology, Series B: Psychological Sciences and Social Sciences, 70*(3), 496–507. doi:10.1093/geronb/gbu060

Wuthrich, V.M., & Frei, J. (2015). Barriers to treatment for older adults seeking psychological therapy. *International Psychogeriatrics, 27*(7), 1227–1236. doi.org/10.1017/S1041610215000241

Wuthrich, V.M., Johnco, C.J., & Loebach-Wetherell, J. (2015). Differences in anxiety and depression symptoms: Comparison between older and younger clinical samples. *International Psychogeriatrics, 27*(99), 1523–1532. doi:10.1017/S1041610215000526

Wyss-Coray, T., & Rogers, J. (2012). Inflammation in Alzheimer disease: A brief review of the basic science and clinical literature. *Cold Spring Harbors: Perspectives in Medicine, 2*(1), a006346. doi:10.1101/cshperspect.a006346

Xue, Q-L. (2011). The frailty syndrome: Definition and natural history. *Clinics in Geriatric Medicine, 27*(1), 1–15. doi:10.1016/j.cger.2010.08.009

Yankner, B.A., Lu, T., Loerch, P. (2008). The aging brain. *Annual Review of Pathology. Mechanisms of Disease, 3*, 41–46. doi:10.1146/annurev.pathmechdis.2.010506.092044

Yeh, C. (2015). Fostering a new (more empowering) world view on aging. *Generations: Journal of American Society on Aging, 39*(1), 10–14. Retrieved from www.asaging.org/blog/fostering-new-more-self-empowering-world-view-aging

Yen, I.H., & Anderson, L.A. (2012). Built environment and mobility of older adults: Important policy and practice efforts. *Journal of the American Geriatrics Society, 60*(5), 951–956. doi:10.1111/j.1532-5415.2012.03949.x

Yen, I.H., Michael, Y.L., & Perdue, L. (2009). Neighborhood environment in studies of health of older adults: A systematic review. *American Journal of Preventive Medicine, 37*(5), 455–463. doi:10.1016/j.amepre.2009.06.022

Yesavage, J.A., Brink, T.L., Rose, T.L., Lum, O., Huang, V., Adey, M.B., & Leirer, V.O. (1982-1983). Development and validation of a geriatric depression screening scale: A preliminary report. *Journal of Psychiatric Residence, 22*(1), 37–49. doi.org/10.1016/0022-3956(82)90033-4

Yi-Yin, L., & Sandmann, L.R. (2012). *Towards a new motivation to learn framework for older adult learners.* Adult education research conference. Retrieved from http://newprairiepress.org/aerc/2012/papers/30

Yun, R.J., & Lackman, M.E. (2006). Perceptions of Aging in two cultures: Korean and American views on old age. *Journal of Cross Cultural Gerontology, 21*(1-2), 55–70. doi:10.1007/s10823-006-9018-y

Zacher, H., McKenna, B., & Rooney, D. (2013). Effects of self-reported wisdom on happiness: Not much more than emotional intelligence? *Journal of Happiness Studies, 14*(6), 1697–1716. doi:10.1007/s10902-012-9404-9

Zarahn, E., Rakitin, B., Abela, D., Flynn, J., & Stern, Y. (2007). Age-related changes in brain activation during a delayed item recognition task. *Neu-robiology of Aging, 28*(5), 784–798. doi:10.1016/j.neurobioaging.2006.03.002

Zarit, S.H. (2009). A good old age: Theories of mental health and aging. In V.L. Bengtson, M. Silverstein, N.M. Putney, and D. Gans (Eds.), *Handbook of theories of aging.* New York, NY: Springer.

Zeigler, M., Cengia, A., Mussel, P., & Gerstorf, D. (2015). Openness as a buffer against cognitive decline: The Openness-Fluid-Crystallized-Intelligence (OFCI) model applied to late adulthood. *Psychology and Aging, 30*(3), 573–588. doi:10.1037/a0039493

Zelinski, E.M., & Kennison, R.F. (2007). Not your parent's test scores: Cohort reduces psychometric aging effects. *Psychology and Aging, 22*(3), 546–577. doi:10.1037/0882-7974.22.3.546

Zelli, A., & Dodge, K.A. (1999). Personality development from the bottom up. In Cervone, D., & Shoda, Y. (Eds.), *The coherence of personality: Social-cognitive bases of consistency, variability, and organization* (pp. 94–126). New York, NY: The Guilford Press.

Zhang, X., Norton, J., Carrière, I., Ritchie K., Chaudieu, I., & Ancelin, M.L. (2015). Generalized anxiety disorder in community dwelling elderly: Prevalence and clinical characteristics. *Journal of Affective Disorders, 172*, 24–29. doi:10.1016/j.jad.2014.09.036

Zhang, X., Xing, C., Guan, Y., Song, X., Melloy, R., Wang, F., & Jin, X. (2016). Attitudes toward older adults: A matter of cultural values or personal values? *Psychology and Aging, 31*(1), 89–100. doi:10.1037/pag0000068

Zhang, Y., Wang, M., Liu, S., & Shultz, K.S. (2009). Bridge employment and retirees' health: A longitudinal investigation. *Journal of Occupational Health Psychology, 14*(4), 374–389. doi:10.1037/a0015285

Zhao, Q.F., Tan, L., Wang, H.F., Jiang, T., Tan, M.S., Tan, L., … Yu, J.T. (2016). The prevalence of neuropsychiatric symptoms in Alzheimer's disease: Systematic review and meta-analysis. *Journal of Affective Disorders, 190*(15), 264–271. doi:10.1016/j.jad.2015.09.069

Zhou, L. (2007). What college students know about older adults: A cross-cultural qualitative study. *Educational Gerontology, 33*(10), 811–831. doi:10.1080/03601270701364545

Zhou, T., Xue, L., & Gao, J., & Kong, J. (2016). Internet-based cognitive behavioural therapy for subthreshold depression: A systematic review and meta-analysis. *BMC Psychiatry, 16*(356). doi:10.1186/s12888-016-1061-9

Zona, S., Guaraldi, G., Luzi, K., Beggi, M., Santi, D., Stentarelli, C., … Rochira, V. (2012). Erectile dysfunction is more common in young to middle-aged HIV-infected men than in HIV-unfected men. *The Journal of Sexual Medicine, 9*(7), 1923–1930. doi:10.1111/j.1743-6109.2012.02750.x

INDEX

CHMS. *See* Canadian Health Measures Survey (CHMS)

CHOICE. *See* Comprehensive Home Option of Integrated Care for the Elderly (CHOICE)

Christianity, 393–395

chronic-care hospitals, 406

chronic disease, 140

chronic illness, 144–146

chronological age, 6

CIHI. *See* Canadian Institute for Health Information (CIHI)

CIHR. *See* Canadian Institutes of Health Research (CIHR)

circumlocutions, 105

cities and communities, 410

classic aging pattern, 112

clinical-pathological entity, 219

Clostridium difficile, 68

CLSA. *See* Canadian Longitudinal Study on Aging (CLSA)

CMHC. *See* Canada Mortgage and Housing Corporation's (CMHC)

coercion, 37

cognitive behavioural therapy (CBT), 184, 186, 191, 200

cognitive changes, 88
  attentional changes in normal aging and, 102
    divided attention, 103
    selective attention, 102–103
    sustained attention, 103–104
  cognitive training and, 108–109
  intelligence and
    and age, 114
    cohort differences in intellectual abilities, 114–116
    factors affecting intelligent scores in older adults, 116
    fluid and crystallized intelligence, 111–113
    meaning of, 110
    primary mental abilities and multiple intelligences, 111
    Spearman's G theory of, 110–111
    variables associated with intelligence maintenance in later years, 117
  language changes with age and, 104–105
    elderspeak, 106–107
    sentence production, 105–106
    word-finding difficulties, 105

lifestyle factor effects on cognition and, 109–110
  memory changes in normal aging and, 93–94
    long-term memory (episodic and semantic memory), 101–102
    sensory memory, 94
    short-term memory/working memory, 94–100
  neuroimaging techniques, 88–90
  normal age-related changes to brain
    bilingualism effects on cognitive reserve, 92–93
    brain structure changes with age, 90–92
  post-formal thought and, 117–118
  wisdom and
    age and, 120
    measurement of, 120
    variations in definition of, 119–120

cognitive development stages, 118

cognitive domains, 92

cognitive enhancers, 229

cognitive epidemiology, 116

cognitive leisure, 359

cognitive neuropsychology, 99

cognitive reserve, 92
  bilingualism effects on, 92–93

cohabitation, 310–311, 317, 318
  effect, 311

cohort, 31
  effects, 29, 203

cohort-sequential design, 35
  advantages and disadvantages of, 36

collagen, 49

collateral, 408

collective dwelling, 403

Collett-Lester Fear of Death Scale, 380

Collip, J.B., 71

Columbia, 382

commission errors, 104

Committee on Aging, 3

co-morbidity, 150–151

Compassionate Care Benefits, 376

compassionate release, 239

compensation, 89, 125, 410, 432

Compensation-Related Utilization of Neural Circuit Hypothesis (CRUNCH) model, 89

competence–environmental press, 410

complex families, 325

complicated grief, 392–393

complicated/prolonged grief, 392

Comprehensive Home Option of Integrated Care for the Elderly (CHOICE), 420, 421

compression of morbidity hypothesis, 150, 166

computerized tomography (CT), 88, 219

concentrated epidemics, 335

conductive hearing loss, 58

Conference Board of Canada, 349, 357

confidentiality of data, 37–39

Confucianism, 14

congenital, 56

Consortium to Establish a Registry for Alzheimer's Disease (CERAD), 289

contextualist model, 284

continuing-care facilities, 423

Continuity Theory, 354

continuous performance test (CPT), 104

conversational language task, 106

Cooper, T., 206–207

coping, 180

coronary artery disease (CAD), 64, 287

Correctional Investigator Canada, 235–237

correspondence principle, 284–285

cosmetic surgery, 51

Costa, P., 30, 279–281, 284–285, 287, 306

Côte d'Ivoire, 132

The Council of Aging of Ottawa, 426

CPAI. *See* Chinese Personality Inventory (CPAI)

CPP. *See* Canada Pension Plan (CPP)

CPT. *See* continuous performance test (CPT)

CR. *See* caloric restriction (CR)

Craik, F.I.M., 93, 98, 101, 125

cremation, 395

Creole language, 256

Criminal Code of Canada, 383

cross-sectional designs, 29, 30–32, 34–36, 43–44
  advantages and disadvantages of, 36

Government of Canada, 234, 355, 358, 365, 376, 383, 386, 403, 407, 408, 426

Grady, S., 93

GRAND. *See* Grandparents Requesting Access and Dignity (GRAND)

grandparent and grandchild (GP–GC) closeness, 22

grandparenting, 326–327

Grandparents Requesting Access and Dignity (GRAND), 327

green burial, 395–396

green-care farm, 426–428

grey divorce, 315

grey matter, 90

grief, 392

grievous and irremediable medical condition, 386

gross domestic product (GDP), 155

GSA. *See* Gerontological Society of America (GSA)

GSS. *See* General Social Survey (GSS)

Guaranteed Income Supplement (GIS), 350, 356–357

Guidelines for Comprehensive Mental Health Services for Older Adults (Mental Health Commission of Canada), 205

Guidelines for Health Professionals and Scientists Working with Older Adults (Lupien), 176

Guidelines for Psychological Practice with Older Adults, 205

A Guide to Long-Term Care Insurance, 424

H

hair changes, with age, 53–54

hair replacement surgery, 54

Hall, E., 154

Hall, G.S., 3

hard plaster hypothesis, 280

HAROLD. *See* Hemispheric Asymmetry Reduction in Older Adults (HAROLD)

Harper, S., 267, 350

Hasher, L., 93, 98, 99, 101

Hayden, S., 207–208

Hayflick, L., 46

Hayflick limit, 46

Hays, H., 377

health
definitions of, 139–140
factors affecting, 142–143
measurement, of older adults, 140–142

Health Council of Canada, 268, 269

Health and Retirement Survey, 160

healthy immigrant effect, 137

hearing aids, 61

hearing changes, with age, 57–62

hearing loss, 58

heart failure, 64

Heart and Stroke Foundation, 67

Hemispheric Asymmetry Reduction in Older Adults (HAROLD), 89

hemorrhagic stroke, 224

HGP. *See* Human Genome Project (HGP)

Hindi, 256

Hinduism, 394

Hitch, G, 95, 99, 128

HIV/AIDS, 335–337

Hoarders (reality show), 194

Hoarding: Buried Alive (reality show), 194

hoarding disorder, 194–197
animal hoarding, 199
hoaders characteristics, 197–198
in older adults, 198
prevalence rates, 197
treatment, 200

Hoarding of Animals Research Consortium, 199

Hogewey dementia village, 426

Hold Me (film), 388

Home Buyer's Plan, 407–408

home care, 421–422

home-equity loan, 409

home maintenance programs, 408

home ownership, 406–407
programs facilitating, 407–409

Hong Kong, 202

Hope for Wellness Help Line, 269

hormone replacement therapy (HRT), 74–75

Horn, J.L., 111–113

hospice care, 374

household wealth, 406

housing options for older adults, 418–419

housing transitions, 418
assisted-living facilities, 422–423

housing options for older adults, 418–419

independent living options, 419–422

long-term-care facilities, 423–425

new models of care for older adults, 426–428

supportive housing availability in Canada, 425–426

HRT. *See* hormone replacement therapy (HRT)

Human Cognitive Abilities (Carroll), 113

Human Genome Project (HGP), 138

humanitarian class immigrants, 255

hypertension, 66

hypodermis, 48

I

IA. *See* Institute of Aging (IA)

IADLs. *See* Instrumental Activities of Daily Living (IADLs)

IAH. *See* Investment in Affordable Housing (IAH) Program

ICA. *See* Inter-Cultural Association of Greater Victoria (ICA)

Iceland, 131

ICF. *See* International Classification of Functioning, Disability, and Health (ICF)

iconic memory, 94

ICR. *See* Index of Cognitive Reserve (ICR)

illness and diseases common in older Canadians
acute illness, 144
chronic illness, 144–146

The Imitation Game (film), 322

immigrants, 13. *See also* ethnic diversity

immune system changes, with age, 68–69

immunological memory, 68

incidence rate, 264

independent living accommodation, 418

independent living communities, 419–420

independent living homes
adult day programs and, 420–421
home care and, 421–422
independent living communities and, 419–420
single-family homes and, 419